PRAISE FOR THE BLOOMSBURY GUIDE TO PHILOSOPHY OF DISABILITY

"This fantastic collection is both long overdue and yet ahead of its time. The essays not only press against the cherished norms of philosophy; they also refract similar dynamics and epistemic violences in other fields. The result is no less than a challenge to the ableist strictures of disciplinarity itself."

Jasbir K. Puar, Professor of Women's and Gender Studies, Rutgers University, USA, and author of *The Right to Maim: Debility, Capacity, Disability*

"This is a lively and wide-ranging collection of essays, offering an enlightening and poignant up-to-date snapshot of the philosophy of disability. The volume showcases a range of philosophical approaches and topics, examining disability and its relationship with philosophy from a variety of angles, which illuminate this new field."

Havi Carel, Professor of Philosophy, University of Bristol, UK, and author of *Illness: the Cry of the Flesh*

"The range in this collection is impressive, from the kinds of disabilities covered, to the domains to which disability connects. From chronic fatigue, substance use, deafness, neurodiversity, speech pathologies, and more, to an exploration of the concept of 'disability' in Africana philosophy, in music theory, assisted reproduction, and more, everyone should find something to learn from this volume."

Barry Lam, Professor of Philosophy, University of California at Riverside, USA, and Founder and Producer of the Hi-Phi Nation podcast

THE BLOOMSBURY GUIDE TO PHILOSOPHY OF DISABILITY

ALSO AVAILABLE FROM BLOOMSBURY

Animaladies: Gender, Animals, and Madness, ed. Lori Gruen and Fiona Probyn-Rapsey
The Right to Sex, Amia Srinivasan
A Philosophy of Struggle, Leonard Harris

THE BLOOMSBURY GUIDE TO PHILOSOPHY OF DISABILITY

Edited by
Shelley Lynn Tremain

BLOOMSBURY ACADEMIC
LONDON • NEW YORK • OXFORD • NEW DELHI • SYDNEY

BLOOMSBURY ACADEMIC
Bloomsbury Publishing Plc
50 Bedford Square, London, WC1B 3DP, UK
1385 Broadway, New York, NY 10018, USA
29 Earlsfort Terrace, Dublin 2, Ireland

BLOOMSBURY, BLOOMSBURY ACADEMIC and the Diana logo are trademarks of Bloomsbury Publishing Plc

First published in Great Britain 2024

A catalogue record for this book is available from the British Library.

A catalog record for this book is available from the Library of Congress.

ISBN: HB: 978-1-3502-6889-0
PB: 978-1-3502-6890-6
ePDF: 978-1-3502-6891-3
eBook: 978-1-3502-6892-0

Typeset by Deanta Global Publishing Services, Chennai, India

Cover description for accessibility: The title of the book appears on two lines across the top. The names of the editor and author of the foreword appear at the bottom. The image is a sculpture by Judith Scott that combines layers of shiny yarn woven vertically on a large cylinder, horizontally around a smaller cylinder, and around a protruding piece at the bottom of it. The sculpture seems to depict the body and head of a being sitting down, a being with one appendage, a fat person, or a little person.

CONTENTS

FOREWORD

LORI GRUEN

In the devastating aftermath of Hurricane Katrina, Neil Smith wrote that it is "generally accepted among environmental geographers that there is no such thing as a natural disaster" (Smith 2006). In the midst of increasing reports about hurricanes, as well as tsunamis, earthquakes, wildfires, and other events linked to climate change, this statement may seem quite odd, at least initially. Smith helps to clarify it by claiming that "In every phase and aspect of a disaster—causes, vulnerability, preparedness, results and response, and reconstruction—the contours of disaster and the difference between who lives and who dies is [*sic*] to a greater or lesser extent a social calculus" (ibid.). He does not deny that these disasters involve natural processes, processes that can be investigated by scientific study. Rather, he points out that the processes themselves are not what constitutes natural disasters: on the contrary, natural disasters are constituted by social forces. Notice that this claim is not reducible to the claim that humans are involved in activities that cause the natural events—that is just one part of the social picture. As Smith puts it, every aspect of the disaster is social.

In my philosophical work on animals, I have made this kind of argument about the concept of species. To be sure, there are animals that behave in a variety of ways and some of these behaviors seem remarkably similar, even identical, among populations of animals; yet, whether a particular population of organisms is classified as a species may change, even quickly, because this seemingly "natural" category is, ultimately, an artifact of certain research needs, needs for specific classifications of populations that enable researchers to answer certain questions. In other words, the concept of species is not a biological or natural given, but rather a social category. So-called natural behaviors are based, in part, on evolved biological capacities, just as weather events involve natural processes. Too often, however, the biological and physical forces seem to occlude the social processes that are at play which, in turn, prevents further investigation into the ways in which social phenomena shape what is regarded as natural. This subtle distinction is often missed, leading to naturalized claims about how zebras or elephants or sharks "function." If species itself is a relatively arbitrary unit in biological terms, it makes little sense to suggest that there is a natural way to describe the function of bodies or behaviors of animals as "species typical." In short, the species concept plays a dangerous role in the naturalization and maintenance of social hierarchies that require much more conscientious critical attention than they currently receive.

Naturalized social hierarchies are central features of problematic ideologies that organize social relations in ways that systematically and routinely harm the beings who are positioned as subordinate. Furthermore, the naturalization of these social relations serves to obscure the power imbalances that both produce them and come to seem "normal." This naturalized, idealized version of "normal" justifies what Shelley Lynn Tremain, the editor of this volume, calls "an apparatus of disability," that is, a network of power relations that elevates certain so-called normal people who can then use their elevated status to control populations that do not fit the ideal. Normal is not merely a description of some bodies or states of affairs, but rather a value-loaded judgment that works to divide people (and other animals) and distribute power.

The ways in which these social hierarchies become invisible through this process of naturalization leads to a range of problems, many of which are taken up in this volume. Most strikingly perhaps, this process of naturalization can lead to two significant problems: first, some people imagine that working toward greater inclusion within the system that is predicated on these hierarchies is possible and desirable; and second, some people who benefit from these social hierarchies often assume that they can speak about the lives of people who are excluded without attending to their distinctive experiences. It can be extremely difficult to track these problems when one is in the grips of the ideologies that support value-rankings between people (and other animals).

The first problem has become quite familiar on college campuses and in popular discussions of diversity, equity, and inclusion ("DEI"). These DEI efforts are based on long-held beliefs according to which expansion of the circle of opportunities, rights, freedoms, and so on in order to encompass those who have historically been excluded will lead to equality. This liberal vision of equality suggests that anyone who shares certain esteemed characteristics (e.g., rationality, autonomy, sentience) with those on top of the hierarchy—usually white, cis-gendered, nondisabled, heterosexual men in North American contexts—should be included in all matters of justice. Ableism, racism, sexism, heterosexism, and trans-exclusion can be rectified, the story goes, by incorporating nonwhite, ciswomen and other genders, queer people, trans people, and disabled people into the social workings of the community or the state. Arguments ensue about which characteristics are the especially salient ones on which to base inclusion and whether, and the extent to which, any group of people, or even any one individual, has these characteristics and thus deserves to be included. But such arguments miss the point. When the social hierarchies that govern these communities are brought to light, it becomes clear that exercises in equity and inclusion are just that—namely, exercises that distract from the reality that there can be no hierarchies without some people situated at the top of these systems of stratification and some people located below them. Rather than fighting for inclusion, we ought to dismantle the hierarchies. Many of the chapters that make up this volume reveal ways in which we might do that.

The second problem with social hierarchies, which becomes vividly clear in the chapters that follow, is this: one of the mechanisms that allows the people on top of the hierarchy to remain on top is the practice of abstraction and generalization. Judgments are made about who has the requisite capacities that are thought to be valuable outside of any particular context. People who are at the top of the hierarchy and, thus, at the center of dominant social, political, and philosophical discourses, rationalize their position in abstraction—their lives are the "best" lives, and they assume that people who are not like them, or who have different sorts of experiences, live lives that have less value. Indeed, abstraction and projection are common problems in philosophical discussions about disabled people. There is an assumption that nondisabled people have the epistemic authority to abstractly assess and compare the lives and experiences of another, however distinctive that other's life may be. The subjective experiences of people outside of the center are not considered; rather, they are reduced to a general category into which these people appear to fit (or not). Focusing on the general category of experience organized hierarchically, both in terms of the experiences of people at the top of the hierarchy and with reference to assumptions about the perceived experiences of people lower in the social hierarchy, reinforces taxonomies of power.

Both of the problems to which I have pointed are so deeply embedded in philosophical discussions and political discourse more broadly that they are often unidentifiable *as problems*. In order to grasp them as problems, critical attention to the rhetorical maneuvers of social groups at the top of the social hierarchy is urgently needed. This very important volume of pathbreaking work in philosophy of disability offers precisely the sort of critical attention required insofar as it centers the social constitution and experience of disability, as well as provides tools with which to de-naturalize, de-pathologize, and re-politicize traditional philosophical understandings and representations of disability.

Reference

Smith, Neil (2006), "There's No Such Thing as a Natural Disaster," *Items: Insights from the Social Sciences*, June 11. Available at: https://items.ssrc.org/understanding-katrina/theres-no-such-thing-as-a-natural-disaster/ (accessed June 11, 2023).

ACKNOWLEDGMENTS

In a number of respects, *The Bloomsbury Guide to Philosophy of Disability* has taken decades to bring to fruition. Indeed, its publication is long overdue. Despite years of struggle and resistance by disabled philosophers, the institutional, political, economic, and sociocultural inequities and exclusions that this book puts front and center persist and, in a variety of philosophical contexts, remain naturalized, have been normalized, and are apparently unrecognizable as entrenched forms of social injustice. In other respects, however, the book has come into being in a relatively short span of time.

In mid-2020—as entire populations globally confronted the isolation and infrastructural segregation with which disabled people routinely contend; as disabled people and elders perished from preventable deaths in nursing homes and other carceral institutions; and as critical insights about the ableism, racism, classism, sexism, colonialism, and nationalism that constitute the government of "public health" entered mainstream cultural discourses—Liza Thompson, the philosophy editor at Bloomsbury Academic, emailed me to ask if I would enter into a conversation with her about philosophy, disability, and publication prospects in the area.

In the course of a brief email exchange in which I responded to Liza's questions about the current state of affairs with respect to work on disability in philosophy, I agreed to put together a Bloomsbury collection of cutting-edge work in philosophy of disability. Thus, the seeds for this book were planted. The authors whose research and writing appear in the book were incredibly excited about its creation and their involvement with it; hence, they diligently adhered to the deadlines that I imposed and earnestly complied with the revision process that my heavy-handed editing style elicits. By the end of 2022, the book had already undergone its final peer review.

I am extremely grateful to Liza for the trust and confidence that she placed in me during our discussions and the enthusiasm for the project that she demonstrated throughout the initial stages of the production process of this book. I would like to extend my thanks to Giles Herman, Ben Piggott, and Emily Drewe, who marshaled the latter stages of the book's production.

I would also like to thank Katrina Calsado, editorial assistant to Liza, who facilitated the peer review of the book, collated contracts, and performed other tasks that precipitated the book's publication. I was deeply moved by the careful consideration that an anonymous reviewer of the book gave to its transgressive political and intellectual dimensions, as well as invigorated by the appreciation that they conveyed for various structural elements of it. I am also very grateful for Judith Scott's evocative artwork, including the sculpture that adorns the cover of this book.

These people have sustained me—politically, philosophically, emotionally, and financially—as I edited the book and even before I endeavored to do so: (in alphabetical order) Ada Jaarsma, Alex Bryant, Amandine Catala, Andrea Pitts, (the) BIOPOLITICAL PHILOSOPHY readership, Catherine Clune-Taylor, Catherine Frazee, Christine Overall, Darleen Burnett, (the) Dialogues on Disability Patreon subscribers, Élaina Gauthier-Mamaril, Eric Winsberg, Evan Simpson, Gabrielle Peters, Isaac Jiang, Jamie Morris, Jane Dryden, Jonathan Wolff, Julie Maybee, Lauren Guilmette, Luvell Anderson, Melinda Hall, Mich Ciurria, Mike Matheson, Nora Berenstain, Robert Chapman, Sally Haslanger, Stephen Yablo, Susan Schweik, Suze Berkhout, Tommy Curry, Trudo Lemmens, Verena Erlenbusch-Anderson, and Will Conway.

The Bloomsbury Guide to Philosophy of Disability is the first edited collection in philosophy of disability. It should not be the last.

INTRODUCTION
NEW MOVEMENT IN PHILOSOPHY

PHILOSOPHY OF DISABILITY

SHELLEY LYNN TREMAIN

Situating Philosophy of Disability in/out of Philosophy

This collection comprises twenty-six bold new chapters that mark the emergence and coalescence of a distinctly insurgent subdiscipline of academic philosophy that, years ago, I initiated and gave the name "philosophy of disability." As the contributions to the collection variously illustrate, specialists in this emerging subfield of philosophy do the following: (1) they examine how philosophy puts into circulation misrepresentations of phenomena that disability comprises and enhances existing misrepresentations of these phenomena; (2) they advance arguments and explanations about how critical and oppositional analyses of disability are marginalized in philosophy, if not entirely excluded from it; (3) they advance arguments and explanations about how disabled philosophers—and disabled philosophers of disability in particular—are vastly underrepresented in the profession; and (4) they articulate up-to-date understandings of disability that construe it as an irreducibly social and political affair.

In other words, philosophy of disability identifies and interrogates how disability has historically been produced, represented, and addressed within the discipline of philosophy and the broader social milieu; it scrutinizes how its own ineluctably critical approach to disability is marginalized in some areas of philosophy and entirely excluded from other areas of the discipline; it documents how disabled philosophers of disability are virtually absent from permanent positions in the profession; and it offers novel discourses about disability that refuse the strategic naturalization and depoliticization of disability by and through the institutional, professional, and disciplinary practices that function as the sedimented scaffolding of philosophy.

Mainstream (nondisabled) philosophy continues to operate under the guise of neutrality, rationality, and objectivity. Nevertheless, the discipline of philosophy—and every other "traditional" discipline that constitutes the modern university—both implicitly and explicitly advances certain ontologies, methodologies, and epistemologies, that is, certain political, social, economic, cultural, and institutional mechanisms condition philosophy and every other discipline of the modern university, even though conventional, established disciplines such as philosophy continue to be represented—and to variously represent themselves—as value neutral, disinterested, detached, and impartial. Indeed, the purported neutrality, rationality, and objectivity which are alleged to be foundational to philosophy disguise the situated and interested nature of philosophical movements, approaches, and argumentative claims.

Throughout the past several decades and in the last several years especially, philosophers who are institutionally, politically, and socially subordinated have steadily challenged the cisgender and heteronormative whiteness and androcentrism of philosophy, persistently working to forge paths for the discipline that make it available to a wider range of constituencies who import an array of hitherto obscured and subjugated identities, perspectives, histories, and values into philosophical discourse and practice. For example, a number of feminist philosophy journals and societies have been created; summer schools and institutes have proliferated that provide mentoring and other support to racialized, 2SLGBTQ+ (two-spirited, lesbian, gay, bisexual, trans, queer plus), and working-class philosophy students; professional philosophy associations increasingly fund projects that promote the interests of underrepresented philosophy faculty; and more and more philosophy conferences prioritize the contributions of members of underrepresented groups in philosophy, while spotlighting marginalized areas of philosophical research.

Despite resistance and outright hostility from certain corners of philosophy, furthermore, an increasing number of philosophy departments offer courses in feminist philosophy, philosophy of race, queer theory, Latinx philosophy, and other areas of inquiry that defy previously accepted ideas about what counts as philosophy and who counts as a philosopher. The subject matter of these courses is designed to transform the discipline of philosophy by subverting the (hetero)sexism, racism, Eurocentrism, homophobia, and transphobia embedded in the claims of mainstream philosophers; by critiquing the methods and "foundational" assumptions of Eurocentric Western philosophy along these lines; and by introducing alternative discourses, methodologies, and thinkers into the so-called canon of philosophy. Some philosophers now deliberately utilize the aforementioned areas of inquiry to redress the androcentrism, Eurocentrism, and whiteness of the discipline of philosophy, as well as to ameliorate the historical underrepresentation of some groups of philosophers within their own respective departments and the profession of philosophy more generally.

Notwithstanding the ways that relations of power within the discipline and profession have begun to shift due to these measures, philosophy of disability and disabled philosophers continue to be systematically left out of many, if not most, of these initiatives or are haphazardly added to them based on assumptions about "inclusion" and "diversity" that take gender and race (construed as mutually exclusive) to be paradigmatic categories of identity and subjection, effectively depoliticizing disability and obscuring how the distinct ways that disabled philosophers are subjected in philosophy complicate myriad constructions of gender and race. The enduring and demoralizing inaccessibility of feminist and other philosophy conferences, for example, drastically constrains the efforts of disabled feminist, racialized, and queer philosophers of disability to desegregate the discipline and profession of philosophy and, indeed, reinforces and reproduces segregationist practices in philosophy. Thus, this collection strives to disrupt the unsatisfactory dimensions of many actions that have been introduced to diversify the discipline and profession of philosophy (and academia more broadly).

One of the features that philosophy of disability has in common with philosophy of gender and philosophy of race, as well as with other oppositional and counter-discourses in the university, is a central reliance on the tools of social constructionism and hence an implicit critique of essentialism. Although philosophers of disability may disagree with each other about what disability is, as well as how, and the extent to which, disability is socially constructed, assumptions about the social constitution of disability more or less lie at the heart of philosophy of disability; that is, regardless of how much practitioners of this relatively recent subfield of philosophical inquiry otherwise disagree with each other, they concur with each other that disability is not a natural state of affairs that exists apart from historically contingent relations of social power. Rather, philosophers of disability provide insights that talk back to the dominant conceptualization of disability that is constitutive of bioethics, cognitive science, and mainstream political philosophy and ethics especially, according to which disability is a natural—that is, prediscursive—deficit, personal misfortune, or pathology that inevitably leads to the social, economic, and political disadvantages that disabled people confront.

Indeed, the questions that mainstream philosophers have asked (and continue to ask) about disability rely on a cluster of motivational assumptions that take for granted the metaphysical status and epistemological character of disability, casting it as a self-evident and thus philosophically uninteresting designation that science and medicine can accurately represent. On the terms of this cluster of assumptions, disability is a transcultural and transhistorical disadvantage, an objective human defect, that is, a non-accidental, biological human property, attribute, or characteristic that ought to be prevented, corrected, eliminated, or cured. That these assumptions are contestable, that disability might be a historically and culturally specific and contingent social phenomenon, a complex apparatus of power rather than a natural attribute or property that certain people possess, is not considered, let alone seriously entertained. Insofar as practitioners of the Euro-American philosophical tradition have (with few exceptions) cast disability as a natural, negative, and inert state of affairs in this way, they have largely removed disability from the realm of philosophical inquiry, precluding it from serious scrutiny and keeping at bay philosophical debate and questioning about its epistemological, ethical, ontological, and political status. The marginalization and exclusion from philosophical discourse of dire social and political matters with respect to disability and the COVID-19 pandemic are a case in point.

Mainstream philosophical discourse about the COVID-19 pandemic has disregarded the structural ableism, poverty, isolation, and other social disadvantages and inequities that have increasingly accrued to disabled people during the pandemic, uniformly attributing these consequences of the pandemic to an inherent natural vulnerability that resides in disabled people themselves rather than to the neoliberal policies that fostered these disadvantages or exacerbated existing inequities. When, over the course of the pandemic, philosophers have (if at all) considered the phenomena that they perceive to constitute disability, they have naturalized these phenomena and sequestered them in the domain of bioethics—as is routinely done in philosophy when issues that pertain to disability arise—directing their attention almost singularly to questions and claims that medicalize and individualize disability, including questions and claims about the development of triage protocols for supposedly scarce health-care goods and resources; questions and claims about whether disabled people can justifiably retain their ventilators if COVID-19 hospital units require them; and questions and claims about which disabled people, in which countries, should or should not be prioritized for vaccination (Tremain 2021).

Nevertheless, philosophy of disability—a widening body of critical philosophical work—denaturalizes disability and, in so doing, politicizes domains of phenomena with respect to disability that (nondisabled) philosophers either naturalize and omit from critical consideration or misrepresent in ways that detrimentally affect disabled people, including the phenomena that have characterized the COVID-19 pandemic: the naturalization and depoliticization of risk, the vulnerabilization of disabled people and elders confined in nursing homes and other carceral congregate settings, and the neoliberal privatization of responsibility for transmission of the virus itself (Tremain 2021).

What Philosophy of Disability Isn't

The publication of *The Bloomsbury Guide to Philosophy of Disability* will undermine prevailing elements of philosophy that naturalize and medicalize disability—regardless of whether they congeal and manifest in mainstream philosophy or in underrepresented oppositional philosophies—by introducing a substantial corpus of philosophical work designed both to subvert the adverse arguments about disability that philosophers articulate and to destabilize the hostile sociocultural discourses about disability from which philosophy draws and to which it contributes. In contradistinction to typical mainstream philosophy, philosophy of disability represents itself as politically motivated in character and socially engaged in content. Like other oppositional and progressive discourses within the university, philosophy of disability has grown out of and remains associated with cultural movement for social justice that endeavors to unsettle current institutional, political, economic, and social arrangements and the power relations that comprise them, reproduce them, and sustain them. A motivational assumption of the collection is, therefore, the contention that the incorporation of certain treatments of disability—certain analytic treatments of disability, especially bioethical treatments of it—under the rubric of philosophy of disability dilutes the radical potential of this area of philosophical practice. These "applications" of analytic philosophy to disability serve, in a variety of ways, to reinstate conventional relations of power with respect to disability.

Indeed, the motivational assumptions of this new subfield—philosophy of disability—are distinct from the assumptions that motivate mainstream philosophical stances on disability according to which disability is a prediscursive human trait or characteristic, a natural flaw or defect that can be adequately and appropriately addressed in the subfield of bioethics and cognate areas of inquiry. The assumptions that motivate philosophy of disability are, moreover, importantly different from the presuppositions that inspire inquiries about disability whose terms of reference are framed as mutually exclusive, dispassionately associated with each other through a conjunction—that is, as philosophy *and* disability (viz. feminist philosophy *and* disability, moral philosophy *and* disability, etc.)—rather than purposively implicated in each other through a preposition—that is, as philosophy *of* disability. Within the terms of the former frame—philosophy and disability—disability is positioned as an object upon which philosophy sets its overbearing inquisitorial gaze, a gaze whose primary research interests remain the questions and concerns about disability that (nondisabled, white, heterosexual, and propertied) mainstream Western and Northern philosophers have generated, largely under the rubric of bioethics. Within the terms of the latter frame—philosophy of disability—by contrast, the ways in which philosophers research and write about the phenomena of disability are assumed to significantly contribute to the very constitution and reproduction of disability; to the ways in which causation with respect to disability is understood; to how the causes and effects of disability are represented; as well as to the constitution, consolidation, representation, and reproduction of philosophy itself.

As the authors in this collection demonstrate, the discursive practices that philosophers use to represent disability, the contexts in which certain forms of representation of disability take place, and the assumptions that underlie the rationale offered for why and how representation takes place as such are fundamental mechanisms of (the apparatuses of) disability and ableism, materializing the contingent phenomena that they comprise, elaborating their parameters, specifying their delineation, and so on. An astute philosophy of disability recognizes that its defining terms of reference are mutually constitutive and mutually reinforcing, entangled, and entwined.

Insofar as a certain strand of philosophers who write about disability have for the most part concentrated on the formulation of responses to a normative agenda that their predominantly nondisabled and white mainstream philosophy interlocutors have essentially determined for them, their philosophical reflections on disability have remained largely wedded to an ableist, racist, speciesist, and cisheterosexist agenda. That is, inasmuch as these philosophers have primarily confined their analyses of disability to (for example) normative concerns with respect to the debate between (outdated conceptions of) justice and care, the most suitable account of distributive justice for what society owes disabled people, the so-called expressivist objection, the distinction between "curative" and "therapeutic" technologies with respect to disability, and mainstream assumptions about the allegedly diminished quality of life of disabled people—all of which matters their interlocutors in mainstream analytic philosophy initiated in the first place—examination of the metaphysical and epistemological status of disability has continued to be neglected in philosophy; naturalization and medicalization of disability have expanded in new directions in certain areas of the discipline; the eugenic impetus of bioethics has been legitimized; the historical emergence of disability and its contingency have remained obscured; denial persists about how certain ontological and ethical commitments condition ableist segregation of the profession; and the ways that disability is intertwined with other apparatuses of power—including settler colonialism, nationalism, white supremacy, class, environmental toxicity, speciesism, and cisheteronormativity—have gone unaddressed. This collection has been configured to move philosophical work about/on disability beyond and outside of the artifactual strictures of research that heretofore predominant philosophical analyses with respect to disability have erected.

Philosophy's Disabling Architecture

The understanding of philosophy's relation to disability, according to which philosophical inquiry into disability involves the application to disability of methodologies, epistemologies, and ethical principles that are external to disability, replicates the infrastructure of traditional Western philosophy whose subfields of metaphysics, value theory, logic, epistemology, and philosophy of language are regarded as foundational to philosophical inquiry and claimed to uniquely distinguish philosophy from other disciplines of research and teaching, self-consciously venerating it as "the queen of the sciences." Philosophers who hold this traditional, conventional view of the discipline maintain that these subfields, and only these subfields, are the necessary, unchanging, and so-called core elements of philosophy. Philosophers who conceive of philosophy in this way assume, furthermore, that other, more recent, areas of philosophical inquiry—such as philosophy of disability, philosophy of race, and feminist philosophy—are merely contingent derivatives of these putatively foundational subfields.

It is this conventional representation of philosophy that provides the scaffolding for the network of the PhilPapers Foundation (n.d.), a consortium that comprises several influential databases of philosophical research and activity—including PhilPapers, PhilPeople, PhilJobs, and PhilEvents—that an initial PhilPapers database spawned. Philosophers visit the PhilPapers and PhilPeople databases to access journal articles and other publications, to gauge the popularity of a given publication, to acknowledge their own interest in and recommendation of certain publications through views and downloads, as well as to otherwise stay abreast of recent developments in philosophy. Both PhilPapers and PhilPeople are, in other words, databases like Academia.edu that are designed specifically to serve the interests of philosophers and advance philosophical research and associated activities. Unlike Academia.edu, however, the content of the PhilPapers Foundation databases is organized into a limited number of predetermined areas of specialization, subfields, and topics in philosophy that are categorized hierarchically in descending order of importance according to prevailing ideas in Eurocentric Western philosophy about which areas, subfields, and topics have the most philosophical import, have the most explanatory power, and should be endowed with the most authoritative status (Tremain 2013, 2017).

Given that the PhilPapers and PhilPeople databases (as well as the other databases in this network) both institutionalize and institute the architecture of mainstream philosophy, the phenomena of disability are treated within the databases as *externalities* of philosophy proper and hence critical philosophical work on disability is chiefly relegated under the databases' category of Applied Ethics—a subcategory of the databases' supreme category of Value Theory—and is thus largely depoliticized, medicalized, and individualized. Philosophers of disability who want to use the databases to publicize and make more widely available their work on disability are therefore compelled to (re)medicalize, and individualize both the work itself and the category of disability in ways that reinforce and reproduce the status quo and the oppression of disabled people; that is, philosophers of disability must situate their critical philosophical analyses (and other work) on disability under one of the subordinate subcategories of the category of Biomedical Ethics, a sub-subcategory of Applied Ethics, alongside and on par with topics such as Drugs, Death and Dying, and Neuroethics; or they must situate the work under the category of Social Ethics, another sub-subcategory of Applied Ethics, alongside and on par with topics such as Deception and Friendship. This medicalized and individualized placement of disability under the rubric of Value Theory depoliticizes the phenomena of disability and circumscribes disability too narrowly, obscuring the fact that the phenomena of disability raise pertinent questions for every subfield of the discipline: disability problematizes the metaphysical status of corporeal, material, and institutional boundaries; disability suggests questions about what counts as oppressive linguistic practice that philosophers of language should consider; disability points to unexamined questions about how the apparatus of ableism and the apparatuses of racism, classism, and sexism (among others) with which disability is inextricably intertwined have shaped the history of philosophy; disability unravels constructs of rationality and objectivity in ways that nondisabled feminist epistemologists have thus far not imagined; and so on.

Indeed, it would be difficult to overstate the constraining effects that the PhilPapers Foundation databases generate for the development of critical philosophical work on disability. Nor could one overstate the deleterious consequences that accrue to disabled philosophers due to a spin-off of the original PhilPapers database, namely, PhilJobs (n.d.), the leading database internationally for jobs in philosophy, whose configuration with respect to a hierarchy of areas of specialization and topics in philosophy mirrors the structure of the original PhilPapers database. To make a long story short, the structure of the PhilJobs database (like the structure of the original PhilPapers database) systematically precludes recognition of philosophy of disability, discouraging the creation of job postings in philosophy of disability and preventing the specification of database searches for jobs in the area. To date, in fact, no advertisement for a full-time philosophy job anywhere in the world has designated philosophy of disability as an area of specialization, although research and teaching in philosophy of disability has been done for decades and close friends of philosophy of disability—namely, critical disability theory and disability studies—are burgeoning interdisciplinary fields of study across the university. Thus, philosophy jobseekers who specialize in philosophy of disability must represent their work in medicalized terms—that is, as a form of bioethics—if they wish to be regarded as viable candidates for positions in philosophy.

In other contexts (e.g., Tremain 2017, 2019, 2020), I have argued that bioethics is first and foremost a technology of modern government whose biopolitical impetus is normalization of the population. My argument in this context is that insofar as philosophers of disability must package their work on disability as bioethics, philosophy of disability, philosophers of disability, and, indeed, disabled philosophers of disability are effectively put in the service of a form of neoeugenics.

Job postings in philosophy influence what philosophers regard as current and emerging research in the discipline and as important areas of the discipline to develop in their own departments. Consider, for instance, the expanding viral sweep of job postings in artificial intelligence (AI) and digital ethics, both exploding areas of the discipline that were virtually unrecognizable and unexplored only a decade ago. Areas of specialization (and competence) in philosophy are made rather than discovered. Hiring departments, insofar as they do not see other departments recruit and hire specialists in the subfield of philosophy of disability, are not inclined to recruit and hire specialists in philosophy of disability themselves. Given that many, if not most, specialists in philosophy of disability are themselves disabled, the current classificatory scheme of the PhilPapers and PhilJobs databases in particular and the PhilPapers Foundation in general ought therefore to be acknowledged as technologies of power that contribute significantly to the underrepresentation of disabled philosophers in the profession of philosophy. In short, the PhilPapers Foundation databases contribute to the perpetuation of the current dismal state of affairs in the discipline with respect to philosophy of disability and its disabled practitioners.

Within philosophy, the pervasive disregard for philosophy of disability and indeed invalidation of it are enabled to persist by the constitutive character of the individualized and medicalized classifications of disability that these databases reproduce. Classification of subfields in philosophy and the questions and concerns that these subfields comprise are not innocent value-neutral representations of objective differences, relations, and similarities that await discovery and recognition. Rather, classification and classification systems in philosophy (as elsewhere) are performative and contribute to the constitution of the value-laden resemblances, distinctions, and relationships between phenomena that they put into place. Although the formula of the

PhilPapers Foundation databases promotes the idea that both the discipline of philosophy and the classification of subfields within the discipline are value neutral, disinterested, and impartial enterprises, political, social, economic, cultural, and institutional force relations influence every aspect of the discipline (and profession) of philosophy. Every philosophical question and concern, as well as every philosophical subfield that these questions and concerns configure, is a politically potent artifact of historically contingent and culturally specific discourse. As discursive artifacts, every philosophical question and concern, as well as every subfield that these questions and concerns constitute, has its own respective history, a respective history whose contingency can be traced genealogically (Tremain 2017, 2020).

An Overview of This Guide

The Bloomsbury Guide to Philosophy of Disability is divided into five parts, which, when taken together, underscore the revolutionary impetus of philosophy of disability as a burgeoning new subfield of philosophy. The book should serve as a compass for everyone who wants to understand this movement from which there should be no turning back. Each of the book's chapters includes an extensive bibliography to enable this endeavor, with the comprehensive index of the book providing additional direction. Though the book is divided into five parts, the separations between these parts should nevertheless be regarded as porous, especially given the extent to which certain themes and insights travel across the chapters of the various parts. Indeed, the overall structure of this collection and the ordering of its parts and their respective chapters aim to disobey the accepted theoretical/applied designation and asymmetrical ranking that actively operate to marginalize critical work on disability in philosophy anthologies and handbooks, as well as in philosophy course syllabi, philosophy department curricula, and philosophy databases.

The first part of the book, "Desegregating the Discipline(s)," comprises six chapters that point to the ways in which philosophy of disability variously operates to break through the artifactual disciplining boundaries and barriers that sideline and exclude critical philosophical work on disability—that is, philosophy of disability.

This part opens with my chapter, "Disaster Ableism, Epistemologies of Crisis, and the Mystique of Bioethics," in which I confront the elephant in the room of any discussion about how philosophy of disability is partitioned from academic philosophy and why: namely, the subfield of bioethics, which, I maintain, is a technology of neoliberal governmentality. By drawing on writing by Naomi Klein and Kyle Whyte, I argue in the chapter that philosophy of disability should identify the claims of bioethicists and other proponents of medically assisted suicide (MAiD) as elements of neoliberal "disaster ableism" and settler colonial presentism.

Critical philosophical analyses of disability also enable recognition of the neoeugenics that underpins the fatphobia that Kristin Rodier and Samantha Brennan examine in their contribution to the collection, "Would You Kill the Fat Man Hypothetical? Fat Stigma in Philosophy." As Rodier and Brennan evocatively point out, the ideals of rationality and objectivity, which motivate mainstream philosophical discourse, create a disabling and hostile workplace environment for fat philosophers.

The third and fourth chapters in this part identify lacunae in both mainstream philosophical accounts of disability and counter-discourses about disability. In his chapter, "Pruriently Feared: Theoretical Erasure of the Disabled Black Male," Tommy J. Curry poignantly argues—using empirical evidence and data about the execution of disabled Black men to do so—that the pain and suffering inflicted upon disabled Black men is largely ignored in white disability studies and theories about the body more generally. Curry's chapter is a historically informed cautionary tale for the development of philosophy of disability. In Licia Carlson's chapter, "Disability, Dissonance, and Resistance: A Musical Dialogue," she, too, explores the ways in which critical analyses of disability and philosophy of disability in particular would be improved if they were to enlarge the purview of their domains of inquiry. Throughout the chapter, Carlson convincingly argues that philosophy of disability would be enriched and historically and culturally contextualized were it to encompass the insights of philosophy of music and, likewise, philosophy of music would be politicized and historically and culturally contextualized were it to incorporate the insights of philosophy of disability.

"Neurodiversity, Anti-Psychiatry, and the Politics of Mental Health," Robert Chapman's contribution to this volume, is designed to establish the place that neurodiversity theory should occupy in the history of philosophical and other critiques of psychiatry and psychiatric pathologization. Chapman's chief purpose in their transgressive chapter is to point out how neurodiversity theory contests both the medical model and the discourse of anti-psychiatry, providing a novel form of critique that both unsettles the current biocentric approach to "mental health" and has the potential to ground a new politics of mental health in the twenty-first century.

In the last chapter of the part, "Disability and African Philosophy," Julie E. Maybee explains how concepts developed in African philosophy of disability demonstrate that Western ideas about disability are not universals, but rather must be recognized as culturally and historically specific. Many of these African concepts about disability, Maybee writes, advance ideas about community and care that contradict the notions of individualism and autonomy that (white) Western disability studies has endorsed and promoted.

The five chapters that make up the book's second part, "Mechanisms of Oppression," articulate the ways in which seemingly nonpolitical phenomena—such as addiction, accommodation requests, algorithms, and assistive reproductive technologies (ARTs)—operate as mechanisms, strategies, and technologies of intersecting relations of power.

The analysis of power as an apparatus that Michel Foucault (e.g., Foucault 1977) introduced and that I (e.g., Tremain 2017) have put to work in the service of philosophy of disability provides the conceptual frame for "The Apparatus of Addiction: Substance Use at the Crossroads of Colonial Ableism and Migration," the fascinating chapter that Andrea J. Pitts has contributed to this volume. A central tactic of Pitts in the chapter is to engage mutually constituting discourses with respect to disability and addiction, uncovering a broad apparatus of relations of power that co-organize the meaning and significance of these discourses.

In "Disability, Ableism, Class, and Chronic Fatigue," Mich Ciurria provides an expansive account of how seemingly value-neutral public policies, routine administrative exercises, and "progressive" activist agendas act as governmental and disciplinary strategies with respect to disabled identification. In particular, Ciurria shows how disabled identity is constituted by and through these regimes, as well as by and through social phenomena such as employment, social assistance benefits, institutional accommodation, and community inclusion and care.

In Johnathan Flowers's pathbreaking chapter, "Algorithms as Ableist Orientation Devices: The Technosocial Inheritance of Colonialism and Ableism," he argues that algorithms, rather than merely measure objective phenomena, both (re)produce and obscure power relations—such as ableism, racism, and colonialism—by naturalizing them through technological means. As Flowers points out, algorithms have increasingly become a source for the governmental production of inequities with respect to (for example) health care, the criminal justice system, online harassment, and hate speech.

The governmental character of technologies is a primary concern of Desiree Valentine in "The ART of Kinship: An Intersectional Reading of Assisted Reproductive Practices." Thus, Valentine offers detailed examples of legal cases to illustrate that the social markers of race, disability, and sexuality are not passive traits of prospective parents in the context of ARTs, but rather come to have their significance precisely through ARTs which operate as kinship devices.

The constitutive character and functions of epistemologies and ontologies that Valentine's chapter highlight resonate in Amandine Catala's contribution to the collection. In "Epistemic Injustice and Epistemic Authority on Autism,"

Catala argues that epistemic injustice undermines Autistic people's epistemic authority about their own experiences of themselves and of the world. Hence, Catala endeavors to establish criteria that bolster Autistic people's claims to this authority. Catala capitalizes the term *Autistic* in order to refer to a political identity and signify this authority.

Entitled "Phenomenologies of Access and Exclusion," the third part of the book comprises five chapters that illuminate various ways in which philosophers of disability employ both phenomenology and first-person narratives to expand our understanding of the disabled subject in a nondisabled world, that is, a world whose infrastructure is constitutive of, constitutes, and reconstitutes the world for nondisabled people.

In Corinne Lajoie's chapter, "Disability, Access, and the Promise of Inclusion: Returning to Institutional Language Through a Phenomenological Lens," Lajoie draws on phenomenology to explicate senses of the terms *access* and *inclusion* that are often obscured. Indeed, Lajoie offers a threefold critique of inclusion rhetoric and its capacity to falsely motivate the impression that lasting change has taken place.

The indisputably political and contextual character of language and speech is the crux of "Stuttering and Ableism: A Study of Eventfulness," Joshua St. Pierre's chapter in this book. St. Pierre focuses on the experience of stuttering to argue that although ableism organizes the perceptual world for the uninterrupted pleasure of the nondisabled world, a robust account of stuttering and "dysfluency" would underline the existential and political stakes of the ableist refusal to hear stuttering on its own terms.

Frantz Fanon's (1986) use of medical metaphors and metaphors about disability constitutes a crucial aspect of Emily R. Douglas's analysis in "Frantz Fanon and Disability: Frictions and Solidarities." In this chapter, Douglas eloquently examines Fanon's position as both a colonized figure and a figure of colonized medicine and charts his existing work—through the phenomenological body schema in particular—in order to identify sites of solidarity between different modes of disablement and becoming-disabled.

Sofia Jeppsson's chapter, "Exemption, *Self*-Exemption, and Compassionate Self-Excuse," interrogates the distinction between excuses and exemptions in moral responsibility philosophy. Madness is typically regarded as grounds for exemption rather than excuses; yet Jeppsson points out that when we exempt someone, we treat them as something to be managed and handled. Jeppsson argues that a better option, for a Mad person, is to adopt a compassionate self-excusing attitude.

In the fifth and final chapter of this part, "Pathologizing Disabled and Trans Identities: How Emotions Become Marginalized," Gen Eickers asserts that "emotional marginalization" (as they refer to it) ought to be recognized as a form of social invalidation. Eickers, evocatively noting that this form of marginalization stems from the long history of pathologization of trans and disabled people, elaborates how emotional marginalization of trans identities and disabled identities is experienced subjectively.

The five chapters that make up "Disabling Normativities," the fourth part of the collection, variously consider how disciplinary norms, social obligations, and ethical standards and principles delimit the possible actions and identities of disabled people (including their subjective identification as disabled), indicating why philosophers of disability should closely attend to these phenomena.

Inspired by Gloria Anzaldúa's (1987) "*mestiza* consciousness," Élaina Gauthier-Mamaril's chapter, "A Crip Reading of Filipino Philosophy," explores the possibilities and tensions of a *mestiza* crip reading of Filipino philosophy. Over the course of the chapter, Gauthier-Mamaril considers the complicated questions of "What is crip philosophy?" and "What is Filipino philosophy?" while engaging in a critical examination of the long tradition of Thomistic virtue ethics in Filipino philosophy to arrive at a crip Filipino philosophy.

Virtue ethics is central to "Recognizing Human Flourishing in the Context of Disability," Jordan Joseph Wadden and Tim Stainton's chapter in what follows. Wadden and Stainton trace a genealogy of the notion of flourishing through the history of philosophy in order to show both how current bioethical defenses of MAiD are antithetical to recognition of the value of disabled people's lives and how the policies and procedures that constitute MAiD itself withhold from disabled people the social capacity for flourishing.

In August Gorman's chapter, "Neurodiversity and the Ethics of Access," he notes that when we adopt a neurodiversity paradigm and thus dispense with the assumption that neurodivergent traits are pathological defects, we seem to relinquish any ground on which to base distinctions between neurodiversity-related claims to entitlement and mere preferences. To resolve this seeming dilemma, Gorman carefully considers several approaches to it that philosophers of disability might take.

In "The Ethics of Disability Passing and Uncovering in the Philosophy Classroom," Joseph A. Stramondo's chapter, he, too, considers a possible dilemma for philosophical thinking about disability, namely, whether one has a moral duty to make known that they are disabled. Over the course of the chapter, Stramondo, taking Peter Railton's well-known Dewey Lecture as his starting point, surveys the options available to the disabled philosophy professor.

In her chapter entitled "Inclusive Ethics: A Precautionary Principle," Stephanie Jenkins draws on both critical disability studies and critical animal studies to argue against two predominant methods used to define the boundaries of moral considerability. Jenkins shows why these approaches are both ableist and speciesist and, by doing so, introduces an innovative embodied ethics that recommends a precautionary principle with respect to moral status.

Each of the five chapters that make up the fifth part of the book, "Resisting Epistemologies," offers radical new ways in which to know disability, to write about it critically, and to organize against forces in the discipline and profession of philosophy that medicalize and individualize disability as means to marginalize it.

Melinda C. Hall's chapter, "Risking Ourselves, Together: The Politics and Persons of Risk," considers the implications of the assertion that both risk and disability are irreducibly political by examining how risk and disability are typically individualized and medicalized in bioethical and public health discourses, as well as how risk is subjectified in the discursive practices surrounding police shootings of Black men in the United States. Hall's project is notably designed to identify opportunities to disrupt harms and take alternative risks through collective action: why we should risk ourselves together and how we should do so.

Christine Overall's chapter, "Disablement and Ageism," extends this exploration of how disability is known through the prisms of dominant epistemologies by considering how ageist conditions of ageing precipitate disablement. Overall's close attention to the ways in which ageism and ableism have shaped public policy with respect to (for example) the incarceration of older people and disabled people in nursing homes and other institutions is especially provocative and timely.

Like earlier chapters in the book, the third and fourth chapters of this part implement arguments in the literature about epistemic injustice, including work in this area that Miranda Fricker (2007) introduced. Josh Dohmen's chapter, "Power-Knowledge and Epistemic Injustice in Employment for Disabled Adults," uses Fricker—in conversation with Foucault's analysis of power-knowledge—to elaborate the forms of epistemic injustice that disabled people confront when they attempt to make choices about work. In "'But You Don't Look Autistic': Resisting Neurotypical Narratives," Nathan Moore teases out the numerous ways that Autistic testimony is rejected and the variety of metaepistemic injustices that accrue to Autistic people, in general, and Autistic philosophers, in particular, due to the omission of these epistemic injustices from the literature of feminist philosophy and social epistemology. Moore's chapter is thus a beacon for fresh areas of inquiry in feminist philosophy (of disability) and social epistemology.

The final chapter of this part (and of the collection in its entirety) puts into greater relief the disruptive character of the subfield of philosophy of disability with respect to the fraught relationship between radical thinking in philosophy with respect to disability and the medicalized understandings of disability that the field of bioethics and cognate areas of the discipline engender. In "Nocebos Talk Back: Marked-Bodied Experience and the Dynamics of Health Inequality," Suze G. Berkhout and Ada S. Jaarsma consider the significance of the nocebo effect for feminist philosophy of disability, linking nocebos with feminist-of-color scholarship in disability studies. As Berkhout and Jaarsma show throughout their chapter, nocebos make palpable how social structures, contexts, and institutional practices produce expectations of harm, pain, and trauma, expectations whose incorporation into feedback loops produces additional harms in the bodyminds of people minoritized and marked in other ways.

The publication of *The Bloomsbury Guide to Philosophy of Disability* is a definitive intervention into philosophy that has tremendous intellectual, political, institutional, and cultural importance. Whether philosophy and, indeed, philosophers will rise to the challenges that this collection of writing poses; will grapple with the expectations that it seeks to have fulfilled; and will enable the provision of the future to which it is directed remain open questions.

References

Anzaldúa, Gloria (1987), *Borderlands: The New Mestiza = La Frontera*, 1st ed., San Francisco: Spinsters/Aunt Lute.

Fanon, Frantz (1986), *Black Skin, White Masks*, trans. Charles Lam Markmann, London: Pluto Press.

Foucault, Michel (1977), *Discipline and Punish: The Birth of the Prison*, trans. A. Sheridan, New York: Vintage Books.

Fricker, Miranda (2007), *Epistemic Injustice: Power and the Ethics of Knowing*, New York: Oxford University Press.

PhilJobs (n.d.), "PhilJobs: Jobs for Philosophers." Available at: https://philjobs.org/ (accessed June 18, 2023).

PhilPapers (n.d.). Available at: https://philpapers.org/ (accessed June 18, 2023).

Tremain, Shelley (2013), "Introducing Feminist Philosophy of Disability," *Disability Studies Quarterly* 33 (4). https://doi.org/10.18061/dsq.v33i4.3877.

Tremain, Shelley L. (2017), *Foucault and Feminist Philosophy of Disability*, Ann Arbor: University of Michigan Press.

Tremain, Shelley Lynn (2019), "Feminist Philosophy of Disability: A Genealogical Intervention," *Southern Journal of Philosophy* 57 (1): 132–58.

Tremain, Shelley L. (2020), "Field Notes on the Naturalization and Denaturalization of Disability in (Feminist) Philosophy: What They Do and How They Do It," *Feminist Philosophy Quarterly* 6 (3): 1–22.

Tremain, Shelley Lynn (2021), "Philosophy of Disability, Conceptual Engineering, and the Nursing Home-Industrial-Complex in Canada," *International Journal of Critical Diversity Studies* 4 (1): 10–33.

PART I

DESEGREGATING THE DISCIPLINE(S)

1 DISASTER ABLEISM, EPISTEMOLOGIES OF CRISIS, AND THE MYSTIQUE OF BIOETHICS

SHELLEY LYNN TREMAIN

Enlarging the Critique

Philosophers increasingly engage in pointed discussions about academic freedom in philosophy and in academia more widely, as well as participate in heated debates with members of the broader public about freedom of speech in society at large. The most impassioned discussions and debates have concerned the philosophical legitimacy of so-called gender-critical feminism, the publication of articles about supposedly innate differences between allegedly natural races, and the extension to Peter Singer and Kathleen Stock of invitations to present their work in light of the former philosopher's remarks about the permissibility of infanticide in the case of disabled infants and the latter philosopher's renown as a leading advocate of "gender critical" feminism and its claims about the immutability of binary sex. Most left-leaning philosophers denounce the transphobia that conditions gender-critical feminism, repudiate the scientific racism that underlies views about innate racial differences, and condemn the claims about infanticide and disability that Singer has articulated. Nevertheless, many philosophers remain resolute that the principle of academic freedom demands that Singer, gender-critical feminists, proponents of scientific racism, and adherents of other disparaged ideas must be allowed to articulate their views without fear of reprisal.

Notice the disparate levels of generality at which these repudiations take place. Although Singer's arguments about disability are repeatedly condemned in the philosophical community, the systemic and structural character of the ableism that precipitated the arguments has gone virtually unaddressed and flourishes unabated. Condemnation of Singer's views about disability is advanced exclusively as the ethical response to egregious claims of an individual philosopher, effectually obscuring and deflecting attention away from the historical conditions of possibility for his claims and the comparatively pernicious ableism that other bioethicists produce. In other words, the singularity conferred upon Singer's arguments—which in turn frames common objections to them—enables both the eugenic impetus of the field of bioethics in toto and the perilous statements of other bioethicists to remain systematically unchallenged, to be neutralized, and to persist, especially insofar as these statements (and the motivational assumptions from which they arise) are routinely reiterated in introductory bioethics classes that are considered to be standard "service" courses and hence a lucrative and vital part of philosophy department curricula and university infrastructure. Indeed, most philosophers treat bioethics as an innocuous "applied" subfield of the discipline that can generally be ignored; that is, although many, if not most, philosophers eschew the arguments that Singer makes, they deem the subfield of bioethics itself—in which the value of disabled people's lives is candidly adjudicated and the ontological status of disability is typically taken for granted—to be harmless, largely inconsequential philosophically, and politically insignificant.

Disability bioethicists (as they refer to themselves) are among the philosophers who insist that Singer's arguments about disabled people are morally reprehensible, culturally harmful, and should therefore be refuted; however, the critiques of Singer that disability bioethicists elaborate—like the critiques of Singer that their more mainstream counterparts author—do not encompass a more comprehensive critique of the subfield of bioethics itself. On the contrary, disability bioethicists generally regard the overall field of bioethics as a progressive and open enterprise within which one can selectively adopt a neutral stance on particular bioethical issues, making the same (neo) liberal assumptions about power, choice, and autonomy that mainstream bioethics promotes (Scully 2021; Stramondo 2022). Thus, philosophers who self-identify as disability bioethicists regularly participate on panels at bioethics conferences, join bioethics associations, collaborate with bioethics institutes, implicitly support mainstream bioethicists whose views are widely regarded among disabled people as detrimental to them, and aspire to publish in the bioethics journals that these mainstream bioethicists produce. Disability bioethicists believe that their work will serve to educate mainstream bioethicists (and the public at large) about the circumstances of disabled people's lives, has the potential to improve the message about disability that the field of bioethics conveys to philosophers and the general public, will broaden the range of materials that bioethicists teach their students about disability, and will shift the focus of research on disability that bioethicists and other philosophers develop (e.g., Stramondo 2022; Reynolds and Wieseler 2022). Yet there is nothing necessary about the subfield of bioethics that demands that it should be reformed rather than abolished. If we can imagine a civic future for society without the police and prisons (and we must do so), then we can surely imagine a professional and intellectual future for philosophy without bioethics.

One of the misguided presuppositions that underlies the efforts of disability bioethicists is the belief according to which the field of bioethics is not itself an instrument of power, not a technology of government. Rather, disability bioethicists aim to modify and strengthen the field of bioethics by correcting and eliminating biases and discriminatory assumptions that they perceive to currently condition some contributions to it. For disability bioethicists, in other words, the governmental and eugenic character of the subfield of bioethics is an accidental feature of the enterprise rather than one of its defining characteristics and the motivation for its very existence. Disability bioethicists—like more evidently mainstream bioethicists and even feminist bioethicists—do not understand that bioethics is an expanding mechanism of the apparatus of disability and institutionalized ableism rather than merely an arena in which discrete instantiations of ableism manifest. The critical analyses of ableism *in* bioethics that disability bioethicists develop are therefore compromised along various dimensions, including that they assume a juridical conception of power in the terms of which power is repressive rather than productive, possessed rather exercised. Insofar as disability bioethicists do not appreciate that power operates primarily through coercion and productive control in constitutive and regulatory ways, they misconstrue how the relation between ableism and the subfield of bioethics should be understood, represented, resisted, and subverted; that is, disability (and feminist) bioethicists continue to frame the relation between power and the subfield of bioethics with reference to the unsavory arguments of certain bioethicists; the eugenic implications of certain practices and technologies; and the misapplication of certain normative ethical concepts (including autonomy, well-being, informed consent, and quality of life), all of which terms of reference individualize and reproduce the institutional and structural social injustices that make possible bioethics.

In *On Being Included* (2012), Sara Ahmed explains how racism is individualized in this way within institutional settings, pointing out the costs of this individualization. Ahmed writes:

> The struggle to recognize institutional racism can be understood as part of a wider struggle to recognize that all forms of power, inequality, and domination are systematic rather than individual. The critique of the psychologizing of racism made by antiracist scholars and activists over generations is thus part of the struggle to recognize institutional racism (see Hesse 2004). In other words, racism should not be seen as about individuals with bad attitudes (the "bad apple model"), not because such

> individuals do not exist (they do) but because such a way of thinking underestimates the scope and scale of racism, thus leaving us without an account of how racism *gets reproduced*. The argument can be made in even stronger terms: the very identification of racism *with* individuals becomes a technology for the reproduction of racism *of* institutions. So eliminating the racist individual would preserve the racism of the institution in part by creating an illusion that we are eliminating racism. Institutions can "keep their racism" by eliminating those whom they identify as racists. (Ahmed 2022: 44, emphasis in Ahmed)

My argument is that the eugenic impetus of bioethics conceals both its origins and its technologies of reproduction thus, that is, the repeated identification of certain bioethicists (such as Singer) as the purveyors of eugenics within bioethics should be recognized as a surreptitious technology that enables the undisrupted reproduction of eugenic ableism as a *fundamental condition of possibility for* the field of bioethics. As I have noted, disability bioethicists do not understand that the subfield of bioethics is an agent of institutionalized ableism, but rather assume that bioethics is a politically neutral arena of inquiry in which occasional instances of systemic ableism occur. These misconceptions of bioethics, that is, conceiving of bioethics as an innocuous, if not progressive, field of inquiry is crucial to the "mystique of bioethics." I use the term *mystique of bioethics* to refer to (1) the technology by which the eugenic impulse of bioethics is concealed; (2) the structural gaslighting that enables this concealment whereby the field of bioethics is cast as the domain of a distinct specialist knowledge that renders bioethicists uniquely qualified to evaluate a purportedly distinctive set of questions and concerns; and (3) the technology of this supposedly specialist knowledge whereby, through practices and strategies of mystification, which are vital to the apparatus of disability, systemic social and political problems are naturalized, individualized, and medicalized.

I concur with Michel Foucault's evocative insight that "power is tolerable only on condition that it masks a substantial part of itself. Its success is proportional to an ability to hide its own mechanisms" (Foucault 1978). Hence, I want to point out that mechanisms and technologies of the apparatus of disability covertly reconstitute and sustain these relations of power in philosophy and beyond; that is, the apparatus of disability thrives in philosophy and society more generally in large part because (1) the materialization, naturalization, and individualization of eugenic ableism in philosophy and the broader social milieu are normalized incrementally, usually with cooperation, complicity, and consent; (2) critical philosophical analyses of the incremental normalization of the apparatus of disability and ableism by and through bioethics remain institutionally marginalized, dismissed, and even discredited; and (3) philosophers of disability who articulate the most thoroughgoing challenges to this normalization and to the subdiscipline of bioethics more widely—that is, articulate critiques directed at the motivational assumptions and putative purposes of bioethics as an enterprise—are openly harassed, ridiculed, and remain excluded from stable employment in philosophy (Tremain 2017, 2019, 2021). Indeed, the profession-wide ableist contract to quash thoroughgoing external critiques of bioethics is the most consequential, entrenched, and obfuscated scandal in philosophy with respect to academic freedom.

In this chapter, I draw upon Kyle Whyte's (2020) work on epistemologies of crisis and Naomi Klein's (2007) writing about disaster capitalism to further elaborate my thesis that bioethics is a neoliberal technology of government, invoking the sixteenth-century sense of the term *government* that Foucault revived to refer to directions of conduct—"the conduct of conduct"—that is, to refer to any form of activity that aims to shape, guide, or affect the conduct of oneself or someone else (Tremain 2017: 72–3; Foucault 1982). Whyte uses the term *epistemologies of crisis* to refer to colonialist narratives and ways of knowing that characterize certain situations and states of affairs as "unprecedented" and "urgent," while obscuring histories of colonization in order to do so. Klein uses the term *disaster capitalism* to describe elements of neoliberalism that variously produce, exploit, and aggravate economic, political, environmental, and social disasters and crises in ways that expand the reach of unregulated economic markets.

My objective in the chapter is to combine both Whyte's insights about epistemologies of crisis and Klein's remarks about disaster capitalism with Foucault's approach to inquiry in ways that enable me to argue that bioethics is an instrument and mechanism of biopower's neoliberal eugenics and, ultimately, an insidious enterprise of colonial power. To wit, Singer did not create bioethics; rather, bioethics produced Singer and other seeming bioethics outliers. As Melinda Hall (2021) has pointed out, the so-called eugenics "fringe" of bioethics is actually its core. "Bioethics," Hall states, "has always been eugenic." Indeed, as an instrument and mechanism of neoliberalism, bioethics, I contend, facilitates the normalization of populations in ways that make them (more) governable, manageable, and cost-effective, that is, bioethics produces strategies and techniques that homogenize populations to maximize their productivity and the efficiency with which they can be governed.

To advance my argument that bioethics is a technology of neoliberal eugenics, I introduce the term *disaster ableism* to refer to strategies and practices that produce, exploit, and aggravate perceived and actual economic, political, environmental, and social disasters and crises in ways that further eugenic goals. As I intend to show, the strategies and practices of disaster ableism in which various Canadian bioethicists, law professors, feminist philosophers, and politicians have participated during the COVID-19 pandemic in particular throw into relief that the neoliberal eugenics agenda, which is at the heart of bioethics, is an integral component of colonialism.

The Apparatus of Disability, Naturally

I shall begin my general discussion of how bioethics furthers its eugenic goals through its contribution to the production of disaster ableism by explaining my assumptions about the metaphysical status of disability and its constitution in philosophy, especially with reference to arguments that I make in *Foucault and Feminist Philosophy of Disability* (2017). My arguments in the book identify the ways in which bioethics and various other domains of philosophy—including philosophy of mind and cognitive science, political philosophy, and feminist philosophy—serve as mechanisms for the political, social, discursive, and material constitution of the apparatus of disability and its naturalized foundation, impairment. The crux of these arguments, when taken together, is this: the conception of disability that continues to predominate in philosophy is inextricably entwined with the exclusion of disabled people from professional philosophy and the marginalization of critical philosophical work on disability from the discipline.

The conception of disability that predominates in philosophy construes disability as a philosophically uninteresting and value-neutral biological trait, that is, as a self-evidently natural and deleterious characteristic, difference, or property that some people embody or possess. Insofar as philosophers hold this naturalized and individualized conception of disability, they assume that disability is a prediscursive entity, with transhistorical and transcultural properties that medicine and science can both astutely recognize and accurately represent and to which universal bioethical and philosophical principles can be applied. Hence philosophers are, in general, genuinely surprised if asked why they overlook disability in their inquiries about, say, social ontology; for, although sex, gender, race, sexuality, and class are now generally regarded in philosophical circles as intriguing social kinds rather than dreary natural kinds, as constructed categories rather than necessary designations, disability rarely receives the compliment of critical attention from philosophers that a social constructionist thesis about it would afford.

Indeed, few philosophers think that critical examination of disability is pertinent to research and teaching in social metaphysics, as the dearth of critical philosophical work about disability on potentially relevant conference rosters, syllabi, and bibliographies amply demonstrates. Nor do philosophers appreciate the critical importance of philosophy of disability for diversification and expansion of the so-called canon of philosophy more generally, for the elaboration of new narratives in philosophy, or for changes to the homogeneous character of the profession that social justice demands. Rather, philosophers remain convinced that any philosophical attention that disability should be paid can be suitably addressed in the subfield of bioethics and cognate fields of inquiry (a position with which disability bioethicists implicitly and even explicitly agree). In these domains of inquiry, too, however, the metaphysical status of disability—that is, the prevailing philosophical understanding of disability as a universally disadvantageous natural human characteristic, attribute, or difference—remains largely unquestioned. Like ethicists, political philosophers, and social metaphysicians (among others), bioethicists typically assume that philosophical examination of disability revolves primarily around deliberation and adjudication about which ethical and political theory or principles can be most aptly "applied" to questions that pertain to this allegedly inert and disadvantageous natural circumstance.

Nevertheless, a different understanding of disability is available according to which the ontology of disability, the ontological status of disability, and the application of philosophical principles and theoretical frameworks to the phenomena of disability are performative and co-constitutive. On this understanding of disability, the ontology of disability is always already a contingent political, and hence, value-laden, state of affairs that should be historicized and relativized. Notice, then, that this understanding of disability suggests an argument according to which the distinction between theoretical philosophy and applied philosophy is both an artifact and a technology of philosophical discourse that enables the naturalization and sedimentation of contingent cultural, social, and political phenomena, including naturalization of disability and the conceptual objects that it comprises. Against the idea that disability is a natural human attribute, personal characteristic, or individuated property of certain people, I argue in the 2017 book and in other contexts (e.g., Tremain 2015, 2020, 2021) that disability should be understood as an apparatus of power in which everyone is entangled and entwined, that is, should be understood as an ensemble of discourses, institutions, scientific statements, laws, administrative measures, and so on, directed at a perceived social requirement deemed urgent in a given historical moment. The urgent requirement to which the apparatus of disability responds in this historical moment is biopolitical normalization of populations and individual subjects in order to make them cost-effective and manageable.

The apparatus of disability is, in other words, a historically specific and dispersed system of force relations that produces and configures practices toward certain strategic political ends, including the performative production and phenomenological experience of impairment as the prediscursive foundation of disability. My articulation of this expansive conception of disability as an apparatus is designed in part to subvert work done in analytic philosophy of disability that both (1) misrepresents how power circulates—casting it in wholly repressive (juridical) terms according to which power is oppositional to the exercise of liberties—and (2) remains wedded to analytic philosophy's methodological preoccupation with the "decomposition of complex phenomena into simpler constituents" (Glock 2008: 154, in Botts 2018: 56); that is, this expansive conception of disability is designed to undermine the atomistic way in which analytic philosophers (of disability) represent disability with so-called rigorous claims about individual "functions," "capacities," types of "disabilities," and levels of "severity," all of which discursive objects and the distinctions that they comprise are strategies of the apparatus of disability that serve to re-decontextualize and re-depoliticize (hence, naturalize) the artifactual phenomena of the apparatus of disability (e.g., Wasserman and Aas 2022).

In short, claims according to which disability is a personal characteristic, biological difference, or property of individuals naturalize and individualize a culturally and historically specific phenomenon, rendering disability an ahistorical and universal fact of the matter rather than a historically contingent and culturally relative apparatus of power, an artifact of force relations. Thus, an outcome of my argument in what follows is the identification of an additional context in which we can recognize that the naturalized ontological status attributed to disability and its conceptual objects is political all the way down. I offer more evidence for the argument that the prevalent understanding of what disability is—that is, the ontology of disability—does not exist apart from, nor prior to, relations of power that bring disability into being as that kind of thing. In short, the ontology of disability and indeed the ontological status of disability are mutually constitutive with and reinforce the power relations that circumscribe them. Hence, an argument for the erosion of the artifactual distinction between theoretical philosophy and applied philosophy is implicitly incorporated into the overall argument of the chapter.

As with the naturalization in philosophy of the subjecting apparatuses of race, gender, age, and sexuality, so, too, with the naturalization of disability in philosophy: the naturalization of these apparatuses in philosophy constitutes structural gaslighting. Nora Berenstain has defined *structural gaslighting* as "any conceptual work that functions to obscure the nonaccidental connections between structures of oppression and the patterns of harm that they produce and license" (Berenstain 2020: 734). As Berenstain explains it, white feminist philosophers enact structural gaslighting when they invoke epistemologies and ideologies of domination that actively and routinely disappear and obscure the actual causes, mechanisms, and effects of oppression in ways that sabotage the efforts and advancement of Black women, women of color, and other minoritized women. As technologies of structural gaslighting, the epistemologies and ontologies of domination in philosophy that persistently naturalize disability are among the historical conditions of possibility for the ongoing reconstitution of disabled people as defective, unreliable, and suboptimal, and thus not viable colleagues. These technologies of gaslighting, these epistemologies and ontologies of domination, repeatedly sabotage attempts to improve the professional situation and position of disabled philosophers and, in addition, have social, economic, and political implications for disabled people in society more broadly (Tremain 2020).

Many bioethicists and other philosophers espouse surreptitious arguments that allegedly sever this causal connection between the conception of disability that prevails in philosophy and the social and political responses whose production this conception generates. For example, although many bioethicists, ethicists, and political philosophers argue that there is a "moral duty" to practice procreative beneficence and produce the genetically "best" offspring (e.g., Savulescu 2001: 415), they adamantly deny that their assertions in this regard thereby provide rationale for authorities to limit the resources—that is, with respect to education, income, employment, housing, etc.—available to already-existing disabled people. These philosophers would therefore eschew the suggestion that their philosophical assumptions and arguments about the best children have implications for the constitution of the discipline and profession of philosophy, that is, contribute to the perpetuation of the homogeneity of philosophy and even exacerbate it. Yet these assumptions and arguments should be recognized as technologies of structural gaslighting that cover over the historical conditions of possibility for the constitution in philosophy of disabled people as defective (unreliable, suboptimal, etc.) from which this purported moral duty and the attendant economic and other inequities that accrue to disabled people derive. These sorts of arguments (this structural gaslighting) according to which there is no causal connection between the conception of disability as a natural misfortune and the inequities and injustice that disabled people confront—including the exclusion of disabled philosophers from adequate employment in philosophy—are strategic elements of the apparatus of disability.

Bioethics (De)Mystified

In "Bioethics as a Technology of Government," the fifth chapter of *Foucault and Feminist Philosophy of Disability*, I assert that bioethics emerged as a technology of government to resolve the problem that the production of disability poses for the neoliberal management of societies (Tremain 2017: 159–202). In particular, disability is constituted as a problem for a central mechanism of (neoliberal) capitalism, namely, biopower, which operates primarily through the exercise of productive forms of coercion and control to maximize the conditions conducive to "life": the life of the species and the life of the individual (Foucault

1978). Note, however, that although bioethics emerged as a technology of government to provide intellectual resources for the resolution of the problem of disability, it is simultaneously implicated in the constitution of disability (and its naturalized foundation, impairment) as a self-evident and, hence, philosophically uninteresting natural deficit and disadvantage.

Indeed, the subdiscipline of bioethics, which relies on an epistemology of domination, is an institutionalized vehicle for the biopolitics of our time, that is, the intellectual resources that bioethics provides facilitate the "strengthening" (read: fitness) of a certain population and the elimination of others. Foucault's remarks about the three major forms that technologies of government take in their development and history can serve as an apt characterization of the emergence of bioethics as a biopolitical subfield of philosophy: first, a given technology of government takes the form of a dream or utopia; then, the dream of the technology of government develops into actual practices or rules to be used in real institutions; finally, the practices and rules of the technology of government become consolidated in the form of an academic discipline (Foucault 1988: 145–62; see also Hall 2015: 166–9, 2016). In the fifth chapter of my monograph, I use Foucault's identification of biopolitical technologies of government as a model with which to trace a genealogy of the introduction and growth of the subfield of bioethics.

The representation within bioethics (and philosophy in general) of disability as an inherently disadvantageous personal characteristic and the eugenic impetus of bioethics that is co-constitutive with this representation—an impetus according to which the appropriate responses to disability are thereby prevention, cure, and elimination—contribute considerably to the antagonistic environment with which disabled philosophers must contend in philosophy, reproducing both our exclusion from the profession and the marginalization of our critical philosophical work on disability from the discipline. That is, bioethics operates as an arena of philosophy, whose guiding assumptions and discursive practices are tremendous obstacles to both acknowledgment that the questions which the apparatus of disability raises are genuinely philosophical and recognition that disabled philosophers who investigate these questions are credible philosophers and worthy colleagues. Disabled philosophers of disability thus confront a wave of epistemic injustice and ridicule if they criticize bioethics too loudly and do so in ways that contest the very consolidation and status of the subfield itself.

Bioethics is a profession unto itself, as well as an academic subfield of philosophy and other disciplines. Hence, many bioethicists are both employees of universities and paid consultants to governments, pharmaceutical companies, TV shows, hospitals, the nursing-home industry, and so on. Insofar as bioethicists are members of the bioethics profession, they are deeply attentive to the preservation and maintenance of the norms that guide this profession, including norms that—through processes of structural gaslighting and mystification—involve attribution to the profession of a distinctly unique expertise and ethical authority, policing the borders of the profession, and reinforcing it internally (Jaggar 1975). As members of the profession of bioethics, that is, a primary allegiance of bioethicists—including disability bioethicists—is to other members of the profession, in addition to the commitment of bioethicists to raise the status and prestige of the profession itself.

Both these loyalties deserve mention because one of the two co-editors of *Bioethics*, the flagship journal of the profession/subfield of bioethics—namely, Canadian bioethicist Udo Schüklenk—is the most prominent proponent of medically assisted suicide (MAiD) in Canadian philosophy, a state of affairs that significantly conditions the contents of the journal and the shape of philosophy in Canada and worldwide. In this regard, note, furthermore, that the status and prestige of the profession of bioethics have looping effects that confer recognition and expertise upon individual bioethicists themselves, improving their odds of accomplishment with respect to employment, publication, funding, and promotion, as well as improving the odds that the universities that employ them will be successful in securing corporate sponsorships, philanthropic endowments, and government grants. Thus, insofar as (disabled) philosophers identify themselves as disability bioethicists and their work on disability as bioethics, they benefit—both personally and professionally—from the status and prestige conferred upon the profession of bioethics, even though (1) their work may, in many respects, closely resemble the work of (disabled) philosophers of disability who do not benefit from these privileges and the opportunities that they afford; and (2) even though their work is likely, given professional norms of bioethics, less original and innovative than the work that philosophers of disability who do not identify as bioethicists produce.

Bioethicists are, in general, extremely protective of their lucrative profession/subfield and its interests and thus reject my critique of bioethics, dutifully fostering the mystique of the bioethics project. For example, bioethicists will not acknowledge that the expansion of their profession coincides with and enables the steadily expanding production and rationalization of biopolitical normalization and its social harms and injustices; instead, bioethicists explain the genealogy of their profession and its steady expansion in terms of discrete events—such as the decades-long involvement of medical ethicists in the Tuskegee Study—casting this expanding governmentality as the necessary antidote to disruptions in the history of an otherwise noble endeavor which strives to ensure that the methodologies and practices of biomedicine and biomedical science uphold the highest ethical standards (e.g., The Hastings Center Timeline Committee, n.d.).

The critiques of bioethics that so-called disability bioethicists and feminist bioethicists make implicitly (and, at times, explicitly) authorize the bioethics agenda by assuming the self-understandings and self-image that the profession/subfield of bioethics represents; hence, the purposes and scope of these critiques are, for the most part, limited to individualized arguments against a certain biomedical practice or technology, the arguments of a certain bioethicist, or a particular application of certain normative principles, all of which critiques are cosmetic fixes to the profession of bioethics that leave unexamined the historical conditions of possibility for the overall enterprise of bioethics and enable its internal reinforcement. In other words, the professional norms of bioethics induce disability bioethicists and feminist bioethicists to comply with the apparatus of disability and the neoliberal eugenics that impels it. For example, disability (and feminist) bioethicists have remained indifferent about the grievous arguments to promote MAiD that Schüklenk and other prominent bioethicists articulate or have defended their right to do so.

Therefore, I want to underscore that my antipathy with the subfield of bioethics constitutes a distinct departure from the reformist critiques of bioethics that disability bioethicists and feminist bioethicists produce (e.g., Stramondo 2022). For my argument is that bioethics (including disability bioethics and feminist bioethics)—as a concerted enterprise—is a neoliberal mechanism and technology of biopower whose increasing institutionalization and legitimation in the university, in the discipline of philosophy, in law, and in public policy (among other contexts) consolidate and conceal the fundamental purpose that this field of inquiry serves in biopolitical strategies of normalization and hence the government of populations and individuals. In short, the field of bioethics is a premier arena for the adjudication of biopower's governmental capacity to make live and let die, as Foucault put it; that is, bioethics is founded on the rationalization of eugenics. For example, the subfield of bioethics rationalizes the proliferation and use of biotechnologies such as prenatal testing and stem cell research and, in doing so, bioethics contributes to the constitution of impairment (among other so-called natural anomalies) through the very identification, evaluation, assessment, classification, and categorization of it, thereby enlarging the purview of the apparatus of disability and extending its reach.

Bioethics, I maintain, comprises a set of strategic discursive practices (tactics) that work in the service of normalization and the government of conduct to eliminate impairments that medical, juridical, and administrative discourses allege to discover and manage, while simultaneously enabling these discourses to enlarge the scope of the broad outlines of the category of impairment itself. As a technology of racism against the abnormal (to use Foucault's insight), bioethics is a modern form of race science. Thus, efforts to decolonize philosophy must take account of the ways in which bioethics is instrumental to the persistence of colonialism within philosophy, within the university, in medicine, in law, and in public policy (Pitts and Tremain 2022).

Robin D. G. Kelley, referencing the lessons of various disabled authors, has pointed out that disability justice embraces a framework of abolitionism, that is, "disability justice," Kelley writes, "demands nothing less than the overthrow of ableism and *all* the structures that undergird it" (Kelley 2022, emphasis in Kelley; also Mingus 2011). My argument is that in order for philosophy to advance justice for disabled people, bioethics—as a mechanism and technology of the apparatus of disability—must be abolished.

As I have pointed out, philosophers regard bioethics as the most suitable domain in philosophy for considerations about disability, as the persistent lack of job opportunities in philosophy of disability and the concurrent proliferation of jobs in bioethics and cognate fields indicate. In so-called Canada, for example, bioethicists have played a vital role in the creation of a culture of eugenics within the discipline of philosophy and in the Canadian milieu at large, both influencing the development and promulgation of legislation in Canada to expand state-sanctioned MAiD and ensuring that disabled specialists in philosophy of disability do not enter the ranks of professional philosophy in Canada. In some respects, Canada now has the most permissive euthanasia/assistive-suicide legislation in the world, thanks in no small part to Canadian bioethicists and other philosophers (Coelho 2022). The Canadian philosophical community continues to virtually exclude disabled philosophers, especially disabled philosophers of disability. These two factors are not coincidental: the legitimation of the MAiD legislation in Canada and the exclusion of disabled philosophers from Canadian philosophy are rather interwoven by the medicalized understanding of (the apparatus of) disability that is mutually constitutive of them.

In addition to the ways in which these bioethicists and philosophers influence and prop up the neoliberal eugenicist arguments of Canadian politicians, they repeatedly generate—in high-profile bioethics journals, on influential bioethics blogs, and for their impressionable bioethics classes—caricatures and sloppy renditions of the arguments against MAiD legislation that disabled Canadian philosophers and other disabled Canadian authors and their allies make. A "feature" article that Schüklenk and Canadian feminist law professor Jocelyn Downie recently published in *Journal of Medical Ethics* is an excellent example of this careless exercise of ableist power. In the article, Downie and Schüklenk (2021) purportedly substantiate—with a single citation to a 1999 article written by an American disabled author—their responses to objections from opponents of MAiD in Canada who argue that the Bill C-7 legislation and Canadian proponents of MAiD ignore the social and political circumstances out of which the legislation and arguments that support it have emerged.

Like Schüklenk, a growing number of bioethicists, both within Canada and abroad, dedicate considerable effort to the task of reconfiguring bioethics in ways that preserve their own disciplinary, professional, and institutional jurisdiction over philosophical claims about disability. Indeed, bioethicists act as gatekeepers for philosophy, shielding the profession from an influx of disabled people and guarding the discipline from the incursion of philosophy of disability. The effectiveness of this gatekeeping and adherence to it throughout the profession can be identified in (for example) a variety of diversity and inclusiveness reports compiled by nondisabled philosophers who (1) express unwarranted satisfaction with and optimism about the current situation of disabled philosophers; or (2) display skepticism about arguments that I and other disabled philosophers of disability make according to which disabled philosophers are excluded from philosophy; or (3) ignore the situation of disabled philosophers altogether.

Exceptions to this exclusion—exemplified by practitioners of disability bioethics—are admissible and serve to disguise and legitimize the subfield of bioethics, typifying the polymorphic character of neoliberalism from which bioethics has emerged and enabling philosophy to proceed under the pretense of political neutrality, objectivity, and disinterest. In other words, the allegedly transformative area of inquiry called "disability bioethics" enhances mainstream bioethics from which it appears to distinguish itself, sustaining the field of bioethics in general and enabling bioethics to enlarge its influence by refashioning itself in the practice of autocritique, that is, to co-opt critical challenges to it in order to achieve its own goals. Indeed, disability bioethics is one of the most effective strategic mechanisms of neoliberalism to emerge from the apparatus of disability and the biopolitical forms of neoliberal power that motivated it to coalesce. As Foucault pointed out in *The Birth of Biopolitics*, the simultaneity of institutional and economic expansion, on one side, and internal integration and consolidation, on the other, is a hallmark of neoliberalism (see also Klein 2007).

Philosophy of disability is, by contrast, a categorically insurgent discourse that neither intersects with bioethics nor is derivative of it. While disability bioethicists jockey for a seat at the table of bioethical discussions, philosophers of disability want to overturn the table. Hence, budding philosophers of disability should conceive their work as oppositional to bioethics and as a form of resistance to its eugenic impetus and medicalizing gaze, both of which phenomena increasingly implicate philosophy in the government of disabled people's lives while purportedly illuminating and informing their putatively self-actualizing choices. Philosophy of disability, among its other pursuits, is motivated to identify the intellectual materials and practices that consolidate the field of bioethics, are produced by it, and enable it to foster popular acceptance of eugenic normalization in certain contexts, to achieve certain aims. For example, philosophy of disability tracks how the consolidation of the field of bioethics has been enabled by and is sustained through the neoliberal touchstones of autonomy (construed as self-governance) and freedom (construed as individual choice), that is, how bioethics both legitimizes and is grounded in neoliberal assumptions about freedom and autonomy that operate by influencing, shaping, and limiting the actions of subjects in accordance with their capacity to choose from a highly circumscribed set of possible actions.

Insofar as bioethics is an instrument and mechanism of neoliberalism, which aims to normalize populations in ways that make them cost-effective and governable, an understanding of the operations of neoliberalism, in a broader sense, can help us identify and understand the power relations that animate bioethics and enable the proliferation of its governmental strategies. If we wish to learn how the episteme of neoliberalism produces values, norms, and practices that capitalize on disasters and crises, we should look to the analysis that Klein develops in her landmark 2007 book, *The Shock Doctrine: The Rise of Disaster Capitalism*.

Disastrous Ableism

In *The Shock Doctrine*, Klein sets out to show how capitalism variously produces and exploits disasters and crises in order to drastically change economies and governments. Klein's goal is to demonstrate that the detrimental impact on disenfranchised and other subordinated social groups of these economic and political swings is both foreseeable and disregarded, if not their desideratum. For Klein, the wizard of this social movement was Chicago-school economist Milton Friedman. It was Friedman who wrote the instruction manual for the contemporary global capitalist economy whose mobility steadily outstrips geopolitical borders through policies of deregulation and a race to the bottom with respect to workers' wages and other benefits. For example, as Klein explains, Friedman used Hurricane Katrina and the flooding of New Orleans in 2005 to facilitate privatization of the city's public education system, a far-reaching policy change that was among the disastrous consequences of Hurricane Katrina that disproportionately affected the city's Black residents. As Harsha Walia has stated, Hurricane Katrina laid bare "the workings of anti-Black warfare through mass displacement and carceral immobility": "Black homes were most vulnerable to the storm, Black people were criminalized during the storm, and Black neighborhoods were abandoned by recovery efforts after the storm" (Walia 2021: 32). Seventy-three percent of the 800,000 people dislocated due to Hurricane Katrina, Walia notes, were Black residents whose neighborhoods became policed and in turn privatized, leaving most of these people permanently displaced.

Three months after the levees broke, Friedman published an op-ed in *The Wall Street Journal* that hailed these consequences of Hurricane Katrina as an occasion to usher in public policy that would further the interests of free-market capitalism (Klein 2007: 5). As Friedman put it at the time: "Most New Orleans schools are in ruins . . . as are the homes of the children who have attended them. The children are now scattered all over the country. This is a tragedy. It is also an opportunity to radically reform the educational system" (Friedman, in Klein 2007: 5). Friedman's "radical" idea (which received financial backing from the George W. Bush administration) was that the American government should distribute vouchers to families that they could in turn spend at state-subsidized, private institutions—"charter schools," as they are called—most of which are run for profit. As Klein points out, many African Americans, especially in New Orleans, regard these charter schools as means to reverse the gains with respect to education that the US civil rights movement made. Yet Friedman emphasized that this elemental change in the way that education in the United States is financed should be regarded as a "permanent reform" rather than merely a temporary, stopgap measure. For Friedman, Klein explains, the idea that the state would run the school system "reeked of socialism" (Klein 2007: 5). In Friedman's right-libertarian view, the sole functions of the state were, in his words, "to protect our freedom both from the enemies outside our gates and from our fellow-citizens: to preserve law and order, to enforce contracts, to foster competitive markets" (Friedman, in Klein 2007: 5). A minimalist government, Friedman had instructed, should guide recovery efforts that followed the storm.

Less than two years after the levees were breached, privately run charter schools had almost entirely replaced the New Orleans public school system, the contract with the New Orleans teacher's union had effectively been torn to pieces, and the union's 4,700 members had been fired. For Klein, this dismantling of the New Orleans public school system post-Katrina exemplifies "disaster capitalism," which she defines as "orchestrated raids on the public sphere in the wake of catastrophic events, combined with the treatment of disasters as exciting market opportunities" (Klein 2007: 6). In this regard, Klein points to Friedman's influential essay in which he articulated the core tenet of disaster capitalism thus: "only a crisis—actual or perceived—produces real change. When that crisis occurs, the actions that are taken depend on the ideas that are lying around. That, I believe, is our basic function: to develop alternatives to existing policies, to keep them alive and available until the politically impossible becomes politically inevitable" (Friedman, in Klein 2007: 5).

This "shock doctrine," as Klein refers to Friedman's dictum, has been instrumental to the expansion of free-market capitalism globally and the neoliberal shakedown of elected socialist governments throughout Central and South America; union busting in the United States; betrayal of solidarity in Poland; ideological pillaging of the African National Congress in South Africa; and installation, the world over, of autocracies and other fascist regimes sympathetic to unfettered capitalism. It is especially pertinent to my argument that Klein eloquently shows how disaster capitalism exploits disasters and crises to mold social values, norms, expectations, and explanations in ways that promote neoliberal social and political agendas among academics, the media, NGOs (nongovernmental organizations), and populations at large, in addition to how it exploits these events to profoundly change governments and economies themselves.

I contend that all levels of government in so-called Canada, as well as various academics, journalists, think tanks, corporations, and foundations, have seized upon the COVID-19 pandemic as an opportune occasion to engage in (what I call) "disaster ableism," that is, have exploited the pandemic and the circumstances that surround it to cultivate norms, values, and beliefs that promote ableist agendas and eugenic goals, further constraining and containing disabled people in Canada. In particular, the Trudeau Liberal government and the bioethicists to whom Canadian politicians regularly defer and appeal have employed disaster ableism to usher into law legislation—namely, Bill C-7—that both significantly expands and more deeply embeds eugenics in Canadian society.

In the midst of a global pandemic, when the residents of Canada were losing their loved ones, their dwellings, and their incomes due to COVID-19; were living in situations of fear, misinformation, and confusion; and were distracted and isolated, the Canadian federal government bypassed adequate public consultation, usurped international treaties, ignored the objections of Indigenous leaders, manipulated parliamentary procedure, and made a mockery of disabled experts invited to participate in its legislative proceedings in order to ensure passage of Bill C-7, legislation that would make sweeping changes to existing Canadian laws on medically assisted suicide. In short, the same (neo)liberal government which, throughout the pandemic, has consistently failed to provide financial and other social supports to disabled people—allowing thousands of them to die from COVID-19 and neglect in nursing homes and other carceral institutions in which disabled people are confined—adopted a pernicious way to (in the words of Friedman) "permanently reform" distribution to disabled people, namely, by providing them with easier access to premature death rather than by providing them with the means to live their lives (Tremain 2021).

During the last months of 2020, I began to write blogposts about MAiD and Bill C-7 at the philosophy blog that I coordinate—BIOPOLITICAL PHILOSOPHY—to inform its international readership about these events in Canada and to explain the links between the events, the disproportionate influence of bioethics in Canadian philosophy, and the eugenic culture in Canadian philosophy that this sway has produced. Early in 2021, furthermore, I conjoined this public philosophy with the resistance of other disabled academics, activists, and policy researchers across Canada. We were loud and persistent, determined to demonstrate how neoliberal arguments about informed consent, personal autonomy, and quality of life with respect to medically assisted suicide for disabled people—and only disabled people—obscure and reinforce the apparatuses of disability, ableism, racism, colonialism, and classism that produced these arguments in the first place.

My blogposts about Bill C-7, in particular, and MAiD, more generally, have met with condescension and derision from bioethicists such as Schüklenk and the editors of *The International Journal of Feminist Approaches to Bioethics* (*IJFAB*), the latter of whom evidently think that bioethics journals should enjoy liberties that are not afforded to philosophy blogs. In a set of hostile interventions, the *IJFAB* editors variously accused me of violating their academic freedom because, in one blogpost in early 2021, I wrote that the journal had implicitly promoted medically assisted suicide by publishing an invited article on the topic authored by Downie, the most zealous proponent of MAiD in Canada. Three of the *IJFAB* editors (one of whom identifies as a disability bioethicist) badgered me on a Facebook post that I shared and persistently demanded that I remove the blogpost or retract the remarks that I had made about the journal. In the course of doing so, the editors inadvertently revealed the rudimentary and outdated nature of their familiarity with arguments advanced to oppose MAiD legislation and MAiD legislation in the Canadian context in particular; they displayed the extent to which their views about academic freedom were misconstrued; and they relied on (neo)liberal and juridical assumptions about power, discourse, and language in order to do so.

The accusations and demands that the *IJFAB* editors made evinced clear examples of *ableist exceptionism*, which is the term that I have coined to refer to the phenomenon whereby disability is uniquely excluded from the production and application of certain values, beliefs, principles, practices, and actions that circulate in political consciousness (Tremain 2017: 28, 33). In the comments on my Facebook post, that is, the editors jointly and separately invoked the "use-mention distinction" to justify their remarks according to which the publication of Downie's invited article in a special issue of *IJFAB* did not signal endorsement of Downie's position on MAiD. When, in response to their invocation of this distinction, I repeatedly asked—jointly and separately—these journal editors whether they would invite an article from Stock on trans women, they collectively and individually ignored my questioning. In other words, the editors refused to acknowledge the ableist exceptionism and value-laden character of their appeals to the use-mention distinction. Hence, I reminded them that (following Foucault and Jacques Derrida) any description was a prescription for the formulation of a given object, subject, and situation to which it seems to innocently refer. As the social and political ramifications and potentially traumatizing personal consequences of a white person's "mention" of the N-word demonstrate (e.g., CBC News 2020), appeals to the allegedly value-neutral use-mention distinction should not be regarded as uncontestably illuminating, compelling, or disinterested. On the contrary, the distinction can incite structural violence and constitute justification for the continued circulation of harmful discursive practices, as well as extend these practices in additional ways.

Indeed, when it became evident to the *IJFAB* editors that I tacitly refused to comply with their demands to delete the blogpost in question, one of them (Scully 2021) wrote a post on *IJFAB*'s own blog entitled, "MAiD and IJFAB: Why Bioethical Discourse Is Not Endorsement." The blogpost invoked the fiction that bioethics is a neutral and objective academic activity that the journal allegedly upholds, pointing out as evidence of this supposedly objective, neutral stance that more than a decade earlier the journal had published an article that questioned the ethics of medically assisted suicide. In addition, the blogpost accused me of failing to respect both the journal's publishing policy and academic freedom insofar as I refused to retract my indisputably publishable remarks. Subsequently, the *IJFAB* editors circulated a Call for Expressions of Interest (CEI) that solicited submissions to an *IJFAB* special issue on academic freedom that linked to the BIOPOLITICAL PHILOSOPHY post in question, explicitly reprimanded me, charged that I had attacked the journal, and referred to my blogpost as the motivation for the special issue. Tellingly, furthermore, *IJFAB*, in issuing this CEI, followed the example of the right-wing libertarian, *Journal of Controversial Ideas*, by advising prospective authors that for the purposes of the special issue on academic freedom, they would be permitted to publish their putatively transgressive ideas anonymously to avoid the sort of recrimination that I had displayed.

In short, the *IJFAB* editors seemed both confused about the position on academic freedom that they had endorsed and notably uninformed about the politically perspicacious arguments that disabled Canadians put forward in opposition to Bill C-7 and MAiD. That these (non-Canadian) feminist bioethicists would harass a Canadian disabled feminist philosopher of disability for her work on the increasing expansion and normalization of euthanasia and medically assisted suicide in Canada, as well as charge that her criticisms in this regard infringe upon their academic freedom, may seem surprising, especially given the grievous underrepresentation of disabled philosophers and disabled philosophers of disability, in particular, in Canadian philosophy and the profession of philosophy more generally. Nevertheless, I maintain that their actions are unsurprising given the strategic purpose that the execution of this exclusion plays in the growing influence of bioethics (including feminist bioethics) in academia, public policy, and social discourse more widely.

Recall that the professional norms of bioethics induce bioethicists to give a certain pride of place both to each other as members of the bioethics profession and to the institutional, political, and social status and prestige of the profession itself. The unwillingness of feminist and disability bioethicists to criticize Downie's and Schüklenk's respective roles in the expansion of MAiD and their implicit endorsement and promotion of Downie's and Schüklenk's claims in this regard are surely due in part to the weight of these professional norms and the complicity among bioethicists that these norms induce. These professional norms and the complicity that they induce have, furthermore, been reaffirmed with the publication of a chapter on MAiD that Downie contributed to *The Routledge Handbook of Feminist Bioethics* (Rogers et al. 2022), one of whose editors is a co-editor of *IJFAB*.

Canadian bioethicists, law professors, politicians, and some very privileged white disabled people maintain that Bill C-7 promises greater equality for disabled people by further enshrining their rights to autonomy and self-determination; however, poor, racialized, Indigenous, trans, and queer disabled people recognize that Bill C-7 constitutes a threat to their collective existence, in addition to the threats that the legislation poses to their personal safety, sense of security, sense of belonging, and self-respect. While Canadian bioethicists, law professors, and politicians have elicited pathos from the Canadian public with poignant speeches about disabled people who require immediate deliverance from the suffering that their lives would impose if Bill C-7 were not passed, disabled activists, academics, policy researchers, and their allies have pointed out that poverty; structural ableism and racism; lack of affordable, accessible housing; and settler colonialism are among the factors that constitute unlivable lives for disabled people in so-called Canada. Insofar as philosophers disregard the expertise of these disabled critics of MAiD—including the expertise of disabled philosophers of disability who critique MAiD—they engage in an especially duplicitous form of epistemic oppression that runs counter to established and emerging feminist and other social epistemologies, serving to reinstate elitist divisions between academics and society at large.

Through medicalization and individualization, bioethics promotes euthanasia/medically assisted suicide by mystifying the socio-discursive and biopolitical origins of the contingent circumstances that surround the enactment of this dreadful intervention, reconfiguring these circumstances to seem as if they require the specialized knowledge that bioethicists are claimed to possess. Although Canadian bioethicists, law professors, and politicians tendentiously assert that Bill C-7 was a unique corrective to past legislative mistakes and, in addition, that arguments to the contrary amount to fallacious "slippery-slope" reasoning, opponents of MAiD adamantly argue that Bill C-7 is of a piece with a long and treacherous history of eugenic policies and practices in Canada—such as forced sterilization and confinement—targeted at disabled people and Indigenous people (among others) that the incremental normalization of the policies and practices depoliticizes and erases (Tremain 2017: 175–7, 2021). Indeed, this preoccupation with supposed errors in the "logical structure" of objections to MAiD is a surreptitious distraction from the eugenic character of the procedure that has enabled bioethicists and other philosophers to repeatedly divert attention away from normalization of the procedure, while continuing to employ outdated notions of social power within which to frame this normalization. In short, the critiques of medically assisted suicide that Downie and Schüklenk (among others) associate with the fallacy of slippery-slope reasoning and thus categorically dismiss are, rather, astute assessments of the incremental normalization of force relations under neoliberalism.

Proponents of medically assisted suicide who charge that disabled activists and authors commit this fallacy (over)confidently argue that the normalization of MAiD about which its critics are concerned can be prevented if the appropriate regulations and safeguards are put in place to ensure that people do not feel coerced to choose this option in response to their respective personal circumstances (see Downie and Sherwin 1996; Tremain 2017). As disabled experts on the legislation have consistently pointed out, however, the enshrinement of Bill C-7 itself constitutes the removal of "safeguards" instituted through previous Canadian legislation on assisted suicide and is precisely one of the ways in which the procedure continues to be stealthily normalized incrementally. The use of the term *safeguards* in the context of this legislation is indeed (1) false reassurance that the MAiD procedure is performed as a last resort after diligent reservation; (2) implicit (and inadvertent) admission that the procedure is, in the first instance, epistemically specious and ethically egregious; and thus (3) a self-referential smokescreen. On a number of occasions, disabled policy researcher and analyst Gabrielle Peters has remarked that the removal of so-called safeguards was clandestinely part of the MAiD plan in Canada all along rather than a corrective afterthought, as Downie, Schüklenk, and other Canadian proponents of expansion of the practice claim. As Peters has put it, "[MAiD] was never meant just for end of life. . . . That was merely their foot in the door" (Peters 2022).

The charge of fallacious slippery-slope reasoning, which Downie, Schüklenk, and other proponents of medically assisted suicide routinely level at critics of the practice, relies on an outdated juridical conception of power that has conditioned Western philosophy. As Foucault pointed out, juridical conceptions of power, which construe it as repressive, as centralized, and as an entity that subtracts from the subject's autonomy and agency, misapprehend the productive and diffuse character of relatively recent forms of subjecting power that operate primarily through the government of subjects and strategic positing of their autonomy, enabling them to act in order to constrain and control them. Hence Downie, Schüklenk, and other proponents of MAiD continue to argue that people who are given the procedure have "freely" chosen it, even as an alarming number of reports appear in the Canadian mainstream press and on social media according to which a given disabled person has opted for MAiD because they (for example) were unable to secure chemical-free, affordable, and accessible housing; could no longer bear to live in an institution; believed that their premature death and subsequent donation of their organs would give their life meaning; or believed that ending their life with MAiD was preferable to continuing it amid grinding poverty.

These proponents of Bill C-7 and of MAiD more generally repeatedly refuse to acknowledge (or, perhaps, to recognize) the productive and coercive elements of the MAiD apparatus for marginalized and vulnerabilized communities but rather are committed to representing these examples of coerced suicide as exceptional cases that can be dismissed or ignored. Insofar as these proponents of medically assisted suicide conceive of power, freedom, and autonomy in terms of negative liberty, they obscure the successful normalization of neoliberal relations of power by and through the effective inculcation and utilization of a relatively recent kind of subjectivity, namely, the self-determining and self-governing individual who is enabled to act in accordance with a narrowly circumscribed set of possible actions. For modern relations of power have already conspired to put in place the options from which one may "autonomously" choose. In other contexts, I have argued that the idea of reproductive autonomy, too, operates in the service of neoliberal governmentality and contributes to the production of liberal subjects in this way (Tremain 2006).

In other words, the charge according to which critics of MAiD invoke fallacious slippery-slope reasoning relies on outmoded ideas about the self-originating character of the neoliberal subject's freedom and autonomy that are integral to this juridical conception of power. Generally speaking, the charge results from the intransigent refusal of these advocates of MAiD to acknowledge that the arguments of their critics address the constitutive nature of force relations under neoliberal governmentality, which includes the constitution of neoliberal subjects whose management and modification of their biological life, through exercise of their supposedly prediscursive autonomy and freedom, is fundamental to their notions of self-hood and responsible citizenship (see Tremain 2017; Pitts-Taylor 2010). In short, the autonomous, informed, and consenting individual in whose name biopolitical arguments that promote MAiD are advanced is a historically and culturally specific artifact of discourse rather than a prediscursive being/self endowed with intrinsic liberties and freedoms. That is to say, the self-determining citizen/patient that neoliberal bioethics upholds and claims to dignify through Bill C-7 in particular and medically assisted suicide more generally has a history, and a relatively recent and culturally specific history at that.

The arguments that feminist proponents of MAiD endorse (and promote) tend to explicitly rely on assumptions about the value of care and compassion rather than convictions about self-determination and individual autonomy, though most of these feminist proponents of the practice (in particular, Downie) are inconsistent and equivocal in this regard. Furthermore, the very powerful lobby group Dying With Dignity Canada, which carries inordinate influence with Canadian politicians and bioethicists, identifies compassion as one of its three core values, along with collaboration and courage, the latter of which—especially when taken together with the organization's motto "It's Your Life, It's Your Choice"—reveals how the group is wedded to the neoliberal values and ideals of a Randist rugged individualism (Dying With Dignity Canada 2022).

As Lauren Berlant has pointed out, compassion is not a clear and simple human emotion, as it is typically taken to be. Indeed, Berlant states that "there is nothing simple about compassion apart from the desire for it to be taken as simple, as a true expression of human attachment and recognition" (Berlant 2004: 7). As Berlant writes:

> [T]he aesthetics of compassion—the cultivation of the senses toward a more nuanced and capacious engagement with scenes of human activity—opens a hornet's nest of problems about what responses should be desired and when private responses are not only insufficient but a part of the practice of injustice. Compassion turns out not to be so effective or a good in itself. It turns out merely to describe a particular kind of social relation. . . . Indeed, it would be possible to make an argument about the image of the human the compassion archive provides for us that could bring down on our heads the whole project of feeling committed to compassion. (Berlant 2004: 9)

Compassion, Berlant explains, implies an asymmetrical social relation between a spectator and a sufferer that privileges the spectator's experience of feeling compassion and attendant (neoliberal) policies which thereby "relocate the template of justice from the collective condition of specific populations to that of the individual" (Berlant 2004: 2). Thus, Berlant rhetorically asks: "What is the relation between becoming capaciously compassionate and becoming distant from responsibility for what one experiences directly and indirectly about the populations relegated to social negativity?" (10). In a genealogical account of the vicissitudes of the term *compassion*, Marjorie Garber supplies a response to Berlant's question by noting how, in the expression of compassion, pleasure and pain intermingle: "the pain of someone else provides an access of pleasure for the compassionate one" (Garber 2004: 20). In this regard, Berlant observes, furthermore, that

> In the liberal society that sanctions individuality as sovereign, we like our positive emotions to feel well intentioned and we like our good intentions to constitute the meaning of our acts. We do not like to hear that our good intentions can sometimes be said to be aggressive, although anyone versed in, say, the history of love or imperialism knows volumes about the ways in which genuinely good intentions have involved forms of ordinary terror (think about missionary education) and control (think of state military, carceral, and police practices). (Berlant 2004: 5)

Sentiments of compassion, although they may seem undeniably natural and intuitive, derive from a particular social training, emerge in particular historical moments, and are shaped by certain aesthetic conventions, none of which is universal, uncontestable, or unmotivated (Berlant 2004: 7).

Presenting Eugenics

The arguments that bioethicists, law professors, and politicians advance about Bill C-7, in particular, and the expansion of medically assisted suicide, in general, are typical of the colonialist presentism that, as Whyte notes, is a characteristic feature of epistemologies of crisis. Recall that Whyte uses the term *epistemologies of crisis* to refer to colonialist narratives and ways of knowing that characterize certain situations and states of affairs as "unprecedented" and "urgent," ignoring histories of colonization and traditional teachings of Indigenous communities to do so. Historically, Whyte states, crises have often been used as both a justification for colonization and a tool with which to obfuscate it. Sometimes, Whyte notes, perpetrators of colonialism imagine that their wrongful practices and actions are defensible because the practices and actions are responses to a given crisis, whether perceived or actual, that is, the perpetrators assume that suspension of certain concerns about justice and morality is justified in response to a crisis. To illustrate this assertion, Whyte offers as an example the way that Americans in the first half of the twentieth century constructed dams that flooded the Seneca and Lakota peoples because they believed that the United States needed energy and irrigation to lessen the threat of the Soviet Union during the Cold War (Whyte 2020: 52).

Thus, Whyte points out that although settlers tend to characterize the current situation with respect to climate change as "unprecedented," "Indigenous peoples of Turtle Island have already passed through human-caused ecological catastrophe at least once in their history" (Whyte 2020: 52). For Indigenous peoples, Whyte remarks, "the current climate change ordeal is bad, but not unprecedented" (Whyte 2019). In this regard, Whyte points to the work of Candis Callison who, in reference to Indigenous peoples in the Arctic, suggests that settler analyses of climate change that characterize the current situation as unprecedented fail to recognize what "climate change portends for those who have endured a century of immense cultural, political, and environmental changes" (Callison 2014: 5, in Whyte 2019). No American or Canadian settler, Whyte states, has offered "an imagined projection of a climate future that is more ecologically dire than what Indigenous peoples have already endured due to colonialism" (Whyte 2019). Indeed, settler analyses of climate change rarely make the connections between climate change, ecological destruction, and settler colonialism. Yet, as Whyte explains, "the infliction of harmful environmental changes on Indigenous peoples" has been an integral part of settler colonialism in the United States (Whyte 2019). Hence, Whyte remarks that settler colonialism must be understood as inextricably entwined with climate change and responded to as such. Whyte is concerned to point out, furthermore, that the belief according to which such acts of colonial oppression are allegedly defensible due to crises is not a relic of the distant past but rather occurs now too. As Whyte puts it,

> Today, people perpetrate colonialism in the name of responding to environmental crises—*climate change* being one prominent case. Responses to scientifically understand and mitigate climate change can harm or threaten Indigenous peoples. From scientific reports that provincialise Indigenous knowledge systems to wind power projects that desecrate Indigenous lands, there is no reason to believe that colonialism today is something other than an evolved practice of a familiar form of power. (Whyte 2020: 52, emphasis in Whyte)

By focusing on climate change, in particular, and environmental destruction, in general, Whyte has elaborated the practices of knowing that enable an understanding of how and why crises are used to mask colonial power. Epistemologies of crisis, Whyte states, involve "knowing the world such that a certain present is experienced as new" (Whyte 2020: 53). As Whyte explains,

> A crisis epistemology, in the context of settler colonialism, might look something like this. A crisis is believed to be happening, whether real, genuine, or perceived. The crisis may be articulated as related to many problems, including health, economic well-being, environmental sustainability, cultural integrity, and religious salvation. But what makes some state of affairs of the world *crisis*-oriented is the automatic assumption of imminence. By imminence, I mean the sense that something horribly harmful or inequitable is impending or pressing on the present conditions people understand themselves to be living in. There is a complexity or originality to the imminent events which suggests the need to immediately become solutions-oriented in a way believed to

> differ from how solutions were designed and enacted previously. (Whyte 2020: 52, emphasis in Whyte)

In other words, crisis epistemologies are "presentist" in their narrative orientation. A narrative is presentist, Whyte explains, if it assumes a certain conception of the unfolding of time as means to achieve power or protect privilege. Presentist orientations favor experiences of time that presume unprecedentedness and urgency; that is, presentism is an exercise of colonial power that effaces the historical realities and conditions of this colonial power. "For Indigenous peoples," Whyte states, "it's by no means a new notion that human societies can inflict ecological catastrophe on one another" (Whyte 2019). As Whyte points out, furthermore, Indigenous Studies scholars have given considerable attention to the temporal assumptions on which settler colonial power relies, critically exposing the liberal assumptions about the primacy of individual autonomy and the settler state that are embedded in national origin stories (Whyte 2020: 53). Whyte refers, for example, to Audra Simpson, who, noting that the "settler colonial present" is one of "purported newness," writes that the settler colonial present is "revealed as the fiction of the presumed neutrality of time itself, demonstrating the dominance of the present by some over others, and the unequal power to define what matters, who matters, what pasts are alive and when they die" (Simpson 2017: 21, in Whyte 2020: 54–5). In this way, Whyte notes, one becomes so preoccupied with the present crisis as new that one questions neither one's own perspective nor the social origins from which the perspective may derive (Whyte 2020: 55). The sense of imminence that accompanies presentism, Whyte says, leads people to obscure or minimize how their actions relate to the persistence of colonialism, capitalism, ableism, racism, and other forms of power (57).

I maintain that the events, justifications, and rationale surrounding the creation and passage of Bill C-7 have been framed within a presentist eugenic narrative of utilitarianism that erases the histories of genocide in Canada. Indeed, the epistemic bases of utilitarianism constitute the quintessential epistemology of crisis. By framing Bill C-7 as a unique and urgent new procedural corrective, Canadian bioethicists, law professors, journalists, and politicians have, again, reconfigured and obfuscated the incremental normalization of eugenic practices in precisely the way that Whyte describes, that is, according to the presentist orientation of an epistemology of crisis that disregards the genesis and evolution of these practices. In other words, the incremental normalization of eugenic bioethical practices and the apparatus of disability from which this strategic presentist mechanism derives have their origins in colonialism and the (white) liberal settler state. In the context of MAiD, the presentist orientation that is characteristic of utilitarian bioethicists and the subfield of bioethics in general implicitly constructs the notions of personal autonomy and quality of life as existing outside of any temporal location, as ahistorical, as timeless, and as universal. In so doing, this presentist orientation conceals the historically contingent and culturally specific character of these politically motivated ideals, as well as the way that these artifacts emerged from and reproduce the (neo)liberal settler state itself.

Epilogue

The geopolitical mobility of neoliberalism and incremental normalization of neoliberal settler eugenics that is facilitated through the production of bioethics are aptly captured in a 2022 article by Nancy Berlinger, research fellow at The Hastings Center, an influential bioethics think tank in the United States with which a number of feminist bioethicists and disability bioethicists have formal and informal ties. As the title of the article—"MAiD Without Borders? Oregon Drops the Residency Requirement"—suggests, the article, which incorporates well-worn arguments about care and compassion with respect to medically assisted suicide and euthanasia, constitutes a sustained rationalization for the provision of MAiD within the US state of Oregon to people who are not residents of the state itself, a previously proscribed practice whose enshrinement in law enlarges the number of disabled people that this mechanism of settler (neo) eugenics will now discipline and govern in a conclusive way.

References

Ahmed, Sara (2012), *On Being Included*, Durham and London: Duke University Press.

Berenstain, Nora (2020), "White Feminist Gaslighting," *Hypatia: A Journal of Feminist Philosophy* 35 (4): 733–58.

Berlant, Lauren (2004), "Introduction. Compassion (and Withholding)," in Lauren Berlant (ed.), *Compassion: The Culture and Politics of an Emotion*, 1–13, New York and London: Routledge.

Berlinger, Nancy (2022), "MAiD Without Borders? Oregon Drops the Residency Requirement," Bioethics Forum Essay, The Hastings Center (blog), April 1. Available at: https://www.thehastingscenter.org/medical-aid-in-dying/ (accessed June 19, 2023).

Botts, Tina Fernandes (2018), "Race and Method: The Tuvel Affair," *Philosophy Today* 62 (1): 51–72. https://doi.org/10.5840/philtoday201828195.

Callison, Candis (2014), *How Climate Change Comes to Matter: The Communal Life of Facts*, Raleigh and Durham: Duke University Press.

CBC News (2020), "Black CBC Journalist Present When Wendy Mesley Used the N-Word Says Her Presence Prompted Disciplinary Action," *CBC News*, June 26. Available at: https://www.cbc.ca/news/canada/wendy-mesley-weekly-imani-walker-1.5629414 (accessed June 19, 2023).

Coelho, Ramona (2022), "Medical Assistance in Dying Overused in Canada Even Before Its Expansion," *The London Free Press*, July 9. Available at: https://lfpress.com/opinion/columnists/coelho-medical-assistance-in-dying-overused-in-canada-even-before-expansion (accessed June 19, 2023).

Downie, Jocelyn and Udo Schüklenk (2021), "Social Determinants of Health and Slippery Slopes in Assisted-Dying Debates in Canada," *Journal of Medical Ethics* 47 (10). Available at: https://jme.bmj.com/content/47/10/662 (accessed June 19, 2023).
Downie, Jocelyn and Susan Sherwin (1996), "A Feminist Exploration of Issues Around Assisted Death," *St. Louis University Public Law Review* 15 (2): 303–30.
Dying With Dignity Canada (2022), "About Us." Available at: https://www.dyingwithdignity.ca/about-us/ (accessed June 19, 2023).
Foucault, Michel (1978), *The History of Sexuality*. Vol. 1, *An Introduction*, trans. Robert Hurley, New York: Vintage Books.
Foucault, Michel (1982), "The Subject and Power," in Hubert L. Dreyfus and Paul Rabinow (eds.), Appended to *Michel Foucault: Beyond Structuralism and Hermeneutics*, 2nd ed., 208–26, Chicago: University of Chicago Press.
Foucault, Michel (1988), *Technologies of the Self: A Seminar with Michel Foucault*, ed. Luther H. Martin, Huck Gutman, and Patrick H. Hutton, Amherst: University of Massachusetts Press.
Garber, Marjorie (2004), "Compassion," in Lauren Berlant (ed.), *Compassion: The Culture and Politics of An Emotion*, 15–27, New York and London: Routledge.
Glock, Hans-Johann (2008), *What Is Analytic Philosophy?* Cambridge: Cambridge University Press.
Hall, Melinda (2015), "Continental Approaches in Bioethics," *Philosophy Compass* 10 (3): 161–72. https://doi.org/10.1111/phc3.12202.
Hall, Melinda (2016), *The Bioethics of Enhancement: Transhumanism, Disability, Bioethics*, Lanham: Rowman and Littlefield.
Hall, Melinda (2021), "Bioethics Has Always Been Eugenic," BIOPOLITICAL PHILOSOPHY (blog), June 4. Available at: https://biopoliticalphilosophy.com/2021/06/04/bioethics-has-always-been-eugenic/ (accessed June 19, 2023).
Hastings Center Bioethics Timeline Committee, The (n.d.), "The Hastings Center Bioethics Timeline," The Hastings Center (blog). Available at: https://www.thehastingscenter.org/bioethics-timeline/ (accessed June 19, 2023).
Hesse, Barnor (2004), "Discourse on Institutional Racism: The Genealogy of a Concept," in Ian Law, Deborah Phillips, and Laura Turney (eds.), *Institutional Racism in Higher Education*, 131–48, Stoke on Trent: Trentham.
Jaggar, Alison (1975), "Philosophy as a Profession," *Metaphilosophy* 6 (1): 100–16.
Kelley, Robin D. G. (2022), "Twenty Years of *Freedom Dreams*," *Boston Review*, August 1. Available at: https://www.bostonreview.net/articles/twenty-years-of-freedom-dreams/ (accessed June 19, 2023).
Klein, Naomi (2007), *The Shock Doctrine: The Rise of Disaster Capitalism*, Toronto: Random House of Canada.
Mingus, Mia (2011), "Changing the Framework," Leaving Evidence (blog). Available at: https://leavingevidence.wordpress.com/2011/02/12/changing-the-framework-disability-justice/ (accessed June 19, 2023).
Peters, Gabrielle (2022), "Comment on Twitter," July 13. Available at: https://t.co/sSctvvFDWM (accessed June 19, 2023).
Pitts, Andrea J. with Shelley Lynn Tremain (2022), "Dialogues on Disability: Shelley Tremain Interviews Andrea Pitts," BIOPOLITICAL PHILOSOPHY (blog). Available at: https://biopoliticalphilosophy.com/2022/05/18/dialogues-on-disability-shelley-tremain-interviews-andrea-pitts/ (accessed June 19, 2023).
Pitts-Taylor, Victoria (2010), "The Plastic Brain: Neoliberalism and the Neuronal Self," *Health* 14 (6): 635–52.

Reynolds, Joel Michael and Christine Wieseler, eds. (2022), *The Disability Bioethics Reader*, New York and London: Routledge.
Rogers, Wendy A., Jackie Leach Scully, Stacy M. Carter, Vikki A. Entwistle, and Catherine Mills, eds. (2022), *The Routledge Handbook of Feminist Bioethics*, Abingdon: Routledge.
Savulescu, Julian (2001), "Procreative Beneficence: Why We Should Select the Best Children," *Bioethics* 15 (5–6): 413–26.
Scully, Jackie Leach (2021), "MAiD and IJFAB: Why Bioethical Discourse Is Not Endorsement," *IJFAB: THE BLOG*, February 11. Available at: http://www.ijfab.org/blog/2021/02/maid-and-ijfab-why-bioethical-discourse-is-not-endorsement/ (accessed June 19, 2023).
Simpson, Audra (2017), "The Ruse of Consent and the Anatomy of 'Refusal': Cases from Indigenous North America and Australia," *Postcolonial Studies* 20: 18–33.
Stramondo, Joseph A. (2022), "How Disability Activism Advances Disability Bioethics," *Ethical Theory and Moral Practice* 25: 335–49.
Tremain, Shelley Lynn (2006), "Reproductive Freedom, Self-Regulation, and the Government of Impairment in Utero," *Hypatia: A Journal of Feminist Philosophy* 21 (1): 35–53.
Tremain, Shelley (2013), "Introducing Feminist Philosophy of Disability," *Disability Studies Quarterly* 33 (4). Available at: https://dsq-sds.org/article/view/3877/3402 (accessed June 19, 2023).
Tremain, Shelley (2015), "This is What a Historicist and Relativist Feminist Philosophy of Disability Looks Like," *Foucault Studies* 19 (1): 7–42.
Tremain, Shelley Lynn (2017), *Foucault and Feminist Philosophy of Disability*, Ann Arbor: University of Michigan Press.
Tremain, Shelley L. (2019), "Philosophy and the Apparatus of Disability," in David T. Wasserman and Adam Cureton (eds.), *The Oxford Handbook of Philosophy and Disability*, 82–99, Oxford: Oxford University Press.
Tremain, Shelley Lynn (2020), "Field Notes on the Naturalization and Denaturalization of Disability in (Feminist) Philosophy: What They Do and How They Do It," *Feminist Philosophy Quarterly* 6 (3): 1–22.
Tremain, Shelley Lynn (2021), "Philosophy of Disability, Conceptual Engineering, and the Nursing Home-Industrial-Complex in Canada," *International Journal of Critical Diversity Studies* 4 (1): 10–33.
Walia, Harsha (2021), *Border and Rule: Global Migration, Capitalism, and the Rise of Racist Nationalism*, Chicago: Haymarket Books.
Wasserman, David and Sean Aas (2022), "Disability: Definitions and Models," in Edward N. Zalta (ed.), *The Stanford Encyclopedia of Philosophy*, Summer 2022 edition. Available at: https://plato.stanford.edu/archives/sum2022/entries/disability/ (accessed July 18, 2022).
Whyte, Kyle (2019), "Climate Change: An Unprecedently Old Catastrophe," BIOPOLITICAL PHILOSOPHY (blog), January 16. Available at: https://biopoliticalphilosophy.com/2019/01/16/climate-change-an-unprecedentedly-old-catastrophe/ (accessed June 19, 2023).
Whyte, Kyle (2020), "Against Crisis Epistemology," in Brendan Hokowhitu, Aileen Moreton-Robinson, Linda Tuhiwai-Smith, Steve Larkin, and Chris Andersen (eds.), *Handbook of Critical Indigenous Studies*, 52–64, New York and London: Routledge.

2 WOULD YOU KILL THE FAT MAN HYPOTHETICAL?

FAT STIGMA IN PHILOSOPHY

KRISTIN RODIER AND
SAMANTHA BRENNAN

I (Rodier) had only just begun to read and work in fat studies, when, in the second year of my Ph.D. in feminist philosophy, I was asked to give a guest lecture to a philosophy of science class about the role of stigmas and stereotypes in dominant understandings of "obesity." I chose to teach two chapters from Kathleen LeBesco's Revolting Bodies? (2014) *because I had previously taught these chapters in feminist philosophy, and they had gone over very well with the students. I knew that some feminist philosophers taught extensive critiques of "obesity" science in their philosophy of science classes and therefore assumed that LeBesco's work would build on these critiques. I was not briefed on the extent to which the students were familiar with the topic, nor did I know how to ask for this information. Nor, furthermore, was I informed about the demographics of the class: namely, that the class comprised forty engineering students, almost all of whom were men. In my disabled fat woman body, teaching about fat bodies, I slowly died in front of this class on that day. When I claimed not that "fat people are fat because they are poor," but rather that "fat people are stereotyped as lower class by virtue of their embodiment," a student raised his hand and said: "I do not get the idea that fat people are poor. Vegetables and lentils are cheap and doing jumping jacks is free. If I was fat, I'd do that until I lost all of the weight." Put as a common-sense solution to fatness, the student had pointed out the irrelevance of the critique, while demonstrating that fat people are widely presumed to lack instrumental rationality. Although I do not remember how I responded, I do vividly recall the shame that washed over me. During the mid-class break after the incident, the student proceeded to have a very loud and demeaning discussion about fat porn with the classmates seated around him, while I was required to teach for another hour.*

I (Brennan) am currently both a fat university administrator and philosophy professor rather than only a fat philosophy professor. As a philosophy professor, I have taught in a variety of areas, including philosophy of sport. When I teach philosophy of sport, I tend to use examples from two of the sports in which I have participated: cycling and rowing. Both sports have their own distinct issues around weight categories, weight stigma, and the pressure to perform. Because of my sports experience, I think, students in philosophy of sport have felt free to share diet tips with me, assuming that I do sports to lose weight. I think that I confront some of this sizeism and fatphobia because I am a smaller fat person. For example, one student shared with me the lightweight rowing team's book of tips to lose weight for the mandatory pre-race weigh-in. No matter what I said in my philosophy of sport class about "movement for all bodies," students in the class assumed that inasmuch as I both engage in sports and am fat, I must be trying to lose weight. In other words, although I am evidently very interested in sports in addition to active in them, students continue to believe that my activity in sports stems from my participation in the weight-loss game; that is, they seem to think that although I am not a lost cause, I am clearly failing at the game. In this regard, the fatphobia that I have experienced in non-sports-related classes has, in some ways, felt more pronounced because the students in these classes had no reason to know about my athletic background. In these non-sports-related classes, that is, I was instead perceived as an overweight, middle-aged white woman who likely eats too much and exercises too little, both of which assumptions are quintessentially fatphobic and ableist.

Introduction

Our world is not a comfortable place for fat people, especially in, but by no means exclusively in, Western, white, and affluent spaces. The levels of discomfort that fat people experience vary among them depending on the ways in which they are positioned with respect to disability, race, gender, class, sexuality, and other forms of subjecting social power. In most academic spaces, to speak of a "fat oppression" puts one on one's heels, defending claims that such a form of oppression exists, even though there is a significant and growing corpus of scholarly literature that argues for fat's place within the aforementioned overlapping and mutually reinforcing oppressions (Puhl and Brownell 2001; Miller and Lundgren 2010; Mollow 2017; Lydecker, O'Brien, and Grilo 2018; Farrell 2011; Strings 2019; LeBesco 2009, 2004). While the notion of fat oppression might call to mind instruments, items, and infrastructure that produce physical discomfort in a world that is not built for fat bodies—including blood pressure cuffs, clothes, school desks, airplane seats, toilet seats, restaurant booths, and bathroom stalls—little attention is paid to less readily perceptible harms, especially social exclusion and emotional discomfort in a culture of intense stigmatization, dehumanization, and violence (Royce 2009; Mollow 2017; Harrison 2021; Rodier 2022a, 2022b). Consider, for example, how routinely the term *fat* is employed as an epithet—despite concerted efforts to reclaim the word—and what the prevalence of this epithet reveals about the continued social disdain for larger bodies. Insofar as philosophers conduct research and teach within and against this cultural and social backdrop of disdain for fat bodies, it is imperative that they ask: How do we engage ethically and critically with fat stigma in our classrooms, our departments, and the profession more generally? In this chapter, therefore, we draw on our experiences as fat philosophers to reflect on the ways in which our embodied presence in the classroom—that is, our fat teaching bodies—raises questions about philosophical and pedagogical credibility, questions that are tangible when we teach canonical Western philosophical ideas and examples that are implicitly and explicitly fat stigmatizing.

Since philosophers are a subset of the general population, we can extrapolate from empirical data on the impacts and pervasiveness of fat stigma (Hatzenbuehler, Phelan, and Link 2013) that this form of stigma and its effects should be reckoned with in all social spaces, including in the institutional and discursive space of academic philosophy. Indeed, philosophy may be uniquely positioned to perpetuate certain dominant norms according to which a thin body is a "good" body, since such a body represents evidence of rational agency. Although fat stigma is, in principle, separable from norms of rational agency, this disassociation is rarely made. Thus, we want to argue that given philosophy's disciplinary preoccupation with reason, there are philosophy-specific ways in which fatphobia is perpetuated. In what follows, therefore, we outline how some canonical texts, contemporary thought experiments, and norms of rational agency in general contribute to fat stigma's specific philosophical contours. This chapter focuses on teaching in particular because of its field-shaping impact and reach with students and because we have extensive experience as fat-bodied philosophy teachers. Pacing, standing, reaching, bending, and sitting—as a fat philosopher/person—in front of a room of philosophy students renders its own epistemological standpoint that until now has seldom been discussed.

Most (mainstream) philosophy faculty and the majority of philosophy students have not encountered the significant critique of fat stigma that one finds in the fat studies literature, though some of them may be familiar with popular online streams of fat acceptance movements/body neutrality. Fat studies initially drew on research rooted in a critique of the cultural turn at the end of the nineteenth century, where fatness in especially elite white contexts came to signify gluttony, ill health, and even a lapse in patriotic duty (Stearns 1997). This critique continues to expand in focus and historical reach in order to better identify how contemporary social concerns about an "obesity epidemic" are linked to eugenics movements, scientific racism, and the transatlantic slave trade (Farrell 2011; Strings 2019; Mollow 2017; LeBesco 2009). In short, fat stigma is not merely the modern result of a predatory diet and weight-loss industry, but rather is a product and effect of the ongoing work of imperialism, scientific racism, and colonialism.

Fatness and disability share intersecting and mutually constitutive histories of marginalization and oppression, given the pathologizing that bodies constructed as fat and as disabled continue to experience with the proliferation of techniques of normalization. This genealogy of fat stigma connects dominant structures and institutions (especially the academy) as part of the perpetuation of the "obesity panic" which, importantly for philosophers, Kathleen LeBesco identifies as a *moral* panic. LeBesco writes: "Moral panics are marked by *concern* about an imagined threat; *hostility* in the form of a moral outrage toward individuals and agencies responsible for the problem; *consensus* that something must be done about the serious threat; *disproportionality* in reports of harm; and *volatility* in terms of the eruption of panic" (LeBesco 2004: 73, emphasis in LeBesco). So-called "obesity" is another culturally constructed category with which to derive and encode the moral worth of persons on the basis of ostensibly natural bodily features (Snyder and Mitchell 2006: 38–9). Fat studies provides a substantial literature that reads "obesity" as a constructed category of bodily difference that has been systematically isolated, measured, and set for eradication. Fat bodies are framed almost exclusively as negative and are overdetermined by medical models that devise interventions—especially targeted at children—that aim to modify behavior and stop the spread of "obesity" (Cooper and Egner 2021). Insofar as this characterization of obesity as an "epidemic" is uncritically adopted in the sociological literature, it is most often framed as a "contagion" that specifically flourishes within immigrant and racialized groups. In terms of this framing of "obesity" as a contagion, these minoritized social groups are represented as "drains on society" insofar as they "accept" larger bodies as sexually attractive. Furthermore, this sociological literature advocates that policy and social supports be directed to the "obese" mothers in these groups and their children in order to stop the spread (Stoll and Egner 2020: 8). In this sociological literature, fat women's psychological fitness to raise healthy children is cast in doubt, demonstrating another way in which eugenics links fatness and disability (Stoll and Egner 2020: 9).

Consider an exercise that Rodier performed multiple times with undergraduates in which students are asked to construct a set of fat/thin binary descriptions of qualities. Here are the most common descriptions on the "fat" side of the binaries: careless, out of control, disordered, uncomfortable, poor, unhealthy, unintelligent/uneducated, depressed, weak-willed, unsuccessful, lazy, and either asexual or hypersexual. These associations vary along intersectional lines by location, culture, and other factors. Literature from controlled settings demonstrates that fat people are perceived as less neat, less productive, less ambitious, less determined, and less disciplined than their thinner counterparts (Larkin and Pines 1979; Lydecker O'Brien, and Grilo 2018; Puhl and Brownell 2001), while fat youth are bullied more often than their thin counterparts (Weinstock and Krehbiel 2009). Fat children suffer from biases since they are more likely to be associated with words such as *stupid* and *bad* than their thin counterparts, whereas thin children are more likely to be associated with words such as *smart* and *good* (Lydecker, O'Brien, and Grilo 2018). Significant discrimination against fat people persists in career and professional development opportunities (Burmeister et al. 2013; Miller and Lundgren 2010; Swami and Monk 2013). For example, in a reckless contribution to Twitter, psychology professor Geoffrey Miller wrote: "Dear obese Ph.D. applicants: if [*sic*] you didn't have the willpower to stop eating carbs, you won't have the willpower to do a dissertation #truth" (Trotter 2013). By publishing his tweet, Miller participated in a presumed consensus around "what we all know" about fat people's respective wills, offering an armchair "science of surfaces" (Snyder and Mitchell 2006). Given this cultural and social climate and backdrop, how do we negotiate topics directly related to both fatness and teaching philosophy in bodies that these topics stigmatize?

"Free-floating Knowers" and Fat-bodied Eaters

Much work has been done in the last twenty-five years to critique a masculinist culture in the discipline of philosophy and increase the participation in philosophy of (white, nondisabled, cisgender) women in the profession of philosophy (Saul 2013; Antony 2012; Alcoff 2003). Earlier landmark feminist texts such as Simone de Beauvoir's *The Second Sex* (1949, 1951) and Genevieve Lloyd's *The Man of Reason* (1993) have shown that philosophy must grapple with the influence of sexism on the philosophical canon, especially in how it formulates "good reasoners." Feminist philosophers have critiqued the refrain in philosophy according to which historical philosophical texts can be discussed and interpreted from a value-neutral lens, both in classrooms in particular and in philosophy journals and the profession more generally (Code 2014). Although some change with respect to the demographics of the academy has taken place, diversity initiatives tend to overrepresent white women with thin body types (Wrenn and Lutz 2016). Behind the failures of a lot of these diversity initiatives are long-standing meta-commitments within philosophy that are difficult to shake loose (Dotson 2012).

Shelley Tremain (2017) has argued that the discipline and profession of philosophy (especially bioethics) makes fundamental ontological and epistemological assumptions—such as the claim that disability is a self-evident and philosophically uninteresting category—that simultaneously condition philosophical inquiry and determine who gets to be a (credible, employed, successful, or celebrated) philosopher. Tremain's thesis is that the conception of disability that currently prevails in philosophy—according to which disability is a naturally disadvantageous property, characteristic, or attribute of individuals—contributes to the perception that disabled philosophers are not viable colleagues and thus contributes to their systemic exclusion from the profession and to the marginalization of philosophy of disability from the discipline (Tremain 2017: 2). In other words, the ontological and epistemological preoccupations and assumptions of the discipline and profession effectively gatekeep whose critical work is of value. Hence, philosophers of disability (especially disabled philosophers of disability) pose a threat to bioethical (and other philosophical) work that leaves the category of disability as a given. The argument about the meta-critical assumptions that philosophers make with respect to fatness, although not the same as the argument about the meta-critical assumptions with respect to disability, follows similar lines to it insofar as both arguments make associations between meta-critical assumptions and assumptions about who is a credible philosopher and who is not. This chapter deals primarily with how influential ideas and teaching techniques use fat in comedic and negative ways. Nevertheless, the chapter also considers why an understanding of how "obesity" is used in bioethics—namely, as an epistemically justified category that can be imported into moral reasoning—is essential for a broader understanding of how fat philosophers experience the discipline.

Feminist initiatives in philosophy have consistently marked a point of reflection on the body for our discipline, in research, in teaching, and in professional and administrative labor. For example, Kate Manne's article on diet culture and philosophy highlights the ways in which metaphors are embedded in philosophy's disciplinary framing, which reveals a politics of the body. As Manne puts it:

> Philosophy, with its characteristic emphasis on reason, often implicitly conceives of rationality as the jurisdiction of the lean, rich, white men who dominate my discipline. . . . We praise arguments for being muscular and compact and criticize prose for being flabby, flowery and, implicitly, feminine. When it comes to our metaphysics—our pictures of the world—we pride ourselves on a taste for austerity, or as W.V.O. Quine put it, "desert

> landscapes." And what is the fat body in the popular imagination but excess, lavishness, redundancy? (Manne 2022)

Manne's focus on lavishness and redundancy is perhaps also tethered to a historical read on fatness in ideas that does not focus on the culture of the discipline, which views fatness as a failure of practical rationality (at the best of times) or as ripe for comedic atavisms which are shot through with elitist, racist, and ableist norms.

Since philosophy characteristically keeps historical ideas alive in the present, we must discuss what it means to responsibly engage with these past ideas. To do so, we must analyze the relationship between contingent forms of bodily valuation and the ways in which canonical ideas and thinkers are treated ahistorically. In Sabrina Strings's book *Fearing the Black Body: The Racial Origins of Fat Phobia* (2019), she argues that fatphobia enforces normative whiteness at the same time as it denigrates and oppresses racialized others. Strings's book outlines how North American race-making projects used fatness as a marker of "savage blackness," an identifiable degenerative trait deemed to prove that Black bodies were inferior (Strings 2019: 88–9). By surveying the Western philosophical tradition from the seventeenth century and onward, Strings details how a very specific white, male, and slender ideal emerges from the epistemologies and metaphysics of several important thinkers. As Strings shows, these white male thinkers have aligned fleshiness in the bodies of white men as evidence that they cannot be proper English intellectuals and, furthermore, that "[t]hinness was seen as more befitting the intelligent, self-possessed white male" (43). These ideas confirm the ongoing philosophical use of fatphobic language that Manne identifies.

Many contemporary philosophers might be squeamish to talk about (our) bodies since our canonical thinkers in the discipline so strongly emphasize *dis*embodied rationality—what Lorraine Code refers to as "free float[ing knowers]" (Code 2014). Although some influential philosophical figures argue for *embodied* rationality, our academic tasks in philosophy—namely, contemplation, argumentation, and writing—primarily revolve around the life of the mind. Yet fat bodies make the body harder to ignore. Along with our highly disembodied tasks, some of Western philosophy's most important historical figures use eating as a recurring example. Consider Epicurus's *Letter to Menoeceus* in which he writes: "And even as men choose of food not merely and simply the larger portion, but the more pleasant, so the wise seek to enjoy the time which is most pleasant and not merely that which is longest." Students regularly understand this passage according to dominant stereotypes that "bad" eaters are unwise—as evidenced by their fat bodies. This analogy about differentiating pleasures is not about an "obesity epidemic," downward mobility, or strains on the health-care system. Epicurus is trying to say that we need to balance our judgments in terms of quality and quantity and become accustomed to the minimum which will ensure less pain if we must go without. Students and philosophers alike are inculcated through diet/weight-loss ideology so strongly that they have a difficult time reflecting on this tight association.[1]

Given that eating is a common topic of discussion in philosophy, the slippage from fat/thin to irrational/rational is always present. Consider how, for Marcus Aurelius, we cause pain because we are ignorant of what nature requires and that the more blameworthy sins relate to desire: "but he who offends through desire, being overpowered by pleasure, seems to be in a manner more intemperate and more womanish in his offences" (*Meditations* 2.9). Notice how, in the passage, desire is represented as under our rational control—it comes from within. In addition, notice how one of the ways in which we do violence to our souls is by acting carelessly. Presumably, one of these ways of acting carelessly would be to engage in careless or "compulsive" eating (something that people of all sizes can do). Consider, for example, Gregory Sadler, a philosophy lecturer at Marist College who shares his lectures online and has berated himself for excessive snacking during a lecture on Aristotle's virtue. Sadler asserts that this excessive snacking has caused the "pain" of being fat, though he is not specific about what kind of pain he means (Sadler 2017). Sadler's teaching technique is understandable, since a form of stigma management is self-deprecation. If we read Sadler's self-interest as *to be perceived as a rational philosopher*, then his self-deprecation could lead to more positive student evaluations, since students respond positively to teachers who seem to argue against their own self-interests (Escalera 2009). So, in short, Sadler has done stigma management to counter the perception that he is a compulsive/irrational eater and thus a bad philosopher. This sort of stigma management makes it extremely difficult for fat-bodied (philosophy) professors to teach their students anything about fatness as an acceptable form of embodiment. While, as we have noted, norms of rationality and a fat body are separable in principle, they are not separable in practice for fat philosophy teaching bodies.

Even when eating is not the core of teaching a concept, fat stigma can inform classroom discussions. Consider a common hypothetical in differentiating moral blame from causal responsibility. A person has a heart attack on the subway platform and collapses, pushing an innocent bystander off the platform and onto the tracks where the bystander is hit by a train. The person who had the heart attack is causally reponsible for the bystander's death but is not morally blameworthy for it. Thus, this example of causal responsibility is contrasted with examples of moral blameworthiness, whereby the person intentionally (rather than accidentally) pushes the bystander/victim off the platform. The example of the distinction between causal responsibility and moral responsibility regularly backfires, however, since students often try to argue that, somehow, the person caused their own heart attack by failing to prevent it. It is possible that one's teaching body primes students to read the example in this way; thus, we get covert messages from students about our blameworthiness. This set of circumstances just raises the question: Who do our students conjure in their minds as the person who has the heart attack? Is it a marathon runner who has an "unexpected" chronic total obstruction, colloquially known as a "widow-maker" (a biased expression that casts heart attacks as primarily a male issue)? Or, is the person in the hypothetical who has the heart attack presumed to be a fat, stressed-out, businessman who eats terribly, perhaps smokes, and drinks too much coffee? We can in fact learn who the students conjure from the hypothetical by what they share in class. Students have said, for example, that the person could well be responsible for their heart attack since they should have exercised and eaten better—inadvertently revealing more about who exactly had the heart attack. Such a remark demonstrates the lengths to which we hold people responsible for their health (neoliberal ideologies of "personal responsibility" name themselves) and illustrates how philosophical discussions according to which the mind controls the body can slip into extreme versions of bodily control with moral implications.

What these teaching traps demonstrate is that dominant norms of rational minds which are evidenced on thin bodies align with contemporary neoliberal ableist values of (among others) individualism, self-sufficiency, discipline, and freedom of the will. The communication of philosophers' ideas to our students demands that we wrestle with cultural understandings that our ideas evoke. Epicurus's emphasis on eating small and simple meals with friends provides a stark contrast and, perhaps, a good corrective to some modern food environments. If, however, we are asking students to consider simple pleasures, then it is important that we reflect on our contemporary historical moment to understand which simple pleasures are even available—how does this requirement land for our students? Even teaching aesthetics (judgments of taste) is salient as stereotypical representations of fat people convey that they eat junky mass-produced food, in contrast to (thinner) people of refined taste (Guthman 2009a, 2009b). In essence, fat people encapsulate those who are not smart enough to tame their desires, nor make enlightened or refined choices, and thus, by implication, if they manage to get there at all, they make subpar philosophers.

Fat Professors and Stereotype Threat

Philosophers who must appear in face-to-face classrooms must do so with their bodies. Christina Fisanick draws on empirical research demonstrating that, unsurprisingly, "the 'normal professor body' shares the same characteristics of the 'normal body' in society. Professors and academics benefit from a specific halo effect, since their normative bodies more easily garner prestige and epistemic authority in the academy more generally (Jenkins 2014: 164). The normal body in society," Fisanick writes, "is legibly heterosexual, able-bodied, white, cisgendered, middle-aged and thin" (Fisanick 2007: 239). It becomes difficult to read a "normal" professor body visually because the practices that sustain a sexuality are not primarily legible. In the same way, what a person eats and their activity levels are not immediately legible from their body, despite strong cultural impulses to read character off of somatotypes (Graham 2005: 178–9). Since dominant understandings project a bundle of failures onto fat bodies, fat philosophers who fail to have a "normal professor body" and may carry character stigma about their life practices experience a credibility gap that they must negotiate in the classroom. For example, having one's intellectual work evaluated fairly is difficult when one's body is taken to signify one's failing practical reason and inadequate intellect. Our argument is that this judgment goes well beyond evaluation of one's presumed habits and, in addition, detracts from perceptions of intellectual reason. Importantly, insofar as philosophy focuses, in unique ways, on teaching reasoning skills—which includes modeling and perceptions of expertise—fat-bodied philosophers experience stereotype threat in this regard.

Stereotype threat is the phenomenon whereby one encounters a stereotype about one's performance, the awareness of which subsequently affects one's performance. In other words, acting within a context of the stereotype—whether it be classrooms, philosophy job interviews, conferences, or professional mingling—leads to self-confirmation of the stereotype threat. As Jennifer Saul (2013) explains it, stereotype threat is both conscious and unconscious, involving ways that a person's awareness of their own group membership, may negatively affect their performance. She writes:

> So, in the case of women in philosophy, implicit biases affect the way we perceive (for instance) the quality of a woman's work, leading us to evaluate it more negatively than it deserves; while stereotype threats may lead a woman to genuinely underperform in philosophy. . . . Victims of stereotype threat underperform on the relevant tasks because they are unconsciously preoccupied by fears of confirming the stereotypes about their group. (Saul 2013)

Our assertions about the impact of stereotype threat on fat philosophers constitute an undesired consequence of our literature review in the relevant areas and our reflections on our own experiences, since they detract from a general claim that we wish to advance—namely, that fatness has no necessary connection to a certain kind of rational mind. Thus, the larger picture tells us that if there are performance gaps, stereotype threat is likely to play a role.

Knowing that students perceive us as less rational than their thinner, normatively bodied male professors, we have discussed with each other how managing this negative perception has led us to experience fuzzy thinking and cognitive dissonance/overload. This experience squares with research on related contexts, such as how women underperform on important job interviews (Shantz and Latham 2012) and how older adults can experience decreased memory and cognitive performance (Kang and Chasteen 2009). Thus far, we have focused on stereotypes with respect to practical rationality because they directly relate to our experiences as fat philosophy teachers; however, as members of wider society, the stereotypes about fatness that we and other fat people experience vary widely, as we pointed out in our remarks at the outset of this chapter with respect to multiple group memberships. Take our social positions with respect to gender, race, and employment status, for example. We share identity factors as fat white women teachers. From this vantage point, we are subject to stereotypes as unruly angry bitches or as matronly caregivers. Given the two options, and insofar as they both cut against credibility, the lesser of the two evils is the latter, that is, to be regarded as "nice" and "friendly" by students. Both of us admit that we have extended additional emotional labor to get students to like us as a way to compensate for stereotypes associated with our bodies while understanding that this process is a form of stigma management. When students do not receive the matronly care from us which they believe that they deserve, the kinds of angry backlashes that we confront have a familiar fatphobic punch.

Navigating classrooms where one's credibility and authority are in question is only damage control, since there is no "right" way to act that will avoid stigma. These epistemic injustices constitute wide-ranging social problems that we must manage individually, contextually, and in the moment. Individual negotiations could involve any one of these responses: losing weight,[2] humor and self-mockery, displays of extreme caring, and allowing intrusive questions or advice. Even in counseling professions and other caring professions (which, it must be said, are profoundly gendered), fat clinicians are perceived by their clients as lacking credibility to help the clients with any issue whatsoever (Moller and Tischner 2019). Following Erving Goffman, Amy Farrell argues that to be stigmatized as fat is to be taken to communicate failure in some way: "a person is gluttonous, or filling a deeply disturbed psychological need, or irresponsible and unable to control primitive urges" (Farrell 2011: 6). Fatness has been, and continues to be, a "discrediting attribute, for which people will go to extraordinary extremes to eliminate" (ibid.). Taken together, stigma and stereotype threat tee up experiences of humiliation in classrooms for fat teachers and students. In order to succeed, fat philosophers must overcompensate, perhaps even over-perform a hyperrationality. For both of us, the first few classes with a new group of students are critical—standing or sitting in front of the room, we start from behind the eight ball.

Credibility is crucial in teaching environments, since students' perception of credibility affects how students approach ideas different from their own (Kretz 2017: 15). While we do not contend that credibility is attained solely through one's embodiment, we nevertheless think that it is an important contributing factor to one's perception of expertise in research and teaching. Strings discusses English philosophers who explicitly state that fatness in elite white men (the *only* intellectuals) signifies a "dull mind." The idea that the most advanced bodies have the highest intellects reiterates eugenic hierarchies, where "lower" bodies are marked for manual labor (Snyder and Mitchell 2006). Contemporary media disproportionately represents fat white men's bodies as signifying a working-class position of downward mobility (Mosher 2001; LeBesco 2004). Furthermore, social concerns about a healthy and industrializing labor pool intersect fatness and disability, since a "healthy" body is independent, self-sufficient, and enterprising. These preoccupations are solidified in institutions and governments with eugenic regimes to purify a nation, such as when, for example, disabled children have been removed from their families because they "drained" parental energy (Snyder and Mitchell 2006). Since philosophy often considers itself to be the highest form of contemplation (intellectual labor), the mind must be of the highest quality and the body is evidence of both intelligence and a rational will. Manne observes that this sizeist and ableist association between the mind and the body appears even in captions in philosophy texts. As Manne writes: "I was recently apprised of a caption on a portrait of David Hume, the 18th-century philosopher, in an introductory philosophy textbook: 'The lightness and quickness of his mind was entirely hidden by the lumpishness of his appearance.' Thus have other fat philosophers been warned that our bodies may similarly mask our intellects" (Manne 2022). While in this chapter we have concentrated on fatness with respect to teaching and disciplinary issues, issues of fat credibility could contribute to important discussions of epistemic trust, testimonial injustice, and so on (see Fricker 2007; Dotson 2011; McKinnon 2017; Daukas 2006).

In short, our argument is not that fat stigma causes stereotype threat only or even primarily when philosophers are teaching about fat, which, strictly speaking, would be relatively rare. We maintain, rather, that being a fat philosopher carries stereotypes that are salient anytime that we teach (full stop) and *especially* when we teach about desire, agency, rationality, aesthetics, and the good life in general, topics central to most teaching in the discipline. While there is literature that discusses the effects of teaching about fat in a fat body (Escalera 2009), negative judgments that influence stereotype threat go beyond individual identity categories. Although we cannot know if weight bias is worse in philosophy unless this issue is directly studied and compared, we do know that other fat philosophers share the experiences of the authors of this chapter. Manne's *New York Times* article on the topic outlines the moral harms of a fatphobic culture as well as her internalization of fatphobia *as a philosopher*:

> I have lately wondered how much my self-directed fatphobia owes to my career as an academic philosopher. . . . I struggle as a philosopher to reconcile my image of my body with its task in the world of being the emissary of my mind. I think of it, tongue in cheek, as my body-mind problem. Often, I cannot bear the idea of sending out my "soft animal" of a body, in the words of the poet Mary Oliver, to fight for feminist views that are edgy and controversial and to represent a discipline that prides itself on sharpness, clarity and precision. I feel betrayed by my soft borders. (Manne 2022)

If we add insights from fat studies scholars, especially Strings, we must go beyond *feminist* framing of fat stigma in philosophy. Fat oppression is *not* sexism extended (Rodier 2022b), but rather an embodied oppression that varies intersectionally. Fat women philosophers may face specific challenges depending on how their fat bodies are shaped and move in academic spaces. Consider April Herndon's experience as a fat woman academic. She recounts that, at a conference on race, she posed a question to a prominent white male academic who, in a reiteration of scientific racism, made a controversial argument about the size of skulls and their association with certain populations. More exactly, Herndon posed a question about feminist standpoint epistemology, which he brushed off by stating that he could "show [Herndon] studies that empirically prove women's hips are wider than men's" (Herndon 2002). He not only missed the point of Herndon's objection, but he did so in a way that upheld scientific purity and, at the same time, invoked Herndon's body to undermine her credibility. Although this response to Herdon could easily be papered over as primarily about gender, its references to wide hips, big thighs, and big rear-ends call forth racist and fatphobic epithets that continue to be used liberally: "fat ass," "thunder thighs," "lard ass," and the list goes on. Reminding Herndon of her size to demonstrate her failed (elite white) womanhood is to effectively silence her as one might do with an epithet. It is not this white male academic's claim per se that demonstrates the gendered fatphobia that Herndon experiences—there may well be differences in hip width on average—but rather the reference to fat on butts and hips *in particular*: it has been an obsession of scientific racism used to construct bodily hierarchies.

Both before and during the Enlightenment, feminine aesthetics valued fleshiness for white women. It was not until the burgeoning "race sciences" used fatness on racialized bodies as evidence of their genetically low status that fleshy white women were no longer desirable. Strings writes,

> The fear of the imagined "fat black woman" was created by racial and religious ideologies that have been used to both degrade black women *and* discipline white women. The . . . ["race sciences"] discourse of fatness as "course," "immoral," and "black" worked to denigrate black women, and it concomitantly became the impetus for the promulgation of slender figures as the proper form of embodiment for elite white Christian women. (Strings 2019: 7, emphasis in Strings)

Strings traces how these ideologies shaped philosophers' views of eating, showing that indulgence in food was not a propensity of the so-called slow-witted, for, as Strings notes, there was now evidence of an "inborn, race-specific propensity for laziness and ease. . . . Such behavior was deemed wholly uncharacteristic of the rational thinkers sitting atop the new racial hierarchy" (Strings 2019: 84).

We maintain that contemporary discourses use "health" to continue the medicalization and stigmatization of fatness, reinforcing that fat people are irrational (because they do not monitor their own health properly) and that it is irrational for fat people to even attempt to be philosophers (precisely because they have limited capacity for rationality). In other words, fatness must be taken together with gender and race (as well as disability, age, and other subjecting categories) in order for us to understand the barriers to credibility in one's particular field of intellectual study.

Philosophical Examples: Magical Train Stopping and Fat Wives

As outlined earlier, wrestling with dominant understandings, stereotypes, and stigmas is a complex task. To address the instances where philosophy evokes fat stereotypes, we can pay attention to particular teaching materials, specifically where nameless fat-bodied people appear in thought experiments. Contemporary analytic ethics courses often revolve around real-life cases and thought experiments about who we can kill (typically older people, disabled people, and drug users, among others) and why (they are a drain on resources, a burden, do not contribute, and so on), probing our biases and generating epistemic and hermeneutical injustices (Tremain 2017, 2021, 2023; Reynolds 2021; Hoffman 2000). Many examples of disability and euthanasia that are used in thought experiments pay little attention to legacies of eugenics that construct disability as an objective, prediscursive bodily inferiority that operates as a model for other acts in which lives deemed to have less value are measured (Tremain 2017; Snyder and Mitchell 2006). Disability and fatness thus share contemporary legacies of this disparagement and disqualification with respect to professions specifically designed for the classification, management, and disciplining oversight of bodily differences, including medicine, charity, social work, public health policy, and so on.

Thought experiments in philosophy that attempt to divorce the context of eugenics from hypotheticals about killing disabled people (utilitarian calculus being but only one methodological context) overlook how disability has historically been used as a natural bodily inferiority to justify mass killing. These hypotheticals continue to be taught despite significant literature in experimentalist philosophy criticizing the use of such thought experiments (Knobe and Nichols 2008), suggesting that they often reinforce stereotypes (Lanphier and McKiernan 2020) and diminish perceptions of harm (Horton 2004: 549), not to mention the objections to them that numerous disabled philosophers of disability have raised (e.g., Hall 2016; Tremain 2017). To return to earlier discussions of heart issues, hypotheticals used outside of ethics can also dehumanize fat people in ways that overlap illness and disability. For example, a critical thinking course might present the fallacy of accident (*ad dictum secundum quid*) where the claim is that cross-country skiing is good for one's heart, therefore, "Mr. Fat Body" should go cross-country skiing. In this hypothetical, the very fact that a body is fat is deployed not only to name and dehumanize the person but also as a sine qua non for cardiac illness. Insofar as Mr. Fat Body is reduced to his body in this hypothetical example, the example and others like it fail and, as we intend to argue, undermine teaching.

A touchstone of so-called lifeboat ethics, "The Trolley Problem," which originates with Philippa Foot (1967), and the "Trolley-ology," which derives from it, are so closely associated with undergraduate-level ethics reasoning that they often appear in popular culture discussions about philosophy (notably, the popular television series *The Good Place* [2017]). In Judith Jarvis Thomson's comment (1985) on Foot's work, she introduces the "fat man" example which was intended to both illuminate and complicate the ethical questions that Foot's trolley problem raises. Standard texts still refer to Thomson's example as "Fat Man" or "The Fat Man." Some philosophers have written books and articles with this example in the title: David Edmonds's 2014 text *Would You Kill the Fat Man*? and Thomas Cathcart's 2013 text *The Trolley Problem: Or, Would You Throw the Fat Guy Off the Bridge?* are but two of them. In the "Fat Man" example (Thomson 1985), one is asked whether a fat person should be thrown over a bridge to stop a train from killing five other people. The idea is that you would be ducking the hypothetical *unless you grant* that the fat man's bulk is sufficient to stop a train. The casual brutal violence in this example works alongside the ubiquitous ways in which violence against fat people is minimized in popular media, media reporting, court cases, and so on (see Mollow 2017; Harrison 2021; Rodier 2022a). While these in-class discussions can be unruly, evoking laughter at the fat person's demise, some students do point out that even the fattest person could not stop a train. In addition, the pedagogical goal may well be undermined since stereotypical short hands—such as pervasive fat stigma—can put one's thumb on the scale. Teaching these examples while fat is especially unpleasant because some students will openly say that insofar as the fat man does not care about himself, he may as well save five people. These kinds of teaching moments are very difficult and synthesize the larger issues that we have outlined about normal philosophy professor bodies. If it is a philosopher's prerogative to teach analytic ethics with highly constructed thought experiments such as these odious hypothetical examples, then the practice itself certainly calls for moral and pedagogical justification.

Studies on "fat man" hypotheticals have now appeared which show that women are less likely than men to judge that they would kill the fat man, while people of all genders are more likely to kill the fat man if they watch a comedy clip of a fat person before they are questioned about the example (Bakewell 2013). Several online teaching materials that we found in our internet searches amp up the stigma that the example entails, using comedic language in their description of the hypothetical fat man. Consider Kai Nielsen's move away from the trolley example and toward a Winnie the Pooh-style example. In prefatory remarks to this example, Nielsen suggests that we think only of the moral imperatives and "forget the levity of the example" (Nielsen 1972: 228):

> [The fat man] was leading a group of people out of the cave when he got stuck in the mouth of the cave and in a very short time high tide will be upon them, and unless he is promptly unstuck, they all will be drowned except the fat man, whose head is out of the cave. But, fortunately or unfortunately, someone has with him a stick of dynamite. The short of the matter is, either they use the dynamite and blast the poor innocent fat man out of the mouth of the cave or everyone else drowns. (Nielsen 1972: 228)

Consider the "levity" that is involved in blowing up a fat person. Why would descriptors such as "poor" and "innocent" be required for the hypothetical?

Recall our remarks about classroom discussions of fatness and blame versus responsibility. As depicted in Nielsen's hypothetical, the fat person's *choice* to be fat positions them differently than a thinner person in the ethical dilemma; thus, the use of the dynamite is better justified. Yet, insofar as the fat man is represented as innocent and poor, he is transformed to a victim of circumstance/happenstance whose dull mind, poor metabolism, and/or disordered eating bring him closer to the moral standing of (thinner) others. The use of the terms *poor* and *innocent* is moral backpedaling, in line with the admonishment to ignore the humor of the example. What should we make of the incessant and repeated violence, alongside humor, that philosophical discourses direct at fat people? It must be that their reduced rational agency is justification for their subhuman status, which makes their brutal deaths easier to stomach. It is one thing to point out that the example epitomizes ineffective pedagogy. It is something else—namely, a matter of justice—to point out the real-world harms of perpetuating fat stigma in teaching.[3]

Consider another ethical dilemma, the discussions of which do not turn on the magical properties of one's girth: truth telling. These discussions in contexts in and out of academic philosophy take this sort of formulation: "Do I look fat in this dress?" or "Do these jeans make my butt look big?" First, these questions should be eradicated due to their emphasis on body size and butts in particular, as Herndon's experience exemplifies. The "real world" context of this dilemma is that the presumed woman (who is likely *not* fat) is asking whether she looks attractive (Nichter 2001), a negative response to which risks hurt feelings. What often elicits laughter about these examples is that the questioners are usually larger than they think, that is, they do not perceive themselves as other people likely perceive them. These ostensible misperceptions push discussion to the self-improvement of the questioners: namely, they need to adjust their self-perception to be motivated to diet. How else could this scenario be interpreted? Is it purely epistemological? In which case, are fat people simply bad perceivers? We think that we can safely say that the crux of the example is that there is a presumption that telling the truth in this situation will be of moral importance because the truth will hurt—and maybe it should (see Callahan's defense of shaming "obesity" in Callahan 2012). This insight reveals that, at a higher level, the discussion was really about whether or not we should hurt a fat person's feelings for their better good.

Conclusions

So, what can we do differently? How one implements any changes to the current state of affairs with respect to fat oppression in philosophy will depend on one's own embodied positionality: there is no one-size-fits-all recommendation for philosophers to reduce fat stigma in their classrooms, for example.

Nevertheless, let's start with some low-hanging fruit in the realm of teaching. An immediate and achievable recommendation is to discontinue teaching thought experiments that explicitly refer to a person's body shape, size, or weight. Given that these thought experiments are meant to elicit intuitions of the moral parameters of the case and, furthermore, given that we know the extent to which widely held intuitions about ability, race, and size can be untrustworthy, there are reasons to avoid characterizing people in these ways. If characterizing people in this way cannot be avoided—for example, when we teach the original thought experiment—perhaps we should brainstorm with students about how to eliminate the (ab)use of the fat person in the hypothetical. A compromise could involve students in a reflection on whether the original thought experiment gets at the moral intuitions that it is intended to illustrate. Some philosophers have changed the fat man to (for example) a "large" man or a 6′5″ football player who is wearing large, heavy equipment, the combined weight of which could stop the train. As we have noted, these adjustments to a well-known problem of the discipline involve risks whose consequences may differ from one philosopher to another, that is, one's relative power and job prospects need to be taken into account when one considers pedagogical adjustments that talk back to the accepted framing of philosophical problems.

Are there other areas of the discipline, beyond applied ethics, which would do well to avoid food/eating examples? And, can we actually ask that philosophers avoid food and eating examples? These questions require rigorous critical discussion that has yet to begin. Nevertheless, we do have a few recommendations for situations when food is relevant. Avoidance of food and appetite altogether when discussing weakness of the will in particular could be helpful. Students have enough opportunities to feel badly about their hunger. Examples that use food and appetite as a measure of self-control and self-mastery can be difficult for students with eating difficulties and/or larger bodies to hear, detrimentally affecting their learning conditions. Enough restrictive frames for thinking about eating exist already. Philosophers contribute to this context with (justified) scrutiny, but they should do so with care. When discussing eating, we recommend that instructors frame food as a positive human need and source of pleasure, full stop. Discussions of environmentalism and veganism seem to dominate philosophy classes about food; yet, what if these discussions were expanded to include consideration of the harms of fat shaming, food shaming, and bodily hierarchies? Who wants to take that on?

This chapter has not specifically addressed professional issues surrounding who we hire and promote, to whom we give teaching awards, and who we invite to present keynotes. To address these issues equitably, tokenism should be avoided, for example, when bringing in guest lecturers to talk about fat, especially if the person is fat-bodied. If it is true that stigma affects job prospects in most professions and if (as we have been arguing) professional philosophy is not immune to this stigma and might be worse than other academic disciplines and other professions in some respects, then philosophers should pause to consider why. Consider, once again, Miller's comments about the willpower of prospective graduate students. Miller defended himself by claiming that his tweet was not actually about one's Body Mass Index (BMI) classification but about "willpower and conscientiousness" (Trotter 2013), confirming what we have been arguing. Notwithstanding that Miller's own field has largely debunked willpower as a useful psychological category (Baumeister and Tierney 2012), the idea that students who have academic achievements sufficient to apply to a Ph.D. program somehow need *additional* bodily screening reveals the truth that entrance requirements and funding decisions are made partially based on reading a motivational profile from a certain kind of body. When a quick Google Search can produce a picture of almost anyone (especially keen graduate students who cultivate professional online presences), attractiveness and normative embodiment are likely to play a role (Swami 2013). Whatever is meant by "professorial appearance"—which includes hairstyle, clothing choices, and weight—has an impact on one's teaching evaluations and job prospects (Wookey, Graves, and Butler 2009). (Let us here not speak of the job interview dinners that elicit demonstrations of one's judgments of taste and fit for the faculty club chairs.) Daniel Hamermesh and Amy Parker (2003) have found that when professors are perceived as attractive, it can account for a move from the tenth to the ninetieth percentile on student evaluations. As teachers, we should ask ourselves whether we hold these same biases and to what extent they affect our evaluation of work that "unattractive" and/or fat students submit. These biases affect formal and informal mentoring, as well as institutionally gatekeep the profession. It will take more than individual reflection to undermine these biases. Indeed, their eventual elimination and transformation require that we continue to foster critical approaches to the structures that maintain and solidify bodily hierarchies.

It would be nice to end this chapter on a positive note by saying, "It is not like philosophers invented fatphobia." Yet the salience of this remark really depends on who one claims in their intellectual tradition. It matters so much what and who we teach and how we frame what we teach (for a discussion of framing fat in women's and gender studies, see Rodier 2022b). Canonical and lesser-known Western philosophers have spurred eugenic intellectual traditions that underpin empire-building and colonialism.[4] The impact of this tradition on current meta-disciplinary norms is germinal in critical work on philosophy as a profession. For we who teach now, the implication is this: How are we bringing critical approaches to these ideas in our classrooms? Given that a fear of fatness has long-standing residency in significant parts of our psyches, government, and medical authorities, this implication cannot be ignored but rather must be handled with care, that is, unless we want our students to learn that fat prejudice is acceptable in philosophy, which would compound intersectional oppressions and lead to—among other things—less credibility for fat professors. Our fat students, who persistently grapple with questions of belonging in our discipline, are paying close attention.

Acknowledgments

A previous version of this chapter appeared under the title "Teaching (and) Fat Stigma in Philosophy" in *Teaching Philosophy*, 2022. The original article received support through the Athabasca University Publications Academic Research Fund. Kristin would like to thank Cressida Heyes, Catherine Clune-Taylor, and Cindy Baker for many discussions that shaped this writing. Thanks are also due to excellent anonymous reviewers at *Teaching Philosophy* and Shelley Lynn Tremain for helping to sharpen the argument.

Notes

1 Rodier taught many spring session ethics courses with a significant Muslim student contingent. These students, fasting sometimes for up to fifteen hours a day depending on the dates of Ramadan, had excellent contributions to these discussions.

2 Not that we are suggesting this as a desirable project, since the science on medium or long-term weight loss demonstrates its relative futility. It is a larger question whether it is fair to ask people with stigmatized bodies to correct their stigmatizing features, even if it is *technically* possible. Any answer to these questions should address whether any project of intentional weight loss is in line with the person's own desires, their community and social values and obligations, and their long-term physical and emotional health (to the extent this is under any control).

3 In a discussion of "experimental philosophy" on the blog Crooked Timber, Brian considers various explanations of the data that people are more willing to sacrifice the lives of "fat men" than others in thought experiments, particularly in cave. He puts forward the hypothesis that people believe fat people are responsible for our sizes, "If the guy in the cave hadn't been so fat, there wouldn't have been a problem. So he isn't really an innocent. So rules against killing the innocent do not count in the minds of some voters in this case." Available at: https://crookedtimber.org/2006/05/02/experimental-philosophy/ (accessed May 22, 2022). Note that while the Crooked Timber blogger Brian considers

that fatness of the thought experimental subject may play a role in peoples' judgments and willingness to kill the subject, fatphobia is not discussed.

4 John M. MacEachran, professor of philosophy at the University of Alberta, Canada, was chair of the Alberta Eugenics Board from 1929 to 1960. He was integral in influencing the implementation of the Sexual Sterilization Act (1928), where he oversaw the authorization of over 2,000 sterilizations of "defectives" in the name of "mental hygiene" and criminality.

References

Alcoff, Linda Martin, ed. (2003), *Singing in the Fire: Stories of Women in Philosophy*, Lanham: Rowman and Littlefield Publishers.

Antony, Louise (2012), "Different Voices or Perfect Storm: Why Are There So Few Women in Philosophy," *Journal of Social Philosophy* 43 (3): 227–55.

Aurelius, Marcus ([167 A.C.E] 1912), *The Thoughts of Marcus Aurelius*, trans. George Long, New York: Dodge Publishing Company.

Bakewell, Sarah (2013), "Clang Went the Trolley," *New York Times*. Available at: https://www.nytimes.com/2013/11/24/books/review/would-you-kill-the-fat-man-and-the-trolley-problem.html (accessed August 24, 2022).

Ball, Natalie (n.d.), MacEachran, John. *Eugenics Archive*. Available at: https://eugenicsarchive.ca/discover/players/512fa14834c5399e2c000 (accessed July 19, 2023).

Baumeister, Roy and John Tierney (2012), *Willpower: Rediscovering the Greatest Human Strength*, New York: Penguin.

Beauvoir, Simone de (2010 [1949, 1951]), *The Second Sex*, trans. Constance Borde and Sheila Malovany-Chevallier, New York: Knopf.

Burmeister, Jacob M., Allison E. Kiefner, Robert A. Carels, and Dara R. Musher Eizenman (2013), "Weight Bias in Graduate School Admissions," *Obesity* 21 (5): 918–20. https://doi.org/10.1002/oby.20171.

Callahan, Daniel (2012), "Obesity: Chasing an Elusive Epidemic," *The Hastings Center Report* 43 (1): 34–40. https://doi.org/10.1002/hast.114.

Cathcart, Thomas (2013), *The Trolley Problem: Or, Would you Throw the Fat Guy off the Bridge: A Philosophical Conundrum*, New York: Workman Publishing Company.

Code, Lorraine (2014), "Ignorance, Injustice, and the Politics of Knowledge: Feminist Epistemology Now," *Australian Feminist Studies* 29 (80): 148–60. https://doi.org/10.1080/08164649.2014.928186.

Cooper Stoll, Laurie and Justine Egner (2021), "We Must Do Better: Ableism and Fat Phobia in Sociology," *Sociology Compass* 15 (4). https://doi.org/10.1111/soc4.12869.

Daukas, Nancy (2006), "Epistemic Trust and Social Location," *Episteme: A Journal of Social Epistemology* 3 (1): 109–24.

Dotson, Kristie (2011), "Tracking Epistemic Violence, Tracking Practices of Silencing," *Hypatia: A Journal of Feminist Philosophy* 26 (2): 236–57.

Dotson, Kristie (2012),"How is this Paper Philosophy?" *Comparative Philosophy* 3 (1): 3–29.

Edmonds, David (2014), *Would you Kill the Fat Man?: The Trolley Problem and What Your Answer Tells Us about Right and Wrong*, Princeton: Princeton University Press.

Epicurus ([341–270 BC] 2016), *Letter to Menoeceus: Epicurus*, trans. Robert Drew Hicks, Scotts Valley: CreateSpace Independent Publishing Platform.

Escalera, Elena Andrea (2009), "Stigma Threat and the Fat Professor: Reducing Student Prejudice in the Classroom," in Esther Rothblum and Sondra Solovay (eds.), *The Fat Studies Reader*, 205–12, New York: New York University Press.
Farrell, Amy (2011), *Fat Shame: Stigma and the Fat Body in American Culture*, New York: New York University Press.
Fisanick, Christina (2007), "'They Are Weighted with Authority': Fat Female Professors in Academic and Popular Cultures," *Feminist Teacher* 17 (3): 237–55.
Foot, Philipa (1967), "The Problem of Abortion and the Doctrine of the Double Effect," *Oxford Review* 5: 5–15.
Fricker, Miranda (2007), *Epistemic Injustice: Power and the Ethics of Knowing*, Oxford: Oxford University Press.
Graham, Mark (2005), "Chaos," in Don Kulick and Anne Meneley (eds.), *Fat: An Anthropology of an Obsession*, 169–84, New York: Penguin.
Guthman, Julie (2009a), "Neoliberalism and the Constitution of Contemporary Bodies," in Esther Rothblum and Sondra Solovay (eds.), *The Fat Studies Reader*, 187–96, New York: New York University Press.
Guthman, Julie (2009b), "Teaching the Politics of Obesity: Insights into Neoliberal Embodiment and Contemporary Biopolitics," *Antipode* 41 (5): 1110–13.
Hall, Melinda (2016), *The Bioethics of Enhancement: Transhumanism, Disability, and Biopolitics*, Lanham: Rowman and Littlefield.
Hamermesh, Daniel S. and Amy Parker (2003), "Beauty in the Classroom: Instructors' Pulchritude and Putative Pedagogical Productivity," *NBER Working Paper* 9853. https://doi.org/10.3386/w9853.
Harrison, Da'Shaun L. (2021), *Belly of the Beast: The Politics of Anti-Fatness as Anti-Blackness*, Berkeley: North Atlantic Books.
Hatzenbuehler, Mark, Jo C. Phelan, and Bruce G. Link (2013), "Stigma as a Fundamental Cause of Population Health Inequalities," *American Journal of Public Health* 103 (5): 813–21. https://doi.org/10.2105/AJPH.2012.301069.
Herndon, April (2002), "Disparate But Disabled: Fat Embodiment and Disability Studies," *NWSA Journal*, 14: 120–37. Available at: https://www.jstor.org/stable/4316927 (accessed July 19, 2023).
Hoffman, Martin (2000), *Empathy and Moral Development: Implications for Caring and Justice*, New York: Cambridge University Press. https://doi.org/10.1017/CBO9780511805851.
Horton, Keith (2004), "Aid and Bias," *Inquiry: An Interdisciplinary Journal of Philosophy and the Social Sciences* 47: 545–61.
Jenkins, Fiona (2014), "Epistemic Credibility and Women in Philosophy," *Australian Feminist Studies* 29 (80): 161–70. https://doi.org/10.1080/08164649.2014.928190.
Kang, Sonia K. and Alison L. Chasteen (2009), "The Moderating Role of Age-Group Identification and Perceived Threat on Stereotype Threat among Older Adults," *International Journal of Aging & Human Development* 69 (3): 201–20.
Knobe, Joshua and Shaun Nichols (2008), "An Experimental Philosophy Manifesto," in Joshua Knobe and Shaun Nichols (eds.), *Experimental Philosophy*, 3–16, New York: Oxford University Press.
Kretz, Lisa (2017), "Debiasing the Philosophy Classroom," *Teaching Philosophy* 40 (1): 11–35. https://doi.org/10.5840/reachphil201732962.
Lanphier, Elizabeth and Amy McKiernan (2020), "Thinking about Thought Experiments in Ethics," *Teaching Ethics* 19 (1): 17–30. https://doi.org/10.5840/tej202022771.

Larkin, Judith Candib and Harvey A. Pines (1979), "No Fat Persons Need Apply: Experimental Studies in the Overweight Stereotype and Hiring Preference," *Work and Occupations* 6 (3): 312–27. https://doi.org/10.1177/073088847900600303.

LeBesco, Kathleen (2004), *Revolting Bodies?: The Struggle to Redefine Fat Identity*, Chicago: University of Massachusetts Press.

LeBesco, Kathleen (2009), "Quest for a Cause: The Fat Gene, The Gay Gene, and the New Eugenics," in Esther Rothblum and Sondra Solovay (eds.), *The Fat Studies Reader*, 65–74, New York: New York University Press.

Lloyd, Genevieve (1993), *The Man of Reason: "Male" and "Female" in Western Philosophy*, London: Routledge.

Lydecker, Janet A., Elizabeth O'Brien, and Carlos M. Grilo (2018), "Parents have Both Implicit and Explicit Biases against Children with Obesity," *Journal of Behavioral Medicine* 41 (6): 784–91. https://doi.org/10.1007/s10865-018-9929-4.

Manne, Kate (2022), "Diet Culture is Unhealthy: It Is Also Immoral," *New York Times*, January 3. Available at: https://www.nytimes.com/2022/01/03/opinion/diet-resolution.html (accessed June 25, 2023).

McKinnon, Rachel (2017), "Allies Behaving Badly: Gaslighting as Epistemic Injustice," in Ian James Kidd, José Medina, and Gaile Pohlhaus, Jr. (eds.), *The Routledge Handbook of Epistemic Injustice*, 167–74, New York: Routledge.

Miller, Beth J. and Jennifer D. Lundgren (2010), "An Experimental Study of the Role of Weight Bias in Candidate Evaluation," *Obesity* 18 (4): 712–18. https://doi.org/10.1038/oby.2009.492.

Moller, N. and I. Tischner (2019), "Young People's Perceptions of Fat Counsellors: 'How can THAT Help Me?'," *Qualitative Research in Psychology* 16 (1): 34–53.

Mollow, Anna (2017), "Unvictimizable: Toward a Fat Black Disability Studies," *African American Review* 50 (2): 105–21. https://doi.org/10.1353/afa.2017.0016.

Mosher, Jerry (2001), "Setting Free the Bears: Refiguring Fat Men on Television," in Jana Evans Brasiel and Kathleen LeBesco (eds.), *Bodies Out of Bounds*, 166–96, Los Angeles: University of California Press.

Nichter, Mimi (2001), *Fat Talk: What Girls and Their Parents Say about Dieting*, Cambridge, MA: Harvard University Press.

Nielsen, Kai (1972), "Against Moral Conservatism," *Ethics* 82 (3): 219–31. Available at: https://www.jstor.org/stable/2380200 (accessed July 19, 2023).

Puhl, Rebecca and Kelly D. Brownell (2001), "Bias, Discrimination and Obesity," *Obesity Research* 9 (12): 788–805. https://doi.org/10.1038/oby.2001.108.

Reynolds, Joel M. (2021), "Conditioning Principles: On Bioethics and the Problem of Ableism," in Elizabeth Victor and Laura Guidry-Grimes (eds.), *Applying Non-Ideal Theory to Bioethics: Living and Dying in a Non-Ideal World*, 1–22, Berlin: Springer.

Rodier, Kristin (2022a), "Taking What you Can Get and Taking Care of Yourself: Mapping Fat Women's Sexual Agency Through Television Stereotypes," in Stephanie Patrick and Mythili Rajiva (eds.), *The Forgotten Victims of Sexual Violence in Film, Television, and New Media: Turning to the Margins*, 101–22, Switzerland: Palgrave MacMillan.

Rodier, Kristin (2022b), "Rethinking Fat Studies and Activism through Women's and Gender Studies Textbooks: Fatspiration, 'Thin Saviours,' and Sexist Beauty Culture," *Canadian Woman Studies* 35 (1–2): 7–15.

Royce, Tracy (2009), "The Shape of Abuse: Fat Oppression as a Form of Violence Against Women," in Esther Rothblum and Sondra Solovay (eds.), *The Fat Studies Reader*, 151–7, New York: New York University Press.

Sadler, Gregory (2017), "March 2017 Webinar - Aristotle on Virtue and Vice," *Youtube*, March 15. Educational video, 50:56. Available at: https://www.youtube.com/watch?v=MThFrkGfpRE (accessed June 25, 2023).
Saul, Jennifer (2013), "Implicit Bias, Stereotype Threat, and Women in Philosophy," in Katrina Hutchison and Fiona Jenkins (eds.), *Women in Philosophy: What Needs to Change?*, 39–60, Oxford: Oxford University Press.
Shantz, Amanda and Gary P. Latham (2012), "The Effect of Stereotype Threat on the Interview Performance of Women," *Advancing Women in Leadership* 32 (1): 1–29.
Snyder, Sharon L. and David T. Mitchell (2006), *Cultural Locations of Disability*, Chicago: University of Chicago Press.
Stearns, Peter N. (1997), *Fat History: Bodies and Beauty in the Modern West*, New York: New York University Press.
Stoll Cooper, Laurie and Justine Egner (2020), "We Must Do Better: Ableism and Fatphobia in Sociology," *Sociology Compass* 1–16. https://doi.org/10.1111/soc4.12869.
Strings, Sabrina (2019), *Fearing the Black Body: The Racial Origins of Fat Phobia*, New York: New York University Press.
Swami, Viren and Rachael Monk (2013), "Weight Bias against Women in a University Acceptance Scenario," *Journal of General Psychology* 140 (1): 45–56.
The Good Place (2017), Season 2, Episode 5. "The Trolley Problem." Directed by Dean Holland. Aired October 19, 2017 on NBC.
Thomson, Judith Jarvis (1985), "The Trolley Problem," *Yale Law Journal* 94 (6): 1395–415.
Tremain, Shelley L. (2017), *Foucault and Feminist Philosophy of Disability*, Ann Arbor: University of Michigan Press.
Tremain, Shelley Lynn (2021), "Philosophy of Disability, Conceptual Engineering, and the Nursing Home-Industrial-Complex in Canada," *International Journal of Critical Diversity Studies* 4 (1): 10–33.
Tremain, Shelley Lynn (2024), "Disaster Ableism: Epistemologies of Crisis and the Mystique of Bioethics," in Shelley Lynn Tremain (ed.), *The Bloomsbury Guide to Philosophy of Disability*, 19–47, London: Bloomsbury Academic.
Trotter, J. K. (2013), "How Twitter Schooled an NYU Professor about Fat-Shaming," *The Atlantic*, June, 3. Available at: https://www.theatlantic.com/national/archive/2013/06/how-twitter-schooled-nyu-professor-about-fat-shaming/313728/ (accessed June 25, 2023).
Weinstock, Jacqueline and Michelle Krehbiel (2009), "Fat Youth as Common Targets for Bullying," in Esther Rothblum and Sondra Solovay (eds.), *The Fat Studies Reader*, 120–5, New York: New York University Press.
Wookey, Melissa L., Nell A. Graves, and J. Corey Butler (2009), "Effects of a Sexy Appearance on Perceived Competence of Women," *The Journal of Social Psychology* 149 (1): 116–18. https://doi.org/10.3200/SOCP.149.1.116-118.
Wrenn, Corey L. and Megan Lutz (2016), "White Women Wanted? An Analysis of Gender Diversity in Social Justice Magazines," *Societies: Gender and Social Change* 6 (2): 12. https://doi.org/10.3390/soc6020012.

3 PRURIENTLY FEARED

THEORETICAL ERASURE OF THE DISABLED BLACK MALE

TOMMY J. CURRY

Introduction

On October 5, 2021, the state of Missouri executed Ernest Johnson by lethal injection. Johnson, a 61-year-old Black man with mental disabilities who suffered from the effects of a lifetime of trauma, had murdered three people during a robbery in 1994. In a decision that disregarded pleas from Pope Francis II, members of Congress, and Bob Holden (the former governor of Missouri), Governor Mike Parson and Attorney General Eric Schmitt ruled that Johnson, despite his intellectual disabilities and looming Eighth Amendment concerns, was culpable for the crime that he had committed (Ferkenhoff 2021). Yet Johnson had lived a life of academic underachievement, adaptive gaps, and societal disadvantage. For example, the mental assessment reports that were disclosed to the Missouri Supreme Court showed that Johnson had "significant difficulties in school with attention, concentration, [and] had evidence of some learning disabilities" (Weis and Kemp 2021: 8). Johnson, who experienced the effects of fetal alcohol syndrome, was placed in special classes at school but eventually dropped out. Fetal alcohol syndrome increased Johnson's propensity for drug and alcohol addiction and depression. Dr. Carl Bell, a pioneer in fetal alcohol syndrome research and its relationship to violence, has found that poor emotional control and affective regulation are related to prenatal alcohol exposure (Bell 2018: 120). Thus, Bell suggests that the neurodevelopmental effects associated with prenatal alcohol exposure "should be a factor a judge or jury should consider before sentencing someone who is found guilty of perpetrating a crime" (ibid.). In fact, Bell argues that the developmental effects of "fetal alcohol exposure may even be a factor to consider when determining if someone is guilty of a crime or not" (ibid.). Although Johnson was mentally disabled from birth and the Eighth Amendment prohibits the execution of disabled citizens, the state of Missouri nevertheless executed him. Why?

Problematic assertions according to which low intelligence and deviance are causally linked have a long history and are well established throughout American academia (Herrnstein and Murray 2004; Hirschi and Hindelang 1977). Despite decades of scholarship indicting reason and rationality for their pretenses as benevolent and effective attributes in assigning blame or arriving at principles of justice, philosophers and legal theorists continue to assert that ethical beings are reasonable or driven by rationality and that ethical matters, specifically analyses of moral culpability, should proceed on this basis (Schlag 1990, 1998). Johnson did murder three people in 1994 but does his guilt render him unworthy of philosophical consideration? Should the violation of his rights by the state be disregarded? Black male studies scholars have argued that no ethos has been attributed to the Black male (Curry 2017a; Neal 2021). He cannot be captured by the tools of legal reasoning; he is incapable of generating sympathy or pathos and demonized by logos (Curry 2017a). The intellectually disabled Black man is already determined to be the expression of the Black male's deviance because of his lower intellectual ability and moral capacities rather than distinguished from it. Disability in the Black male is thought to diminish what is assumed to be the naturally occurring capacity for reason in human beings. Black men were, on this basis, historically denied the fortuity of humanity throughout the nineteenth and twentieth centuries and continue to be dehumanized in the present. Legal and moral philosophers have consistently failed to consider how the constitution of Black males—as social beings—fundamentally differs from the humanist supposition and the intersectional categories believed to dictate processes of recognition. Black males are assumed to be less intelligent than both white Americans and their female counterparts, that is, Black women. This supposed intellectual deficit which is associated with Black men and boys renders ethicists and jurors alike indifferent to the vulnerabilities that disabled Black men experience due to the combination of ableism, white supremacy, and misandry.

The humanity of disabled Black men cannot be reclaimed within a white supremacist society that defines Black men according to racist caricatures that are used to justify lethal engagement with them and their extermination (Curry 2017a). Empirical, historical, and theoretical evidence from a range of researchers overwhelmingly demonstrates that the Black male is thought to be a demonic and characterologically vacuous existence (Curry 2017a; Headley 2022; Neal 2021; Curtis 1975, 1976). The Black male is what non-Black males say he is regardless of intent, act, or disability (Curry 2017a). Philosophy elides the theorization of his victimization and death because the tools of philosophical investigation almost solely depend on recognition and political consensus to activate shame, guilt, and liberal consensus around groups and individuals who are deemed worthy to be seen as victims. The philosopher is enamored by abstractions of intersectional categories that depend on the politics of the practitioner and the recognition of subjects from their peers rather than the evidence of racial and ethnic crises in society. The data that demonstrates the deliberate executions of intellectually disabled Black men, including the evidence of their death and the suffering that they endured from lethal injection, suggests that we cannot trust philosophical methodology and analysis to unveil the silenced positionality of racialized men and boys, especially Black males (Kitossa 2021; Yancy 2022).

Within a variety of philosophical discourses and traditions, the Black male is both implicitly and explicitly conceived as a dehumanized object, as the unthought (Curry 2017a). He is not a subject, has no somebodyness or being, and has no character that makes any accusation against him impossible rather than a typical example or extension of his deviant nature and lust for violence (Curry 2018). Even within the theoretical terms of intersectionality, the Black male has been depicted as a savage rapist driven to violence by his lack of manhood and positive self-worth (Curry 2021c; Oluwayomi 2020; Stone 2019). Contemporary intersectional feminist thinking claims that the focus on the deaths of Black men—their slain Black male bodies—is a zero-sum calculus waged against the visibility of other Black groups (Curry 2018, 2021c; Purdie-Vaughns and Eibach 2008; Threadcraft 2021). In order to argue in this way, these scholars ignore the sexual vulnerabilities of Black males, insisting that Black men and boys are primarily, if not exclusively, only victims of racism. This perspective discourages and indeed politically condemns theoretical interrogations that engage Black male death and sexual vulnerabilities analytically. I argue in what follows that given this framework, mental disability in toto is, within the United States, indistinguishable from the pathology attributed to Black men and boys rather than simply an unrecognizable example of it.

Mental Disability and the Stay of Execution

In the first years of the twenty-first century, intellectually disabled Black men have been the subjects of a number of Supreme Court decisions that have tested the constitutionality of executing American citizens with intellectual disabilities. The Eighth Amendment of the U.S. Constitution prohibits the cruel and unusual punishment of criminal defendants. Unlike many constitutional amendments, the Eighth Amendment has not been engaged as a static doctrine that dictates the positive or negative rights of citizens. On the contrary, the Eighth Amendment is dynamic and articulates one example of the changing standards of decency within democratic constitutional societies. As Chief Justice Earl Warren wrote in 1958 in *Trop v. Dulles*, the Eighth Amendment "is not static but must draw its meaning from the evolving standards of decency that mark the progress of a maturing society" (Warren in Brown 2018). Unfortunately, the American society in which the meaning of the Eighth Amendment is determined is a racist society, where Black males who comprise a mere 6 percent of the U.S. population comprise 41 percent of the population on death row in men's prisons (Fins 2022). The sordid history of the death penalty in the United States is saturated with the blood of Black men who were falsely accused, executed although innocent, or sentenced to the death penalty when whites who committed similar offenses were given prison sentences (Ogletree 2002; Ross 1994; Hattery and Smith 2022). In a review of more than 130 cases, Robert Dunham (2020), Executive Director of the Death Penalty Information Center, said:

> [t]he numbers further confirm what researchers have repeatedly documented in other contexts: that vulnerable defendants who belong to communities that have historically been discriminated against by the criminal legal system face an elevated risk of being wrongfully sentenced to death. The findings are especially significant now, as the federal government and several states are rushing to execute a number of intellectually disabled Black men without affording them meaningful judicial review of legal claims that, if proven, would require their death sentences to be vacated.

The disproportionate rate of Black men sentenced to the death penalty and executed makes the disregard of their intellectual disability or other impairments relevant for how the criminal justice system considers the moral culpability of disabled offenders and how critical race theorists and philosophers assess the failure of these institutions to stay the execution of disabled Black males who have been unjustly convicted and, subsequently, are unconstitutionally executed.

In *Atkins v. Virginia*, the Supreme Court concluded that the Constitution puts a "substantive restriction" on the government's power to end the life of an intellectually disabled person (Weis and Komp 2021: 47). Indeed, the *Atkins v. Virginia* decision created a Supreme Court precedent according to which to exact the death penalty on individuals with intellectual disabilities violates the cruel and unusual punishment clause of the Eighth Amendment. The precedent recognized that the execution of people with intellectual disabilities violated this clause of the Eighth Amendment because many mentally disabled people cannot be deemed morally culpable for the acts that they commit or the injuries that they cause to others. It would be unjust to punish members of this group with death, that is, although every use of the death penalty is pernicious, it seems especially pernicious to use the most severe punishment that the state has at its disposal with intellectually disabled people who cannot understand the full consequences of their actions.

Daryl Atkins was a Black man born in 1977 in Hampton, Virginia. He was an only child who was born with polydactyly, a hereditary condition that gave him six fingers on each hand and six toes on each of his feet. He was in addition burdened with poverty and a history of academic underachievement and substance abuse (Walker 2009). In 1996, Atkins and William A. Jones were charged with killing Eric Nesbitt. As with cases of intellectual disability and the death penalty, the ethical considerations of courts and theorists reside in the culpability that the individual has as a member of a disabled and disadvantaged group, not on the injury created by their actions. Atkins was eighteen years old when he was convicted of killing Nesbitt, though he insists that he did not pull the trigger and that Jones orchestrated the kidnapping, robbery, and murder of Nesbitt. In 1988, Atkins was sentenced to death after a series of Supreme Court appeals on the basis of intellectual disability that were ultimately unsuccessful.

The defense showed how Atkins's recollection of the murder of Nesbitt was evidence of his intellectual disability. According to Attorney Mark Olive, there was irrefutable proof that the prosecution coaxed Jones into identifying Atkins as the shooter with a deal that would spare the former from the death penalty if he implicated Atkins (Olive 2014: 369–79). As Atkins was sentenced to death for his alleged role in this murder, the central issue concerned his "mental capacity" and the coercive influence that Jones had over him. The defense brief argued that Atkins's sentence did not simply claim that he suffered from a mental disability but rather demonstrated it through a reconstruction of the testimony which Atkins gave of the events that culminated in the murder of Nesbitt. The brief

> describes how the older Jones, unlike Atkins, did not give a statement upon his arrest but waited a year and then, in the presence of counsel, provided what prosecutors wanted—a statement against Atkins—in return for not being eligible for the death penalty; quotes Jones's clear, grammatically correct description of being subservient to Atkins during the crime, juxtaposed with Atkins's version which is "convoluted and ungrammatical;" carefully selects quotes in which Atkins "repeats himself, he refers to himself in the third person, and his grammar is poor," and quotes in which Jones's version is presented in "an active voice

> with short, grammatically correct sentences;" and excerpts quotes from Atkins "that reveal Atkins's simple character," and quotes from Jones which suggest "a self-serving purposefulness and manipulation to his recollections." (Olive 2014: 370)

The brief argued that Mr. Atkins's testimony shows that his culpability was in question and, given his mental impairment, the death penalty sentence would violate his constitutional rights. Following *Hall v. Florida* (2014), the state is prohibited from making determinations of intellectual disability solely from IQ (intelligence quotient) test scores, especially given that these tests have been repeatedly shown to implicitly rely upon racist, ableist, sexist, and classist biases and assumptions. In *Hall*, the Supreme Court clarified its stance in *Atkins v. Virginia* by challenging the use of rigid IQ test scores to deny individuals with intellectual disabilities protection under *Atkins*. Hall, a Black male convicted of murder and rape, tested between 60 and 80 on IQ tests over the course of his life (Bazelon 2014). The Supreme Court decided that the Florida law, which determined intellectual disability (and, by effect, moral culpability) in accordance with an IQ score of 70 or below, was unconstitutional. In the words of the Supreme Court: "This rigid rule, the Court now holds, creates an unacceptable risk that persons with intellectual disability will be executed, and thus is unconstitutional" (Ellis 2014: 391). These precedents should have offered constitutional protections and judicial scrutiny in the case of the execution of Johnson. Johnson was a victim of disregard and the failure of state decisions to protect his rights as a disabled Black man from a severely disadvantaged background.

Johnson was born in 1960, in Steele, Missouri. In a petition for the writ of habeas corpus to the Supreme Court of Missouri (Weis and Komp 2021), it was noted that since the third grade Johnson had been administered seven IQ tests. In every one of these intelligence tests, except for one, Johnson's assessment revealed that he was intellectually disabled. The intellectual assessment reports disclosed to the Missouri Supreme Court state that at the age of twelve, Johnson had an IQ of 63. As a child, Johnson was physically abused and neglected. He sustained head injuries, his caregivers neglected him, he grew up impoverished, and was a victim of child abuse and domestic violence (Weis and Komp 2021: 13). As a young boy, Johnson's mother would allow older women (ages thirty to forty) to exploit him sexually in exchange for money or alcohol. In order to ensure Johnson's compliance with these arrangements, his mother would encourage Johnson himself to drink alcohol or smoke marijuana (Weis and Komp 2021: 42). The rape of young Black boys by older women is rarely discussed throughout the American academy, despite evidence that child sexual abuse leads to multiple negative health consequences and antisocial behavior (Curry and Utley 2018; Curry 2023).

Surgical complications that arose during the removal of a tumor from Johnson's brain compounded his history of traumatic experiences. In a petition for the writ of habeas corpus submitted to the Supreme Court of Missouri, his lawyers demonstrated that Johnson's intellectual capabilities, as evidenced by eight intelligence assessments administered between 1968 and 2009, were diminished and demonstrated that he had a low IQ over the course of his life. Johnson's cognitive impairment was also compounded by a surgical procedure to remove the brain tumor. In an affidavit assessing brain images of Johnson, Dr. Joel Zivot explained that insofar as only some of the brain tumor was removed, and given the amount of brain tissue excised (roughly 15–20 per cent), it was likely that Johnson would experience seizures during the execution. Zivot stated, "As a result of Mr. Johnson's brain tumor, brain defect, and brain scar, a substantial risk of serious harm will occur during his execution as a result of a violent seizure that is induced by Pentobarbital injection. Generalized seizures, such as the one that would occur in Mr. Johnson, are severely painful" (Zivot 2016: 8). Given the severity of the seizures that Johnson would experience due to the lethal injection, the execution clearly violated his constitutional right to not endure cruel and unusual punishment. In short, following *Atkins v. Virginia*, Johnson should not have been executed. In this chapter, I am concerned to analyze why the state-sanctioned death of disabled Black men such as Johnson is considered permissible and how it is rationalized, that is, how the constitutional directive and societal compassion to stay execution is invalidated for disabled Black men and how racist stakeholders (judges, juries, lawyers, and the public at large) use their executions to confirm racialized scenarios of their violent acts.

The Construction of Low IQ and the Crimogenetic Black Male Position

While philosophers began understanding cognitive disability as an area of ethical concern and care during the late twentieth century (Carlson and Kittay 2010: 4), cognitive disabilities among Black males continued to be attributed to an innate racial predisposition that expressed itself as violence: homicide, rape, armed robbery, and so on. Throughout the 1960s, psychologists and ethicists debated whether prisons or mental health facilities were the proper institutions in which society should, with some exceptions, put mentally disabled children who committed offenses (Klaber 1969). For Black Americans, especially Black males, prisons were the preferred institution of confinement. Mental illness was used to assign differences and criminalize the behavior of racialized groups by suggesting that cultural behaviors and beliefs were the manifestation of maladjusted psychological frames (Szasz 1969).

Presumptions concerning the cultural psychology of racial-ethnic minorities proliferated throughout the mid-twentieth century, suggesting that the experiences of disadvantaged racial groups in the United States were the product of their violent and pathological cultures rather than white racism or the inequality of American society in general.

In the 1950s, Oscar Lewis introduced the idea of the culture of poverty to explain why poor Black and brown men were particularly violent and sexually aggressive (Lewis 1966: xlii–lii). In *La Vida*, Lewis argued that poor Black and brown populations had cultural dispositions toward poverty and pathological group behavior, claiming that members of these racial groups expressed individual malfeasance and deviance because they reflected the values and accepted behaviors of their subcultures. According to Lewis (1966), the traits of these groups include

> a high incidence of maternal deprivation, of orality, of weak ego structure, confusion of sexual identification, a lack of impulse control, a strong present-time orientation with relatively little ability to defer gratification and to plan for the future, a sense of resignation and fatalism, a widespread belief in male superiority, and a high tolerance for psychological pathology of all sorts. (Lewis 1966, xlviii)

Lewis's research provided the basis for ghetto studies (Hannerz 1969) and subculture of violence theories (Wolfgang and Feracutti 1967; Amir 1971) by enabling white social theorists to link violent crime to the psychology of Black men and boys. By the 1970s, the lower intelligence of Black men was cast and represented in criminological terms.

In 1967, Marvin E. Wolfgang and Franco Ferracuti published *The Subculture of Violence: Towards an Integrated Theory in Criminology* in which they argued that Black Americans had a particularly violent subculture that tended toward physical aggression and homicide. Based on a study of homicide rates in Philadelphia, Pennsylvania, Wolfgang and Ferracuti argued that the rates of homicide among racial groups that accounted for sex and class could both explain and identify subcultural populations within the same geographical areas. Because the rates of physical aggression and homicide were claimed to be linked to one's race and sex, Menachem Amir (1971) argued that Wolfgang and Ferracuti's findings about homicide and a population's general proclivity toward violence could easily explain Black men's propensity to commit acts of sexual violence and rape. In *Forcible Patterns of Rape*, Amir argued that "The Negro male's aggressive sexuality seems to be more problematically due to the strong need to overcome problems of masculinity and of sexual identity. This is so because of the Negro family structure (mother-based family) and the need to overcome general social disadvantages by substituting sexual aggressive masculinity for failures as a man in the economic and social status spheres" (Amir 1971: 330). Amir suggested that disproportionate rates of criminal perpetration indicated general group tendency and temperament. As such, his theories claimed to *predict* that members of certain social groups would behave in particular ways because of their internal psychosocial and cultural elements, in addition to the ways that the theories described the behaviors of disaggregated race, sex, and class groupings.

> The Negro subculture is a historically unique subculture which embodies all the characteristics of a lower-class subculture but has some of its features in a more pronounced form. . . . The Negro subculture is characterized by the revolving of life around some basic focal concerns which include a search for thrills through aggressive actions and sexual exploits. . . . The emphasis is given by males to masculinity, and their need to display and defend it through brief and transitory relations with women. Such needs and the subsequent concerns with sex stem from growing up in a family in which the mother is dominant and the father has a marginal position. . . . Young boys are imbued with negative, or at least ambivalent, feelings toward masculine functions. Sexual and aggressive behavior becomes the main vehicle for asserting their worthiness. They, therefore, idealize personal violence and prowess which substitute for social and economic advantages. (Amir 1971: 327–8)

Similar to Lewis's culture of poverty research, criminologists and psychologists emphasized the subcultural proclivities of family organization, Black male deviance, and maladjusted psychology as the foundation of Black violence. By the mid-twentieth century, sociologists and ethnographers dedicated themselves to linking the patriarchality of Black males and the inability of Black men to peacefully coexist within or lead the traditional nuclear family as a pathway to street culture, drug addiction, alcoholism, and deviance (Hannerz 1969). The presumed absenteeism of adult Black males within the Black home was linked to sex-role confusion and hypermasculinity, which was an internalized "female personality disorder" among Black boys (Burton and Whiting 1961; Barclay and Cusumano 1967), gangsterism (Miller 1958; Rohrer and Edmonson 1960), and deviant behaviors (Hannerz 1969; Mosher 1969). These anthropologists, psychologists, and criminologists aimed to create an interpretive framework of Black male pathology and deviance that could be observed throughout various disciplines and observationally confirmed ethnographically.

From the 1960s on, both the claim that Black males lack intellect because of their genetic makeup and a growing consensus among psychologists that the deviance of Black males was linked to an antisocial disorder and schizophrenia were used to criminalize Black males and helped manufacture societal support for the lethal extermination of Black male deviants. The psychiatric diagnosis of Black males as schizophrenic made criminality synonymous with theft or militant revolt against state-sponsored segregation. In an article entitled "The Protest Psychosis: A Special Type of Psychosis," Walter Bromberg and Franck Simon (1968) argue that Black deviance and its relationship to nationalist thinking and militancy was "guided in content by African subcultural ideologies and is colored by a denial of Caucasian values and hostility thereto. This protest psychosis among prisoners is virtually a repudiation of 'white civilization'" (Bromberg and Simon 1968: 155). The medical historian Jonathan Metzl, in documenting the relationship between mental illness and American racism, explains that

> American assumptions about the race, gender, and temperament of schizophrenia changed beginning in the 1960s. Many leading medical and popular sources suddenly described schizophrenia as an illness manifested not by docility, but by rage. Growing numbers of research articles from leading psychiatric journals asserted that schizophrenia was a condition that also afflicted "Negro men," and that black forms of the illness were marked by volatility and aggression. (Metzl 2010: xiii)

Cognitive impairment was a feature of the sociological explanation for Black racial inferiority and the place that Black people occupied in the social hierarchy of American society.

The Moynihan Report of 1965 drew from this previous literature concerning the failure of Black males in order to proclaim the backwardness of Black Americans as a group. In the report, Daniel P. Moynihan is clear that the Black community has been forced into a matriarchal structure because American racism "seriously retards the progress of the group as a whole and imposes a crushing burden on the Negro male and, in consequence, on a great many Negro women as well" (Moynihan 1965: 29). Moynihan recognizes that the racial oppression of America specifically targeted Black males and concedes John Dollard's (1937) analysis that the sexual stratification of Jim Crowism created a border between Black men and civil society. "Keeping the Negro 'in his place' can be translated as keeping the Negro male in his place: the female was not a threat to anyone," writes Moynihan. Moynihan explains it in this way: "Unquestionably, these events worked against the emergence of a strong father figure. The very essence of the male animal, from the bantam rooster to the four-star general, is to strut. Indeed, in 19th century America, a particular type of exaggerated male boastfulness became almost a national style. Not for the Negro male: The 'sassy nigger' was lynched" (Moynihan 1965: 17).

Black male underperformance academically and economically was used as evidence of suboptimal group consciousness. Moynihan argues that the underclass status of the Black race, specifically its lack of upward mobility, was due to family structure rather than some innate racial trait. As Moynihan points out, the middle-class Black family "has managed to save itself, but for vast numbers of unskilled, poorly educated, city working class the fabric of conventional social relationships has all but disintegrated" (Moynihan 1965: Introduction). The Negro family of the urban ghetto remains confined to cycles of poverty and disadvantage because Black men have no aspiration for class mobility and Black women's educational and economic success cannot ignite racial uplift. The lower IQs of Black males make them more prone to value immediate gratification over delayed gratification, according to Moynihan. Moynihan, influenced by the work of Walter Mischel, interprets Black male academic underperformance as a larger personality type of Black men. In previous studies, Mischel (1961) had introduced an achievement measure to evaluate cross-cultural achievement studies among nonwhite children. Mischel claims that previous research shows that in nonwhite cultures the

> preference for DelR [delay larger reinforcements] as opposed to ImR [immediate smaller reinforcements] has been found to relate positively to social responsibility and to accuracy of time statements, negatively to delinquency, positively to intelligence, and positively to the presence (as opposed to the absence) of the father within the home under some conditions. (Mischel 1961: 543)

Years later, Mischel (2014) would author *The Marshmellow Test* as a summary of his decades of research, which found that children with impulse control who tended to delay gratification were higher achieving academically and more successful over the course of their lives.

While *The Bell Curve* (1994) is popularly associated with the pseudoscience of the IQ and the claim that low IQ is linked to social deviance and high IQ is related to civility, throughout the 1970s intelligence was often thought to be a proxy for social integration, class elevation, and deviance. Black men were thought to constitute the least integrated social group in the United States, the group least capable of sustained employment or educational attainment, the most criminal group, and consequently, also thought to constitute the least intelligent group in the United States. Psychologists such as Arthur R. Jensen (1971) suggested that Black males were problems for society because their lower intelligence drove them toward deviance and underperformance. What made Jensen's intervention into intelligence testing novel was that he wanted to disaggregate Black IQ scores according to sex. Jensen concluded that Black males generally have a lower IQ than

Black females across the board (Sowell 1977). Similar to the work of his contemporary Lynn A. Curtis (1975), Jensen argued the deviance of Black males was not a shared racial trait that could be applied to Black females. Because Black females had higher IQs compared to their Black male counterparts, according to Jensen, and were less contracultural, according to Curtis, they were more able to succeed socially and economically in the United States. Travis Hirschi and Michael Hindelang (1977) shared the concern that contemporary social scientists had about the disproportionate rates of deviance among lower-class and Black populations, though they believed that IQ was a definitive variable that dictated the perpetration of and propensity to commit acts of violence. In this regard, Hirschi and Hindelang wrote that "it seems reasonable to conclude on the basis of currently available data that IQ is related to official delinquency and that, in fact, it is as important in predicting official delinquency as social class or race. We know of no current research findings contrary to this conclusion" (Hirschi and Hindelang 1977: 575).

In 1977, the American Association on Mental Deficiency (AAMD) understood the term *mental retardation* to refer to "significantly subaverage general intellectual functioning existing concurrently with deficits in adaptive behavior and manifested during the development period (the upper age of the developmental period is set at eighteen)" (Edgerton 1979: 2). Notice that while the 1977 AAMD definition of mental disability (or cognitive impairment) refers to a below-average intelligence—an IQ score below 70—the definition also emphasized cognitive disadvantages produced by deficient adaptive behaviors. Adaptive behaviors in this framework are defined as "standards of personal independence and social responsibility expected in a person's age and cultural group" (ibid.). Racial differences among white Americans indicated endemic cultural conditions that could not be treated through psychiatric or medical intervention. In short, Blackness was a contraindication for therapeutic approaches to mental illness. The racial effect left little room for ameliorative care. Robert Edgerton maintained that racial differences produced different sociocultural psychologies that produced individual deficits. Edgerton wrote:

> This emphasis [on adaptive behaviors] is obviously needed in the United States because of the recognition that children or adults from ethnically different backgrounds (say Afro-Americans or Puerto Ricans) . . . may do poorly on IQ tests and yet behave in a manner that is entirely appropriate for the expectations of people in their subculture. (Edgerton 1979: 2–3)

The growth of racist sociological and psychological explanations for Black male deviance culminated in sex-specific projects that justified the mass incarceration of Black males, increased police management of them, and state execution of them as a way to control them as a supposedly deviant population (Curry 2017a; Del Zotto 2004; Sidanius and Pratto 1999). This aversion toward Black men and boys in the United States culminated in interdisciplinary projects throughout American universities that attempted to explain Black male deviance and aggression by linking low intelligence, criminalization, and other biostatistical markers to gender theory (Lemelle 2005, 2010; Curry 2021c, 2022). In other words, Black male deviance was a political stratagem that concretized the core of America's anti-Black racism, as well as a theoretical invention of American intellectuals and scholars (Lemelle 1995, 2010) who feared association with poor Black communities throughout the United States, both culturally and biologically (Curry 2017a). Black male deviance and criminality is an ideological construct—an interpretive schema that the political economy and institutional practices dictate in order to ensure the maintenance of a Black male underclass. Not only is the label of "Black male deviance"—like the label of "mental illness"—a deleterious construct, it is also a projection on to Black males, a caricature used to justify racist misandry, fear, and moral spite against their existence (Curry 2018). Racist misandry is the "cumulative assertions of Black male inferiority due to errant psychologies of lack, dispositions of deviance, or hyper-personality traits (e.g., hyper-sexuality, hyper-masculinity) which rationalize the criminalization, phobics, and sanctioning of Black male life" (Curry 2018: 267). Substituted for the nature of Black men and boys, these anti-Black stereotypes of Black males as violent, sexually predatory, and incompetent are the basis of how individuals throughout American society *perceive* Black men and boys and how academics interpret this group within *theory* (Curry 2017a, 2018). The American psychological establishment's use of schizophrenia, low IQ, and cultural deprivation to demonize Black males as criminals, sociopaths, and rapists has conditioned not only academic explanations of Black male deviance but the popular conceptualizations that everyday Americans employ to interpret Black men and boys as a group. The disabled Black male, who is burdened by mental illness, becomes what this racist research anticipates: an antisocial deviant and murderer who must be confined and killed by the state to protect white life and American society.

Mental Disability as the Confirmation of Black Male Deviance and Worthlessness

Very little literature exists that discusses the consequences of disability on the Black male body (Curry 2017b). As I have demonstrated, Black males are often depicted in medical literature, psychological studies, criminology, and even philosophical feminist literature (e.g., hooks 2004; Brownmiller 1975; Crenshaw 1989) as violent abusers of women and children, as sexual predators, or as aspiring patriarchs, with little exploration of the particular race-sex vulnerabilities that Black men experience (Curry 2021a, 2021c), a lacuna exacerbated by an emphasis on discrimination in the literature on social justice. In short, a discrimination framework prevails that assumes that discrimination and individual bias unjustly marginalize groups and individuals burdened by negative stigmas and stereotypes. These post–civil rights era views of discrimination suppose that at the base of all individual and group stereotypes is a humanity denied, that is, the discrimination framework gains moral and political force through its insistence that we are all human beings and, as such, should have equal standing in a democratic society. Discrimination, on this view, is usually due to a mark of racial, ethnic, sexual, or physical difference, which prevents human beings from enjoying equal standing in a democratic society and, hence, is wrong: it creates injustice. Indeed, this liberal democratic idea has been a dominant assumption in much of the disability literature produced to date, at least in the Global North. Yet, an understanding of disability among Black men and boys requires that we begin our analyses in a much different register that identifies presumptions about the absence of humanity and social standing in a democratic society in addition to assumptions currently made with respect to difference.

What is humanity to the nonhuman? What is negated in the disabled Black male given that he is already negated—made into nothing—as a Black male? Philosophical explorations and theorizations of Black maleness often lack substance and meaningful conceptualization of Black men and boys because these inquiries and theories do not often occupy the place of persons or moral beings in *thought*. "It is to humans that we extend the mantles of equality, dignity, justice, responsibility, and moral fellowship. Reason, in philosophical accounts, is generally taken to be the ground for human dignity, hence the special accord and moral status we attribute to humans. But people with cognitive disability are individuals who have at best a diminished capacity for rational deliberation?" ask Licia Carlson and Eva Feder Kittay (2010: 1). Insofar as one analyzes the social situation and position of disabled Black males, one is left with an ineffable problem of thought that forces one to declare a tentative humanity for them that enables recognition and inclusion of them as the basis of doing philosophy. Theory cannot capture the humanity of Black men, because humanity is absent—taken—from Black men and boys. As a *negation* of the human, Black males were never thought to be rational or capable of deliberate moral actions. For philosophers, the claim that Black males are human is an untenable and unthinking starting point for theory, since "philosophers conceive of the mark of humanity as the ability to reason" (ibid.). Moral philosophers have represented the notions of freedom, rationality, and individuality, as well as liberal philosophical anthropology as the preconditions of conceptual analysis. The flourishing democratic society and the expectation of a (white) humanity that can be cared for and considered, even if disabled in ways that diminish the grand human standing of the rational individual, do not suppose the nullification of the human being (Warren 2018) and the imposition of sub-personhood (Mills 1998) as is the case with disabled Black males.

Steele, Missouri, is a midwestern city with southern politics. It is in the bootheel of Missouri, which was historically segregated and violent. Johnson was born into a racial warzone. The violence, poverty, and terror that Black Americans experienced throughout the bootheel of Missouri were similar, if not identical, to the experiences of Black Americans in the Deep South of the United States where a virtually identical social structure and organization existed for them. The bootheel of Missouri is part of the Mississippi Delta and reproduced the class conflicts between poor uneducated whites and the Black populations throughout Pemiscot County (Wyllie 1954: 185). Poor whites at the time, fearing competition (for wealth, land, employment, prestige, etc.) from Blacks, used terrorism, lethal violence, and criminalization to target Blacks in an attempt to drive them out of neighborhoods, schools, and industries throughout the region. The historian Irvine G. Wyllie, when describing the racial terrorism of Pemiscot County toward Blacks during the mid-twentieth century, noted that whites rationalized their violence against Blacks as a conflict "between the 'best citizens' and 'bad Negroes.' Best citizens were white, law-abiding, and God-fearing, upholders of moral law and defenders of civil peace. Bad Negroes were identified with every crime from drunkenness and theft to murder and rape" (Wyllie 1954: 186). Lynchings, which, at the time, were not uncommon throughout the bootheel of Missouri, targeted Black men and boys as criminals and rapists who were deemed a threat and incompatible with civil society (McCulley 2014).

Outside of the southern states, Missouri had the second highest number of lynchings in the United States between 1877 and 1950 (Equal Justice Initiative 2017: 44–5). Like the Jim Crow system of the southern states, the myth of the Black rapist and the Black male as a social deviant was rampant. Black men were not allowed to develop or participate in self-improvement or succeed in education. Black men who defied *the place* that whites had mandated that they occupy were lynched or murdered for public display. Black males were confined to a race-sex caste system that forbade interracial interaction and social mobility. This system created a qualitatively different situation for Black males than for their female counterparts where any attempt on the part of Black men to improve their condition was "perceived by the white caste as an affront" (Dollard 1937: 298). This cultural and political schema created the foundation of the racist ideologies that deemed Johnson a threat from birth and unable to be anything other than a deviant. The particular history of Missouri aligns with much of what scholars know of this period in

U.S. history, but the philosopher needs to understand the specific context of the region that prefixed Johnson's presumed nature—his unchanging and inevitable disposition. Johnson was the object of neglect due to deleterious assumptions made about his Black maleness and structurally confined to the social strata—that is, the social conditions—of inferiority. In short, Johnson was neglected by social workers and educators, as well as by a society that saw no need to invest in his improvement because, as a poor Black boy, he could only be managed and was expected to, one day, be imprisoned and eventually executed by the state to protect the white citizens of American society (Curry 2018).

The disabled Black male finds himself defined negatively by the lack of human qualities attributed to him. The philosophical anthropology of the Black male has never presumed rationality or intelligence as belonging to his particular genre. On the contrary, the "normal" Black male is intellectually deficient and amoral. He is a savage being that must be controlled through legal repression and extra-legal terror. In other words, the "normal" Black male has no attributes that intellectual disability would diminish because the "disabled" Black male is the expected expression of Black men and boys in the United States (and throughout North America more generally). This casting of the Black male as without rationality, as a sensuous beast, predetermines the levels of violence and disregard that many whites think that the Black male body deserves. As I have previously argued, "The primitivity imposed upon the Black male robs him of the potential to ever be innocent, rational, or human" (Curry 2017a: 326). When perceived by white society, the Black man is not recognized as what he truly is. This perceptional imprisonment disrupts the presumed benefits of recognition and the presumption of intersubjectivity found throughout the epistemic injustice literature. The Black male is constructed not by misperceptions of his being but rather by the projection of his being into what is represented as body and self before the mind of the white perceiver. To know the Black male is to fear and detest him. He is the perennial threat to life, liberty, one's person, and society. Consequently, caricature *is* the being of Black males. It is all that he can be and what he has always been to the white onlooker. As I have previously explained:

> The Black male is caricatured in being perceived. He is not recognized by the white but distorted by white apperception. The caricature created by white anxiety is imposed upon him and is his actual (non)being to the white mind. He (his physical existence) is subsumed by the various negativities of Blackness housed in the white mind; the caricature is what emerges from this conceptual consumption. Although these delusions do not belong to him and have no actual correspondence

> to his physical body, the reality—the material fact—that the caricature is not being him has no effect on white perceptions of what he in fact is. In defining him as savage, he is imagined to not only be outside civilization but a threat to it. He is not simply othered, but made nonexistent; reconfigured as whites see fit to justify his subjugation or extermination. (Curry 2017a: 326)

Historically, mental disability in the Black male was thought to both confirm his racial inferiority and indicate his primitivism/savagery as a Black male; that is, Black males, who are thought to be at a lower stage of human evolution, have been depicted as savages and violent predators primed to kill at the slightest offense. Not only did this stereotype exist during Reconstruction and the Jim Crow era, it was adopted by white liberals from the mid-1950s forward as a set of cultural arguments used to describe the psychology of poor Black males throughout the United States (Staples 1982; Curry 2021c).

In Black males, cognitive impairment and mental illness are stereotype-enhancing attributes that confirm the negative social capital of the group. In short, Black males are thought to be less intelligent than whites and their Black female counterparts. This lack of intelligence is racial and subcultural insofar as it is a peculiar feature of poor Black male psychology. As I have indicated throughout this chapter, the disproportionate rates of crime among Black males in the United States are believed to be a feature of their peculiar masculinity. Furthermore, hypermasculinity and the psychosis of their Black male personality are thought to explain the underclass status of Black men and boys in the United States. Anthony Lemelle (1995) has shown that the criminalization of Black men and boys by the American citizenry, be they Black or white, is rooted fundamentally in the political resistance and rejection of American values. The militancy of working-class and poor Black males against the established racial order of the United States has led to the systematic demonization of Black men and boys at various levels of society. Consequently, mental disability confirms the negativity (the savagery) of the Black male as a less evolved and irrational beast (Curry 2017b). The violence that the Black male perpetrates against others is thought to be the product of his presumed lack of intelligence and moral competence. In this racist social context, low IQ in Black males is not a disability, but rather an observable trait. It is a naturally occurring deficit in Black maleness, the appropriate social responses to which should be incarceration and lethal deterrence rather than compassion and care. White Americans do not believe that the Black male is human but rather imagine him to be a wild beast or ape (Goff et al. 2008). This inhuman being is therefore excluded from the moral community and his existence is believed to be a threat.

Conclusion

In *The Man-Not: Race, Class, Genre, and the Dilemmas of Black Manhood* (2017a), I argue that Black males are a population excluded from civil society and marked for death. Throughout their life course, Black men and boys experience higher rates of violence, trauma, and lethal engagement from the state, white Americans, and their caretakers. Like many other Black males who are sexually abused and raped over their life course (Curry 2019; Curry and Utley 2018; Curry 2023), Johnson was a victim of childhood physical and sexual abuse. Contrary to the presumptions of intersectional feminism and gender theory, racialized males are an out-group population that are the primary victims of white patriarchal violence and are targeted for state elimination through police executions (Curry 2021a), institutional decimation (Stewart and Scott 1978), and the death penalty. For males racialized as Black, maleness is not a privilege but rather a deleterious category that excludes them from the moral community and ethical deliberation (Curry 2021b). As a dehumanized being, a caricature of the terrors that the white society fears, the Black male's pain and suffering are disregarded. He exists as America's object of dread. He is a criminal because he is a danger to civil society. It is in his nature to harm and kill. A predator that was not gifted with human reason. Consequently, he is not subject to ethical deliberation. His threat to others is to be controlled, his existence in society managed. As such, the Black male's death is perceived to be righteous, and his suffering is thought to be his penance.

Once one admits that racism is misandric aggression in the United States that targets racialized out-group males to both manage and control the population growth and political militancy of the subordinate group (Curry 2017a, 2021a; Sidanius and Pratto 1999; Ghavami and Peplau 2012; Miller 1991, 1994, 2004), the execution of disabled Black males becomes expected rather than exceptional. Mental disability does not detract from the Black man's savagery, but rather confirms it and is interpreted as a universal trait among Black men and boys (Curry 2017b). The criminality of Black men and boys arises from this congenital defect. While the sociological evidence is clear that it is poverty and the social ostracization that Black males experience that produces disparate rates of crime, "the standard theories of black male deviance obscure the historical reality of Black males being forced into criminality. Forced criminality, viewed as a historical process, results in a Black counterculture that will likely fail to correct itself through economic solutions" (Lemelle 1995: 17). Johnson did commit murder, but rather was a victim of the conditions of poverty and the repetitive hatred the world had toward him as a poor Black man (Blum, Li, and Naranjo-Rivera 2019; Johnson, Blume, and Hritz 2018). As a jurisprudential matter, the execution of Johnson was illegal and unconstitutional. From a philosophical and ethical perspective, Johnson was negated and dehumanized by the collective fear and disregard that American society has for Black males generally.

References

Amir, Menachem (1971), *Patterns in Forcible Rape*, Chicago: University of Chicago Press.

Barclay, A. and D. R. Cusumano (1967), "Father Absence, Cross-Sex Identity, and Field-Dependent Behavior in Male Adolescents," *Child Development* 38 (1): 243–50.

Bazelon, Emily (2014), "The Death Penalty Just Got a Tiny Bit Saner," *Slate.com*, May 27. Available at: https://slate.com/news-and-politics/2014/05/hall-v-florida-the-supreme-court-rules-against-floridas-rigid-iq-standard.html (accessed June 20, 2023).

Bell, Carl C. (2018), *Fetal Alcohol Exposure in the African-American Community*, Chicago: Third World Press.

Blum, Robert William, Mengmeng Li, and Gia Naranjo-Rivera (2019), "Measuring Adverse Child Experiences Among Young Adolescents Globally: Relationships with Depressive Symptoms and Violence Perptration," *Journal of Adolescent Health* 65: 86–93.

Bromberg, Walter and Franck Simon (1968), "The Protest Psychosis: A Special Type of Reactive Psychosis," *Archives of General Psychiatry* 19 (2): 155–60.

Brown, Eric (2018), *Advocacy for Insights*, New York: The Atlantic Philanthropies.

Brownmiller, Susan (1975), *Against Our Will: Men, Women, and Rape*, New York: Fawcett Columbine.

Burton, Roger V. and John W. M. Whiting (1961), "The Absent Father and Cross-Sex Identity," *Merrill-Palmer Quarterly of Behavior and Development* 7 (2): 85–95.

Carlson, Licia and Eva Feder Kittay (2010), "Introduction: Rethinking Philosophical Presumptions in Light of Cognitive Disability," in Licia Carlson and Eva Feder Kittay (eds.), *Cognitive Disability and Its Challenge to Moral Philosophy*, 1–15, Malden: John Wiley and Sons.

Crenshaw, Kimberlé (1989), "Mapping the Margins: Intersectionality, Identity Politics, and Violence against Women of Color," *Stanford Law Review* 43 (6): 1241–99.

Curry, Tommy J. (2017a), *The Man-Not: Race, Class, Genre and the Dilemmas of Black Manhood*, Philadelphia: Temple University Press.

Curry, Tommy J. (2017b), "This Nigger's Broken: Hyper-Masculinity, the Buck, and the Role of Physical Disability in White Anxiety Toward the Black Male Body," *Journal of Social Philosophy* 48 (3): 321–43.

Curry, Tommy J. (2018), "Killing Boogeymen: Phallicism and the Misandric Mischaracterizations of Black Males in Theory," *Res Philosophica* 95 (2): 235–72.

Curry, Tommy J. (2019), "Expendables for Whom: Terry Crews and the Erasure of Black Male Victims of Sexual Assault and Rape," *Women Studies in Communication* 42 (3): 287–307.

Curry, Tommy J. (2021a), "Disaggregating Death: George Floyd and the Significance of Black Male," in George Yancy (ed.), *Black Men from Behind the Veil: An Ontological Interrogation*, 65–79, Washington, DC: Lexington Books.

Curry, Tommy J. (2021b), "Black Maleness as a Deleterious Category," in Tamari Kitossa (ed.), *Appealing Because He is Appalling: Black Masculinities, Colonialism, and Erotic Racism*, xi–xxvi, Alberta: University of Alberta Press.

Curry, Tommy J. (2021c), "Decolonizing the Intersection: Black Male Studies as a Critique of Intersectionality's Indebtedness to Subculture of Violence Theory," in Robert K. Beshara (ed.), *Critical Psychology Praxis: Psychosocial Non-Alignment to Modernity/Coloniality*, 132–54, New York: Routledge.
Curry, Tommy J. (2022), "Reconstituting the Object: Black Male Studies and the Problem of Studying Black Men and Boys within Patriarchal Gender Theory," in Shirley Anne Tate and Encarnación Gutiérrez Rodríguez (eds.), *The Palgrave Handbook of Critical Race Theory and Gender*, 525–44, New York: Springer International Publishing.
Curry, Tommy J. (2023), "He Didn't Want Any of That: Considerations in the Study and Theorization of Black Boys Sexual Victimization," in Aisha K. Gill and Hannah Begum (eds.), *Child Sexual Abuse in Black and Minoritised Communities: Improving Legal, Policy, and Practical Responses*, 273–301, New York: Palgrave MacMillan.
Curry, Tommy J. and Ebony A. Utley (2018), "She Touched Me: Five Snapshots of Adult Sexual," *Kennedy Institute of Ethics Journal* 28 (2): 205–41.
Curtis, Lynn A. (1975), *Violence, Race, and Culture*, Lexington: Lexington Books.
Curtis, Lynn A. (1976), "Rape, Race, and Culture: Some Speculations in Marcia J. Walker and Stanley L. Brodsky (eds.), Search of Theory," in *Sexual Assault: The Victim and the Rapist*, 117–34, Lexington: Lexington Books.
Dollard, John (1937), *Caste and Class in a Southern Town*, New York: Doubleday.
Dunham, Robert (2020), "DPIC Analysis--Intellectually Disabled Defendents of Color, Foreign Nationals, Disproportionately Subject to the Death Penalty," December 4. Available at: https://deathpenaltyinfo.org/news/dpic-analysis-intellectually-disabled-defendants-of-color-foreign-nationals-disproportionately-subject-to-the-death-penalty (accessed July 18, 2022).
Edgerton, Robert B. (1979), *Mental Retardation*, Cambridge, MA: Harvard University Press.
Ellis, James W. (2014), "Hall v. Florida: The Supreme Court's Guidance in Implementing Atkins," *William and Mary Bill of Rights Journal* 23 (2): 383–92.
Equal Justice Initiative (2017), "Lynching in America: Confronting the Legacy of Racial Terror," Alabama.
Ferkenhoff, Eric (2021), "Ernest Lee Johnson Murdered Three People with a Claw Hammer. Why Are Experts and the Pope Questioning His Execution?" *USA Today*, October 7. Available at: https://www.msn.com/en-us/news/crime/ernest-lee-johnson-murdered-three-people-with-a-claw-hammer-why-are-experts-and-the-pope-questioning-his-execution/ar-AAPevFU?li=BBnbcA1 (accessed June 20, 2023).
Fins, Deborah (2022), *Death Row the USA*. NAACP Legal Defense and Educational Fund. Available at: https://www.naacpldf.org/wp-content/uploads/DRUSAWinter2022.pdf (accessed June 20, 2023).
Ghavami, Negin and Letitia Anne Peplau (2012), "An Intersectional Analysis of Gender and Ethnic Stereotypes Testing Three Hypotheses," *Psychology of Women Quarterly* 37 (1): 113–27.
Goff, Phillip Attiba, Jennifer L. Eberhardt, Melissa J. Williams, and Matthew C. Jackson (2008), "Not Yet Human: Implicit Knowledge, Historical Dehumanization, and Contemporary Consequences," *Journal of Personality and Social Psychology* 94 (2): 292–306.
Hall v Florida (2014), SC10-1335 (Supreme Court, May 27).
Hannerz, Ulf (1969), *Soulside: Inquiries into Ghetto Culture and Community*, Chicago: University of Chicago Press.
Hattery, Angela and Earl Smith (2022), "Victimizing the Innocent: Racism, Wrongful Convictions, and Exonerations of Black Men in the Criminal Legal System," in Nicky

Ali Jackson, Kathryn M. Campbell, and Margaret Pate (eds.), *The Victimology of a Wrongful Conviction*, 35–54, New York: Routledge.
Headley, Clevis (2022), "Philosophy as Excited Delirium and the Credibility Deficit," in George Yancy (ed.), *Black Men from Behind the Veil: Ontological Interrogations*, 27–37, Lanham: Lexington Books.
Herrnstein, Richard J. and Charles Murray (2004), *The Bell Curve: Intelligence and Class Structure in American Life*, New York: The Free Press.
Hirschi, Travis and Michael J. Hindelang (1977), "Intelligence and Delinquency: A Revisionist Review," *American Sociological Review* 42 (4): 571–87.
hooks, bell (2004), *We Real Cool: Black Men and Masculinity*, New York: Routledge.
Jensen, Arthur R. (1971), "The Race x Sex x Ability Interaction," in Robert Cancro (ed.), *Intelligence: Genetic and Environmental Influences*, 107–61, New York: Grune & Stratton.
Johnson, Sheri Lynn, John H. Blume, and Amelia Courtney Hritz (2018), "Convicions of Innocent People with Intellectual Disability," *Albany Law Review* 82 (3): 1031–62.
Kitossa, Tamari (2021), *Appealing Because He Is Appalling: Black Masculinities, Colonialism, and Erotic Racism*, Edmonton: University of Alberta Press.
Klaber, M. (1969), "Mental Retardation: A Question of Ethics for the Consultant Psychologist," *Community Mental Health Journal* 5 (2): 180–5.
Lemelle, Anthony (1995), *Black Male Deviance*, Westport: Praeger.
Lemelle, Anthony (2005), "Africana Studies and the Crisis of Black Masculinity," in James E. Conyers (ed.), *Afrocentric Traditions*, 63–82, New York: Routledge.
Lemelle, Anthony (2010), *Black Masculinity and Sexual Politics*, New York: Routledge.
Lewis, Oscar (1966), *La Vida: A Puerto Rican Family in the Culture of Poverty–San Juan and New York*, New York: Random House.
McCulley, Jessica LeKay (2014), "Rape, Lynching, and Mythmaking in Missouri, 1804–1933," Theses. St. Louis: University of Missouri St. Louis.
Metzl, Jonathan (2010), *The Protest Psychosis: How Schizophrenia Became a Black Disease*, New York: Beacon Press.
Miller, Errol (1991), *Men at Risk*, Kingston: Jamaica Publishing House Ltd.
Miller, Errol (1994), *Marginalization of the Black Male: Insights from the Development of the Teaching*, Kingston: Canoe Publishing.
Miller, Errol (2004), "Male Marginalization Revisited," in Barbara Bailey and Elsa Leo-Rhynie (eds.), *Gender in the 21st Century: Caribbean Perspectives, Visions, and Possibilities*, 99–113, Kingston: Ian Randle Publishers.
Miller, Walter (1958), "Lower Class Culture as a Generating Milieu of Gang Delinquency," *Journal of Social Issues* 14 (3): 5–19.
Mills, Charles (1998), *Blackness Visible: Essays on Philosophy and Race*, Ithaca: Cornell University Press.
Mischel, Walter (1961), "Delay of Gratification, Need for Achievment, and Acquiescence in Another Culture," *Journal of Abnormal and Social Psychology* 62 (3): 543–52.
Mischel, Walter (2014), *The Marshmallow Test: Mastering Self-Control*, New York: Little, Brown, and Company.
Mosher, Loren R. (1969), "Father Absence and Antisocial Behavior in Negro and White Males," *Acta Paedopsychiatrica: International Journal of Child & Adolescent Psychiatry* 36 (6–7): 186–202.
Moynihan, Daniel P. (1965), *The Negro Family: The Case for National Action*, Washington, DC: U.S. Department of Labor.

Neal, Ronald (2021), "Troubling the Demonic: Anti-Blackness, heterosexual Black Masculinity, and the Study of Religion in North America," in Caroline Starkey and Emma Tomalin (eds.), *The Routledge Handbook of Religion, Gender, and Society*, 428–41, London: Routledge.
Ogletree, Charles J. (2002), "Black Man's Burden: Race and the Death Penalty in America," *Oregon Law Review* 81 (1): 15–38.
Olive, Mark E. (2014), "The Daryl Atkins Story," *William and Mary Bill of Rights Journal* 23 (2): 363–81.
Oluwayomi, Adebayo (2020), "The Man-Not and the Inapplicability of Intersectionality to the Dilemmas of Black Manhood," *Journal of Men's Studies* 28 (2): 183–205.
Purdie-Vaughns, Valerie and Richard P. Eibach (2008), "Intersectional Invisibility: The Distinctive Advantages and Disadvantages of Multiple Subordinate-Group Identities," *Sex Roles* 59 (5–6): 377–91.
Rohrer, John and Munro S. Edmonson (1960), *The Eighth Generation Grows Up: Cultures and Personalities of New Orleans Negroes*, New York: Harper & Row.
Ross, Michael (1994), "Is the Death Penalty Racist," *Human Rights* 21 (3): 32–40.
Schlag, Pierre (1990), "The Problem of the Subject," *Texas Law Review* 69: 1627–743.
Schlag, Pierre (1998), *The Enchantment of Reason*, Durham: Duke University Press.
Sidanius, Jim and Felicia Pratto (1999), *Social Dominance: An Intergroup Theory of Social Hierarchy and Oppression*, Cambridge: Cambridge University Press.
Sowell, Thomas (1977), "New Light on Black I.Q," *New York Times*, March 27, 221.
Staples, Robert (1982), *Black Masculinity: The Black Male's Role in American Society*, San Francisco: Black Scholar Press.
State v Johnson (1998), 78282 (Supreme Court of Missouri, May 26, 1998).
State vs Johnson (2011), SC 90582 (Supreme Court of Missouri, March 1).
Stewart, James B. and Joseph W. Scott (1978), "The Institutional Decimation of Black American Males," *Western Journal of Black Studies* 2 (2): 82–92.
Stone, Brad Elliot (2019), "Studying Black Men Seriously: A Reading of Tommy Curry's The Man-Not," *American Studies* 58 (2): 67–77.
Szasz, Thomas (1969), "The Uses of Naming and the Origin of the Myth of Mental Illness," *American Psychologist* 16 (2): 59–65.
Threadcraft, Shatema (2021), "Making Black Femicide Visible," *Philosophical Topics* 49 (1): 35–44.
Walker, Thomas G. (2009), *Eligible for Execution: The Story of the Daryl Atkins Case*, Washington, DC: CQ Press.
Warren, Calvin (2018), *Ontological Terror: Blackness, Nihilism, and Emancipation*, Durham: Duke University Press.
Weis, Jeremy S. and Laurence Komp (2021), "Petition for Writ of Habeus Corpus for Ernest Johnson v. Anne Precythe," Kansas City, Missouri, June 21.
Wolfgang, Marvin and Franco Feracutti (1967), *The Subculture of Violence: Towards an Integrated Theory in Criminology*, London: Tavistock Publications.
Wyllie, Irvine G. (1954), "Race and Class Conflict on Missouri's Cotton Frontier," *The Journal of Southern History* 20 (2): 183–96.
Yancy, George, ed. (2022), *Black Men from Behind the Veil: Ontological Interrogations*, Lanham: Rowman and Littlefield.
Zivot, Joel (2016), "Affadavit of Joel Zivot," Atlanta, Georgia, October 20.
Zotto, Augusta Del (2004), "Gendercide in a Historical-Structural Context: The Case of Black Male Gendercide in the United States," in Adam Jones (ed.), *Gendercide and Genocide*, 157–71, Nashville: Vanderbilt University Press.

4 DISABILITY, DISSONANCE, AND RESISTANCE

A MUSICAL DIALOGUE

LICIA CARLSON

Over the past few decades, philosophers have increasingly paid critical attention to disability. Yet few philosophers have ventured into the arena of disability aesthetics, disability arts and culture, or disability and music, despite the fact that extensive research is done in these areas within disability studies and other associated fields of inquiry. Indeed, philosophical treatments of disability have given relatively little attention to the musical lives of disabled people and to the relations between disability, disabled people, and the arts and aesthetics more generally.[1] In particular, philosophers of music rarely address disability nor does disability appear to be a prominent theme in either analytic or Continental work in this area. In this chapter, I map some connections between philosophies of music and philosophies of disability in part to show how a dialogue between these fields is important and generative, referring to both fields in the plural because there is neither a single philosophy of disability nor a single philosophy of music. Just as the voices of disabled philosophers are having a profound effect on the profession[2] (as this volume affirms), disabled musicians, composers, musicologists, scholars, and performers are transforming scholarship on music and the lived experience of music. I begin my argument in the chapter by discussing why philosophers of music should consider disability and, in turn, explain how philosophies (and philosophers) of disability would benefit if they were to formulate and address questions about disability and music and topics in aesthetics more generally. I then conclude by identifying a number of resonances between these subfields of philosophy, including the ways in which bringing music and disability together can produce forms of resistance to ableism and the exclusion of disabled people from philosophy.

Cripping the Philosophy of Music

Philosophies of music cover a vast terrain, spanning historical periods and philosophical traditions. Some questions and concepts recur, like a theme with many variations: What is music? Where is its place among the other arts? What is the nature of musical perception? What effect does music have on us, including on our emotions, our bodies, our behavior, and our character? What is the nature of musical genius? From a historical standpoint, we can also ask what specific philosophers have said about music and what role it plays in their philosophical work. Still other questions have emerged more recently, such as: What is the relationship between music and technology? How do gender, race, sexuality, and class inflect and define the experience, production, consumption, and evaluation of music? How are advances in neuroscience and cognitive science changing what we know about music and the brain? Although I cannot possibly cover all of these areas in this chapter, I want to consider what it would mean to bring a critical disability lens to philosophies of music. In *Disability Aesthetics*, Tobin Siebers writes, "To argue that disability has a rich but hidden role in the history of art is not to say that disability has been excluded. It is rather the case that disability is rarely recognized as such" (Siebers 2010: 4). Though Siebers is focused on modern visual art, the same can be said of much work in the philosophy of music. In this investigation of the presence and absence of disability in music, I will explore two kinds of figures that appear in philosophical discussions of it—namely, musical normates and musical prototypes—and consider how "cripping" philosophies of music has implications for a number of areas of inquiry, including music and emotion, embodiment, musical understanding, research ethics, and language.

In *Extraordinary Bodies*, Rosemarie Garland-Thomson introduces a new term: "the normate names the veiled subject position of cultural self, the figure outlined by the array of deviant others whose marked bodies shore up the normate's boundaries. The term *normate* usefully designates the social figure through which people can represent themselves as definitive human beings" (Garland-Thomson 1997: 8). This concept of the normate has been taken up in a variety of ways within disability studies, including in work on art and music (Reynolds 2022; Straus 2011). In the context of philosophies of music, I will define the "musical normate" as the (stated or unstated) "normal" or species-typical human musical subject, whether a listener or a performer, who is the object of philosophical investigation. One does not have to search far for musical normates, as they populate a broad range of historical and contemporary topics and texts. In some cases, philosophers explicitly appeal to the musical normate in their work on philosophy of music. For example, Jenefer Robinson, in her discussion of music and emotion in her book

Deeper than Reason (2005), often makes reference to the "qualified listener" or "normal folk." In addition, one can find many more indirect and implicit instances in philosophical discourse on music in which disability serves to define the contours of what constitutes the musical normate.

Consider, for example, Roger Scruton's *The Aesthetics of Music* (1999). Though disability does not appear in the subject index of the book and is not thematized in any sustained way, it appears multiple times and implicitly delineates who the normal musical subject *is* and clearly *is not*. It becomes immediately apparent that Scruton deems the "deaf" and people who are not "rational" to be unable to fully engage with and appreciate this art form in its truest and most elevated sense. In the opening pages Scruton writes, "A deaf person could recognize sounds by sensing the vibrations that produce them: this would be a kind of tactile lip-reading. But *sounds* (the sounds of things) would nevertheless be absent from his experience . . . a deaf person could know much about sounds, and about the particular sounds emitted by objects, while not knowing *sound*" (Scruton 1999: 1, emphasis in Scruton). Indeed, Scruton invokes deafness a number of times in the ensuing chapters, though without reference to any sources that explicitly address the nature of deafness or Deaf musicians. Scruton also addresses the limitations that deafness imposes in relation to the perception of chords: "It seems that deaf people can discriminate concords from discords, in the acoustical sense; but they cannot hear consonance or dissonance, for the simple reason that they cannot hear" (71). Music is a distinct form of ordered sound, Scruton goes on to explain, and, in this context too, provides an example intended to illustrate what features constitute the normal musical subject:

> The order of music is a perceived order. When we hear tones, we hear their musical implications in something like the way that we hear the grammatical implications of words in language. . . . It is possible, as I shall argue, to make too much of the analogy with language. But it is a useful analogy. . . . It also reminds us of an all-important fact about sounds, which is that they have a *primary* occurrence in the lives of rational beings, as instruments of communication. (Scruton 1999: 18, emphasis in Scruton)

Later in his book, Scruton invokes deafness in a broader context, saying, "Although music can be used in communication . . . it is not used to convey information. Moreover, there are rational beings who are tone-deaf; certainly many who are deaf to the meaning of music" (Scruton 1999: 172). This statement signals a double exclusion: both people who lack hearing *and* people who are "rational" but lack the capacity to hear tones are "deaf to music." Furthermore, the statement points to deeper questions about how the meaning of music is defined and who is capable of fully perceiving and understanding it. I will return to this point later in the chapter.

Disability does not figure prominently in Scruton's book, nor does he offer any discussion of the definitions and meanings of "deafness" or "rationality." Yet the presence in the book of the musical normate is established early on and thus readers of the book can assume that the musical subject—that is, one who fully engages with music—is not "deaf" or "irrational," the latter stipulation presumably meaning that the musical subject is *not* cognitively disabled. In fact, the opening lines of Scruton's book invoke two examples that draw upon the commonplace association between disability and deficit. The first example appears in the first chapter on "Sound" which begins: "Like colours, sounds are presented to a single privileged sense-modality. . . . They are objects of hearing in something like the way that colours are objects of sight, and they are missing from the world of deaf people just as colours are missing from the world of the blind" (Scruton 1999: 1). Interestingly, the second example appears at the end of the book which closes with an appeal to a conception of a "true community" forged through music in the context of a discussion of culture. The discussion begs for clarification with respect to who is included and excluded from this community forged through music. Scruton writes:

> Music is free from the obligation to represent the empirical world; hence it can gesture to the true community, precisely when that community is vanishing. The implied community which can be glimpsed in music is finer, nobler, and more generous in its feelings than anything that we could know. The encounter with it leads to the peculiar, quasi-religious reverence of the recital room and the concert hall. . . . [A]rt endorses life only through the 'we' of the implied community. (Scruton 1999: 489–95)

Who is included in this musical "we"? In my book *Shared Musical Lives: Philosophy, Disability, and The Power of Sonification*, I offer a very different account of what a community or relationship based on the "musical we" might mean (Carlson 2022: ch. 5). In the space of this chapter, I want to suggest that one should wonder whether there is room for deaf people and nonrational people in this "finer, nobler, true" community insofar as they cannot fully appreciate and partake in music as Scruton has defined it. I am reminded of Angela Davis's statement in *Blues Legacies and Black Feminism*, which offers a stark counterpoint to Scruton's idealized and, arguably, exclusionary vision of a community formed through music. "Art," Davis states, "never achieves greatness through transcendence of sociohistorical reality" (Davis 1999: 183).

I present this reading of Scruton's work as simply one example of how the presence/absence of disability can contribute to the creation of the musical normate. For he is by no means an outlier in this regard. In fact, one aim of this chapter is to encourage philosophers to bring this critical perspective to other works in the philosophy of music, as disability seems to be unthematized and undertheorized in this field. Thankfully, there exists a rich body of critical work on disability and music, produced in other domains, upon which to draw.

Deaf musicians, composers, and scholars of disability and d/Deafness have challenged what Anabel Maler has called the "hearing-centric view of music" in which "deaf people live in a world of silence, cut off both from musical expression and from receiving pleasure from musical works" (Maler 2015: 73). In "Musical Expression Among Deaf and Hearing Song Signers," Maler argues that

> d/Deaf song signers embody music differently than the hearing by creating a visual, kinetic form of music in sign language, rather than using sign language to express something about sound. In exploring the differences between how hearing and Deaf performers interpret music using sign language, I have raised the possibility that deafness can be a source of musical ability rather than a source of impairment and that hearing can even be seen as a disability in the context of Deaf musical performance and practice. (Maler 2015: 88)

In short, Maler has articulated a reversal of sorts that signifies the shifting boundaries of disability and points to the important notion of disability and deaf gain. Disability does not, by necessity, imply an impoverished existence (or in this case, the absence of a musical life), but rather can be positive and generative. As Maler puts it, "I propose that deafness, rather than being disabling in the context of musical experience, actually enables distinctive musical performances. . . . Deafness, I argue, is not a deficit for musical experience; rather, it is a source of musical ability" (Maler 2015: 73).

Music and disability scholar Joseph Straus has critiqued the existence of musical normates by proposing alternatives to "normal" hearing or "qualified listeners." He writes, "Normal hearing is the way in which normally embodied people make sense of music. I would like to counterpoise this with what I will call 'disablist hearing,' that is the way in which people with disabilities make sense of music" (Straus 2011: 160). One example that Straus addresses is deaf hearing (167–70). Although deaf hearing has distinct features—such as its reliance on the tactile and the visual—Straus argues that it is not a form of art and experience that is exclusive to people who are deaf. Echoing this idea, Jeannette DiBernardo Jones writes,

> Hearing is something many musicians take for granted. Few hearing musicians stop to consider what it means to hear deafly. As hearing musicians increasingly become aware of the physiological experience of deaf bodies, hearing deafly is something that all types of bodies can do. Yet musicians and listeners can also participate in hearing Deafly, with a capital D that signals the cultural minority of those with hearing loss,

as we become more aware of the political implications of the history of language and Deaf culture. (Jones 2015: 54)

The seemingly essential and exclusive connection between hearing and music is, in short, an artifact of ableist discourse.

As I have indicated, Scruton's construction of the normal (or perhaps ideal) musical subject as rational also raises questions about whether people who are not "rational"—such as cognitively or intellectually disabled persons—can engage in and enjoy music. Consider the example of an individual who has what have been called "profound intellectual and developmental disabilities," someone who is not able to express herself in language, to read, or to write. Many philosophers might assume that this person could never appreciate the sophisticated works of Brahms and Beethoven. Yet some individuals, such as philosopher Eva Kittay's daughter Sesha, who cannot use language nor read or write, are extremely responsive to music and can clearly express distinct musical preferences (Kittay 2019; Vorhaus 2016; Vorhaus and Ockelford 2017). These instances challenge assumptions about music and cognition, as well as call into question the means by which we define and assess intelligence and cognitive ability (Carlson 2022).

One can likely find the musical normate lurking in many other places in philosophies of music. By drawing upon phenomenological approaches to music, and to art more generally, for example, a critical disability studies approach can open up new questions and avenues of inquiry.[3] Music is often considered the most temporal of all the arts and, not surprisingly, interesting phenomenological investigations into the ways in which time structures musical experience are underway. Yet what assumptions may be at work in discussions of how ("normal") individuals experience time? Work on disability and temporality in which philosophers and disability studies scholars are engaged could make important contributions to discussions of time in philosophies of music. Thus, we might ask these preliminary questions: How could taking disability and "crip time" (Kafer 2013) into consideration challenge and enhance theories of musical time? How does crip time change and challenge discourses within philosophies of music about musical performance (Carlson 2022)?

In *Music and Ethical Responsibility*, Jeff Warren (2014) takes a phenomenological approach to musical experience, arguing that musical experiences are relational, context-based, and embodied, as well as asserting that we have ethical responsibilities within these musical experiences. Warren recognizes that musical experience constitutes encounters with difference and, in a Levinasian vein, considers the ethical responsibilities that follow from this fact. Music, he explains, leaves a "trace" of the other. As he puts it:

> Music is not autonomous. Composing, performing and listening to music are not separate from other activities in the world. Music is always linked with human beings, because in creative and experiential acts we leave traces . . . since our musical experiences leave traces that affect other people, we are responsible to other people in the ways that we create, perform, and experience music. (Warren 2014: 162)

As I argued in *Shared Musical Lives*, however, it is important to consider how disability shapes these musical encounters and how it informs the ethical obligations that attend them. By bringing a critical philosophy of disability lens to phenomenological ethical analyses such as Warren's, philosophers of disability can offer new ways to examine the nature of the "trace" and the concept of otherness, as well as provide insights about how forms of ableism impede these ethical encounters in musical and other contexts.

In addition to the ways in which a critical philosophy of disability approach to music can problematize and subvert notions of the "normal listener," such an approach can problematize and expand philosophical theories of music and embodiment. In her book *The Sonic Self*, the late violinist and philosopher Naomi Cummings writes about her unique embodied relationship to her violin and the surrounding space: "In the process of changing my relationship to space, I discover a new possibility of 'self,' a new construction of my embodied position. . . . No one can know 'what it is like' to experience my particular body, working with my particular violin, in this particular space, unless I give my own first-person report" (Cummings 2000: 12–13). Although Cummings does not address disability directly in the book, it is nevertheless a rich source of insights that can be used to consider questions about embodiment and musical performance that many disability scholars have explored in other contexts. Blake Howe, for example, calls disablist music "a musical practice that rejects the normal performance body and instead molds its performance practices around the impairments of its performers. Rather than concealing or silencing a disability, disablist music audibilizes disability—asserts disability, even claims disability as a fundamental component of its sonic identity" (Howe 2015: 202). To take another example, composer and performer Molly Joyce writes about how her disability has shaped her compositions, her choice of instrument (a Magnus electric toy organ), and her performances:

> Disability informs my practice in that it compels me to produce work only a disabled body can produce; work that can't be compared to standard notions of ability but can rather be without juxtaposition. As a composer and performer largely working in the classical music tradition, which involves instruments that have been around for centuries for very specific

> bodies of specific abilities, disability from a social model perspective frees me from conforming to such instruments and tradition. It allows me to consider the lived experience first and foremost and then find the resulting musical material. (Joyce, in Hambrook 2019)

Joyce's remarks raise broader questions for philosophers of music. What connections can be drawn between philosophies and theories of embodiment, performativity, and identity and philosophies of music? How do assumptions about the normal bodymind (Price 2014) govern philosophical investigations of embodied musical experience? And how can the experiences of disabled performers challenge and enhance these explorations?

Another broad area of debate that a critical understanding of disability should inform concerns the role of emotion in musical experience. Philosophical questions about music and emotion span the ages, ranging from Plato's discussion of musical modes in *The Republic* through to contemporary research in psychology and cognitive neuroscience. In his famous book *On the Musically Beautiful*, for example, the nineteenth-century philosopher of music Eduard Hanslick defines what aesthetic experience of music should be by setting it apart from the abnormal in no uncertain terms, defining purely hedonic experiences of music as "pathological" (Hanslick 1996: 60). As Hanslick's appeals to the pathological to distinguish allegedly abnormal aesthetic experiences of music indicate, philosophers of disability and of music should examine how ableist assumptions about "normal musical subjects" shape philosophical arguments regarding the relationship between music and emotions. How might alternate modes of hearing (such as what Straus defines as "autistic hearing") inflect the experience of music? For example, many of the autistic persons in the book *Music and Autism: Speaking for Ourselves* describe the connections between their rich emotional and musical lives in ways that challenge dominant assumptions about autism (Bakan et al. 2018). Works like Straus's, and the voices of autistic people who describe their relationship to music, should prompt philosophers of music, of disability, and of emotion to critically examine how "normal" or "desirable" emotional states have been defined and described in the history of philosophy of music and the arts, as well as motivate them to investigate the extent to which disability is present and/or absent in these definitions and descriptions.

A critical perspective on disability must also be directed at the burgeoning area of research on music and the brain. In "Music, Philosophy, and Cognitive Science," Diana Raffman (2014) identifies a number of issues in cognitive science research that are of interest to philosophers of music, including the relationship between music and emotion and the nature of musical understanding. Thanks in part to technology such as fMRI (functional magnetic resonance imaging) and PET (positron emission tomography) scans, philosophers interested in musical perception and experience have been brought into dialogue with neuroscientists and cognitive scientists. Yet Straus's assessment a decade ago is no less true of research in cognitive science and music today. Indeed, as Straus puts it: "The relatively new field of music cognition . . . both describes and enforces *normal hearing*. That is, music cognition enshrines a notion of how people who are understood as normal—physically, psychologically, and cognitively—make sense of music" (Strauss 2011: 150, emphasis added). To be sure, some of this work has offered new perspectives on music and the emotions. As Raffman explains, cognitive scientists are examining perception of emotion in music, the expression of emotion by a musical work, and the evocation of emotion in the listener (Raffman 2014: 596). Although these new ways to examine music and emotions have expanded the purview of philosophers of music and of emotion, it is important nevertheless that researchers in these areas consider who their research subjects are, how the inclusion of disability as a conceptual lens might reshape this research, and how attention to the experience of disabled musicians might transform it.

Raffman also identifies the nature of musical understanding as another area of research in cognitive science that is philosophically germane (Raffman 2014: 592). Here, too, we can turn our critical lens to identify how and where disability has been left out of this research or incorporated into it in deleterious ways. Consider the relationship between vision and musical perception. Though, as the earlier dissonances revealed, many people assume music to be an aural art rather than a visual art, musical understanding can rely upon visual cues and engagement in many ways. One question that philosophers have considered is how tonal space is part of the nature of musical perception. As Raffman writes: "Philosophers have argued over whether talk of movement in space is metaphorical when applied to music. The scientists' thought is that the tonal pitch relationships in a musical work are isomorphic to, and hence can be theoretically modeled and psychologically represented, as certain spatial relationships" (598). Yet if disability, specifically blindness, is introduced into the analytical framework of the research, how might this idea of musical space and movement be challenged or reshaped? How might Straus's notion of "blind hearing" (Straus 2011) transform the philosophical questions and answers regarding musical perception and understanding?

In "Understanding Is Seeing: Music Analysis and Blindness," Shersten Johnson considers the activity of music analysis through the lens of blindness "in both its somatic and metaphorical guises" (Johnson 2015: 131). She explains,

> music analysis, often geared toward prescriptive norms, is an ideal place where norms can be questioned. . . . [W]e might suspend our visually

> centered biases in order to understand how individuals with disabilities engage with music. The more we expand the sensorium of understanding and consider analysis through the lens of disability, the richer become our conceptualizations of how music works. (Johnson 2015: 147)

A concrete example of this enriching expansion concerns the idea of how melodic movement can be perceived spatially. As Johnson remarks: "When musicians speak of high and low pitches, the terms correspond more closely with the orientation of notes on the printed page than, say, notes on the piano where higher is to the *right* of the keyboard." This observation raises the possibility that "pitches moving up and down over time, thus creating a melodic contour, is a learned cultural norm" (Johnson 2015: 133). Insofar as philosophers of music are interested in the relationship between movement, music, and metaphor, considering the ways that blind musicians understand melodic contour is instructive and valuable, particularly if attempts are made to claim that there is something universal about the nature of musical perception.

We can also find examples of the musical normate in how the "musical mind" is defined. In *Reflections on the Musical Mind*, neuroscientist Jay Schulkin (2013) explores the evolutionary and cognitive features of musical experience. In doing so, Schulkin relies on an underlying assumption according to which the characterization of the "musical mind," unless otherwise specified, is one that reflects normal cognitive, physiological, and biochemical processes. This assumption is punctuated by discussions throughout Schulkin's book of various disabilities that play a role in the investigations of the cognitive bases of our musical experience. For example, references to blindness, Williams syndrome, autism, and conditions specific to music (such as amusia) play various roles in how Schulkin and other cognitive scientists define the complex nature of musical perception. In other words, disability is clearly present in the discussions. Yet Schulkin's treatment of disability and the representation of disability in much of the research upon which his work relies raise a number of questions, including these: To what degree do investigations of music in disabled populations remain rooted in a medical model of disability as pathology? Are there ways in which the presence of disabled people in the research and examples of disability in it further entrench certain ableist assumptions or forms of othering? How do assumptions about normal cognition, cognitive capacities, intelligence, and brain function shape this research? And how do forms of cognitive ableism inform the questions that are asked by cognitive scientists in this kind of research (Carlson 2001)?

While one could still characterize the treatment of disability as marginal in Schulkin's book, the late neurologist Oliver Sacks's book *Musicophilia: Tales of Music and the Brain* (2008) places the experience of disability and music at its center. In his introduction to this compendium of musical case studies, Sacks explains his approach to the topic in this way: "Above all, I have tried to listen to my patients and subjects, to imagine and enter their experiences—it is these which form the core of the book" (Sacks 2008: xiv). Notwithstanding Sacks's remarks, we should consider the degree to which this chronicle of individuals who diverge from what might be called "species-typical" *musical* lives remains rooted in the pathological model of disability. How do Sacks's narratives reinforce the line between normal and abnormal and, in doing so, perpetuate, rather than challenge, aberrant musical prototypes? Sacks can be read from a critical disability perspective in a number of ways. His work, in places, seems to be producing (and re-producing) a kind of cabinet of curiosities that enfreak his subjects. Yet some disability theorists view Sacks's work in *Musicophilia* as consonant with the values of disability studies. Leonard Cassuto, for instance, writes, "Sacks is a doctor by training and trade, but he rejects the 'find and solve' model that turns disability into disease. *Musicophilia* shows more clearly than ever the common ground that Sacks shares with thinkers in disability studies, their concern with the same problems, and their shared value of human difference" (Cassuto 2007: 63). Other authors in disability studies and philosophy of disability take a less enthusiastic stance on Sacks's writing about disabled people.

This kind of scientific and clinical research on musical subjects—upon which many philosophers rely—prompts additional questions about research ethics that go beyond questions about how disability is defined and represented. In the context of intellectual disability, specifically, I (2013b) have argued that there is a double danger of the inclusion and exclusion of disabled persons in research. While it is important that disabled subjects be *included* in research, there are complex issues of consent, autonomy, vulnerability, and risk that attend their participation in it, including their participation in musical research. As philosophers of music engage with the expanding research on music and the brain, it is crucial to keep these questions in the foreground: (How) Do ableist norms shape research on music and cognition? What does it mean to pursue this research in ways that resist master narratives and that do not objectify or enfreak these individuals? How can disabled people (including musicians, music and disability theorists, and philosophers) play a more direct and empowered role in shaping the nature of this research?

The preceding discussion maps out only a few of the places within the philosophies of music where one might go in search of the musical normate and where existing work on music and disability and the perspectives of disabled people who engage with music can be enormously useful. Just as presumptions about the "musical normate" point to deeper problems of ableism in philosophies of music that must be challenged, so too certain musical prototypes exist in discussions about disability and music. Certain ableist figures have assumed mythical or dominant status in these discussions that philosophers of music must also interrogate. In *The Faces of Intellectual Disability*, I (2009) discuss the ways that certain prototypical examples of "the intellectually disabled" can be found in both philosophical and bioethical discourse. These examples illustrate how a particular kind of person (in this case, kinds based upon stereotypes and ableist assumptions) becomes representative for the whole group. I shall now briefly consider two examples of musical prototypes that disability scholars have exposed.

In her fascinating exploration of the intersection of art and blindness, *More than Meets the Eye: What Blindness Brings to Art*, Georgina Kleege talks about the dissonance people experience when they are confronted with the idea of a blind visual artist or blind museumgoer (Kleege 2018). As discussed earlier, "deaf musician" may seem equally strange to many nondisabled people. These apparent contradictions, which reveal underlying assumptions about the nature of both art and disability, arise due to the gap between ableist expectations and the artistic lives of disabled people. In some cases, it is precisely because of these dissonances that certain examples of disabled artists take on an iconic status. Consider deaf Beethoven or an increasingly blind Monet. The narrative that surrounds these artistic contradictions is often one of astonishment and wonder that these artists, *in spite of* their disabilities, were able to continue to produce. Musical prototypes, however, can be understood to function in the opposite way: they are familiar tropes that *wed*, rather than separate, certain disabilities and art forms.

The "blind musician" and, even more specifically, the "blind African-American musician" are examples of this phenomenon. Important work has been done on the complex ways in which disability, as well as race, has shaped the reception of nondisabled audiences to blind musicians (Honisch 2019; Krentz 2005; Rowden 2009). As Terry Rowden says in the beginning of his book *The Songs of Black Folk*, "for these [blind and visually impaired African American] musicians and the audiences who have sought them out, their blindness, like their blackness, has been a 'difference that has made a difference' in both the music they produced and the ways that music has been received" (Rowden 2009: 1). Rowden examines why it is that these musicians generated such a range of (often contradictory) responses, revealing the importance of an intersectional approach to theorizing disability and race together. For example, in the case of blind Tom Wiggins, assumptions about blindness, "feeblemindedness," and Blackness were intertwined and served to shape the perceptions of his musical identity and performance.

The example of Wiggins points to another musical prototype, perhaps the most well-known prototype in the context of cognitive and intellectual disabilities: the musical savant. Straus, who has extensively critiqued the notion of the musical savant, argues that it is imperative to recognize these individuals in a "realistic mode" rather than enfreak them. Straus puts it this way: "People who have been labeled as savants are not otherworldly super-crips or bizarre freaks; rather they are people who, like the rest of us, are good at some things and not so good at others" (Straus 2014). In short, the generation and perpetuation of these prototypical cases serve to "other" these musicians and present them in an attenuated and erroneous way. Insofar as philosophers of music address disability, it is crucial to be aware of these musical prototypes and challenge them, as well as move beyond them.

The examples that I have discussed point to the othering of disabled people in three ways: first, by virtue of their exclusion from the musical normate which they simultaneously serve to shape; second, by virtue of the apparent contradiction between their capacity and their disability (the unexpected or "oxymoronic" blind painter, deaf musician, etc.); and finally, through an exoticized version of the disabled artist—such as the musical savant—who is remarkable in spite of their disability.

Like theorists such as Straus and Kleege, many disabled artists are challenging these depictions and dominant ableist narratives about the relationship between disability and art, including the many examples of blind visual artists that Kleege documents in her book, deaf musicians such as Scottish timpanist Evelyne Glennie (Glennie, Gilman, and Kim 2019), the members of the rock band Beethoven's Nightmare, Deaf rappers Signmark and Sean Forbes (Jones 2015: 62–6), and musical subjects with cognitive and intellectual disabilities (Carlson 2022; Straus 2014). As Garland-Thomson has urged, if we adopt a "because-of-rather-than-in-spite-of" framework, it becomes possible to see how disability can be enriching and generative in unique ways (Garland-Thomson 2012: 343).

Attention to the ways that disability functions linguistically and metaphorically within philosophical discourses about music is vitally important. Where, in both historical and contemporary works, does the language of disability play a role in philosophical discussions of music? When, furthermore, do these invocations of disability function as what David Mitchell and Sharon Snyder have called "narrative prostheses"? When might they be provocative and empowering (Silvers 2000)? Philosopher and musicologist Peter Szendy's book *Phantom Limbs: On Musical Bodies* (2015) provides a good example of how disability is used as a narrative prosthetic within philosophical discourses on music. Szendy's philosophical and historical examination of the complex relationship musicians have with their instruments, that is, his use of language and concepts associated with disability—such as phantom limbs and "idiotisms"—invites a closer analysis.

Philosophies of disability can contribute to and amplify philosophies of music in both critical and constructive ways. Moreover, the breadth and depth of musical research in disability studies and the contributions of disabled composers and musicians have revealed alternate modes and models of musical experience that can inform philosophical approaches to music (Cheng 2016; Lubet 2011; Howe et al. 2015; Straus 2011, 2018; Lerner and Straus 2006; Carlson 2013a, 2022; Kim and Gilman 2009). Yet, as I will argue in the next section, philosophers of disability can learn equally as much from work on music, aesthetics, and disability.

Sonifying Philosophies of Disability

In "Music as Philosophy," Philip Alperson acknowledges that "music has had a substantive role to play in the practice of philosophy from the time of Pythagoras to our own" (Alperson 1994: 206). In considering what it might mean to think more broadly about the connections between music and philosophy, Alperson offers a "typology of roles which music might play in the construction of philosophical theories" (204). I think these roles—genetic, illustrative, emblematic—can be useful tools with which to consider how music can contribute to philosophies of disability specifically. Alperson says music serves a genetic role in philosophy when "some aspect of musical practice motivates a philosopher to construct a philosophical theory" (205). An example of this genetic role, I would argue, is Canadian philosopher Jan Zwicky's notion of *lyric* philosophy, which is, in large part, founded upon music in myriad forms. In my own work, informed in part by Zwicky's approach, attention to music played this genetic function insofar as it led me to recast old arguments and develop new ones with regard to philosophy and intellectual disability.

In *Shared Musical Lives*, I argue that musical experience can have both epistemic and ethical significance. Musical experience can reveal dimensions of ourselves and of others that may go unrecognized. Shared musical experience, or what I call the "musical we," can transform relationships, expand our moral imagination, and cultivate virtues. I use the concept of sonification—which in a scientific and technological context means the translation of data into audible sound or musical tones—as an organizing tool for my philosophical claims about music and disability. I first encountered the idea of sonification at a conference on music cognition in a presentation on sonification and epilepsy. Researchers sonified patients' electroencephalograms (EEGs) by assigning musical tones to them in order to better perceive when one of the patients was about to have a seizure. The researchers found that doing so made it easier to "hear" the imminent seizure in the EEG than to see it. The notion of sonification was helpful to me in clarifying my book's main argument; hence, I transposed it into a philosophical key thus: "*sonification* is the process by which musical experience reveals dimensions of the self and transforms our relationships to others; . . . on a more theoretical level, *philosophical sonification* refers to the analysis of these concrete forms of sonification and the knowledge they yield and involves a critical (re-)examination of philosophical concepts, arguments, and theories with a musical attunement" (Carlson 2022: 5).

While much philosophical work on intellectual and cognitive disability has been rooted in discussions of political philosophy, ethics, and bioethics, very little connection has been made between philosophies of disability and philosophies of art and music. Yet attention to the musical lives of disabled people promises to have a generative and transformative impact on philosophical theories and discussions of intellectual disability. There is epistemic value in considering musical lives insofar as they can reveal forms of flourishing and modes of cognition, emotional engagement, and alternate ways of performing identity that may have otherwise been undetected. Musical experience, and artistic expression more generally, can challenge, reconceptualize, and expand conceptions of personhood and flourishing; expose ableist dualisms (such as normal/abnormal, active/passive); reconfigure relationships; reveal and cultivate musical virtues; and interrogate sites and forms of musical production (Carlson 2022).

Alperson says that music can play an illustrative role, where "the use of a musical example is apt but not indispensable to the theory" and, furthermore, can serve as what he calls a "component" capacity, "occupying an important place in a philosophical system" (Alperson 1994: 204–5). In the case of philosophers (either past or present) for whom music is a part of their larger works—including Plato, Rousseau, Nietzsche, Adorno, Davis, and West—this specific dimension of their work may generate pertinent questions for philosophers of disability. For example, how is musical experience relevant to theories of flourishing, personhood, and community? How is disability relevant to debates regarding music as a language? How do theories of the commodification of art and music intersect with work on disability? In the case of intellectual disability specifically, musical examples can be illustrative insofar as they challenge assumptions about global deficit and reveal capacities that may not otherwise be present (Vorhaus 2016; Vorhaus and Ockelford 2017; Kittay 2019; Carlson 2022).

Philosophers of disability can also draw upon musical concepts and metaphors to expand their lexicon. In this regard, music can serve as what Alperson calls an "emblematic function," "serving as a model or guiding metaphor for a philosophical concept or principle in the construction of a theory" (Alperson 1994: 205). I began this chapter with a discussion of some "problematic" dissonances, but dissonance in music (as in disability and life) need not be a negative term; like silence, dissonance can be productive. Counterpoint, improvisation, harmony, resonance, syncopation—all of these musical terms might find a welcome home in philosophies of disability, and in doing so, expand our philosophical imagination.

Alperson concludes by saying that "to the extent that we are willing to regard music as philosophical," it can "continue to heighten our sense of wonder and advance our understanding of the universe and of ourselves" (Alperson 1994: 206). I would add that philosophers of music and of aesthetics more broadly can contribute to a fuller understanding of disability and to the work of philosophers of disability through discussions of embodiment, emotion, flourishing, performance, and beauty.

Resonance and Resistance

Thus far, I have addressed how philosophies of music and disability can mutually benefit from a critical dialogue. I would like to conclude this chapter by identifying a number of resonances that I have found between them.

Critiques of essentialism, autonomy, and the epistemic authority of science are likely familiar to philosophers of disability whose work aims to challenge the dominance of both medical models of disability and the myth of the independent, autonomous subject. I want to note that some philosophers of music have made roughly analogous arguments in a musical context. The first resonance is between ontological debates about the "musical work" and critiques of essentialism with respect to the status of disability in philosophies of disability. In the philosophy of music, the ontological status of the musical work has long been a topic (Alperson 1994; Ingarden 1998). How exactly should we conceive of it? Is it a kind of Platonic form? Does its essence reside in the score, the composer's intention, or in each individual performance? Lydia Goehr, in *The Imaginary Museum of Musical Works* (2007), explains how the very concept of the musical work is historically contingent. In "Voices from the Margins," Alperson uses the example of illness to make a similar argument:

> Musical works are not natural kinds but rather human productive activities fraught with intentional meaning, contextual pressures, enabling conditions and forces, and the accretions of history. . . . We might compare our understanding of musical works with our understanding of human illnesses. Illnesses of course have underlying physiological conditions but the full human meaning of illnesses in the context of human affairs can only be fully understood in the context of the complexities of lived human experience. (Alperson 2009: 93)

In the spirit of Alperson's comparison, we can consider the parallels between how philosophers of music and philosophers of disability have challenged the assumption that music and disability, respectively, are unproblematic natural kinds (Carlson 2022). Disability scholarship on music has added another dimension to this debate regarding the ontological status of the musical work by exploring how disability can be present *in* musical works themselves. For example, in *Broken Beauty: Musical Modernism and the Representation of Disability*, Straus (2018) shows how modernist music represents various forms of disability through rhythmic, harmonic, and melodic structures.

Philosophers of music have also critiqued the idea of the musical work as an autonomous entity, generally with a focus on purely instrumental music, or "absolute music." In *The Philosophy of Music* (2004), Aaron Ridley, like Alperson, imports medicalized language to characterize this obsession with autonomy in a musical context. He defines the "syndrome" of autonomania as follows: "the autonomaniac begins by assuming that music is, essentially, pure sound, and then sets about investigating it in accordance with a method which reinforces that assumption" (Ridley 2004: 13). He goes on to say: "[We] should think about music not as autonomous patterns of sound, but perhaps rather as patterns of sound that are embedded in the rest of the world, shot through with history." He adopts a "baggy musical ontology" and, in doing so, rejects this obsession with the musical work as autonomous (ibid.). Philosophers of disability have critiqued the idea of disability as a pathological state rooted solely in the individual. Feminist disability theorists, too, have challenged the notion of the self as an independent, autonomous, and atomistic entity by acknowledging the ways that dependency, interdependence, and material power dynamics define our subjectivity. Many of the models of disability that philosophers have proposed—for example, social, materialist, postmodern, minority, historicist, and relativist models—though different in many respects, share a commitment to a contextualist approach that eschews the idea that disability is a neutral, natural kind. This resonance between philosophies of disability and philosophies of music that ground both the experience of music and of disability in material, social, political, and economic conditions is a connection worthy of further exploration.

A third resonance between philosophies of music and philosophies of disability is that both areas of inquiry necessarily engage with and problematize scientific authority and knowledge. In the context of disability, a vast body of work challenges the medical model of disability and other forms of medical authority, epistemic injustice, and ableism in bioethical and clinical contexts. Philosophers of music also increasingly contend with the burgeoning research in music cognition and forms of "musical pathologies" (as I discussed earlier) and thus must address similar questions of authority and critically consider presuppositions that underlie this scientific research.

The field of music therapy, an area of research that few philosophers of music or philosophers of disability have addressed, explicitly brings music and disability together. As I have argued elsewhere, there is tremendous philosophical value in critically engaging with both the benefits and drawbacks of music therapy (Carlson 2022). Although some disability scholars have rightly been critical of this field because of its grounding in a therapeutic, rehabilitative, and often normalizing model (Straus 2011, 2014), there are many different approaches to music therapy, some of which may be consonant with a critical philosophy of disability approach. Indeed, I think that philosophers of disability and philosophers of music can make valuable contributions to these worthwhile cross-disciplinary conversations and can also gain valuable knowledge about the relationship between music and disability from within this field of practice.

A final resonance can be found in the ways in which philosophers of music and philosophers of disability are engaging in acts of resistance. Philosophers from both fields (and the few who bridge them) have theorized and articulated commitments to gender, racial, economic, social, and disability justice. In both fields, furthermore, they have also worked to move marginalized groups and philosophical approaches from the margins to the center.

One shift in philosophies of music has been to expand the purview of what kinds of music and musical activities are considered. Musicologist Christopher Small has introduced a term (which I have adopted) that speaks to this more capacious understanding of our musical lives; "musicking," he says, is "to take part, in any capacity, in a musical performance, whether by performing, by listening, by rehearsing or practicing, by providing material for performance (what is called composing), or by dancing" (Small 1998). Yet this conception of musical experience is not in line with traditional approaches in the philosophy of music. In the introduction to *The Music of Our Lives* (2011), Kathleen Higgins writes, "Contemporary American philosophy has little place for music, let alone for the music of everyday life. Musical aesthetics is a marginal phenomenon within aesthetics, and the whole field of aesthetics is treated as a fringe of philosophical concern. . . . Conservatism, ethnocentrism, and divorce from experience characterize the now established philosophical approach to music" (Higgins 2011: xiv, xv). Some philosophers of music (such as Small) have, however, cleared new paths for philosophical work in their field that is more diverse, politically grounded, and intersectional; that is, they are broadening the boundaries of what kinds of music are worthy of philosophical consideration and transforming the way that musicking is understood, expanding the purview to include non-classical forms of music and engaging with philosophical work on race and gender (Davis 1999; Darby and Shelby 2005; Skitolsky 2020). In a similar vein, feminist philosophies of disability consider gender and disability through a variety of methods and, in doing so, continue to move feminist philosophy and philosophies of disability in new directions (Tremain 2013, 2015; Carlson 2001, 2021; Wendell 1996; Hall 2011). At the same time, work in feminist and disability aesthetics is challenging boundaries and forms of exclusion, as well as underscoring the transformative and political power of art and music (Eaton 2021; McClary 1991; Silvers 2000; Siebers 2010). Enabling cross-pollination and dialogue between the intersectional work in all of these areas has considerable potential.

Another resonance between philosophies of disability, disability studies, and philosophies of music can be found in work that exposes the whiteness of the fields. In "Decolonising Disability: Thinking and Acting Globally," Helen Meekosha advocates for the "process of intellectual decolonization" of disability theory (Meekosha 2011). How might this process be relevant to philosophies of music? And what philosophical challenges and solutions emerge when theorizing music, race, and disability together?

In his foreword to *Hip Hop to Philosophy: Rhyme 2 Reason*, Cornel West writes that "philosophers of all stripes must break their relative silence on two pressing topics in their academic discipline—race and music. . . . Though hip-hop music has yet to produce a figure of the stature of a Mozart, Coltrane, or Aretha Franklin, many towering hip-hop artists deserve our philosophical attention—and the hip-hop phenomena itself warrants examination" (West 2005). Jesse Steinberg and Abrol Fairweather introduce their edited volume *Blues: Philosophy for Everyone, Thinking Deep About Feeling Low* in this way: "Blues and philosophy are definitely not one and the same. Yet the essays in this book make the case that there is a lot of connective tissue. These connections have to do with a shared approach and response to the many profound and enduring questions of human nature, knowledge, and existence" (Steinberg and Fairweather 2012: xvi). Though these anthologies are not directly centered upon disability, many of the chapters address relevant themes, including emotional trauma, adversity, loss, political empowerment, and resistance. Lissa Skitolsky's book *Hip-Hop as Philosophical Text and Testimony*, on the other hand, explicitly theorizes the relationship between hip-hop, anti-Black racism, and trauma as a form of disability. Skitolsky's work is an important corrective to both the exclusion of hip-hop music in philosophies of music and to medical and individual models of disability and trauma. She argues,

> Shifting the focus from trauma as individual pathology to a psycho-social space helps us better understand trauma as a product of contingent and unnatural social conditions. . . . Hip-hop culture illustrates that the trauma of systematic anti-black violence represents both a pathology of American history and collective memory that perpetuates its reoccurrence through its dis-appearance in thought,

perception, discourse, and understanding about race and American society. (Skitolsky 2020: 61)

Higgins has argued that music has the power to bridge cross-cultural divides and foster better understanding across differences (Higgins 2014). Skitolsky's analysis of hip-hop offers one example of what this might mean in practice. While there are reasons to be suspicious of an overly romanticized notion of music's harmonizing effect (Carlson 2022), new connections and forms of communication can emerge by including disability culture and disability arts in this conversation. Disabled artists and disabled philosophers, by drawing upon lived experience and critiquing forms of ableism, racism, marginalization, and exclusion, are expanding the very boundaries and definitions of philosophy, music, culture, and artistic expression.

Although the theoretical possibilities of these dialogues and resonances are exciting, they mean very little if they remain abstract and exclusionary, and if music, philosophy, and the arts are inaccessible. Disability justice must be predicated on a commitment to inclusion and to combatting forms of material and structural oppression. This commitment must include conversations and anti-oppression measures implemented in academic disciplines and higher education more generally, as well as the provision of the necessary material and creative resources for musical and artistic expression. Disability justice through the arts must include the commitment to inclusive music and arts education in all communities; the development of creative opportunities and spaces that are accessible, safe, affordable, empowering, and stigma-free; and the welcoming cultivation, celebration, and respect of *all* forms of musical and artistic lives.

Notes

1 She argues that its "depiction of traumatic violence . . . departs from and contests the depiction of trauma in professional academic and clinical discourse," and thereby challenges conceptions of disability rooted in individual pathology (2020: 163). Largely ignored in academic discussions of philosophy of music, genocide studies, and analyses of race and anti-Black racism, Skitolsky contends that hip-hop is essential to understanding systemic forms of epistemic injustice, whiteness, and the nature of trauma and violence.

2 The chapters in this volume are a testament to this movement, as is the Dialogues on Disability series of interviews with disabled philosophers conducted by Shelley Tremain. See the Dialogues on Disability archive. Available at: https://biopoliticalphilosophy.com/dialogues-on-disability/ (accessed June 19, 2023).

3 Joel Michael Reynolds's article "The Normate: On Disability, Critical Phenomenology, and Merleau-Ponty's Cézanne" is an example of this in the context of visual art.

References

Alperson, Philip (1994), "Music as Philosophy," in Philip Alperson (ed.), *What is Music: An Introduction to the Philosophy of Music*, 195–210, University Park: University of Pennsylvania Press.

Alperson, Philip (2009), "Facing the Music: Voices from the Margins," *Topoi* 28 (2): 91–6.

Bakan, Michael, with Mara Chasar, Graeme Gibson, Elizabeth J. Grace, Zena Hamelson, Dotan Nitzberg, Gordon Peterson, Maureen Pytlik, Donald Rindale, Amy Sequenzia, and Addison Star (2018), *Music and Autism: Speaking For Ourselves*, New York: Oxford University Press.

Carlson, Licia (2001), "Cognitive Ableism and Disability Studies: Feminist Reflections on the History of Mental Retardation," *Hypatia: A Journal of Feminist Philosophy* 16 (4): 124–46.

Carlson, Licia (2009), *The Faces of Intellectual Disability: Philosophical Reflections*, Bloomington: Indiana University Press.

Carlson, Licia (2013a), "Musical Becoming: Intellectual Disability and the Transformative Power of Music," in M. Wappett and K. Arndt (eds.), *Foundations of Disability Studies*, 83–103, London: Palgrave Macmillan.

Carlson, Licia (2013b), "Research Ethics and Intellectual Disability: Broadening the Debates," *Yale Journal of Biology and Medicine* 86 (8): 303–13.

Carlson, Licia (2021), "Feminism and Disability Theory," in Kim Q. Hall and Ásta (eds.), *The Oxford Handbook of Feminist Philosophy*, 517–30, New York: Oxford University Press.

Carlson, Licia (2022), *Shared Musical Lives: Philosophy, Disability, and the Power of Sonification*, New York: Oxford University Press.

Cassuto, Leonard (2007), "The Uncanny Symphony of Oliver Sacks," *The Chronicle of Higher Education* 54 (10): 63.

Cheng, William (2016), *Just Vibrations: The Purpose of Sounding Good*, Ann Arbor: University of Michigan.

Cummings, Naomi (2000), *The Sonic Self*, Bloomington: Indiana University Press.

Darby, Derrick and Tommie Shelby, eds. (2005), *Hip Hop to Philosophy: Rhyme 2 Reason*, Chicago: Open Court.

Davis, Angela (1999), *Blues Legacies and Black Feminism*, New York: Vintage.

Dialogues on Disability (n.d.), BIOPOLITICAL PHILOSOPHY (blog). Available at: https://biopoliticalphilosophy.com/dialogues-on-disability (accessed October 8, 2022).

Eaton, A. W. (2021), "Feminist Aesthetics," in Kim Q. Hall and Ásta (eds.), *The Oxford Handbook of Feminist Philosophy*, 295–311, New York: Oxford University Press.

Garland-Thomson, Rosemarie (1997), *Extraordinary Bodies*, New York: Columbia University Press.

Garland-Thomson, Rosemarie (2012), "The Case for Conserving Disability," *Journal of Bioethical Inquiry* 9: 339–55.

Glennie, Evelyne, Sander Gilman, and Youn Kim (2019), "Is there Disabled Music? Music and the Body from Dame Evelyn Glennie's Perspective," in Youn Kim and Sander Gilman (eds.), *The Oxford Handbook of Music and the Body*, 318–30, New York: Oxford University Press.

Goehr, Lydia (2007), *The Imaginary Museum of Musical Works: An Essay in the Philosophy of Music*, Oxford: Oxford University Press.

Hall, Kim Q., ed. (2011), *Feminist Disability Studies*, Bloomington: Indiana University Press.

Hambrook, Colin (2019), "Molly Joyce on the Influence of Disability Studies on Her Music Making," *Disability Arts Online*, June. Available at: https://disabilityarts.online/magazine/opinion/molly-joyce/ (accessed June 24, 2023).

Hanslick, Eduard (1996), *On the Musically Beautiful*, trans. G. Payzant, Indianapolis: Hackett Publishing.
Higgins, Kathleen (2011), *The Music of Our Lives*, Lanham: Lexington Books.
Higgins, Kathleen (2014), *The Music Between Us: Is Music a Universal Language?* Chicago: University of Chicago Press.
Honisch, Stefan Sunandan (2019), "Virtuosities of Deafness and Blindness: Musical Performance and the Prized Body," in Youn Kim and Sander Gilman (eds.), *The Oxford Handbook of Music and the Body*, 276–94, New York: Oxford University Press.
Howe, Blake (2015), "Disabling Music Performance," in Blake Howe, Stephanie Jensen-Moulton, Neil Lerner, and Joseph Straus (eds.), *The Oxford Handbook of Music and Disability Studies*, 191–209, New York: Oxford University Press.
Howe, Blake, Stephanie Jensen-Moulton, Neil Lerner, and Joseph Straus, eds. (2015), *The Oxford Handbook of Music and Disability Studies*, New York: Oxford University Press.
Ingarden, Roman (1998), *Ontology of the Work of Art*, Athens: University of Ohio Press.
Johnson, Shersten (2015), "Understanding is Seeing: Music Analysis and Blindness," in Blake Howe, Stephanie Jensen Moulton, Neil Lerner, and Joseph Straus (eds.), *The Oxford Handbook of Music and Disability Studies*, 131–52, New York: Oxford University Press.
Jones, Jeannette DiBernardo (2015), "Imagined Hearing: Music-Making in Deaf Culture," in Blake Howe, Stephanie Jensen Moulton, Neil Lerner, and Joseph Straus (eds.), *The Oxford Handbook of Music and Disability Studies*, 54–72, New York: Oxford University Press.
Kafer, Alison (2013), *Feminist, Queer, Crip*, Bloomington: Indiana University Press.
Kittay, Eva Feder (2019), *Learning From My Daughter: The Value and Care of Disabled Minds*, Oxford: Oxford University Press.
Kleege, Georgina (2018), *More Than Meets the Eye: What Blindness Brings to Art*, New York: Oxford University Press.
Krentz, Christopher (2005), "A 'Vacant Receptacle?' Blind Tom, Cognitive Difference, and Pedagogy," *PMLA: Publications of the Modern Language Association of America* 120 (2): 552–7.
Lerner, Neil and Joseph Straus, eds. (2006), *Sounding Off: Theorizing Disability in Music*, New York: Routledge.
Lubet, Alex (2011), *Music, Disability, and Society*, Philadelphia: Temple University Press.
Maler, Anabel (2015), "Musical Expression Among Deaf and Hearing Song Signers," in Blake Howe, Stephanie Jensen Moulton, Neil Lerner, and Joseph Straus (eds.), *The Oxford Handbook of Music and Disability Studies*, 73–91, New York: Oxford University Press.
McClary, Susan (1991), *Feminine Endings: Music, Gender, and Sexuality*, Minneapolis: University of Minnesota Press.
Meekosha, Helen (2011), "Decolonising Disability: Thinking and Acting Globally," *Disability and Society* 26 (6): 667–82.
Mitchell, David and Sharon Snyder (2000), *Narrative Prosthesis: Disability and the Dependencies of Discourse*, Ann Arbor: University of Michigan Press.
Price, Margaret (2014), "The Bodymind Problem and the Possibilities of Pain," *Hypatia: A Journal of Feminist Philosophy* 30 (1): 268–84.
Raffman, Diana (2014), "Music, Philosophy, and Cognitive Science," in Theodore Gracyk and Andrew Kania (eds.), *The Routledge Companion to Philosophy and Music*, 592–602, New York: Routledge Press.

Reynolds, Joel Michael (2022), "The Normate: On Disability, Critical Phenomenology, and Merleau-Ponty's Cézanne," *Chiasmi International: Trilingual Studies Concerning Merleau-Ponty's Thought* 24: 199–218.

Ridley, Aaron (2004), *The Philosophy of Music: Theme and Variations*, Edinburgh: Edinburgh University Press.

Robinson, Jenefer (2005), *Deeper Than Reason: Emotion, and Its Role in Literature, Music, and Art*, New York: Oxford University Press.

Rowden, Terry (2009), *The Songs of Blind Folk: African American Musicians and Cultures of Blindness*, Ann Arbor: University of Michigan Press.

Sacks, Oliver (2008), *Musicophilia: Tales of Music and the Brain*, New York: Vintage.

Schulkin, Jay (2013), *Reflections on the Musical Mind: An Evolutionary Perspective*, Princeton: Princeton University Press.

Scruton, Roger (1999), *The Aesthetics of Music*, New York: Oxford University Press.

Siebers, Tobin (2010), *Disability Aesthetics*, Ann Arbor: University of Michigan Press.

Silvers, Anita (2000), "From the Crooked Timber of Humanity, Beautiful Things Can Be Made," in Peg Zeglin Brand (ed.), *Beauty Matters*, 197–221, Bloomington: Indiana University Press.

Skitolsky, Lissa (2020), *Hip-Hop as Philosophical Text and Testimony: Can I Get a Witness?* Lanham: Lexington Books.

Small, Christopher (1998), *Musicking: The Meanings of Performing and Listening*, Middletown: Weslyean University Press.

Steinberg, Jesse R. and Abrol Fairweather, eds. (2012), *Blues: Philosophy for Everyone, Thinking Deep about Feeling Low*, Malden: Wiley-Blackwell.

Straus, Joseph (2011), *Extraordinary Measures: Disability in Music*, New York: Oxford University Press.

Straus, Joseph (2014), "Idiots Savants, Retarded Savants, Talented Aments, Mono-Savants, Autistic Savants, Just Plain Savants, People with Savant Syndrome, and Autistic People Who Are Good at Things: A View from Disability Studies," *Disability Studies Quarterly* 34 (3). https://doi.org/10.18061/dsq.v34i3.3407.

Straus, Joseph (2018), *Broken Beauty: Musical Modernism and the Representation of Disability*, Oxford: Oxford University Press.

Szendy, Peter (2015), *Phantom Limbs: On Musical Bodies*, trans. Will Bishop, New York: Fordham University Press.

Tremain, Shelley (2013), "Introducing Feminist Philosophy of Disability," *Disability Studies Quarterly* 33 (4). https://doi.org/10.18061/dsq.v33i4.

Tremain, Shelley (2015), "This is What a Historicist and Relativist Feminist Philosophy of Disability Looks Like," *Foucault Studies* 19: 7–42.

Vorhaus, John (2016), *Giving Voice to Profound Disability: Dignity, Dependence and Human Capabilities*, London: Routledge.

Vorhaus, John and Adam Ockelford (2017), "Identity and Musical Development in People with Severe Profound and Multiple Learning Disabilities," in Raymond Macdonald, David J. Hargreaves, and Dorothy Miell (eds.), *The Oxford Handbook of Musical Identities*, 642–67, New York: Oxford University Press.

Warren, Jeff (2014), *Music and Ethical Responsibility*, Cambridge: Cambridge University Press.

Wendell, Susan (1996), *The Rejected Body: Feminist Philosophical Reflections on Disability*, New York: Routledge.

West, Cornel (2005), "Foreword," in Derrick Darby and Tommie Shelby (eds.), *Hip Hop to Philosophy: Rhyme 2 Reason*, xi–xii, Chicago: Open Court.

5 NEURODIVERSITY, ANTI-PSYCHIATRY, AND THE POLITICS OF MENTAL HEALTH

ROBERT CHAPMAN

Introduction

The neurodiversity movement is a disability rights and justice movement that emerged in the late 1990s when greater numbers of autistic people gained access to the internet and began to form online autistic communities (Singer 2017). These events constituted an initial period of consciousness raising that eventually led to the key theoretical innovations of the movement, including the emergence of the "neurodiversity paradigm" (Walker 2021) which aims to provide an alternative to the medical conception of neurological disability. As an alternative framework, the neurodiversity paradigm has been increasingly adopted by people with a range of psychiatric or learning disability diagnoses in addition to its initial endorsement within autistic communities. In other words, both the neurodiversity movement and its theories encompass a growing range of mentally disabled people and distressed people.

An examination of the meaning and significance of the neurodiversity movement must, at its outset, take into consideration that there is no leader of the movement, nor is it grounded in a foundational textbook or other official founding document. Nevertheless, the claims of certain influential theorists and activists, as well as a range of themes and issues, have emerged that typify neurodiversity advocacy (Singer 2017; Walker 2021). Most notably, neurodiversity proponents push back against the default pathologization and control of a variety of neurocognitive disabilities. They have engaged in this resistance in part by adopting social and relational models of disability, which frame disablement as the product of oppressive social environments rather than the consequence of a brain defect. As part of this resistance, furthermore, they have critiqued the very idea of the "normal" brain or mind. In this regard, the heart of the idea of neurodiversity (and hence the neurodiversity movement) is that neurological diversity functions more like biodiversity than like pathological dysfunction: cognitive ecosystems require a diversity of minds to function. Hence, such cognitive diversity is important to support or conserve rather than eliminate or cure.

While the vocabularies used to refer to this cognitive diversity remain contested, many activists and authors have adopted Nick Walker's (2021) terminology, which synthesizes terms that a variety of advocates for people disabled in the relevant ways have developed. Walker's terminology distinguishes between marginalized "neurodivergent" people, who depart from neuronormative ideals, and "neurotypicals," who fall roughly within what is considered the "normal" range of neurological functioning of a given society. On this neurodivergent framing, specific groups such as dyslexics or autistics become "neurominorities" rather than people with specific mental disorders. Furthermore, these terms and assumptions constitute what Walker has called the "neurodiversity paradigm," the broader framework that offers a way in which to fundamentally reframe neurodivergent disablement. The neurodiversity paradigm shifts analysis away from a focus on measurement of each person's abilities in relation to and distance from the species norm—whereby certain people are marked as naturally defective—and moves analysis toward a focus on how normality and defect, as well as enablement and disablement, are relationally constituted.

Historically, members of various medicalized and pathologized groups have pushed back against medicalization, over-pathologization, and psychiatric social control of them. This long history includes lesbian and gay rights activists who mobilized to combat the pathologization of homosexuality, the formation of the psychiatric survivor's movement, and the efforts of the Mad Pride movement, to name just a few. Perhaps the most notable element of this activist history is the anti-psychiatry movement, the theory of which was formed in the 1960s and has since underpinned a range of critiques of psychiatric over-pathologization and social control. Because both the neurodiversity movement and the anti-psychiatry movement resist what they regard as over-pathologization, critics of the former movement have often conflated it with anti-psychiatry or characterized it as an offshoot of the latter movement (e.g., Ruffalo 2018). No historical evidence supports this characterization. In fact, neurodiversity theory primarily grew out of disability studies, which has an entirely different analysis of disablement than anti-psychiatry (Singer 2017). In contrast to anti-psychiatry, which emphasizes that people labeled "mentally ill" are wholly unlike people with "real" (i.e., bodily) illnesses, moreover, neurodiversity proponents stress the similarities between cognitively and physically disabled people. This emphasis means that the theory and politics of neurodiversity are quite different from previous theoretical and political critiques of psychiatric pathologization.

In this chapter, I situate the rise of the neurodiversity movement and what I call "neurodiversity theory" (Chapman 2019) in the broader historical context of the aforementioned discussions. My aim is, in part, to show the place and originality of neurodiversity theory in the history of critiques of psychiatric pathologization. In addition, I want to show how neurodiversity theory challenges both the medical model, on the one hand, and anti-psychiatry, on the other. Part of what neurodiversity theory brings into mental health discourse is an anti-ableist analysis that is grounded in the tenets of disability studies, an analysis lacking in anti-psychiatry. In doing so, the neurodiversity movement provides a new theoretical critique that in turn allows (or so I argue) new possibilities for emancipatory mental health politics in the twenty-first century.

To make the case that neurodiversity theory offers these emancipatory possibilities, I begin my discussion by describing the Freudian model of mental illness that dominated thinking about mental pathology in the post–World War II era of the twentieth century. In turn, I explain the critique that anti-psychiatrist Thomas Szasz developed of this model. At least partly in light of Szasz's critique, the medical model morphed into a more biocentric model, associated with the "father" of biological psychiatry, Emil Kraepelin. I point out some problems that both the Szaszian position and the biocentric medical model encounter, that is, share in common. Finally, I argue that neurodiversity has emerged to both resist the biomedical model and avoid the problems that I associate with the Szaszian position. I end the chapter by reflecting on neurodiversity theory and politics.

The Freudian Medical Model

The medical model in psychiatry dates back at least to Kraepelin who, widely regarded as the father of modern psychiatry, was among the most influential psychiatrists of the late nineteenth and early twentieth centuries (Shorter 1996). Today, Kraepelin is known for introducing the division of types of patients in accordance with meticulously observed clinical symptoms, development of symptoms, and progression of diseases, while attempting to map these divisions onto underlying biological markers. By the early twentieth century, German biological psychiatry led the world, and Kraepelin's approach was regarded as the most viable scientific way of understanding and responding to mental health problems. Indeed, it was this approach and the practices that surrounded it that neurodiversity proponents would later come to critique.

The anti-psychiatry movement arose for different reasons. During a brief period between 1945 and the 1960s, biological psychiatry retreated and indeed was largely abandoned in liberal societies. The key problem for biological psychiatry was that Kraepelin and its leading proponents were eugenicists, whose eugenic ideals were intimately bound into their theories (Harrington 2019). Prior to the rise of Hitler, both governments and populations in liberal democracies had widely accepted and even promoted eugenics, and thus the centrality of eugenics to biological psychiatry was not considered a problem. Although people within these jurisdictions were not generally exterminated, thousands of people with disabilities within them were sterilized, especially women, working-class people, and Black people. In this historical context, the Kraepelinian approach to psychiatry reigned unchallenged. It is especially relevant to note that the first targets of Nazi eugenic policy were people deemed mentally ill or disabled, both of which groups were brutally exterminated in huge numbers (see, e.g., Torrey and Yolken 2010). It was only toward the end of the Second World War that authoritarian eugenics lost widespread public support as more and more people became aware of the extent of the horrors of the Holocaust and the earlier eugenics policies that had precipitated them. (Notably, however, Indigenous, poor, disabled, and other marginalized people in Canada and the United States have even recently continued to be sterilized under the guise of medical necessity.)

The retreat of German biological psychiatry and authoritarian eugenics allowed Freudian psychoanalysis to briefly take biological psychiatry's place (Harrington 2019). In contrast to Kraepelin, Sigmund Freud focused on the mind, understanding mental illness as the product of an upset balance between conscious and unconscious drives rather than as subnormal biological functioning. In addition, Freud hypothesized that mental health problems stemmed from early childhood experiences, traumatic events, or repressed instincts rather than individual biological defects. In other words, the Freudian approach to psychiatry was far more psychosocial than Kraepelin's biological approach, helping to move psychiatry away from eugenic approaches and to become grounded in new talking therapies. By 1950, the Freudian approach had indeed established a fragile hegemony in psychiatric theory and practice.

Although the Freudians did help facilitate a move away from eugenics, other problems persisted with the psychiatry of this period. Thus, the Freudian approach to psychiatry rather than the Kraepelian approach became the focus of the critique that anti-psychiatry proponents advanced. They identified several key problems. First and foremost: the asylums. As Andrew Scull details:

> publicly-funded asylum systems underwent explosive growth throughout the nineteenth and well into the twentieth century. In England, for instance,

> the number of officially certified lunatics doubled between 1844 and 1860, while the general population grew by only 20 per cent, and increase in their numbers continued to outstrip the growth of the population as a whole by a large margin for the remainder of the century, rising to over 100,000 by the early 1900s. Expansion was equally dramatic in France and in the United States, and not just the total number of patients, but the size of the receptacles within which they were confined grew remorselessly. (Scull 2006: 117)

While, in the postwar era, asylums were no longer used to exterminate inmates, they continued to be places with terrible living conditions where patients were often bound and otherwise restrained, were physically assaulted, deprived of social contact, and abused in a variety of other ways. They were also subjected to invasive and harmful treatments, including lobotomy. The mistreatment of patients in asylums was central to what anti-psychiatry proponents campaigned against, especially after Michel Foucault detailed the history of asylums and exposed their function as a form of social control in his classic 1961 book *Madness and Civilization* (Foucault 1965). By framing asylums as prisons that locked up innocent people (most of whom had not committed any crimes), critics raised awareness and helped to shift public opinion toward the elimination of these institutions.

As, simultaneously, the civil rights movements in the 1950s and 1960s pushed back against racist, patriarchal, and heteronormative systems of domination, it became increasingly clear that psychiatric practices had merged with these systems to pathologize social deviance and resistance: Black civil rights protestors were framed as mad; women who reacted to systemic sexism and other oppressive social conditions were framed as hysterical; and, perhaps most starkly, "homosexuals" were framed as mentally ill in need of conversion therapy (Bayer 1985). Given these issues and, furthermore, given worries about the scientific status of psychoanalysis, researchers, professionals, and members of the general public increasingly turned against Freudian psychiatry. It was in this social and political context that anti-psychiatry theory was developed.

Szaszian Anti-psychiatry

The term *anti-psychiatry*, which remains controversial, is generally used to refer to a number of rebel psychiatrists and critical social theorists who challenged psychiatric pathologization and social control in the 1960s. Prominent figures included Ronald Laing, a Scottish psychiatrist who argued that schizophrenia was an understandable reaction to painful family dynamics; Franco Basaglia, the psychiatrist who campaigned to close the asylums in Italy; and Foucault, who analyzed the history of what he called "the great confinement" of mad people during the Enlightenment. I shall continue to focus on the Hungarian-American libertarian psychiatrist Szasz, who argued that mental illness is a "myth" and psychiatric diagnoses are "lies." I want to focus on Szasz's account because it has, arguably, remained the most influential in mental-health politics and provides a helpful contrast with the neurodiversity movement, as I demonstrate later in this chapter.

Szasz himself was a psychiatrist and professor working in the United States. After initially training in medicine and in turn becoming a professor in 1956, he published his seminal critique of psychiatry in his 1960 article "The Myth of Mental Illness." The following year, he published a book with the same title and built upon the arguments detailed in the book until his death in 2012. Even today, critics of psychiatry continue to regularly echo these arguments which, in fact, underpin the contemporary offshoot of anti-psychiatry called "critical psychiatry," arguably the dominant movement of resistance to psychiatric pathologization in the United Kingdom and the United States currently (Davies 2013).

I refer to Szasz's argument as the "comparativist critique" (Chapman 2023) because it relies on a comparison between psychiatry and bodily medicine, as well as a comparison between the concepts of the normal body and the normal mind. The comparative critique applies to the concept of mental illness (or disorder) and to psychiatric diagnostic classifications. The most basic form of the critique concerns the very concept of mental illness or disorder. For Szasz, we can tell mental illness is a "myth" because, unlike bodily conceptions of illness, it does not reflect objective abnormalities in the structure or functioning of the body and indeed is purely a normative matter. On this view, illness has, since the nineteenth century, been correctly understood as a biological issue in which a part of the body has malfunctioned. For Szasz, the notion of "mental" illness is rather a metaphor that we have come to forget is a metaphor. On this view, that we forgot that so-called mental illness is a metaphor is why psychiatry came to treat it as if it was a real illness, even in cases where there is no tangible evidence of illness in the literal sense.

The second form of the comparativist critique regards specific diagnoses such as schizophrenia and depression. For Szasz, these diagnoses are "lies" that comprise clusters of socially disvalued traits rather than specific disease processes that biological tests can objectively verify. Unlike medical illness, which can often be distinguished through scientific processes in the lab, psychiatric diagnoses are based on conjecture. Indeed, the classifications themselves are decided by committee vote and the application of these classifications by clinicians is based on their own subjective judgment. Hence it is false, for Szasz, to think of these psychiatric diagnoses as real illnesses.

Szasz did accept that neurological illnesses exist. He regarded these illnesses as real and no less objective than other illnesses of the body. His disagreement concerned specifically the notion of "mental" illness. In fact, he stressed, most psychiatric disorders do not have evidence of anything like a biomarker in the brain. Furthermore, whenever biological causes have been found—for instance, as happened with syphilis in the 1890s or with neurological disorders—then these disorders get moved out of psychiatry and instead given to (what Szasz took to be) legitimate branches of medicine that deal with them as illnesses. Either way, though, Szasz's comparativist critique leaves no room for the concept of mental illness in the Freudian sense, that is, of illness as psychic imbalance.

Taken together, Szasz's comparativist critique depicted psychiatric pathologization as stemming from social and ideological norms, as opposed to what he saw as the objective functional and structural norms on which general medicine relied. In other words, by comparison to objective illnesses and disabilities of the body, Szasz dismissed psychiatric concepts of disorder. On this basis, he reasoned, psychiatric conjecture functions as a disguise; for instead of calling attention to conflicting human needs, aspirations, and values, the notion of mental illness provides an amoral and impersonal "thing" (an "illness") as an explanation for problems in living (Szasz 1960; 1974: 116).

For Szasz, such problems were just ordinary, everyday problems that psychiatric diagnosis mystifies and obscures. To the extent that Szasz's argument in this regard is convincing, the implications of accepting it are that mental illness is a myth, psychiatry is not a legitimate branch of medicine, and that psychiatry's institutions should be closed.

Problems with Anti-psychiatry

Szasz's critics quickly recognized that his theories ran into significant problems of their own. One theoretical issue that poses problems for the theory is that it both relied on and reinforced untenably rigid binaries between the mind and body, political and scientific, and real and mythical. In fact, things are much less clear cut: biological illnesses such as common colds can cause mental disablement or distress, while mental illnesses such as anxiety or eating disorder are intimately bound up with bodily functioning. Politically, the rigidity of Szasz's binary thinking was important because acceptance of his arguments leads to a wholesale denial of the reality of mental disability or illness as genuine disability or illness. Although it is true that some patients found Szasz's arguments freeing, for many others, Szasz's reduction of these issues to mere individual problems in living erased their experiences of illness or disablement, not to mention the utility of diagnosis or treatment in many instances. Thus, while some clinicians, activists, and researchers have taken the Szaszian perspective as a basis for liberation, many others regard it as theoretically untenable and no less epistemically harmful than the medical model.

In his 1982 book *Psycho-Politics*, the socialist and psychologist Peter Sedgwick identified another issue with Szasz's critique, an issue that is highly pertinent to our concerns. In the book, Sedgwick provided a detailed analysis of Szasz's work and emphasized that the Szaszian position relied on the assumption that bodily disablement, illness, and diagnosis were based on purely objective discoveries, free from ideology. In Sedgwick's words:

> In seizing on the value-laden, subjective, "political" elements of psychiatric diagnosis and treatment, [Szasz and his followers] have implicitly—and sometimes, indeed, explicitly—conceded the value-free, apolitical and "objective" character of medicine-in-general: their dismissal of positivism in psychiatry is founded on a contrast with non-psychiatric medicine which actually depends on the acceptance of positivism as a possible method in vital areas of human decision-making. (Sedgwick 2015/1982: 27)

In short, the comparativist critique reifies the idea of the normal body (including the brain) to lend support for the argument that the notion of mental normality is comparatively lacking in objectivity. Yet, as Sedgwick detailed, this position is quite untenable, since bodily conceptions of health, illness, normality, and so forth are also intertwined with social norms and ideological baggage. After all, different cultures pathologize different bodily states, have different conceptions of normal functioning, and so forth. Sedgwick thus argued that the comparativist critique was based on a flawed analysis that made mental and bodily pathologization and disablement seem more different from each other than they actually were.

Importantly, Sedgwick was concerned with both the theoretical validity of Szaszian arguments and their political implications. Szasz himself was open that his theorizing was grounded in his hard-right, libertarian politics. For Szasz, the implications of his claim according to which mental illness is a "myth" was that asylums should have to release their inmates (an implication to which Sedgwick was sympathetic) and that patients who claimed to be mentally ill were essentially malingerers. For Szasz, in other words, patients ultimately used mental illness and disability concepts to deny responsibility for their ordinary "problems in living." As Szasz himself put it: "So-called mentally ill persons [. . .] pretend to be disabled by illnesses that do not exist" (Szasz 2008: 110). In short, the implication of accepting Szasz's argument is that people who claim to be schizophrenic, autistic, and so on are not broken in a medical sense but rather are expressing failures of moral character—that is, a failure to take responsibility for their situations.

For Sedgwick, the problems with Szasz's argument about the mythical character of mental illness were these: that it was wrong; that it would lead to victim-blaming mentally impaired and unwell people; and that abolition of the concept of mental illness would, if taken seriously, primarily lead to depletion of funding for mental health facilities and the incarceration of former asylum patients in prisons instead of asylums. After all, if there is no mental illness or disability, then it is hard to get a government to offer support. For Sedgwick, the primary problem was capitalism, and if it could not use one state mechanism to control, it would simply use another. This point is important to note because, in retrospect, Sedgwick turns out to have made a correct prediction. The asylums did close, with some patients returning to their communities. Many of them struggled to find work, however, were insufficiently supported, and ended up in prison. Thus, although Szaszian rhetoric had helped pave the way to free some former inmates from asylums, many of them went from one form of social control to another. Equally, Szaszian rhetoric functioned to enable the early neoliberal governments of the 1980s to justify the implementation of austerity measures in mental health services. Because Szaszians saw the problem as primarily residing in one idea, mental illness, rather than providing a broader analysis of social and material conditions, their critique was unable to be used as the basis for liberation.

The Modern Concept of Mental Disorder

Despite these problems, Szasz's critique—along with the critiques of the other anti-psychiatrists—gained enough support to push psychoanalytic psychiatry to the hazy fringes of psychiatric discourse. Yet psychiatry did not cease to exist even following the height of anti-psychiatry critique. Following the Szaszian critique, psychiatry simply shifted back to a Kraepelinian model, focused on cognitive deficit and underlying biological dysfunctions. Psychiatry was easily able to make this reversal because Szasz would happily acknowledge the reality of illness if it had a verified neurological basis. His critique applied only to purely "mental" illnesses. This return to the Kraepelinian model left psychiatry open to develop the new concept of mental disorder that was adopted from 1980 onward, along with new research programs that focused on the identification of underlying biological disorders. From this time forward, psychiatry massively expanded.

The shift back to a Kraepelinian model was formalized in the third edition of *The Diagnostic and Statistical Manual* (*DSM-III*) published in 1980. While psychoanalysis had conceived of mental illness as a clash between conscious and unconscious drives, the neo-Kraepelinian view held that mental disorder was an individual defect in neurological or cognitive functioning, which caused disability or distress for the individual. This neo-Kraepelinian view later came to be known as the "harmful dysfunction" account of disorder, since it takes both harm and dysfunction to be necessary, and together sufficient, for the ascription of disordered status. In this context, the term *dysfunction* was Darwinian and conceptualized as a matter of subnormal ability when compared to the fitness of the typical person. Harm was conceptualized as distress or disability and determined clinically. If someone was taken to have a dysfunction that caused harm or disability, they were thus understood to have a genuine mental disorder.

As new cognitive and biomedical frameworks rapidly expanded, new hopes of biological cures drove much psychiatric research (Andreasen 1984). The new project of psychiatry was to find individual cognitive deficits, group these deficits into clear types, and then find underlying biological dysfunctions associated with them. This new approach brought about changes in how specific conditions were understood. Depression, for example, was no longer regarded as caused by trauma or unresolved conflicts but rather was understood to stem from a chemical imbalance. Given my purposes in this chapter, I want to consider the case of autism, which had first been defined in the 1940s but radically changed in line with this broader shift to a neo-Kraepelinian approach. Understanding how this shift conditioned claims about autism will enable our understanding of what the neurodiversity movement arose to resist.

In the United States in the 1940s, autism was taken to be a relatively rare and highly disabling social and communication condition, perhaps caused by uncaring mothers who upset their children's emotional development (Silberman 2015). This characterization of autism by psychoanalytically oriented psychiatrists entailed both that mothers were wrongly blamed for their children's autism and families were split apart. Following the *DSM-III*, and especially by the 1990s, autism had been expanded into a broad "spectrum" construct, not defined in relation to communication and social understanding deficits and restricted interests. This characterization of autism as a spectrum allowed recognition that many more people shared experiences (albeit in a less apparent way) than the more specific group that had been recognized earlier.

By the 1990s, a number of studies on twins had shown that autism was highly heritable, since siblings with greater genetic similarity were also more likely to both be autistic (e.g., Bailey et al. 1995). Autism was also increasingly associated with neurocognitive deficits rather than regarded as an emotional disorder. While no specific biomarker had been found, researchers hypothesized that autistic people might share a broken empathizing mechanism or deeper problems in general cognitive functioning. Because of the popularity of this hypothesis, biomedical research was focused on the discovery of autism genes to develop prenatal tests to terminate autistic fetuses, while practice focused on the use of intensive behavioral interventions intended to make autistic children more "normal." This therapeutic practice was focused primarily around Applied Behavior Analysis (ABA), where the therapist punished the autistic child for "abnormal" behaviors and rewarded them for performing "normally." And so, it was this approach, rather than the Freudian approach, that the neurodiversity critique was developed to resist.

The Neurodiversity Critique

When autistic people began to connect online in the 1990s, they realized that quite a few of them shared some similar worries. Many of these people did not want to be cured of their autism, since they saw their autistic sensory processing style as integral to who they were and their personal identity. Despite this self-understanding, many of these autistic people had nonetheless been put through coercive and harmful behavioral interventions that aimed to make them more "normal." In addition, many of these autistic people were worried about the drive to develop genetic tests for autism, which seemed premised on the assumption that mass termination of autistic fetuses was desirable. Autistic people had not rallied for the development of this research and regarded its development as a horrifying return to eugenics.

Many autistics began to realize, furthermore, that the extent to which they were disabled relied on the environment as much as on their individual cognitive styles. For instance, although autism was widely regarded as a pervasive social and communication disorder, many autistic people found that when they engaged in online communication from their own homes, and especially when they talked to other autistic people, the communication was much easier for them. They also recognized that non-autistic people, who were purportedly socially able, had problems understanding and communicating with autistic people. This observation raised the question of whether the problems with respect to communication were intrinsic to autistic people (as they were assumed to be) or whether the problems involved arose due to relational issues between autistics and other people or environments.

Autistic people also realized that although they were disabled by society, many of them had specific abilities that were hard to separate from their autistic cognition. For instance, many autistic people excelled in certain forms of creativity or in highly technical subjects. This insight led autistic people to question the practice of dividing up different brains and minds into the normal or abnormal, functional or dysfunctional; that is, they began to consider whether there might be a multitude of optimal forms of functioning, which are unrecognized given the hegemony of the ideal of cognitive normality.

The anti-psychiatry critique was of little utility to autistic people who wished to formulate theoretical claims about their new self-understandings. For these autistic self-advocates did not see the diagnosis of autism as a "lie," since it was clear to them that they did process information, think, and behave in ways that were different to the ways in which most people engaged in these acts. Although these self-advocates did contend that autism was not an illness, they nevertheless held that they were disabled rather than individuals with "problems in living" for which they had failed to take responsibility. Insofar as many autistic self-advocates had experienced depression and anxiety, they were happy to think of these experiences as medical conditions that required support. In other words, their critique was not meant to be a rejection of the concept of mental disorder as such. Rather, they wished to critique the idea of "normal" brain or mind and the idea of "normal" functioning, which underpinned modern conceptions of mental disorder. They also aimed to critique coercive therapies designed to normalize the population.

Out of these online groups, new concepts began to emerge among group members. The earliest of these concepts was the notion of the "neurotypical," which was first popularized on autistic advocate Laura Tisoncik's satirical website Institute for the Study of the Neurologically Typical (ISNT). The ISNT website was essentially a spoof of neurotypical researchers who studied autism. On the website, autistic writers thus "picked apart characteristics of neurotypical individuals in the same patronizing, pathologizing, voice in which traits commonly held by autistic people are described, with feigned obliviousness to how such traits might also be useful" (Tisoncik 2020: 73). Despite the satirical beginnings of the term *neurotypical*, the term had political utility, and autistic and other neurologically disabled people began to use it to refer to people with close proximity to the idealized "normal" person.

A more serious political counterpart concept also began to emerge. As Marjtin Dekker, an autistic advocate active at the time, recalls:

> A new idea came up in the group, based on the evidence and lived experience that autistic brains are wired differently from the mainstream on a fundamental level. Biological diversity of all kinds is essential to the survival of an ecosystem—so why should neurological diversity, which is one aspect of biological diversity, be any different? (Dekker 2020: 46)

Although, initially, autistic people developed this discourse collectively, Judy Singer, who is sometimes credited with coining the term *neurodiversity*, and Harvey Blume, a journalist who had been keenly listening in and reporting on emerging neurodiversity discourse, were the first people to publish theory about neurodiversity. In the late 1990s, that is, both Singer and Blume published on the concept of neurodiversity, thus bringing the idea of it out from autistic email lists, where it had proliferated, and into the wider world.

The first articles to appear in the wider culture came from Blume, who had a journalist's knack for quickly grasping the essence of complex ideas. Thus, the term *neurodiversity* first appeared in a 1998 article he published in *The Atlantic*. In Blume's words:

> The common assumption in cognitive studies these days is that [in] the human brain . . . the occasional bug is inevitable: hence autism and other departures from the neurological norm. [Autistics are suggesting] another way of looking at this. Neurodiversity may be every bit as crucial for the human race as biodiversity is for life in general. Who can say what form of wiring will prove best at any given moment? (Blume 1998)

On Blume's understanding, the shift to neurodiversity represented a transition from the view that mental functioning is either normal or abnormal to the view that different minds have different cognitive specializations. For instance, "computer culture," he wrote, "may favor a somewhat autistic cast of mind" (Blume 1998). To the extent that this turns out to be so, for Blume, the idea that minds can be divided into functional or normal, on the one side, and abnormal or dysfunctional, on the other, seemed to miss something important about human nature.

Singer, a working-class autistic woman and daughter of a Holocaust survivor, was more interested than Blume in the emancipatory political implications of this emerging discourse. Thus, she combined Blume's framing with theoretical work from disability studies. In particular, Singer drew on the social model of disability that physically disabled activists in the United Kingdom developed in the 1970s and disability studies scholars later elaborated (Oliver 1990). This model framed disablement as arising, in at least significant part, from societal organization, such as inaccessible physical structures, exclusionary norms and expectations with respect to education, and discriminatory requirements for employment. Singer proposed a "politics of neurological diversity, or neurodiversity . . . as an addition to the familiar political categories of class/gender/race" (Singer 1999: 64). Singer, rather than focus on cognitive specializations as Blume had done, envisioned the development of an "ecological" society that supports divergent individuals to construct their own "ecological niche," in the sense of helping their cognitive functioning and thriving (67). In Singer's ecological society, autistic people would no longer be pathologized and marginalized but be seen as part of a broader collectivist cognitive ecosystem.

Significant interventions were later made by Kasianne Asasumasu, who coined the term *neurodivergence*, and Walker, who coined the term *neurominorities*. The introduction of these terms allowed disabled people to reclaim psychiatric and psychological diagnoses as well as to take control of how they were conceptualized and represented, while using the terms as categories around which to organize and push for societal change. As Steven Kapp and Ari Ne'eman (2020) of the Autistic Self Advocacy Network (ASAN) clarify:

> Some associated with the "anti-psychiatry" movement even reject the idea that diagnoses represent actual underlying neurological differences from the norm as opposed to purely responses to trauma. ASAN's perspective is different and is instead rooted in the idea of "neurodiversity," which challenges the "medical model" that assumes that the goal of service provision or "treatment" is to restore autistic people to "normalcy" [or] indistinguishability from peers. While we reject the idea that interventions should stress "indistinguishability" and often challenge the idea of exclusive medical authority, we do not reject the utility of the autism diagnosis itself or the well-documented reality that it constitutes a real divergence from "typical" neurology. (Kapp and Ne'eman 2020: 188–9)

Thus, on this account, autism could be recognized as a genuine disability continuous with physical disability, while the idea that autism can be reduced to a medical problem inherent to a given individual could be resisted. The articulation of the neurodiversity account heralded the beginning of a mass project, in which psychiatric classifications were reclaimed as bases around which to organize, resist, and demand rights or accommodations. Hence, the neurodiversity movement began to rapidly grow as more and more people with a vast range of diagnoses adopted its frameworks and vocabularies to redescribe their disablement and push back against coercive normalizing practices.

Neurodiversity and the Concept of Mental Disorder

At least two key issues arise for neurodiversity proponents. The first issue regards how viable it is that neurodiversity is vital for functioning at the group level and how we should understand this claim and the nature of its significance. In another context (Chapman 2021), I point out that the limited research on group functioning so far shows that diversity of neurological or cognitive functioning does indeed tend to aid group functioning up to a certain point, after which communication breaks down because the differences are too great. Other factors also impact communication, including group management and social and material environments. This research, in my view, supports the basic claim of neurodiversity according to which an approach to brains or minds that takes as its yardstick "normal" functioning is not a particularly accurate or useful way to frame mental functioning and, furthermore, that how well any given person functions will largely be contextual and be influenced by a variety of contingent social factors. Insofar as this argument is convincing, it presents a conceptual and empirical challenge to Kraepelinian and Szaszian conceptions of normal neurological functioning, as well as undermines the implication that the default should be to develop treatments that enforce normalcy on people who fall outside the norm.

One issue could potentially arise here, however. If widely accepted within a capitalist system, the neurodiversity framework could lead to a society in which people are valued for their instrumental utility to the collective, which may be as bad as a society in which people are valued on the basis of their perceived proximity to normality. Although I think that this outcome would be highly undesirable, it should be noted that big businesses and tech firms already utilize the concept of neurodiversity in this way in order to mine and exploit neurodivergent cognition as an untapped resource. On the one hand, this outcome reduces neurodivergent people who can be economically useful to mere instrumental utility and, on the other hand, it leaves behind all the people who are not currently able to aid in production. Yet I see this outcome as due to a co-option of the concept of neurodiversity by capital rather than due to a legitimate use of it. Insofar as capitalism will commodify anything, including concepts, the prospect that capitalism might commodify neurodiversity is not a reason to reject neurodiversity but rather a reason to understand neurodivergent liberation as at odds with capitalism.

The distinction between the concepts of use value and exchange value can help us to make sense of how the core idea of neurodiversity should be understood (Marx 1990). The former concept concerns how humans are able to reconstruct the external world for our own collective benefit, while the latter concept is about what is profile determined by the market. For me, the neurodiversity claims are about use value; that is, they allow us to acknowledge the material fact that we are organisms who need sufficient diversity to solve complex problems in a fluctuating environment. In short, it seems a fact to me that it is collectively and individually good for us to be part of neurologically diverse societies. The concept of neurodiversity does not, in my view, support reduction of any human at any given time for their perceived economic dis/utility, as determined by exchange value. To suggest otherwise would be to co-opt the neurodiversity construct in a way that is in direct opposition to the spirit of the movement. Of course, attempts to co-opt or commodify neurodiversity have occurred and will inevitably continue to occur; however, these attempts occur with virtually everything under capitalism and thus are not an issue specific to neurodiversity theory.

I should emphasize that the move toward the neurodiversity concept is generally forwarded as one half of the conceptual shift that neurodivergence urges and the move away from medical models of disability (or, equally, relational models) is the other half of the shift that neurodivergence compels. Because these moves come in tandem, the neurodiversity approach is intimately bound up with the basic principle that the world should be adjusted to accommodate disabled people. Hence, the neurodiversity approach provides both a challenge to the dominant medicalized approach with its focus on normalization and a stark alternative to it. Furthermore, insofar as the neurodiversity approach emphasizes the reality of disability and the need for changes in broader social conditions, it does not involve the problem that Szasz's approach did, which (as I have shown) switched one form of social control to another.

The second key issue that the neurodiversity approach raises for its critics is this: it may go too far, that is, may end up wrongly depathologizing disabilities that are best seen as inherently pathological. This issue is reminiscent of the problems that I associated with anti-psychiatry earlier, since it may be harder to justify state support for medical support while denying that anything is medically wrong. Perhaps the key issue from critics of neurodiversity regards the way in which some autistic people, or parents of autistic children, prefer to view autism as a pathology. This issue has been especially contested in cases where the autistic person is non-speaking, has high support needs, and has additional learning disabilities. While many autistic people who fall into this demographic do prefer the neurodiversity approach, many critics of the approach believe that this issue undermines the neurodiversity paradigm (for e.g., Hughes 2020). Similar issues have also emerged with regard to other diagnoses than autism, as more and more people adopt the neurodiversity framework.

The more general issue that the neurodiversity approach raises for neurodiversity proponents concerns how they would determine what counts as healthy or not once they reject the notion of normal functioning. Most proponents of neurodiversity are happy to acknowledge that, say, dementia is a neurological illness or that anorexia is an illness (or, if they do not use the word *illness*, then something that means much the same, i.e., a harmful state that it is better to recover from and which the government should provide clinical care for, etc.). Yet neurodiversity proponents have not clarified exactly how we are to navigate the boundaries of health once we reject the notion of "normal functioning." Whether they can do so in a way that is both convincing for researchers, clinicians, and policymakers and liberatory for neurodivergent people will largely determine whether the movement ends up mired in the same kinds of issues that I associated with Szasz or is able to go beyond this dilemma to something truly new. Since most neurodiversity proponents seem committed to retaining at least some notion of mental and neurological pathology—for example, in situations where people find it helpful to self-identify as having an illness—the problems that I have associated with Szasz will likely be avoided. With respect to the details of this conceptualization, neurodiversity theorists can work them out in the coming years.

The Politics of Neurodiversity

Let me summarize what I have tried to show in this chapter. The Szaszian critique of psychiatric pathologization was designed specifically to combat the psychoanalytic understanding of mental illness. While the Szaszian critique provided a forceful argument against this pathologization, I have identified at least two key problems with it. First, Szasz held that conceptions of neurological abnormality were objective and apolitical. These assumptions of his critique opened the door to the return of Kraepelian psychiatry to focus on neurological abnormalities. Second, the Szaszian critique led to an overly rigid denial of recognition of mental disablement or illness in a way that is epistemically harmful for many people, especially people who find recognition of illness or disability useful or vital.

The neurodiversity critique is different insofar as its primary challenge is to the Kraepelinian approach, whereby mental disorder is harmful dysfunction, and to the Szaszian approach, which equally relies on the notion of normal functioning. Against the notion of "normal" neurological functioning that makes implicit reference to singularity and homogeneity, proponents of neurodiversity argue that neurodiversity is more like biodiversity and hence that diversity itself constitutes normal functioning. By applying social models of neurological disability, neurodiversity proponents have in addition challenged the "harm" component of mental disorder. On this view, neurodivergent people are often harmed and some neurodivergent traits are rightly associated with harm. To the extent that the challenge is convincing, however, it disrupts the notion that these forms of neurodivergence are simply defective in relation to the neurotypical norm in such a way that brings inherent distress.

I want to end this chapter with some remarks about the political significance of neurodiversity for the future of the politics of mental health. This political significance has been examined by Steve Graby (2015), who suggests that the neurodiversity movement may provide a bridge between the psychiatric survivors movement and the broader disabled persons movement. Notably, while psychiatric survivors have long resisted pathologization, they have often relied on anti-psychiatry theory to conceptualize this resistance to it. This reliance on anti-psychiatry, however, leads to denial of the fact that neurodivergent people are disabled and has been highly divisive for psychiatric service users since a great many others want increased support. Furthermore, anti-psychiatry, which was largely premised on the conviction that people with psychiatric diagnoses are fundamentally unlike people with bodily disabilities, leaves little room within which to build shared understandings and solidarity between psychiatric survivors and the broader disabled persons movement.

By contrast, neurodiversity theory allows an increasing variety of psychiatric survivors (or, service users) to resist pathologization and control, while recognizing the reality of their disablement. In this way, these neurodivergent people stress their similarities to people with bodily disabilities rather than their difference from them. By doing so, they make room for a shared analysis of disablement and a shared basis for resistance. Neurodiversity theory, although in relative infancy, might indeed expand in ways that enable it to help ground a new politics of mental health that allows for an analysis of ableism rather than disability erasure. In order to establish its place in the history of the politics of mental health, neurodiversity must find a way in which to build bridges and acknowledge the reality of disablement and nonetheless resist wrongful pathologization and social control.

References

Andreasen, Nancy (1984), *The Broken Brain: The Biological Revolution in Psychiatry*, New York and London: Harper and Row.

Bailey, A., A. Le Couteur, I. Gottesman, P. Bolton, E. Simonoff, E. Yuzda, and M. Rutter (1995), "Autism as a Strongly Genetic Disorder: Evidence from a British Twin Study," *Psychological Medicine* 25 (1): 63–77. https://doi.org/10.1017/S0033291700028099.

Bayer, Ronald (1985), *Homosexuality and American Psychiatry: The Politics of Diagnosis*, Princeton: Princeton University Press.

Blume, Harvey (1998), "Neurodiversity. On the Neurological Underpinnings of Geekdom," *Atlantic*, September 1998 Issue.

Chapman, Robert (2019), "Neurodiversity Theory and Its Discontents: Autism, Schizophrenia, and the Social Model of Disability," in S. Tekin and R. Bluhm (eds.), *The Bloomsbury Companion to the Philosophy of Psychiatry*, 371–90, London: Bloomsbury Academic.

Chapman, Robert (2021), "Neurodiversity and the Social Ecology of Mental Functions," *Perspectives on Psychological Science* 16 (6): 1360–72. https://doi.org/10.1177/1745691620959833.

Chapman, Robert (2023), "A Critique of Critical Psychiatry," *Philosophy Psychiatry and Psychology* 30 (2): 103–19. Available at: https://muse.jhu.edu/article/899938 (accessed June 29, 2023).

Davies, James (2013), *Cracked: Why Psychiatry is Doing More Harm than Good*, London: Icon Books.

Dekker, Marjtin (2020), "From Exclusion to Acceptance: Independent Living on the Autistic Spectrum," in S. K. Kapp (ed.), *Autistic Community and the Neurodiversity*

Movement, 41–9, Singapore: Springer. Available at: https://link.springer.com/10.1007/978-981-13-8437-0_3 (accessed June 28, 2023).
Foucault, Michel (1965), *Madness and Civilization*, New York: Pantheon.
Graby, Steve (2015), "Neurodiversity: Bridging the Gap between the Disabled People's Movement and the Mental Health System Survivors' Movement?" in *Madness, Distress and the Politics of Disablement*, Policy Press. https://doi.org/10.1332/policypress/9781447314578.003.0017.
Harrington, Anne (2019), *Mind Fixers: Psychiatry's Troubled Search for the Biology of Mental Illness*, New York: W.W. Norton and Company.
Hughes, Jonathan A. (2020), "Does the Heterogeneity of Autism Undermine the Neurodiversity Paradigm?" *Bioethics* 35 (1): 47–60. https://doi.org/10.1111/bioe.12780.
Kapp, Steven K. and Ari Ne'eman (2020), "Lobbying Autism's Diagnostic Revision in the DSM-5," in Steven K. Kapp (ed.), *Autistic Community and the Neurodiversity Movement: Stories from the Frontline*, 167–94, Singapore: Springer. https://doi.org/10.1007/978-981-13-8437-0_13.
Marx, Karl (1990), *Capital: A Critique of Political Economy*, vol. 1, trans. Ben Fowkes, New York: Penguin.
Oliver, Michael (1990), *The Politics of Disablement*, London: Macmillan.
Ruffalo, Mark (2018), "Neurodiversity: A Dangerous Extension of a Discredited Philosophy." Available at: https://www.psychotherapy.net/blog/title/neurodiversity-a-dangerous-extension-of-a-discredited-philosophy (accessed June 28, 2023).
Scull, Andrew (2006), *The Insanity of Place / The Place of Insanity Essays on the History of Psychiatry*, Abingdon: Routledge.
Sedgwick, Peter (2015/1982), *Psycho Politics: Laing, Foucault, Goffman, Szasz, and the Future of Mass Psychiatry*, London: Unkant.
Shorter, Edward (1996), *A History of Psychiatry: From the Era of the Asylum to the Age of Prozac*, New York City: John Wiley and Sons.
Silberman, S. (2015), *Neurotribes: The Legacy of Autism and the Future of Neurodiversity*, New York: Avery Publishing.
Singer, Judy (1999), "'Why Can't You Be Normal for Once in Your Life?' From a 'Problem with No Name' to the Emergence of a New Category of Difference," in Mairian Corker and Sally French (eds.), *Disability Discourse*, 59–67, Buckingham and Philadelphia: McGraw-Hill Education.
Singer, Judy (2017), *Neurodiversity: The Birth of an Idea*, Amazon.
Szasz, Thomas (1974), *The Myth of Mental Illness: Foundations of a Theory of Personal Conduct*, New York: Harper and Row.
Szasz, T. S. (1960), "The Myth of Mental Illness," *American Psychologist* 15 (2): 113–18. https://doi.org/10.1037/h0046535.
Szasz, T. S. (2008), *Psychiatry: Science of Lies*, Syracuse: Syracuse University Press.
Tisoncik, Laura A. (2020), "Autistics.Org and Finding Our Voices as an Activist Movement," in Steven Kapp (ed.), *Autistic Community and the Neurodiversity Movement*, 65–76, Palgrave Macmillan. Available at: https://link.springer.com/book/10.1007/978-981-13-8437-0 (accessed July 20, 2023).
Torrey, E. F. and R. H. Yolken (2010), "Psychiatric Genocide: Nazi Attempts to Eradicate Schizophrenia," *Schizophrenia Bulletin* 36 (1): 26–32. https://doi.org/10.1093/schbul/sbp097.
Walker, Nick (2021), *Neuroqueer Heresies. Notes on the Neurodiversity Paradigm, Autistic Empowerment, and Postnormal Possibilities*, Fort Worth: Autonomous Press.

6 DISABILITY AND AFRICAN PHILOSOPHY

JULIE E. MAYBEE

African philosophy is a branch of Africana philosophy, a still-developing subfield of philosophy that, as Lucius T. Outlaw, Jr. and Chike Jeffers have defined it, focuses on philosophizing "engaged in by persons and peoples African and of African descent who were and are indigenous residents of continental Africa and residents of the many African Diasporas worldwide" (Outlaw Jr. and Jeffers 2022). As a branch of Africana philosophy, African philosophy focuses on the philosophizing in which indigenous residents of continental Africa engage.

Historically, the field of African philosophy has seldom addressed the topic of disability and the issues that surround it (Onazi 2020: 14). A cursory search for the terms *disability*, *disabilities*, and *disabled* in the search fields for the *Journal on African Philosophy*—one of the core journals in African philosophy—turned up zero results for these terms. A search for the same terms, as well as the terms *Africa* and *African* in any search field of the *Philosopher's Index*, which indexes works published in the field of philosophy since 1902, returned only fifteen results in total—a number of which were included only because one of the search fields contained the term *African-American*.[1] Nevertheless, philosophers who work in African philosophy have increasingly addressed disability, often publishing their research in disability studies journals, in journals in Africana studies, and in books aimed at interdisciplinary audiences.

Philosophers who work in the field of African philosophy have begun to address disability for two main reasons. First, many disabled people in Africa today experience extreme poverty, exclusion, and stigma. Although the experience of disability across Africa's fifty-four countries is not monolithic, Oche Onazi—whose book, *An African Path to Disability Justice: Community, Relationships and Obligations*, draws on African philosophy to develop an account of disability justice—points out that "people with disabilities across

Africa are confronted with similar, if not worse, experiences of the type found in Jos, Nigeria" (Onazi 2020: 8), where he grew up, experiences that inspired him to write his book (7). Onazi describes Jos as a city in which a range of disabled people beg for their daily needs, are avoided by other people on the street, are subjected to dehumanizing treatment in various institutions, and are subjected to negative and exclusionary cultural attitudes, as well as rank among the poorest and most marginalized residents of the city with respect to food, health care, shelter, employment, and access to other public goods and services. "Indeed," Onazi writes, summarizing his research for the book, "immersing myself in the literature and in some of the most horrific stories of the injustices or experiences of people with disabilities in Africa in media news reports, documentary films, and photographs in newspapers and magazines has made this book very difficult to write" (9). The pressing condition of many disabled people in Africa has inspired philosophers, such as Onazi, to address issues of disability—and to do so in ways that mobilize indigenous African philosophical thought in the search for solutions. As Paul Lekholokoe Leshota and Maximus Monaheng Sefotho have suggested, however, negative perceptions and evaluations of at least some disabled people in the indigenous philosophical thought of some African cultures and traditions require that an African philosophy of disability, in addition to affirming African views and values, must critique some of these views and values (Leshota and Sefotho 2018: 101, 103).

I want to suggest that philosophers who work in African philosophy have been inspired to address disability for another reason: African philosophical thought provides a rich set of resources with which to rethink conceptions of disability and disability justice, as well as to contribute to the liberation of disabled people—both within Africa in particular and around the world more widely.

Rethinking the Concepts of Disability and Impairment

Cross-cultural (and, indeed, cross-historical) comparisons of philosophical thought and concepts help to reveal the degree to which concepts and reasons are tied to languages and cultures. As Leshota and Sefotho remark in a discussion of African intercultural philosophy,

> there is a cultural dimension to all philosophy. People who philosophize, do so as humans who do not exist on a universal plane, but are immersed in a particular social, cultural and spiritual context. Philosophical assumptions together with language (metaphors, images) that is often

> carried into our analysis are created within and informed by specific ontological assumptions informed by specific cultural worldviews. People who philosophize are created and shaped within specific cultures. (Leshota and Sefotho 2018: 107)

All philosophy has a cultural dimension because, as I have argued elsewhere, words and the concepts and facts that they express cannot be understood apart from the web of other concepts and beliefs to which they belong and the cultural practices through which they are enacted (Maybee 2019: 100–10; 2017).

This argument about the mutually constitutive character of language and culture for the conceptual tools of philosophy is no less true of the Western concepts of disability and impairment (or handicap), which are highly abstract categories that conflate a number of different sorts of situations and conditions and which, as anthropologists Benedicte Ingstad and Susan Reynolds White have remarked, were invented in Europe under particular historical circumstances. "In many cultures," they write, "one cannot be 'disabled' for the simple reason that 'disability' as a recognized category does not exist. There are blind people and lame people and 'slow' people, but 'the disabled' as a general term does not translate easily into many languages" (Ingstad and Whyte 1995: 7). Leshota and Sefotho have suggested, for instance, that the Basotho use of the Sesotho word *bokooa* as a generic term to refer to all forms of disability is a recent phenomenon and a usage that was intended "to match Western categorization, which creates, through surveys, projects, public systems and policies, the disabled as a social category." Historically, they add, the Basotho had only "specific terms and conceptual categories for persons who had this or the other perceived difficulty or problem." To the degree that the Basotho did regard people in more abstract terms as normal or abnormal, Leshota and Sefotho suggest, they defined abnormality in terms of what they regarded as *moral* defects or unresponsiveness "to society's usual expectations," as well as what they viewed as mental or physical defects (Leshota and Sefotho 2020: 5). Rather than cut up the world into categories of normal and abnormal in which abnormality is defined in terms of bodily differences (whether mental or physical), the Basotho cut up the world into categories of normal and abnormal in which abnormality included *moral* differences too.

Even in the West, according to historian Irina Metzler, the concepts of disability and impairment as we understand them today are a fairly recent phenomenon. During the Middle Ages in Europe, no single term existed that corresponded to today's concept of disability (Metzler 2015: 4). Rather, medieval people offered various interpretations of what, today, we would think of as different disabilities. To the degree that medieval people did employ a generalized category, disabled people were part of a "multiform category" of *pauperes* or paupers—a group of people that included widows, sick people, pilgrims, and physically disabled people who were socially disempowered or economically poor and so required support from others (155). Unlike many people who are defined as disabled today, people who belonged to this category during the Middle Ages were not excluded from society, Metzler says, but rather were integrated members of it (156). Moreover, the abstract terms that were used to refer to what, today, we would think of as physical conditions or impairments—terms such as *infirm, debilitated, weak,* and *impotent*—referred, in that historical context, to people who were, as Metzler puts it, "suffering from poverty" or were powerless because of a lack of economic ability, in addition to people who lacked physical ability due to orthopedic impairments, paralysis, or old age (4–5). Thus, medieval people in Europe employed categories of identity that centered around capturing a generalized need for social support from others, rather than around capturing bodies or bodily differences.

Today's concepts of disability and impairment belong to a pattern of thought, developed later in the West, in which people are defined primarily in terms of their bodies. In Western society, Oyèrónkẹ́ Oyěwùmí has remarked, "the body is the bedrock on which the social order is founded" (Oyěwùmí 1997: 2). As she explains it, Western "society is constituted by bodies and as bodies—male bodies, female bodies, Jewish bodies, Aryan bodies, black bodies, white bodies, rich bodies, poor bodies" (and, we could add, disabled or impaired bodies)—where the term *bodies*, Oyěwùmí says, refers to both physicality and biology (1). Unlike in Western "body-reasoning" or "bio-logic" (8), she argues, the traditional Yoruba social order was "not focused on the body" (14) or was not based on the body (36, 42). Traditional Yoruba did not employ a biological conception of sex, for instance. They recognized, of course, that people had different roles in the process of human reproduction, and they had words to distinguish those roles: *obinrin* (the ones who have babies) and *okùnrin* (the ones who do not have babies). Since children have no role in reproduction, however, these words applied only to adults, and never to children (33–4). The Yoruba word for "offspring," *ọyọ*, was also sex- and gender-neutral (40–1), as were most other nouns and pronouns, and even proper names (40–2). Indeed, Samuel Johnson, an early twentieth-century cultural anthropologist, reported in 1921 that when Yoruba translators tried to use the Yoruba language to express the idea of sex, they had to invent words that made no sense to ordinary Yoruba people at the time (41; Johnson and Johnson 2010: xxxvii). Because the terms *obinrin* (the ones who have babies) and *okùnrin* (the ones who do not have babies) applied only to adults, being an *obinrin* or *okùnrin* was not understood as a biological or sexual essence that determined an individual's identity.

Traditional Yoruba society, rather than define people in terms of bodies or biology, Oyěwùmí notes, defined them in terms of social relations (Oyěwùmí 1997: 12–13, 36). The most important determinant of someone's identity in traditional Yoruba society was seniority (42), which was defined in terms of when someone joined (came inside) the compound or lineage, through either birth or marriage (46). Because one could come inside the compound as either a child or an adult, this conception of seniority was not linked to age. It was, Oyěwùmí suggests, a "relational and situational" concept rather than a bodily or biological one: whether one is senior or junior depended on social relations as well as on who happened to be present at any particular time (42). Since this notion of seniority is grounded in a social relationship that is not connected to age or sex, it is neither physical nor written on bodies.

Thus, African philosophy describes systems of thought in which people are identified not in terms of their bodies or biology, but rather in terms of social relationships or other characteristics that are less readily apparent to the eye. As Lieketseng Yvonne Ned has observed, "many indigenous people do not identify with the concept of disability because indigenous communities focus on strengths and abilities in relation to communal responsibility, with impairment seen as a part of the individual. . . . This is reflective of the communal living characteristic in African societies" (Ned 2022: 493). I will return to the communalistic aspects of many indigenous African societies in the next section of this chapter.

Still, indigenous African societies have expressed a range of views, both negative and positive, about different conditions that would be included under today's Western concepts of disability or impairment. As I have explained, the Basotho, for instance, have historically regarded mental and physical (and moral) differences as defects. According to Mary Nyangweso, among the Asante, children born with physical "deformities"—including having six fingers—would be killed at birth (Nyangweso 2021: 119; cf. Kyei 1992: 52) and chiefs who acquired an illness—such as epilepsy—would be destooled (Nyangweso 2021: 119). Although the Igbo lack a word that is equivalent to *disability*, they regarded having an impairment (which is conceived of as a dent or lack of wholeness) as a misfortune (Nwokorie and Devlieger 2019: 5). Furthermore, the mistreatment of people with albinism in many indigenous African societies—which is often supported by cultural and spiritualistic beliefs—is severe (Nyangweso 2021: 120–2; Imafidon 2019: 19–23, 80, 82, 98–109; Ndlovu 2016: 34–5). By contrast, according to Nyangweso, the Ga regarded intellectually disabled people with awe and treated them with kindness, gentleness, and patience, believing them to be reincarnations of a deity. The Chagga regarded physically disabled people to be pacifiers of evil spirits and so would not harm them. In Benin, children born with disabilities were often revered, accepted, and protected, as it was believed that supernatural forces produced them and that they brought good luck (Nyangweso 2021: 119).

Sometimes, an indigenous African society's attitudes toward disabled people are not clear and straightforward. In Yoruba thought, disabled people were believed to have been created by the deity, *Òrìṣà-ńlá* or *Ọbàtálá*, who was tasked by *Olódùmarè*, the Supreme Being, with forming people's physical being. On some accounts, *Òrìṣà-ńlá* created deformed physical bodies to punish people who violated a taboo or whose ancestors committed some offense. On some accounts, *Òrìṣà-ńlá* created such bodies in error after drinking too much palm wine. And on other accounts, *Òrìṣà-ńlá* created such bodies according to their (*Òrìṣà-ńlá* is regarded as gender-neutral or asexual) own fancy, as an expression of their own, original definition of human physicality (Adegbindin 2018; Imafidon 2021: 52; Nyangweso 2021: 119–20). While the Yoruba account of disabled people as the creation of a deity ensures that disabled people in Yoruba society receive recognition and protection as companions to *Òrìṣà-ńlá*—particularly "hunchbacks," "cripples," "albinos," and "dwarves," who are specifically named in various divinations (Adegbindin 2018)—Elvis Imafidon suggests that the overall Yoruba attitude toward disability is negative, insofar as it is largely grounded in notions of "curse, anger, or error" (Imafidon 2021: 52).

Alternatively, Omotade Adegbindin argues that *Òrìṣà-ńlá*'s status as a highly valued divinity, who is ethically pure (without moral fault), morally neutral, or impartial (as symbolized by *Òrìṣà-ńlá*'s neutral gender or asexuality), and associated with material safety, leads to a positive identity for disabled people as favored by the gods. It also leads to an image of human beings according to which they have a variety of valued bodily configurations that are pluralistic in terms of ability—an image that undercuts the Western dichotomy between "normal" and "deformed"/"abnormal" (Adegbindin 2018).

African philosophical thought thus shows that the concepts of disability and impairment are highly abstract products of certain cultures' histories that do not necessarily translate into other cultures' languages or systems of thought. These concepts categorize people in a particular way, namely, in terms of bodies rather than social relations or other characteristics that are less apparent to the eye—ways that are not replicated in many indigenous African societies. While indigenous African societies had various views about a variety of conditions that would fall under today's Western concept of disability—some of which must rightly be rejected—African philosophical thought also points toward ways in which to conceptualize human beings that would help to undercut the Western emphasis on bodies as well as the negative valuation of people who would be considered disabled today. Since the concepts of disability and impairment are human-made, they could also be *un*made. Following African philosophical thought, different categories could be used to define or categorize people and in turn there could be different facts (Maybee 2019: chs. 6 and 7).

Communalistic Conceptions of Personhood

One of the most important debates in African philosophy has been about the concept of the person. In particular, African philosophers have proposed communitarian conceptions of the person that the indigenous thought of many African societies has inspired. Philosophers who work in African philosophy of disability have disagreed over the degree to which these communitarian conceptions of personhood contribute to the exclusion and mistreatment of disabled people in Africa or can be mobilized to help liberate disabled people.

Many societies and languages draw a distinction between what in English would be called a "human being" and what would be called a "person." While the concept of human being captures the kind of being that people are as natural creatures (i.e., "human" beings rather than, say, "cat" beings), the concept of person, as Imafidon has pointed out, concerns who is understood to have intrinsic worth or value and thus who is accorded power in society (Imafidon 2021: 47–8).

For Immanuel Kant, for instance, only rational beings are "persons," that is, beings who are capable of genuine morality and so have intrinsic worth and value. As he puts it in the *Groundwork for the Metaphysics of Morals*, beings "whose existence rests not on our will but on nature nevertheless have, if they are beings without reason, only a relative worth as means, and are called things; rational beings, by contrast, are called 'persons' because their nature already marks them out as ends in themselves, i.e., as something that may not be used merely as means" (Kant 2018: 41 [Ak 4:428]). While some passages in this text—for example, "Now I say that the human being and in general every rational being exists as end in itself" (ibid.)—suggest that Kant regarded all human beings as rational and therefore as persons, as Emmanuel Chukwudi Eze pointed out, in other texts Kant associated black skin color with poor rational capacities (Eze 1998: 215). Such claims about the supposed rational capacities of Black people would suggest that for Kant, Black people would be, at the very least, *lesser* persons than whites or, at worst, *not* persons at all—in which case they would fall outside of Kant's class of beings who are covered by morality, who must be treated as "ends in themselves" and never merely as means, or whose interests must be taken into account in any moral decision-making. Taken together, Kant's views about personhood and race effectively provide a moral justification (or cover) for the enslavement and colonial exploitation of Black people, as Eze suggests (ibid.). These views, which were influential at both the time that they were written and thereafter, have therefore had consequences in terms of who was accorded social power: whites were accorded power, while Blacks were not.

In the West, too, people who have been classified as "disabled" have had a diminished personhood status and so reduced social power (Szántó 2020: 131). In a study conducted by English professor and disability studies scholar Marilynn J. Phillips in the 1980s, for instance, disabled people in the United States reported that they are largely regarded as "damaged goods." Although "the phrase 'damaged goods' more often refers to products than to people," Phillips writes, "it can be metaphorically transferred from product to person in a society which idealizes commodity uniformity and functional predictability. . . . Those failing to meet such standards are reclassified as irregulars, seconds, damaged goods" (Phillips 1990: 850). The study's participants associated their status as "damaged goods" with a reduction in social power, including the perception of them as unmarriageable and unemployable (853). Indeed, on a larger scale, disabled people's status as diminished persons helps to explain their increased incarceration in institutions under inhumane conditions in Western countries during the nineteenth and twentieth centuries, as well as the rise of the eugenics movement, during which forced sterilization and restrictive marriage laws systematically excluded disabled people from the valued social roles of sexual partner and of parent (Maybee 2019: 49–61, 80–6).

Imafidon criticizes communitarian conceptions of personhood in African philosophical thought on the grounds that these conceptions of personhood define disabled people as nonpersons and so lead to the exclusion of disabled people from the protections of the community—an exclusion that is all the more consequential precisely because these societies are communitarian. As Imafidon suggests, conceptions of the person in African philosophical thought have typically included social and normative criteria in addition to ontological criteria. In terms of the ontological criteria, one is a person in virtue of having a certain kind of being—a being composed of certain elements or that has a certain description. According to Kwame Anthony Appiah, for instance, in Akan thought, "a person consists of a body (*nipadua*) made from the blood of the mother (the *mogya*); an individual spirit, the *sunsum*, which is the main bearer of one's personality; and a third entity, the *okra*," which is "a sort of life force" whose presence is associated with breath (Appiah 2004: 28; cf. Imafidon 2021: 51–2).[2] The Yoruba conception of the person is tripartite, Imafidon suggests: a person consists of *ara* (body), *emi* (vital principle)—which, like the Akan *okra*, is associated with breath—and *ori* (destiny), which guides the life of the person (Imafidon 2012: 5). In Igbo thought, a human being is a person, not because they are made up of certain elements but rather because they have an extra, outside element, namely, a *chi*, or double, in the realm of the spirits (Achebe 1976: 132–3; cf. 1998: 68).

In terms of the social and normative criteria, in many indigenous African belief systems, being a person is a status that, as Ifeanyi A. Menkiti suggested, must be *achieved* (Menkiti 1984: 172). According to this view, being a person requires a *process* in which one is expected to live up to one's social and communal responsibilities over time. As Kwasi Wiredu has summarized the view, a person is "a morally sound adult who has demonstrated in practice a sense of responsibility to household, lineage and society at large" (Wiredu 2009: 16). This conception of personhood, as Ned suggests, leads indigenous African communities to define people largely in terms of "strengths and abilities in relation to communal responsibility," which, as she notes, reflects the communalism of many African societies (Ned 2022: 493). As I have pointed out, Imafidon suggests that African thought typically requires that one satisfy both social/normative criteria and ontological criteria to be considered a person. Someone who meets all the ontological criteria will not be considered a person if they consistently fail to live up to the community's social/moral expectations and will, by consequence, be ostracized or excluded. Conversely, a disabled person who does not satisfy the ontological criteria of personhood that these conceptions of the person assume will be excluded, even if they do live up to all the community's social/moral expectations (Imafidon 2021: 53).

In fact, Imafidon argues, disabled people are often excluded from the category of persons for both ontological and social/normative reasons. Either they are believed to lack some required ontological feature for personhood or they may be excluded due to a community's perception that they are unable to satisfy its social/moral expectations (Imafidon 2021: 52–3). The consequences of being labeled a "nonperson" in a communalistic society is particularly dire, because the communalism of the society means that people rely on one another for mutual care. Insofar as disabled people are labeled as "nonpersons" within African thought, they are cast outside of the community of beings that members of the community have a duty to care for, which negatively impacts them in a host of ways. To take one example, this exclusion has reduced the extent to which disabled people have had access to health care during the COVID-19 pandemic (53).

Imafidon offers a two-pronged approach to address the denial of personhood to disabled people. One solution that he proposes is that educational programs must challenge "the deeply entrenched and ubiquitous paranormal theories of disability" that circulate in many African communities and replace these theories with biological and scientific theories (Imafidon 2021: 54). I want to argue, however, that there are two problems with this solution. First, the solution ignores the long history of criticisms of medical and biological accounts of disability that disability activists and scholars of disability have advanced.[3] Abandoning the problematic views of one set of cultures for the problematic views of another set of cultures does not seem like the best solution. Indeed, such a solution ignores some of the resources in African philosophical thought that could be mobilized to create inclusive societies. As Hebron L. Ndlovu suggests, although "there is a need to rethink all religious doctrines, ethics, and attitudes (emanating from both African religions and Christianity) that militate against the full participation of persons with disabilities in the mainline activities of any given society," such a rethinking "should be done simultaneously with retaining those positive beliefs and values that foster the creation of inclusive societies" (Ndlovu 2016: 36). Ndlovu notes that indigenous African beliefs about identities that fall under today's Western concept of disability have often been mixed or ambivalent (32–6). As I have noted, for instance, although some aspects of the spiritualistic beliefs in Yoruba society reinforce negative perceptions of disabled people, other aspects support positive identities for disabled people. These beliefs could also, as Adegbindin has suggested, be used to support pluralistic understandings of ability that undercut the Western dichotomy between "normal" and "deformed"/"abnormal" (Adegbindin 2018)—a dichotomy arguably invented, maintained, and regulated by Western medicine.[4]

Recall that one positive aspect of the communalistic beliefs of many African societies is that people are often defined in terms of social relationships rather than physical characteristics. In African conceptions of personhood, Ndlovu suggests, "Communal membership entails, among other things, belonging to an endless chain of interpersonal relationships and collective responsibility for the general well-being of other members of the community" (Ndlovu 2016: 36). The emphasis on communal or interpersonal relationships (child/son/daughter, nephew/niece, fellow member of the compound, etc.) could be used to help promote the inclusion of disabled people in communities' activities (Maybee 2019: 166–70).

Imafidon's second solution to the denial of personhood to disabled people is that African societies should adopt what he calls a "broad sense of community," in which communalism and definitions of personhood are based on "general, flexible, and tolerant principles of humanity and solidarity that accommodate differences rather than . . . on very specific and rigid forms, features, or qualities of being." Such a communalism would be "less hostile to, more tolerant of, and more open to, differences in general" rather than assume a narrow set of values or beliefs, a culture, a religion, a language, or an ethnicity (Imafidon 2021: 55).

Other African philosophers have also criticized the ableist implications of African conceptions of personhood—particularly in relation to the social/normative criteria that regard personhood as a process or achievement (Manzini 2018; Onazi 2020). In his book on disability justice, for instance, Onazi argues that to the degree that such conceptions emphasize the fulfillment of obligations and mutual reciprocity as conditions for personhood, disabled people who are unable to fulfill certain obligations or who cannot achieve full reciprocity in social relationships may be considered less of a "person" and so less worthy of moral consideration (Onazi 2020: 16, 19, 24–5). Onazi therefore proposes an account of communalism in which the required social obligations are regarded as *asymmetrical*, rather than reciprocal (26–8, 130–3). On this view, the only criterion of personhood is to be a human being who is the *recipient* of obligation (26). Such an account of personhood is consistent with the importance that many indigenous African societies place on human dependency generally (130)—a topic to which I will return in the next section. Onazi therefore proposes "an account of disability justice that takes the value of community relationships and asymmetrical obligations as its core feature to serve as a criterion for evaluating existing laws, policies, practices and legal and political institutions" (28). In a similar vein, borrowing from feminist disability theory, Imafidon recommends adopting an ethics of communalism or of caring for others that is connected to a notion of mutuality rather than to a notion of reciprocity. Unlike reciprocity, Imafidon suggests, mutuality does not require an equal or balanced return, or a return of services of the same kind, but only a mutual recognition within or given a person's "capacity to show love, friendship and appreciation" (Imafidon 2019: 83–5).

We must also consider the degree to which negative understandings of the personhood or moral status of disabled people in Africa today are products of colonial oppression, capitalism, and poverty more generally. Historically, as societies have moved away from more subsistence-based economies to capitalist, wage-based economies, the definition of what counts as work or genuine economic activity narrows, reducing the number, variety, and economic significance of tasks that disabled people are able to carry out, thereby reducing disabled people's social value (Maybee 2019: 28–33). In Botswana, for instance, according to Julie Livingston, the introduction of migrant wage work in the mines, as well as the introduction of colonial medicine, led disabled people to become socially weaker (Livingston 2005: 128). Changes in work and a new system of medical examinations led to the marginalization of "myopic, deaf, club-footed, epileptic and arthritic men," who "in earlier times may have been quite 'able' and successful farmers and herders" (14). The introduction of capitalism and Western medicine thus made it more difficult for many disabled people to fulfill communal responsibilities and so achieve personhood according to traditional, social/normative definitions. Moreover, as Ned has suggested, the capitalist economic system disintegrated traditional, communal living arrangements and structures of caring generally and created conditions of poverty that undercut the ability of communities to care for disabled members in general (Ned 2022: 495).

In sum, although conceptions of the person in many African societies have sometimes relied on religious or spiritualistic views that improperly deny personhood to some disabled people, they can nevertheless provide resources for designing or redesigning societies and social institutions to foster inclusion. Furthermore, we must also take into consideration the degree to which the colonial encounter and the introduction of capitalist wage systems have undercut the ability of people both to achieve personhood status according to traditional, social/normative criteria—redefining these people as "disabled" and as "nonpersons"—and to care for disabled members of their communities.

Overlapping Values

Disability scholars and activists in the West have sometimes noted that the values that disabled people support and promote are opposed to the values that dominate in many Western societies. Paul K. Longmore has suggested, for instance, that, in their attempt to build a disability culture, "Deaf and disabled people have been uncovering or formulating sets of alternative values derived from within the Deaf and disabled experiences" (Longmore 2003: 222). These efforts "have been collective rather than personal efforts. They involve not so much the statement of personal philosophies of life as the assertion of group perspectives and values" (ibid.). For example, he says, people with physical disabilities have been affirming values from their own experience that "are markedly different from, and even opposed to, nondisabled majority values" (ibid.). In particular, Longmore explains, "They declare that they prize not self-sufficiency but self-determination, not independence but interdependence, not functional separateness but personal connection, not physical autonomy but human community. This values[-]formation takes disability as the starting point. It uses the disability experience as the source of values and norms" (ibid.). These sorts of alternative values, Longmore suggests, are good for both disabled people in particular and American culture generally, the latter of which, he says, is "in the throes of an alarming and dangerous moral and social crisis, a crisis of values" (ibid.). Indeed, Longmore argues that the disability movement's commitment to these alternative values

> can offer a critique of the hyperindividualistic majority norms institutionalized in the medical model and at the heart of the contemporary American crisis. That analysis needs to be made, not just because majority values are impossible for people with disabilities to match up to, but, as important, because they have proved destructive for everyone, disabled and nondisabled alike. They prevent real human connection and corrode authentic human community. (Longmore 2003: 222)

(The destructiveness of America's hyperindividualism has been well illustrated by responses to the COVID-19 pandemic in many parts of the United States, where people have insisted that it is their individual right to refuse to wear a simple cloth or paper covering over their nose and mouth to prevent unnecessary disease and death for other US residents.)

The alternative values that Longmore lists—"not self-sufficiency but self-determination, not independence but interdependence, not functional separateness but personal connection, not physical autonomy but human community"—are reflected in the value systems that many African philosophers, cultures, and societies promote. African philosophical thought can therefore play a crucial role in helping disability activists and scholars as well as philosophers of disability think through these values and provide theoretical foundations for them.

I have shown how some of these values are reflected in African philosophical thought. The communalistic emphasis of many indigenous African societies leads them to define people primarily in terms of personal and social connectedness rather than functional or physical abilities. These values are often grounded in an appreciation of the basic dependency of human beings on others. For instance, Wiredu suggests that although conditions and practices have been changing as a result of urbanization and commercial farming, the Akan still have "an acute sense of the essential dependency of the human condition." The Akan conception of the person recognizes that humans are "radically self-insufficient" at birth and holds that, although the acquisition of skills and abilities can reduce dependency, human dependency is never completely eliminated. While self-reliance is "understood and recommended by the Akans," Wiredu adds, "its very possibility is predicated upon this ineliminable residue of human dependency." On this view, no human being is really self-sufficient, since whatever self-sufficiency one has is always predicated on a background context of mutual support. "Human beings, therefore, at all times," Wiredu concludes, "in one way or another, directly or indirectly, need the help of their kind". This notion of basic human dependency undergirds the Akan's commitment to practices of mutual aid and to a communalistic ethic (Wiredu 2003: 293–4).

The ethics of *ubuntu/buntfu/botho* found in a number of indigenous African societies also emphasizes human interdependency. As Ndlovu summarizes it, *ubuntu/buntfu/botho* "embraces communalistic notions of a holistic personhood, partnership, mutuality, the dignity of the Other, and that cardinal principle that 'I am because we are; and since we are therefore I am'" (Ndlovu 2016: 35). Tsitsi Chataika and Judy McKenzie suggest that the ethics of *ubuntu* can be used to support disabled children, for instance, because of its emphasis on "care and interdependency." Nevertheless, foregrounding care and dependency often "restricts individual agency," they suggest, thus placing it "in opposition to a discourse of autonomy and human rights" (Chataika and McKenzie 2013: 158). Hence, approaches to disability justice that may work well in the West may not work well in many African contexts (ibid.). Mary Berghs has suggested that Africans' interpretation and application of *ubuntu* to activist struggles for disability justice are still in development (Berghs 2017: 7). Nevertheless, I would suggest that an ethics of *ubuntu* that values "the dignity of the Other" or a diversity of human experiences and ways of being in addition to interdependence could help disabled people hone systems of value that balance human interdependency not with self-*reliance* but with self-*determination* within their social contexts.

Cultural anthropologist and activist Diana Szántó's discussion of "polio-homes"—self-supporting, communal dwellings managed by polio-disabled people—in Freetown, Sierra Leone, provides an excellent example of how one group of disabled people in Africa has negotiated the values of communalism and self-determination within their context. The discussion also exhibits the role that African philosophical thought plays in this negotiation. Between 2008 and 2011, Szántó worked with fourteen organizations connected to thirteen different "polio-homes" (Szántó 2020: x, 51).

Despite attempts—by both international nongovernmental organizations (which emphasize individual rights) and Sierra Leone's government—to suppress the collectivist values of the country's traditional belief systems (or "backward culture," as the Sierra Leone government put it) in favor of more Western, neoliberal individualistic values, groups of polio-disabled people in Sierra Leone established and manage cooperative dwelling places dedicated to the values of communalism, mutual responsibility, and collective solidarity (Szántó 2020: 93, 148). "[T]he most important function of a polio-home," Szántó writes, "is the maintenance of a strong net collective of solidarity. This net substitutes for institutional forms of social insurance" (68). In the polio-homes (as Szántó refers to them), residents employ *ososu*—a trust-based, traditional, rural savings and credit system that allows individuals to draw on pools of resources on a rotating basis—and share resources generally. The daily earnings produced by collective begging—which is only one of the ways in which residents supported themselves—are also shared. "Selfish is a person who does not want to share," Szántó writes, "and not only is this morally wrong, there is almost an element of pity for such a person: he surely misses out on something, both materially and socially" (141). This emphasis on communalism and collective solidarity means that, in the "polio-homes," people support one another. "It is not easy to have a full stomach in the squat," Szántó says, "but it is also impossible to die of starvation" (64). Szántó calls these dwellings "squats" because they are constructed in part out of less permanent materials inside once-abandoned buildings on land to which the residents often have no clear claim. But, for Szántó, the term *squat* also captures the agency that residents express by taking control of previously closed, urban spaces that belonged to private owners or to the state. "To squat is to self-organize and invent forms of collective government, decision-making and responsibility-sharing," she explains. "It is in this sense that all the polio-homes, no matter the strict legal status of the individual places, can be considered 'squats': proofs of the agency, agility and creativity of their founders, caretakes and members" (50).

Szántó argues that these residences of polio-disabled people challenge the Western disability movement's model of integration, according to which integration must be individualistic, while collective cohabitation is associated with segregation (Szántó 2020: 83, 118). For, while the "polio-homes" are collective dwellings for disabled people, they are also integrated (60, 70), as they draw in and support nondisabled family members, including spouses or intimate partners, children, family members who come to the city from rural areas, and other nondisabled members of the surrounding communities. The "collective organization of the polio-homes" meant that many of the residents had "gone farther than their siblings [who remained in the rural areas] in terms of education, geographical mobility and social mobility" (147). Being in the city and being a member of the polio-home meant that the disabled residents' "chances of joining networks that included diverse, high status persons" were also greater than they were for siblings who remained in the provinces. Life in the urban polio-home thus meant that disabled residents "could benefit their families in the hinterland" (ibid.), Szántó says, and these city-dwelling polio-home residents were often called upon to do so. Disabled residents of the polio-homes also paid nondisabled people from the community for various goods and services, including for assistance when collectively begging (141). "[A]s communities," Szántó asserts, the polio-homes "actually integrate a much larger public than that of the permanent members" (72). In short, "polio-squats are open places, which, instead of isolating disabled people, constantly draw social life from the exterior" (ibid.).

The "polio-homes" thus also challenge the Western disability movement's emphasis on the dichotomy between disabled and nondisabled people, Szántó suggests (Szántó 2020: 118, 260). The disabled members of the polio-homes have more or less stable, intimate relationships, often with nondisabled people, become parents, and maintain rich social networks (130–8). Echoing African philosophical thought's emphasis on the role of social connectedness in defining the person, for the disabled polio-home residents, it is relational ties that confer social value. Parenthood, in particular, is regarded as "a basic measure of social personhood," Szántó remarks (137). To be "normal" means to raise a child and be surrounded by family. "The stigma which cannot be washed away," she writes, "is not the polio, but the social incapacity reflected directly by the lack of being embedded in society by communal, family and relational ties" (138). Sierra Leone is a non-welfare society that supports few of its citizens (82); hence, poor people who are disabled and poor people who are not disabled are less distinct from each other than they may be in Western welfare societies. The needs of the residents of the polio-homes, Szántó suggests, are not different from the needs of the nondisabled poor in the city (245–6). Although the polio-homes do have occasional disputes with members of their surrounding communities, they have a great deal in common with the nondisabled members of the surrounding communities, interact with these community members, and are often protected by them (223). The emphasis that the Western disability movement places on the disabled/nondisabled dichotomy is therefore not very useful for understanding Freetown's polio-homes.

Szántó tries not to idealize these residences for polio-disabled people. They are "not utopias," she writes, and are marked by violence, alcohol addiction, the sexual abuse of young girls, as well as everyday quarrels and disputes (Szántó 2020: 277). They are also subjected to structural violence by the state—including occasional forceable removals or raids by the police—and to the structural effects of predatory capitalism by multinational corporations, which has impoverished most of the country's population (175–6, 191). Still, Szántó writes, "I sometimes think that in Sierre Leone I discovered the most individualistic form of collectivism" (256)—a collectivism in which the self-development of individual residents was just as important as living in community. The "polio-homes" of Freetown, Sierra Leone, thus exemplify one way in which disabled people in Africa have balanced the values of human interdependency and self-determination (both individual and collective) in their social context—values that are often reflected in and supported by African philosophical thought.

Conclusion

African philosophy has a great deal to contribute to thinking about disability and disability justice. It helps to show how the concepts of disability and impairment can be rethought in ways that would promote more positive attitudes toward, and greater inclusion of, people currently defined as "disabled" according to today's Western concept of disability. Communalistic conceptions of personhood found in many indigenous African societies and explored by African philosophers can also be mobilized to advocate for more positive attitudes toward disabled people and justice for them. In addition, African philosophical thought can be used to support the values of interdependence, personal connection, and human community that disability activists and scholars often champion, as well as to negotiate definitions of self-determination in light of these values.

Notes

1 Searches for more specific African groups (Akan, Yoruba, Igbo, etc.) did not produce any results that were not already included in the search for *Africa* or *African*.

2 As Imafidon points out elsewhere (Imafidon 2012: 4–5), there has been disagreement about the account of the person in indigenous Akan philosophy. Kwame Gyekye has argued that while the Akan are generally regarded as having a tripartite conception of the person, their account is really dualistic (Gyekye 1998: 59, 65). Joseph I. Omoregbe and Kwasi Wiredu, by contrast, have suggested that, for the Akan, a person has five parts (Omoregbe 1998: 6; Wiredu 1998: 197). These sorts of disagreements helped to inspire Paulin Hountondji to suggest that the very idea of there being collective "philosophies" at all is a myth (Hountondji 1996: 34–6, 43, 44; 2003: 125–7, 131). My own view, as suggested by the aforementioned discussion, is that we can speak generally of collective "philosophies" or systems of belief insofar as those philosophies are embedded in the words, concepts, and commonly held beliefs of cultures and societies, though we must be careful to keep in mind that such collective philosophies are never entirely clear and that there may not be univocal agreement about beliefs in any given society.

3 The literature criticizing medical models of disability is too large to cite here. For a summary of some of the arguments, see Maybee (2019: 4–15). For a discussion of arguments against biological conceptions of disability (or impairment), see Maybee (2019: ch. 5).

4 For arguments for the view that Western medicine invented, maintains, and regulates the Western distinction between "normal" and "deformed"/"abnormal," see, for instance, Maybee (2019: 41–2, 44–8, 116–19, 180–1, 195), Tremain (2001: 618–20).

References

Achebe, Chinua (1976), *Morning Yet on Creation Day: Essays*, Garden City: Anchor Press.

Achebe, Chinua (1998), "'Chi' in Igbo Cosmology," in Emmanuel Chukwudi Eze (ed.), *African Philosophy: An Anthology*, 67–72, Malden: Blackwell Publishers.

Adegbindin, Omotade (2018), "Disability and Human Diversity: A Reinterpretation of Ẹni-Òòṣà1 Philosophy in Yorùbá Belief," *Yorùbá Studies Review*, Fall (December). Available at: https://news.clas.ufl.edu/yoruba-studies-review/ysr-fall-2018/ (accessed June 21, 2023).
Appiah, K. Anthony (2004), "Akan and Euro-American Concepts of the Person," in Lee M. Brown (ed.), *African Philosophy New and Traditional Perspectives*, 21–34, Oxford: Oxford University Press.
Berghs, Maria (2017), "Practices and Discourses of Ubuntu: Implications for an African Model of Disability?" *African Journal of Disability* 6: 292.
Chataika, Tsitsi and Judy McKenzie (2013), "Considerations of an African Childhood Disability Studies," in Tillie Curran and Katherine Runswick-Cole (eds.), *Disabled Children's Childhood Studies: Critical Approaches in a Global Context*, 152–63, London: Palgrave Macmillan.
Eze, E. Chukwudi (1998), "Modern Western Philosopohy and African Colonialism," in E. Chukwudi Eze (ed.), *African Philosophy: An Introduction*, 213–21, Malden: Blackwell Publishers.
Gyekye, Kwame (1998), "The Relation of Okra (Soul) and Honam (Body): An Akan Conception," in E. Chukwudi Eze (ed.), *African Philosophy: An Anthology*, 59–66, Malden: Blackwell Publishers.
Hountondji, Paulin J. (1996), *African Philosophy: Myth and Reality*, 2nd ed., Bloomington: Indiana University Press.
Hountondji, Paulin J. (2003), "An Alienated Literature," in P. H. Coetzee and A. P. J. Roux (eds.), *The African Philosophy Reader*, 2nd ed., 125–36, New York: Routledge.
Imafidon, Elvis (2012), "The Concept of Person in an African Culture and Its Implication for Social Order," *Lumina: Journal of Interdisciplinary Studies* 23 (2): 19 pages.
Imafidon, Elvis (2019), *African Philosophy and the Otherness of Albinism: White Skin, Black Race*, London and New York: Routledge.
Imafidon, Elvis (2021), "African Communitarian Philosophy of Personhood and Disability: The Asymmetry of Value and Power in Access to Healthcare," *International Journal of Critical Diversity Studies* 4 (1): 46–57.
Ingstad, Benedicte and Susan Reynolds Whyte (1995), *Disability and Culture*, Berkeley: University of California Press.
Johnson, Samuel and Obadiah Johnson (2010), *The History of the Yorubas: From the Earliest Times to the Beginning of the British Protectorate*, Cambridge: Cambridge University Press.
Kant, Immanuel (2018), *Groundwork for the Metaphysics of Morals: With an Updated Translation, Introduction, and Notes*, trans. Allen W. Wood, New Haven: Yale University Press.
Kyei, T. E. (1992), *Marriage and Divorce Among the Asante: A Study Undertaken in the Course of the Ashanti Social Survey (1945)*, Cambridge: African Studies Center, Cambridge University.
Leshota, Paul Lekholokoe and Maximus Monaheng Sefotho (2018), "Philosophy of Disability: African Perspectives," in Maximus Monaheng Sefotho (ed.), *Philosophy in Education and Research: African Perspectives*, 93–111, Pretoria: Van Schaik Publishers.
Leshota, Paul Lekholokoe and Maximus Monaheng Sefotho (2020), "Being Differently Abled: Disability through the Lens of Hierarchy of Binaries and Bitso-Lebe-Ke Seromo," *African Journal of Disability* 9: 1–7.
Livingston, Julie (2005), *Debility and the Moral Imagination in Botswana*, African Systems of Thought, Bloomington and Indianapolis: Indiana University Press.

Longmore, Paul K. (2003), *Why I Burned My Book and Other Essays on Disability*. American Subjects, Philadelphia: Temple University Press.

Manzini, Nompumelelo Zinhle (N. Z.) (2018), "Menkiti's Normative Communitarian Conception of Personhood as Gendered, Ableist and Anti-Queer," *South African Journal of Philosophy* 37 (1): 18–33.

Maybee, Julie E. (2017), "Em'Body'Ment and Disability: On Taking the (Biological) 'Body' out of Em'Body'Ment," *Journal of Social Philosophy* 48 (3): 297–320.

Maybee, Julie E. (2019), *Making and Unmaking Disability: The Three-Body Approach*, Lanham: Rowman and Littlefield.

Menkiti, Ifeanyi A. (1984), "Person and Community in African Traditional Thought," in Richard A. Wright (ed.), *African Philosophy: An Introduction*, 171–81, Lanham: University Press of America.

Metzler, Irina (2015), *A Social History of Disability in the Middle Ages: Cultural Considerations of Physical Impairment*, New York: Routledge.

Ndlovu, Hebron L. (2016), "African Beliefs Concerning People with Disabilities: Implications for Theological Education," *Journal of Disability and Religion* 20 (1–2): 29–39.

Ned, Lieketseng Yvonne (2022), "African Renaissance as a Premise for Reimagined Disability Studies in Africa," *Journal of Black Studies* 53 (5): 485–504.

Nwokorie, Okechukwu V. and Patrick J. Devlieger (2019), "'We Only Got Coca-Cola': Disability and the Paradox of (Dis)Empowerment in Southeast Nigeria," *African Journal of Disability* 8 (April): 1–13.

Nyangweso, Mary (2021), "Disability in Africa: A Cultural/Religious Perspective," in Nic Hamel and Toyin Falola (eds.), *Disability in Africa: Inclusion, Care, and the Ethics of Humanity*, 115–36, Rochester: University of Rochester Press.

Omoregbe, Joseph I. (1998), "African Philosophy: Yesterday and Today," in E. Chukwudi Eze (ed.), *African Philosophy: An Anthology*, 3–8, Malden: Blackwell Publishers.

Onazi, Oche (2020), *An African Path to Disability Justice: Community, Relationships and Obligations*, Cham, Switzerland: Springer.

Outlaw Jr., Lucius T. and Chike Jefffers (2022), "Africana Philosophy," in Edward N. Zalta (ed.), *The Stanford Encyclopedia of Philosophy*, Fall edition. Available at: https://plato.stanford.edu/archives/fall2022/entries/africana/ (accessed September 7, 2023).

Oyěwùmí, Oyèrónkẹ́ (1997), *The Invention of Women: Making an African Sense of Western Gender Discourses*, Minneapolis: University of Minnesota Press.

Phillips, Marilynn J. (1990), "Damaged Goods: Oral Narratives of the Experience of Disability in American Culture," *Social Science and Medicine* 30 (8): 849–57.

Szántó, Diana (2020), *Politicizing Polio: Disability, Civil Society and Civic Agency in Sierra Leone*, Singapore: Palgrave Macmillan.

Tremain, Shelley (2001), "On the Government of Disability," *Social Theory and Practice* 27 (4): 617–36.

Wiredu, Kwasi (1998), "How Not to Compare African Thought with Western Thought," in Emmanuel Chukwudi Eze (ed.), *African Philosophy: An Anthology*, 193–9, Malden: Blackwell Publishers.

Wiredu, Kwasi (2003), "The Moral Foundations of an African Culture," in P. H Coetzee and A. P. J Roux (eds.), *The African Philosophy Reader a Text with Readings*, 2nd ed., 287–96, New York: Routledge.

Wiredu, Kwasi (2009), "An Oral Philosophy of Personhood: Comments on Philosophy and Orality," *Research in African Literatures* 40 (1): 8–18.

PART II

MECHANISMS OF OPPRESSION

7 THE APPARATUS OF ADDICTION

SUBSTANCE USE AT THE CROSSROADS OF COLONIAL ABLEISM AND MIGRATION

ANDREA J. PITTS

In recent decades, scholarly work within disability studies has begun to explore how licit and illicit substance use—including substances such as alcohol, cocaine, opioids, amphetamines, cannabis, caffeine, tobacco, and other related substances—have long served as reference points within historical and contemporary health discourses to differentiate human behavior that is perceived to be "normal" from human behavior that is perceived to be "abnormal." For example, Melinda Hall's genealogical engagement with discourses of human enhancement marks views about the use of caffeine as a potential strategy "to augment human traits" (Hall 2006, 3). Additionally, David Houston Wood (2009) traces the relationship of late sixteenth/early seventeenth-century European views of alcohol and its social effects to medicalized discourses of alcoholism in the twenty-first century. Through a reading of William Shakespeare's works and the associated discourses of humoralism at the time,[1] Wood notes that in *Hamlet* and other works by Shakespeare, readers are confronted with questions pertaining to "alcoholism's status as a disability: should society pity the 'drunkard' as the sufferer of a genetic disease? Alternatively, should society blame the individual for his or her weakness? Is it in fact within that person's scope of willpower to amend such a fault, or sin?" (Wood 2009, n.p.). Wood concludes that within this early modern European period, there were strikingly modern models of drunkenness that appear to consider alcoholism as akin to contemporary views regarding the social and political dimensions of disability.

In a parallel, but largely separate, strand of research, addiction discourses have also grown in recent decades, including specifically major biomedical and social programming efforts across the globe that are designed to support the study of and treatment for differing forms of addiction behavior. In response to this proliferation in addiction science and institutional development, Craig Reinarman and Robert Granfield (2015) note in *Expanding Addiction: Critical Essays* that

> beyond the flagship of Alcoholics Anonymous, there are now dozens of other such groups including Overeaters Anonymous, Gamblers Anonymous, Shoppers Anonymous, and Clutterers Anonymous. So-called "behavioral addictions" include "Internet addiction disorder" suffered by "onlineaholics," which is seen as a serious problem in the U.S., as it is in China, South Korea, and elsewhere.... At the very least addiction has become an all-purpose meta-metaphor for the often troubling relationships we have with what we love, enjoy, desire, or require, and thus find hard to control. (Reinarman and Granfield 2015: 1)

Against the medicalized approaches within much of this discourse, Reinarman and Granfield also note that "Despite its prominent place in our lexicon, however, addiction is a relatively recent invention" (Reinarman and Granfield 2015: 1). They offer a historicized framing of addiction discourses, which seeks to denaturalize the prevailing view of addiction as a "brain disease"—a view which has grown to prominence in the twenty-first century. Rather than assuming the discovery of a preexisting biological etiology for addiction, as researchers in the biomedical sciences might have it, authors within the field of "critical addiction studies" interpret the clustering of behaviors and social conditions often characterized as addiction as itself a "historical accomplishment" that warrants critique and ongoing political and theoretical scrutiny (Reinarman 2005: 310).

Notably, while important genealogical explorations of concepts such as disease, illness, and impairment have likewise circulated within philosophy of disability (Tremain 2017) and disability studies (Mitchell and Snyder 2015) in recent decades, much of this work has yet to develop a substantive engagement with addiction discourses and related discourses of substance-use disorders and their affiliated institutional responses. As such, this chapter offers an exploratory engagement at the intersection of these discourses. In particular, the chapter seeks to uncover a broad apparatus of related medical, academic, legal, cultural, and geopolitical sets of relations that co-constitute the meaning and significance of addiction and substance-use discourses. Furthermore, I aim to show that this apparatus of addiction is located across a vast network of causal and contributory relations with patterns of transnational and internal migration that mark the exceedingly global dimensions of disability discourses. Importantly, these global dimensions of disability, also, I argue, demonstrate the colonial dimensions of ableism, including systemic patterns of criminalization, economic exploitation, military interventionism, and heightened neoliberal proclivities toward individualization and naturalization.

In what follows, I begin, first, by describing several approaches to disability that guide my analysis throughout this chapter. Namely, I situate the chapter within the context of two genealogical approaches to disability discourses—the genealogical approach of Shelley Tremain (2017) and the genealogical approach of David Mitchell and Sharon Snyder (2015). I focus on these works, in particular, as they provide important contextual and historicized approaches to disability that I use to frame addiction discourses in the two remaining sections of the chapter. In these two sections of the chapter, I demonstrate how we can identify addiction and substance-use discourses as intertwined with disability in both national and transnational policy in the United States. To do so, I turn to several contexts through which we can see such a genealogical co-imbrication of disability and addiction discourses. That is, in the second section, I underscore the development of the Americans with Disabilities Act (ADA) in the United States and outline the legislative precursors to this policy that show how addiction discourses and other peripheral embodiments become formally separated from addiction discourses in the late 1980s and the early 1990s. In the final section, I turn to two transnational migration contexts that are linked to drug policy to show the implications of addiction and substance-use discourses and their affiliated transnational impacts on disability. Such contexts demonstrate both that disability discourses themselves are not divorced from addiction and substance-use discourses and that their mutual co-constitution shapes how migrants move as disabled and debilitated populations. While the scope of the apparatus of addiction is remarkably expansive, I nevertheless suggest a few exploratory connections between addiction discourses and genealogical approaches to disability that, in my view, warrant further research and consideration.

Historicizing and Contextualizing Addiction Discourses

Tremain's groundbreaking work on disability and impairment discourses has engaged carefully with a variety of sociohistorical conceptions of disability, all of which developed as challenges to more conventional medical models of disability (Tremain 2017: 85–6). Notably, Tremain traces the historical emergence of disability scholarship and anti-ableist activism in the United States and the United Kingdom to explore nuanced differences among the social models of disability developed throughout the last several decades of the twentieth century. Importantly, Tremain argues, furthermore, that both the British social model of disability and the minority-group model of disability initiated in the United States rely on epistemological and ontological assumptions that "bear a remarkable resemblance to assumptions made on the conventional, medicalized, conception of disability" (91). She points out that

> insofar as disability theorists have assumed that impairment is a transhistorical and universal phenomenon . . . they have been concerned to formulate arguments about (among other things) why social responses to impairment vary between historical periods and cultural contexts, that is, why people with impairments are included in social life in some places and periods and excluded from social life in some places and periods. Notice that impairment is represented in these claims as nonhistorical (biological) matter of the body, which is molded by time and class, is culturally shaped, or on which culture is imprinted. In other words, the category of impairment has remained the passive, politically neutral foundation of disability on both the BSM [British social model] and minority-group model, as well as the conventional, medicalized conception of disability. (Tremain 2017: 91)

Tremain's work seeks to denaturalize impairment discourses in opposition to the epistemological and ontological assumptions that she perceives to prevail in late twentieth-century disability discourses. She thus develops a robustly historicized and relativized philosophy of disability that explains why views about embodiment, space, movement, institutions, and academic knowledge production are themselves sociohistorical phenomena that constitute an "apparatus" of disability. To do this, she argues that the concept of impairment has been "an element of the apparatus of disability . . . all along" (Tremain 2017: 93). That is, she states, "disability is an apparatus of force relations, a product of human invention and intervention all the way down" (18). Drawing from the methodological direction of Michel Foucault, Tremain argues that a "diagnostic style of reasoning" developed in the late 1700s, which relies on statistical measurement and perceived regularities to materialize "impairments as universal attributes (properties) of subjects through the iteration and reiteration of rather culturally specific regulatory norms and ideals about (for example) human function and structure, competency, intelligence, locomotion, and ability" (93). Furthermore, Tremain's approach defends the claim that this apparatus of disability is "inextricable from and mutually constitutive" of other apparati of power such as gender, race, sexuality, ethnicity, class, age, and various nationalisms (37–8).

I consider Tremain's approach to be a useful framing of the related sociohistorical and geopolitical force relations that constitute contemporary addiction discourses, including their associated medical, legal, academic, colonial, and affective dimensions. That is, I propose that addiction discourses likewise make up a related and overlapping set of force relations with disability discourses, although their specific iterations, as we will see in the following section, have, at times, been distinguished from disability discourses. As Reinarman (2005), quoting the work of Peter Cohen (2010), outlines:

> Once the Protestant Reformation and market capitalism gave rise to the notion of "the autonomous individual" in the West somewhere around the 17th century . . . we began to see the development of its opposite—a modern sort of devil which takes the form of people who are thought to have lost the capacity for the self-regulation, independence, and entrepreneurial activity which were considered the essence of the autonomous individual. (Cohen 2010, in Reinarman 2005, 310)

If we consider this development of the autonomous individual within the context of seventeenth-century European discourses of modernity, we must also, as I mention through my use of Tremain's work, put such discourses in relation with racial, gendered, sexual, and colonial discourses. For example, as global disability theorist Shaun Grech (2015) notes, Latin American decolonial theorists such as Aníbal Quijano and Ramón Grosfoguel have long highlighted that the invention of European modernity was itself dependent on colonial projects and their continued organizing logics. In this sense, there would be no European forms of modernization, industrialization, and civilization without accompanying forms of European colonization, dehumanization, land dispossession, and exploitative labor and enslavement.

Grech argues that colonialism and its afterlives shape the emerging concepts of the body, normalcy, consciousness, and normativity, all of which operate within and through conceptions of disability (Grech 2015: 10). Tracing the writings of Olaudah Equiano, a formerly enslaved Igbo abolitionist author of the eighteenth century, Grech points out, for example, "[t]he trafficking of slaves was an early example of the creation of the 'ideal' colonised body. . . . Disabled people were always worth less as productive slaves, and in fact slave traders went to quite some length to even hide their illnesses or impairments, since this would push down their value upon sale" (ibid.). Accordingly, as we will see in the third section of this chapter, addiction discourses, too, rely on such colonial dimensions of an ideally self-controlled, self-regulating, moderate, and law-abiding individual. This framing of the "temperate" modern subject has also led to serious negative implications for colonized peoples, including the condemnation, dehumanization, and annihilation of peoples deemed uncivilized precisely in this manner.

Consider, for example, as Siobhan Senier (2012) notes, that colonial officials "pathologized Native bodies and Native cultures. Even today, we continue to hear that Indians were too weak to resist New World microbes, that they have some kind of genetic predispositions to diabetes or alcoholism, they need intervention and management in the form of the Indian Health Service, substance abuse programming, and so forth." In this same vein, alongside alcohol, we see addiction discourses around gambling and gaming seeking to control and condemn Indigenous communities and their economic and political strategies. For example, Nakoda scholar of Native American studies Kathryn Shanley puts the issue in the following manner:

> Gambling, or its more dignified terminological brother gaming, straddles that nebulous line between legal and illegal, moral and immoral, healthy and sick in the consciousness of many mainstream American citizens and policy makers. And nothing brings out that ambivalence in the American cultural mind more than Native American gaming. Indians continue to suffer the dichotomized thinking that would have them be simply good Indians or bad Indians. When associated with the "natural" world, Mother Earth, we are good Indians, but when we are involved in the business of making money from gambling, we are bad Indians. (Shanley 2000: 93)

In this chapter, I similarly follow these threads of analysis by scholars within philosophy of disability, disability studies, and decolonial studies to underscore the continued co-constituting force relations between settler and extractive colonization and addiction discourses. In the third section, I trace how drug policy and interventionism place colonized peoples within a devastating economy of colonial extraction, exploitation, and violence. These examples, I claim, demonstrate the transnational dimensions of the apparatus of addiction, including its connections to colonial ableism and migration.

I also want to briefly mention the methodological—that is, genealogical—approach of Mitchell and Snyder (2015), whose framings of "ablenationalism" and "peripheral embodiment" provide helpful concepts through which to consider the relationships between addiction and disability discourses. *Ablenationalism* is a term that marks, as Mitchell and Snyder state, "where ableism and nationalism meet" (Mitchell and Snyder 2015: 11). They describe ablenationalism as a product of post-Fordist economies that have implemented neoliberal patterns of inclusionism. Specifically, they write:

> As people with disabilities encounter the inflexibilities of key social institutions such as health care, religious gatherings, communities, workplaces, schools, families, and so on, such encounters increasingly depend upon the ability of some to "fit in" by passing as nondisabled, or, at least, not too disabled. Inclusionism requires that disability be tolerated as long as it does not demand an excessive degree of change from relatively

> inflexible institutions, environments, and norms of belonging. (Mitchell and Snyder 2015: 14)

In this sense, ablenationalism has both domestic and international dimensions. Due to domestic forms of ableism and nationalism (as Mitchell and Snyder note in the previous quote), many nondisabled people consider disabled people and people who, according to legislation such as the ADA, do not meet established criteria of the designation "disabled," to be parasitic on the aims and stability of the nation-state. Alternatively, people who are designated as "appropriately" disabled or "not too" disabled are regarded as the "able-disabled," Mitchell and Snyder point out (Mitchell and Snyder 2015: 14). Often, such able-disabled populations are used as representatives of the technological and biomedical achievements of the nation-state. Consider, in this regard, the national pride placed in disabled athletes who are described within heroic narratives of overcoming through access to new technological enhancements in prosthetics and medical intervention. Mitchell and Snyder remark on this point: "This new era of disabled athleticism—an era of buffed, muscular, yet technologically supplemented bodies—promises all of the transcendent capacity a hyperreal, medicalized culture could offer" (56). Relatedly, people who fall outside of this form of acceptable inclusionism inhabit what Mitchell and Snyder refer to as occupying "peripheral embodiments," due to "exclusions [that] result from equality denied to a majority of crip/queer bodies based on determinations of their excessive deviance from culturally inculcated norms" (14). Accordingly, able-disabled populations are folded in the neoliberal aims of nation-state market demands while receiving less and less access to the redistribution of material and social resources within the state. In short, if one is unable to respond to these market demands for inclusionism, then one is considered a "burden" on the state and thereby "somehow outside of its best interests" (17).

Ablenationalism has important international dimensions as well, including dimensions linked to nationalist obsessions with technological advancement and neoliberal economic strategies; that is, the forms of inclusionism impacting some disabled and debilitated populations support forms of nationalism that negatively evaluate noncapitalistic geopolitical contexts. For example, as Mitchell and Snyder consider in this regard, forms of American exceptionalism such as remarks that John Kerry—former Secretary of State in the Obama administration and Special Presidential Envoy for Climate under President Biden—made in 2013 according to which the ADA sets the "gold standard for the rest of the world . . . and [that] we must export that gold standard" across the globe (Kerry 2013, in Mitchell and Snyder 2015: 59). Kerry continues:

> In four simple words, [the Convention on the Rights of Persons with Disabilities] says to other countries that don't respect the rights of

> disabled people: Be more like us. To countries that warehouse children with disabilities—be more like us. To countries that leave children to die because they have a disability—be more like us. To countries that force children with disabilities to abandon education—be more like us. (Kerry 2013, in Mitchell and Snyder 2015: 59)

As Mitchell and Synder point out, this self-referential exportation of rights-based inclusionism overlooks the neoliberal paradigms of austerity and cost-cutting that continue to imprison, neglect, and abuse disabled populations within the nation-state's own legal jurisdictions and indeed seeks to strengthen these paradigms. An exportation model of this kind illustrates the important concept of homonationalism. Introduced by Jasbir Puar, the concept of homonationalism signifies a form of American nationalism associated with protections for lesbian, gay, bisexual, and trans (LGBT) people that condemns foreign nation-states for their homophobic and transphobic practices while bolstering and fetishizing the United States's own economic and institutional efforts (Puar 2007: 43–4).

When we take this geopolitical, institutional, and social backdrop into account, we can begin to recognize how addiction discourses in (for example) the United States are encompassed within the framing of peripheral embodiment. The following section, in which I trace the legislative formation of the ADA, provides an extended example of this form of ablenationalism.

Ablenationalism, Addiction, and the ADA

In the decades since the passage of the ADA in the United States, philosophers (among others) have considered whether addiction is itself a disability. For example, Katherine Jenkins and Aness Kim Webster defend a definition of disability as "marginalised functioning," which they characterize as "the social situation of being unable to physically function in the ways that are presupposed by the norms that govern the construction of common social environments and the structuring of common social interactions" (Jenkins and Webster 2021: 736). Within this framing of disability, they briefly consider whether "alcohol intolerance" (which appears as interestingly distinct from alcoholism) is a form of marginalized functioning in the manner that they describe. They note in this regard,

> there may be some contexts—business entertainment contexts, perhaps—in which the expectation that people will drink alcohol is so strong that refraining from drinking alcohol constitutes a serious social problem. In such contexts, a person who cannot drink alcohol counts as having marginalised functioning because the norm "people can drink

> alcohol" is serving as a default in structuring social interactions. (Jenkins and Webster 2021: 737)

In this context, Jenkins and Webster have considered alcohol intolerance, which is medically described as "caused by a genetic condition in which the body can't break down alcohol efficiently . . . [and] the only way to prevent these uncomfortable reactions is to avoid alcohol" (Mayo Clinic 2022). Other philosophers and theorists, too, have defended accounts according to which addiction is a form of disability, including Bennett Foddy and Julian Savulescu (2010) and David Wasserman (2004). Although Jenkins and Webster have chosen a metabolic condition to distinguish which socially marginalized factors warrant consideration, we could, however, add (albeit not uncontroversially) that alcoholics who violate the norm that "people can drink alcohol" could also be categorized under the descriptions that they provide.

Against these other thinkers, my aim in this chapter is not to outline definitive framings of disability or questions regarding "weakness of will," "autonomy," "functioning," or related concepts that circulate in much of the extant philosophical literature on addiction. Rather, my central aim in this chapter is to identify the biopolitical dimensions of addiction discourses, a task that, in my view, can be best accomplished genealogically. Tremain has made these remarks regarding Foucault's conception of biopower:

> The configuration of power centered on life (biopower) through which life itself becomes the ground for political struggle—in a word, biopolitics—is, in short, a strategy of liberal governmentality. Insofar as the phenomena toward whose management biopower is directed emerged as urgent within the frameworks of liberalism and capitalism, such a strategic movement of power must operate in ways that maximize the efficiency of the state and minimize its political, economic, and social costs, while at the same time guiding, influencing, and limiting people's actions in ways that seem to enhance their capacity to be self-determining. (Tremain 2017: 74)

Like Tremain, I am skeptical of how academic institutions—including professional philosophy itself—operate within the biopolitical reach of liberal governmentality. While I do not have the space in this chapter to fully elaborate these academic dimensions, suffice it to say that addiction-related discourses—including discourses associated with alcohol recovery programming, the racialized stigmatization of Black and brown peoples during the crack-cocaine epidemic of the 1980s and the 1990s (Reinarman and Levine 2004), and expanding patterns of bioconsumptive models of agency that limit social and individual forms of action, including illicit drug sale and use to consumption (Valencia 2018: 141)—deeply complicate any ethics pertaining to addiction behaviors. That is, as Tremain suggests in her work on the biopolitics of disability, the seeming "capacity to be self-determining" must be considered within the broader apparati of disability, colonialism, racism, and other co-enabling force relations.

To underscore how addiction discourses overlap and diverge with disability discourses in domestic contexts, I shall now examine the legislative precursors to the ADA. Wasserman's (2004) description of the relationship between the ADA and addiction provides a helpful historical framing for this purpose. He writes:

> Under current disability law in the United States . . . drug addiction is classified as an impairment, and many or most drug addicts qualify as disabled. The partial list of physical and mental impairments in the regulations accompanying the ADA includes "drug addiction." A current, former, or suspected addict is classified as an "individual with a disability" if her addiction "substantially limits one or more major life activities"; if she has a record of (past) addiction that substantially limits her, or if she is substantially limited because she is "regarded as having" an addiction. . . . The self-inflicted character of some addictions is no bar to their inclusion under the ADA. There is no exception for impairments acquired through voluntary conduct—the person who becomes addicted because of reckless abuse is as eligible for the protections of the ADA as the person who becomes paraplegic because of reckless driving. But a drug addict enjoys the protection of the ADA only if she has stopped using the drug: the law specifically disqualifies those currently engaged in "illegal use of drugs" as individuals with disabilities. There is no exclusion for those currently engaged in the legal use of alcohol. (Wasserman 2004: 463–4, quoting Americans with Disabilities Act of 1990)

Wasserman's last remarks regarding access to protections under the ADA mark a significant shift between the Rehabilitation Act and the ADA. Under a 1978 amendment to Section 504 of the Rehabilitation Act, the US Congress confirmed that alcoholics and drug addicts—current or former substance users—were "handicapped individuals" within the scope of federal law (Goff 1993). However, as Reese Henderson points out, Section 504 "does not protect employees whose alcohol or drug abuse problems impair their ability to function on the job, particularly when their condition might threaten the lives or well-being of others" (Henderson 1991: 728). In court cases following the 1978 amendment, judges did not interpret this legislation consistently (ibid.). Rather, differential protections were offered under the amendment. For example, in *Nisperos v. Buck* (1989) an Immigration and Naturalization Service attorney qualified for protections under Section 504 due to his ongoing cocaine addiction. However, in other cases, such as in *American Federation of Government Employees v. Dole* (1987), it was deemed lawful that all employees—regardless of job performance—could be subject to random drug screenings by their employer and eventually terminated if drugs were found in their urine samples (Henderson 1991: 729). To regulate these discrepancies, Section 104(a) of the ADA effectively tightened the language of "qualified individuals with a disability" to hold that any persons who are *currently* using illegal drugs or alcohol *are not* protected by the ADA. If a person with an addiction history or history of illegal substance use seeks rehabilitation and is thereby no longer "currently" using illegal drugs, they are regarded as entitled to protections under the ADA.[2]

Given these shifts and inconsistencies, some scholars such as Dean Spade (2015: 176) and other legal analysts note that the ADA of 1990 "appears to exclude more addicts from the protections of the ADA than the 1978 Amendment excluded under the Rehabilitation Act" (Henderson 1991: 737). While the Rehabilitation Act regulated who was worthy of protection according to standards regarding job performance, the ADA effectively denied illegal drug users any protections, regardless of their potential contributions to labor markets or performance metrics. In this sense, we see a curious biopolitical limit: regardless of the value of someone's labor, their status as a "current drug user" precludes them from employment protections and accommodations under extant disability law in the United States.

One means through which to show the biopolitical operations of this shift, and thus trace some dynamics of the apparatus of addiction, is to look back at the congressional records whereby members of the US Senate publicly debated the ADA and the scope of its protections. My aim in doing so is to show how the public deliberations about those who are deemed worthy of protections under the ADA exhibit the ablenationalist tropes that Mitchell and Snyder describe. Namely, current drug users come to occupy "peripheral embodiments" that, elaborating on Mitchell and Snyder's claims, "cannot be adequately accommodated even under the most liberal, fluid, and flexible diversity doctrine given the in-built limits of community infrastructure, reasonable tolerance, limited economic resources, and traditional historical expectations about who will share the rapidly dwindling commonwealth represented by public and private spaces" (Mitchell and Snyder 2015: 4). What such peripheral embodiment entails, I suggest, is that we can identify domestic patterns of internal movement and migration within the United States, including forced relocation and circulation among racialized, colonized, and gendered peoples through courts, prisons, jails, detention facilities, child welfare services, court-ordered rehabilitation, and the enactment of legislated health services. In short, the lack of legal protections under the ADA afforded to people who currently use drugs renders them importantly distinct in terms of governance and desert of material resources from the able-disabled persons who are either not addicted to illegal substances or who voluntarily seek rehabilitation services.

Consider, on these points, the remarks by Republican Senators Jesse Helms (North Carolina) and William Armstrong (Colorado) who, in deliberations about the proposed ADA legislation in September 1989, appear to demarcate some of these very distinctions between peripheral embodiment and able-disabled populations. Notably, at one point in the Senate deliberations with Democratic Senator Tom Harkin (Iowa), who authored and sponsored the proposed ADA legislation, Armstrong asks Harkin this question: "if a person is a consumer of illegal drugs, does he gain a protected status under this bill?" (Congressional Record-Senate 1989: 19853). Harkin replies, "I can answer definitively to the Senator that current users of illegal drugs are not, and we are working out a couple of amendments with the Senator from North Carolina and a couple of others to better clarify that" (ibid.).[3] Armstrong continues:

> May I read a list of related items? I think perhaps the Senator is going to allay some of my fears. Mental disorders, such as alcohol withdrawal, delirium, hallucinosis, dementia with alcoholism, marijuana, delusional disorder, cocaine intoxication, cocaine delirium, disillusional disorder. I have a whole list of these. Am I correct in assuming that these would not be covered as disabilities? (Congressional Record-Senate 1989: 19853)

Harkin responds that he is "obviously not familiar with these disorders" and then a few moments later clarifies that some additional amendments to the bill would be forthcoming to definitively clarify that such disorders will not be protected.

While this dialogue tracks the distinction actually found between the ADA and the Rehabilitation Act, it also points our attention to other peripheral embodiments and thus to a broader purview of the scope of the "in-built limits" by which disability law in the United States has distinguished between disabilities and other pathologized behaviors. Tellingly, Armstrong continues: "How about homosexuality and bisexuality? . . . How about exhibitionism, pedophilia, voyeurism, and similar? . . . How about compulsive kleptomania, or other impulse control disorders?" (Congressional Record-Senate 1989: 19853). At each step, Harkin assures the senator from Colorado that these conditions would not be covered by the ADA.

Helms subsequently takes the floor and questions Harkin. Like Armstrong, Helms begins by making queries about employment conditions—such as asking whether businesses will be unable to terminate employees due to "schizophrenia" or because one of them is "a manic-depressive" or "a pedophile." Harkin responds by distinguishing someone whose disability is "controlled by drugs, [is] under a doctor's care, and [is] qualified for the job" from someone who is not (Congressional Record-Senate 1989: 19864). If those conditions are met and the person is still not hired, then that person would have the right to file a claim under the ADA. Undeterred, Helms continues to ask whether "homosexuals," "transvestites," and "those who are HIV positive or who have active AIDS disease are covered" (19865). In particular, Helms asks whether such persons can qualify for public accommodations under Title III of the ADA, including specifically whether they should be protected in cases of the adoption of children. In Harkins's replies to Helms, he clarifies that "homosexuality is not a disability" covered under the ADA and that a subsequent amendment will make explicit that "the term 'disabled' or 'disability' shall not apply to an individual solely because that individual is a transvestite" (19875). Regarding HIV/AIDS status, Harkin, during the course of the deliberations, asks Helms why HIV-positive status would be a relevant consideration for an adoption agency, to which Helms replies: "You want to put a child up for adoption and subject him to a terrible risk. Bear in mind, Senator, that approximately 85 percent of the HIV-positive people in this country are drug users and/or homosexuals" (19865).

Activist collectives such as MindFreedom International—a group that describes itself as largely made up of "people who have personally experienced human rights violations in the mental health system" (MindFreedom 2022)—have protested against the terms outlined in this congressional record, terms that demand that people be forced into biopsychiatric models of health and wellness through pharmaceutical control and compulsory rehabilitation. In their statement to the American Psychiatric Association (among others), MindFreedom protestors from a 2003 hunger strike based in California state:

> We respect the right of people to choose the option of prescribed psychiatric drugs. Many of us have made this personal choice.... However, choice in the mental health field is severely limited. One approach dominates, and that is a belief in chemical imbalances, genetic determinism and psychiatric drugs as the treatment of choice. Far too often this limited choice has been exceedingly harmful to both the body and the spirit. (MindFreedom 2003, quoted in Lewis 2013: 123-4)

As MindFreedom and other disability scholar-activists argue, the concessions made by Harkin and prompted by Helms distinguish between people who are considered properly "controlled" by biopsychiatric drugs or properly rehabilitated by therapeutic interventions for illegal drug use from those people who are not managed in these ways. The latter group of people are thereby placed beyond the pale of the ADA's legal protections and thus come to occupy peripheral locations relative to people deemed more appropriately controlled and regulated by biopsychiatry and medical interventions. Liat

Ben-Moshe (2020) extends this point in her work on the carceral connections to this distinction. She writes:

> even when the budget of mental health does not go directly into institutionalization, it still goes into expanding biopsychiatry and medical intervention, which often intersect with surveillance and punishment, especially for racialized and low-income populations. This contributes to what I call *carceral sanism*, which are forms of carcerality that contribute to the oppression of mad or "mentally ill" populations under the guise of treatment. (Ben-Moshe 2020: 58, emphasis in Ben-Moshe)

Accordingly, these deliberations about the ADA and their subsequent distinctions regarding applicable protections under the law foreground the functions of the ADA within overlapping apparati of disability and addiction. Within such overlapping discourses, as Mitchell and Synder note, "the calculated provision (and purposeful nonprovision) of services based on principles of detecting qualifying bodies as 'too impaired' for meaningful labor underscores the degree to which even a catchall category of 'surplus labor' operates as a highly guarded space of state-sanctioned ostracization" (Mitchell and Snyder 2015: 16–17).

Within this challenge to both traditional Marxist and liberal discourses of disability, such distinctions between able-disabled people and people existing in peripheral statuses to rights-based inclusion and participation in labor markets serve as hallmark characteristics of ablenationalism. As Ben-Moshe's work and the works of other scholar-activists attuned to the carceral, racial, and colonial dimensions of ableism attest, the development of carceral sanism thereby places racialized and colonized communities within networks of surveillance, criminalization, and compulsory rehabilitation. As such, while patterns of incarceration and institutionalization are not usually considered to fall under the umbrella of "migration," more geographers are now suggesting, for example, that we could and should consider mass incarceration, psychiatric institutionalization, and other forms of confinement as forms of forced migration (Mitchelson 2013). From prison gerrymandering to the devastating community effects of incarceration and its collateral consequences, the movement of racialized, disabled, and colonized peoples into, between, and through forms of state-sanctioned confinement is a shared feature within a given nation-state of the joint apparati of disability and addiction. That is, liberal governmentality and its rights-based and medicalized distinctions and interventions within addiction discourses and disability protections harbor the needed infrastructure (such as "drug-free workplaces") to massively displace Indigenous, Black, and brown communities within and across borders of the United States.

Lastly, let us not forget that "To this day, almost any drug law violation, including simple possession, subjects legal permanent residents to deportation and makes people ineligible for lawful status" (Drug Policy Alliance 2021). Indeed, the numbers of deportations due to drug-related crimes have skyrocketed along with other forms of mass incarceration in the United States. For at least the past ten years, driving under the influence of alcohol (DUI) and illegal drug-related crimes have constituted the second most common criminal conviction for the more than 3.2 million people forcefully removed by Immigration and Customs Enforcement (TRAC Immigration 2022), with illegal entry/reentry the most common conviction. In fact, in 2009, DUIs outpaced even illegal entry as the most prevalent criminal conviction held by people who were deported from the United States.[4]

These last points regarding the circulation and movement of people within the legal jurisdiction of a settler nation-state such as the United States direct our attention to the patterns of movement of people across settler borders due to the co-constituting force relations between addiction and disability discourses. In the last section of this chapter, therefore, I turn to these mechanisms of governmentality by briefly examining transnational relations between the United States, Mexico, and China in order to underscore how transnational migration patterns are shaped through the apparati of addiction and disability.

Colonial Ableism and the War on Drugs

Regarding transnational migration discourses and disability, we can note, following Mansha Mirza, that "both disability and displacement represent a disruption of the 'natural order of things,' [that is,] the social categories that modern societies tend to be grounded in" (Mirza 2014: 217). Referring to both displaced refugees and disabled people, Mirza notes that assumed natural categories like "nation-states" and "national boundaries," as well as notions of personhood and normative ideals of health and embodiment, often seem to present themselves as givens. Mirza criticizes political responses and humanitarian approaches that seek to return disabled and displaced peoples into whatever the terms of normalcy are for categories such as "citizenship" and "able-bodiedness" (ibid.). Such humanitarian responses, she argues, are also at the heart of systems of confinement, institutionalization, assimilation, "mainstreaming" within schools and labor sectors, refugee camps, asylum detention, and transnational aid industries, all of which seek to direct these populations back into an assumed status of belonging within the legal and normative relations of a given nation-state.

To understand this process, Mirza and other scholars examining the interconnected relationship between disability, displacement, racism, and colonialism—such as Nirmala Erevelles (2011), Puar (2017), and Rachel da Silveira Gorman (2016)—develop concepts that describe *processes* of disablement and debility. These terms shift conceptions of disability away from identity-based categorizations and focus instead on the social relations through which we can interpret disability. These approaches likewise critique the dominance of white settler and often middle-class narratives within disability studies by examining how racism, colonialism, and processes of disablement are intertwined. As Gorman states:

> [The] bifurcation of disabled subjects into "disabled already" and "disabled because of" leads to an implicit assumption of disability as a fixed ontological state (rather than a social relation), and defines the "deserving" or "innocent" disabled over and against those harmed through violence, poverty, and incarceration. In part, this bifurcation echoes and reinforces a preoccupation in white-focused disability studies with proving that disabled people (read as white) are "as oppressed as" racialized people, or colonized people (read as non-disabled). (Gorman 2013: 271)

Following Gorman's approach, Mary Jean Hande (2019) argues with respect to migrants:

> "This bifurcation [also] enables poor, racialised and immigrants' experiences of disablement through colonial and imperialist violence—such as trauma, criminalisation, homelessness, and displacement through gentrification—to be read as a 'moral failing', 'inherent characteristic', or 'just life' rather than as a disability that may be conceptualised as injustice" (Hande 2019: 564).

These approaches are thus assemblages or processes by which people are subject to patterns of racialization, capitalistic exploitation, expendability, and norms of embodied difference and functionalism. A processual framework of this kind (rather than simply an individualistic rights-based or identity-based framework) seeks to explain the piecemeal and often normalizing patterns of inclusion for disabled people within neoliberal logics of market expansion and nationalism, as I discussed in the previous section.

Following these methodological considerations, it is not difficult to find historical examples of migration patterns that have been shaped to rely on notions of health, civic and economic stability, and moral norms in order to condemn conditions of addiction and substance use. For example, prohibition and temperance movements of the nineteenth century and the sponsors and administrators of early almshouses, asylums, and jails that characterize eugenics in US and Canadian history considered alcoholism a vice, defect, and threat to social stability. For example, as Laura I. Appleman notes:

> California asylums were built not only to incarcerate and treat the mentally ill, but also to provide "detention facilities for 'imbeciles, dotards, idiots, drunkards, simpletons, fools,' [and] for 'the aged, the vagabond, [and] the helpless." In part, this desire to contain and control segments of the population stemmed from the influx of domestic migrants flooding the state from the East, along with high numbers of Mexican and Asian immigrants, making state inhabitants anxious about all forms of "deviance" and difference. (Appleman 2018: 431)

Considering this last point about immigration into the United States by Mexican and Asian migrants, we can easily find archival evidence of postcards circulated in the early twentieth century that depict Chinese men lounging in opium dens in San Francisco's Chinatown (New York Public Library 2022). These postcards of opium dens were quite popular during the late nineteenth and twentieth centuries, with the racializing images linking the moral vice of opium addiction to Chinese migrants in the United States at the time.

Notably, the proliferation of these postcards followed a peak period of migration of Chinese people occurring during the Opium Wars of the mid-nineteenth century, leading some ten million Chinese migrants to leave the country during massive upheavals between Britain and China (Zhu 1994). China was at a trade advantage in the late eighteenth and early nineteenth centuries because British markets demanded tea from Chinese exporters (Hanes and Sanello 2002). Given that the British had little interest in Chinese markets at the time, the British began importing opium from India in mass quantities, first legally, then illegally to allow the British to regain control of markets in Canton ports at the time. The outcome of the Opium Wars was not only drastic economic consequences for China but also the British colonization of Hong Kong, which began in 1841 and lasted over 150 years (Ngo 1999). Later waves of Chinese migrants eventually relocated to the Americas, including the United States and Canada, where laws such as the 1882 Chinese Exclusion Act and the 1885 Chinese Immigration Act in the United States and Canada, respectively, sought to limit Chinese migration into both settler nations. Importantly, the authorities of both Canada and the United States considered Chinese migrants to be carriers of infectious disease, a long-term and vicious stigma that continues to harm Chinese- and other Asian-descended populations as witnessed in recent public attention to ongoing patterns of anti-Asian violence during the COVID-19 pandemic (Le et al. 2020). Accordingly, such associations between disease, addiction, race, and culture thereby bring into perspective the colonial dimensions of ableism. Namely, the white, settler, middle-class narratives of liberal forms of disability inclusionism, as well as the constricted normativity, violence, and patterned exclusions of systemic ableism, each leave unacknowledged this "underside" of the modern era (to borrow a phrase from decolonial theorist Enrique Dussel [1996]).

If we wish to further emphasize how the apparatus of addiction operates within transnational contexts and impacts migration flows, we can consider the "war on drugs" and its ablenationalist implications. While the war on drugs has had tremendously racialized implications, the extent of which I cannot fully explore in this chapter, we can briefly consider what Sayak Valencia (2018) describes as "gore capitalism." Following Hande's and Mirza's claims that rights- and identity-based disability discourses often fail to consider how trauma, criminalization, and displacement become naturalized as features that seemingly separate such embodied conditions from disability, Valencia highlights how drug cartels and settler states such as Mexico and the United States have become participants within a new "episteme of violence" (Valencia 2018: 22). Valencia notes that Tijuana, Mexico, a bordertown where the "effects of gore capitalism are most obvious and brutal," is "the crystallization of an episteme of violence that makes [violence] into a fantasy shared by the entire country" (127–8). In this regard, Valencia quotes Mauricio Bares who states:

> Unfortunately, the game played by authoritarian governments with this bloody spectacle we have suffered through has ended up getting out of their hands, and this has turned us into a violent society all-to-familiar with crime. A society that even when not involved directly in crime still accepts it at some level. What's more it quietly anticipates that one day it might be able to capitalize on it somehow. (Bares 2008, in Valencia 2018: 127–8)

With these remarks, Valencia describes "gore capitalism" as the "undisguised and unjustified bloodshed that is the price the Third World pays for adhering to the increasingly demanding logic of capitalism. It also refers to the many instances of dismembering and disembowelment, often tied up with organized crime, gender and the predatory uses of bodies" (Valencia 2018: 12). Under this view, capitalism is transformed through a form of biopower wherein our bodies and agential capacities are considered largely through our habits of consumption. This form of biopower no longer "infiltrat[es] from the outside"; rather, as Paul B. Preciado writes, "it is the body desiring power to consume, seeking to swallow it, eat it, administer it, wolf it down, more, always more" (Preciado 2013: 207, quoted in Valencia 2018: 140). The "gore" element takes its meaning from this new episteme of violence that, as Bares mentions, now "capitalizes" on violence: the extreme displays of violence by drug cartels and the nation-state participate within the "undisguised and unjustified bloodshed" of gore capitalism; military research into methods of torture and interrogation techniques circulate as new forms of knowledge and expertise that shape transnational anti-trafficking and anti-terrorism; and Mexican drug traffickers "enact . . . particular style[s] of violence that they link to a signature or a brand" that circulates as forms of necroempowerment. Such a form of empowerment under this new episteme of violence "transform[s] contexts and/or situations of vulnerability and/or subalternity into possibilities for action and self-empowerment, and . . . reconfigure[s] these situations through dystopian practices and a perverse self-affirmation achieved through violent means" (Valencia 2018: 191). Within this framing, the distinctions between persons who are "disabled already" and "disabled because of" no longer appear as morally or politically meaningful. Rather, the desire to produce and materially benefit from violence present in narco-trafficking and inflicted through the nation-state to curb the possession and trafficking of illicit drugs thereby renders obvious and inevitable the market demand to maim, torture, and traumatize.

Accordingly, ablenationalism when taken to this extreme, perpetuated through the war on drugs and its financial and enfleshed circulation of violence, reconfigures what Puar (2017) calls the "right to maim." Gore capitalism is not only, as Puar notes, a "source of value extraction from populations that would otherwise be disposable," wherein "maiming is a sanction tactic of settler colonial rule justified in protectionist terms and soliciting disability rights solutions that, while absolutely crucial to aiding some individuals, unfortunately lead to further perpetuation of debilitation" (Puar 2017: xviii–xix). Rather, gore capitalism reconfigures disablement, death, and snuff as dynamic and open-ended markets that demand continued circulation and protection for the preservation of the nation-state. In this framing, the estimated 12.4 million disabled migrants (Migration Data Portal 2022)—who move across border-zones, through military and immigration checkpoints, under the shadow and whim of coyotes and smugglers, and risking life, limb, and violation on Mexico's "death train," *La Bestia*—too are part of this economic circuit of violence. In this sense, consider a group of Honduran amputee activists who were maimed during their journeys on *La Bestia* and who demand to raise the awareness of the governments of Honduras, Mexico, and the United States about the harms that migrants face. *La Caravana de los Mutilados*, as they call themselves—the Caravan of the Mutilated—journeyed for eight months in 2015, as Eric Vásquez writes, "travers[ing] three national borders in the hopes of raising a transnational public consciousness concerning the plight of migrants and to entreat President Barack Obama to end US deportation programs" (Vásquez 2022: 48). The media spectacle of the journey of the Caravan of the Mutilated, as well as their detainment within the private for-profit facility in Pearsall, Texas, each operate as nodes within the economy of violence that these men negotiate. Notably, José Luís Hernandez Cruz, the Caravan's president, stated that *La Caravana*'s main request to then-president Obama and to the Honduran government was for assistance with job creation for people with disabilities in Honduras. In this same vein, José Jeremias Gamez, another member of *La Caravana*, states of the comments that he endured after deportation back to Honduras: "Ya no sirves para nada," many told him, or "Now you're not good for anything" (64). Rather than vanish into peripheral status within the paradigms of inclusion/exclusion across the three nation-states, these activists engage in the very necropolitical economy of their violation. Namely, they migrate again across the three countries, open to full public spectacle, scrutiny, and risk. However, this time, in their words, "*Nuestra visa es nuestra mutilación*" or "Our visa is our mutilation" (Wilkinson 2015).

Importantly, among the factors impacting emigration from Honduras, we must also acknowledge that "the pressure of the American drug war rerouted most trafficking [from] its previous route[s] and instead [sent them] directly through Central America" (Mackey 2017). The stories of the men of *La Caravana*, or of the woman in Olancho, Honduras, who gave birth to a child with a gunshot wound in the infant's leg due to police crossfire during state suppression measures to quell anti-corruption protests (Mackey 2017) constitute *testimonios* that demonstrate the circulation of life and death, violence and pleasure, pity and spectacle, through the distribution, sale, and control of narcotics. As we seek additional language and expression to understand the apparatus of disability, I ask that we, too, keep the relations of proximity and distance with drugs, alcohol, addiction, and other substance-related force relations within frame. This call for deliberation about, and resistance to, the ways in which the apparatus of addiction and the apparatus of disability are co-constitutive is, of course, nothing like a call for temperance, sobriety, or a demand for more medicalized options for the many of us who face addiction. Rather, this call for deliberation and resistance is a call for justice in the midst of colonialism and ableist markets of violence, as well as an attempt to wage countermeasures with whatever means that we have left.

Notes

1 According to Wood, early modern English humoralism can be traced from Aristotle to Avicenna and eventually Renaissance theorists such as Marcilio Ficino (1489), Philip Barrough (1596), Thomas Wright (1603), and Robert Burton (1621). He states: "The principal caution these early modern treatises present with regard to alcohol and its effects centers upon its propensity to emotional rousing through sudden caloric escalations. The relationship of time, temperature, and the humors thus lies at the root of these matters. . . ." (Wood 2009).

2 Interestingly, alcoholism remains somewhat ambiguous under the ADA. That is, current alcohol users *are* subject to the previous protections offered under the 1978 amendment of the Rehabilitation Act, and thus deemed an "individual with a handicap" and the legal protections that that entails, including being protected from termination for their addiction and offered "reasonable accommodations" to seek rehabilitation while remaining employed (Henderson 1991: 737).

3 Armstrong also asks about alcoholism, and Harkin responds that they would be subject to the same policy, a statement which did not end up being applied following the passage of the ADA.

4 To be clear, I would like to highlight, however, that nearly half of the people deported from the United States (47 percent) have no criminal convictions on their records at all (Bier 2018).

References

American Federation of Government Employees v. Dole, 670 F. Supp. 445, 447, D.D.C. 1987.

Americans with Disabilities Act of 1990. Public Law 101–336. 108th Congress, 2nd session, July 26, 1990.

Appleman, Laura I. (2018), "Deviancy, Dependency, and Disability: The Forgotten History of Eugenics and Mass Incarceration," *Duke Law Journal* 68 (3): 417–78.

Bares, Mauricio (2008), "Violencia Ancestral," *Reforma*, suplemento cultural, México, D. F.

Ben-Moshe, Liat (2020), *Decarcerating Disability: Deinstitutionalization and Prison Abolition*, Minneapolis: Minnesota University Press.

Bier, David J. (2018), "60% of Deported 'Criminal Aliens' Committed Only Victimless Crimes," Cato Institute. Available at: https://www.cato.org/blog/60-deported-criminal-aliens-committed-only-victimless-crimes-few-violent-crimes (accessed May 7, 2022).

Cohen, Peter (2000), "In the Addiction Doctor the Voodoo Priest of Western Man?" *Addiction Research and Theory* 8 (6): 589–98.

Congressional Record—Senate (1989), "Senate—Thursday, September 7, 1989," *Proceedings of Congress and General Congressional Publications*. Available at: https://www.govinfo.gov/app/details/GPO-CRECB-1989-pt14/ (accessed May 7, 2022).

Drug Policy Alliance (2021), "The War on Drugs Meets Immigration," *Uprooting the War on Drugs.org*. Available at: https://uprootingthedrugwar.org/wp-content/uploads/2021/02/uprooting_report_PDF_immigration_02.11.21.pdf (accessed May 5, 2022).

Dussel, Enrique (1996), *The Underside of Modernity: Apel, Ricoeur, Rorty, Taylor, and the Philosophy of Liberation*, trans. and ed. Eduardo Mendieta, Atlantic Highlands: Humanities Press.

Erevelles, Nirmala (2011), *Disability and Difference in Global Contexts: Enabling a Transformative Body Politic*, New York: Palgrave Macmillan.

Foddy, Bennett and Julian Savulescu (2010), "Relating Addiction to Disease, Disability, Autonomy and the Good Life," *Philosophy, Psychiatry and Psychology* 17 (1): 35–42.

Goff, J. Larry (1993), "The Legislative Response to Alcoholism and Drug Addiction in the Americans with Disabilities Act of 1990," *The Journal of Psychiatry and Law* 21 (1): 77–107.

Gorman, Rachel da Silveira (2013), "Mad Nation? Thinking through Race, Class, and Mad Identity Politics," in Brenda A. LeFrançois, Robert Menzies, and Geoffrey Reaume (eds.), *Mad Matters: A Critical Reader in Canadian Mad Studies*, 269–80, Toronto: Canadian Scholars' Press.

Gorman, Rachel da Silveira (2016), "Disablement in and for itself: Towards a 'Global' Idea of Disability," *Somatechnics* 6 (2): 249–61.

Granfield, Robert and Craig Reinarman (2015), *Expanding Addiction: Critical Essays*, New York: Routledge.

Grech, Shaun (2015), "Decolonising Eurocentric Disability Studies: Why Colonialism Matters in the Disability and Global South Debate," *Social Identities: Journal for the Study of Race, Nation, and Culture* 21 (1): 6–21.

Hall, Melinda (2016), *The Bioethics of Enhancement: Transhumanism, Disability, and Biopolitics*, Lanham: Lexington Books.

Hande, Mary Jean (2019), "Disability Consciousness on the Frontlines of Urban Struggle," *Antipode* 51 (2): 558–78.

Hanes III, W. Travis and Frank Sanello (2002), *The Opium Wars: The Addiction of One Empire and the Corruption of Another*, Naperville: Sourcebooks, Inc.

Henderson, Reese J. J. (1991), "Addiction as Disability: The Protection of Alcoholics and Drug Addicts under the Americans with Disabilities Act of 1990," *Vanderbilt Law Review* 44 (3): 713–40.

Jenkins, Katharine and Aness Kim Webster (2021), "Disability, Impairment, and Marginalised Functioning," *Australasian Journal of Philosophy* 99 (4): 730–47.

Kerry, John (2013), "Our Disabled Deserve Access Abroad," *USA Today*, July 21. Available at: https://www.usatoday.com/story/opinion/2013/07/21/secretary-of-state-kerry-disabities-treaty-column/2573513/ (accessed May 4, 2022).

Le, Thomas K., Leah Cha, Hae-Ra Han, and Winston Tseng (2020), "Anti-Asian Xenophobia and Asian American COVID-19 Disparities," *American Journal of Public Health* 110: 1371–3.

Lewis, Bradley (2013), "A Mad Fight: Psychiatry and Disability Activism," in Lennard J. Davis (ed.), *The Disability Studies Reader*, Fourth edition, 115–31, New York: Routledge.

Mackey, Danielle (2017), "The Election Fraud in Honduras Follows Decades of Corruption Funded By the U.S. War on Drugs," *The Intercept*, December 23. Available at: https://theintercept.com/2017/12/23/honduras-election-fraud-drugs-jose-orlando-hernandez/ (accessed May 8, 2022).

Mayo Clinic (2022), "Alcohol Intolerance," *Diseases and Conditions, MayoClinic.org*. Available at: https://www.mayoclinic.org/diseases-conditions/alcohol-intolerance/symptoms-causes/syc-20369211 (accessed May 27, 2023).

Migration Data Portal (2022), "Disability and Human Mobility," *Migrationdataportal.org*. Available at: https://www.migrationdataportal.org/themes/disability-and-human-mobility (accessed May 8, 2022).

MindFreedom (2003), "Original statement by the Fast for Freedom in Mental Health to the American Psychiatric Association, National Alliance for the Mentally Ill, and the US Office of the Surgeon General," *MindFreedom.org*. Available at: https://mindfreedom.org/kb/act/2003/mf-hunger-strike/original-statement-by-the-fast-for-freedom-in-mental-health/ (accessed May 7, 2022).

Mirza, Mansha (2014), "Refugee Camps, Asylum Detention, and the Geopolitics of Transnational Migration: Disability and Its Intersections with Humanitarian Confinement," in Liat Ben-Moshe, Chris Chapman, and Allison C. Carey (eds.), *Disability Incarcerated*, 217–36, New York: Palgrave Macmillan.

Mitchell, David T. and Sharon L. Snyder (2015), *The Biopolitics of Disability: Neoliberalism, Ablenationalism, and Peripheral Embodiment*, Ann Arbor: University of Michigan Press.

Mitchelson, Matthew L. (2013), "Up the River (from Home): Where Does the Prisoner 'Count' on Census Day?" in Dominique Moran, Nick Gill, and Dierdre Conlon (eds.), *Carceral Spaces: Mobility and Agency in Imprisonment and Migrant Detention*, 77–92, Surrey: Ashgate.

New York Public Library (2022), "The Miriam and Ira D. Wallach Division of Art, Prints and Photographs: Photography Collection." "An Opium Den, Chinatown, San Francisco, Calif," *New York Public Library Digital Collections*. Available at: https://digitalcollections.nypl.org/items/510d47d9-a583-a3d9-e040-e00a18064a99 (accessed May 7, 2022).

Ngo, Tak-Wing (1999), "Colonialism in Hong Kong Revisited," in Tak-Wing Ngo (ed.), *Hong Kong's History: State and Society Under Colonial Rule*, 1–12, New York: Routledge.

Nisperos v. Buck, 720 F. Supp. 1424, N.D. Cal. 1989.

Preciado, Paul (2013), *Testo Junkie: Sex, Drugs, and Biopolitics in the Pharmacopornographic Era*, New York: The Feminist Press.

Puar, Jasbir K. (2007), *Terrorist Assemblages: Homonationalism in Queer Times*, Durham: Duke University Press.

Puar, Jasbir K. (2017), *The Right to Maim: Debility, Capacity, Disability*, Durham: Duke University Press.

Reinarman, Craig (2005), "Addiction as Accomplishment: The Discursive Construction of Disease," *Addiction Research and Theory* 13 (4): 307–20.

Reinarman, Craig and Harry G. Levine (2004), "Crack in the Rearview Mirror: Deconstructing Drug War Mythology," *Social Justice* 31: 182–99.

Reinarman, Craig and Robert Granfield (2015), "Addiction is Not Just a Brain Disease: Critical Studies of Addiction," in Craig Reinarman and Robert Granfield (eds.), *Expanding Addiction: Critical Essays*, 1-21. New York: Routledge.

Senier, Siobhan (2012), "Rehabilitation Reservations: Native Narrations of Disability and Community," *Disability Studies Quarterly* 32 (4). https://doi.org/10.18061/dsq.v32i4.1641.

Shanley, Kathryn (2000), "Lady Luck or Mother Earth? Gaming as a Trope in Plains Indian Cultural Traditions," *Wicazo Sa Review* 15 (2): 93–101.

Spade, Dean (2015), *Normal Life: Administrative Violence, Critical Trans Politics, and the Limits of the Law*, Durham: Duke University Press.

TRAC Immigration (2022), "Latest Data: Immigration and Customs Enforcement Removals: Ice Data through June 2020," *TRAC Immigration*. Available at: https://trac.syr.edu/phptools/immigration/remove/ (accessed May 7, 2022).

Tremain, Shelley L. (2017), *Foucault and Feminist Philosophy of Disability*, Ann Arbor: University of Michigan Press.

Valencia, Sayek (2018), *Gore Capitalism*, Cambridge, MA: MIT Press.

Vásquez, Eric (2022), "'Your Life Is One-Hundred-Percent at Risk': The Caravan of the Mutilated and the Internationalism of the Vulnerable," *Public Culture* 34 (1): 47–70.

Wasserman, David (2004), "Addiction and Disability: Moral and Policy Issues," *Substance Use and Misuse* 39 (3): 461–88.

Wilkinson, Tracy (2015), "Migrantes hondureños, mutilados por el tren, protestan por su situación," *The Baltimore Sun*, May 17. Available at: https://www.baltimoresun.com/hoyla-mig-hondurenios-story.html (accessed May 8, 2022).

Wood, David Houston (2009), "'Fluster'd with Flowing Cups': Alcoholism, Humoralism, and the Prosthetic Narrative in Othello," *Disability Studies Quarterly* 29 (4). https://doi.org/10.18061/dsq.v29i4.998.

Zhu, G. (1994), "A Preliminary Study of International Migration of the Chinese People," *Chinese Journal of Population Science* 6 (4): 403–15.

8 DISABILITY, ABLEISM, CLASS, AND CHRONIC FATIGUE

MICH CIURRIA

Introduction

In this chapter, I identify and explain some of the exclusions that I and other people with myalgic encephalomyelitis/chronic fatigue syndrome (ME/CFS) confront, including restricted access to government-issued disability benefits, rejected requests for accommodations, and conditional acceptance by the disabled community. I will argue that Marxist feminism lends insight into how we can best respond to the economic, social, cultural, and political exclusions with which people with ME/CFS must grapple. In my view, an adequate response to such exclusions must explicitly address the capitalistic notion of "scarce resources" that leads to the gatekeeping of ME/CFS in particular and disability in general. Finally, I will argue that the construction of post-work imaginaries would both "trouble" (to use Judith Butler's neologism) the capitalist definition of disability as a productivity-impairing pathology—that is, a pathology that positions the disabled body as an economic and moral risk—and destabilize the ability/disability binary that underwrites this definition and privileges the nondisabled subject.[1]

ME/CFS

The US Centers for Disease Control (CDC) describes ME/CFS as a "disabling and complex illness" with the following features:

> People with ME/CFS are often not able to do their usual activities. At times, ME/CFS may confine them to bed. People with ME/CFS have overwhelming fatigue that is not improved by rest. ME/CFS may get worse

> after any activity, whether it's physical or mental. This symptom is known as post-exertional malaise (PEM). Other symptoms can include problems with sleep, thinking and concentrating, pain, and dizziness. People with ME/CFS may not look ill. (Centers for Disease Control 2022a)

I experience most of these features of ME/CFS. I am tired most of the time. Sometimes, I cannot get out of bed. I have aches and pains, brain fog, difficulty concentrating, and post-exertional malaise. I also experience positive effects of ME/CFS, such as privileged insight into ableist oppression, heightened compassion, and meaningful relationships with other disabled people (Ciurria 2022). Nevertheless, none of these positive experiences counts toward the medical definition of chronic fatigue syndrome that the CDC relies upon and thus none is included in its authoritative description. Instead, medical discourse reductively defines ME/CFS, and indeed all "disabilities," according to their negative symptoms. This approach (as I will argue) denies the multiplicity and complexity of chronically fatigued people's circumstances and begs the question of whether ME/CFS in particular and disability in general are, essentially, pathology.

ME/CFS is medically controversial, which poses problems for people who try to obtain a diagnosis of it. The CDC (2021) notes that "researchers have not yet found what causes ME/CFS, and there are no specific laboratory tests to diagnose ME/CFS directly"; partly for this reason, although "an estimated 836,000 to 2.5 million Americans suffer from ME/CFS . . ., about 90 percent of people with ME/CFS have not been diagnosed." Eleanor Alexandra Byrne adds that "since no bio-marker or causal mechanism has been uncontroversially identified for CFS/ME, the status of the CFS/ME patient is unclear. This poses many epistemic challenges" (Byrne 2020: 372). Doctors, Byrne explains, are reluctant to diagnose people with ME/CFS due to a combination of skepticism about the credibility of their testimony and skepticism "of whether or not [ME/CFS] is a legitimate illness category" (474). These forms of epistemic marginalization present barriers to diagnosis, which in turn create barriers for people with ME/CFS to gain access to certain services that may (and usually do) require that they have official medical certification.

Ableist Exclusions

In short, many people with ME/CFS do not receive and cannot acquire the services that they need and to which they are patently entitled. To be sure, the CDC admits that millions of people with ME/CFS have a (theoretically) medically diagnosable disability, which would make them eligible for support services *if* their condition were medically unambiguous. Due to their liminal medical status, however, these people are routinely deemed ineligible for the services and thus cannot avail themselves of them. In this section of my chapter, I will focus briefly on the exclusion of people with ME/CFS from (i) disability benefits, (ii) educational accommodations, and (iii) broad acceptance by the disabled community.

Benefits

In the United States, most people with MS/CFS do not qualify for government disability benefits that require a diagnosis corroborated by "medically acceptable clinical and laboratory findings," according to the US Social Security Administration (SSA), which further stipulates that "symptoms alone cannot be the basis for a finding of disability" (Social Security Administration 2018). Neither of these conditions is met in most cases of ME/CFS. The SSA stipulates, furthermore, that applicants must be "unable to do any substantial gainful work activity because of a medical condition(s) that has lasted, or can be expected to last, for at least 12 months." Like most disabled applicants for these benefits, many people with ME/CFS can do *some* work. For example, I myself have taught one university course per semester for the last three years. Yet this part-time employment would make me ineligible for benefits that I could receive, all else being equal, were a diagnosis forthcoming.[2]

Accommodations

Nor do most people with ME/CFS qualify for educational accommodations, which also typically require a diagnosis or other professional verification. The University of Missouri-St. Louis (UMSL), where I currently work, is a case in point. The accommodations request form provided by Disability Access Services (DAS) at UMSL disclaims that the university "cannot provide accommodations to a student without verifiable supporting documentation from a qualified professional." Yet, as I have indicated, a medical diagnosis is unavailable to approximately 90 percent of people with ME/CFS, while other forms of documentation can be just as difficult to obtain. This inability to provide the required documentation is especially a problem for young people, that is, most university students, as "ME/CFS is often thought of as a problem in [older] adults" and "not as much is known about ME/CFS in children [under 18] because there have been few studies in this age group" (Centers for Disease Control 2022b). In other words, most students with ME/CFS at UMSL (and other institutions of higher education with similar policies) cannot procure (through the stipulated procedures)[3] the accommodations that they need to obtain an education on equitable terms with their nondisabled peers.

Inclusion and Exclusion in the Disabled Community

The disability community largely does not recognize people with ME/CFS as disabled but rather assumes that ME/CFS is somehow an entirely natural phenomenon, that is, an impairment due to its association with physical pain and the (often) unrecognizable disabling circumstances that surround it. On the social model of disability developed in the United Kingdom, disability and impairment are completely separate phenomena: "disablement is nothing to do with the body," while impairment is "*nothing less than* a description of the physical body." For proponents of this social model, disability is the social disadvantage that people with impairments confront (Oliver 1990: 35, quoted in Tremain 2001: 62, emphasis in Tremain). Because ME/CFS ranges from uncomfortable to painful, it is often assigned to the category of impairment alone. Indeed, when I presented at a disability conference in 2020, an audience member asked how we are to distinguish between a disability such as Deafness and an impairment like ME/CFS, implying (perhaps unwittingly) that I should not have been invited to present because I am not truly disabled. Whereas the medical model conflates disability and impairment, the social model, in Dan Goodley's words, separates them in a way that reduces "the complexities of dis/ableism [and] dis/ability to simple models [and] categorizations" (Goodley 2014: xi). Both models ignore the biopolitical context that constructs disability and impairment as contingently related aspects of a capitalist system.

Exclusion from the disabled community usually means denial of resources that could help mitigate other forms of exclusion, including the exclusions that ensue due to ineligibility for benefits and lack of accommodation. People with ME/CFS are ambiguously disabled subjects, who straddle the boundary between "ability" and "disability," and who (as I have noted) inhabit a liminal space in which they may lack access to economic benefits and a range of other government disability services, while they may simultaneously lack access to peer support systems that might help offset the costs of these exclusions. I use the term *queerly disabled* to refer to people who exist at this nexus.

Insights from Marxist Feminism

What is the best way to address these exclusions? One possible response is this: people with ME/CFS could advocate for more diagnostic testing and better access to (i), (ii), and (iii). This response, however, is an individualistic strategy that would work only for the most unambiguous cases—namely, cases with discernable biomarkers of illness and a documented record of unemployment. Worse, this strategy could incite the SSA to impose *even stricter* restrictions on benefits to protect (needlessly) scarce taxpayer dollars (as it has seemingly done for the last ten years according to SSA data on the number of disabled people in current payment status per year [Social Security Administration 2022]). Moreover, better access to diagnoses would not convince social modelists that ME/CFS entails disability. On the contrary, medical validation could simply be taken to *confirm* the view that ME/CFS is a wholly natural, that is, biological, state of the body. This approach would, in other words, reinforce the notion that impairment is separate from disability and can be medically defined.

In addition, individualistic/diagnostic solutions to the exclusions that people with ME/CFS face fail to address the underlying (biopolitical) causes of the exclusions in question, including the capitalist, "scarce resources" ideology that favors austerity measures and gatekeeping. A scarce-resources policy seeks to conserve an artificially restricted pool of taxpayer dollars for the "most" or "truly" disabled claimants rather than expand the pool of resources to meet existing demand. This sort of policy is a deliberate neoliberal strategy, not an accident. As Marta Russell puts it, "the definition of disability is not static but fundamentally linked to the needs of capital accumulation. . . . When the welfare state entered into 'crisis' [due to unnecessary cuts], governments attempted to narrow the definition of disablement and to cut entitlement levels" (Russell 2019: 20). This exclusionary approach to disability benefits generates competition for funding and services while simultaneously positioning disabled people as either "deserving" burdens on society or "undeserving" swindlers who are trying to "milk the system." This scarce-resources ideology is so deeply entrenched in neoliberal society that it has been internalized by many disabled people, who may question their dis/ability status only due to the hegemony of overly narrow, bureaucratic, and neoliberal criteria. As disabled blogger Rosie Pacey observes, "'Stealing resources' is where the ableist narrative [about who counts as disabled] intersects with austerity. Austerity tells us that there is only enough money in the pot to help those with the very worst conditions. It tells us that we're not disabled enough and to say otherwise would be to steal limited resources from those who really need it" (Pacey 2018).

The scarce-resources mentality has infiltrated the disabled community in the form of gatekeeping and infighting. Members argue about who is really disabled or dysfunctional enough to deserve recognition and support. Disability theorists sometimes contribute to the gatekeeping problem by defining disability too narrowly, thereby failing to "acknowledge that there are important evaluative differences between disabilities that complicate some of the simplifying tendencies in the literature" (Nadelhoffer 2022). The adherence of disability theorists to an exclusionary definition of disability supports metaphysical obfuscations which, in turn, lead to epistemic harms. As Shelley Tremain points out,

> a disabled people's movement that grounds its claims to entitlement in the identity of its subject ("people with impairments") can expect to face similar criticisms [to the feminist movement] from an ever-increasing number of constituencies that feel excluded from and refuse to identify with those demands for rights and recognition; in addition, minorities internal to the movement will predictably pose challenges to it, the upshot of which are that those hegemonic descriptions [of disability] eclipse their respective particularities. (Tremain 2001: 635)

In short, hegemonic and totalizing definitions of disability evoke resentments and hostilities from both minorities within the disabled community and people definitionally excluded from its remit. An adequate solution to the gatekeeping of disability, which is itself a product of neoliberal capitalism, must contradict the neoliberal construction of disability as a diagnosable illness that impairs wage-generating productivity (Russell 2019). Demanding equal access to economic supports, accommodations, and community, without demanding changes to the overarching capitalist apparatus of disability, would not challenge this system of ableist exclusions. I want to suggest that a better solution to ableist oppression—including the ableist oppression that accrues to people with ME/CFS and other queerly disabled people—can be found in Marxist feminism's response to patriarchal capitalism.

Marxist feminism emerged as a reaction to the exclusion of women from certain sectors of the economy, worker's compensation, welfare, and other benefits. In the first half of the twentieth century, only 20 percent of women were classified by the US Census Bureau as "gainful workers" and only 5 percent of married women in the United States belonged to this category (Yellen 2020). When John F. Kennedy signed the Equal Pay Act in 1963, women as a group earned 60 percent of the average male income (Daugherty 2022; U.S. BLS 2013). White and Asian women, however, earned significantly more than Black and Hispanic women due to the double race/gender gap (Daugherty 2022; U.S. BLS 2013). Women were also highly susceptible to domestic violence, which was widely accepted and even encouraged. This state of affairs resembles disabled people's situation today, in which only 20 percent of disabled people participate in the American workforce (U.S. BLS 2022), and many of them are paid a subminimum wage of as little as pennies an hour (U.S. Department of Labor 2021) under conditions in which they face high rates of violence and harassment (Alfonseca 2021). Other structural inequalities compound these exclusions, resulting in intersectional oppressions. For example, Black, male, low-income, and non-English-speaking claimants are less likely to be awarded disability benefits when they are not represented by a lawyer, compared to more privileged groups (U.S. General Accounting Office Report 2003). This inequitable situation reveals one of the intersections of ableism and other systems of oppression. Marxist feminism provides a blueprint for how to address these kinds of structural inequalities.

In *The Trouble with Work*, Kathi Weeks analyzes (and ultimately rejects) two early-wave feminist strategies in response to patriarchal capitalism. The first strategy "was to accept the lesser value accorded to unwaged domestic labor and seek to secure women's equal access to waged work" (Weeks 2011: 12). The thought was that wage labor would liberate women from mandatory domestic service and grant them financial independence. The second strategy was to "revalue unwaged forms of household-based labour, from housework to caring work" by redefining these tasks as productive or "gainful" work (13). This second strategy mainly took the form of a demand for wages for housework. Both strategies challenged the notion that women's labor is a private service to the family, whereas men's labor is "real work" that contributes to the nation's gross domestic product (GDP).

Although well-meaning, both strategies, Weeks argues, "failed to challenge the dominant legitimating discourse of work," which defines work as a necessity, a moral duty, and a raison d'être (Weeks 2011: 13). Thus, the proposed strategies tacitly reinforced the ethic of compulsory wage labor. The first proposal sought to integrate women into the (exploitative, alienating) workforce, while the second proposal sought to extend the workforce into the home. Neither approach challenged the capitalist organization of labor, the necessity of producing surplus value for employers at the expense of the worker's autonomy, the valorization of work as a moral duty, the vilification of nonworkers, or the many other downsides of compulsory capitalism. Today, women make more money than their predecessors but work harder than ever, as they are increasingly expected to juggle the "double burden" of housework and wage work.[4] Similarly, Black and Hispanic women continue to work harder than white and Asian women and get paid less than them due to the double gender-race gap (Patten 2016). That is, more wage labor has not resolved the problems of exploitation and structural injustice that early-wave feminists sought to mitigate.

As an alternative to the proposed strategies, Weeks defends the refusal to work as a "model of resistance, both to the modes of work that are currently imposed on us and to their ethical defense [in the productivist work ethic]" (Weeks 2011: 25). This strategy is part of a broader anti-work feminist program (which targets quantity of work, in contrast to the more popular versions of Marxist feminism that focus on quality of work). Anti-work feminism addresses not only the poor quality of work but also, and to a greater extent, the increasing scope and overvaluation of work. To this end, anti-work proposals seek to change both the nature of work under capitalism (i.e., as alienating, exploitative, exhausting drudgery) and its compulsoriness (i.e., its tendency to organize and subjectify people as either docile and disciplined workers or else disabled and deviant nonworkers). Indeed, one of the most insidious aspects of capitalism, from a liberatory feminist perspective, is its ability to "construct docile subjects" who identify primarily as workers (53). The capitalist ethic, Weeks notes, "is advice not just about how to behave but also *about who to be*; it takes aim not just at consciousness but also at the energies and capacities of the body, and the objects and aims of its desires" (54, emphasis added). This productivity ethic is also gendered and raced such that workers are expected to identify with group-specific occupations and industries—for example, "pink collar" jobs for women, manual labor for Black men—but the work ethic is supposed to apply to everyone. To reject wage labor or to be excluded from it thus positions one as morally deviant or economically inexpedient—a problem, in general, for moral, economic, and political systems of valuation. Yet refusal of the compulsoriness and valorization of work is precisely what we must do.

The refusal to work, says Weeks, can be realized in two policies that more effectively address the problems targeted by first- and second-wave feminism's demands. The first policy that Weeks recommends is a universal basic income (UBI) sufficient to liberate people from the need to work while enhancing the bargaining power of workers. This provision would make work a choice rather than a necessity, empowering workers to refuse to work for wages lower than they should accept. UBI would also allow workers to take parental leave, sick leave, and other types of leave at will without fearing financial penury. Clearly, a policy of UBI would address the circumstances of the lives of people with ME/CFS by reducing the need to undertake exhausting labor. UBI would allow workers in general to take control of their labor power and sell it, if they choose, on their own terms, not under the pressures of neoliberal economics. Even more importantly, UBI would provide an opportunity to "contemplate the shape of a life beyond work, the kind of freedom that, as Marx speculates, 'begins only when labour determined by necessity and external expediency ends,' in a sphere of existence that lies 'beyond the sphere of material production proper'" (Weeks 2016: 146, quoting Marx 1981: 959). The free time that a policy of UBI affords would, if implemented, allow us to reconsider our values, roles, and relationship to labor, independent of the ideological influences and material constraints of the capitalist matrix.

The second proposal that Weeks recommends is a thirty-hour full-time workweek with no decrease in pay compared to the standard forty-hour workweek. This adjustment in work life would liberate workers to imagine post-capitalist futures, enjoy unstigmatized rest and relaxation, articulate radical political demands, cultivate hopes and dreams that transcend the confines of work culture, and enjoy other activities that are subversive to the productivist ethic. This strategy, rather than demand more work for more pay, demands *less* work for more pay.[5]

One of the greatest advantages of anti-work policies, from a feminist perspective, is that they trouble the enforcement of binary and hierarchical gender roles constructed by the structured workplace. As Weeks observes, labor relations produce distinct genders, as well as distinct classes:

> Waged work and unwaged work alike continue to be structured by the productivity of gender-differentiated labor, including the gender division of both household roles and waged occupations. But the gendering of work is not just a matter of these institutionalized tendencies to distinguish various forms of men's work and women's work, but a consequence of the ways that workers are often expected to do gender at work. Gender is put to work when, for example, workers draw upon gendered codes and scripts as a way to negotiate relationships with bosses and co-workers, to personalize impersonal interactions, or to communicate courtesy, care, professionalism, or authority to clients, students, patients, or customers. (Weeks 2011: 9)

Work is a site of subjectification, producing distinct gender roles, relations, and identifications. Within work culture, femininity and masculinity are binary and oppositional categories. Genderqueer kinds, as a result, appear as a problem and an expense, because they disrupt the operating procedures of the standard (gender-normative) workplace. The recognition of genderqueer workers requires changes to the built environment, such as introducing nonbinary bathrooms, pronoun policies, uniforms, and other "accommodations" that threaten the operational efficiency and growth of capital that neoliberalism requires. (Neoliberalism favors status and resists any type of accommodations.) In short, nonbinary gender destabilizes work culture, while post-work spaces liberate us to imagine and inhabit queer genders that are suppressed by capitalist scrips.

Anti-work strategies thus destabilize patriarchal capitalism by both liberating us from work-regimented gender roles and providing us with post-work spaces in which to imagine gender on our own terms. In our free time, we can daydream about the roles and relationships that we would like to have outside of the capitalist gender matrix. Indeed, Weeks identifies daydreaming as a generative site of post-work imaginaries. The practice of daydreaming, Weeks writes, is "often treated as an embarrassment," in part because it "represents a lapse in concentration [and productivity]," which is a violation of the productivist work ethic, and in part because it "reveals . . . our immoderate desire to be and have more," to play with social roles and relationships outside of the capitalist regime (Weeks 2011: 191). Daydreaming along with other anti-work practices like sleeping, socializing, and "just chilling" defy work's rules and regulations, make space for us to imagine and construct alternative genders, sexualities, and dis/abilities.

Weeks's anti-work strategies can be leveraged against the barriers imposed on disabled people, particularly people with ME/CFS and other medically ambiguous, boundary-crossing disabilities.

Simple Solutions

The simplest solution to ableist exclusions, as stated earlier, is to demand better access to diagnostic testing, disability benefits, accommodations, and community support. I call the solution "simple" because it leaves intact the bureaucratic systems that police disability. Like early-wave feminist solutions to patriarchal capitalism, that is, this strategy fails to disrupt the capitalist definition of disability and the scarce-resources thinking that leads to the policing of it. Before I offer a superior Marxist feminist solution to the problem of ableist exclusions that capitalism produces, I want to clarify why I am opposed to the simple solution to such exclusions.

Benefits

First, disability benefits and other forms of conditional welfare force disabled people into a position of marginalization and dependency, which, as Iris Marion Young explains, is a paradigm case of oppression. Young writes:

> Today the exclusion of dependent persons from equal citizenship rights is only barely hidden beneath the surface. Because they depend on bureaucratic institutions for support or services, the old, the poor, and the mentally and physically disabled are subject to patronizing, punitive, demeaning, and arbitrary treatment by the policies and people associated with welfare bureaucracies. Being a dependent in our society implies being legitimately subject to the often arbitrary and invasive authority of social service providers and other public and private administrators, who enforce rules with which the marginal must comply, and otherwise exercise power over the conditions of their lives. (Young 1990: 50)

The demand for better access to disability benefits fails to challenge the coercive management and marginalization of welfare recipients. Benefits-holders are denied civil liberties that most nondisabled people enjoy, such as the ability to administer their own lives without supervision. They are also treated as "charity cases" who should be grateful for the scant public income that they receive, although it is much less than the average wage. According to the US Center on Budget and Policy Priorities (2021), the average disabled-worker benefit is about US$1,200/month, whereas the average real wage is US$65,000/year: almost five times higher. Disabled benefits-holders are allowed to earn an additional US$1,300/month, which places them at the threshold of "gainful employment" (US$30,000/year), a level far below the average wage. The Center on Budget and Policy Priorities (2021) adds that "most . . . beneficiaries can't work [at all]," and benefits will be "terminated because of sustained work"; additionally, "most . . . applications are rejected" in the first place. Even if more disabled people could gain access to benefits, they would still be much worse off than nondisabled workers and they would, in addition, be under the coercive control of government bureaucracies. As Russell similarly argues, "the bureaucratism of the welfare state . . . transformed people into objects of state policy called 'clients' [and] lead to a 'dictatorship over needs'" (Russell 2019: 18). Hence, better access to disability benefits would not eliminate the governmental and bureaucratic gatekeeping and policing of disabled people's lives.

Accommodations

The "accommodationist strategy" (Tremain 2017), which favors conditional accommodations over universal accessibility, raises similar concerns about equity and inclusion. Accommodationist university policies force disabled students to do more work than their nondisabled counterparts to acquire an education that is on a par with the education that their nondisabled peers receive. Although UMSL (like most universities) publicizes that it is committed to "equal access to education," disabled students must register with DAS, contact their health-care provider, meet with a DAS staff member, complete tests and interviews, notify professors of their disability, and fulfill other requirements, before they can use the accommodations that grant them this "equal access." As Tremain explains,

> The administrative recognition of . . . requests for accommodation almost always depends upon some sort of medical validation and certification. Hence, insofar as universities and colleges operate with this accommodationist approach, people in the latter group—namely, disabled people—must usually medicalize their circumstances and enter a bureaucratic morass in order to get the social goods that they require, that is, must make more effort (and usually considerably more effort) to get the services and resources that they require. (Tremain 2017: 31)

These requirements are especially vexing for students with ME/CFS, whose main symptom is fatigue, for the application process that is required to obtain accommodations could exacerbate the very condition that the accommodations are meant to alleviate in the first place. This predicament could, and does, compel some students with ME/CFS to leave academia altogether.

Aimi Hamraie agrees that the accommodationist approach "forces disabled people to carry out the labor of requesting and creating access—often constantly," leading to an inequitable workload (Hamraie 2016: 264). They also raise two additional objections to this approach: first, the approach "positions disabled students as exceptional 'misfits'"; and second, the approach is "often premised upon 'retrofitting' a material arrangement after the fact, rather than building a commitment to access into the process of designing a conference, event, or classroom" (264). In other words, accommodationist policies impose extra, invisible work on disabled students, stigmatize disability (as deviancy), and offer piecemeal, post hoc solutions to systemic and structural problems with respect to the distribution of resources and the pervasiveness of ableism.

Peer Support

All disabled people should have access to the disabled community and are entitled to feel a sense of belonging within it. The peer support and other social goods that this community can provide to disabled people are important; thus, potential members of the community should not be required to "prove" that they have a certain kind of disability or are disabled enough in order to avail themselves of these goods. By imposing these sorts of demands on each other, we validate the scarce-resources ideology that sustains divisions and hierarchies within disabled communities.

Structural Solutions

Marxist feminism provides a better solution to the ableist exclusions that have been the focus of this chapter than the responses that I have discussed thus far, a solution that takes the form of the refusal to work. This refusal can be realized in a number of anti-work policies and proposals.

Government

First, a UBI sufficient to support a comfortable lifestyle would liberate disabled people from the arduous application processes that one must endure in order to receive disability benefits. Under a system of UBI, everyone would receive a livable income regardless of dis/ability status. This provision would eliminate the need to complete applications, go to appointments, submit diagnostic tests and laboratory findings, and fulfill a variety of other arbitrary, invasive, and exhausting criteria and conditions. A shorter workweek, in addition to UBI, would allow more disabled people to participate in the workforce if they so choose, since shorter shifts are more manageable for many bodies, including some chronically fatigued bodies. More flexible hours would also reduce the incidence of relapses, flare-ups, post-exertional malaise, and injuries caused by work-related stress and overexertion, thereby reducing the very need for institutional support.

Education

In higher education, the refusal to work (in a standardized way) could be realized in Universal Design (UD) and ungrading. The Center for Universal Design defines UD as "the design of products and environments to be usable by all people, to the greatest extent possible, without the need for adaptation or specialized design" (Center for Universal Design 2008). UD, thus, strives to make accommodations superfluous by designing education to be accessible to all. UD principles include equitable use (design should be useful to people with diverse disabilities), simplicity (design should be easy to understand), and low physical effort (design can be used with minimum fatigue).[6] In ways such as this, UD strives to reduce the need for accommodations by increasing accessibility for a variety of disabilities. The implementation of UD in universities and other workplaces would address the excessive work and workload inequities that typical accommodations policies cause, particularly to chronically fatigued and multiply-oppressed people.

Tekla Babyak (2022) points out that completely eliminating accommodations may be impossible, since disabled people's access needs can come into conflict. Similarly, Hamraie notes that "the critique of accommodationism should not imply that flexibility toward individual access needs is unnecessary" (Hamraie 2016: 265). Rather, disabled people should be invited to articulate their individual needs as part of a collective conversation and continuous negotiation about the design of shared spaces. The goal of UD is not to replace one one-size-fits-all paradigm with another paradigm but rather to "build . . . in mechanisms for accountability that hold space for critical questions about material arrangements—the kind of spaces offered by iterative design processes" (265). That is, UD seeks to create mechanisms for conversation and accountability around disability.

Ungrading is another work-reducing strategy that may be especially beneficial to disabled people with ME/CFS. Ungrading involves the elimination or significant reduction of the number of graded assignments per course, as well as the use of alternative grading schemes such as self-assessment and peer assessment (Stommel 2020). Ungrading reduces the need for accommodations by giving students more control over their education, including their grades and workloads. Grades can be used, similar to wages, to increase productivity while alienating students from the act of production, the product of their labor, and each other. Indeed, Stommel claims that "grades . . .

are currency for a capitalist system that reduces teaching and learning to a mere transaction. Grading is a massive co-ordinated effort to take humans out of the educational process" (Stommel 2017). A grade-based economy turns assignments into commodities rather than learning experiences. Ungrading, in contrast, entices students to value learning for its own sake and to pursue their own interests in ways that the academic-industrial complex does not encourage and even discourages.

The Disabled Community

Within the disabled community, one of the forms that the refusal to work should take is the refusal to demand evidence of illness, pathology, and other markers of "real disability." These demands create more work, competition, and gatekeeping within the community, and in society in general. Not only are these transactions taxing for "ambiguously" disabled people, but they incorrectly "posit [disability] as a preexisting and stable entity" (Tremain 2001: 633), thereby denying the variability and diversity of disabled people's circumstances and experiences. In this connection, ME/CFS is described by the CDC as having diverse "presentations" and "clinical courses," which can vary widely from one person to the next and from one circumstance to another (Centers for Disease Control 2019). In terms of contextual variability, the term *ME/CFS* did not exist until the 1950s, nor did it receive widespread recognition until the 1980s, at which time it was disparagingly referred to in the national media as "Raggedy Ann Syndrome" and "Yuppie Flu," due to its (mis)perceived association with wealthy white women (Siegel et al. 2018). Since then, studies have shown that ME/CFS is more prevalent in racialized and low-income groups (Jason et al. 2009), partly due to the conditions of oppression that these groups must navigate (Ciurria 2020). As debates around ME/CFS continue to evolve, its criteria continue to change. Hence, the demand that disabled people provide evidence that they meet a specific set of criteria to count as disabled ignores the cultural and subjective specificity of ME/CFS in particular and disability in general. This demand ignores that, in Tremain's words, disability is "a historically and culturally specific and contingent social phenomenon, a complex apparatus of power rather than a natural attribute or property that certain people possess" (Tremain 2017: 2).

Marxist feminist strategies would serve to undermine the totalizing and ahistorical (medical) apparatus of disability by refusing to reduce disabilities to a set of impairments, leaving open the possibility of diversity and difference in the circumstances of disabled people. The framework of historicized Marxist feminist approaches to disability, in addition, erodes the firm line between ability and disability. Indeed, from a Marxist feminist perspective, one of the main advantages of the anti-work approach is that it troubles the definition of disability as (nothing more or less than) a productivity-impairing pathology—a definition that emerged under a capitalist regime. Capitalist ideology posits disability as inherently deviant and subordinate relative to ability, and an anti-capitalist approach is needed to disrupt this reductive definition.

The Social Construction of Disability, Impairment, and the Relationships Between the Two

Sarah F. Rose traces this genealogical construction in her analysis of the category of disability in industrial, urban societies. In the remainder of this chapter, I will use Roses's work to expose and explain (a) the problematic construction of disability under capitalism, (b) the parallel construction of impairment under the same capitalist regime, and (c) the contingent relationship between impairment and disability. In turn, I will examine how anti-work feminism deconstructs the capitalist apparatuses of disability, impairment, and the dis/ability binary, as well as offers a more complex understanding of the meanings of these concepts and the relationships between them.

Disability

In *No Right to Be Idle: The Invention of Disability, 1840s-1930s*, Rose traces the historical construction and contestation of disability during the transition from agrarian society to industrial, urban economy. During this transitional period, Rose explains, disability was increasingly identified with concepts of impairment and unproductivity. That is, disabled people were seen as defective in such a way that they could not produce surplus value for an employer, as demanded by the emerging capitalist economy. This defectiveness constituted deviance and disposability in the cultural imagination. As disabled people were therefore pushed out of the workforce in greater and greater numbers, disability "became synonymous with reliance on public dependency, poor citizenship, and the inability to care for oneself or work productively. In other words, disability was believed to pose risks both to individuals' own morals and to those of the nation as a whole" (Rose 2017: 3). Several factors contributed to this eugenics paradigm.

First, the transition to an urban economy simultaneously disabled workers and forced disabled people into a position of dependency. As Rose explains, "Within working-class communities, disabling injuries were often so common that they served at least as a marker of poverty, if not class itself." Workplace injuries were especially common in already-oppressed groups due to intersections of class, gender, and race. Women, for instance, were recruited to paint "radioactive radium on watch faces"; migrant workers were hired to dig dam tunnels through carcinogenic silica rocks (Rose 2017: 4); Black workers were "concentrated in the lowest-paying, dirtiest, and most hazardous jobs"; and so on for other marginalized populations (Jones 2000). At the same time, "'policy makers' racialized and gendered assumptions about health, 'fitness,' accidents, and the nature of 'breadwinners' and family often barred nonwhites and women from gaining equal access to compensation and rehabilitation programs and, in some cases, life outside institutions for the feeble-minded" (Rose 2017: 4). The confluence of workplace injuries and denials of public support coalesced to construct disability as a raced and gendered category, which, in turn, compounded the hardships imposed on disabled people as such.

Prior to the introduction of worker's compensation, which provides money to certain categories of workers who are injured while performing their jobs, disability was not seen in a negative light, as it is today. As Rose notes, "Early twentieth-century Pittsburgh steel mills were so dangerous, for example, that missing a finger [along with more noticeable disabilities] was *considered normal* and did not prevent laborers from finding employment. *Nor did such an impairment cause stigma* within working-class communities; rather, such injuries were often seen as indicating manly mastery of a dangerous workplace" (Rose 2017: 7, emphasis added). Indeed, some men regarded workplace injuries as a badge of honor and a sign of masculine strength. This attitude changed, however, when employers began to select interchangeable, that is, "unimpaired," bodies to work the machines. Rose explains that "as mechanized factory labor became increasingly central to the economy, employers in nearly all sectors began to demand workers who . . . had intact, interchangeable bodies" (2). Workers became "cogs in a machine," fungible parts of an assembly line. People with non-fungible bodies were designated as unemployable and, as their numbers grew, they became an "unproductive" surplus population.

The introduction of workman's compensation, whose purpose was to help unionized (white, male) workers remain in the workforce, had the perverse effect of fueling discrimination against disabled people by strengthening associations between disability and risk. As Rose puts it: "what had been a 'normal' [disabled] working body instead became read as a sign of carelessness or inefficiency, and ultimately a reason to keep people out of the workplace" (Rose 2017: 7). Major companies began to screen workers for disabilities and to implement rigorous physical examinations to exclude disabled workers, even though many disabled people could and did work in alternative economies. Yet employers, rather than take responsibility for disabling workplace conditions, attributed blame for accidents and injuries to disabled workers. Doing so contributed to the perception of disability as a risk to both the disabled person and the economy.[7]

As disabled people were increasingly screened out of the mainstream economy, some moved to sheltered workshops which, to this day, pay less than the minimum wage; others entered unregulated gray markets; and still others were institutionalized in "asylums for idiots" and similar facilities. In asylums, disabled inmates did most of the upkeep of the institutions, performing tasks that ranged from cooking, to gardening, to caring for other inmates, to printing the inmate newsletter. This labor was also gendered and raced insofar as women were typically assigned to "feminine" roles such as caring for children, while men were typically assigned to "masculine" roles such as gardening (Carlson 2009), and Black inmates were historically assigned to segregated asylums with harsher living conditions or were given harsher tasks within desegregated asylums (Davis 2010; McWhorter 2009). None of this labor was recognized or compensated as productive work, nor did it count as training for the paid workforce, although this invisible productivity often garnered profits for the institutions and wardens of these facilities. In this way, disabled people's labor was expunged from the recorded history of work.

Through these processes, work came to be defined as productive labor done by unimpaired bodies. Disabled people's labor was "ungainful," perceived as outside of the realm of productive work. This ableist logic explains why the current Social Service Administration requires that applicants provide evidence of impairment and inability to work in order to be eligible for benefits. If either condition is unmet, the applicant is insufficiently "disabled" to warrant support. This apparatus is also reflected in educational policies that, as I have indicated, demand verifiable documentation of underlying illness, as well as the social model's conception of impairment as an illness that impedes normal functioning. Although the social model, as developed in the United Kingdom, rejects the medicalization of disability, it merely displaces this apparatus onto impairment. Impairment on the social model, more precisely, is seen as a personal medical affliction. All three apparatuses neglect the historical contingency and variability of disability.

Anti-work strategies disrupt the prevailing capitalistic construction of disability as productivity-impairing pathology. If everyone receives a UBI sufficient to liberate them from both poverty and the need to work, if a multiplicity of (noninterchangeable) bodies can participate in the paid workforce, if UD principles replace accommodationist policies, then disability will no longer be a marker of subordinate status, public dependency, and inability to work. Nondisabled people will receive welfare and more disabled people will hold paying jobs. In contrast, advocating for better access to (conditional) benefits, accommodations, and community—to all of which disabled people are, I should emphasize, entitled—will not disrupt the capitalist marking of disability as a site of deviancy, dependency, and risk, although it may assist certain disabled people. Nor will easier access to these benefits and supports help the millions of undiagnosed disabled people who are categorically barred from such services by virtue of diagnostic criteria. Some disabled people may be granted benefits but the majority will remain barred from doing so.

Just as the wages-for-housework movement and the masculine/feminine binary have reinforced the perception of women as domestic servants, special dispensations to disabled people tacitly reinforce both the negative perception of disability as a moral and economic risk and the ability/disability binary that underwrites this conception. Anti-work policies disrupt both binaries by rebuking work culture and its rigid class, gender, and disability axes. The refusal to work liberates us from preconceived notions about social roles and social hierarchies (seen as natural and necessary in the capitalist imaginary) and generates post-work spaces in which to reimagine and reconstruct our roles and relationships, imagining new ways of "doing" gender, dis/ability, and so on.

Like genderqueer kinds, queerly disabled kinds pose a threat to the dis/ability binary. Robin Dembroff describes "genderqueer" as a "gender critical kind . . . whose members collectively destabilize the binary axis, or the idea that the only possible genders are the exclusive and exhaustive kinds *men* and *women*" (Dembroff 2020: 1). Similarly, queerly disabled or "cripqueer" is a crip critical kind whose members destabilize the binary dis/ability axis. (Some people use the term *cripqueer* to refer to disabled-and-queer people but I prefer to use this term to designate queerly disabled people who transgress the dis/ability binary. Using this terminology, I am a queer cripqueer person.) To be sure, these two critical kinds—that is, genderqueer and cripqueer—may not be perfectly analogous. For instance, one's social recognition as disabled depends much more heavily on institutional apparatuses and their disciplinary techniques (e.g., diagnostic tests) and, in this regard, is policed to a greater extent than is gender. Nevertheless, both cripqueer and genderqueer kinds destabilize their respective binary axes. Taking a cue from queer theory, crip philosophers should ask ourselves this question: Why do we allow institutions—which are overwhelmingly controlled by nondisabled professionals—to define disability? Should we not rather define it ourselves through playful "world-traveling" and "loving perception" (Lugones 1987)? If institutional authorities are today widely recognized as lacking the authority to define sex, gender, and race, then why should they be permitted to define dis/ability? How can we *play* with dis/ability if it is an *institutional* concept?

Play is an important notion in queer theory. In Butler's formative work (1990), they proposed that gender is performative, that we can do gender in a variety of ways, and that playing with gender gives rise to a multiplicity of gender formations. Through play, we can imagine and construct new genders outside of the binary axis. The same argument can be applied to disability: playing with dis/ability can allow us to do dis/ability on our own terms and can lead to a multiplicity of dis/ability formations, including ones that defy medical categorization and institutional specification. Note that this playful approach is not compatible with a capitalist apparatus that defines disability in narrow, binary, and invariant terms. Indeed, dis/ability play should be understood as acts of resistance that run directly counter to professionally determined and exclusively negative diagnostic criteria of disability. Disability play destabilizes medical categories and exposes the positive sides of disability, which are extensively documented in crip theory.[8] The advantages of being disabled include crip kinship (Kafai 2021), crip joy, and crip creativity (Ljuslinder, Ellis, and Vikström 2020; Ciurria 2022), which are component parts of "crip culture," "a daring space of shameless flaunting," in which "we find fellow crips who affirm and reflect our originality and beauty back at us," and in which "internalized ableism begins to crumble" and "uppity crips [defy] mainstream culture's insistence on subordination and [do] it with style and humor" (Wood 2014: 2). The generative, affirmative, and joyful side of crip culture—indeed, its very existence—is dismissed and obfuscated by symptomatic definitions of disability. Thus, symptomatic discourse perpetrates a form of ableist structural gaslighting in that it denies and pathologizes disabled people's testimony about their culture and their affirmative experiences.[9]

The notion of queer disabilities is sure to be controversial, but it gains support from Dembroff's defense of queer genders. Dembroff argues that the exclusion of genderqueer kinds "creates a gap of metaphysical explanation and understanding" by denying the existence of nonbinary people (Dembroff 2020: 2). This refusal to acknowledge genderqueer kinds leads to epistemic injustice, specifically, a silencing or smothering of nonbinary people's testimony. Similarly, the dis/ability binary erases people who exist at the border of ability and disability. This ontological positioning, in turn, casts doubt on queerly disabled people's testimony. The recognition of cripqueer kinds is thus a step toward resolving these metaphysical and epistemic gaps.

In "Dis/ability Studies: Theorizing Disablism and Ableism," Goodley (2014) prefigures part of the current debate about the dis/ability dichotomy in the following way. Like me, he seeks to "acknowledge . . . the ways in which disablism and ableism (and disability and ability) can only ever be understood simultaneously in relation to one another" (Goodley 2014: xiii). One of the key tasks of disability studies, he says, is to "keep disablism and ableism, disability and ability in play with one another, to explore their co-construction and reliance upon one another" (9), as I have done here. Another point of overlap is that Goodley argues that the dis/ability binary is, in effect, a disciplinary apparatus intended to reduce government spending by distinguishing between nondisabled people who do not deserve benefits and disabled people who do, as well as dividing the "deserving" disabled from the "undeserving" disabled. The "deserving disabled" are granted access to services but are also, by the same token, positioned as "welfare-dependent . . . , passively reliant upon social security payments, draining the public coffers, unprepared to do a day's hard work" (ibid.). The "undeserving" disabled, meanwhile, are positioned as crooks trying to pilfer money and privileges to which they are not entitled. This predicament is a classic double bind insofar as the "deserving" disabled are treated as burdens while the "undeserving" disabled are treated as thieves. Disability in either guise is a liability that harms the disabled person and the general social good.

Using resources from Marxist feminism and queer theory, I have attempted to vindicate Goodley's critique by illuminating how disability came to be defined in reductive and exclusionary terms under capitalism and have defended anti-work feminism as a solution to this problem.

Impairment

Like disability, impairment is a social construct that has been shaped by capitalist forces. Rose notes that prior to the Industrial Revolution, there was no standard definition of disability or impairment, nor any clear relationship between the two. The term *impairment* was a catchall for a range of conditions that included "blindness, idiocy, amputations, withered limbs, shell shock, even tuberculosis—that occurred at various ages and stemmed from very different origins, both acquired and congenital" (Rose 2017: 3). The category of impairment has evolved, along with disability, in response to the fluctuations of market capitalism and waves of public resistance.

The diagnosis of idiocy, for example, is no longer seen as a valid medical construct. Yet in the Enlightenment era, as Stacy Simplican explains, it played a "key role . . . in defining the meaning of personhood and limiting political membership" (Simplican 2015: 26). John Locke applied the term to "savages, women, [and] madmen," as political liberals such as him sought to exclude these groups from citizenship (28). The concept of idiocy was later extended to the uneducated, the unemployed, and the poor, all of which were deemed incapable of contributing to a "well-ordered society." The notion of idiocy, in other words, had no biological basis but was engineered as a tool to distinguish between "worthy citizens" and "natural subordinates." The term *idiocy* was replaced by *mental retardation* in the mid-twentieth century, which itself was superseded by *developmental disabilities*, a blanket term designed to cover a range of diagnoses, including attention deficit hyperactivity disorder (ADHD), autism spectrum disorder (ASD), cerebral palsy, deafness, blindness, and "other developmental delays" (Centers for Disease Control 2021). These classifications, however, continue to be contested and reconfigured, which speaks to the inherently political nature and mutability of medical classifications, which I have clarified.

Simplican argues that although the concept of developmental disability seems to be an improvement over idiocy, it bears more in common with its predecessor than one might think. As Simplican explains it, the designation of "developmental disability" still functions as a barrier to citizenship, namely, as a tool to distinguish between citizens proper and subordinates. Simplican points out, furthermore, that "severely developmentally delayed" people, in particular, are a paradigm case of marginalization, excluded by a "capacity contract" that "bases political membership on a threshold level of capacity and excludes anyone who falls below" (Simplican 2015: 4). The fear of disability under the capacity contract functions to punish disabled people and, by the same token, to discipline nondisabled people into a regime of compulsory, docile, and even enthusiastic productivity. Hence, the categories of disability and impairment are not completely distinct but rather function as part of a capitalist regime that employs dynamic strategies to extract labor power from workers. This dynamic system produces social categories for functional purposes.

The genealogy of the notion of idiocy—that is, its descent from impairment, to mental retardation, to developmental disability—exemplifies the sociohistorical contingency and mutability of impairment, its variable relation to disability, and the relation of both concepts to a capitalist apparatus that produces docile workers and subordinated nonworkers. What was once deemed impairment morphed into learning disability, which later multiplied into a range of highly variable formations (vision impairment, ADHD, ASD, etc.), which continue to emerge in the present as part of an ever-evolving discourse informed by mechanisms of power and resistance.

The Relationship Between Disability and Impairment

The relationship between the categories of impairment and disability is analogous to the relationship between sex and gender. As Tremain argues, the categories of sex and impairment are "historical artifact[s] of [the same] regime of knowledge/power. . . . Both 'natural sex' and 'natural impairment' have circulated in discursive and concrete practices as nonhistorical (biological) matter of the body, which is molded by time and class, is culturally shaped, or on which culture is imprinted" (Tremain 2001: 623). I have tried to corroborate this claim by showing, through a specific genealogical interpretation, that impairment, disability, sex, and gender are, every one of them, historical artifacts of the same capitalist regime of knowledge and power.

As Tremain has noted, Donna Haraway argued that early-wave feminists "did not question the sex-gender distinction because it was a useful tool" to advance women's rights (Tremain 2001: 625). Feminists could, and did, use the essentialized category of gender to demand protections for female-bodied people. Nevertheless, this useful distinction indirectly also served to erase nonbinary genders and reinforce the primacy of maleness and masculinity. That is, it reinforced the naturalization of a political binary that essentializes gender as a function of birth-assigned sex.

So, too, with impairment. The concept of impairment (as a marker of the disabled body) exists to support contingent biopolitical arrangements, including capitalistic ones. It can be useful to conflate disability and impairment for instrumental reasons, though doing so homogenizes and oversimplifies the category of disability. As a case in point, Tremain (2001) has pointed out that the United Kingdom's Disability Living Allowance (DLA) has forced applicants to conceal the heterogeneity of their lived experience and identify with a homogenizing definition of impairment that is designed to, among other things, protect allegedly scarce public resources and deny allegedly fraudulent applications. Like other government schemes of distribution that are targeted at disabled people, the DLA forces disabled applicants to "confess" to disabling experiences that reinforce the public perception of impairment as natural, homogenous, and wholly negative. In this way, government bureaucracies totalize and homogenize the definition of disability so as to manage the disabled population. The medical definition of disability adopted by the DLA grants support to some disabled folks while writing others out of existence, which is, indeed, the purpose of the policy. That is, the DLA seeks to metaphysically invalidate and epistemically silence queerly disabled people in the pursuit of economic efficiency and labor control.

Anti-work strategies trouble the medicalization, homogenization, and marginalization of disability by liberating disabled people from the paternalistic control and ideological influence of governments, academic administrators, and other (predominantly nondisabled) institutional authorities. If everyone were to receive UBI, if noninterchangeable bodies could participate in the workplace, and if special dispensations for disabled people were thus no longer prioritized, then the obligation to comply with the dictates of the capitalist market, and to identify uniquely with one or the other side of the dis/ability binary, would be lifted. Disabled people would be liberated to play with the notion of disability outside of identity-regimenting institutional spaces.

Conclusion

People with ME/CFS are largely excluded from (i) receipt of benefits, (ii) provision of accommodations, and (iii) a sense of belonging and inclusion in the disabled community. The simple solution to these exclusions is to pursue better access to diagnoses and (i)–(iii). Yet Marxist feminism suggests a better strategy, namely, that we could refuse to comply with the logic of capitalism by demanding freedom from work, an unconditional basic income, a shorter workweek, and universally accessible spaces. Implementation of these policies would liberate us from oppressive governmental bureaucracies and would empower us to question the capitalistic engineering of disability as a moral and economic risk, a wholly negative set of symptoms, and a singular, uniform experience. Furthermore, these policies, if implemented, would create post-work spaces in which to play with dis/ability outside of the capitalist regime and its rigid dualisms.

Notes

1 In a blog post on the same topic (2020), I said that I identify as chronically fatigued rather than "someone with ME/CFS," just as I identify as queer rather than "someone with queerness." In this chapter, however, I often use the term *ME/CFS* (and the phrase "someone with ME/CFS") because it is more widely recognized and simpler to use. Nevertheless, I continue to maintain that, as a social construct and a subject position, ME/CFS is more accurately captured in disability-first language.

2 In my case, my immigration status and other factors pose additional barriers to my ability to receive benefits, but even if these factors were not present, I would not be eligible for benefits due to my employment history and illness category.

3 It is possible that some university administrators will shirk the official policy and defer to a student's testimony, but the policy itself is discriminatory and may deter students from believing that they are eligible or would be seriously considered for accommodations.

4 Note that Black and Hispanic women have always done more paid labor that white women, typically in low-paying service jobs. But the rate of workforce participation for these groups has still increased over the last fifty years.

5 These are not the only possible anti-work strategies. They are simply two that Weeks suggests as suitable to address the demands of early-wave feminism. Other strategies might include giving workers a cooperative stake in their companies, extending the social safety net more broader (including implementing and expanding universal health care), and nationalizing private and semiprivate services like medicine and banking. I support all of these strategies. My defense of a UBI and a shorter workweek should not be taken to exhaust the range of desirable anti-work reforms.

6 Viz. Burgstahler (2009) for a more extensive list of UD principles.

7 See Hall (2021) for a longer explanation on how risk is a social construct used to oppress disabled people.

8 See Ciurria (2022) for a broader description of the positive dimensions of, and misconceptions about, crip culture.

9 My concept of ableist gaslighting is influenced by Berenstain's account of racial gaslighting (2020).

References

Alfonseca, Kiara (2021, November 21), "Crime against Disabled People is Rising and Advocates Say More Needs to be Done," *ABC News*. Available at: https://abcnews.go.com/US/crime-disabled-people-rising-advocates/story?id=81210410 (accessed August 24, 2022).

Babyak, Tekla (2022, May 27), "On Being a Killjoy Canon Crip in Philosophy," Presented at the Philosophy and Activism Conference, University of Missouri-St. Louis.

Berenstain, Nora (2020), "White Feminist Gaslighting," *Hypatia: A Journal of Feminist Philosophy* 35 (4): 733–58.

Bureau of Labor Statistics (2013, March 11), "Women's Earnings, 1979–2012." Available at: https://www.bls.gov/opub/ted/2013/ted_20131104.htm (accessed August 24, 2022).

Bureau of Labor Statistics (2022, February 24), "Persons with a Disability: Labor Force Characteristics – 2021." Available at: https://www.bls.gov/news.release/pdf/disabl.pdf (accessed August 24, 2022).

Burgstahler, Sheryl (2009), "Universal Design of Instruction (UDI): Definition, Principles, Guidelines, and Examples," *Do-It (Disabilities, Opportunities, Internetworking, and Technology)*. Available at: https://www.washington.edu/doit/sites/default/files/atoms/files/Universal_Design_04_12_21.pdf (accessed August 24, 2022).

Butler, Judith (1990), *Gender Trouble*. New York and London: Routledge.

Byrne, Eleanor A. (2020), "Striking the Balance with Epistemic Injustice in Healthcare: The Case of Chronic Fatigue Syndrome/Myalgic Encephalomyelitis," *Medicine, Health Care and Philosophy* 23 (3): 371–9.

Carlson, Licia (2009), *The Faces of Intellectual Disability: Philosophical Reflections*, Bloomington: Indiana University Press.

Center on Budget and Policy Priorities (2021, December 2), "Chart Book: Social Security Disability Insurance." Available at: https://www.cbpp.org/research/social-security/social-security-disability-insurance-0 (accessed August 24, 2022).

Centers for Disease Control (2019), "Presentation and Clinical Course of ME/CFS." Available at: https://www.cdc.gov/me-cfs/healthcare-providers/presentation-clinical-course/index.html (accessed July 20, 2023).

Centers for Disease Control (2021), "Facts about Developmental Disabilities." Available at: https://www.cdc.gov/ncbddd/developmentaldisabilities/facts.html (accessed August 24, 2022).

Centers for Disease Control (2022a), "Myalgic Encephalomyelitis/Chronic Fatigue Syndrome." Available at: https://www.cdc.gov/me-cfs/index.html (accessed August 24, 2022).

Centers for Disease Control (2022b), "ME/CFS in Children." Available at: https://www.cdc.gov/me-cfs/me-cfs-children/index.html (accessed August 24, 2022).

Center for Universal Design (2008), "About UD." Available at: https://projects.ncsu.edu/ncsu/design/cud/about_ud/about_ud.htm (accessed August 24, 2022).
Ciurria, Mich (2020), "Capitalism and Chronic Fatigue (blog)," BIOPOLITICAL PHILOSOPHY. Available at: https://biopoliticalphilosophy.com/2020/12/18/capitalism-and-chronic-fatigue-guest-post-by-michelle-ciurria/ (accessed August 24, 2022).
Ciurria, Mich (2022), "The Tragedy of Nondisability: A Sad and Boring Life," BIOPOLITICAL PHILOSOPHY (blog). Available at: https://biopoliticalphilosophy.com/2022/07/06/the-tragedy-of-nondisability-a-sad-and-boring-life/ (accessed August 24, 2022).
Daugherty, Greg (2022), "Women Still Earn Less than Men for Comparable Work in 2022 America," *Investopedia*. Available at: https://www.investopedia.com/history-gender-wage-gap-america-5074898 (accessed August 24, 2022).
Davis, King (2010), "Special Report: America's First Asylum for African Americans Marks 150th Anniversary," *Psychiatric News*. Available at: https://psychnews.psychiatryonline.org/doi/full/10.1176/appi.pn.2020.8a23 (accessed August 24, 2022).
Dembroff, Robin (2020), "Beyond Binary: Genderqueer as Critical Gender Kind," *Philosopher's Imprint*. Available at: https://philsci-archive.pitt.edu/16317/ (accessed July 20, 2023).
Department of Labor (2021), "Subminimum Wage." Available at: https://www.dol.gov/general/topic/wages/subminimumwage (accessed August 24, 2022).
General Accounting Office (2003), "SSA Disability Decision Making [Report]." Available at: https://www.gao.gov/assets/gao-04-14.pdf (accessed August 24, 2022).
Goodley, Dan (2014), *Dis/ability Studies: Theorising Disablism and Ableism*, London and New York: Routledge.
Hall, Melinda (2021), "Projecting Risk: Doing Risk Together and Disability Justice," Philosophy, Disability, and Social Change 2 Conference, Blavatnik School of Government, University of Oxford.
Hamraie, Aimi (2016), "Beyond Accommodation: Disability, Feminist Philosophy, and the Design of Everyday Academic Life," *PhiloSOPHIA: A Journal of Trancontinental Feminism* 6 (2): 259–71.
Jason, Leonard A., Nicole Porter, Molly Brown, Valerie Anderson, Abigail Brown, Jessica Hunnell, and Athena Lerch (2009), "CFS: A Review of Epidemiology and Natural History Studies," *Bulletin of the IACFS/ME* 17 (3): 88.
Jones, Jacqueline (2000, November 30), "Black Workers Remember," *The American Prospect: Ideas, Politics, and Power*. Available at: https://prospect.org/features/black-workers-remember/ (accessed August 24, 2022).
Kafai, Shayda (2021), *Crip Kinship: The Disability Justice & Art Activism of Sins Invalid*, Vancouver: Arsenal Pulp Press.
Ljuslinder, Karin, Katie Ellis, and Lotta Vikström (2020), "Cripping Time: Understanding the Life Course through the Lens of Ableism," *Scandinavian Journal of Disability Research* 22 (1): 35–8.
Lugones, Maria (1987), "Playfulness, 'World'-Travelling, and Loving Perception," *Hypatia: A Journal of Feminist Philosophy* 2 (2): 3–19.
Marx, Karl (1981), *Capital: A Critique of Political Economy*, vol. 3, trans. David Fernbach, London: Penguin.
McWhorter, Ladelle (2009), *Racism and Sexual Oppression in Anglo-America: A Genealogy*, Bloomington: Indiana University Press.
Nadelhoffer, Thomas (2022), "Chronic Pain, Mere-Differences, and Disability Variantism," *The Journal of Philosophy of Disability*. https://doi.org/10.5840/jpd20223110.

Oliver, Michael (1990), *Politics of Disablement*, London: Macmillan International Education.
Pacey, Rosie (2018), "Gatekeeping Disability: The Intersection of Ableism, Austerity, and Capitalism," *Medium* (blog post). Available at: https://medium.com/disability-acts/gatekeeping-disability-853ea804d98f (accessed August 24, 2022).
Patten, Eileen (2016), "Racial, Gender Wage Gaps Persist in U.S. Despite Some Progress," Pew Research Center. Available at: https://www.pewresearch.org/fact-tank/2016/07/01/racial-gender-wage-gaps-persist-in-u-s-despite-some-progress/ (accessed August 24, 2022).
Rose, Sarah F. (2017), *No Right to Be Idle: The Invention of Disability, 1840s–1930s*, Chapel Hill: UNC Press.
Russell, Marta (2019), *Capitalism and Disability: Selected Writings by Marta Russell*, Chicago: Haymarket Books.
Siegel, Zachary A., Abigail Brown, Andrew Devendorf, Johanna Collier, and Leonard A. Jason (2018), "A Content Analysis of Chronic Fatigue Syndrome and Myalgic Encephalomyelitis in the News from 1987 to 2013," *Chronic illness* 14 (1): 3–12.
Simplican, Stacy C. (2015), *The Capacity Contract: Intellectual Disability and the Question of Citizenship*, Minneapolis: University of Minnesota Press.
Social Security Administration (2018), "Providing Medical Evidence for Individuals with Myalgic Encephalomyelitis/Chronic Fatigue Syndrome (ME/CFS) [Fact Sheet]." Available at: https://www.ssa.gov/disability/professionals/documents/64-063.pdf (accessed August 24, 2022).
Social Security Administration (2022), "Selected Data from Social Security's Disability Program." Available at: https://www.ssa.gov/oact/STATS/dibGraphs.html (accessed August 24, 2022).
Stommel, Jesse (2017), "Why I Don't Grade," Jesse Stommel's Website (blog). Available at: https://www.jessestommel.com/why-i-dont-grade/ (accessed May 27, 2023).
Stommel, Jesse (2020), "Ungrading: A Bibliography," Jesse Stommel's Website (blog). Available at: https://www.jessestommel.com/ungrading-a-bibliography/ (accessed August 24, 2022).
Tremain, Shelley (2001), "On the Government of Disability," *Social Theory and Practice* 27 (4): 617–36.
Tremain, Shelley L. (2017), *Foucault and Feminist Philosophy of Disability*, Ann Arbor: University of Michigan Press.
University of Missouri-St. Louis, Disability Access Services Accommodations Request Form. Available at: https://docs.google.com/forms/d/e/1FAIpQLScVkR9xOgwzB0QqwXX1VpQljDMdDs1K-tlxTJomE1RPMLLTxA/viewform (accessed August 24, 2022).
Weeks, Kathi (2011), *The Problem with Work*, Durham and London: Duke University Press.
Wood, C. (2014), "Introduction: Criptiques: A Daring Space," in C. Wood (ed.), *Criptiques*, 1–5, Minneapolis: May Day Publishing.
Yellen, Janet L. (2020, May), "The History of Women's Work and Wages and How it has Created Success for Us All," *Brooking* (blog post). Available at: https://www.brookings.edu/essay/the-history-of-womens-work-and-wages-and-how-it-has-created-success-for-us-all/ (accessed August 24, 2022).
Young, Iris Marion (1990), *Justice and the Politics of Difference*, Princeton: Princeton University Press.

9 ALGORITHMS AS ABLEIST ORIENTATION DEVICES

THE TECHNOSOCIAL INHERITANCE OF COLONIALISM AND ABLEISM

JOHNATHAN FLOWERS

Algorithmic Technologies as Orienting Devices

Langdon Winner (1980) begins his pathbreaking article "Do Artifacts Have Politics?" by rejecting what he regards as traditional views of the social organization and political nature of technology according to which socioeconomic systems determine the politics of technology embedded in them. For Winner, this view of the politicization of technology ignores the technological object itself in favor of an analysis of social structures which purportedly result in the technology. In contrast, Winner provides two new perspectives on the politics of technology: the perspective that technologies are "flexible" in their politics and the perspective that technologies are "inflexible" in their politics. His first perspective, that technologies are politically "flexible," underscores how technology can be designed and organized to establish and maintain systems of power and authority. On this view, the social contexts of the technology are extended through the organization of the technology and its intended purposes. Technology, on this construal, is "flexible" and the social consequences of it cannot be understood apart from the individuals and structures involved in its design and implementation. Thus, the politics of the technologies are as "flexible" as the politics of the social contexts that they extend.

Winner's second perspective, that technologies are politically "inflexible," indicates how technology is tied to institutionalized structures of power and authority that drive the decisions about what kinds of technologies are produced and adopted. On this view, the social consequences of a technology cannot be divorced from the politics of the decisions involved in developing, deploying, and adopting a technology. To adopt a technology is to adopt a social and cultural organization that conditions how human relations are formed and maintained. This view assumes that the politics of technology are inflexible, as to understand the consequences of technology, we must also understand the social organization that ultimately enables the social consequences of the technology. Insofar as these social and cultural organizations themselves are "inflexible," are predetermined, the politics of the technologies themselves are "inflexible."

Technologies orient individuals in line with the histories that precede the technologies. In this regard, Winner points out that the disability justice movement (though he does not refer to it as such) made clear the politics of the organization of the built environment by demonstrating the ways in which the built environment denied the capacity for disabled persons to fully participate in society. Although Winner remarks that architects and city planners have not engaged in intentional neglect (Winner 1980: 125), the organization of the world around ability has entailed this "politics of neglect." It constitutes the naturalization of a history of assumptions about who should be able to access public spaces and who should not, about who will use public spaces and who will not, that leads to the technological institution of inaccessible spaces. The assertion that this institutional inaccessibility is the product of "longstanding neglect" rather than the product of the naturalization of ableist assumptions in design indicates how technology inherits ableist assumptions. As a way of ordering the world, determining social relations, and prescribing forms of social organization, technology's inheritance of ableism is made manifest through who is intended to use forms of technology and who is not (Ahmed 2007). It is this nature of technology that enables it to become what Sara Ahmed calls an "orientation device."

According to Ahmed (2006, 2007), an orientation device supplies the orientations of persons within the world and structures how the world unfolds to place objects in reach through their proximity. The orientation device reveals the nature of the object, the tasks for which the object is to be used, and who is to perform these tasks. Orientation devices enable the alignment of persons with modes in which to occupy space that histories, which organize the world in ways proximate to the histories and which preexist the extension of the body in space, deem appropriate. These orientation devices may need to be prepared or made ready for use through a history of use and development that precedes a given object into the world—making it familiar to users upon arrival—and is continuous with the histories of the spaces in which it is used.

To illustrate this point, Ahmed uses the example of her desk: "The object on which and through which I work hence leaves its impression: the action, as intending, as well as tending toward the object, shapes my body in this way and that. The work of repetition is not neutral work; it orients the body in some ways rather than others" (Ahmed 2006: 57).

Combining Ahmed's insights with Winner's two perspectives on the politics of technology, we can understand "flexible" technologies to orient individuals through their extension of the social and cultural contexts and histories that precede their development. By extending these contexts, flexible technologies presuppose an unfolding of the world through their design, thereby orienting the persons upon which the technology is deployed. Winner's second perspective on technology seems more straightforwardly aligned with Ahmed's understanding of technology as an orientation device. Thus, the choice to adopt a technology that denies access based upon the organization of people determines the proximity of the technology to people and the human relations that it maintains to them. Following Ahmed, however, it is not the case that technologies as orientation devices simply orient people through the ways in which they extend social contexts or force the adoption of a social context, but rather through the ways in which the extension and adoption of a social context is also the extension and adoption of a history of orienting persons toward or away from "objects" in social, cultural, and physical space.

The histories that precede and serve to shape the body in large part determine how orientation devices orient it: for example, an orientation device developed within a space organized around ability and whiteness should be regarded as the product of histories of colonialism and ableism, which thus serves to maintain the proximities of whiteness and ability to objects in the world. Bodies that do not "fit" the shape of whiteness and ability may, through the disciplinary structures of technology, be disoriented, that is, may be "brought in line" with a world organized around ableism and colonialism (Ahmed 2007). As ways of organizing the world, these technologies continually remake the world in the image of whiteness and ableism and, in addition, produce individuals whose ideological construction maintains this world. Algorithms are quintessentially world-makers. As technologies that are increasingly involved in the ordering of social relations, algorithms enable the maintenance of a world organized around colonialism and ableism, especially through the ways in which they organize conceptions of "intelligence" and the world that proceeds from them.

Following Emily Tucker (2022), in this chapter, I will not use the terms *artificial intelligence* and *machine learning* (or even synonyms of them), except in relation to direct quotations. Rather, I will refer to these technologies as "algorithms." Insofar as the term *artificial intelligence* conceals how algorithmic technologies maintain the organization of the world around ableism and colonialism, as well as how power dynamics structure this world, it implicitly enables the ableist, eugenicist, and racist purposes to which the technologies are put to be perceived as unmitigated goods and advancements in society. By refusing to use the terms *artificial intelligence* and *machine learning*, I aim to point to the histories of colonialism and ableism that are implicit in the deployment and design of algorithms. As Cathy O'Neil (2016) and Winner (1980) have separately noted, we must attend to the political and social purposes that motivate the introduction of these technologies rather than simply try to understand the technologies themselves. In other words, we must try to discern what it is that the persons who design and deploy the technologies seek to accomplish, as well as what the technologies themselves seek to accomplish through their deployment.

Mike Annany (2016) describes an algorithm as a generic solution to a well-defined problem articulated through the language of computer programming. Algorithms, for Annany, serve to filter and sort information by means of the computational and cultural logics of the societies that create them (Annany 2016: 98). On this view, an algorithm is a cultural achievement, operating in line with the narratives that organize the world. Recalling that technology functions as an "orientation device," we can say that algorithms supply orientations through the automation of the social and cultural beliefs that preexist their development, despite the claims that developers of algorithms advance according to which they automate objectivity. Automation is not regurgitation; rather, automation is the imposition of a certain cultural logic upon a given cultural space through the way in which the algorithm organizes the world in application. As Tarleton Gillespie writes, "The algorithmic assessment of information, then, represents a particular knowledge logic, one built on presumptions about what knowledge is and how one should identify its most relevant components" (Gillespie 2014: 168); in other words, the algorithmic assessment information is a way in which to orient people toward what they know about the world, what it is possible to know about the world, and why they should understand the world in this way.

Knowledge, on this critical construal of the logic of algorithms, encompasses everything from the products that a user purchases, to their driving or social media habits, and on to the results of a functional magnetic resonance imaging (fMRI) scan of their brain as compared with a presumed baseline of a "normal" brain with a "normal" neurological structure. In the context of disability and race, these knowledge logics are engaged in the production and classification of people in line with the logics of a world organized around colonialism and race: once deployed, these logics place objects in reach through the orientations supplied. Thus, algorithms construct raced and disabled persons out of a thousand different data points in line with the cultural logics that structure how the world unfolds. Insofar as these technologies are aimed at prediction, algorithms orient raced and disabled persons toward prescriptive outcomes for their lives within a society organized by and around racism and ableism.

It is the automated nature of these platforms that obfuscates how these cultural logics serve to enable algorithms to perform their orienting function. Indeed, the automation of processes of decision-making, of ordering the world, is taken to be one of the defining benefits of these platforms. In describing search engines, Safiya Noble argues that the results of user queries are "delivered to users through a set of steps (algorithms) implemented by programming code and then naturalized as 'objective.' One of the reasons this is seen as a neutral process is because algorithmic, scientific, and mathematical solutions are evaluated through procedural and mechanistic practices" (Noble 2018: 51), all of which purport to remove the human from the process of evaluation and thus reduce the biases of the machine. In the context of disability, this tendency toward objectivity is reflected in the aims of algorithms intended to function as diagnostic aids or predictive technologies. As Sarah Itani and her co-authors observe with reference to the use of machine learning platforms,

> ML [machine learning] methods differ from standard statistical ones in some respects. On the one hand, ML is perceived as a promising alternative way of conducting exploratory data analyses which are inductive and assumption-free. . . . ML has thus attracted growing interest in the sphere of translational neuroscience over the last years, in the hopes of solving questions which currently remain pending—including the etiological basis of ADHD [attention deficit hyperactivity disorder]. (Itani et al. 2019: 2)

As a philosopher of disability, I do not share this optimism about the potential benefits of machine learning for understanding disability.

Typically, there are two types of algorithms: supervised and unsupervised. Supervised platforms rely upon data that a user or developer has labeled as the input material to produce—by classifying and sorting the appropriately labeled data—a desired output. In contrast, unsupervised platforms rely upon existing properties of data supplied to an algorithm in order to perform an analysis according to the "rules" of the algorithm that a programmer has established. In both cases, the human element remains salient: as the means whereby appropriate "rules" are established in unsupervised learning and as the means whereby the appropriate curation of data occurs in supervised learning. Both supervised and unsupervised approaches to algorithmic development and training do not result in true intelligences: they are algorithms configured to sort and process data in increasingly sophisticated ways in line with cultural logics rather than autonomous agents free of human input. As models, they execute processes whereby input is transformed into output results which solve the problems that the developer seeks to resolve through the deployment of the algorithm (Russel and Norvig 2022).

It is in this mode that Itani and her colleagues (2019) have developed an interpretable algorithmic model that seeks to predict attention deficit hyperactivity disorder (ADHD) with a high degree of explanatory power. Described as an "expert aware" approach, the study that produced this model aimed to cultivate clinical trust in explainable models. As the authors have explained, an initial predictive model is developed on unsupervised data, which is subsequently assessed by a domain expert. Although the qualifications and expertise of the domain expert are not explicitly identified in the article that Itani and co-authors have written, the domain expert is likely a clinician trained in the neurophysiology of ADHD, given that the study itself relied upon the ADHD-200 collection, a database of more than 700 resting-state fMRI and other phenotypical datasets. That is, this two-stage approach relies on human expertise to provide more credibility to the results that the predictive model produces, because the machine analysis of neurophysiology may produce errors in interpreting the data. In other words, when an algorithm is combined with human expertise, the algorithm presumably becomes a more effective aid in the prediction of ADHD insofar as this combination increases the credibility of the model or at least the faith that the model will return accurate results and serve as an effective diagnostic aid.

Yet this mode of "training" an algorithm introduces an additional way in which algorithms impose order, that is, serve as orientation devices: medicalization. Insofar as medicalization entails the orientation of the disabled person as a problem to be fixed, as someone who possesses a "malfunctioning" natural capacity, algorithms trained according to a medicalized understanding of the disabled person will limit the capacity of any given disabled person to articulate their lived experience with disability; instead, orientations toward ADHD will rely entirely upon the authoritative prescriptions of medicine and the results of analytic platforms. As Cynthia Bennett and Os Keyes put it, "By adding technical and scientific authority to medical authority, people subject to medical contexts are not only not granted power, but are even further disempowered, with even less legitimacy given to the patient's voice" (Bennett and Keyes 2020).

Medicalization—the institutional process that controls access to diagnosis, treatment, and accommodation of disability—has become what Adele Clarke and her co-authors (2010) call "biomedicalization," which they define as "the increasingly complex, multisited, multidirectional processes of medicalization that today are being both extended and reconstituted through the emergent social forms and practices of a highly and increasingly technoscientific biomedicine" (Clarke et al. 2010: 48). Biomedicalization further extends the operation of algorithms as orientation devices that maintain the organization of the world around racism and ableism. For biomedicalization increasingly determines access to housing, employment, education, and health-care treatments, in service of ordering human relations, on the basis of the computational and cultural logics of an algorithm as an orientation device. In this regard, Clarke and co-authors describe one mode of orientation through the deployment of risk assessment tools and their production of the class of individuals described as "at risk." As these authors explain, biomedical risk assessment tools collate statistical data at the population level and then algorithmically transform this data into meaningful recommendations for individuals who are then classed according to the calculated risk that they will develop diseases such as breast cancer or disabilities such as autism and ADHD.

This point is valuable as traditional statistical methods are often inapplicable for diagnosis, given the complexities of disability as an experience. Insofar as disability itself unfolds in line with the orientations of race, gender, and sexuality, the experience of disability may manifest in ways that traditional statistical analysis is unable to capture. Following Candice Lanius (2015), statistical analysis and the algorithms built upon it constitutes a "technology of mistrust" that operates to question self-reporting about the lived experience of disability. For Lanius, "statistics are used when personal experience is in doubt because the analyst has no intimate knowledge of it. Statistics are consistently used as a technology of the educated elite to discuss the lower classes and subaltern populations, those individuals that are considered unknowable and untrustworthy of delivering their own accounts of their daily life" (Lanius 2015). Given the biomedicalization of disability and health, algorithms—by reducing health and disability to a statistical analysis—provide the means whereby the lived experiences of disabled people are subordinated to the ideological and technological structures of the biomedical-industrial complex and to the ways in which the statistical models that these platforms generate determine how the world unfolds. In doing so, these programs project a "line" for an individual who is dubbed "high risk," a line that, if interrupted early, can save the assessed individual from the inevitability of an undesirable life. Indeed, as Bennett and Keyes note:

> AI systems in this domain are built on the premise that an early diagnosis is a good outcome, that diagnosis leads to possibilities of treatment, support and consideration. Notwithstanding the already-discussed biases in who can access diagnosis (and how diagnostic tests

> are constructed), there are serious questions about whether an earlier diagnosis is a better one. Rather than helping people, earlier diagnoses may harm them. (Bennett and Keyes 2020)

Early detection and prediction platforms serve as a means with which to reorient the disabled body toward appropriate objects prior to its emergence into the world so that the life that the disabled person leads will more closely align with a world organized around ability. The (medicalized) detection and prediction algorithm imposes an orientation that places objects in reach through the ways in which it predetermines the nature of disabled life in advance of arrival of any given disabled person. Thus, these technologies serve to situate a disabled person in line with what Joseph Stramondo describes as an "ideology of pity" (Stramondo 2022) while simultaneously presupposing a naturalized "misfit" (Garland-Thomson 2014), that is, a natural inability of the disabled person to "fit" into the world due to their disability, thereby retaining the organization of the world around ability and obscuring the power relations and politics of technology that indeed make possible this world through these technologies.

In short, an algorithm does not function alone: it is embedded within a social context upon which it relies for the data that it uses to make its predictions. Indeed, as Gillespie notes, "Algorithms are inert, meaningless machines until paired with databases on which to function" (Gillespie 2014: 169). For Gillespie, the automated nature of algorithms requires data to be prepared, organized, and classified so that the algorithm can be applied to it. And so, it is to datasets that I now turn in this chapter.

Datasets, Disability, and Race

The curation of a dataset, the collection of data to which the algorithm is applied, is the process through which an algorithm "learns" to order the world. How datasets are compiled and organized, as well as the cultural logics that govern this organization, supply the initial orientation of the algorithm, which shapes the world that the platform maintains and reproduces through its organization and production of data. That is, the decision about which method of data collection that developers will use is informed by cultural logics that structure what should and should not be included. Second, the process of data collection and transformation into an input suitable for use by an algorithm ignores the world from which the data is drawn, the same world that is organized around ableism and racism. Data collection and organization practices reproduce the orientations of the world and thereby reproduce the inequalities that these orientations maintain.

As Gillespie (2014: 171) notes, the process of categorization and classification of the data that constitute the datasets that algorithms use is itself a political act, albeit one that proceeds from both the orientations that the developer inherits and the algorithm through the purposes to which the platform will be put. The organization of the data to be used by an algorithm is itself an assertion about the nature of the world and the persons within it, an assertion that proceeds from the proximity of the algorithm to the people to whom it is applied. Thus, the cultural logics that inform what should be included in a dataset or in training data and what should not often inform how data is prepared for inclusion in algorithmic decision-making processes. Choices about what to include or how to organize data are also choices that determine how the world should and should not unfold and, hence, choices about the kinds of relations and proximities that any given algorithm enables.

Most algorithms that claim to predict criminality are trained upon the statistical data of criminality for a given location, data that is over-representative of people of color both with respect to how such data is collected and with respect to how the criminal justice system makes manifest institutionalized racism. O'Neil (2016) points to the Level of Service Inventory-Revised (LSI-R), a questionnaire offered to incarcerated persons that has been used to develop models that predict risks of recidivism among incarcerated and formerly incarcerated individuals. This questionnaire comprises a series of questions that classify incarcerated individuals as high, medium, or low risk of reoffense based on the points scored for each response. In a world organized around whiteness, the nature of the questions asked can stand in as a proxy for race. Consider, for example, that Black men are incarcerated at a rate of 2,724 per 100,000 persons and Black offenders serve longer felony sentences on average than white offenders (Oleson 2016). Hence, incarcerated Black people are more likely to have an incarcerated family member or friend than their white counterparts, which adds weight to their scores on the questionnaire. In other words, the LSI-R questions that are asked about friends and family members who have criminal records act as a racial proxy for reoffending. Thus, "Thanks in part to the resulting high score on the evaluation, [the Black offender] gets a longer sentence, locking him away for more years in a prison where he's surrounded by fellow criminals—which raises the likelihood that he'll return to prison" (O'Neil 2016: 28).

While the LSI-R is one example of how data collection reproduces the organization of a world around whiteness, Angwin and co-authors (2016) found that the Correctional Offender Management Profiling for Alternative Sanctions, or COMPAS, recidivism system assessed non-reoffending Black individuals as high risk for reoffense at nearly twice the rate of their white counterparts. In contrast, COMPAS also assessed Black reoffenders as low risk at nearly half the rate of their white counterparts which resulted in more false positives for Black individuals than for white individuals, a finding that maintains whiteness as a default orientation. Despite objections on behalf of Northpointe (Dieterich et al. 2016), the company that developed COMPAS, error rates cannot be used as a measure of fairness. Alexandra Chouldechova (2017) demonstrates that COMPAS has disparate impacts on marginalized populations, and Black individuals specifically, regardless of the choice of fairness measure. Put another way, because of the organization of the world around whiteness, the choice of fairness measure is irrelevant when the data used itself is drawn from a world that presumes in advance the criminality of Black persons.

I want to underscore that the point of this analysis is not to contest fairness measures or to indicate how fairness as a concept proceeds from whiteness as a starting point; rather, the point of this analysis is to indicate how algorithms serve to maintain a world organized around whiteness. Algorithms reproduce and extend an orientation toward Black persons that maintains their subordinated status by positioning them as inherently deviant and criminal. This attribution of deviance and criminality leads to the production of a world organized around whiteness through datafication, converting lived experience into datapoints which can then be fed to an algorithm. Once converted into data, lived experience that only proceeds from whiteness will serve to produce, or reproduce, a world made white. Thus, as Ruha Benjamin notes, "If we consider that institutional racism in this country is an ongoing unnatural disaster, then crime prediction algorithms should more accurately be called crime production algorithms" (Benjamin 2018: 86). Individuals who live within zones designated as potential hotspots for crime by predictive policing algorithms will be judged as potential criminals through the deployment of the algorithm. Predictive policing algorithms thus produce a world that takes whiteness as the point from which it unfolds by imposing an order continuous with the assumption of inherent Black criminality. The designation of a crime "hotspot" is a way in which to order the social relations into which individuals can enter and invites modes of interaction with law enforcement officers on the basis of the claim to "know" the inherent criminality of a given location. This speculative racism increases the possibility that police brutality will take place, exacerbates the production of inherent criminality as a fact of Blackness, and reinforces the maintenance of a world made white through institutionalized racism.

Algorithms also produce health inequalities and disparities in health care. A 2019 study of a health-care algorithm found that its design, which used cost of care to predict future health-care needs, prioritized the health needs of white patients over Black patients with more severe health needs (Obermeyer et al. 2019: 447–53). Because Black patients in the system typically had lower incomes than white patients and therefore spent less than white patients on health care, the algorithm treated the Black patients as if they were at a lower health risk, despite the fact that they had significantly more health-care needs than white patients. The study found that these Black patients were excluded from extra care programs and specialist referrals because their estimated risk score (based on their health-care spending) did not rise to the levels where they would be considered for such programs. In short, this supposedly race-neutral health-care program reinscribed racial and economic disparities by design, despite the intention to avoid such disparities, due to the way in which race as an orientation structures the proximity of persons toward health care. As the social determinants of health care—such as income—are organized by a world with whiteness at its center, inequality is thus a product of how datasets inherit the orientations of the worlds that supply the data that they use.

Algorithms, rather than measure an objective phenomenon, obscure the power relations of racism and ableism by naturalizing, through technological means, poorer outcomes as an inevitability. This naturalization disconnects the data from actual social contexts in which it is embedded. The choices in the kinds of data supplied to the algorithm maintain how it produces results both socially and technologically, which reifies inequalities through the representation of a "ground truth," that is, the "truth" that underlies the data on which the platform is trained and which structures the result produced by the platform. As the purported "truth" that the algorithm claims to produce through its classification of data, a ground truth is indicative of how the world unfolds. Thus, the applications of an algorithm and the production of a ground truth through data curation are an additional way in which algorithms order the world and maintain ability and race at its center.

Ground truths emerge in accordance with the ways in which developers label training data. Consider, for example, how an algorithm would distinguish a dog from other animals. Such a platform might succeed at recognizing a corgi, beagle, husky, and a wolf as dogs or canines. However, this hypothetical platform might fail were it tasked with determining domesticated dogs from wolves if the given dataset lacked a sufficiently robust ground truth that determined its outputs; that is, the platform would likely fail if the reality upon which it was trained were not nuanced enough with respect to the question asked. Put simply, as Osman Aka, Ken Burke, Alex Bauerle, Christina Greer, and Margaret Mitchell (2021) indicate, "If the ground truth annotations in a sparsely labelled dataset are potentially biased, then the premise of a fairness metric that 'normalizes' model prediction patterns to ground truth patterns may be incomplete" (Aka et al. 2021: 327). In essence, if the reality of the developers proceeds from a world organized around their orientation and the organization of that data proceeds from that orientation, the product that the algorithm generates will be a world that is distant from the worlds of people whose orientations the developers do not share.

Aka and co-authors (2021) are primarily concerned with how improper labeling of datasets creates inaccurate ground truths that result in a concept of fairness that would not resolve bias; however, this failure is better understood as ground truths whose concept of fairness maintains a single orientation as the point from which the world unfolds. Ground truths may be inaccurate insofar as they exclude certain persons from the worlds that algorithms organize. Datasets, like the bodies that make them up, are shaped by what is near to them. The determination of proximity, in the context of a dataset, is a determination made through how the world unfolds from the orientation that the programmer adopts. If the orientation of the programmer does not place certain people in proximity to them, these people will not be included in the dataset, resulting in an algorithm that develops a "ground truth" which does not include some persons, some ways of being in the world. As an example, facial recognition and emotional identification platforms trained on publicly available datasets often reproduce ableist and racist assumptions about the expression of emotion because these datasets are drawn from images of predominantly white, Western, nondisabled men. So, for example, these technologies will attempt to masculinize the features of Black women (Guest and Birhane 2020) in line with an orientation toward beauty that takes whiteness as its default. These same technologies often fail to recognize the facial expressions of many people with disabilities (such as people with cleft lip or palate, achondroplasia, Down syndrome, or Parkinson's disease) because individuals with these disabilities are not included in the datasets of facial expression and emotional display (Guo et al. 2019). Insofar as public datasets are circulated among algorithms and their developers in a form of "citational politics," or a politics of who is included in what corpus, the repetition of exclusion generates a politics of data curation in which some people simply do not exist.

In this vein, Jutta Treviranus (2018) presents a case wherein she sought to see how machine vision technologies, intended to help algorithmically guided (or "driverless") automobiles navigate busy intersections, would respond to individuals who acted unexpectedly within intersections. In this context, the idea that something is "unexpected" may be reframed as "out of line" or "does not conform to the familiarity with the world" that the training data for these algorithmically guided vehicles has organized. Thus, Treviranus displayed to the vehicles a capture of a disabled friend navigating the intersection in her wheelchair, albeit backward. The backward motion of the friend is valuable, for, as Treviranus notes, this manner of locomotion was the most effective way for the friend to navigate the world through her disability, despite it being out of line with the normative assumptions for how she should navigate the world. As Treviranus writes:

> When I presented a capture of my friend to the learning models, they all chose to run her over. I was told to try again once the learning models had been exposed to more data about people using wheelchairs in intersections. I was told that the learning models were immature models that were not yet smart enough to recognize people in wheelchairs, they would expose them to learning data that included many people using wheelchairs in intersections. When I came back to test out the smarter models they ran her over with greater confidence. I can only presume that they decided, based on the average behavior of wheelchairs, that wheelchairs go in the opposite direction. (Treviranus 2018)

These remarks from Treviranus indicate two things: first, the immature models of the algorithmically guided vehicles were trained using a dataset that did not include wheelchair users, thereby resulting in the institution of an order that did not include wheelchair users. Therefore, the reality that the algorithm claimed to represent placed intersections out of reach for wheelchair users through their lack of inclusion; it was a world where wheelchair users did not exist, a world that could have resulted in the deaths of wheelchair users. Second, when the algorithm was updated to include data of wheelchair users, this data included the average behavior of wheelchair users only, such that individuals who might use wheelchairs in non-normative ways were excluded: only wheelchair users who appeared in line with dominant assumptions about how a wheelchair should be used were "visible" within the world that unfolded through the technology. The "invisibility" of non-normative wheelchair users in the so-called smarter model resulted in the model's higher confidence to run over non-normative wheelchair users.

Algorithms also inherit structures of marginalization according to the ways in which language maintains and reifies the orientations of ability and whiteness. As I pointed out, algorithms generate a "ground truth" through the association between the data supplied to the platform and the labels assigned to that data, a "ground truth" that results in a negative meaning that emerges between the label and what is labeled. Data labels emerge from an orientation toward the world, resulting in outputs that align with the orientation of the world around ableism and racism. Thus, "if we build an intelligent system that learns enough about the properties of language to be able to understand and produce it, in the process it will also acquire historic cultural associations, some of which can be objectionable. . . . If machine learning technologies used for, say, resumé screening were to imbibe cultural stereotypes, it may result in prejudiced outcomes" (Caliskson 2017: 10). That so-called intelligent systems which learn the properties of language adopt cultural stereotypes has significant implications for algorithms known as "natural language processors" (NLPs) that a variety of applications use to (for example) combat online abuse by identifying objectionable language, predict hate speech, and assess applicants for employment or education. Used properly, NLPs can be a key element in our information ecosystem, capable of preventing violence against the most marginalized communities. Like all algorithms, however, this function of NLPs is constrained by how the world unfolds as a product of the histories of ableism and racism.

In the context of content moderation, Thomas Davidson, Debasmita Bhattacharya, and Ingmar Weber (2019) found that the language classifiers applied to content on X (formerly Twitter)—"tweets"—that is conveyed in African American Vernacular English (AAVE) are flagged as sexism, hate speech, harassment, and abuse at higher rates than tweets conveyed in Standard American English (SAE), which is taken to be the "default" form of English. In this regard, it is important to note the long history of linguistic marginalization of AAVE (previously referred to as "ebonics") through a perceived association of AAVE with poverty, criminality, and a lack of intelligence. For example, Fern Johnson and Richard Buttny's (1982) study found that if a speaker used AAVE, white participants in the study described the speaker in negative terms and relied upon stereotypical descriptions of African Americans to supplement this judgment more than they did if a speaker used SAE. In addition, John Russell Rickford (1997) notes that even research that seeks to reaffirm the value of AAVE, specifically its grammatical structure, can rely upon linguistic data that maintains negative stereotypes of the African American community, stereotypes that themselves have their ground in the histories of colonialism that seek to, as Ahmed notes, remake the world in the image of whiteness. This history of treating AAVE as marginal, broken, associated with poverty, criminality, and illiteracy remakes the English language in the image of whiteness, thereby positioning SAE as the point from which appropriate communication can unfold. NLP platforms inherit this bias insofar as they, too, take SAE as the point from which a linguistic world unfolds. This orientation positions AAVE as a "misfit" within such a world. Databases of ordinary language, upon which NLP platforms are trained, retain this bias and serve to orient users away from AAVE as an appropriate form of English.

Further, Davidson, Bhattacharya, and Weber's 2019 study on NLP algorithms found that the classifiers disproportionately penalize "Black-aligned tweets," including one classifier who flagged close to 18 percent of the assessed corpus of Black tweets as abusive compared to 8 percent of the white corpus that they assessed. This elevated classification of AAVE tweets as more abusive or as a more violent form of speech than tweets in SAE persisted even when these language classification programs were applied to

AAVE and SAE tweets which contained language that was more clearly related to negative or abusive language. In short, the NLP platforms used in the study relied on a "ground truth" that aligned with the historical perception and treatment of Black people as more violent than white people and associations of Black speech with violence, criminality, and illiteracy. These perceptions and associations are especially problematic in the context of Black Twitter, as André Brock Jr. describes it:

> Black Twitter is an online gathering (not quite a community) of Twitter users who identify as Black and employ Twitter features to perform Black discourses, share Black cultural common places, and build social affinities. While there are a number of non-Black and people of color Twitter users who have been "invited to the cookout," so to speak, participating in Black Twitter requires a deep knowledge of Black culture, commonplaces, and digital practices. . . . While their use of Twitter accrues to them a technological identity that intersects with their racial and gendered selves, Black Twitter users are as heterogeneous as the community they hail from. (Brock 2020: 81)

Insofar as membership in Black Twitter requires a deep understanding of "Black culture, commonplaces, and digital practices" (Brock 2020: 81), how NLPs position Black tweets has implications for the entire community space that emerges through Black Twitter. To take the example of digital practices, we may understand their emergence as how Black offline customs are translated through the medium of Twitter into a unique mode of conduct. Black digital practices are therefore the transformation of cultural customs of Blackness through computing technologies that enable the legibility of users *as Black* rather than simply as generic users of generic digital practices and platforms.

Brock continues: "Black Twitter illuminates the service's role as a cultural communication medium, transcending the size limitations and conversational incoherence of chat rooms while allowing users to participate in open-ended community-building discourses in near real time" (Brock 2020: 121). Black Twitter is the result of the legibility of Twitter users as Black through the translation of their offline customs into online digital practice and is itself actively engaged in the collective resistance against a world made white. Thus, insofar as NLPs flag the majority of Black tweets as hate speech or violent speech, they entail an orientation toward the Black struggle for liberation and Black community-building, particularly in online spaces, as hostile (toward whites). Indeed, Black Lives Matter and Black feminism, which themselves are responses to a culture of white supremacy, or whiteness generally, have been transformed in an online space due to the creation of Black Twitter as a space "to perform Black discourses, share Black cultural common places, and build social affinities" (81). NLPs and language classification platforms orient these communities as, at best, "misfits" and, at worst, oppositional to the appropriate unfolding of the world.

Analogously, NLP programs "learn" the biases against disabled people that are embedded in everyday language. The negative affect of language about disability emerges from language habits of a world that takes disability to be an objective feature of the body that predicts negative life outcomes. In their respective feminist work on disability and language, Vivian May and Beth Ferri (2005) and Sami Schalk (2013) examine the constitutive effects of ableist language. May and Ferri trace a history of feminist scholarship that uses disability metaphors to convey the effects of inequitable power relations. As they explain, blindness, immobility, paralysis, and other disabilities have historically been metaphorically associated with the inequalities that women experience. Read through Ahmed's work, this history forms a citational practice of language that orients feminist scholarship toward disabled people through the association of disability with negative power structures. This citational history, as an orientation device, maintains the discriminatory attitudes that Stramondo and Rosemarie Garland-Thomson point to as emerging from the perception of disability as inherently negative.

Schalk (2013), through an analysis of various feminist writings, highlights the systemic character of this linguistic use of disability: not only do these metaphors emerge from the ableism of the broader society, they are obstacles to building solidarity between the feminist community and the disabled community. Thus, as Schalk puts it, "This use, in feminist texts, of disability to represent stigma—or, in the case of the two metaphors analyzed above, restriction, or woundedness—could alienate disabled readers from these texts and, therefore, prevent effective cross-group and ally actions" (Schalk 2013), thereby rendering coalitions in the face of the intersecting threats that both feminist and disabled communities confront more difficult. This history of disabled metaphor is simultaneously a history of raced metaphor: Schalk points to the ways in which both Charlotte Perkins-Gilman and Margaret Sanger deployed "positive" eugenic rhetoric and rhetoric about women's roles as breeders in order to encourage better education and treatment of white, middle-class, able-bodied women who would give birth to the next generation of eugenically sound, rather than "weak" or "feeble-minded," "children," a deployment of eugenics that was itself in the service of a world that unfolded along lines of colonialism and ableism, despite the supposedly progressive aims of the (predominantly white) feminist movement. Put another way, the citational politics of the use of ableist metaphors within feminist scholarship and feminist history result in a world that unfolds from the orientations of ableism and colonialism such that disability and race attain a negative affect which is circulated through these communities.

Ableist metaphors in feminist scholarship are not an anomaly: they are an intensification of the negative associations of disability that emerge in ordinary language and are indicative of how language in its entirety is oriented around ableism as a norm that positions some bodies as "at home" within the spaces that language organizes. It is this orientation that NLPs, trained on ordinary language datasets, learn when they learn the negative associations of disability that emerge due to the assumption that disability leads to negative life outcomes. Given the deployment of such programs in the context of a variety of applications—including content moderation and resumé analysis—when NLP programs inherit this orientation, the result is a world wherein disabled persons are relegated to the status of "misfit."

In a study of the Bidirectional Encoder Representation from Transformers (BERT)—an NLP platform whose uses include inferring the intention of search text when supplied to a search engine (such as Google Search) or for content moderation (such as Facebook's own RoBERTA)—Ben Hutchinson and his co-authors found that "for queries derived from most of the phrases referencing persons who do have disabilities, a larger percentage of predicted words produce negative sentiment scores. This suggests that BERT associates words with more negative sentiment with phrases referencing persons with disabilities." Among the words associated with persons with disabilities were these: *homelessness*, *addiction*, *violence*, and *unemployment* (Hutchinson et al. 2020). As Hutchinson and his co-authors note, although these associations are in part a consequence of the contexts in which NLP data is gathered, they are also products of the historical associations of disability with deficiency and a lower quality of life that shape the discursive contexts in which disability is discussed in everyday language.

The "downstream" consequences of this inheritance are the marginalization of disabled people's ability to participate and gather in online communities. Insofar as NLP programs like BERT associate disability with negative sentiment, and "Since the primary intended use of this model is to facilitate the moderation of online comments, higher scores when mentioning disabilities can result in non-toxic comments mentioning disabilities being flagged at a disproportionately high rate. In practical terms, this might result in innocuous sentences discussing disability being suppressed" (Hutchinson et al. 2020). In other words, through their generation and inheritance of negative associations with disability, NLP programs (such as RoBERTA) and search platforms (such as Google Search) result in the suppression of information related to disability and the marginalization of online communities organized through the online discourses of disabled persons. While there is little literature on the formation of online cultural spaces organized around disability, there is considerable literature on online activism as enabling community formation. The #CripTheVote movement has resulted in forms of social movement unique to the disability community by leveraging the unique properties of social media and other online fora, simultaneously enabling the emergence of disabled persons and a vital and engaged political constituency oriented toward enabling the political advocacy of disabled persons (Mann 2018; Trevisan 2019). With respect to the #CripTheVote hashtag, furthermore, Christina Cedillo notes that "the hashtag also allows disabled users to connect with others, facilitating the formation of disabled communities. That is, disabled users can decide for themselves how they wish to come together to constitute a community and with whom" (Cedillo 2021).

Cedillo's point is twofold: first, the online nature of digital activism allows disabled persons, who cannot navigate a world wherein they are a misfit, to participate in advocacy on behalf of their community and their political needs. Second, this participation results in the cultivation of spaces and communities that are defined on the terms of the disabled person. This access to options pushes back against a blanket organization of the disabled community as a uniform mass with identical needs (Cedillo 2021). The nature of online community formation results in a sharing of experience across differences of disability in an environment of support and validation that minimizes the possibilities of ableist stigma and rejection by enabling users to manage and determine exactly which aspects of their disabled identity they disclose, to whom, and in what way. Moreover, the nature of online community formation also allows users to withdraw from the community on their own terms, which may not be possible in offline spaces or spaces that are primarily organized around the perceptions of able-bodied individuals (Miller 2017). Thus, as Cedillo notes: "This results in the formation of communities that may or may not be as easily identifiable to outsiders as those composed of people who share cultural or other characteristics, but they are communities, nonetheless" (Cedillo 2021). As communities, they extend the disabled body through space without hindrance while simultaneously providing support for the activities of disabled people.

How algorithms maintain the centrality of ableism makes it more challenging to discover and engage with disabled communities. Google Search results for the query "disabled community" more often return results for organizations, spaces, and places that take able-bodied or neurotypical orientations toward disability as the default, rather than return results for digital community spaces that unfold from the orientations of disabled persons. Furthermore, Google Search returns results for community spaces that proceed from the perspectives of caregivers, parents, physicians, or other nondisabled "experts" on the experiences of disabled persons (Cedillo 2021). Google's search algorithm, itself one of the downstream applications of NLP technology such as BERT, maintains the centrality of ability in organizing the world, even when the world that is sought is one in which disabled persons are "at home." NLP applications such as Google Search and RoBERTA thus suppress the experiences of disabled persons by ensuring that the understandings of disability and the communities found unfold in line with the orientations of ableism. These online communities supply an orientation toward disability that does not proceed from the experience of disability itself, but rather from the narratives about disability that nondisabled people supply. Insofar as algorithms and NLPs inherit the orientations of disability from culture at large, they impose an order upon the world that results in a world organized around ability.

The preceding discussion demonstrates how the combination of algorithms and datasets that are organized around race and ability as a dominant orientation toward the world entails a world that unfolds to maintain ableism and racism as a central orientation (in Ahmed's sense). My discussion thus far also indicates that the organization of a dataset is not simply the collection of objective, unbiased data: it is the imposition of an order upon the world. This order takes as its starting point the orientations of the people responsible for determining the ends, the kinds of social relationships that should emerge through the deployment of technology. Taken in the conjoined context of Winner and Ahmed, the process of compiling and generating a database, as well as connecting it to an algorithm, is a process that determines how the world should unfold, who should be included in this world, and in what way. As I have pointed out, furthermore, these platforms also determine how disability unfolds in the world, the extent to which it is included in the world, and in what way.

Algorithms and the Orientation of Disability

While the previous discussion points to how the technical aspects of algorithms serve to maintain a world organized around whiteness and ability, the application of algorithms to disability also organizes disability along whiteness and medicalization. Under a medical model of disability, disability is represented as a deviation from "normal" human functioning that negatively impacts the life outcomes of the person diagnosed as disabled. On this view, disabled persons suffer from biological abnormalities or dysfunctions in need of treatment or assessment by medical or scientific authorities and institutions (Siebers 2008). The medical model of disability constructs both disability and normality through the orientations that scientific and medical fields produce which, as Shelley Tremain (2017) notes, casts impairments and abnormalities as the allegedly prediscursive foundations of disability that exist outside of historical locations and cultural conditions. Disability, itself represented as an objective biological feature or characteristic, is treated as an inherent or intrinsic property of a given disabled person rather than as an assignation that is shaped by social, cultural, or political forces that have already structured how disability should be understood and in what way society should respond to it

Our "models" of disability are abstract representations of processes that are used to determine how we respond in the world and serve to order the world. Algorithms, too, are models: how and what they model are, as demonstrated in the previous sections, grounded in the kinds of data they are supplied. Insofar as algorithms draw statistical correlations between data to supply a range of predictive actions, some ways in which to model disability are more amenable to algorithms than others. To create a model, we must first choose what to include in the model which involves the simplification of the world into a form that we can easily deploy in a variety of situations (O'Neil 2013). In the context of disability, this simplification requires the determination and selection of what will count as the relevant features of disability for inclusion in datasets. For example, data scientists rely on simplified versions of disability as represented through "objective" measures such as electroencephalograms (EEGs) and other neurological data gathered through biomedical technologies. This reliance on medical diagnoses to identify the relevant features of disability would enable only actors with access to the institutionalized structures of diagnosis to form the ground that trains the algorithm. In contrast, data that draws upon more social determinants of disability—for example, how a given disabled person identifies as disabled, the nature of their understanding of disability, even their choice about "person-first" or "diagnosis-first" language—can structure how they are included and thus positioned within the models of disability that algorithms generate.

The reliance on the medical model of disability is due to the simplicity of medicalized data and the ease whereby this data can be entered into an algorithm. Sociocultural determinants of disability are harder for algorithms to model and process than medical diagnoses that derive solely from the medical model of disability (Tilmes 2022). The emphasis on medical data as inputs into algorithms thus colludes to position the medical model as the hegemonic orientation of disability which, as Nicholas Tilmes writes, "crowds out analysis of the socio-political processes that inform it. After all, that disability becomes legible to AI in terms of measurable diagnoses does not entail that AI is objective but highlights its alignment with the medical model" (Tilmes 2022: 21).

It is this alignment with the medical model that prevents algorithms from adequately modeling disability. In the context of chronic pain, Rhonda Moore,

Ross Smith, and Qi Liu (2020) note that individuals who experience chronic pain may also experience invisible disabilities that existing diagnostic tools do not easily capture. Insofar as chronic pain is also an encultured, subjective experience (Tremain 2017) that varies according to the lived experience of the disabled person, current data curation methodologies—such as numerical pain scales and behavioral assessments of pain which rely upon a disabled person's self-report—may not adequately capture the experience of chronic pain (Moore, Smith, and Liu 2020). Even in the context of data-driven pain assessment methodologies—such as assessment tools that rely upon facial recognition or analysis of EEG data from individuals who experience pain—self-assessments continue to be used as a comparison for the results of the data-driven methodologies (Levitt and Saab 2019; Lötsch and Ultsch 2018). Thus, the effect of data-driven analysis of chronic pain remains subject to data gaps due to (for example) subjective clinical interpretations of pain states, the correlation of self-assessments of pain states with data, and the cultural context in which the pain is assessed.

Racist beliefs about the nature of pain persist in medical contexts. For example, Todd and co-authors found that Black patients are routinely prescribed less pain management treatment than their white counterparts for severe fractures in emergency room situations, a finding that parallels their earlier (1993) work reporting that nonwhite Hispanic patients also received less pain medication for similar injuries. Additionally, Black children are less likely to be prescribed any pain medication for moderate pain, and physicians are, in general, more likely to underestimate the pain that Black patients experience relative to the pain that their white counterparts experience (Goyal, Kuppermann, and Cleary 2015). Further, both white physicians and nonphysicians have been shown to endorse age-old racist beliefs about Black people's relation to pain and about their bodies in general, including the beliefs that Black people feel less pain, have thicker skin, and clot more quickly than their white counterparts. Put plainly, as Kelly Hoffman and her colleagues note, "a substantial number of white people—laypersons with no medical training and medical students and residents—hold beliefs about biological differences between blacks and whites, many of which are false and even fantastical in nature" (Hoffman et al. 2016: 4300). In short, the organization of the world—including the medical world—around whiteness remakes even the perception of a patient's pain in the image of whiteness, thereby resulting in the presumption that Black pain is, itself, out of line with the "normal" experience of pain as experienced from within the orientation of whiteness.

The persistence, in medical contexts, of racist beliefs about pain conditions the algorithmic assessment of pain, which relies on the cultivation and organization of a "ground truth" for pain experiences, creating data gaps and, ultimately, health-care disparities along lines of race. As Moore, Smith, and Liu note:

> Existing data curation methods reinforce these data gaps, drawing lines between clinically verifiable pain and disability experiences, rendering others as invisible, marginalized, or as outliers. Consequently, patients may suffer for years due to misclassification of symptoms, leading to delayed diagnosis, treatment and poor pain and disability outcomes. . . . All these issues contribute to different types of bias at different points across the life course of the data—as integral parts of the data inputs and outputs—in the thought of what data is relevant to the problem, in curation decisions around what data to collect or exclude, in processes of screening, assessments, exclusions and analyses of patient social and clinical data based on the perceived visibility and judgement of the validity of the pain and disability. (Moore, Smith, and Liu 2020)

Chronic pain is not the only disability oriented around whiteness. Neurotypicality, for example, is also oriented around whiteness. In the context of algorithmic assessment, analysis, and prediction of Autism, Os Keyes (2020) notes that although race was rarely mentioned in the corpus of articles that they used in their analysis of the application of algorithms to the experience of Autistic persons, this apparent absence did not imply that the framing of Autism was not itself gendered and racialized. Indeed, it is the organization of Autism as proximate to whiteness as an orientation with respect to diagnosis of certain marginalized persons that enables algorithms to reproduce Autism as disability in the image of whiteness. This proximity is demonstrated by: first, children of color are typically seen by at least six clinicians before they are given an Autism diagnosis; and, second, children of color are more likely to receive some diagnosis other than Autism due to a lack of clinician training in the recognition of symptoms of Autism in children of color, implicit bias among providers, and the (mis)attribution of Autism symptoms to behavioral difficulties that are stereotypically associated with children of color (Aylward, Gal-Szabo, and Taraman 2021). The contents of the datasets upon which these platforms are trained, and curation of these datasets results in a citational practice that produces Autism in proximity to whiteness. Algorithms reinforce and maintain this proximity through their application and connection with these datasets. Thus, as Bennett and Keyes note, "Dependence on diagnostic tools which are based on the experiences of those already diagnosed thus risk replicating these biases, providing seemingly-objective rigor to determinations that a child presenting inconsistently with (white, assigned male at birth) autistic children cannot be autistic, and should be gatekept out of support systems" (Bennett and Keyes 2020: 2). In short, the reliance on these diagnostic tools results in both an inability to correctly diagnose children of color as Autistic and the orientation of Autism as proximate to whiteness, such that Autism shares a likeness with whiteness that erases, or renders marginal, Autistics of color.

Attempts to algorithmically predict and assess other forms of neurotypicality also contribute to the organization of the world and disability around whiteness through the curation of datasets used in the development of these platforms. The ADHD-200 competition dataset is one example of this phenomenon. As described by the competition website, the ADHD-200 sample consists of "776 resting-state fMRI and anatomical datasets aggregated across 8 independent imaging sites, 491 of which were obtained from typically developing individuals and 285 in children and adolescents with ADHD (ages: 7-21 years old). Accompanying phenotypic information includes: diagnostic status, dimensional ADHD symptom measures, age, sex, intelligence quotient (IQ) and lifetime medication status" (ADHD-200). A global competition that included twenty-one international teams, the ADHD-200 competition was an attempt to provide a global, field-wide effort to advance neuroscientific understanding of the etiology of ADHD through the application of algorithms to the ADHD-200 sample. Of note, while the sample included gender and IQ measures, it did not include a quantifier for race. Importantly, children of color are more than 69 percent less likely to receive an ADHD diagnosis than their white counterparts, thereby resulting in an underdiagnosis of ADHD among children of color and, among Black children, a higher likelihood of misdiagnosis due to racial stereotypes (Rizvi and Mrini 2022).

Researchers in algorithmic applications to ADHD have not critically engaged the possibility of racial bias in their research programs nor have they considered the effect of racial bias on data collection, including the demographics of research participants, selection of results, and applications of technology (Rizvi and Mrini 2022). Additionally, extant research has not addressed questions of access to technological modes of assessment nor the culturally specific nature of how these technologies engage in their assessment. This failure to account for racial bias is also a concern with algorithmic detection of Autism insofar as cultural distinctions in interpersonal communication, one way in which algorithms determine the presence of autism, can vary across cultures. Algorithms that are not trained on culturally sensitive clinical assessments for Autism or deployed in conjunction with culturally competent clinicians can result in lower predictive accuracy when the algorithm is deployed (Tariq et al. 2019). The limited availability of culturally sensitive clinical assessments due to both the proximity of disability to whiteness—a proximity maintained by the ways in which histories of colonialism shape access to assessment and diagnosis—and the research agendas of programmers and institutions with a vested interest in algorithmic prediction of disability (though not in the critical appraisal of these programs), as well as the ongoing organization of the fields of medicine and computing sciences around whiteness serve to continue to structure disability as both a product of medicine and of whiteness.

References

Ahmed, Sara (2006), *Queer Phenomenology: Orientations, Objects, Others*, Durham: Duke University Press.

Ahmed, Sara (2007), "A Phenomenology of Whiteness," *Feminist Theory* 8 (2): 149–68. https://doi.org/10.1177/1464700107078139.

Aka, Osman, Ken Burke, Alex Bauerle, Christina Greer, and Margaret Mitchell (2021), "Measuring Model Biases in the Absence of Ground Truth," in *Proceedings of the 2021 AAAI/ACM Conference on AI, Ethics, and Society*, 327–35.

Angwin, J., J. Larson, S. Mattu, and L. Kirchner (2016), "Machine Bias," *ProPublica*, May. Available at: https://www.propublica.org/article/machine-bias-risk-assessments-in-criminal-sentencing (accessed July 21, 2023).

Annany, Mike (2016), "Toward an Ethics of Algorithms," *Science, Technology, and Human Values* 41 (1): 93–117. https://doi.org/10.1177/0162243915606523sthv.sagepub.com.

Aylward, Brandon S., Diana E. Gal-Szabo, and Sharief Taraman (2021), "Racial, Ethnic, and Sociodemographic Disparities in Diagnosis of Children with Autism Spectrum Disorder," *Journal of Developmental and Behavioral Pediatrics: JDBP* 42 (8): 682–9. https://doi.org/10.1097/DBP.0000000000000996.

Benjamin, Ruha (2018), *Race after Technology: Abolitionist Tools for the New Jim Code*, Cambridge: John Wiley and Sons.

Bennett, Cynthia L. and Os Keyes (2020), "What is the Point of Fairness? Disability, AI and the Complexity of Justice," *ACM SIGACCESS Accessibility and Computing* 125. https://doi.org/10.1145/3386296.3386301.

Birhane, Abeba and Olivia Guest (2020), "Towards Decolonising Computational Sciences," arXiv preprint arXiv:2009.14258.

Brock, Andre (2020), *Distributed Blackness: African American Cybercultures*, New York: New York University Press.

Caliskan, Aylin, Joanna J. Bryson, and Arvind Narayanan (2017), "Semantics Derived Automatically from Language Corpora Contain Human-Like Biases," *Science* 356 (6334): 183–6. https://doi.org/10.1126/science.aal4230.

Cedillo, Christina V. (2021), "#cripthevote: Disability Activism, Social Media, and the Campaign for Communal Visibility," *Reflections: A Journal of Community-Engaged Writing and Rhetoric*, Summer, Special Issue: "Activism and Academia in Community Work," Jasmine Villa, Yndalecio Isaac Hinojosa, and Isabel Baca, eds. Available at: https://reflectionsjournal.net/2021/06/cripthevote-disability-activism-social-media-and-the-campaign-for-communal-visibility/ (accessed July 21, 2023).

Chouldechova, Alexandra (2017), "Fair Prediction with Disparate Impact: A Study of Bias in Recidivism Prediction Instruments," *Big Data* 5 (2): 153–63. https://doi.org/10.1089/big.2016.0047.

Clarke, Adele E., Laura Mamo, Jennifer Ruth Fosket, Jennifer R. Fishman, and Janet K. Shim, eds. (2010), *Biomedicalization: Technoscience, Health, and Illness in the U.S.*, Duke University Press. https://doi.org/10.2307/j.ctv125jk5c.

Davidson, Thomas, Debasmita Bhattacharya, and Ingmar Weber (2019), "Racial Bias in Hate Speech and Abusive Language Detection Datasets," arXiv preprint arXiv:1905.12516.

Dieterich, William, Christina Mendoza, and Tim Brennan (2016), "COMPAS Risk Scales: Demonstrating Accuracy Equity and Predictive Parity," *Northpointe Inc* 7 (4): 1.

Garland-Thomson, Rosemarie (2014), "The Story of My Work: How I became Disabled," *Disability Studies Quarterly* 34 (2). https://doi.org/10.18061/dsq.v34i2.4254.

Gillespie, Tarleton (2014), "The Relevance of Algorithms," in T. Gillespie, P. Boczkowski, and K. Foot (eds.), *Media Technologies: Essays on Communication, Materiality, and Society*, 167–95, Cambridge, MA: MIT Press.

Goyal, Monika K., Nathan Kuppermann, Sean D. Cleary, Stephen J. Teach, and James M. Chamberlain (2015), "Racial Disparities in Pain Management of Children with Appendicitis in Emergency Departments," *JAMA Pediatrics* 169 (11): 996–1002.

Guo, A., Ece Kamar, Jennifer W. Vaughan, Hannah Wallach, and Meredith R. Morris (2019), "Toward Fairness in AI for People with Disabilities: A Research Roadmap," arXiv preprint arXiv:1907.02227.

Hoffman, Kelly M., Sophie Trawalter, Jordan R. Axt, and M. Norman Oliver (2016), "Racial Bias in Pain Assessment and Treatment Recommendations, and False Beliefs about Biological Differences between Blacks and Whites," *Proceedings of the National Academy of Sciences* 113 (16): 4296–301.

Hutchinson, Ben, Vinodkumar Prabhakaran, Emily Denton, Kellie Webster, Yu Zhong, and Stephen Denuyl (2020), "Social Biases in NLP Models as Barriers for Persons with Disabilities," arXiv preprint arXiv:2005.00813.

Itani, Sarah, Mandy Rossignol, Fabian Lecron, and Philippe Fortemps (2019), "Towards Interpretable Machine Learning Models for Diagnosis Aid: A Case Study on Attention Deficit/Hyperactivity Disorder," *PLoS ONE* 14 (4): e0215720. https://doi.org/10.1371/journal.pone.0215720.

Johnson, Fern and Richard Buttny (1982), "White Listeners' Responses to 'Sounding Black' and 'Sounding White': The Effects of Message Content on Judgments about Language," *Communication Monographs* 49: 33–49.

Keyes, Os (2020), "Automating Autism: Disability, Discourse, and Artificial Intelligence," *Journal of Sociotechnical Critique* 1 (1): 1–31. https://doi.org/10.25779/89bj-j396.

Lanius, Candice (2015), "Fact Check: Your Demand for Statistical Proof is Racist." Available at: https://thesocietypages.org/cyborgology/2015/01/12/fact-check-your-demand-for-statistical-proof-is-racist/ (accessed July 21, 2023).

Levitt, Joshua and Carl Y. Saab (2019), "What does a 'Pain Biomarker' mean and can a Machine be taught to Measure Pain?" *Neuroscience Letters* 702: 40–3. https://doi.org/10.1016/j.neulet.2018.11.038.

Lötsch, Jörn and Alfred Ultsch (2018), "Machine Learning in Pain Research," *Pain* 159 (4): 623–30. https://doi.org/10.1097/j.pain.0000000000001118.

Mann, Benjamin W. (2018), "Rhetoric of Online Disability Activism: #CripTheVote and Civic Participation," *Communication, Culture and Critique* 11 (4): 604–21.

May, Vivian M. and Beth A. Ferri (2005), "Fixated On Ability: Questioning Ableist Metaphors in Feminist Theories of Resistance," *Prose Studies* 27 (1/2): 120–40.

Miller, Ryan A. (2017), "'My Voice is Definitely Strongest in Online Communities': Students Using Social Media for Queer and Disability Identity-Making," *Journal of College Student Development* 58 (4): 509–25.

Moore, Rhonda, Ross Smith, and Qi Liu (2020), "Using Computational Ethnography to Enhance the Curation of Real-World Data (RWD) for Chronic Pain and Invisible Disability use Cases," *ACM SIGACCESS Accessibility and Computing* 1–7. https://doi.org/10.1145/3412836.3412840.

Noble, Safiya Umoja (2018), *Algorithms of Oppression. How Search Engines Reinforce Racism*, New York: New York University Press.

Obermeyer, Ziad, Brian Powers, Christine Vogeli, and Sendhil Mullainathan (2019), "Dissecting Racial Bias in an Algorithm Used to Manage the Health of Populations," *Science* 366 (6464): 447–53. https://doi.org/10.1126/science.aax2342.

Oleson, James C. (2016), "The New Eugenics: Black Hyper-Incarceration and Human Abatement," *Social Sciences* 5 (4): 66. https://doi.org/10.3390/socsci5040066.

O'Neil, Cathy (2013), *On Being a Data Skeptic*, Sebastopol: O'Reilly Media, Inc.

O'Neil, Cathy (2016), *Weapons of Math Destruction: How Big Data Increases Inequality and Threatens Democracy*, New York: Crown Publishinig Group/Broadway Books.

Rickford, John R. (1997), "Unequal Partnership: Sociolinguistics and the African American Speech Community," *Language in Society* 26 (2): 161–97. Available at: https://www.jstor.org/stable/4168760 (accessed July 21, 2023).

Rizvi, Naba and Khalil Mrini (2022), "Using HCI to Tackle Race and Gender Bias in ADHD Diagnosis," arXiv preprint arXiv:2204.07900.

Russel, Stuart and Peter Norvig (2022), *Artificial Intelligence: A Modern Approach Fourth Edition*, Upper Saddle River: Pearson Education Limited.

Schalk, Sami (2013), "Metaphorically Speaking: Ableist Metaphors in Feminist Writing," *Disability Studies Quarterly* 33 (4). https://doi.org/10.18061/dsq.v33i4.3874.

Siebers, Tobin (2008), *Disability Theory*, Ann Arbor: University of Michigan Press.

Stramondo, Joseph A. (2022), "How Disability Activism Advances Disability Bioethics," *Ethical Theory and Moral Practice* 25: 335–49.

Tariq, Qandeel, Scott Fleming, Jesse Schwartz, Kaitlyn Dunlap, Conor Corbin, Peter Washington, Haik Kalantarian, Naila Khan, Gary Darmstadt, and Dennis Wall (2019), "Detecting Developmental Delay and Autism Through Machine Learning Models Using Home Videos of Bangladeshi Children: Development and Validation Study," *Journal of Medical Internet Research* 21 (4): e13822. https://doi.org/10.2196/13822.

Tilmes, Nicholas (2022), "Disability, Fairness, and Algorithmic Bias in AI Recruitment," *Ethics and Information Technology* 24: 21. https://doi.org/10.1007/s10676-022-09633-2.

Tremain, Shelley L. (2017), *Foucault and Feminist Philosophy of Disability*, Ann Arbor: University of Michigan Press.

Treviranus, Jutta (2018), "Sidewalk Toronto and Why Smarter is not Better," *Medium*. Available at: https://medium.datadriveninvestor.com/sidewalk-toronto-and-why-smarter-is-not-better- b233058d01c8 (accessed July 21, 2023).

Trevisan, Filippo and Derrick Cogburn (2019), "Technology and Grassroots Inclusion in Global Governance: A Survey Study of Disability Rights Advocates and Effective Participation." Available at: https://scholarspace.manoa.hawaii.edu/bitstream/10125/59659/0219.pdf (accessed May 31, 2022).

Tucker, Emily (2022), "Artifice and Intelligence," Tech Policy Press. Available at: https://techpolicy.press/artifice-and-intelligence/ (accessed September 7, 2023).

Winner, Langdon (1980), "Do Artifacts Have Politics?" *Daedalus* 109, no. 1 (Winter): 121–36.

10 THE ART OF KINSHIP

AN INTERSECTIONAL READING OF ASSISTED REPRODUCTIVE PRACTICES

DESIREE VALENTINE

We tend to conceive of assisted reproductive technology (ART) in terms of its intended outcome—that is, the making of a future baby. But, as many scholars have shown over the past few decades, ARTs participate in the transformation of our conceptions of (for instance) social and biological kinship roles, the interpersonal and institutional organization of society, and legal and commercial relations, in addition to the role that they play in making future babies. ARTs involve the performative art of what Charis Thompson calls "ontological choreography," or the "dynamic coordination of the technical, scientific, kinship, gender, emotional, legal, political, and financial aspects of ART clinics" (Thompson 2005: 8). The interpersonal, the political, and the technoscientific operate together through a range of literal and metaphoric maneuverings, creating *parents* alongside babies in the process. In so doing, ARTs help construct and conscript the social, legal, biogenetic, and identity-based accoutrements needed to produce and sustain such kinship legibility.

In this chapter, I explore the intersection of contemporary assisted reproductive practices with a host of social identity markers, including race, disability, region, class, gender, and sexuality. I show how such markers operate not only as social positionings but as productive forces in the reproductive process. My aim is to show that an intersectional reading of ART illuminates how social and political norms and values are communicated and consolidated through practices that surround the technology and use of the technology itself, as well as how these practices make various patterns of kinship legible. To make patterns of kinship legible is to construct—via shared norms and social schemas—a way in which to perceive and comprehend a relation *as one of kin*. Legibility thus relies on institutional norms and supports that help make it possible to decipher what counts as kin or kinship relations. This process requires the production of stories, mythos, ideologies, policies, definitions, value schemas, and forms of resource distribution that communicate how kinship is to be identified.

In the first section of the chapter, I provide an overview of the relation between assisted reproductive practices and understandings of kinship and family-making. In the second section, I refer two case studies of sperm donor negligence to argue that social markers such as race and disability operate not only as status outcomes in the reproductive process (i.e., in the form of markers that inhere in the child that is produced) but as *kinship devices*, organizing and producing value schemas regarding how kin is made intelligible and how it ought to be sustained. Both cases rely on dominant norms and power relations to be legally cognizable, individualizing harm by locating it at the site of the child rather than in the persistence of structures of oppression. I conclude in the third section by appealing to three activist-scholarly approaches that work to reveal and transform structures of oppression as they are expressed through ARTs, namely, reproductive justice, queer reproductive justice, and disability justice frameworks.

ART and Constructions of Kinship

The term *assisted reproductive technology* (*ART*) refers to the technological means of manipulating gametes and/or creating embryos outside the body to help foster conception. Examples of ART include in vitro fertilization (IVF), intrauterine insemination (IUI), artificial insemination, and gestational and traditional surrogacy. Such procedures will sometimes use donor sperm, donor eggs, or embryos that were previously frozen. While, historically, ARTs were marketed as a treatment for "infertility," ARTs have in recent decades been increasingly used by single people, gay and lesbian couples, and others wishing to build alternatives to the two-parent, heteronormative family structure (Thompson 2005). They have also been increasingly used for genetic-screening purposes.

ARTs illustrate that conception, gestation, and birth are not merely biological events, but rather are social events that create new relationships, new actors, new terms, and new ways to conceptualize the shared event of conceiving, having, and raising a child. As Thompson writes, "assisted reproductive technologies demand as much social as technological innovation to make sense of the biological and social relationships that ARTs forge and deny" (Thompson 2005: 5). Take, for example, the multitude of terms that have emerged to capture various roles and positions within the assisted reproductive process: *sperm donor, birth mother, intended parents, gestational carrier*, and so on. The basis of kinship has, in short, become more blurred between the biological and the social. Yet biological relatedness remains a potent force for grounding kinship and narrativizing connection. For example, in assisted reproduction that uses a sperm donor, it is commonplace for donors to be chosen based on what are thought to be heritable biological features that match a gestator, their partner, or reflect broader familial likenesses. Typically, sperm banks will provide donor profiles that include characteristics of the donor such as race/ethnicity, height, weight, eye color, hair color, and health history of the donor and his immediate family. In so doing, sperm banks "market sperm differences and, thus, provide an opportunity to re-materialize, reconstitute, and reproduce the body of the donor" (Mamo 2005: 246).

Selection processes like these do not occur in a societal vacuum. As discussed earlier, what is created through ARTs is not simply a baby but rather families themselves. And families themselves are continually socially *legitimized.* Part of the "creations of families" that occurs in the fertility clinic thus involves, as Camisha Russell notes, "ensur[ing] that the *correct* couple or person comes to be understood as the parent(s) of that child" (Russell 2018: 106, emphasis added). Identifying the "correct" couple or person to be matched with the "correct" child necessitates, Russell notes, the use of "ideas of race, ethnicity, and culture . . . as resources available to fertility patients in their construction of naturalizing narratives" of parenthood (107). And yet this transparency of choice in creation is covered over by assumptions about what choices are self-evident. As Seline Szkupinski Quiroga writes, "what remains unspoken is the desire to create a certain type of family, one that closely matches, and thus reproduces, the heteropatriarchal model of a white nuclear family" (Quiroga 2007: 144). To this sexual and racial critique of US fertility projects, I want to add a disability critique, one which outlines the uninterrogated desire to reproduce both in ways oriented toward normative ability and through aspirations of physical, social, and intellectual fitness. Especially in what can be called non-normative family structures (e.g., those with single parents, same-sex parents, more than two parents, or other nonparent family members caring for children), the imperative to gain normative status by closely modeling the "norm" (read: two-parent household, middle-to-upper-class economic status, racially "matching" kin, etc.) is particularly strong. Thus, the gender, sexuality, race, and socioeconomic status of prospective parents who utilize assisted reproduction intersect in ways that can work against or consolidate attachments to dominant power structures. While assisted reproductive practices showcase a seemingly more transparent array of choices and control in manifesting specific procreative outcomes and therefore highlight the active social-constructedness of kinship, the sociopolitical and economic structures of society—the values, norms, and beliefs related to what constitutes *responsible* assisted reproduction—constrain and enable such reproductive choices. Made under constraints of respectability and legibility, these so-called choices tend to bolster ongoing systems of power, reproducing purportedly new kinship in familiar ways.

Identification of the "correct" or "best" arrangement of parent and child plays out in interpersonal interactions within the clinic and broader structural arrangements of society that limit the use of ARTs to particular social groups, especially financially well-off individuals and those who can prove infertility (i.e., heterosexual couples). Such economic restrictions often correspond to stratified and hierarchical racial, region, and gender-based dynamics that exclude non-white, non-Western, and non-partnered individuals. Consider, too, what some commentators have referred to as the "gay tax" in the United Kingdom which restricts same-sex couples, single women, and non-cis people with wombs from accessing IUI or IVF through the National Health Service (NHS). This "gay tax" requires that these prospective parents first pay the NHS an estimated £30,000 (out of their own pockets) for twelve treatments that will "prove" their medical infertility before they are eligible to access IUI or IVF, something that cisgendered heterosexual couples can prove by simply trying to conceive over a two-year period (Hutton 2021).

Stratified reproduction[1] results in the continued concentration of power by, and support in reproduction for, people who are the most economically and otherwise privileged. Concerns about the affordability and accessibility of ARTs therefore abound in feminist, queer, and racial justice-oriented scholarship, as do issues surrounding the various bioeconomies of ART and the bodies and labors that are both commoditized and excluded in the process. Take, for instance, the transnational fertility marketplace wherein intimate life is "outsourced" through "surrogate services, egg donors and women surrogates," which are "often drawn from the world's most 'vulnerable' [to fill] this need" (Mamo 2005: 28). ARTs help generate and participate in a biosocial system of reproduction, wherein "labour is called upon to support life in one place at the potential expense of the lives in another" (27). This exchange is not one between actors of equal standing but rather is dependent on value systems and social schemas that *expect* and *accept* the exploitability and disposability of certain populations—namely, poor and racialized populations of the Global South.

Any understanding of ART's relation to kinship must be focused through the lenses of intersectionality and the structural dynamics of society, which include analyses of social and legal norms concerning family legitimacy, wealth stratification and access to ARTs, and the uneven distribution of supports (and harms) regarding family-making. In the next section of this chapter, I explore specific legal cases about sperm bank negligence that relied on the social markers of race and disability in their constructions of kinship. I then return to a general discussion of ARTs, kin-making, and social structure.

Disability and Race as Kinship Devices in ARTs

In ARTs that involve donor sperm usage, there is an increased sense of control in generating a particular *type* of child—specifically, a child with certain racial and ability statuses that are believed to emerge from choosing sperm with a certain "biogenetic" makeup. This air of control has led to both an increased sense of personal responsibility on the part of parents to make the best choices for their future kin and the idea that reproductive damages accrue when this control is not achieved due to negligent medical and/or business practices. In what follows, I focus on two legal instances in which plaintiffs argued that they ought to be compensated after sperm bank negligence led to the production of children with unwanted biological and so-called genetic characteristics. These tort claims focus on sperm bank mix-ups that, as argued, resulted in race and disability-related damages.

The first case, from 2014, is that of *Cramblett v. Midwest Sperm Bank*.[2] Here, Jennifer Cramblett, a white lesbian woman, sued for wrongful birth and breach of warranty against Midwest Sperm Bank. As the complaint alleged, Cramblett had chosen the sperm of a white, blue-eyed man and instead received the sperm of a Black man. It was only after a successful insemination that Cramblett was made aware of the "mix-up." By this point, she was already four to five months pregnant. She carried the pregnancy to term and, in 2012, gave birth to a healthy, Black/mixed-race girl. Originally heard in an Illinois Circuit Court, the case was dismissed in 2015. Newspapers reported that "[her] claim of wrongful birth 'could not be legally sustained in a case where a healthy child was born' given that wrongful birth case law largely revolves around the birth of a child deemed to have a significant impairment" (Lenon and Peers 2017: 142).

Around the same time as *Cramblett*, a slew of cases began emerging in relation to one of the largest and longest operating sperm banks in the world, Xytex Corporation. In 2007, Margaret Elizabeth Hanson and Angela Collins conceived a child using sperm from Xytex Donor 9623, a donor that the Atlanta sperm bank lauded, both verbally and in their literature, as having a high IQ, multiple degrees, and an impressive health history (Associated Press 2015). In 2014, Xytex mistakenly sent emails revealing this sperm donor's name to individuals who had conceived using Donor 9623, leading parents to google the name and discover that much of what they were told about the Donor was untrue; instead, he had dropped out of college, been arrested for burglary, and was diagnosed with "schizophrenia." Hanson and Collins filed a lawsuit[3] in 2015, alleging that the sperm bank misled them about the health of their donor and seeking financial compensation related to monitoring their son's mental health, given the possibility of him developing schizophrenia. This lawsuit was dismissed by a Fulton County, Georgia Superior Court judge because the suit was interpreted as a "wrongful birth"[4] claim, a type of tort claim that is not recognized by Georgia law. Several other, similar, lawsuits have subsequently emerged, as Donor 9623 helped produce at least thirty-six children across Canada, the United States, and Britain. Most recently, in 2020, Wendy and Janet Norman's lawsuit[5] against Xytex, first filed in 2017 and dismissed by a Georgia Court of Appeals, was allowed to go forward by the state's Supreme Court.

Narratives of kinship underlie the plaintiff's complaints in both *Cramblett* and the Xytex cases. Race and disability do not function as incidental features of the child created via ART, but rather as kinship devices that help make and unmake connective ties. In the case of donor sperm and insemination, the making and unmaking of connective bonds are mediated by technoscientific practices and their imbrication with human meaning-making processes based in naturalizing and deterministic social understandings of genes and biology. Laura Mamo calls these collaborations "affinity-ties" which involve "imagining shared social and cultural characteristics with potential children, and sperm banks' investment of the biomaterial, sperm, with an ability to create relatedness" (Mamo 2005: 237–8). In her study, Mamo found that affinity-ties were articulated by anthropomorphizing sperm as having an ethnic background, health history, and variety of personality characteristics. Cultural understandings of inheritance featured prominently here, with would-be parents relying "less on conceptions of their own nurturing as parents when imagining their children . . . than on cultural understandings of heredity and genetics" (247–8). These cultural understandings of heredity and genetics involve what Abby Lippman calls "geneticization," or the "ongoing process by which differences between individuals are reduced to their DNA codes, with most disorders, behaviours and physiological variations defined, at least in part, as genetic in origin" (Lippman 1991: 19). Consumers select sperm donors against the backdrop of geneticization, despite the ambiguous connection between genes and human development. Many of the traits selected or deselected are not genetically heritable; furthermore, even traits known to be genetically *linked* remain deeply social in their expression. Key here is that the process of kinship via affinity-ties, as situated within cultural practices of geneticization, results in an interpretive move that translates social and cultural characteristics into presumed genetic hereditary traits.

As we see with ARTs, kinship is continually constructed and *naturalized*. What happens when the veil of control that naturalizing processes provide is exposed? In *Cramblett* and the Xytex cases, the effect of race and disability as kinship-*un*making devices becomes apparent. While in both scenarios the plaintiffs express that they love their children very much, they seek damages related to the negligence that generated (or might generate) undesired characteristics in their kin. Implicit in these claims is the idea that the plaintiffs were harmed in ways related to their kinship-making abilities. In Cramblett's complaint, the claims for damages are associated with Cramblett and her partner's ability to relate to their daughter and how they, as a family, relate to broader society. Such "damages" included how the town to which Cramblett and her partner moved is all white, "too racially intolerant," and far from any area where Cramblett can take her child to get a "decent haircut." Additionally, Cramblett expressed worries about her "unconsciously insensitive family members" and noted her "limited cultural competency relative to African Americans, and steep learning curve" given the fact that she "did not know African Americans until her college days." Cramblett appeals to a loss of "shared genetic traits," which she presents as an implicit—or "natural"—desire, describing her daughter as "*obviously* mixed-race" and herself as "*obviously* different in appearance" (emphasis added), followed by a list of difficulties that this presents. And yet, Cramblett is *no less genetically related* to her daughter than if she had received any other donor's sperm. This "loss" (as it were) is actually about the fact that she now exists in a parental relationship to her genetically related but "racially distant" kin. In addition, the putative loss to Cramblett seems to be that she can no longer maintain her sense of (white) self and the social power that affords.

For Hanson and Collins, a break in kinship ties is articulated through what Zohar Freeman describes as "a litigative method for delineating between disabled and non-disabled seminal . . . and potential bodies . . . [that implicitly] refuse[s] kinship between non-disabled parent and disabled child" (Freeman 2019: 127–8). The prospect that their son will be diagnosed with schizophrenia figures as a "haunting" of "risky genetics" that now mandates strict oversight and control. Understanding their son's life in this way partakes in what Kelly Fritch and Anne McGuire call the "spectralization of disability" or "the idea that disability is not a singular ontological trait or category of being but is rather a graded, tenuous and flexible state of becoming" (Fritsch and McGuire 2019: 32). The problem, Fritch and McGuire identify, is not the idea of disability as a spectrum or even as spectral. The problem lies in a *response* to the spectralization of disability that "upholds disability (or a more severe or intense form of disability) *as an object of dread*" (33, emphasis added). In seeking monetary compensation and support in the form of a fund that would help monitor and test their son for signs of mental illness, the mother's suit transforms the possibility of human variation into a pathology to be guarded against. "From Collins and Hanson's perspectives," Fritch and McGuire write, "the 'quality biology' promised by the sperm bank failed to materialize . . . [and was] thus wrongly valued" (44). If, as Freeman writes, "sperm sold by Xytex is marketed as a capital investment whose return is in the child's resemblance to . . . its consumers," then compensation is thought to be required (Freeman 2019: 126). Not only was the sperm deemed a failure in its ability to "re-materialize" bodymind traits assumed to be genetically heritable, but it interrupted the process of building affinity-ties. Collins and Hanson's son is now "marked" and will continue to be marked via strategies of surveillance that make "risk" an "illness in and of itself" (Conrad 2007: 163). When disability is cast as an always looming *threat* in this way, the social response to it is individualized medical intervention. The loss or damage Collins and Hanson articulate is individualized and embodied in their son, forging a barrier to the social and cultural understanding of inheritance and kinship in which they had been invested.

There is no doubt that practices of negligence occurred in both *Cramblett* and the Xytex cases. The question that I have pursued thus far is how this negligence was interpreted via underlying notions of kinship, particularly in assisted reproduction using donor sperm. Both Cramblett's lawsuit and Hanson and Collins's lawsuit geneticize race and disability, locating the source of their harm and due compensation in the bodies of their children, severing kinship ties imagined via social and physical likenesses. The limitations of this line of thinking lie in its inability to foreground the sociopolitical dynamics of race and disability and the structural injustices wrought through each of these social categories.

In a world that lacks both social awareness and structural supports for living and flourishing amid disability, it is unsurprising that disability continues to function largely as *inherently* negative, as it does in the Xytex cases. Note that the origins of the negative perception of disability are a *structural* problem, as many disability scholars and disability justice activists helpfully articulate. Yet, there are few, if any, legally and socially cognizable ways to articulate this structural injustice. Hence, parents such as Collins and Hanson use legal interpretive strategies that tend to rely instead on the hyper individualization and medicalization of disability. However, disability is not simply something that one is or has but rather, as Fritch and McGuire put it, "something we participate in" (Fritsch and McGuire 2019: 49). Recall the earlier discussion of the spectralization of disability. The problem with both the spectralization of disability and the Xytex cases is the way that the "disability to come" is figured as an object of dread, something that haunts individual bodies. The idea that disability is a flexible and dynamic mode of *becoming* has greater liberatory potential than the idea that disability inheres in the bodymind as a singular ontological trait. As Fritch and McGuire write,

> The possibility of the spectrum of disability lies in the ways it exposes an inherent connectivity, relationality, and interdependency between bodies and their social and physical environments. Indeed, the notion of a relational and responsive disability spectrum promises that we can together make a world that can embrace variegations of embodied difference such that confronting the biosocial limits of ourselves is met with collective commitments to creating infrastructures of access, care and supports for flourishing. (Fritsch and McGuire 2019: 48)

Key here is the sense in which genuine connection requires infrastructures of support that can lead to flourishing. In framing their losses as individual, Cramblett and Hanson and Collins, each in their own way, resolidify the structures of ableism and racism that in part give birth to their "harms" in the first place. For example, Cramblett describes a personal loss generated by structural problems (such as her all-white neighborhood, insensitive white family members, and the psychological impacts of racism on their daughter), while refusing to vilify these structures as problems in themselves. For example, it apparently was not a problem for Cramblett to raise a white child in a racially intolerant neighborhood or among racially insensitive relatives. Cramblett did not receive the whiteness that she bargained for and, so, sued under terms that suggested that she is due compensation because she now has to deal with racism personally, not because racism exists per se. This inference, in turn, implicitly suggests that there is a "rightful" racism, establishing the effects of structural racism as the status quo.

Similarly, the argument from Hanson and Collins is that they should not have to sustain the "risk" that inheres in their son—that they are wrongfully now impacted by (the potential of) disability and the difficulties that disability may present, especially in an ableist society that lacks structural supports, both financial and social. What drops out of frame here, however, is the idea that there are people for whom risk *is* socially and politically *sanctioned*. Under current structural conditions, certain risks for certain populations are par for the course, so to speak. These risks might include "increased rates of incarceration and institutionalization, police and state surveillance, violence, poverty, suicide, social isolation, and so on" (Fritsch and McGuire 2019: 47). In Hanson and Collins's case, an individual, biological "solution" is sought, in the form of medicalized surveillance of their son's behaviors, reactions, emotions, and so on, leaving to the side analysis of social structures and the potential of substantively altering our "collective social, political, economic, environmental and cultural living conditions" (45).

In short, both cases are individualizing in part due to a commodification system of donor sperm promising certain "results." The defense in each case relies on the breach of a promise to have been given sperm with the capability of building imagined kinship ties, a capacity narrativized through a "re-materialization" of the donor body and his given traits that are presumed to be biogenetically heritable. Insofar as this process is assumed to have failed due to negligence on the part of the sperm banks, the plaintiffs in effect argued that they should not—rightfully—be required to contend with race and disability-based hardships and therefore should be compensated. Notice that such claims are legible only if there is a category of people who—*rightfully*—must deal with illness and disability, that is, a category of people that should not include the plaintiffs who "responsibly" participated in a market capitalist schema whose design should have precluded these possibilities.

Rather than individualize and privatize the "damages" in these cases, we ought to acknowledge *structures* as the source of harm so that we do not reproduce oppressions in the process of trying to alleviate them. If we acknowledge unjust social structures in this way, kinship practices related to race and disability can begin to function in liberatory ways rather than work to sediment dominant ideals and forms of power. If race and disability are productive forces—kinship devices rather than merely kinship features—then we must transform their uses toward the construction of a more just society and reproductive future for all.

ARTs and Liberatory Reproductive Frameworks

I want to conclude this chapter with a brief discussion of the frameworks of reproductive justice, queer reproductive justice, and disability justice in order to help forge a more liberatory, intersectional approach to ARTs and the process of making kin. These justice frameworks are integral to the creation of a world that centers on structural concerns and engages in structural transformation.

Reproductive justice is both an analytical framework and a sociopolitical movement invested in an intersectional and historical approach to understanding reproductive politics today. The language of reproductive justice emerged in 1994 as an oppositional response to the dominant and narrow reproductive rights platform which focused primarily on the rights to abortion of middle-class white women, neglecting to take account of Black, Latinx, and Indigenous people of color who experience *reproductive oppression*, that is, practices of institutional control, hyper-surveillance, coercion, exploitation, and negligence concerning their bodies, sexuality, and reproduction (Ross 2006). Three main principles animate calls for reproductive justice: (1) the right to *have* or *not to have* a child; (2) the right to control birthing options; and (3) the right to raise children in safe and healthy environments conducive to flourishing. By pursuing economic justice, quality education, accessible health care, affordable childcare, and environmental safety measures—avenues not typically connected with the dominant reproductive rights platform—reproductive justice aims to build the conditions wherein one can *genuinely enact* the above rights. As Mamo writes,

> This framework explicitly reconciles individual rights and autonomy principles, specifically a right to self-determine reproductive futures—to have children, to not have them, to time them and space them, free of coercion, patriarchy, racist policies, heterosexual mandates, etc., with social justice principles which ensure that all people cannot only have and raise children in a context of economic, educational and just resource allocation, but also live in conditions free of oppression. (Mamo 2018: 28)

Importantly, continued efforts to enact reproductive justice go beyond rights-based discourse that individualizes and privatizes harm and negligence. Reproductive justice encourages us as a society to reckon with a variety of state-sponsored and state-enacted violations of reproductive freedom and develop more comprehensive responses.

In a context of increasing use of ARTs by gay, lesbian, and queer families such as the plaintiffs in the cases discussed previously, it is imperative that we both recognize the demand of non-normative families for access to ARTs and refuse the consolidation of hegemonic power structures in the process. Mamo therefore proposes a *queer* reproductive justice framework that "does not (necessarily, nor only) advocate for increased access to and affordability of ART, but instead understands these as constitutive of bioeconomies of inequalities" (Mamo 2018: 30). Queer reproductive justice therefore demands that one be accountable to such social relations, to "recognize how one's actions are made legible in these contexts as well as how they rely on and affect the lives of others" (ibid.) and to be willing to advocate for social policies that make possible more just relations within the use of ARTs. This advocacy may include the collection of data related to surrogates and egg donors, the development of legal and monetary protections for reproductive laborers, and the transformation of value systems in order to forge queer forms of family creation and kinship based "not only on biological relatedness but also . . . an ethic of care" (ibid.). Joshua Gamson refers to the latter as family justice, or the "centering [of] insights of diverse family forms [to] bring forward resources that current policy reads as mainly deficits" (Gamson 2018: 2). This "family justice" may include turning toward "multigenerational 'extended kin ties'" often found in lower socioeconomic status households or "chosen family" often forged within queer networks.

A queer reproductive justice framework—rather than emphasize the biogenetic or social traits of individuals that are used to cultivate and protect relational ties—helps to center the inherent relationality of kin-making. Such a framework attends to the ongoing construction of access, forms of care, and meanings of kinship. Even with the overriding *force* of the biological as the default for understanding kinship in dominant US paradigms, sociality and social connectedness are always part of the picture. As Mamo writes, "who is included in the family and who 'drops out' are shaped by patterns of sociality and senses of alliance and affiliation that are not determined by the crude criteria of blood connection" (Mamo 2005: 259). Think, in this respect, of the denial by slave owners of their biological kin who emerged from the rape of enslaved women or, more generally, of the history (and present) of disabled, racialized, and non-normatively gendered biological kin who are cast out of the familial domain. Relationality is always contextualized, and biogenetic renderings of relationship will never be value free. As Lippman writes, "No strictly objective . . . view of the biological world exists. Any attempt to explain or order it will be shaped by the historical and cultural setting in which it occurs" (Lippman 1991: 112). Keeping this fact in mind encourages a more expansive rendering of the meaning of disability—moving analyses of disability away from medicalized or biologized definitions of it and toward recognition of its sociopolitical and relational nature.

Alongside reproductive justice and queer reproductive justice, the framework of disability justice is thus key to generating an intersectional, structural response to the reproduction of harms and systemic oppression within uses of ARTs. Developed in 2005 by queer women of color working within progressive and radical movements fighting ableism, disability justice commits to anticapitalist, intersectional solidarity-building and includes a "commitment to cross-movement organizing" and "cross-disability solidarity" (Sins Invalid 2015). As the authors of "10 Principles of Disability Justice" write,

> We cannot comprehend ableism without grasping its interrelations with heteropatriarchy, white supremacy, colonialism, and capitalism, each system co-creating an ideal bodymind built upon the exclusion and elimination of a subjugated "other" from whom profits and status are extracted. (Sins Invalid 2015)

The ten principles of disability justice include the intersectional commitment to reconceiving access and liberation *collectively*—forging solidarities across what currently tends to be understood as separate movements, including movements for racial justice, economic equity, and gender equality. The principles also importantly challenge dominant ontological assumptions about persons, moral values, and worth. For example, they embrace a recognition of "wholeness," "sustainability," and "interdependence"—centering the value of the whole person and the specific teachings of one's embodied existence in relation to a world in which communities and living systems are fundamentally intertwined and reliant upon one another for opportunities of flourishment. Ultimately, disability justice understands all bodies as "unique and essential" and as "[having] strengths and needs that must be met" (Sins Invalid 2015). This incredible heterogeneity is not a problem to be overcome but rather the position from which we must generate new ways of relating and belonging. In the context of increased use of ARTs and related prenatal screening and selective reproductive practices, disability justice activists challenge eugenic agendas that define who is "fit" or "not fit" to reproduce or be reproduced, while engaging in cross-movement organizing to build societal conditions in which ARTs are both accessible and accessed within social schemas premised on awareness, appreciation, and support for a variety of bodyminds.

The histories of reproductive justice, queer reproductive justice, and disability justice scholarship and activism point to a vibrant alternative to narrow approaches to kin-making within assisted reproduction that rely on individualization, commodification, geneticization, and privatization. Placing the use of ARTs in conversation with these three justice approaches provides avenues for retooling dominant narratives of social markers like race, disability, and sexuality in the service of more liberatory forms of kinship-building.

Examination of ARTs through a structural—rather than individualized—lens enables us to recognize that race and disability are not merely features that may be selected to inhere in the bodyminds of kin, but rather operate in the context of ARTs as kinship *devices* or productive forces themselves. Furthermore, although conventional understandings of kinship appear limited to the personal or domestic sphere, it is important to recognize that these kinship devices are supported (or opposed) via more comprehensive structural conditions of social power and legitimacy. Therefore, we must expand our kinship imaginary to include practices intent on building the conditions in which genuine connection and just treatment of racialized, disabled, and other currently marginalized people can occur.

Notes

1 *Stratified reproduction* is a term coined by Shellee Colen (1995) to refer to the privileging of certain reproductive futures over others.

2 Cramblett v. Midwest Sperm Bank, LLC, No. 1:2016cv04553—Document 29 (N.D. Ill. 2017), (N.D. Ill. 2017). Available at: https://law.justia.com/cases/federal/district-courts/ illinois/ilndce/1:2016cv04553/325662/29/ (accessed June 20, 2023).

3 Collins v. Xytex Corp., et al. A16A1139, A16A1141. Available at: https://www.leagle.com/decision/ingaco20160317200 (accessed July 21, 2023).

4 For more information on the legal claim of wrongful birth see Valentine (2022).

5 Norman et al. v. Xytex Corp., et al. S19G1486. Available at: https://cases.justia.com/georgia/supreme-court/2020-s19g1486.pdf?ts=1601294526 (accessed July 21, 2023).

References

Colen, Shellee (1995), "'Like a Mother to Them': Stratified Reproduction and West Indian Childcare Workers and Employers in New York," in Faye Ginsburg and Rayna Rapp (eds.), *Conceiving the New World Order: The Global Politics of Reproduction*, 78–102, Berkeley: University of California Press.

Conrad, Peter (2007), *The Medicalization of Society: On the Transformation of Human Conditions into Treatable Disorders*, Baltimore: Johns Hopkins University Press.

Freeman, Zohar (2019), "Refusing Kinship via 'Wrongful Birth' Tort Law: A Case Study of Collins et al. v. Xytex et al." *Knots: An Undergraduate Journal of Disability Studies* 4 (1): 122–30.

Fritsch, Kelly and Anne McGuire (2019), "Risk and the Spectral Politics of Disability," *Body and Society* 25 (4): 29–54.

Gamson, Joshua (2018), "Kindred Spirits?," *Reproductive Biomedicine and Society* 7: 1–3.

Hutton, Alice (2021), "Married Lesbian Couple Launch Discrimination Action against NHS," *The Guardian*, November 7. Available at: https://www.theguardian.com/world/2021/nov/07/married-lesbian-couple-launch-discrimination-action-against-nhs (accessed April 25, 2022).

Lenon, Suzanne and Danielle Peers (2017), "'Wrongful' Inheritance: Race, Disability and Sexuality in *Cramblett v. Midwest Sperm Bank*," *Feminist Legal Studies* 25: 141–63.

Lippman, Abby (1991), "Prenatal Genetic Testing and Screening: Constructing Needs and Reinforcing Inequities," *American Journal of Law and Medicine* 17 (1–2): 15–50.

Mamo, Laura (2005), "Biomedicalizing Kinship: Sperm Banks and the Creation of Affinity-ties," *Science as Culture* 14 (3): 237–64.

Mamo, Laura (2018), "Queering Reproduction in Transnational Bio-economies," *Reproductive Biomedicine and Society* 7: 24–32.

Quiroga, Seline S. (2007), "Blood Is Thicker than Water: Policing Donor Insemination and the Reproduction of Whiteness," *Hypatia: A Journal of Feminist Philosophy* 22 (2): 143–61.

Ross, Loretta (2006), "Understanding Reproductive Justice," *Off Our Backs* 36 (4): 14–19.

Russell, Camisha (2018), *The Assisted Reproduction of Race*, Bloomington: Indiana University Press.

Sins Invalid (2015), "'10 Principles of Disability Justice," September 17. Available at: https://www.sinsinvalid.org/blog/10-principles-of-disability-justice (accessed June 20, 2023).

The Associated Press (2015), "Sperm Bank Sued Over Donor's Profile, Mental History," *CBS News*, April 20. Available at: https://www.cbsnews.com/news/sperm-bank-sued-over-donors-profile-mental-history/ (accessed June 20, 2023).

Thompson, Charis (2005), *Making Parents: The Ontological Choreography of Reproductive Technologies*, Cambridge, MA: MIT Press.

Valentine, Desiree (2022), "The Wrongs of Wrongful Birth: Disability, Race, and Reproductive Justice," in Joel M. Reynolds and Christine Wieseler (eds.), *The Disability Bioethics Reader*, 125–34, New York: Routledge.

11 EPISTEMIC INJUSTICE AND EPISTEMIC AUTHORITY ON AUTISM

AMANDINE CATALA

Introduction

"Nothing About Us Without Us." This slogan from the disabled people's movement, which has also become the slogan of the neurodiversity movement, makes clear that policies, theories, and other endeavors that focus on neurodiversity should not be formulated and carried out without the leadership, input, and involvement of neurominoritized people. I use the term *neurominoritized* rather than the term *neurodivergent* and the term *neuronormalized* rather than the term *neurotypical* to highlight that these categories are not natural kinds, but rather the products of neuronormative power relations, as emphasized by the neurodiversity movement. Let me unpack, first, the notion of neurodiversity, then turn to the notion of neuronormativity. The term *neurodiversity* refers to the natural range of variation among neurocognitive profiles across the human species (Singer 2017). It is from these naturally occurring neurocognitive variations that the socially constructed and normatively loaded categories of "neurotypical" and "neuroatypical" or "neurodivergent" are subsequently produced. Neurodiversity thus comprises *both* neuronormalized ("neurotypical") and neurominoritized ("neuroatypical" or "neurodivergent") profiles. Starting from the recognition of human neurodiversity and the neuronormative power relations that underlie the distinction between "neurotypical" and "neuroatypical," the neurodiversity movement advocates for the inclusion and equal consideration of neurominoritized individuals in all spheres of social life, whether educational, professional, medical, or cultural, for example.

This chapter will focus on one type of neurominoritized profile, namely, autism. Most Autistic self-advocates (including myself) prefer to use what the disabled people's movement calls "identity-first language"—that is, use the terms *Autistic person* and *Autistic*—which represents autism as a positive source of identity, as exemplified by the neurodiversity movement. In contrast, both the medical sphere and the broader social sphere generally rely on "person-first language"—that is, use phrases such as "person with autism" or "person who has autism"—which betrays a negative view of autism as a disorder or a set of deficits.

By understanding autism as a neurocognitive variation rather than a neurocognitive deficit, the neurodiversity movement denaturalizes and politicizes neurotypicality and exposes neuronormativity. In previous work, my co-authors and I defined *neuronormativity* as follows:

> Neuronormativity refers to the prevalent, neurotypical set of assumptions, norms, and practices that construes neurotypicality as the sole acceptable or superior mode of cognition, and that stigmatizes attitudes, behaviors, or actions that reflect neuroatypical modes of cognition as deviant or inferior. Neuronormative assumptions, norms, and practices uphold standards regarding, for example, (what is neurotypically considered) appropriate eye contact, facial expressions, prosody, conversational flow, processing speed, and responsiveness—all of which can be difficult for autistic [and other neurominoritized] individuals to understand, sense, or apply, due to neurological differences. (Catala, Faucher, and Poirier 2021: 9016)

Neuronormativity is reflected in, for example, the medical and social language used to refer to autism, language that is replete with stigmatizing and subordinating terms such as *epidemic, disorder, deficit, lack, abnormalities, impairment, risk, cure, treatment, victim*, and *burden*, as well as stigmatizing and subordinating phrases such as "affected by autism" and "suffers from autism." Neuronormativity includes common stereotypes and beliefs about Autistics such as that we lack social motivation, empathy, or humor (Jaswal and Akhtar 2018). Neuronormativity also upholds pedagogical and academic standards that do not take into account our different ways of processing information, sensory stimuli, and social interactions in a world built by and for neuronormalized individuals to the detriment of neurominoritized people (Catala 2022a, 2022b). Even philosophical debates that aim to denounce unjust power relations in the production, circulation, and validation of knowledge rely on neuronormative ideals for the formulation of criteria with which to allocate credibility and intelligibility. These debates suggest, for example, that it is not unjust not to be taken seriously if one does not look one's interlocutor in the eyes or if one appears nervous or anxious when expressing oneself (e.g., Fricker 2007: 41–2; Saul 2017: 237–8).

Otherwise put, neuronormativity creates epistemic injustice for Autistics. Epistemic injustice arises when members of nondominant groups are not adequately believed or consulted, or when they are not adequately understood or represented, that is, when they receive levels of credibility or intelligibility that are unduly diminished because of biases. Miranda Fricker has identified two main types of epistemic injustice: testimonial injustice and hermeneutical injustice (Fricker 2007). Fricker uses the term *testimonial injustice* to refer to an undue credibility deficit that accrues to someone because of conscious or unconscious biases on the part of their interlocutors. For example, if a teacher dismisses the contributions of an Autistic student because the student avoids eye contact, appears nervous, or takes a moment to process and respond, the student thereby suffers testimonial injustice because the diminished level of credibility that they receive from their teacher stems from neuronormative biases on the part of their teacher. Note that this credibility deficit can occur *regardless* of whether the teacher knows that the student is Autistic, because their diminished credibility judgment still relies on neuronormative biases regarding what is neuronormatively taken to be an appropriate way to interact or react in an epistemic exchange.

Fricker uses the term *hermeneutical injustice* to refer to an undue intelligibility deficit that accrues to someone because of biases in a society's mainstream pool of interpretive or hermeneutical resources, such as common concepts, shared understandings, social meanings, and collective representations. Because nondominant groups are often marginalized in the processes that shape mainstream hermeneutical resources, these resources tend to be largely shaped by dominant groups. As a result of the hermeneutical marginalization of nondominant groups, mainstream hermeneutical resources tend to obscure, minimize, or stigmatize the experiences, perspectives, and realities of nondominant groups, which therefore remain largely misunderstood or misrepresented. For example, the common understanding of autism as a disorder or a set of deficits unduly stigmatizes Autistics by representing us as deficient, which obscures both that autism is a natural variation among the range of neurocognitive profiles that make up neurodiversity and that the pathologization of autism is the result of neuronormativity. By marginalizing the neurodiversity model of autism that Autistic self-advocates promote, the dominant deficit model of autism misrepresents the reality of autism, which therefore remains largely misunderstood as a disorder. That is, Autistics suffer hermeneutical injustice because the lack of intelligibility that they face stems from neuronormative biases in mainstream hermeneutical resources. These biases, in turn, both result from the hermeneutical marginalization of Autistics and serve to maintain it: if the dominant understanding of autism as a disorder or a set of deficits is correct—that is, if indeed we are fundamentally flawed, deficient human beings—why should we be included in the production of hermeneutical resources that aim to describe us or interpret our experiences?

In addition, Autistics face what I have called *metaepistemic injustice* (Catala 2020). Metaepistemic injustice arises when scholars theorize the very notions of epistemic injustice and agency in ways that discriminate against or are detrimental to members of nondominant social groups. For example, when philosophers construe reliable epistemic agency as requiring that one look their interlocutors in the eyes or not appear nervous or anxious in an epistemic exchange, they commit metaepistemic injustice with respect to Autistics, who typically utterly dislike and, hence, avoid eye contact and who often experience social anxiety. On this neuronormative conception of epistemic agency, Autistics are not taken seriously as knowers because of neuronormative biases regarding eye contact and anxiety. Here, Autistics face an undue deficit in both credibility and intelligibility, not in an actual epistemic exchange but at the metalevel of philosophical methodology. Indeed, on this neuronormative conception of epistemic agency, Autistics are both dismissed as epistemic contributors (i.e., they face an undue credibility deficit) and misrepresented as unreliable epistemic agents (i.e., they face an undue intelligibility deficit). Because these undue credibility and intelligibility deficits occur at the metalevel of philosophical methodology, Autistics can be said to face both metatestimonial and metahermeneutical injustice.

Metaepistemic injustice is normatively problematic because it directly affects how we normatively assess actual epistemic exchanges. Recall the previous example of the teacher who dismisses an Autistic student's valuable or truthful epistemic contribution because the student does not look their teacher in the eyes. The teacher, in this example, clearly grants the student a diminished level of credibility because of the lack of eye contact. That is, the Autistic person should be said to face testimonial injustice in this case, because of the (conscious or unconscious) neuronormative biases that underlie the teacher's diminished credibility judgment. Yet if our philosophical theories stipulate that reliable epistemic agency requires making eye contact, *and that it is therefore not unjust* to dismiss someone who does *not* make eye contact in an epistemic exchange, then it seems like the correct normative assessment of the situation is that the Autistic student in the previous example does *not* in fact face testimonial injustice in this case, even though they clearly do. This neuronormative conception of epistemic agency, then, effectively excludes Autistics from the scope of epistemic (in)justice. Thus, while metaepistemic injustice occurs at the level of philosophical theorizing independently of any actual epistemic exchange, it affects how we (fail to) recognize instances of epistemic injustice in actual epistemic exchanges.

Otherwise put, this neuronormative conception of epistemic agency mistakenly justifies the exclusion of certain classes of epistemic agents by legitimizing the diminished level of credibility that they are unduly granted.

Another form of metaepistemic injustice stems from autism researchers who define autism as involving a lack of theory of mind (Baron-Cohen 1997; Yergeau and Huebner 2017) or a lack of understanding of others' mental states. This inaccurate assumption can lead researchers to the further inaccurate assumption that Autistics also lack understanding of their own mental states (Hens, Robeyns, and Schaubroeck 2018; Yergeau and Huebner 2017). Taken together, these assumptions create metaepistemic injustice for Autistics since they are thereby construed as deficient and unreliable epistemic agents, including with respect to their understanding of their own experience (Legault, Bourdon, and Poirier 2021; Yergeau and Huebner 2017), *before* they even make any contributions to an actual epistemic exchange. This conception of autism as involving a lack of access to one's own mental states is instituted at the metalevel of research on autism and has an impact on the normative assessment of actual epistemic exchanges with Autistics. Indeed, this flawed conception of autism effectively *justifies* both the dismissal of the first-person testimonies of Autistics (i.e., Autistics supposedly do not face testimonial injustice) and their marginalization in the process of developing more adequate understandings and representations of autism and Autistics (i.e., Autistics supposedly do not face hermeneutical injustice). That is, the credibility and intelligibility deficits that Autistics face are supposedly not undue but rather are warranted since Autistics, on this flawed conception, *are* deficient and unreliable epistemic agents. Autistics, on this view, do not face epistemic injustice. They are effectively excluded from the circle of subjects of epistemic justice. In other words, the metaepistemic injustice that occurs at the level of research on autism—which consists in construing Autistics as unreliable epistemic agents—has a direct impact on the (mis)recognition of instances of epistemic injustice that Autistics confront in everyday life.

In short, Autistics face several forms of epistemic injustice in multiple spheres, whether medical, clinical, social, educational, professional, scientific, or scholarly. In this context, the neurodiversity movement's injunction—adopted from the disabled people's movement—to do or say "Nothing About Us Without Us" is effectively a call to reclaim epistemic authority: to insist on guiding the way in which Autistics (and other neurominoritized individuals) are talked about and represented, as well as to require that we be consulted and taken seriously—especially, though not exclusively, on matters that directly pertain to us. In this sense, "Nothing About Us Without Us" involves working toward greater epistemic justice, both hermeneutical and testimonial.

In sum, by exposing neuronormativity, by invalidating the stigmatizing and subordinating language and representations that pervade the medical and social spheres, and by centering the perspectives and experiences of Autistics, the neurodiversity movement empowers Autistics, as members of a community built around their shared and positively valued social identity, to reclaim their epistemic authority in the face of epistemic injustice and, hence, to denounce and resist neuronormativity.

The remainder of this chapter proceeds as follows. In the next section, I introduce the distinction between perceived and actual epistemic authority and connect this distinction to the notion of epistemic injustice. I then introduce two further analytical tools, namely, the notion of neuronormalized avoidance and the distinction between propositional and experiential knowledge. I argue that these analytical tools allow us to formulate criteria for legitimate epistemic authority on autism. Finally, I argue that epistemic authority should be construed as a process rather than an outcome and identify some important implications that this construal of epistemic authority has for diagnosing or recognizing autism.

Epistemic Injustice and Perceived versus Actual Epistemic Authority

Epistemic injustice undermines one's perceived epistemic authority, which, in turn, undermines one's epistemic agency. Indeed, when one is not adequately believed or consulted (i.e., faces testimonial injustice) or is not adequately understood or represented (i.e., faces hermeneutical injustice), one is seriously undermined in one's epistemic agency or one's ability to use, produce, or convey knowledge. Epistemic injustice undermines our perceived epistemic authority. By *perceived epistemic authority*, I mean whether one *is viewed* as qualified or competent to speak on a given topic. In this sense, perceived epistemic authority is a descriptive notion or an empirical matter. Perceived epistemic authority is to be contrasted with *actual epistemic authority*, or whether one *should be viewed* as qualified or competent to speak on a given topic because one is actually competent or adequately positioned to speak about the topic. In this sense, actual epistemic authority is a prescriptive notion or a normative matter.

Let me unpack the distinction between perceived and actual epistemic authority further. The first thing to note is that one can have the former without the latter, and vice versa. To some extent, this variance is precisely what the concept of epistemic injustice captures, namely, the mismatch between perceived and actual epistemic authority. Indeed, the classic case of testimonial injustice is one in which a person who has *actual* epistemic authority and, hence, should be believed and granted the appropriate level of credibility is not *perceived* as such due to their interlocutor's biases and, hence, is disbelieved and granted a diminished level of credibility. In this case, the person suffers an undue credibility *deficit*. As José Medina has shown, however, the reverse scenario, of credibility *excess* rather than deficit, is also possible (Medina 2013). Take, for example, the gap between first-person versus third-person accounts of what autism is like. Whereas the third-person accounts of researchers, doctors, parents, or practitioners often describe Autistics as lacking social motivation, empathy, or humor, first-person accounts of Autistics ourselves often contradict these third-person descriptions of autism (Catala, Faucher, and Poirier 2021; Jaswal and Akhtar 2018). Although Autistics are best positioned to describe what autism is like, non-Autistic researchers, doctors, parents, or practitioners are often granted more credibility than Autistics to talk about autism. That is, non-Autistics often enjoy a credibility excess: they are *perceived* as having epistemic authority on autism, when in fact they do not *actually* have epistemic authority on autism—at least not if their perspectives are not thoroughly informed by Autistics' perspectives on autism, which is too rarely the case.

Note that Medina's claim is not that members of dominant groups who enjoy credibility excesses thereby face testimonial injustice. Rather, Medina's point is that credibility allocations are always comparative and contrastive. To the extent that non-Autistics enjoy more credibility on autism than they should and, moreover, that their perspectives on autism tend not to be informed by Autistic perspectives, the credibility excesses that non-Autistics enjoy go hand in hand with the credibility deficits that Autistics confront. In other words, much like subordination and privilege are two sides of the power imbalances that define oppression, credibility deficits and excesses are two sides of the credibility imbalances that define epistemic injustice.

In sum, credibility deficits arise when a person has actual epistemic authority but is not perceived as such, whereas credibility excesses arise when a person is perceived as having epistemic authority even though they do not. Both credibility deficits and excesses are defined relative to the actual epistemic authority that a person has: a person faces a credibility deficit when they receive less credibility than their actual epistemic authority warrants; a person enjoys a credibility excess when they receive more credibility than their actual epistemic authority warrants. In both cases, the mismatch between actual versus perceived epistemic authority generates epistemic injustice, in the form of either credibility deficits or credibility excesses. Because both credibility deficits and excesses contribute to maintaining the epistemic oppression of members of nondominant groups, they are epistemically unjust.

Epistemic Privilege and Neuronormalized Avoidance

The distinction between perceived versus actual epistemic authority is connected to the idea, central to standpoint theory, that social location matters for knowledge production (Hartsock 1983; Harding 1986; Wylie 2003). More precisely, standpoint theory makes the case for three main claims (Toole 2019). First, knowledge is *socially situated*. The particular positions that we respectively occupy in the social structure as members of dominant and nondominant groups affect the experience that we have of the social world and, by extension, the knowledge that we have of the social world. Second, members of nondominant groups will tend to have an *epistemic privilege*. The knowledge that they have of certain aspects of the social world and, in particular, of the oppressive realities that they experience will tend to be more accurate and reliable than the knowledge that dominant groups have, precisely because nondominant groups experience oppression in an unjust society in ways that dominant groups do not. Third, however, this epistemic privilege is not automatic simply in virtue of one's membership in a nondominant social group. Rather, epistemic privilege is a *collectively mediated and critically generated* achievement. To avoid internalized oppression or false consciousness and achieve epistemic privilege, members of nondominant groups must adopt a critical stance with respect to the power relations that unjustly structure society and produce their oppressed social position.

Much as members of nondominant groups will tend to have an epistemic privilege because they experience oppression firsthand, members of dominant groups will tend to have what Charles Mills calls "epistemic ignorance" because they do not directly experience oppression (Mills 1997, 2007, 2015). Because the term *ignorance* has ableist connotations (Simplican 2015; Tremain 2017), I instead use the term *avoidance* to refer to the phenomenon Mills calls "ignorance." Let me say a bit more about this terminological substitution. The term *ignorance* refers both to a lack of knowledge (as when one is ignorant about, say, astrophysics) and to a form of denial, refusal, or resistance (as when one person ignores another or when one ignores a certain type of reality, like climate change or racial injustice, despite readily available and pervasive evidence). The term *ignorance* can thus connote both a lack and an active kind of attitude or behavior. Similarly, the term *avoidance* connotes both the lack of facing up to or recognizing the person, situation, or knowledge one is avoiding, as well as the fact that one is actively, though not always consciously nor explicitly, seeking to avoid this confrontation or recognition. While the term *avoidance* may be an imperfect substitute for the term *ignorance*, it has the merit of not perpetuating the latter's ableist connotations. For the sake of clarity and accuracy, I retain the term *ignorance* when referring to Mills's own work, but I add an asterisk after the term to signal that the term is ableist.

Ignorance* or avoidance here is construed not as a mere lack of knowledge or the absence of beliefs, but rather as inaccurate knowledge or the presence of false beliefs about some area of the social world—for example, about the oppressive realities or different experiences that characterize the lives and situation of members of nondominant groups. Ignorance* or avoidance might include, for example, the false belief that systemic racism or neuronormativity does not exist. Ignorance* or avoidance is a pernicious phenomenon for at least two reasons. First, it generates an illusion of knowledge on the part of dominant groups, who believe that their perception and understanding of social realities are accurate, even though they are inaccurate. That is, dominant groups will typically not know that they do not accurately know (Medina 2013; Mills 1997), because ignorance* or avoidance is not a gap in knowledge of which dominant knowers are readily aware, but rather a set of false beliefs that dominant knowers take for granted and are not spontaneously inclined to question. Second, ignorance* or avoidance can be resistant to counterevidence or the narratives of members of nondominant groups, because the false beliefs or inaccurate knowledge that dominant groups have about the social world both justify the status quo from which they directly benefit and, hence, comfort them in their privileged position. In other words, ignorance* or avoidance serves the vested interests of dominant groups in systemic racism or neuronormativity, for example. It is nonetheless possible for members of dominant groups to overcome the ignorance* or avoidance that typically characterizes their privileged social position, if they adopt a critical stance with respect to their privileged positionality and the unjust status quo.

Let me now connect the notions of epistemic privilege and avoidance to the distinction between perceived and actual epistemic authority, as well as to epistemic injustice. As explained earlier, a key insight from standpoint theory is that the positions that dominant and nondominant groups respectively occupy in the social structure differentially affect the (lack of) experience and, hence, the (lack of) knowledge that they respectively have of the unjust or oppressive aspects of the social world. More precisely, because members of nondominant groups experience oppression firsthand and do not have the same interest as dominant groups in preserving the status quo or in denying its unjust character, their knowledge of the unjust or oppressive aspects of the social world will tend to be more accurate and reliable. In other words, their *experiential* knowledge of the social world will tend to generate more accurate *propositional* knowledge about the social world. This link between experiential and propositional knowledge is indeed what the notion of epistemic privilege captures. The epistemic privilege of nondominant groups, however, will not be recognized by dominant groups, whose social position tends to generate avoidance. This gap between epistemic privilege and avoidance directly contributes to the mismatch between perceived and actual authority outlined previously. Despite their epistemic privilege and, hence, their *actual* epistemic authority about certain aspects of the social world, members of nondominant groups will often be *perceived* by members of dominant groups as lacking epistemic authority about these aspects. Conversely, despite their avoidance and, hence, their lack of *actual* epistemic authority about certain aspects of the social world, members of dominant groups will often be *perceived* among themselves as having epistemic authority about these aspects. In other words, with regard to their respective epistemic contributions regarding oppression or the unjust status quo, members of nondominant groups will often face undue credibility deficits, whereas members of dominant groups will often enjoy undue credibility excesses.

How, then, can members of dominant groups overcome avoidance? To answer this question, it is useful to look more closely at Mills's account of ignorance* or avoidance. In the context of race relations, Mills defines ignorance* as "a particular pattern of localized and global cognitive dysfunctions (which are psychologically and socially functional), producing the ironic outcome that whites will in general be unable to understand the world they themselves have made," and adds that "[p]art of what it means to be constructed as 'white' [. . .] is a cognitive model that precludes self-transparency and genuine understanding of social realities" (Mills 1997: 18). While Mills does not use these terms, his characterization of ignorance* effectively articulates two related levels of ignorance* or avoidance, namely, subjective and objective ignorance* or avoidance (Catala 2019).

Subjective avoidance refers to the fact that members of dominant groups tend to lack self-transparency with respect to their privileged social location. That is, they are often unaware of their own social positionality or their privilege. They experience their privileged position as so natural or normal that it becomes imperceptible and unquestionable to them. In the context of autism, the subjective avoidance of non-Autistics is readily noticeable through the fact that the word *autistic* is much more well-known (if rarely adequately understood) than the word *allistic*, which refers to non-Autistic people. In other words, the default social position of allism is taken for granted, so much so that it is essentially considered *not even worth naming or recognizing* (much as White subjects do not typically view themselves as racialized because of the assumption of Whiteness as the norm). This example of the limited use and understanding of the term *allistic* on the part of allistics themselves is a stark illustration of subjective avoidance. Subjective avoidance is thus characterized by a lack of self-transparency of the knower or the *subject* of knowledge—here, allistics or members of dominant groups.

Objective avoidance refers to the fact that as a result of subjective avoidance, members of dominant groups will have inadequate understandings and, hence, misunderstand or misinterpret significant aspects of the social world. In the context of autism, the objective avoidance of allistics is manifested in the countless persistent myths that they circulate about autism and the neuronormative status quo. These myths include: that we lack empathy, social motivation, or humor; that we are generally defective human beings and deficient epistemic agents; and that the neuronormative status quo is a just state of affairs. This latter myth, about the justice of the neuronormative status quo, is reflected in a variety of largely taken-for-granted, dominant expectations, including the following: Autistics should be grateful to be "allowed" in predominantly allistic public spaces and other settings; Autistics should refrain from making "unreasonable" requests, including that allistics respect the way in which most of us want them to refer to us (namely, as Autistic people rather than as people with autism or people who suffer from ASD) and that they not force us to act as supercrips or pass as neuronormalized by imposing (for example) participation in countless meetings or social gatherings, the use of synchronous means of communication, or the use of loud, crowded, bright, smelly, hot, or cold spaces that are overwhelming for the senses; and other neuronormative expectations regarding conversational pace or work productivity. All of these expectations can lead to Autistic meltdowns, shutdowns, or burnout. Neuronormativity in neuroableist societies is something neurominoritized people know experientially in ways that neuronormalized people do not, much as Black people, Indigenous people, and people of color experientially know White supremacy in a racist society in ways that Whites do not. Because neuronormalized people occupy a privileged social position that does not come with direct experiences and understandings of neuronormativity, their position will be characterized by objective avoidance. Objective avoidance thus corresponds to a lack of (and, often, resistance to) an adequate understanding of the relevant *object* of knowledge—here, neuronormativity or oppressive social realities.

Following Mills's suggestion that ignorance* or avoidance can arise in contexts other than that of racial oppression (e.g., male ignorance* or avoidance in the context of gender oppression [Mills 2007: 22]), we might adopt the notion of neurotypical ignorance* or neuronormalized avoidance in the context of neuro-oppression (Catala, Faucher, and Poirier 2021). In the context of race, the system of oppression that is racism both produces and is maintained by a particular set of assumptions, norms, and practices, namely, White supremacy. White supremacy, in turn, generates White ignorance* or avoidance in both its subjective and objective components. Similarly, in the context of neurodiversity, the system of oppression that is neuroableism both produces and is maintained by a particular set of assumptions, norms, and practices, namely, neuronormativity. Neuronormativity, in turn, generates neurotypical ignorance* or neuronormalized avoidance in both its subjective and objective components. Subjective avoidance entails that due to the lack of self-transparency of most neuronormalized subjects to themselves, they will be unaware of both their social positionality and how their positionality generates objective avoidance, that is, affects or limits their understanding of certain aspects of the social world—for example, about neurodiversity or neuronormativity.

We are now in a position to identify the first criterion for legitimate or actual epistemic authority on autism: namely, awareness of subjective and objective avoidance. That is, one must recognize that one's social position limits one's understanding of certain social realities. In other words, one must adopt a posture of epistemic humility (Medina 2013). This is true for both allistics and Autistics. It is true for allistics, who, by definition, do not experientially know what autism is like because they do not experience it firsthand. It is also true for Autistics, because any one of us in the Autistic community is only one Autistic person, whose experiential understanding of autism is also shaped by and limited to our own intersectional social position. For example, experiencing autism as a cis, White, settler, physically nondisabled, oralizing woman with no intellectual disability and no material or financial precarity makes for qualitatively different experiences of autism than the experiences of Autistics who are differently situated along axes of gender identification, race, indigeneity, physical or intellectual dis/ability, non/orality, and class. While Autistics each have legitimate or actual epistemic authority over our own experience of autism, any one of our perspectives, on its own, is not sufficient to achieve a more complete and accurate understanding of autism. In this sense, it is always important for Autistics not to make claims to spokespersonhood on behalf of the Autistic community as a whole. Of course, the adoption of a posture of epistemic humility in light of intersectionality and mereology does not preclude the simultaneous recognition of the possibility of coalition-building across the Autistic community and sensitivity to the contextual and intersectional differences that give rise to different needs and claims.

Another risk of which one should be aware is the possibility of power dynamics within the community of Autistic self-advocacy itself. These power dynamics are at play whenever, for example, White, oralizing Autistics end up—often inadvertently but nonetheless problematically—dominating the self-advocacy conversation on autism. Non-oralizing Autistics can communicate through writing, text-to-speech, letter boards, images, and other means of augmentative and alternative communication (AAC). Nevertheless, non-oralizing Autistics can easily be overlooked even within the Autistic community, in a way that runs directly counter to the neurodiversity movement's and disabled people's movement ideal of saying or doing "Nothing About Us Without Us." Unless intersectionality thoroughly informs and shapes the discourses and practices of the Autistic self-advocacy community, epistemic oppression in the forms of non-consultation, non-inclusion, non-recognition, and non-representation threatens to cause problems with respect to the production of knowledge, theories, and representations about autism within the Autistic community as it has done within the dominant allistic society.

To address the subjective aspect of avoidance, then, we—allistics and Autistics alike—must be aware of our respective social positions and intersectional identities, as well as the epistemic limitations that these positions and identities often entail. Importantly, allistics and Autistics who are privileged along other axes of social identity must understand that occupying their particular social position means that they do not readily have access to certain social experiences or realities. This recognition of their respective epistemic limitations should prompt allistics and Autistics alike to look for people who are better positioned to account for these experiences or realities, such as: what autism is like, what it is like to be Autistic in a neuronormative world, and what it is like to be Autistic at other intersections of social identity and oppression than one's own. These better-positioned people are Autistics ourselves, from across a range of intersectional social positions. By seeking out the first-person perspectives and accounts of differently situated Autistics, allistics and Autistics can address the objective aspect of avoidance and acquire more accurate and reliable understandings of the social experiences and realities to which we do not ourselves have access. In order to be more accurate and reliable, propositional knowledge should be informed by experiential knowledge.

Experiential and Propositional Knowledge

Within the epistemic realm of what we know, propositional knowledge is but one type of knowing. Nonpropositional or experiential types of knowing include tacit, embodied, and affective knowing (Catala 2020; Shotwell 2011, 2014). Tacit knowing refers to what we implicitly know, learn, or find out from moving through the social world. Tacit knowing can be articulated propositionally but is not typically conveyed propositionally nor made explicit. In general, one can easily notice gaps in one's tacit knowledge when one moves into a new context or an unfamiliar environment for the first time, whether a new country, school, neighborhood, workplace, organization, institution, and so on. People who are accustomed to these contexts or environments will generally know how to interact and get around with a level of ease that is not readily available to newcomers. Embodied knowing is what we know through our bodies; affective knowing, what we know through our affects. To illustrate embodied and affective knowing along with tacit knowing, consider the case of social anxiety. One may have propositional knowledge about social anxiety without ever experiencing it. By contrast, one might have experiential knowledge of social anxiety because of what they experience and know through their body and affects. For example, one's body tenses up; one's chest becomes tight; one's heart starts racing; one feels fear, stress, or nervousness; one feels an urge to disappear, hide, or leave; and so on. Additionally, one's social anxiety might be triggered by one's tacit knowledge that a particular social context is not friendly to nor welcoming of people in one's intersectional position—for example, insofar as one is an Autistic woman or a racialized, trans, or nonbinary Autistic person. Note that our propositional knowledge of what social anxiety is or feels like will be more complete, accurate, and reliable if it is informed by the perspectives of people who experience social anxiety firsthand and who therefore have experiential (tacit, embodied, affective) knowledge of social anxiety.

In the context of autism, experiential knowledge is crucial for more accurate and reliable propositional knowledge about both what autism is or how it is characterized, as well as what autism is like or how it is experienced in a neuronormative world. The necessity for propositional knowledge about what autism is or how it is characterized to be informed by the experiential knowledge of Autistics can be appreciated if one turns to some of the most common myths about Autistics, such as that we lack empathy and social motivation. These myths have rightly been called into question by Autistic and non-Autistic researchers alike (e.g., Milton 2012; Yergeau and Huebner 2017; Jaswal and Akhtar 2018). In both cases, however, the critique of these myths is fundamentally informed by the first-person propositional accounts of Autistics, which is based on the affective knowledge that they have of their capacity for empathy and social motivation. Another common characterization of autism that has repeatedly been denounced by Autistic self-advocates is that Autistics can accurately and definitively be sorted into different levels of "functioning."

Again, experiential knowledge of autism contradicts this arbitrary system of classification. Our abilities and levels of so-called functioning vary tremendously, both synchronically across the sheer variety of skills that define "functioning" and diachronically across the course of our day and of our lives. To illustrate synchronic variability, consider the fact that some extremely bright Autistic scientists may be unable to cook or clean (due to executive difficulties rather than lack of time or effort) or that some non-oralizing Autistics may have rich and meaningful social lives. With respect to diachronic variability, we may experience significant shifts, in a single day or throughout our lifetime, in our ability to tolerate spaces that are taxing on the senses; to engage in social interactions; or to execute complex tasks. Note that fanciful claims according to which Autistics can accurately and definitively be sorted into different "functioning" levels are problematic, not simply because they are false but also because they are used to deny some of us appropriate access to help or services based on our actual, rather than perceived or arbitrarily defined, support needs. Moreover, the ableist hierarchy that is implied in functioning labels creates a stigmatizing and subordinating differentiation both among Autistics specifically and among humans generally—a differentiation that historically has served as a justification for various wrongs such as eugenics and forced sterilization.

The necessity for the experiential knowledge of Autistics to inform propositional knowledge about what autism is like and how it is experienced can be brought into relief by considering the effects of neuronormativity on Autistics. As mentioned earlier, neuronormative expectations and environments can lead to various forms of collapse, such as Autistic meltdowns (saturation leading to hyperreactivity), Autistic shutdowns (saturation leading to hyporeactivity), or Autistic burnout (the utter exhaustion that results from living in a neuronormative world as an Autistic person). As these various forms of collapse demonstrate, neuronormativity in neuroableist societies is something that Autistic people know experientially through our bodies and affects. In other words, the production of accurate and reliable propositional knowledge about autism and neuronormativity requires seeking out and heeding the experiential knowledge of Autistics about our own experience of autism and neuronormativity.

Similarly, propositional knowledge about autism and neuronormativity will be more complete, accurate, and reliable if it is informed by the critical and diverse perspectives of Autistics, who directly experience autism and neuronormativity from a range of social positions and intersectional identities. I say the "critical" perspectives of Autistics because, as explained previously in the context of standpoint theory, Autistics do not automatically have an epistemically privileged perspective on autism or neuronormativity simply in virtue of being Autistic. A critical stance is required in order to avoid the very real and problematic phenomenon of internalized neuroableism and, hence, the perpetuation of epistemic oppression. Neuroableist beliefs that may be internalized by Autistics and that would contribute to our epistemic oppression might include, for instance, the beliefs that we are defective or deficient, that we do not have access to our own mental states, or that non-oralizing Autistics have nothing to contribute. These assumptions essentially cast Autistics as unreliable epistemic agents and thereby reinforce our epistemic oppression. I also say the "diverse" perspectives of Autistics because the Autistic community, like any other community, is internally diverse along axes of gender identification, sexual orientation, race, class, education, physical and intellectual dis/ability, age, culture, indigeneity, national origin, and immigration status (Ballou, daVanport, and Onaiwu 2021; Bruno 2022; Garcia 2021; Price 2022; Simmonds 2020; Srinivasan 2021; Walker 2021). As mentioned earlier, furthermore, experiencing autism as someone who is privileged along other axes of social identity such as gender identification, race, or class is very different from experiencing autism as someone who is oppressed along these other axes of social identity. Intersectionality inevitably affects and, hence, fundamentally shapes our respective experiential knowledge of autism and neuronormativity when neuroableism intersects with other systems of oppression such as racism or cisgenderism, for example. Whereas a cis White Autustic woman might feel safe stimming in certain publc spaces, a Black, Indigenous, trans, or nonbinary Autistic person might feel utterly unsafe doing so because of the risk of being perceived as a threat or even subjected to physical restraint or violence, including from law enforcement (Garcia 2021; Price 2022; Simmonds 2020). In other words, interlocking systems of oppression affect our respective experiential (tacit, embodied, affective) knowledge of what it is like to be Autistic in a world where neuroableism is compounded by other systems of oppression.

Propositional knowledge about autism, then, will be incomplete, inaccurate, and unreliable if it is not informed by the experiential, critical, and diverse knowledge of Autistics from across the range of intersectional social positions. Note, importantly, that this kind of incomplete, inaccurate, and unreliable propositional knowledge both stems from and maintains the exclusion of minoritized perspectives and therefore contributes to epistemic oppression by producing multiple forms of epistemic injustice (Catala, Faucher, and Poirier 2021; Legault, Bourdon, and Poirier 2021). Specifically, dismissing or failing to solicit the testimonies of Autistics due to neuronormative biases creates testimonial injustice insofar as Autistics are not taken seriously as knowers or not viewed as knowers at all (Fricker 2007; Dotson 2011). Moreover, marginalizing the contributions of Autistics creates contributory hermeneutical injustice (Dotson 2012) by preventing them from contributing to the pool of mainstream understandings and representations of autism, which perpetuates inaccurate interpretations of autism and the experience of Autistics.

We are now in a position to identify the second criterion for legitimate or actual epistemic authority on autism: namely, propositional knowledge must be informed by the experiential, critical, and diverse knowledge of Autistics. Together, the two criteria of awareness of subjective and objective avoidance, as well as experientially informed propositional knowledge, highlight the necessity of revising one's previous beliefs when they turn out to be false in the face of counterevidence. For example, when studies repeatedly show that Autistics do not lack theory of mind, researchers should revise their beliefs accordingly (Yergeau and Huebner 2017). Failing to adjust one's beliefs despite counterevidence is a sign of active ignorance* (Medina 2013) or avoidance, whereby members of dominant groups actively resist evidence that challenges their biased beliefs. Moreover, the two criteria are conducive to greater epistemic justice for Autistic people, as they signify that Autistics should be taken seriously as epistemic agents: as relevant interlocutors and as contributors to mainstream interpretive resources regarding autism.

Epistemic Authority as a Process and "the Diagnosis Question"

I have argued that legitimate or actual epistemic authority on autism depends on two criteria: (1) the person's awareness of subjective and objective avoidance and (2) the person's reliance on experiential, critical, and diverse knowledge. It seems to me that these two criteria are jointly necessary and perhaps also jointly sufficient. However, I want to leave open the possibility that there might be other relevant criteria for determining legitimate or actual epistemic authority on autism that might further improve or specify the two criteria that I have identified. In this final section, I want to argue furthermore that legitimate or actual epistemic authority should not be construed as a one-off outcome that can easily be checked off or that, once achieved, is permanently secured and retained. Rather, legitimate or actual epistemic authority should be viewed and approached as a process, something that must be continually practiced, repeated, updated, and developed. As a process, epistemic authority is a way to consistently approach how one produces and validates knowledge, namely, in a careful, epistemically humble way. Epistemic humility and epistemic authority are compatible rather than in conflict. Indeed, as I argued earlier, epistemic humility may be required for epistemic authority.

That epistemic authority should be construed as a process, rather than an outcome, can be appreciated by looking at the implications that this epistemological and methodological shift has for diagnosing or recognizing autism. After all, the question of legitimate authority on autism also involves the important question of legitimate authority for diagnosing or recognizing autism. I say "recognizing" autism for two main reasons. First, using the term *recognizing* allows us to observe a critical distance from the medical model of *The Diagnostic and Statistical Manual of Mental Disorders*, to avoid the pathologization of autism and, ultimately, to destabilize the monopoly that professionals often exert over the recognition of autism. This monopoly essentially amounts to a problematic form of gatekeeping with respect to both who gets to be recognized as Autistic and who has the legitimate epistemic authority to recognize autism. Second, the term *recognizing* means both "being able to tell or identify" (as when you recognize an object or a person) and "acknowledging or respecting" (as when you recognize a peer as an equal). In the context of autism, recognizing autism means both being able to identify an Autistic person as Autistic (typically through a professional or personal process) and acknowledging the fact that Autistic phenotypes can vary greatly across other axes of social identity, such as gender identification or race. Indeed, recognizing autism in the sense of identifying autism requires recognizing autism in the sense of acknowledging the variety of Autistic phenotypes. This acknowledgment requires being familiar with up-to-date research on Autistic phenotypes and demographics, as well as with first-person accounts of autism from across a range of social identities (i.e., the experiential and diverse knowledge of Autistics). Many professionals do not meet either of these requirements. By contrast, many Autistics, who were not previously aware that they are Autistic, come to recognize themselves as Autistic by meeting these requirements. Here we can see the significance of construing actual epistemic authority as a process that needs to be updated and that can be developed and, hence, the importance of questioning the monopoly that professionals often have over the recognition of autism. Let us look more closely at several factors that support these claims.

The question of seeking and receiving a professional diagnosis is a question both of accessibility and of socio-personal circumstances. Not every Autistic person can easily have access to a professional diagnosis (a matter of accessibility). Nor does every Autistic person want a professional diagnosis (a matter of socio-personal circumstances). Let me say a bit more about each of these two scenarios. Accessing a professional diagnosis is not always possible for various reasons including, but not limited to, age, income, geographical region, language, immigration status, gender, and race. Autistic adults who were born before the 1980s are referred to in the scientific literature as "the lost generation" because professional understanding and public awareness of autism were (even more) limited prior to that time (Lai and Baron-Cohen 2015). Depending on the context, waitlists for professional assessments can be long and the financial cost prohibitive. Even when one makes it to the stage of a formal assessment, one may not be properly diagnosed as Autistic due to the gender and racial biases that often interfere with the interpretation of relevant traits or behaviors and with the application of diagnostic criteria. For example, it is common for Autistic girls and women to fly under the diagnostic radar because their Autistic traits manifest differently than boys' or men's do. Many Autistics—especially women, people who were assigned female at birth, and racialized people—are also known to mask their Autistic traits, which means professionals who are not aware of the phenomenon of masking (also known as camouflaging) might fail to recognize them as Autistic (Bargiela, Steward, and Mandy 2016; Dean, Harwood, and Kasari 2017; Lai et al. 2017; Tierney, Burns, and Kilbey 2016). Additionally, Autistics who are Black, Indigenous, or people of color are more likely than their White peers to be diagnosed with behavioral disorders instead of autism (Garcia 2021; Price 2022).

In addition to the fact that a professional diagnosis is far from accessible to every Autistic, not every Autistic wants to have a professional diagnosis, usually due to their socio-personal circumstances. Many Autistics recognize themselves as Autistic (i.e., self-diagnose) by reading up on autism from scholarly and autobiographical sources, blogs, forums, social media, and the like. Some Autistics deem that recognizing themselves as Autistic is sufficient and do not feel the need to seek a professional confirmation of what they already know from extensive reading or engagement with fellow Autistics. Some, especially women, Indigenous and racialized people, and trans or nonbinary people, may even be vigorously opposed to seeking a professional diagnosis because of a deep distrust of the professional system due to past adverse experiences with medical, clinical, and other practitioners, such as institutional violence or gaslighting.

The foregoing factors, then, highlight the significance of construing actual epistemic authority as a process that needs to be updated and that can be developed. Moreover, these factors point to the need to call into question the monopoly that professionals often exert over the recognition of autism. Professionals who may at one point have been up to date in their knowledge about autism continue to rely on what are now outdated, partial, and, hence, inaccurate and misleading beliefs about how to recognize autism. Because of their professional status, these professionals retain perceived epistemic authority even though they no longer have actual epistemic authority for recognizing autism. This, then, is a clear case of credibility excess. By contrast, previously unidentified Autistics who acquire the relevant knowledge to be able to recognize themselves as Autistic typically lack perceived epistemic authority for recognizing autism (especially outside the Autistic community), even though they have actual epistemic authority to do so based on their newly acquired propositional knowledge and their ability to match it to their own experiential knowledge of autism. This, then, is a clear case of undue credibility deficit. The mismatch between actual and perceived epistemic authority that these credibility excesses and deficits capture is also reflected in the fact that self-recognition (or self-diagnosis) of autism is granted a second-class status compared to the first-class status that is granted to professional recognition (or diagnosis) of autism. In light of all the factors surveyed, this prioritization of professional over personal recognition of autism seems plainly unwarranted.

Indeed, this unwarranted prioritization gives rise to two gatekeeping problems. The first problem concerns who gets to be recognized as Autistic and takes the form of a concern that autism is "over-diagnosed." The second problem, which might be called "the Diagnosis Question," concerns who has legitimate epistemic authority to recognize autism. Let me begin with the "over-diagnosing" objection, which might as well be called the "over-inclusion" objection (as if there were ever such a thing in the context of social justice). Autism is part of neurodiversity, which is part of biodiversity. Like biodiversity, neurodiversity and autism are found all over the world. Autism is also present across all age groups, gender identities, socioeconomic classes, and cultural or racialized groups. It is crucial for all Autistics to be properly identified or recognized as Autistic so that their specific needs can be adequately addressed and so that they can thrive regardless of the intersectionality of their respective social positions. Autism is a heterogeneous reality that does not admit of quotas. To think that autism is overdiagnosed simply because a better understanding of autism makes the diagnosis or identification accessible to more people than just White boys is to unduly try to control who has access to recognition as Autistic and the positive things that can come from it, including self-understanding and self-acceptance, a sense of belonging to a community, empowerment, access to certain services or inclusion measures, and so on. "The Diagnosis Question" asks whether someone who identifies as Autistic does so as a result of a professional or a personal assessment. "The Diagnosis Question" creates both the illusion that the question is justifiably asked and the expectation that every Autistic should be willing to answer it so that recognition by the relevant "authorities" of their autism can be granted or denied accordingly. In neuronormative societies, professional recognition of autism may be necessary for insurance or "accommodations" purposes. Yet this institutional requirement tells us less about the importance or validity of a professional assessment than it does about the neuronormativity and pervasive lack of universal accessibility that characterize our (neuro)ableist world.

References

Ballou, Emily Paige, Sharon daVanport, and Morénike Giwa Onaiwu, eds. (2021), *Sincerely, Your Autistic Child: What People on the Autism Spectrum Wish Their Parents Knew about Growing up, Acceptance, and Identity*, Boston: Beacon Press.

Bargiela, Sarah, Robyn Steward, and William Mandy (2016), "The Experiences of Late-Diagnosed Women with Autism Spectrum Conditions: An Investigation of the Female Autism Phenotype," *Journal of Autism and Developmental Disorders* 46 (10): 3281–94. https://doi.org/10.1007/s10803-016-2872-8.

Baron-Cohen, Simon (1997), *Mindblindness: An Essay on Autism and Theory of Mind. Learning, Development, and Conceptual Change*, Cambridge, MA: MIT Press.

Bruno, Grant (2022), "Pîtoteyihtam: A Nehiyaw Perspective on Autism." Available at: https://www.casda.ca/cals/event-info/agenda/ (accessed June 17, 2023).
Catala, Amandine (2019), "Multicultural Literacy, Epistemic Injustice, and White Ignorance," *Feminist Philosophy Quarterly* 5 (2): 1–23. https://doi.org/10.5206/fpq/2019.2.7289.
Catala, Amandine (2020), "Metaepistemic Injustice and Intellectual Disability: A Pluralist Account of Epistemic Agency," *Ethical Theory and Moral Practice* 23 (5): 755–76. https://doi.org/10.1007/s10677-020-10120-0.
Catala, Amandine (2022a), "Academic Excellence and Structural Epistemic Injustice: Toward a More Just Epistemic Economy in Philosophy," *Journal of Social Philosophy* 1–24. https://doi.org/10.1111/josp.12465.
Catala, Amandine (2022b), "Toward Greater Neuroinclusion in Philosophy," Blog of the APA (blog), April 4. Available at: https://blog.apaonline.org/2022/04/04/toward-greater-neuroinclusion-in-philosophy/ (accessed June 17, 2023).
Catala, Amandine, Luc Faucher, and Pierre Poirier (2021), "Autism, Epistemic Injustice, and Epistemic Disablement: A Relational Account of Epistemic Agency," *Synthese* 199: 9013–39. https://doi.org/10.1007/s11229-021-03192-7.
Dean, Michelle, Robin Harwood, and Connie Kasari (2017), "The Art of Camouflage: Gender Differences in the Social Behaviors of Girls and Boys with Autism Spectrum Disorder," *Autism* 21 (6): 678–89. https://doi.org/10.1177/1362361316671845.
Dotson, Kristie (2011), "Tracking Epistemic Violence, Tracking Practices of Silencing," *Hypatia: A Journal of Feminist Philosophy* 26 (2): 236–57. https://doi.org/10.1111/j.1527-2001.2011.01177.x.
Dotson, Kristie (2012), "A Cautionary Tale: On Limiting Epistemic Oppression," *Frontiers: A Journal of Women Studies* 33 (1): 24–47. https://doi.org/10.5250/fronjwomestud.33.1.0024.
Fricker, Miranda (2007), *Epistemic Injustice: Power and the Ethics of Knowing*, Oxford: Oxford University Press.
Garcia, Eric (2021), *We're Not Broken: Changing the Autism Conversation*, Boston: Houghton Mifflin Harcourt.
Harding, Sandra G. (1986), *The Science Question in Feminism*, Ithaca: Cornell University Press.
Hartsock, Nancy C. M. (1983), "The Feminist Standpoint: Developing the Ground for a Specifically Feminist Historical Materialism," in Sandra Harding and Merrill B. Hintikka (eds.), *Discovering Reality*, 161: 283–310, Synthese Library, Dordrecht: Kluwer Academic Publishers. https://doi.org/10.1007/0-306-48017-4_15.
Hens, Kristien, I. Robeyns, and K. Schaubroeck (2018), "The Ethics of Autism," *Philosophy Compass* 14 (1): 1–11.
Jaswal, Vikram K. and Nameera Akhtar (2018), "Being vs. Appearing Socially Uninterested: Challenging Assumptions about Social Motivation in Autism," *The Behavioral and Brain Sciences* 42: 1–84.
Lai, Meng-Chuan and Simon Baron-Cohen (2015), "Identifying the Lost Generation of Adults with Autism Spectrum Conditions," *The Lancet Psychiatry* 2 (11): 1013–27. https://doi.org/10.1016/S2215-0366(15)00277-1.
Lai, Meng-Chuan, Michael V. Lombardo, Amber N. V. Ruigrok, Bhismadev Chakrabarti, Bonnie Auyeung, Peter Szatmari, Francesca Happé, Simon Baron-Cohen, and MRC AIMS Consortium (2017), "Quantifying and Exploring Camouflaging in Men and Women with Autism," *Autism* 21 (6): 690–702. https://doi.org/10.1177/1362361316671012.

Legault, Mylène, Jean-Nicolas Bourdon, and Pierre Poirier (2021), "From Neurodiversity to Neurodivergence: The Role of Epistemic and Cognitive Marginalization," *Synthese*, August. https://doi.org/10.1007/s11229-021-03356-5.

Medina, José (2013), *The Epistemology of Resistance: Gender and Racial Oppression, Epistemic Injustice, and the Social Imagination*, New York: Oxford University Press. https://doi.org/10.1093/acprof:oso/9780199929023.001.0001.

Mills, Charles (1997), *The Racial Contract*, Ithaca: Cornell University Press.

Mills, Charles (2007), "White Ignorance," in Shannon Sullivan and Nancy Tuana (eds.), *Race and Epistemologies of Ignorance*, 13–38, Albany: State University of New York Press.

Mills, Charles (2015), "Global White Ignorance," in Matthias Gross and Linsey McGoey (eds.), *Routledge International Handbook of Ignorance Studies*, 217–27, London and New York: Routledge, Taylor & Francis Group.

Milton, Damian E. M. (2012), "On the Ontological Status of Autism: The 'Double Empathy Problem'," *Disability and Society* 27 (6): 883–7. https://doi.org/10.1080/09687599.2012.710008.

Price, Devon (2022), *Unmasking Autism: Discovering the New Faces of Neurodiversity*, First edition, New York: Harmony Books.

Saul, Jennifer (2017), "Implicit Bias, Stereotype Threat, and Epistemic Injustice," in Ian James Kidd, José Medina, and Gaile Pohlhaus Jr. (eds.), *The Routledge Handbook of Epistemic Injustice*, 235–42, New York: Routledge.

Shotwell, Alexis (2011), *Knowing Otherwise: Race, Gender, and Implicit Understanding*, University Park: Pennsylvania State University Press.

Shotwell, Alexis (2014), "Implicit Knowledge: How It Is Understood and Used in Feminist Theory: Implicit Knowledge," *Philosophy Compass* 9 (5): 315–24. https://doi.org/10.1111/phc3.12130.

Simmonds, Melissa (2020), "Missing Voices: The Black Autistics Journey." Available at: https://www.youtube.com/watch?v=UkKwT-3IWfg (accessed July 21, 2023).

Simplican, Stacy Clifford (2015), *The Capacity Contract: Intellectual Disability and the Question of Citizenship*, Minneapolis: University of Minnesota Press.

Singer, Judy (2017), *NeuroDiversity: The Birth of an Idea*, Lexington: Judy Singer.

Srinivasan, Hari (2021), "A Boy Like Me," Disability Visibility Project (blog). Available at: https://disabilityvisibilityproject.com/2021/02/06/a-boy-like-me/. (accessed July 21, 2023).

Tierney, Siobhan, Jan Burns, and Elizabeth Kilbey (2016), "Looking behind the Mask: Social Coping Strategies of Girls on the Autistic Spectrum," *Research in Autism Spectrum Disorders* 23 (March): 73–83. https://doi.org/10.1016/j.rasd.2015.11.013.

Toole, Briana (2019), "From Standpoint Epistemology to Epistemic Oppression," *Hypatia: A Journal of Feminist Philosophy* 34 (4): 598–618. https://doi.org/10.1111/hypa.12496.

Tremain, Shelley L. (2017), *Foucault and Feminist Philosophy of Disability*, Ann Arbor: University of Michigan Press.

Walker, Nick (2021), *Neuroqueer Heresies: Notes on the Neurodiversity Paradigm, Autistic Empowerment, and Postnormal Possibilities*, Fort Worth: Autonomous Press.

Wylie, Alison (2003), "Why Standpoint Matters," in Robert Figueroa and Sandra G. Harding (eds.), *Science and Other Cultures: Issues in Philosophies of Science and Technology*, 339–51, New York: Routledge.

Yergeau, Melanie and Bryce Huebner (2017), "Minding Theory of Mind," *Journal of Social Philosophy* 48 (3): 273–96. https://doi.org/10.1111/josp.12191.

PART III

PHENOMENOLOGIES OF ACCESS AND EXCLUSION

12 DISABILITY, ACCESS, AND THE PROMISE OF INCLUSION

RETURNING TO INSTITUTIONAL LANGUAGE THROUGH A PHENOMENOLOGICAL LENS

CORINNE LAJOIE

In the opening pages of her seminal study of the question of access in higher education, Tanya Titchkosky proposes that "the academy is part of a neoliberal context where it is generally assumed that 'we all' value access and desire inclusion" (Titchkosky 2011: x). Access and inclusion are commonly framed as synonymous with modern democratic ideals and tasked with overturning the historical exclusion of disabled people from all dimensions of public life, including from educational settings. On this common-sense view, that is, access is framed as a necessary condition for the inclusion of disabled people and as a solution to the problems caused by the people whose bodyminds must be absorbed into the smooth, predictable course of institutional life.

This general set of assumptions, however, belies deeper problems. At a political level, the experiences and priorities of disabled people still take a back seat to the authority of policymakers, administrators, and large institutions in determining conditions for inclusion, standards of legal compliance, and the forms of access that are available. Although in the past thirty years significant advancements have been made in US civil rights legislation that protects disabled people against discrimination in educational institutions, patterns of discrimination persist (Colker 2007; Maroto and Pettinicchio 2015). The conflation of access with the promise of inclusion also raises a host of conceptual questions, starting with: What does inclusion promise? How, if at all, do the forms of inaccessibility that disabled people experience inform this promise as opposed to, say, what able-bodied people imagine access barriers to be? In what ways do institutional worlds congeal around words and bodyminds that do *not* pose a problem? What happens when claims for access and inclusion no longer generate friction? By whom, for what purpose, and at what cost are disabled people welcomed into a more "inclusive" world? This set of questions steers my phenomenological analysis of institutional language in the chapter that follows.

In the contemporary university, layers of familiarity conceal the senses of the terms *access* and *inclusion*. Insofar as they are obscured, these notions remain largely unexamined and have acquired the status of "ordinary" words. That which is perceived as ordinary usually seems self-evident and necessary. In fact, ordinariness can serve to dissimulate the ways in which (or the reasons why) certain things have become ordinary in the first place, as well as obscure the possibility of things becoming otherwise. A critical analysis of the status quo requires that we refuse to leave ordinary conceptions of access and inclusion unexamined. This chapter takes as its starting point the claim that the very ordinariness of the terms *access* and *inclusion* signals the need for a more careful appraisal of what these notions represent than currently exists in most institutional settings. In order to embark on this critical examination of them, I offer a phenomenological investigation of institutional language that brings to the foreground what typically recedes to the background of institutions. Drawing on resources in the work of Sara Ahmed (2012) and other authors, I study the gaps between what institutions do and what they say they do. My examination of these gaps centers the relationship between institutional language, commitments, and the lived experiences of disabled people in higher education.

In the first section of this chapter, I introduce phenomenology as a key methodological resource with which to study features of our lives that typically remain unnoticed. These typically unnoticed features—what phenomenologists call the "background" features of experience—play a constitutive role in the establishment of the conditions for worldly engagement, intersubjective sense-making, and understanding. Insofar as the background is rarely perceived for itself, however, it must be disoriented to come into view. Disorientations can shift our attention and allow us to return in a new light to what is taken to be ordinary. Building on these insights, I call into question taken-for-granted understandings of access and inclusion and show how words can form the "rhetorical background" of institutional lifeworlds. On this account, words are not merely higher-level entities divorced from lived experience. Rather, they are instruments that help constitute how we orient ourselves in worlds shared with others. In the second section, I examine how, by withdrawing from scrutiny, the notions of access and inclusion happily circulate in academic worlds. In turn, I offer a threefold critique of the rhetoric of inclusion, arguing that

(1) this rhetoric does not identify or seek to disrupt underlying oppressive structures; (2) this rhetoric can falsely motivate the impression of change and lead us to underestimate both the traction of sedimented institutional habits *and* the institution's ability to adapt strategically its mechanisms of exclusion; and (3) this rhetoric is always conditional and often relies on unspoken distinctions between "undeserving" (i.e., "problematic") and "deserving" disabled people.

Starting with the Background: Returning to Institutional Language through a Phenomenological Lens

Phenomenology offers us tools to re-orient our attention toward what is least noticeable and nonetheless shapes the worlds that we inhabit. As a practice of attention, phenomenology allows us to uncover (or recover) what recedes to the background and transform it into an object of study. By studying the background conditions that make our experience of the world coherent and meaningful, phenomenology can help us interrogate *how* and *which* things become ordinary. In what follows, I ask how, by becoming the unquestioned background of our experience, or simply "the way things are," the familiarity of institutional language functions to conceal ideals, values, and commitments that recede from view. I submit that a phenomenology of institutional language gains its critical edge by asking how institutional power is served by words that have become ordinary.

An example of this practice of critical attention to institutional language is offered by Ahmed's *On Being Included* (2012). Ahmed turns to the notions of diversity and inclusion as sites of inquiry for understanding the relationship between racism, whiteness, and institutional life. As Ahmed explains it, diversity and inclusion have become common-sense goods on the neoliberal marketplace of higher education. Many universities count at least one committee dedicated to the implementation of these values. It might appear to be an odd choice, then, to study notions that have become so widely embraced as to become familiar. Yet it is precisely the familiarity of these notions—and what this familiarity dissimulates—that motivates Ahmed's project. Ahmed investigates how the ease with which the language of diversity and inclusion circulates in institutions contributes to creating the barriers and blockages that minoritized others encounter in these spaces.

When notions of social reconfiguration such as diversity and inclusion circulate without any resistance and do not come up against institutional walls, we should be wary of the work that they are in fact doing. Notions that are "detached from histories of struggle over inequality" (Ahmed 2012: 80) might be enabled to circulate more easily by virtue of this detachment. These notions might become empty vessels that merely reproduce the status quo. Put another way, words might seem to be doing transformative work but in fact actively work to keep things exactly the way they are. Ahmed coins the term *non-performatives* to describe how words can deliberately fail to bring into effect what they promise. As Ahmed defines it, a non-performative is "happy" (i.e., successful) in institutional contexts when it does not do what it says it does, thereby allowing institutions to "make commitments without being behind them" (119). To actually get behind these commitments (e.g., to diversity or inclusion) would require institutions to override past commitments (e.g., to racism, sexism, ableism, or classism), which they are often not genuinely willing to do. Ahmed notes that supposedly new commitments to diversity and inclusion on the part of university can be a way to bring the past into the future "by sheer force of habit" (127). That is, the past can be smuggled into the present under the cover of a willingness to transform institutions, including through appeals to non-performatives.

To better recognize how institutional language upholds the status quo, we need what Ahmed calls a "politics of reattachment" (Ahmed 2012: 80). A politics of reattachment investigates the meaning and use of certain notions and allows them "to be shared as a question" (81) precisely by calling them into question. In order to reattach words to meanings that they may have lost, or which may have become obscured through repeated use, we must take a phenomenological approach to institutional language. The task of phenomenology, in this context, is to help us identify how language, bodies, and worlds coalesce, while refusing to take for granted or naturalize the relationship between them. Indeed, as a method, phenomenology is a particularly helpful tool with which to call into question institutional language. In order to engage in a phenomenological politics of reattachment, however, we must deliberately reverse the order of priority between the background and the foreground of our purview and begin our inquiry with what recedes from view. Bringing the background elements of our lives into view effects a type of disorientation that allows us to better understand why certain things are made to disappear and what is lost when they do.

Phenomenology offers us multiple accounts of the relationship between background and foreground as foundational to perception and bodily life. In the first book of *Ideas*, Husserl analyzes conscious acts as possessing an intentional structure: consciousness is always "consciousness of something" (Husserl 2014: 162). Husserl describes the directionality of consciousness through the image of a halo radiating from the pure ego and toward its object. Consciousness singles out an object in directing itself toward it. The elements that surround this object continue to be present for consciousness;

however, they are relegated to the margins of the halo as the material thing "stands out [from] this background" (162). Husserl offers the example of the perception of a piece of white paper: "Around the paper lie books, pens, inkwell, and so forth; they are also 'perceived' in a certain way [. . .] but while I am turned to the paper, they dispense with any such turn to them and apprehension of them" (61). The piece of paper itself is given in a clear intuition, while its surroundings are only dimly lit by consciousness's halo and are not themselves apprehended.

The focus of consciousness can readily change. The books, pens, and inkwell on Husserl's desk (one may suppose) can be brought into focus and become explicitly perceived for their own sake. From one moment to the next, the halo of consciousness can glide over the paper and onto the inkwell—for example, when the inkwell is knocked over and spills on the desk. In more conceptual terms, non-actualized perceptual possibilities can be actualized through a reorganization of our mode of attention or of the perceptual field itself. The background can become foreground through a shift in focus. What constitutes the foreground and background of our awareness is as much defined by our engagement with the world as it is by the world itself as a horizon that both precedes and exceeds our engagement with it. We learn from Husserl that the relationship between background and foreground is dynamic rather than fixed. It involves a movement of oscillation as our focus shifts with new elements brought into focus and others placed out of focus.

Husserl and Maurice Merleau-Ponty also describe the shifting relationship between background and foreground through the lens of operative intentionality. Where act-intentionality describes explicit conscious acts such as judgments and decisions, a more latent intentional structure supports pre-reflective forms of bodily activity. Operative intentionality denotes a practical, non-representational orientation to the world as a sphere for action and perception. Rather than limiting intentionality to mental representations, both authors theorize intentionality as fully embodied and describe how our bodies move through the world against a spatial and temporal background. Habitual movements, for example, recede from our conscious awareness and sediment in our body schema. Once incorporated into our body schema, they are available to be re-activated and do not require that we call them forth explicitly. Habits of movement and perception become the background against which we perceive the world and interact with others. Just as Merleau-Ponty describes that some parts of our body trail behind "like a comet's tail" (Merleau-Ponty 2012: 102) when we are absorbed in a task, we might say that the subject trails behind its own habitual bodily responses to the world, engaging its bodily past to foreground only the necessary aspects of a lived situation. At an organic level, many vital bodily functions also operate below the level of conscious awareness (e.g., the autonomic nervous system regulates our heart rate, respiration, arousal, and digestion). It would be both impossible and undesirable for one to be fully aware of every feature of our environment and every bodily function that allows us to exist in the world. One's feet need to recede from consciousness to ride a bike smoothly. So, too, does our breathing recede from our immediate awareness at most moments of the day. Most simply, some aspects of ourselves and our world must recede for other aspects of them to become manifest.

The diacritical structure of background and foreground does not merely operate at an individual level. The background of our experience includes organic bodily functions, personal embodied histories, and forms of bodily self-awareness; however, these elements are always embedded in richly intersubjective social, cultural, institutional, affective, and political horizons which help constitute them. Phenomenological analyses of racialization as a habit of perception show, for example, how racialization structures our interactions with the world and with others in largely unconscious ways, by receding to the background of our awareness (Alcoff 2006; Al-Saji 2010, 2014; Ngo 2019). Within this habitual embodied perceptual framework, whiteness becomes the invisible norm according to which objects, others, and environments are perceived and some of them are marked as inherently "deviant" or "dangerous" (Curry 2006; Fielding 2006; Guenther 2019; Yancy 2017; Tremain 2017). Whiteness can—and often does—provide the unquestioned background against which intercorporeal relations, relations of property, and social and political relations emerge and are interpreted.

We might also think of what Tobin Siebers (2011) names "the ideology of ability" as unconsciously structuring our perceptions of and engagement with the world and with our own bodyminds. Siebers straightforwardly describes this ideology as a general "preference for able-bodiedness" (Siebers 2011: 8). The ideology of ability plays a central role in how human status and worth are attributed to persons. It motivates desires to both transcend and perfect the human body, which desires are both contradictory and complementary. As Siebers explains, this ideology is "imbricated [. . .] in our thinking and practices" (9), but largely remains unnoticed. If we extend Sieber's argument in a phenomenological direction, we can argue that the tendency to repress or reject an awareness of our bodies as vulnerable to ailment, aging, decay, or impairment is intertwined with a socially embedded ideology of ability that equates disability with inferiority and lack. With this phenomenological approach, we can recognize how the ideology of ability functions as background to our conceptions of and lived experiences of embodiment, often without our explicit or conscious awareness.

Building on the insights of Ahmed, Husserl, Merleau-Ponty, and Siebers (among others), I offer the notion of "rhetorical background" to describe how linguistic expressions, sets of concepts, turns of phrase, signs and symbols, and modes of speech can sediment and form the unthematized background against which bodily action and perception unfold. Institutional statements offer a relevant case study for this claim. In 2016, the Pennsylvania State University adopted an official statement in which it elaborated its commitment to diversity and inclusion. The central expressed aim of the statement is to provide units within the university with a clear sense of direction as they devise their own diversity plans and statements. Marcus Whitehurst, the university's Vice-Provost for Educational Equity, explains the university's goal in drafting this statement as follows: "When anyone asks, 'Where does Penn State stand when it comes to diversity?', we can point to our diversity statement, and say, 'This is where we stand, these are the actions that we want to take as an institution, as a community'" (Waldhier 2016). The statement, which can be found on the university's website, outlines a set of commitments to diversity, equity, and inclusion in areas such as recruitment, retention, representation, and review. In particular, the statement identifies the centrality of inclusion as "a core strength and an essential element of [the university's] public service mission" (ibid.). In turning to this statement, I do not wish to single out the Pennsylvania State University in any way. Both in form and in content, the Penn State statement resembles the statements issued by many other learning institutions across North America in recent years. I am rather interested in how a statement of this kind can function as a background against which decisions are made, actions are performed, and orientations (both symbolic and material) are adopted. The statement can be brought again to the foreground and made thematic, such as, for example, when someone asks, "Where does the university stand when it comes to diversity?" It functions most efficiently, however, as an unthematized background that an institutional community implicitly shares and in relation to which various objects and experiences acquire meaning. When the words fade into the background, they are passively carried into individual and collective habits and perceptions.

In an evocative formulation, Ahmed names the elements that come to form the background of our lives "points of recession" (Ahmed 2012: 38). For Ahmed, institutions cohere through a movement of recession, which is another way of saying that things are institutionalized by "[becoming] part of the background for those who are part of an institution" (21). Certain things become ordinary features of institutional life and constitute its background. Modes of functioning and communication, forms of bodily interaction, practices of silencing, hierarchies, values, types of humor, institutional commitments, attitudes, and material barriers become *the way things are* by receding to the background. Ahmed further suggests that "[to] share a world might be to share the points of recession" (38). In other words, sharing a world with others could mean sharing what gets looked over and becomes part of the background; entire worlds may be built on the commonality of points of recession. Sharing points of recession can even be a way to gain inclusion into these worlds: we may need to accept what gets passed over as a *condition* for belonging in a particular world. Words, for example, can become conditions. When we adopt, or even enthusiastically embrace, certain words (e.g., *diversity*, *inclusion*, and now *access*), we are seen as "fitting in." Embracing these words becomes a way for one to signal institutional fit. Alternatively, those who call into question the ordinariness of institutional language, forcing the background into the foreground, are seen as being out of place. Some points of recession are necessary: one's feet when walking, the ground when rushing to a meeting. Other points of recession are a function of the contingent social and political organization of shared lifeworlds and contribute to the normalization of systems of violence.

It can be difficult to notice points of recession, given that the background is precisely that which recedes from view in order to make *other* things visible. To borrow Merleau-Ponty's example in *Phenomenology of Perception*, we do not typically notice the lighting in a room, but rather only the objects it illuminates (Merleau-Ponty 2012: 324–6). When we are absorbed in a situation, the background itself remains invisible. The lighting in the room, for Merleau-Ponty, functions as a level. Merleau-Ponty's technical term *levels* refers to norms that recede and organize our perceptions of and actions in the world. Levels are not themselves perceived. Rather, levels, too, recede from our immediate awareness; they make worldly engagement possible by remaining between (or behind) things. Levels are also highly adaptable, for, like Husserl before him, Merleau-Ponty adopts a view of bodily life as inherently mutable and temporally open-ended. Shifts in levels are required to meet the changing demands of our situation. Consider, for example, how the spatial level tilts when we lay down on the ground, or how the visual level of lighting adapts as we walk into a building after being out in the sun for hours. Although levels offer up the sedimentation of a particular way of being in the world, they change to allow our bodies to gear into a new situation, or for this situation to meet our bodies in ways that orientate us. Furthermore, Merleau-Ponty's theorization of levels centrally considers the possibility of these background levels themselves coming into view. For Merleau-Ponty, levels allow us to establish an equilibrium between body and world in which worldly engagement is nevertheless constantly re-negotiated and susceptible to moments of surprise, latent tension, hesitation, loss, or disruption. In other terms, the lability of levels fundamentally engages the possibility of disorientations.

Disorientations draw our attention to what previously receded to the background: a person may notice the ground under their mobility device when a wheel gets stuck in a pothole; someone else may notice their breathing when it becomes strenuous after performing a task; and another person may notice the light in the corner of the room when it begins to flicker. More pointedly, and as feminist, queer, disability, and critical race scholars have argued in various contexts, people whose bodies and minds position them obliquely in relation to hegemonic norms and practices may notice that which typically gets overlooked in the process of creating worlds by virtue of their exclusion from them (Ahmed 2006; Garland-Thomson 2011; Harbin 2016; bell hooks 2000; Hill Collins 2022; Lugones 2003; Ortega 2016). When we find ourselves being out of sync with the level assumed by others, the level itself becomes visible. Similarly, when points of recession no longer function as the background against which other things appear, they appear for themselves and can be examined.

Phenomenological attention to such processes of disorientation is central to my use of phenomenology as a method for reflecting on institutional language. As Ahmed's work repeatedly emphasizes, we learn about worlds and institutions by refusing to tacitly accept—or, to borrow an expression favored by Ahmed, "get behind"—the points of recession that they involve. With respect to the case that concerns us in this chapter, interrogating the language of access and inclusion involves throwing into relief a rhetorical background that produces harmful social, political, and institutional arrangements. This rhetorical background functions most effectively when it is taken for granted. By refusing to uncritically *get behind* it, I seek to disorient the meanings of access and inclusion and call these notions into question. In making this claim, I wish to recognize that refusing to get behind the habits of an institution is itself disorienting. The effects of these disorientations are felt in very concrete, embodied ways by the people who occupy the margins of the institution. For many people, including scholars of color, and trans or gender nonconforming, disabled, and chronically ill scholars, being disoriented in and by higher education takes a considerable physical and mental toll. At the same time, however, the act of refusing the ways in which some things that serve as background to our lives are made to seem both necessary and ordinary can give us critical leverage and allow us to better understand how we might transform institutions. The next section turns to the conceptual pair of access and inclusion to examine the gaps between the happy promise of inclusion and the lived experiences of disabled people in higher education.

Access and the (Happy) Promise of Inclusion

Access is commonly viewed as a cornerstone of disability inclusion. Accessibility is required to facilitate the inclusion of disabled students, faculty, and staff in every aspect of institutional life. Eventually, the rhetorical contiguity of these notions—often alongside the notion of diversity—in mission statements, official letters, annual reports, and grant applications, generates a sense of conceptual continuity. To borrow a formulation by Ahmed, "one word seems to follow, almost automatically, the other," such that "the association between them becomes stronger" (Ahmed 2019: 50) as a function of repeated use. When words trail innocuously behind one another, they acquire a particular shine. Together, they bounce around pleasantly like a familiar jingle that is "in tune, in time, not abrasive because it is [shiny and happy]" (Ahmed 2014). When some words sound shiny, happy, and melodic, other words, like *sexism*, *racism*, or *ableism* sound dull, angry, and noisy. Even more, these words appear to "have lost their utility" (ibid.). The uses of institutional language teach us about how institutions function and about what is useful to them. In the case of the notions of access and inclusion, the rhetoric of inclusion covers over the complexity of disability as a phenomenon and furthers practices of exclusion under the cover of institutional change.

In her study of diversity, Ahmed examines how the buzz around this notion in higher education serves to cancel out the (white) noise of institutional racism. When the notion of diversity is buzzing around, the racism of institutions is less noticeable. More perniciously, faculty and students who expose the racism of so-called diverse institutions are accused of being angry, paranoid, or pathologically stuck in a racist past that has been overcome. By naming racism, they become a problem for institutions rather than institutional whiteness being named as the problem. The mere act of "bring[ing] a problem to institutional attention can mean [. . .] becoming what 'gets in the way' of institutional happiness" (Ahmed 2012: 146–7). This "getting in the way" of institutional happiness, however, is necessary when happiness "allows inequalities to be concealed and thus reproduced" (72). In a similar manner, I suggest that the recent buzz around access and inclusion in institutional settings can serve to cover up the noisy complaints of those who denounce the inaccessibility of ableist social worlds. In short, disabled people who request accommodations or point out inaccessibility are perceived as the problem when they refuse to get behind the institution's rhetorical background and instead point at the gaps between institutional discourse and practice.

Inspired by Ahmed's fruitful notion of the feminist killjoy, scholars of disability offer the notion of the crip killjoy to describe how the bodyminds, sensations, affects, and needs of disabled people put them at odds—at times, willingly and at other times, unwillingly—with cultural demands for happiness. The crip killjoy, as Lisa Merri Johnson and Robert McRuer (2014) suggest, can kill joy simply by virtue of refusing to apologize for relinquishing fantasies of hyper-ability and demands for productivity. The tired body, the ill body, or the body in pain are often seen as killing joy and as disturbing happiness when their fatigue, illness, or pain challenge ideals of health, fitness, and ability (Mollow 2013). The pressure from the neoliberal university to be "happy, flexible, and productive employee[s]" (Apelmo and Nordgren 2021: 119) frequently casts disabled people's requests for access (or even the fact of disability itself) as burdensome and as synonymous with negative affects such as resentment, bitterness, peevishness, entitlement, or jealousy. Insofar as one refuses institutional happiness by questioning the institution's commitment to creating access, one positions oneself as a crip killjoy. In this case, killing joy *cripply* involves refusing to turn access and inclusion into "happy" words for the institution. If happiness describes an affective and sensorial orientation toward objects, situations, values, and persons, as Ahmed suggests (2010), then refusing institutional happiness involves staying *out of line* with institutions by calling them into question.

Symbols, much like words, also perform affective work. The International Symbol of Access (ISA) depicts a white stylized outline of a person sitting in a wheelchair against a blue background. First adopted at the eleventh World Congress of Rehabilitation International in 1969, it has quickly become a ubiquitous symbol of disability in everyday life. The symbol can be found anywhere: from bathroom stalls, to elevators, parking spots, doors, or vehicles. It serves to indicate the presence of access, or, perhaps more accurately, it signals a legalized, compliance-based commitment to accessibility. Kelly Fritsch analyzes the ISA as implicated in "a happy affective economy" (Fritsch 2013: 135) that produces disability as "an individualized problem that can be known and solved." The affective economy in which the ISA circulates primarily caters to the comfort of nondisabled people and eases their minds. The symbol is intended to indicate that "the difference of disability [has been] taken care of" (ibid.). The ISA's presence eliminates the challenge and unease that would arise through an examination of the difference that disability makes: "With the appearance of the ISA, happy affects of having 'done our duty for the disabled' circulate" (144). When duties have been performed, disability can once again recede to the background.

The logic of the ISA that Fritsch describes echoes my earlier discussion of the relationship between background and foreground. The ISA symbol appears—or is foregrounded—to allow disability to "happily" recede to the background. In Fritsch's terms, the ISA is "a symbol of inclusion and accommodation [that] allows disability to appear in order to disappear." More precisely, what disappears is "the difference and uncomfortableness of disability" (Fritsch 2013: 135); it is replaced with a symbol that placates concerns about inaccessibility. As a result, the problem of disability is no longer a problem. Instead, disabled people complaining about inaccessibility themselves become the problem. Disabled people are expected to be happy with what they get, even if what they get are merely crumbs, as Mia Mingus

(2017) brilliantly puts it, and even if what they get is not in fact accessible. In the end, disabled people who insist on complaining about inaccessibility are seen as getting in the way of the circulation of happy affects.

Happy words and happy symbols produce effects that transform how disabled people inhabit institutional spaces. For both Ahmed and Fritsch, a critical analysis of happy words and symbols reveals gaps: between words and worlds and between symbols and worlds. There are gaps between what institutions say they do and what they in fact do; there also exist gaps between what symbols serve to indicate and what really is there. Paying attention to these gaps is a crip phenomenological practice that re-orients us toward how worlds are in fact experienced by disabled people. Investigating how these words and symbols circulate helps us understand where disabled people are imagined as belonging (or not) and how economies of inclusion structurally depend on the capacitation of only certain types of disability and disabled people.

The rhetoric of inclusion offers one example of a happy site that reveals concerning gaps upon closer analysis. Discourses of inclusion are central to contemporary neoliberal academic cultures. Inclusion purports to transform the architecture of higher education, both materially and symbolically. While metrics of diversity appraise the inclusion of non-normative bodies in spaces that they did not previously inhabit and from which they were previously excluded, inclusion names the process by which "diverse" bodies are "welcomed in." On this view, one is either included in—"inside"—or excluded from—"outside"—the university. Images of closed doors, glass ceilings, or institutional walls come to mind. Those who previously stood on one side of the closed door are newly invited to cross its threshold. As Ahmed evocatively puts it, the open door "becomes a gift: come in, come in!" (Ahmed 2012: 243). Making the university accessible opens new doors for disabled people.

The reality of inclusion, however, is far more complex. Titchkosky and Rod Michalko explain that the inclusion of disabled students, faculty, and staff in universities relies on their ambiguous position as both insiders and outsiders: disabled people are "present yet absent or included as an excludable type" (Titchkosky and Michalko 2012: 137). The aim of disability services, for example, is to ensure that disabled people who are *already* a part of the lifeworld of a university—albeit as a "naturally excludable type" (Titchkosky 2007: 149)—are fully included in this world. Yet when disabled people do show up, they show up as a problem. Disabled bodyminds become interrogation points, bold, conspicuous punctuation marks on a blank page, stringing together a series of questions: "What are they doing here anyway?" (Titchkosky 2011: 78). What do they want? What do we *do* with them now? As question marks, they become barriers in the course of everyday institutional life, a site of perplexing uncertainty. Meanwhile, the surface inclusion of disabled people consistently elides the question of what has made disability exclusion ordinary in the first place.

I am guarded about the rhetoric of inclusion for at least three reasons, all of which are interrelated. To begin, this rhetoric fails to identify and disrupt underlying oppressive structures. More simply, the inclusion of disabled bodies in able-bodied spaces does not transform the status quo. For this reason, the inclusion of disabled people also does not necessarily change how they experience these spaces. While the aim of inclusion is to make room for disabled people in the able-bodied world, this process does not disrupt widespread assumptions about the neutrality and normality of nondisabled, hearing, and neurotypical spaces. To be "invited in" the room when the room does not change may produce the *impression* that things are different. However, at the level of lived experience, the room still *feels* like it was never intended for disabled people in the first place. In many cases, those who are welcomed in are still figured as outsiders.

Nirmal Puwar (2004) cleverly appropriates the term *space invaders* to describe how the inclusion of some racialized and gendered bodies in academic and professional spaces is perceived as an intrusion. Beneath the shiny veneer of an inclusive rhetoric that is deployed to justify their presence, gender nonconforming, Black, Indigenous, fat, poor, disabled, and chronically ill people are regularly made to feel out of place in academia. Space invaders may very well, in theory and in practice, be included, but they are still figured as "belonging elsewhere" (Puwar 2004: 42). While inclusivity has become a pillar of modern neoliberal educational systems, the inclusion agenda does not necessarily (or even often) translate into concrete changes to the harmful structures that it seeks to correct or to the felt experiences of the people who were previously excluded. Furthermore, because the root causes of ableist exclusion remain unchallenged, the institutional promise of inclusion offers no guarantees that disabled people will receive adequate support—be it financial, material, academic, psychological, or professional—once they are employed or become students. Margaret Price's (2014) fascinating study of independent scholarship shows that many disabled scholars are forced into the highly precarious, grossly underpaid, and unrecognized margins of academic spaces due to institutional inaccessibility, despite the fact that universities worldwide have embraced diversity and inclusion as core values. In short, the contributions of disabled scholars and students are regularly sidelined within supposedly inclusive academic spaces.

Very simply, the institutional worlds that auxiliary measures such as accommodations purportedly made more inclusive never anticipated the presence of disabled people in the first place. Inclusion is always temporally retroactive: some people are perceived to legitimately belong in certain spaces, while others must be welcomed in after the fact. As presently conceived, the promise of inclusion functions as what Jay Dolmage (2017) calls a "retrofit." Dolmage identifies spatial metaphors that reflect how spatial and material arrangements produce some aspects of disability. The first of these linguistic devices is the metaphor of the "steep steps," which reflects how social hierarchies are mirrored in the construction of spaces as inaccessible to people who are considered inferior or unworthy. Dolmage explains that the steep steps of the university have historically conveyed a message about the privileged status of the people who belonged in it, for example, by reflecting eugenic beliefs about the superior cognitive abilities of white cisgender men.

The "retrofit," by contrast, is a corrective intervention that supplements, improves, or amends existing structures. A retrofit might be employed to adapt a building to new codes or regulations. The addition of wheelchair-accessible ramps to centennial university buildings is a prime example of such adaptations. For Dolmage, the retrofit communicates the idea that "disability is supplemental to society, that it is an afterthought or imposition" (Dolmage 2017: 105). Returning to the image of inclusion as a new door that opens, we might say (with Dolmage) that the door that opens is never the main door. Instead, "disability as an identity category can come in the side or the back entrance if it is to be included at all" (106). In similar terms, Fritsch writes that "disability is included as an afterthought; welcome, but only by way of the side entrance" (Fritsch 2013: 141). Consider these powerful remarks by R. Tina Catania, a disabled graduate student writing about her experiences in academia:

> Classes, programs, and TA responsibilities are not designed with accessibility in mind. Just like the university, which was created by and for rich, white men in a racist-sexist-heteropatriarchal society; women, people of color, people with disabilities, and so on, have been "added in." They try to add us in and stir us into their already ableist "diversity soup." But why can't classes be designed to be accessible from the start? We were never conceived of as belonging; we were never meant to be citizens of the university. So it is no wonder that we hit walls and continually encounter the limits of disability offices and "reasonable" accommodations. (Carter et al. 2017: 103)

The people who are added in (or, more strikingly, *stirred in*) to the "ableist diversity soup" that Catania describes were never perceived as belonging in higher education spaces in the first place. Catania's impression of being added into spaces that were never designed with disability in mind is an experience of coming up against walls and encountering the limits of "accommodationist" (Tremain 2013) frameworks. The experience of coming up against walls and limits does not strictly (or even primarily) operate at a reflective level but rather is felt in our everyday interactions with people, objects, and places within and outside the university. When we come up against these walls, we learn about the ableism of institutions and about what access and lack of access feel like, both corporeally and affectively.

My second worry about the rhetoric of inclusion is that the current deployment of it has deeply pernicious effects. I maintain that the rhetoric of inclusion does not in fact disrupt the status quo with respect to the exclusionary homogeneity of the university but rather, in many ways, serves to both sustain and guard it under the cover of institutional change. This view requires us to recognize that institutions are not merely passive, ossified structures with closed doors, glass ceilings, and walls that function as inert roadblocks to inclusion. To be sure, universities (and other institutions) often employ such images of inert roadblocks—including staircases, gates, doors, bathroom stalls, and sidewalks—as symbols of architectural barriers to access. If we accept these images at face value, however, we risk perpetuating the idea that institutions are static and monolithic: they are not. Instead, the closed doors, glass ceilings, and brick walls that guard the status quo move strategically. They reflexively track the resistant and resisting initiatives of bodies within the institution and outside of it. We must remember that power is highly permutable and adaptable. Inclusion can become institutionalized precisely through the adaptation of past practices of exclusion to emerging demands for democratization, tolerance, and flexibility. Institutions can claim that they are changing without in fact changing. They can act as if they are doing "everything right" or "all that they can" without in fact doing anything at all. The rhetoric of inclusion can erect new walls that are less visible and that falsely motivate the impression of change.

My view of institutions as both carrying over the weight of the past and dynamically shifting to meet emerging patterns of use and practice is indebted to Merleau-Ponty's (2010) own thinking about institutionality. Merleau-Ponty's use of the notion of institutionality departs from our everyday understanding of institutions as establishments or ritualized conventions. Inspired by Husserl, Merleau-Ponty describes institution as the creative establishment of a field of meaning that is temporally open-ended rather than determined in advance. This field of meaning, once it has been instituted, is available to be taken up and reworked, always in relation to its past. Although Merleau-Ponty did not develop a sustained account of social or political institutions, his analysis of the temporal logic of institutions is helpful because it tracks the ways in which the past is reworked in and by the present rather than being discretely separated from it. For Merleau-Ponty, what we think of as sense (or meaning) does not emerge spontaneously out of thin air. Even the most original work of art is embedded in a thick expressive history which it seeks to surpass only by entering into dialogue with it. Furthermore, we can think of the Merleau-Pontyan movement of institutions as involving both stability *and* sedimentation. Rather than an entity that is defined once and for all, an institution is something that emerges over time and against a background of practices, values, histories, and embodiments that constantly shift. Merleau-Ponty's account foregrounds the dynamic movement by which that which is instituted coalesces, at certain times by giving more weight to sedimented habits, and at other times by espousing new forms that better meet emerging demands.

Ahmed embraces a view of institutions that is compatible with Merleau-Ponty's own view of them insofar as she reminds us of the activity that goes into the process of institutionalization. Drawing on early sociological theories of institutions, Ahmed warns against "the [stabilization of] institutions as things" (Ahmed 2012: 21). In this regard, she is concerned to theorize "how institutions acquire the regularity and stability that allows them to be recognizable as institutions in the first place" (ibid.). Institutions are not fixed objects or unmarked containers for human action. They are the products of our engagement with them and offer resources for thinking critically about how bodies and worlds are mutually shaped. Institutions offer what Ahmed aptly terms an "institutional sense" (ibid.), which I understand phenomenologically as involving direction, fit, meaning, and orientation. Understanding the forces that lie behind the directions in which superficial institutional commitments to inclusion sway can help us understand how these commitments routinely mask a deeper, persistent, and highly adaptable allegiance to the preservation of inherited vectors of power and privilege. When one door opens, another door closes.

My third and final concern about the rhetoric of inclusion is that inclusion is necessarily conditional. Only forms of difference that can benefit the institution merit inclusion. The incorporation of some "privileged" minoritized subjects (rather than all minoritized subjects) necessarily produces an excess. This excess creates a class of "undeserving" minoritized subjects who remain excluded from dominant social and political arrangements. This view of the rhetoric of inclusion, according to which it implicitly distinguishes between deserving and undeserving institutional subjects, is indebted to broader feminist, queer, crip, and antiracist critiques of inclusion that illustrate how practices of and discourses about inclusion are tied to capitalist standards of productivity and to classed, gendered, and racialized demands for labor (Dolmage 2018; Erevelles 2016; Ferguson 2004; Puar 2017). David T. Mitchell and Sharon L. Snyder (2015), in a nod to Jasbir Puar's (2007) earlier notion of homonationalism, offer the concept of "ablenationalism" to describe how some disabled people have been accepted into the fold of mainstream society on the condition that they satisfactorily integrate into global consumer culture. The authors demonstrate that the formation of the "exceptionalized" category of the "able-disabled," whose integration in mainstream society is considered profitable, produces new sites of exclusion. Think, for instance, of the contrast between the staggering rates of incarceration of Black and brown disabled people, on the one hand, and, on the other, discourses of disability pride that foreground issues that concern and benefit white, wealthy, heterosexual, and cisgendered disabled people living in the Global North. In brief, the rhetoric of inclusion can be entirely indifferent to a critique of power and divorced from it. The inclusion of some minoritized subjects can be fully intertwined with the reproduction of systems of power that mark other minoritized subjects for social death, impoverishment, and disenfranchisement.

Forms of conditional inclusion that produce exclusions govern academic settings. In particular, the expansion of economic rationality to many aspects of higher education has imported notions of efficiency, productivity, competitiveness, and flexibility as standards of inclusion into academic spaces. The impact of capitalist logics of performance and profitability on contemporary public higher education systems cannot be overstated. Many scholars have noted how universities have progressively aligned themselves with neoliberal ideology in the past decades (Mintz 2021; Saunders 2010; Slaughter and Rhoades 2000). This shift coincides with a massive defunding of public education, significant increases in the number of adjunct and part-time faculty, and the rise of a culture of individual responsibility that frames education as a personal investment marketed to students *qua* consumers. I do not want to oversimply the many variations in structure, mission, or modes of governance between educational institutions. However, a common thread runs through much of public higher education, at least in the United States, which transforms students into customers, administrators into managers, and faculty members into entrepreneurs.

The standards of performance review that universities employ are "encoded with ableism" (Waterfield, Beagan, and Weinberg 2017: 329) from the start. Disabled academics are expected to replicate the ideal of an "optimal (nondisabled) academic" (345) through forms of self-governance that ultimately determine their worth to the institution. As a result, disabled people who are not considered "predictably productive under neoliberalism" (Fritsch 2013: 142) face substantial barriers to success and flourishing. The disabled faculty members whom Waterfield and colleagues interviewed, for example, report making studied efforts to provide their colleagues and deans with assurances that they are as "hardworking and productive" (Waterfield, Beagan, and Weinberg 2017: 338) as their nondisabled colleagues. One of these disabled interviewees described how, for years, she worked to build her image as a productive and involved scholar before she disclosed her disability. Earning this recognition allowed her to stave off potential concerns about her performance when her disability began to affect her work. Another interviewee reported grading papers from a hospital bed. Overall, the disabled faculty members interviewed by the authors reported feeling tremendous pressure to prove themselves to be as valuable to the university as their nondisabled colleagues.

In my experience as a disabled graduate student, I have come to understand what I am calling "conditional inclusion" through the lens of an unspoken distinction between "good" and "bad" disabled students. Universities and departments *happily* include people whose disabilities do not interfere with their "productivity" but hold people whose disabilities do affect their academic outcomes as individually responsible for their situations, further stigmatizing these disabled people and casting them aside. In other words, disabled graduate students who are not "productively" disabled and who experience conditions that interfere with their capacity to meet departmental benchmarks become expendable. Although disabled students are formally encouraged to apply to higher education programs that focus on "diversifying" academia, they (like disabled faculty members) often find themselves with little to no support and are forced to fend for themselves once they have been included in these supposedly inclusive programs. Students experiencing traumas, chronic health crises, or psychological distress that impact their work—and especially students of color and first-generation students—often suffer quietly and become known as "bad" students or "lost causes" when it is informally decided that they will not positively contribute to the department's "happy" image and reputation. To reiterate, manifestations of disability are considered tolerable only when they do not disrupt idealized standards of performance.

The manifestations of disability that so-called inclusive universities will tolerate are also contingent on the identity categories through which given disabled subjects are perceived. Conditional inclusion occurs at the intersection of vectors of race, class, gender, ability, sexuality, size, and nationality. For example, Theri A. Pickens argues that although some forms of madness are seen as "germane to [a person's] identity as a professor" (Pickens 2017: 243) (think, for example, of the "crazy" genius of the white tenured male professor), other forms of madness are perceived as threatening. Pickens shows that "madness cannot be marshaled for gain when yoked to a body already associated with it" (253). The bodies of trans, queer, disabled, Black, and Indigenous scholars and scholars of color are already perceived as antithetical to scholarly thinking; these subjects cannot legitimately embrace madness as a professional quirk. Pickens's claim is not that the university is safe for Mad and psychiatrically disabled people who hold privileged identities (e.g., if they are white). Rather, her suggestion is that the attribution of madness to non-normative bodies functions as a "disciplining practice" (254) that marks them as fundamentally antithetical to norms of reason, emotional detachment, coherence, and even morality. Recognition of these distinctions is another way in which to expose the fact that disability inclusion can be fully complicit with other forms of oppression and, indeed, can require them to become digestible.

Epilogue

In this chapter, I have approached institutional language phenomenologically to uncover and investigate what composes the unexamined, taken-for-granted rhetorical background (as I refer to it) of institutional life. This background can be thrown into relief, but doing so requires that we disorient ordinary ways of talking about access and inclusion. The concerns that I have raised should not be understood to imply that I advocate a wholesale rejection of all attempts to foster the inclusion and participation of disabled people in higher education. Creating access is necessary for transforming both the worlds in which we live and the ones that we can imagine, as well as for eliminating the forms of exclusion and harm that disabled people routinely experience. However, I have argued throughout this chapter that the ways in which the notions of access and inclusion circulate must both concern us and be resisted when they are deployed to placate the killjoy complaints of disabled people, when they sideline disabled people's experiences of coming up against institutional walls, and when they generate expectations of conformity to ableist standards of performance and productivity.

References

Ahmed, Sara (2006), *Queer Phenomenology: Orientations, Objects, Others*, Durham: Duke University Press.

Ahmed, Sara (2010), *The Promise of Happiness*, Durham: Duke University Press.

Ahmed, Sara (2012), *On Being Included: Racism and Diversity in Institutional Life*, Durham: Duke University Press.

Ahmed, Sara (2014), "Dated Feminists," Feminist Killjoys (blog). Available at: https://feministkilljoys.com/2014/04/08/dated-feminists/ (accessed July 21, 2023).

Ahmed, Sara (2019), *What's the Use?: On the Uses of Use*, Durham: Duke University Press.

Alcoff, Linda (2006), *Visible Identities: Race, Gender, and the Self*, New York: Oxford University Press.

Al-Saji, Alia (2010), "The Racialization of Muslim Veils: A Philosophical Analysis," *Philosophy and Social Criticism* 36 (8): 875–902.

Al-Saji, Alia (2014), "A Phenomenology of Hesitation: Interrupting Racializing Habits of Seeing," in Emily Lee (ed.), *Living Alterities: Phenomenology, Embodiment, and Race*, 133–72, Albany: State University of New York Press.

Apelmo, Elisabet and Camilla Nordgren (2021), "Still Waiting for the Hand to Be Raised: On Being Crip Killjoys at an Ableist University," in Hannah Egard, Kristofer Hansson, and David Wästerfors (eds.), *Accessibility Denied. Understanding Inaccessibility and Everyday Resistance to Inclusion for Persons with Disabilities*, 107–22, London: Routledge.

Carter, Angela M., Tina Catania, Sam Schmitt, and Amanda Swenson (2017), "Bodyminds Like Ours: An Autoethnographic Analysis of Graduate School, Disability, and the Politics of Disclosure," in Stephanie L. Kerschbaum, Laura T.

Eisenman, and James M. Jones (eds.), *Negotiating Disability: Disclosure and Higher Education*, 95–113, Ann Arbor: University of Michigan Press.
Colker, Ruth (2007), *The Disability Pendulum: The First Decade of the Americans with Disabilities Act*, New York: New York University Press.
Curry, Tommy J. (2006), "Revealing Whiteness: The Unconscious Habits of Racial Privilege," *Newsletter of the Society for the Advancement of American Philosophy* 34 (105): 43–7.
Dolmage, Jay T. (2017), *Academic Ableism: Disability and Higher Education*, Ann Arbor: University of Michigan Press.
Dolmage, Jay T. (2018), *Disabled Upon Arrival: Eugenics, Immigration, and the Construction of Race and Disability*, Columbus: Ohio State University Press.
Erevelles, Nirmala (2016), *Disability and Difference in Global Contexts: Enabling a Transformative Body Politic*, New York: Palgrave Macmillan.
Ferguson, Roderick A. (2004), *Aberrations in Black: Toward a Queer of Color Critique*, Minneapolis: University of Minnesota press.
Fielding, Helen A. (2006), "White Logic and the Constancy of Color," in Dorothea Olkowski and Gail Weiss (eds.), *Feminist Interpretations of Maurice Merleau-Ponty*, 71–89, University Park: Pennsylvania State University Press.
Fritsch, Kelly (2013), "The Neoliberal Circulation of Affects: Happiness, Accessibility and the Capacitation of Disability as Wheelchair," *Health, Culture and Society* 5 (1): 135–49.
Garland-Thomson, Rosemarie (2011), "Misfits: A Feminist Materialist Disability Concept," *Hypatia: A Journal of Feminist Philosophy* 26 (3): 591–609.
Guenther, Lisa (2019), "Seeing Like a Cop: A Critical Phenomenology of Whiteness as Property," in Emily Lee (ed.), *Race as Phenomena: Between Phenomenology and Philosophy of Race*, 189–207, London: Rowman & Littlefield.
Harbin, Ami (2016), *Disorientation and Moral Life*, New York: Oxford University Press.
Hill Collins, Patricia (2022), *Black Feminist Thought: Knowledge, Consciousness, and the Politics of Empowerment*, London: Routledge.
hooks, bell (2000), *Feminist Theory: From Margin to Center*, Cambridge: South End Press.
Husserl, Edmund (2014), *Ideas Pertaining to a Pure Phenomenology and Phenomenological Philosophy. First Book*, Indianapolis: Hackett Publishing.
Johnson, Merri Lisa and Robert McRuer (2014), "Cripistemologies: Introduction," *Journal of Literary and Cultural Disability Studies* 8 (2): 127–48.
Lugones, Maria (2003), *Pilgrimages = Peregrinajes: Theorizing Coalition against Multiple Oppressions*, Lanham: Rowman and Littlefield.
Maroto, Michelle and David Pettinicchio (2015), "Twenty-Five Years After the ADA: Situating Disability in America's System of Stratification," *Disability Studies Quarterly* 35 (3): n.p.
Merleau-Ponty, Maurice (2010), *Institution and Passivity: Course Notes from the Collège de France (1954–1955)*, trans. Leonard Lawlor and Heath Massey, Evanston: Northwestern University Press.
Merleau-Ponty, Maurice (2012), *Phenomenology of Perception*, trans. Don Landes, London: Routledge.
Mingus, Mia (2017), "Access Intimacy, Interdependence and Disability Justice," *Leaving Evidence* (blog). Available at: https://leavingevidence.wordpress.com/2017/04/12/access-intimacy-interdependence-and-disability-justice/ (accessed July 21, 2023).

Mintz, Beth (2021), "Neoliberalism and the Crisis in Higher Education: The Cost of Ideology," *American Journal of Economics and Sociology* 80 (1): 79–112.

Mitchell, David T. and Sharon L. Snyder (2015), *The Biopolitics of Disability: Neoliberalism, Ablenationalism, and Peripheral Embodiment*, Ann Arbor: University of Michigan Press.

Mollow, Anna (2013), "Bellyaching – Social Text," *Social Text*. Available at: https://socialtextjournal.org/periscope_article/bellyaching/ (accessed June 23, 2023).

Ngo, Helen (2019), *Habits of Racism: A Phenomenology of Racism and Racialized Embodiment*, Washington: Lexington Books.

Ortega, Mariana (2016), *Between Worlds: Latina Feminist Phenomenology, Multiplicity, and the Self*, Albany: SUNY Press.

Pickens, Therí A. (2017), "Satire, Scholarship, and Sanity; or How to Make Mad Professors," in Stephanie L. Kerschbaum, Laura T. Eisenman, and James M. Jones (eds.), *Negotiating Disability: Disclosure and Higher Education*, 243–54, Ann Arbor: University of Michigan Press.

Price, Margaret (2014), *Mad at School: Rhetorics of Mental Disability and Academic Life*, Ann Arbor: University of Michigan Press.

Puar, Jasbir K. (2007), *Terrorist Assemblages: Homonationalism in Queer Times*, Durham: Duke University Press.

Puar, Jasbir K. (2017), *The Right to Maim: Debility, Capacity, Disability*, Durham: Duke University Press.

Puwar, Nirmal (2004), *Space Invaders: Race, Gender and Bodies Out of Place*, Oxford: Berg.

Saunders, Daniel (2010), "Neoliberal Ideology and Public Higher Education in the United States," *The Journal for Critical Education Policy Studies* 8 (1): 41–77.

Siebers, Tobin (2011), *Disability Theory*, Ann Arbor: The University of Michigan Press.

Slaughter, Sheila and Gary Rhoades (2000), "The Neo-Liberal University," *New Labor Forum*, no. 6: 73–9.

Titchkosky, Tanya (2007), *Reading and Writing Disability Differently: The Textured Life of Embodiment*, Toronto: University of Toronto Press.

Titchkosky, Tanya (2011), *The Question of Access: Disability, Space, Meaning*, Toronto: University of Toronto Press.

Titchkosky, Tanya and Rod Michalko (2012), "The Body as the Problem of Individuality: A Phenomenological Disability Studies Approach," in Dan Goodley, Bill Hughes, and Lennard Davis (eds.), *Disability and Social Theory: New Developments and Directions*, 127–42, London: Palgrave Macmillan.

Tremain, Shelley (2013), "Introducing Feminist Philosophy of Disability," *Disability Studies Quarterly* 33 (4).

Tremain, Shelley (2017), "Knowing Disability, Differently," in Ian James Kidd, José Medina, and Gaile Pohlhaus, Jr. (eds.), *The Routledge Handbook on Epistemic Injustice*, 175–83, New York: Routledge.

Waldhier, Laura (2016), "New Statement Underscores University's Commitment to Diversity," February 21. Available at: https://www.psu.edu/news/administration/story/new-statement-underscores-universitys-commitment-diversity/ (accessed June 23, 2023).

Waterfield, Bea, Brenda Beagan, and Merlinda Weinberg (2017), "Disabled Academics: A Case Study in Canadian Universities," *Disability and Society* 33 (4): 1–22.

Yancy, George (2017), *Black Bodies, White Gazes: The Continuing Significance of Race in America*, Lanham: Rowman and Littlefield.

13 STUTTERING AND ABLEISM

A STUDY OF EVENTFULNESS

JOSHUA ST. PIERRE

I once heard a speech-language pathologist (SLP) make this sneering remark in response to critical disability theory: "If I have to work my ass off to speak to you *or* listen to you, and you can fix the problem, why should I bother trying to communicate with you at all?" In my experience as a stutterer, the sentiment that underlies this remark is typically reserved for someone's inner voice and veiled behind plausible deniability. Yet when the sentiment is expressed overtly and bluntly in this way, it conveys so well the everyday ableism that I and other stutterers encounter. Thus, I intend to use this reply from our ableist SLP as the critical opening to examine the eventfulness of stuttering suppressed by ableism. While not all SLPs are ableist, the sentiment that this ableist SLP expressed is especially useful for my purpose insofar as the *discipline* of speech-language pathology, as a dominant authority about stuttering, subtends ableist commitments.

But first things first: what is ableism? Fiona Kumari Campbell offered a definition over twenty years ago that remains a sound place to begin. For Campbell, ableism describes "a network of beliefs, processes and practices that produces a particular kind of self and body (the corporeal standard) that is projected as the perfect, species-typical and therefore essential and fully human. Disability then is cast as a diminished state of being human" (Campbell 2001: 44). Ableism makes an ontological distinction between humans "fit" and "unfit" to inhabit the world. Campbell indicates that ableism is more than an "ideology" in the Marxist sense of a dominant set of beliefs and representations. Ableism is also a set of processes and practices that traverse the discursive and the material register to establish and maintain (the desire for) a corporeal standard of ability. Understood as a network that assigns value to and sorts human beings using eugenic categories such as normal versus abnormal or "fit" versus "unfit," ableism always cuts two ways: it values able-bodiedness while de-valuing disabled modes of being.[1] In early twentieth-century eugenic practices, the categorization of "intelligence"—allegedly represented by intelligence quotient (IQ) scores—played a central role in dividing (along fault lines of disability, race, gender, sexuality, and class) people deemed "fit" to live from people deemed "unfit" to live. Today—in addition to IQ—a "neoliberal ableist" (Goodley 2014) society employs various metrics like Emotional Intelligence, fluency levels, capacities of attention, and Body Mass Index (BMI) to construct and maintain valued corporeal standards.

If we ask *where* ableism is produced, some currents of critical disability theory would emphasize institutional policies, structures, and built environments that classify, sort, and surveil human subjects (e.g., Schweik 2009; Hamraie 2017; Malhotra 2012). Others might highlight rhetorical sites like media and other cultural representations of disability that foment and perpetuate eugenic ideals (e.g., Schalk 2018; Dolmage 2013, 2018). Still others might draw attention to affective drives and psychological dispositions that circulate through bodies and get expressed as pity or disgust (e.g., Overboe 2012). All of these critical approaches are necessary, since ableism weaves together multiple forces, including formal and informal practices, cultural representations, affective flows, and psychological dispositions. A stutterer, for example, experiences the demand for fluency in strict timetables and deadlines that rationalize and limit time, as well as in dominant social rhythms of conversation; cheap comedic gags; mocking names; and split-second, unconscious looks of revulsion from interlocutors that feed negative self-conceptions and demarcate a shared world.

In this chapter, I use our ableist SLP as a frame to interrogate the relational dynamics of ableism and stuttering. Ableism, I argue, organizes the perceptual world for the uninterrupted pleasure of the able-bodied, though it hides its perceptual formation behind a coat of neutrality. Ableism is, moreover, a contractive force that ties stuttering to an individual body as a way to stifle the eventfulness of stuttering. In contrast, I suggest that stuttering is best understood as a dynamic event that emerges *between* beings. By "event," I mean, first, that stuttering is an irreducibly temporal phenomenon that coagulates time in unexpected and sometimes uncomfortable ways. Second, I mean that the happening (event) of stuttering is a collaboration of multiple agents, only some of whom are representable as individual speakers and listeners. By offering a more robust account of speech and speech disability than ableism produces, I aim to both underscore the existential and political stakes of the ableist refusal to hear stuttering on its own terms and nurture responsiveness to the potentially uncomfortable possibilities that can emerge within the dysfluent event.

Atomism, Holism, and Connectionism

Allow me to state it again: "If I have to work my ass off to speak to you *or* listen to you, and you can fix the problem, why should I bother trying to communicate with you at all?" The disdain for nondominant modes of being is clear; nevertheless, allow me to bracket this contempt for the moment in order to consider the ableist expectations of communication that are built into this message. In other words, under what conditions *is* one worthy of being heard? It seems that verbal communication, for the ableist SLP, is a type of contract between self-contained and autonomous individuals, where no labor is expected of the unmarked speaker or the unmarked listener and, furthermore, where any interruption to easy listening (or speaking) nulls the responsibility of the listener (or speaker) to communicate, especially if the disabled party is capable of fixing the problem and chooses not/fails to do so.

I suggest that this schema distributes responsibility among interlocutors unjustly—with belonging within a shared world predicated upon compulsory fluency and therapeutic intervention—and, more fundamentally, misconstrues the ontology of the voice and its event of communication. One goal of this chapter is thus to elaborate a central, though as-of-yet undertheorized, concept within dysfluency studies. This concept is the idea, stated colloquially, that "it takes two" to stutter. In 2012, I wrote that "stuttering cannot be understood apart from expectations of 'normal' hearing," and suggested that "stuttering [is] constructed by a hearer prejudiced against 'broken' speech as well as its speaker, and thus a product of ableism" (St. Pierre 2012: 6). Jerome Ellis, in reference to his own voice, notes that "sometimes I refer to it as *my* stutter, but sometimes I refer to it as *the* stutter because to me stuttering is not bound t-t-t-t-to my body. It is a phenomenon that occurs between me and whoever I'm speaking to. . . . I like to think of it as something we share" (Cole and Ellis 2020). Later in the same interview, Ellis articulates this methodological distinction even more clearly as the difference between "oh, he's stuttering" and—in the passive voice—"there is a stutter happening."

As I will detail throughout this chapter, Ann Cahill and Christine Hamel's fruitful concept of "intervocality" gives additional support to the idea that stuttering is necessarily shared, highlighting the irreducible in-betweenness of the voice. For Cahill and Hamel, stuttering is merely one instance of the more general point that voice *itself* is a shared capacity:

> Voice is a fundamentally interactive event. Vocal emanations do not exist as self-contained, self-defined phenomenon, but always vibrate between and among entities (human bodies, built and found infrastructure, etc.). The meanings and evaluations of those vocal

> emanations—whether they are viewed as disruptive or impressive, or shrill, or beautiful—are never inherent to the emanations themselves, but are the products of power and value discourses masquerading as natural or given. (Cahill and Hamel 2022: 64)

Cahill and Hamel understand the sonorous voice to be thoroughly relational at the registers of both materiality and meaning. Value discourses that masquerade as natural or given, as Cahill and Hamel write, obscure the active role that the listener plays in the construction of the meaning (let alone sounding) of the stuttering voice. Ableist sentiments such as "Why, if I have to work my ass off, should I bother trying to communicate with you?" can pass as politically neutral—akin to the way that Cahill and Hamel note that aesthetic judgments of voices as shrill or grating are taken to be "neutral responses to inherent qualities of certain voices" (Cahill and Hamel 2022: 69)—rather than the product of unconscious listening practices. To use their example, a tone that signifies assertive qualities in men is often heard as shrill or bossy when voiced by women. As Cahill and Hamel assert, "Shrillness happens, at least sometimes, when a receiving body that expects (and constitutes itself as having the right to expect, and the right to have that expectation fulfilled) female-identified voices to be marked with a certain gentleness finds their expectations dashed. In an important way, then, the receiving body produces the shrillness of the voicing body" (70). Ableist habits have likewise shaped the capacities of listening bodies to expect voices identified as human to be (un)marked with fluency. The posture assumed by our ableist SLP is the right to expect fluency and the right to have that expectation fulfilled. As such, one fundamental difference between myself and our ableist SLP is whether the individual or the communicative relation itself takes methodological primacy. Did *I* stutter? (Are vocal capacities bound to individual bodies?) Or is there a stutter happening?

To propose "there is a stutter happening" releases the stutter from the restrictions of what Lisbeth Lipari (2014) calls the "atomistic paradigm" of communication. Lipari contests that research within disciplines of communication, psychology, linguistics, and yes, speech-language pathology, often remain stuck in a classical scientific paradigm that, among other moves, makes the wholes servants of the parts. The methodological commitment to atomism, she argues, has inverted the relation between communicative parts and the whole such that the individual interlocutor—rather than the dynamic shared between—has become the basic unit of communication. I agree with Lipari insofar as she argues that starting with discrete parts (speaker/listener) offers an insufficient account of both the phenomenon of communication and its political and existential stakes. In the final section of this chapter, however, I will part ways with her suggestion that holism can offer a sufficient replacement. As an alternative to both atomism and holism, I follow the line of thought that William Connolly (2011) calls "connectionism."

Intervocality

A fundamental reason why the atomistic paradigm lacks explanatory force around speech and speech disability is that the material voice does not respect the basic terms of atomism. The sonorous qualities of the voice must vibrate *between* entities to exist. "In an ontological sense," Cahill and Hamel write, "the material intersubjectivity of voice consists of the interactions that any given sound . . . necessarily involves" (Cahill and Hamel 2022: 28–9). To sound, a voice must release into *something*, and the ecology of bodies (including human bodies) that receive the vibrations of the voice in particular ways give shape to and mark the voice in particular ways. Voice is thus a necessarily shared capacity. "'The' voice that is 'mine,'" they remark, "is composed of a plentitude of sonorous experiences entwined and enmeshed with the other—other surfaces, other materials, other receiving bodies without which the released voice could not come into existence" (31). That is to say, the voice, the stutter, only becomes "mine" in the act of sharing and becoming entangled with the world. The voice emerges from the contributions of multiple actors as a "shimmering field" that is "both constructed by and constructing those beings" (36) rather than as a self-contained capsule transferred from one individual to another.

Stutterers know that differentials of personal energy, acoustic dynamics, mood of the room, or the receptiveness of listeners all mold and mark stuttering vocalizations in dramatic ways. We share our stutter with such materials. I habitually register the sonorous contours of any situation where I might have to speak. How big is the space? What are the surfaces like? How much additional breath and force would be required to sound a voice here? What are the temporal rhythms and breaks in the soundscape? Where and when might interruptions emerge? Stutterers learn to pay particular attention to the receptive capacities and states of human listeners, since human bodies are likely the most important entities that are needed to sound a human voice and thus they are, in addition, the entities that are most capable of denying it. Marty Jezer writes: "Are we making our listeners uncomfortable? Even as I'm speaking I'm monitoring how I'm speaking, how the listener is reacting to my speaking, and how I'm reacting to my perception of the listener's reaction. Is their pursing of his lips a reaction to the tension in my voice? Why did he blink? Why is he averting his eyes?" (Jezer 1997: 13)

Jezer notes that while stutterers can overestimate the negative attitudes toward their stuttering, fluent speakers can be self-conscious. Yet the point stands that such anxious surveillance toward listening bodies is born of necessity when the voice always articulates and reinforces social relations: yet another tax that ableism levies upon the dysfluent. "Voices are sonorously marked by the particular other to whom they are directed" (Cahill and Hamel 2022: 68) and, in the case of my voice, I internalized disableist responses early on by learning to stutter to most everyone with deference and shame: my body made small and my voice almost apologetic for sounding in a fluent world. Impatient, patronizing, or otherwise rude listeners shift the affordances of a moment and diminish the capacity of the situation to let a stutter resonate as such.

Ableist Perception

A distinction may be useful at this point: namely, hearing versus listening. While these terms tend to get used interchangeably (and while they pour into each other), Jean-Luc Nancy explains that "[e]very sensory register . . . bears with it both its simple nature and its tense, attentive, or anxious state" (Nancy 2007: 12). *To hear* is to perceive the general form or sense of a sound: "to hear a siren, a bird, or a drum is already each time to understand to least the rough outline of a situation, a context if not a text." *To listen* is the tense, attentive, or anxious state of hearing: "to be straining toward a possible meaning, and consequently one that is not immediately accessible" (6). It is important to note that Nancy's definition of listening does not depend upon sound. Humans also listen via American Sign Language (ASL), touch, reading, feeling, and *especially* in the flows between the modalities. In any case, our ableist SLP jumps right to the refusal to listen to stuttered speech, which already implies a background reluctance to encounter the rough outlines of stuttering; a reluctance to hear its sounds, see its sights, and be stirred by its affect. Ableism functions at both registers and I will attempt, for my own part, to maintain the partition between hearing and listening.

Any phenomenology worth its salt must attend to the dynamics of power that discipline the senses to shape experience and, in our case, render some voices more perceptible—and more worthy of attunement—than others. I, again, take my lead from Connolly, who, although he recognizes the differences between phenomenology and critical theory, invites us to think generously in this space. He writes:

> We note immediately a difference in rhythm between the sentences of Foucault and those of Merleau-Ponty. Merleau-Ponty's sentences

> convey an implicit sense of belonging to the world, while Foucault's often mobilize elements of tension, resistance, and disaffection circulating within modern modalities of experience. . . . The initial connection between these two thinkers across difference is that both see how perception requires a prior *disciplining* of the senses in which a rich history of sensory inter-involvement sets the stage for later experience. (Connolly 2011: 52, emphasis in Connolly)

Paying attention at the level of perceptual formation, we can trace how ableism, as an ongoing process, designs and enacts worlds in which some people can belong and exercise freedom more fully than others can.

It might thus come as bad news to our ableist SLP to learn that hearing is necessarily laborious; all perception arrives to consciousness through highly disciplined senses, to say nothing yet of the reflexive labor of attuned listening. Lipari explains that "perception is a process of distilling sensations into culturally distinct patterns" (Lipari 2014: 45), which means that we slosh through mountains of sensation each moment and would be left continually overwhelmed if we could not distill this flux into quickly recognizable patterns and forms. Thus, within the ordinary, everyday mode that Connolly calls "action-orientated perception," perception does not represent the world in-itself but is instead tuned to possible action in any given moment. "Because it is oriented to dictates of action in a world marked by speed, risk, surprise, need, and opportunity," Connolly writes, "perception *subtracts* from the incoming sensory material a surplus irrelevant to a small set of action possibilities" (Connolly 2002: 27, emphasis added). Put otherwise, during the split-second delay in which sensation becomes perception, the "body/brain/culture network" (ibid.) subtracts all those sensations that it takes to be unimportant to the needs of the moment and organizes the remainder into culturally distinct forms. The preconscious speed by which perception occurs is both vital and stained with the possibility of injustice. As Lipari puts it:

> It's one thing when we jump back and recoil at the sight of a big snake, only to realize it's an old, tattered piece of rope. It's quite another when we unconsciously (or consciously) make presumptions about a person's ability on the basis of the color of their skin, the tones of their accent or dialect, or the style and quality of their clothing. (Lipari 2014: 46)

Ableism is manifest and reproduced in these preconscious habits and dispositions that pattern human sensation. There is no doubt that stuttering can be a spectacle for the fluent interlocutor. Our bodies can shake, faces can wince, tongues can wave, lips can tremble, voices stretch, spittle can escape. Dis-ease or disgust is a common response. But what hinges upon the formation of generous perceptual dispositions, rather than ones that are reductive and cruel, is political belonging for groups marked by vocal difference. The feeling of disturbance that can emerge when a stutter happens can either re-circulate ableist commitments or become a site of transformation—a moment where things can happen.

Connolly, drawing upon the neuroscientific work of Antonio Damasio, terms these perceptual dispositions "somatic markers" and insists that they reduce neither to biology nor culture. A somatic marker, for Connolly, describes "a culturally mobilized, corporeal disposition through which affect-imbued, preliminary orientations to perception and judgment scale down" the flux of sensation. While Connolly notes that somatic markers both aid quick judgment and can spark new lines of thought, he cautions, like Lipari, that "they also fold into these subtractions and accentuations elements that sometimes turn out to be dangerous, unwise, or cruel" (Connolly 2002: 35). To return to Lipari's example, although ableist (and/or racist) presumptions about a person's capacity and value that have been formed on the basis of preconscious dispositions toward a disability (and/or racialized) accent are culturally mobilized, they reside in gut feelings (i.e., are resistant to argumentation) such that disgust or dis-ease *feels* like an apodictic moral guide. Connolly would amplify the point that the perception of a vocal emanation is never inherent to its sound and might in addition remind our ableist SLP that "the weight of somatic markers also generates a need for tactics and techniques by which to work on them when their compressions of experience become too restrictive or destructive" (35–6). "Why should I bother trying to communicate with [a disabled person] at all?" is an *excellent* heuristic to begin work on individual and collective habits and dispositions.

Shared World-Building

Though ableist formations of perception are masked behind a veneer of neutrality, practitioners of the medical model are hard-pressed to avoid biosocial norms in their attempt to define stuttering. For example, Ehud Yairi (2013), in an effort to produce an objective measure of stuttering—one that can differentiate between real, pathological, stuttering and "Stuttering-Like Disfluencies" that invade even normal speech—argues that methods of counting dysfluencies or relying upon self-perception (i.e., does one self-identify as a stutterer?) are insufficient and must ultimately be tested against the fluent listener's judgment. Yairi affirms the suggestion made by K. L. Moll in 1964 about nasal vocalizations that "the ultimate test of the acceptability of speech involves its perceptual acceptability to listeners," and he adds that "stuttering, unlike nasality or hoarseness, occurs almost only during interpersonal communication; it rarely occurs when not talking to listeners. Hence, the case for listeners' judgment as the ultimate test of what is normally fluent sound speech and what is not, is even stronger" (Yairi 2013: 296). Yairi and I might agree on this point: stuttering vocalizations become meaningful only in the context of interpersonal communication and are constituted as abnormal by listeners who, I would add, have been disciplined by biosocial norms to police the boundaries of acceptability. Although Yairi and our ableist SLP might thus concede that stuttering happens and finds meaning in material, social, and political relations—at least in this regard, stuttering is co-generated in the ear of the beholder—they would nevertheless maintain that stuttering is not *ontologically* relational.

Notice that as soon as we admit even a crack of the interlocutor's habits and judgments inside the event of stuttering, the failure to hear stuttering on its own terms can be even more readily recognized as value laden and should no longer be enabled to pass as neutral. For communication is not, as the American Speech-Language Association (ASHA) claims, the "active process of exchanging information and ideas" (American Speech-Language-Hearing Association n.d.), but, more robustly, is "the way humans collaboratively construct our shared social worlds" (Lipari 2014: 113). Put otherwise, speech does not merely "represent" ideas and "express" individual "needs, wants, feelings, and preferences that others can understand" (American Speech-Language-Hearing Association n.d.). Speech is, rather, also a creative (and thus possibly destructive) force. Consider how Connolly describes the act of thinking:

> Thinking is not merely involved in knowing, explaining, representing, evaluating, and judging. Subsisting within these activities are the inventive and compositional dimensions of thinking. To think is to move something. And to modify a pattern of body/brain connections helps to draw a habit, a disposition to judgment, or a capacity of action into being. *Thinking not only expresses our identities; it participates in composing, strengthening, and modifying them.* (Connolly 2002: 104, emphasis added)

Speech, much like thinking in this broad sense, is an act that composes, strengthens, and modifies the constitutive relations of self and world. (Note that the distinction between speech and thinking is only a partition: speech acts as a mode of thinking both with others and with oneself.)

To refuse to hear and listen to stuttering is thus to refuse much more. Jill Stauffer insists, by way of Emmanuel Levinas, that "[s]elves and worlds are not essences but are, rather, cooperatively authored achievements and, as such, may be destroyed" (Stauffer 2015: 22). People who conform to biosocial norms and experience a tight "fit" with a world designed for them can forget that selves and worlds are not the inevitable products of a sovereign author, but fragile collaborations that often fail. Drawing upon the testimonies of survivors of mass violence in the twentieth century, Stauffer argues that what she calls "ethical loneliness" consists of two compounding events: "being abandoned by humanity and then not being heard" (77). (Not being *listened to* fits more neatly with Nancy's distinction.) If oppression and the force of dehumanization pushes people "beyond the confines of the shared human world into a space of abandonment" (29), what such a person needs is a rebuilt world and, moreover, rebuilt trust in their world. None of this rebuilding can be accomplished alone. The refusal of family to recognize abuse, the unwillingness of a community to bear witness to injustice, or as Stauffer explores in detail, the failure of a Truth and Reconciliation Committee to hear stories on their own terms—each failure to listen does not only do nothing to rebuild, but indeed goes further to pilfer the resources from which selves and worlds arise.

Stauffer moves between examples of horrific and mundane violence to make her point that, for good or for ill, the fabric from which selves and worlds are made is collectively woven: we are radically dependent on each other. We can thus recognize, without having to draw equivalencies between social harms, that stutterers often experience abandonment from a common world and a form of ethical loneliness by way of a thousand cuts rather than a single traumatic incident (though momentous trauma can also occur). So poignantly articulated by our SLP, a central experience of stuttering in an ableist world is feeling unheard and unworthy of the labor of listening. Our speech—that is, cooperative acts of world-building that include self-composition—is ignored, talked over, circumvented, side-eyed, paraphrased, patronized, and pitied. "People react to stuttered speech differently than they react to fluent speech. They fidget, they cover their eyes, their interrupt, they say the word they think you are trying to say, they give advice, they make faces, they mimic, they laugh, they look away, they walk away" (Jezer 1997: xix). These responses can happen so frequently for stutterers that over time we can expect *not* to be heard and *not* to share in world-building. Without a receptive world, a stutterer can begin to wonder if "I still have a voice" and if "I'm still here" (Schick 2014).

My point is this: one of the quirks of stuttering vis-à-vis ethical loneliness is that its two movements of estrangement from a common world and then not be listened to trace back to the same fount. Reflecting on personal experience, Jezer writes that "The actual violation [of stuttering] cuts much deeper than the temporary interruption of the ability to communicate. Stuttering is not only a blockage of speech; it is a blow to the psyche, an impediment to the fulfillment of a basic inner need" (Jezer 1997: xix). Read through Stauffer, I suggest that Jezer refers to the basic need to be encountered and listened to; that is, he recognizes, and thus worries, that the self is a collectively composed achievement that others can deny bit by bit, and whittle away interaction by interaction. "For the child who stutters and for the adult whose stuttering has become chronic, speech is not a medium for communication but a recording of humiliation, a confirmation of ineptitude, an indication of abnormality, a violation of what everyone else in the world considers fully human" (ibid.). Without a sufficiently receptive world, what ought to be a medium for communication, for shared world-building, becomes instead a medium of vocal injustice and ethical loneliness. Why, the ableist interlocutor shrugs, should a world that stutters even exist?

Of course, insofar as being unheard and unlistened to are practices that mark social hierarchy, the voices of many different marginalized people besides stutterers are devalued and ignored. Vocal injustice abounds. "That vocal code-switching is required by members of disadvantaged groups (but never or rarely by members of dominant groups) in order to participate more fully in social life should be recognized as an unjust tax, not just in time and energy, but of existential vulnerability" (Cahill and Hamel 2022: 58). The stutterer must attempt to pass as fluent to participate in a fluent world; it is the stutterer, hardly the fluent listener, who works their ass off and risks parts of themselves within the event of communication. This tax of time, energy, and vulnerability compounds if one's stuttering voice is also marked as dangerous by systems of white supremacy, patriarchy, and/or cisnormativity. Pleasing the dominant ear is a full-time job.

Allow me to take stock. From our current position, the complaint of our ableist SLP comes down to a few issues. First, insofar as ableism organizes the perceptual world for the uninterrupted pleasure of the able-bodied, our SLP is angered that the spell of non-labored listening has been broken. Second, they are angered that speakers who do not please the fluent ear would still expect—let alone demand—full participation within a common world. This ableist anger is moralized insofar as subjects who ought to take proper responsibility for themselves choose instead to contaminate the purity of the fluent public world with their difference from this fluent world. The third matter gestures to the previous two and concerns responsibility for the event of stuttering. "Why," I can imagine the SLP ask with exasperation, "are you trying to make *your* problem *my* problem?" "Why should I strain myself to communicate [i.e., listen] when the problem could be fixed for me?"

Within a sufficiently narrow framework, this position makes sense. For example, the liberal tradition, which limits culpability to the intentions and actions of individual subjects, provides an escape for our SLP who protests the unexpected labor of listening. Put otherwise, our SLP can disavow any responsibility for the stutter, let alone for the destruction/repair of a stutterer's world because they have been failed by a moral framework—whether it be contractual or deontological—that cannot take into account the dynamics of intervocality. Within an intervocal event, to share responsibility is to loosen attachment to individual ownership of voice and instead become responsive to the contingencies of the moment that continually recreate "the possibilities for intelligibility, recognition, and communication" (Cahill and Hamel 2022: 66). It is, in short, ableism, not disability, that forecloses entangled modes of being and agency. Cahill and Hamel gesture toward this point when they write that "the responsibility for [stuttering's] social meaning (as defective, problematic, in need of medical or therapeutic attention) is mystified by ableist political structures, which construct the receiver of the broken speech as neutral, and the stuttering body as the sole generator of the stutter *qua* stutter" (69). When a stutter happens, ableist political structures (which include reductive somatic markers and methodological commitments) shrink from the contingencies of the moment by which responsiveness could be forged and fall back instead upon pre-set and individualizing logics such as the social contract or the scapegoat.

The (Failed) Eventfulness of Stuttering

I anticipate an objection from interlocutors who are dedicated to the medical model of disability and, by extension, to atomism. "All this philosophy of voice is fine," I can imagine them interjecting, "but it misunderstands what stuttering *really is* such that the critique misses its mark." At this point, our ableist SLP might double-down on methodological atomism by appealing to its kin—biological reductionism—and seek to distinguish between causative (etiological) and mere reactive factors of stuttering. ASHA, for instance, insists that "genetics and neurophysiology appear to be related to the *underlying causes* of stuttering, [while] environmental factors, temperament, and speaking demands may *influence* a child's *reactions* to stuttering" (ASHA n.d., emphasis added). The few dynamics of intervocality that do not fall through the cracks of this definition get swept into the pile of reactive factors such as mood and environment. To be sure, ASHA concedes that "each child who stutters develops stuttering as a result of his or her own unique factors" and that "causes of stuttering are multifactorial and include certain genetic and neurophysiological factors that are thought to contribute to its emergence" (ibid., emphasis added). Notice, however, that although the account of stuttering that ASHA advances acknowledges the emergence of stuttering into a network of contingent social and material relations, the account reserves the attribution of the causes of stuttering—that is, the *true* meaning of stuttering—for biomedical markers like genes and neurophysiology.

The split between causative and reactive, agential and non-agential forces is tidy because ASHA fails to recognize its own methodological commitments, let alone the limits of these commitments. Zara Richter traces the diagnosis of speech disability across the nineteenth and twentieth centuries and finds two polar kinds of problematization. The first kind of problematization comprises the "symbolic interactionist" accounts of stuttering that psychoanalysis has mobilized in which "symbol errors are connected to emotional-interpersonal histories" (Richter 2020: 100). Stuttered speech, on these accounts, indicates unresolved psychopathology. The second kind of problematization comprises the "biological deterministic" accounts of stuttering that "mechanistic psychology" has mobilized to identify physical causes for both speech and speech disability. This debate remains unsettled, although, as Richter explains, biological reductionism nevertheless manages to claim victory of it:

> The form in which speech has primarily settled for it to be the subject of diagnosis and self-help activism has been overtly bio-reductionist. Not because such can be demonstrated as the core element of speech disability, but because of American culture, where bio-determinist psychology has been most successful and has, in turn, demanded all disorders under study to be biologically locatable in genetics, in the body, or in another physical explanation. (Richter 2020: 109)

To demand that the phenomenon of speech disability match the form of bio-reductionism is to require that physical causes of stuttering (genetics and neurophysiological development) be elevated and cut from their mutual, contextual, and constitutive relations. It follows that SLPs and kin suppress their ability to explain what is happening in the moment of speech.

For example, *The Diagnostic and Statistical Manual of Mental Disorders* (*DSM-V*) now labels stuttering as "childhood-onset fluency disorder" and classifies it as a Communication Disorder under the superordinate category of Neurodevelopmental Disorders. An exemplar of ableism, this definition posits a corporeal standard of speaking lifted to the status of universality in order to mark less-than-fully-human speech: "The essential feature of childhood-onset fluency disorder (stuttering) is a disturbance in the normal fluency and time patterning of speech that is inappropriate for the individual's age. . . . The disturbance in fluency interferes with academic or occupational achievement or with social communication" (APA 2013).

The word *disturbance* describes a change in a plan or process with a typically negative connotation. Like a boat jammed in a canal, stuttering, on the *DSM-V* account, is imagined to be an ailment of failed eventfulness. Although disturbances emerge from within complex processes to which they contribute, they are often subject to what Alfred North Whitehead calls "misplaced concreteness" (Whitehead 1967: 51), the mistake, as Ada Jaarsma explains, of confusing "being for becoming, the static for the dynamic, the map for the territory, the causative for system-entangled relations" (Jaarsma 2017: 11), such that stuttering becomes knowable only through abstractions-turned-objects—such as "disturbances"—that *subtract* from the dynamism of communication to arrive at predictable genetic, neurophysiological, and developmental markers. Yet the biological reductionist is stuck, for to give real credence to the compositional dimensions of speech would allow too much plasticity into being and risk the neutrality and hegemony of biosocial norms.

Perhaps the most questionable premise upon which the reification of stuttering (as an age-inappropriate disruption of normal fluency and time patterning of speech) rests is the notion of a normal trajectory of human development—a trajectory that queer and crip theorists have insisted is never pre-cultural and pre-discursive, but rather is invested with heterosexist and ableist desire. Alison Kafer, for instance, writes that "straight time" signifies "a firm delineation between past/present/future or an expectation for a linear development from dependent childhood to independent reproductive adulthood" (Kafer 2013: 34). What the stutter "disturbs" is thus not development itself but rather the expectation of a linear movement from full dependence to full independence via school, work, and social (ultimately reproductive) relations. Speech, on this heteronormative and ableist developmental account, is *quasi*-compositional insofar as distinct patterns of speech correspond with (both reflect and aid) each stage of development. Fluent speech helps compose the self along a normalized trajectory; dysfluent speech derails the process. When adolescent and adult humans vocalize (age-inappropriate) dysfluency, they enact, straight time says, a form of moral inappropriateness that degrades them and is even dangerous both to themselves and to the wider society. In other words, a body that is tuned to straight time will expect repetitions like "da-da-da" from infants and young children but will likely feel disturbed in the gut when adults vocalize dysfluency. Hence, the maintenance of zones of non-disturbance for the ableist listener is an essential, though invisibilized, service thrust upon disabled speakers of every age.

While Richter takes issue with the hegemony of biological reductionism, their point is slightly more general: insofar as *both* physicalist and symbolic accounts hunt for discrete causes within isolated domains, they are both essentialist discourses. In contrast, Richter affirms a non-essentialist position of stuttering that is useful to consider in this context. The first premise of this position is that speech is a multilayered power that straddles *both* symbolic *and* physicalist domains. The second premise of the position is that "speech disability must ultimately be navigated as a volitional condition of bodily agency itself" (Richter 2020: 107). Maurice Merleau-Ponty's concept of gesture is key to understand Richter's position.

Merleau-Ponty, too, was unsatisfied with the choice between intellectualist and physicalist accounts of speech, both of which drain speech of its embodied and lived significance. As I have explained elsewhere:

> Much like perception, speech is a means of "communion," calling forth (and being called forth by) meaning from situations around us. For Merleau-Ponty, the categorical distinction between gestural behavior and the rational, signifying activity of speech gives way to a continuity of "expressive" actions enacted by the body. Dividing the speech act into thought and language or bodily act and external meaning relies upon an unphenomenological fracturing of the intentional arc of the speaking body. (St. Pierre 2015: 51)

Speech, for Merleau-Ponty, is but one moment within the intentional arc of being-with another in a common world. Here, the very possibility of speech flows from a suprapersonal coordination of preconscious and nonverbal gesture that suggests "a form of semi-intentional cohesion between all speaking human subjects" (Richter 2020: 97). That is to say, nonverbal gestures performed via somatic imitation and habit enact a common world of meaningfulness, a shared context "in which expressions embody our understanding" (Engelland 2014: 74) and out of which speech can bubble to the surface. The idea that "it takes two" to stutter is thus an artificial abstraction as well, since antecedent even to the relational dynamic between speaker and listener is a shared belonging to a common context reproduced through the habituation/discipline of sensitive and interrelated bodies.

It is important to note that, for Merleau-Ponty, what a self encounters in nonverbal gesture is not mechanical behavior but rather reversibility. Chad Engelland explains that "[b]ehavior is not itself a thing but the manifestation of another self to whom things are present" (Engelland 2014: 82). This reversibility is why, as Richter reminds us, Merleau-Pontyan gesture does not reduce to biology or culture but instead mediates the two (Richter 2020: 98). To perceive is to be perceptible insofar as "our bodies enable us both to have a world and to be had by others as one having a world" (Engelland 2014: 82). Stauffer's conception of ethical loneliness does problematize the sense of automatic belonging that derives from Merleau-Ponty. As I indicated earlier, inclusion within a shared world is a coordinated achievement of world-building that can be denied in multiple ways.

Nevertheless, with Richter, the first point that I want to emphasize is that speech, "composed preconsciously of gesture" (Richter 2020: 98), spans two categorical domains and is thus predisposed to reductionism. To understand the eventfulness of speech disability without collapsing this eventfulness in the process of understanding it requires (as I have urged throughout this chapter) an awareness of the "compounding nature of the sensory, gestural, social structural, and inner aspects of speech" (109). But if the logic of our ableist SLP rejects the complex multimodality of stuttering, they will surely rebuff Richter's additional point that "speech disability must ultimately be navigated as a volitional condition of bodily agency itself" (107). The reversibility of the sensitive body of "flesh"—as Merleau-Ponty will call it (1969)—means that ableism can never have the final say. Engelland, quoting Merleau-Ponty, writes that "Flesh is not only a passive part of the world; it is also an active point of view on the world 'capable of gestures, of expression, and finally of language, *it turns back on the world to signify it*'" (Engelland 2014: 76, emphasis added). Human bodies (to say nothing here of nonhuman animals) secrete meaning and call it forth in communion with the world, which makes speech disability an active force of material differentiation and resignification rather than a collapse of agency and meaningfulness.

Listening Beyond Atomism and Holism

My central claim in this chapter has been that the reductive beliefs, processes, and practices constitutive of ableism stifle the eventfulness of stuttering. Within an ableist framework, stuttering becomes a non-event, a failed composition, a happening where nothing manages to happen, move, or change (at least in the right way). For our ableist SLP, stuttering does not even register as a happening, a gathering of shared time, but is rather reduced to a mere individual trait: an ailment that drains meaning from the world and that can be scrubbed from the human condition altogether with enough effort. Against such reduction, how might we affirm that a stutter "is happening" and, moreover, nurture the eventfulness of stuttering? How might we collectively hold time to let stuttering do its work? Both Cahill and Hamel, as well as Lipari, might in this regard gesture toward reflexive listening practices as a transitive goal—necessary, but not sufficient, to the task. Lipari, for example, writes:

> Today, most research about listening takes a largely atomistic perspective that aims to improve listening processes so that we may become more effective and better listeners. Without a doubt, these are noble goals that can offer great benefit to individuals and society, particularly in relation to disabilities such as traumatic brain injuries, neurological disorders,

> auditory processing disorders, hearing impairments, and so forth. But unfortunately, they also, at the same time, tend to perpetuate the very mechanistic and transmission views of language and thought that keep us from understanding or engaging with other ways of being. (Lipari 2014: 98)

"Good listening" does seem to be in short supply. Especially for marginalized voices, the dissemination of practices such as not interrupting; providing feedback; asking questions; and being patient, honest, helpful, and caring (Imhof 2003) would shift communication toward dysfluent territory. Resonant with Lipari's concern, however, I worry that "good listening" becomes a technocratic fix for vocal injustice that further individualizes and further mystifies the relational and sociopolitical dynamics of communication. "Good listening" is easily packaged as a set of skills, a medium of self-improvement in the form of "listening capital" for neoliberal ableist societies. Inversely, "bad listening" is too easy a scapegoat for ableism. The ableist listener is indeed "the poor listener [who] focuses on the speaker's voice, clothes, or looks and, in so doing, discounts whatever they might say due to a critical stance on the speaker" (Campbell 2011: 67). Furthermore, the habits of perception of the ableist listener can indeed cut across all eight of Les MacLeod's modes of "negative" listening: biased, selective, insulated, disruptive, narcissist, defensive, pseudo (pretending to listen), and concern for only the words being spoken (MacLeod 2016: 17). Yet I contend that the goal of "better listening" reifies the individual and mystifies political difference. To single out qualities inherent to individual listeners deflects attention from the contingent process of world-building by which dispositions and habits are made.

Lipari offers as an alternative a holistic account of listening. For the holist, the parts of a system are always constituted by and serve the whole. For example, "the heart is nothing without the larger organism in which it functions; the conscious self requires an intersubjective web of language to be; an anthem is situated within a nation that gives it meaning" (Connolly 2011: 32); to which, I imagine, Lipari would add that interlocutors are nothing without a conversation that gives it meaning, and a conversation is situated within a cultural habitus itself that comprises worlds of meaning past, present, and future.

Given this gesture toward the larger whole, Lipari's answer to the question of what a holistic paradigm of listening—what she calls "interlistening"—would encompass is unsurprising: "In short, everything. Perhaps it would begin with the understanding that listening requires an awareness of our habitual categories and a willingness to go beyond them" (Lipari 2014: 99). How might this happen? "One suggestion is to listen from a space of emptiness and unknowing, to be strong enough to relinquish our perceived mastery, control, and foreknowledge while remaining attentive and aware" (ibid.). Much like improving individual listening practices, holistic listening is a noble goal. When, to pick up a point discussed earlier, pre-reflective dispositions lead to reductive and cruel forms of listening, an individual and collective willingness to go beyond such dispositions becomes necessary for dysfluent folk to sound and belong within a common world.

While the goal of perceptual reformation is noble, I suggest that holism, like atomism, is conceptually insufficient to accomplish this task. The problem, to quote Hasana Sharp, is that "whole is another word for individual, that which is not divided" (Sharp 2011: 36). Like the individual, a unified whole is also an artificial abstraction from the dynamic interrelations of a multitude of beings. Sharp and Connolly, even though they engage different interlocutors—Spinoza and Gilbert Simondon for Sharp versus Nietzsche and William James for Connolly—arrive at similar conclusions with respect to the insufficiencies of the conceptual paradigms of holism and atomism and (each in their own way) chart a middle path through them. Connolly calls this position "connectionism." It is important to note within the context of disability that Sharp, in conversation with Simondon, links the impossibility of a unified whole to an ontological excess rather than deficit: "Being is a system of relations that is excessive, always incomplete and uncompleted, and perpetually differentiating. [Being] is not a unity because it is '*supersaturated*,' replete with energetic force that is composing and recomposing in new formations, in response to new tensions, at all times" (Sharp 2011: 36, emphasis added). Ableism rests upon the specific conceit of a "whole" body (both individual and collective) that disability diminishes. Perhaps what our ableist SLP protests, even more than labored listening, is the condition of existence—a condition emphasized when a stutter happens—that being is too excessive to coalesce into self-sufficient unities.

For William James, Connolly explains, the parts of a system can never add up to a complete whole because the constitutive relations are "punctuated by 'litter' circulating in, between, and around them" such that "the connections are typically loose, incomplete, and themselves susceptible to potential change" (Connolly 2011: 35). For the connectionist, the self—like any complex being—is neither a bounded individual nor a part defined by its relation to the whole, but rather a set of supersaturated relations variably open to change. Crips know quite well that everyday existence hinges upon the collaboration of multiple agents. Nevertheless, the individual and the unified whole are such powerful abstractions that they make the affirmation of a world in constant recomposition an ongoing task. Jaarsma puts this point well and bends the discussion back to our ableist SLP when she writes: "We face the challenge of affirming our own becoming, as relational and porous selves that develop within specific ecologies. Responsive to cues from the environment, inherited tendencies as well as ecological factors, our selves are developmental, constitutively. At stake, politically, is our subjective willingness to tune into these relational dynamics" (Jaarsma 2017: 79). Our ableist SLP demonstrates that the unwillingness to tune into relational dynamics leads to an existential "leveling" (57) where universal categories and imperatives run free and, of crucial significance, difference and becoming cease to matter. Listening for such relational dynamics, for the tensions into which something new might flow into being, is a political, and specifically counter-eugenic, practice.

Although the matter is unsettled, I find that connectionism offers a compelling account of "the stutter that happens" insofar as it centers the relational dynamic of communication while proposing an alternative to the questionable premise of a whole (i.e., undivided) conversation and, further upstream, an undivided social world within which Lipari situates "holistic" listening. Lipari insists that the critical listener "must notice the gaps and fissures that occur when one voice speaks in place of another, or when another is silenced" (Lipari 2014: 203) and, to reiterate, offers the practice of listening from a space of emptiness and unknowing as a way to relinquish our perceived mastery over the world, while still remaining attentive to the situation. Although I do not disagree with this technique to relinquish mastery, I want to recommend a slight alternative that both offers more affordances for listeners and affirms a world of becoming: namely, to listen *in the mode of ontological excess* for gaps and fissures. Because "there are vibrations, bits of noise, and litter in each system that do not fit perfectly into it," Connolly points out, "new things can come into being, ruffling an established set of connections or throwing them into crisis" (Connolly 2011: 36). Perhaps our ableist SLP knows this. Perhaps they understand that radical listening will decompose the bounded self, ruffle perceptual formations, and open a fissure for something new. Perhaps they do not know this. Either way, the time has come for ableist listening to experience discomfort and some crisis.

Conclusion: Sharing Time

This chapter has skirted a direct discussion of time; nevertheless, in what remains, allow me to gather a few threads. Speech is an event that occurs at once in linear and nonlinear time: while, as Lipari explains, an utterance may unfold in linear, diachronous time: "successive words shape the meaning of future and previous words in an eternal blending of past, present, and future" (Lipari 2014: 146). Ableist formations of relation and thought are marked by an obsession with linear time that corresponds with the demands of action-orientated perception. Yet while humans coordinate perception and organize verbal speech within straight time, these are punctuated experiences that draw from a more basic experience where "human lives unfold with a kind of spiraling and branching recursivity and synchrony" (152). To think, speak, or act is to vibrate a thread of meaning always already in conversation with others (past, present, or future). For the dysfluent or otherwise, it is not uncommon to catch oneself mid-conversation, tripped up on a word three sentences ago that triggered a past experience and is flooding the present with anticipation that could open multiple futures.

The event of communication is thus always layered: it always unfolds at once in the register of measurable, chronological time, and in a non-chronological register defined by synchrony and recursivity that Connolly (drawing from Henri Bergson) calls "durational time." This combination of chronological time and durational time is "the flow of time as becoming. It is waves of memory protracted into a present unfolding toward an altered future" (Connolly 2005: 102). Due to the pressures of everyday life and the possession of a human sensorium, it is easy to forget, Connolly insists, that clock time is not literal time but rather a human artifice sustained by its connection to durational time (114). When stretched along just one dimension of time, the stutter seems inhospitable, riddled with temporal sinkholes and dead-ends. Perhaps we are inclined to forget that clock time is not literal time because modernity and ableism have been busy peddling this lie in the effort to control (i.e., put in their place) elusive experiences like daydreaming, stuttering, or mystical states that suspend operational time and can invite a shared attunement to time as becoming.

The ableist interlocutor who is caught in operational time and disciplined both by the clock and by a normative grammar to fixate on the prediction of linear meaning is lost at this point: either unable or unwilling to dwell in the thickness of time and, moreover, in the *politics* of becoming that emerges from the "dissonant conjunction between new swerves of time and the ethical uncertainty they engender" (Connolly 2005: 120). Clock time is not something that we can share but rather can only co-manage and co-participate within, such that to share time—to share stuttered time—requires a willingness to suspend operational time, and moreover, a willingness to deepen our *attachment* to dissonant rhythms found within the push and pull of nonhuman time.

Note

1 Some disability theorists like Dan Goodley (2014) accordingly use the term *disableism* to disambiguate the negative from the positive face of ableism. Others

like Gregor Wolbring (2008) contend that the nomenclature is unnecessary insofar as formations of power like ableism or racism always already imply this dual characteristic of inclusion/exclusion. I take Wolbring's point but find the distinction between ableism and disableism useful to describe lived experience within ableist formations of power.

References

American Psychiatric Association (2013), *Desk Reference to the Diagnostic Criteria from DSM-V (R)*, Arlington: American Psychiatric Association Publishing.

American Speech-Language-Hearing Association (n.d.), "Definition of Communication." Available at: https://www.asha.org/njc/definition-of-communication-and-appropriate-targets/ (accessed May 12, 2022).

American Speech-Language-Hearing Association (n.d.), "Fluency Disorders." Available at: www.asha.org/practice-portal/clinical-topics/fluency-disorders/ (accessed May 12, 2022).

Cahill, Ann J. and Christine Hamel (2022), *Sounding Bodies: Identity, Injustice, and the Voice*, New York: Methuen Drama.

Campbell, Fiona Kumari (2001), "Inciting Legal Fictions: Disability's Date with Ontology and the Ableist Body of the Law," *Griffith Law Review* 10: 42–62.

Campbell, Robyn (2011), "The Power of the Listening Ear," *English Journal* 100 (5): 66.

Cole, Sean and Jerome Ellis (2020), "Made to be Broken" [Audio podcast episode], in *This American Life*, WBEZ Chicago, August 7. Available at: https://www.thisamericanlife.org/713/made-to-be-broken/act-one-10. (accessed July 22, 2023)

Connolly, William E. (2002), *Neuropolitics: Thinking, Culture, Speed*, Minneapolis: University of Minnesota Press.

Connolly, William E. (2005), *Pluralism*, Durham: Duke University Press.

Connolly, William E. (2011), *A World of Becoming*, Durham: Duke University Press.

Dolmage, Jay Timothy (2013), *Disability Rhetoric*, Syracuse: Syracuse University Press.

Dolmage, Jay T. (2018), *Disabled Upon Arrival: Eugenics, Immigration, and the Construction of Race and Disability*, Columbus: The Ohio State University Press.

Engelland, Chad (2014), *Ostension: Word Learning and the Embodied Mind*, Cambridge, MA: The MIT Press.

Goodley, Dan (2014), *Dis/Ability Studies: Theorising Disablism and Ableism*, New York: Routledge.

Hamraie, Aimi (2017), *Building Access: Universal Design and the Politics of Disability*, Minneapolis: University of Minnesota Press.

Imhof, Margarete (2003), "The Social Construction of the Listener: Listening Behavior across Situations, Perceived Listener Status, and Cultures," *Communication Research Reports* 20 (4): 357–66.

Jaarsma, Ada (2017), *Kierkegaard after the Genome: Science, Existence, and Belief in this World*, New York: Palgrave MacMillan.

Jezer, Marty (1997), *Stuttering: A Life Bound Up in Words*, Toronto: Harper Collins.

Kafer, Alison (2013), *Feminist, Queer, Crip*, Bloomington: Indiana University Press.

Lipari, Lisbeth (2014), *Listening, Thinking, Being: Toward an Ethics of Attunement*, University Park: Penn State University Press.

Malhotra, Ravi (2012), "Has the Charter Made a Difference for People with Disabilities?: Reflections and Strategies for the 21st Century," *The Supreme Court Law Review: Osgoode's Annual Constitutional Cases Conference* 58: 273–97. Available at: https://digitalcommons.osgoode.yorku.ca/sclr/vol58/iss1/10 (accessed July 22, 2023).

MacLeod, Les (2016), "Listening: More than What Meets the Ear," *Physician Leadership Journal* 3 (4): 14–19.

Merleau-Ponty, Maurice (1969), *The Visible and the Invisible*, Evanston: Northwestern University Press.

Nancy, Jean-Luc (2007), *Listening*, New York: Fordham University Press.

Overboe, James (2012), "Theory, Impairment and Impersonal Singularities: Deleuze, Guattari and Agamben," in Dan Goodley, Bill Hughes, and Lennard Davis (eds.), *Disability and Social Theory*, 112–26, London: Palgrave Macmillan.

Richter, Zara (2020), "Speech: Speech Disability's Awkward Late Modernity: A Multimodal Historical Approach," in David T. Mitchell and Sharon L. Snyder (eds.), *A Cultural History of Disability in the Modern Age*, 95–109, New York: Bloomsbury Academic.

Schalk, Sami (2018), *Bodyminds Reimagined: (Dis)Ability, Race, and Gender in Black Women's Speculative Fiction*, Durham: Duke University Press.

Schick, Erin (2014), "Honest Speech," *Button Poetry*, August 21. Available at: https://www.youtube.com/watch?v=j8XOyY54-Ew (accessed July 22, 2023).

Schweik, Susan M. (2009), *The Ugly Laws: Disability in Public*, New York: New York University Press.

Sharp, Hasana (2011), *Spinoza and the Politics of Renaturalization*, Chicago: University of Chicago Press.

St. Pierre, Joshua (2012), "The Construction of the Disabled Speaker: Locating Stuttering in Disability Studies," *The Canadian Journal of Disability Studies* 1 (3): 1–21.

St. Pierre, Joshua (2015), "Distending Straight-Masculine Time: A Phenomenology of the Disabled Speaking Body," *Hypatia: A Jorunal of Feminist Philosophy* 30 (1): 49–65.

Stauffer, Jill (2015), *Ethical Loneliness: The Injustice of Not Being Heard*, New York: Columbia University Press.

Whitehead, Alfred North (1967), *Science and the Modern World*, New York: The Free Press.

Wolbring, Gregor (2008), "Is There an End to Out-Able? Is There an End to the Rat Race for Abilities?" *M/C Journal* 11 (3). https://doi.org/10.5204/mcj.57.

Yairi, Ehud (2013), "Reply to Letter to the Editor," *Journal of Fluency Disorders* 38: 294–8.

14 FRANTZ FANON AND DISABILITY

FRICTIONS AND SOLIDARITIES

EMILY R. DOUGLAS

Introduction: Reading with Fanon

Frantz Fanon (1925–61), a philosopher, psychiatrist, and revolutionary, has long been recognized for his careful discussions of the impacts of racism and colonization upon embodiment. Born in Martinique in 1925, Fanon served in the Free French Forces in the Second World War and, after earning a medical degree in Lyon, was posted at Blida-Joinville psychiatric hospital in Algeria. Both inside and outside the clinic, Fanon's work, articulated in dialogue with phenomenologists, existentialists, psychoanalysts, and politicians, grapples with colonial madness, alienation, and corticovisceral (psychosomatic) disabilities. During the 1950s, Algeria—which had been colonized by the French for more than a century—entered into a war for independence that was characterized by the French army's use of torture and the use of guerilla tactics by Algerian liberation groups (Clancy-Smith 1998; Zack 2002). Amid the Algerian revolution, Fanon resigned from his post and joined forces with the *Armée de libération nationale* (ALN), eventually moving his medical practice and political activism to Tunis. He survived an assassination attempt on his life while hospitalized in Rome due to a land-mine injury, subsequently returning to Tunis to act as a representative for the Algerian provisional government at various meetings and conferences across Africa. His death in 1961 from leukemia occurred as his final manuscript, *The Wretched of the Earth*, was published and became a decolonial standard.[1]

This chapter takes Fanon as a fully fledged philosopher in his own right who makes significant unique contributions to thinking about disability. As Tommy Curry (2011) has pointed out, even "the most studied Black philosophers are read as the embodiment of their white associates: W. E. B. DuBois is read as the Black Hegel, the Black James, the Black Dewey, Frantz Fanon as a Black Sartre or Black Husserl"—or, increasingly, as the Black Merleau-Ponty (Curry 2011: 315–16). My argument in the chapter assumes that Fanon's work is not a *prosthetic* to other forms of phenomenology, but rather fundamentally modifies the assumptions of embodiment that white and European phenomenologists have advanced.

A large amount of scholarship on Fanon, particularly from the 1990s and 2000s, engages the psychiatric without engaging disability. Indeed, Fanon's work has seldom been taken up in philosophy of disability, nor, for the most part, has Fanon himself been recognized as a philosopher of disability. Although, to be sure, the word *disability* appears few times in Fanon's work, he persistently considered its neighbors—madness, alienation, suffering, pathologies, tension, and spasms—in his writing. Thus, I read Fanon with a methodological note that Nirmala Erevelles (2011) inspires. Erevelles argues that Black feminist Hortense Spillers's work "is as much about disability as it is about race," and should be seen as a corrective to the whiteness of mainstream disability theory. Though Fanon's texts address different questions than Spillers's, his writings (not unlike Spillers's) provide insights into experiences of racialized disability and debilitation, notably in colonial and (so-called) postcolonial situations. This chapter can thus serve as a guidepost with which to consider Fanon as engaged with disability, thematically mapping orientations in his work with disability scholarship. My aim in the chapter is not to posit Fanon's understandings of disability as overarching or universal, but rather to draw out the particular benefits of his work for thinking about disability.

Fanon is well known for both his work in, and modifications of, social therapy (which is sometimes translated as institutional therapy) and his emphasis on context in psychiatric treatment.[2] His exhortations for situational diagnosis indicate that he recognizes how social and political forces have psycho/physical implications. A Black Martinician, Fanon is careful to articulate both his own specificity and the ways that his alienation relates to other racialized others who are differentially sorted in terms of perceived abilities and capacities and, thus, differentially sorted in terms of the surveillance and pathologization to which they are subjected. Indeed, the colonial situation fundamentally remakes the medical encounter and, thus, acknowledgment of the context (intersubjective, political, and communal) in which it takes place is crucial. By affirming the social causes and configurations that lead individuals to be diagnosed as sick, Fanon establishes a critical point of view on disability and illness. Mad studies and Black studies theorists have begun to develop critical frameworks for thinking about madness, following the threads of Fanon's sociogenic method (Pickens 2019; Bruce 2021). I maintain that philosophers of disability should join this wave by appreciating and working with Fanon's insights.

Fanon's proposal of sociogeny as a method significantly alters the way that both "mental" and "physical" disabilities are recognized and treated. The term *sociogeny* more generally gained attention in early sociological texts as a way to explain society as an origin of certain pathologies (Ward 1898). In clinical realms, sociogeny remains associated with "mass sociogenic illness" and hysteria—in other words, to psychosomatic medicines. The term is often used interchangeably with *psychogenesis* (Müller-Vahl et al. 2022; Tsekoa and Mugomeri 2015). However, Fanon's conception of sociogeny is not psychologically bound, allowing us to think fruitfully across the scale of individual/collective and beyond the binary of mind/body. He invokes the term *sociogeny* early in *Black Skin, White Masks*:

> Reacting against the constitutionalist tendency of the late nineteenth century, Freud insisted that the individual factor be taken into account through psychoanalysis. He substituted for a phylogenetic theory the ontogenetic perspective. It will be seen that the black man's alienation is not an individual question. Beside phylogeny and ontogeny stands sociogeny. . . . [L]et us say that here it is a question of sociodiagnostics. (Fanon 1986: 13)

Sociogeny is understood in various ways.[3] Rinaldo Walcott (2006) argues that sociogeny is a key way of broaching interior and exterior, individual and the collective: "What is at stake in articulating sociogeny or the sociogenetic is an attempt to think the group and the individual at once . . . Fanon most forcefully reconnects mind and body in their social and political contexts to offer us an analysis of the stakes of rethinking the category of the Human" (Walcott 2006: 34). Carolyn Urena writes of "the theoretical framework of sociogenesis, which links the self to society as a way to understand the kind of transformation needed to heal [colonial] wounds" (Urena 2019: 1649). On her reading, sociogeny enables deeper understanding of the body's suffering as well as its healing (1651). Without a sociogenic method, Urena claims, philosophies of oppression and decolonization miss the "human-made social contexts" and so will constantly disappoint any attempts at reparations (1653). Andrea Pitts, in turn, sees sociogeny as a tool for the "revaluation of the therapeutic, preventative, and palliative functions of clinical medicine" (Pitts 2021: 622). These understandings of sociogeny, though themselves diverse, all serve to foreground the entangled relationship of pathologization and healing with social context.

In sum, sociogeny leads to knowledge and understanding about the structuring of racialization and the pathologizations of racialized and colonized disabled people, in addition to the knowledge and understanding it affords about the etiology of specific unexplained/new illnesses, diseases, and disability. Note that sociogeny is not merely additive but rather transforms the articulations of ontogeny and phylogeny (not that they were fully impartial). In some respects, a sociogenic approach to disability resembles the social model of disability, according to which disability is not an individualized, embodied trait, but rather a product of our inaccessible and rigid environments (Oliver 1990; Shakespeare 2010). My argument is that Fanon's work goes beyond the social model of disability insofar as it assumes that society is a causal agent in colonial pathologies and alienation rather than merely the site of misfitting and mismatching in relation to dominant social, political, and architectural norms. Viewing disability through a sociogenic lens allows us to deconstruct several assumptions of dominant ableist imaginaries, including the illusion of a neat and clean line between disabled and nondisabled.

Levels of Analysis: From the Body Schema to Debilitation

During the last several years, a turn has taken place within Fanon's studies that better acknowledges his medical and psychiatric writings, a turn prompted in part by Jean Khalfa's and Robert C. Young's collection, *Alienation and Freedom* (2018). Critical phenomenologists have also increasingly used Fanon's writing to elaborate the ongoing effects of colonization and racism upon embodiment. By drawing robustly upon Fanon, George Yancy (2008), Helen Ngo (2012), Alia Al-Saji (2020, 2021), and other authors have connected the material stresses on the body to racializing atmospheres. As Ngo puts it, "a [racialized] body is laden with the work of managing others' racialized anxieties" (Ngo 2012: 58). This work is physical, physiological, and affective. It is also often disabling.

For example, many theorists have taken up Fanon's critique of the phenomenological body schema that Maurice Merleau-Ponty proposes. Fanon argues that Merleau-Ponty's body schema tacitly assumes a white subject, falsely universalizing our relations to our bodies and their motilities (Fanon 1986: 83–5). Instead, Fanon feels fixed by racialization in his body, which he names the historical-racial and racial-epidermal schemas. He asserts that the universalized idea of the body schema fails to apply to him because a "historico-racial schema," woven by the white man, changes his sensations, perceptions, and sense of body. The piercing cry "*Tiens, un nègre*!" from a small child on the train fixes him, exposing a "racial epidermal schema" (110–11).

Fanon's critique of the body schema is interpreted in multiple ways. Ngo reads Fanon's encounter as an experience of fragmentation, exposing how "the racialized body teeters constantly on the brink of dissolution and undoing," but not total dissolution (Ngo 2012: 70, 73). Kristin Zeiler reads Fanon's critique of the body schema as excorporation, where "something that has been part of one's lived body on a pre-reflective and practical level becomes a thematic object of one's attention . . . it is unwanted and typically painful" (Zeiler 2013: 75). Shiloh Whitney reads the body schema as a "theory of affect," where Fanon then shows us "the collapse of the racialized body schema is not only a disabling of motor intentionality but a depletion of affective agency: a diminishing of the forcefulness and influence racialized people's affects have on the bodies of others" (Whitney 2018: 506). Al-Saji (2020) argues that the Black subject's body schema was never a universalized embodied experience, but rather always already fragmented.

These existing analyses get much right: they correctly place the affective and political atmospheres as part of the causal structures of sociogeny. However, none of them links the body schema to disability, capacity, or injury. One way to view body schema alterations is as disabling, in the broader sense in which Iris Marion Young (1980) argues that women are "physically handicapped" in patriarchal societies according to their motility and comportment. Scholars have yet to take up either the historico-racial or epidermal schemas in terms of their utility in understanding racialized disability. A simplified analogy of the historical-racial or racial-epidermal body schema to disability, however, does a disservice to the complex imbrications of racialization and disability. Indeed, to focus on only the body schema as representative of Fanon's contributions to philosophy of disability is insufficient: there are numerous experiences of disability and injury that do not occur at the scale of the body schema alone. If the lived body is not elaborated beyond the body schema, we miss out on the modulations and variations of anatomy and physiology, which are absolutely crucial for doing justice to disabled experience.

Much of Fanon's work takes as a starting point the many colonial pathologies that were theorized, produced, and used to justify ongoing settlement, both in French colonization and more broadly. Throughout Fanon's career, he came up against naturalization of criminality and violence to the racialized and colonized, in specific formations according to context, whether in Martinique, France, Algeria, Tunisia, or elsewhere. He consistently argues against theories such as Octave Mannoni's dependency complex of the colonized, refusing the individualized psychoanalytic framework (Fanon 1986; Dhavantari 2020). In short, Fanon's work both pushes back on these naturalizations of pathology, showing them to be social constructs, and simultaneously demonstrates the actual harms of colonialism. Indeed, "disability is central to Fanon's arguments: one of the main features of colonialism which he identifies is the creation of specific mental 'pathologies' and 'disorders' as a result of the colonial relationship. . . . Fanon believes that colonial wars create specific sorts of mental distress" (Sherry 2007: 14). My argument is that the scalar work of debilitation is one level to which we can attend beyond the body schema.

Fanon's work prefigures queer theorist Jasbir Puar's recent writing on debilitation and the uses of injury for colonialism (2017, 2021). Puar introduces the notion of "debilitation"—the colonial production and maintenance of injury and disability—construed as the exercise of a right to maim.[4] This technique, "justified as moral because it doesn't kill, is a mode of producing value from disposable bodies while all but ensuring a slow death" (Puar 2021: 396). To understand some instances of disability as maiming is not to say that to be disabled is to be maimed; rather to understand disability as maiming is to highlight the different and graduated modes of becoming disabled. Both disability and debility carry connotations of impairment, yet debility points to injury rather than accident. Further, debility puts into question the very binary in which injury is understood as either accidental or intentional, insofar as many modes of debilitation are excused as unintentional: debilitation "as a normal consequence of labouring, as an 'expected impairment'" (Puar 2017: xvi). Part of Puar's point is that debilitation is intensely useful for colonialism. Maimed subjects are the outcome of processes that produce "permanent disability via the infliction of harm and the attrition of the life support systems that might allow populations to heal from this harm" (143). Maiming humans *and* a given geopolitical region's economic, social, and industrial infrastructure are beneficial for settler colonization: they ensure that the individuals who are impaired cannot receive adequate treatment and care, while also slowly debilitating "able-bodied" subjects over time through the compromised infrastructure. Fanon's work gives us insight into an early exercise of this right to maim.[5]

Debilitation is a widely shared condition, and yet its mechanisms are specifically dispersed. White residents of Martinique, France, and North Africa developed distinctly colonial pathologies: nevertheless, these white colonial pathologies did *not* constitute debilitation in Puar's sense. Fanon speaks of the pathologies of whiteness in *Black Skin, White Masks*, especially affective ankylosis, the Prospero complex, and negrophobia (Fanon 1986: 22, 107–8, 154–66). In *The Wretched of the Earth*, many of the psychopathologies that Fanon treats in white people are related to torture and the exercise of violence by themselves or family members. A wide literature on the pathologies of whiteness exists which could be used, for example, to understand the distress of the torturers that Fanon treats: distress coming from a foreseen "natural result" of the work of torture.[6] I decenter these white pathologies in this chapter both as a matter of scope and as part of the broader project to disrupt the whiteness of disability studies (Meekosha 2011; Bell 2017). With this reflection on the Fanonian literature complete and the theme of debilitation to track, we can turn to Fanon's medical work.

Fanon as Physician and Psychiatrist

As noted earlier, Fanon was trained as a psychiatrist within French colonial systems, including in Lyon; as such, he was deeply embedded within French colonial medical institutions as well as a medical gaze in general. Fanon's insights about the medical realm apply in cases of institutionalization, individual medical treatment and appointments, and the ways in which colonialism directly hampers and produces certain kinds of medical situations. He was hired as *Chef de service* for a wing of the psychiatric hospital Blida-Joinville, Algeria. There, Fanon was the only racialized doctor, working with a population of around 2,000 segregated Muslims and Europeans. No physicians spoke Arabic or other local languages, relying on the incomplete translations of Arab nurses (Gordon 2015: 81). Examining Fanon's medical practice and medical writings reveals an ambivalent attitude toward many of the mainstays of the medical model of disability.

We know that Fanon used and took part in electroshock, insulin shock, and forced sleep therapies (Fabris and Aubrecht 2014; Tosquelles and Fanon 2018a, 2018b). His participation in these practices reflects both a remaining faith in organicity and a concern for those interested in radical change of our institutions. In terms of institutionalization, Fanon is said to have greatly transformed Blida-Joinville upon his arrival, removing physical restraints in a recapitulation of the Pinel myth (Gordon 2015: 81). Fanon pushed sociotherapy at Blida-Joinville, continuing Tosquelle's vision, but noticed that it worked imperfectly. He also fought for the establishment of day-program-only hospitalization, which he eventually established at the *Hôpital Charles-Nicolle* in Tunis (Fanon 2018b; Fanon and Geronimi 2018). Nevertheless, he also promoted both the inclusion of psychiatric hospitals in general hospitals and the alignment of psychiatry with less politicized branches of medicine. As Chloë Taylor (2010) notes, mad people and particularly mad activists usually do not welcome this kind of re-medicalization of madness.

Throughout the last century, medicine has been, and remains, marked by a significant attachment to lesion that Michel Foucault (2003) identifies as a technique of the medical gaze that coalesced within European medicine at the end of the eighteenth century. Whereas previously, a doctor might ask a patient, "What is the matter with you?" the anatamo-clinical mode of perception asks "Where does it hurt?" (Foucault 2003: xxi). Importantly, the medical gaze "contains within a single structure different sensorial fields. . . . A gaze that touches, hears, and moreover, not by essence or necessity, sees" (202). Physical examinations such as palpating are part of this "sight."

These observations both articulate the framework that Fanon worked *within* and are prefigured in his own observations. His writings about medicine serve as both corrective texts to pathologization and expose the lesion-focused assumptions in medicine that block effective treatment. Still, his position within the gaze is ambivalent and fraught. Femi Eromosele (2022) argues that Fanon's work cannot mesh easily with Mad Studies due to his use of this framework, more medical than social. As Eromosele puts it, "he is never in doubt that what he is dealing with are mental disorders, palpable aberrations in human functioning" (Eromosele 2022: 172). In contrast, Esme G. Murdock argues that "the social model of disability is directly related to Fanon's work in contextualizing the way a settler colonial society rooted in land theft and occupation is the foundational situation that triggers and/or worsens the traumatic disorders of the colonized he encountered" (Murdock 2022: 115). We can examine Fanon's stance closely through his own writings.

In "The 'North African Syndrome'" (1967) Fanon examines a diagnostic construct built on colonial psychiatry that was in circulation during his time in Lyon. When a North African in France in the early 1950s was seen by a French doctor, medical dogma about lesion-centric medicine met with racist assumptions and racializing pathologized notions of North Africans in general. Fanon imagines a medical encounter and examination with, what it seems are, scraps and pieces of his own experiences. The essay helps us to understand both Fanon's view on the psychosomatic or hysterical, as well as the ways in which symptoms of illness and disability in North Africans are capacitated toward maintaining colonial conditions.[7]

Fanon observes that "doctors continue to be taught that every symptom requires its lesion" (Fanon 1965: 8), as an "inflexible" rule. In this way, medical professionals have brought a static, assumed true, Eurocentric framework to bear. He maintains that, on the whole, medicine as Western colonial medicine presupposes that there must exist a physical lesion in the body which explains, acting as cause or etiology, all the symptoms seen. This assumption keys into the medical, individualized model of disability, framing the problem as something to be "fixed" within a single body, isolatable. Fanon notes that a doctor can more easily find a patient at fault than modify traditional medical thinking (ibid.). Hence, in his analysis of the text, David Macey writes that the "North African syndrome" affected French doctors, not North Africans (Macey 2000: 469). Thus, descriptions of pain, often incompletely translated—such as the descriptions of vague, generalized, and whole-body symptoms mentioned—absent any temporal or spatial delimitation, are filtered through a medical mode of apprehension.[8] Distrust, mistrust, and the requirement for objective measurable criteria all result in reinforcing racial hierarchizations: "In the face of this pain without lesion, this illness distributed in and over the whole body, this continuous suffering, the easiest attitude, to which one comes more or less rapidly, is the negation of any morbidity. When you come down to it, the North African is a simulator, a liar, a malingerer, sluggard, a thief" (Fanon 1965: 7).

The patient is a metonym, a stand-in for a mass, rather than a subject with particularities: all his contours are shared and generalized, either the site of pity (if he is primitive and ignorant), the site of fear (if he is dangerous), or both; hence, the patient "bears the dead weight of all his compatriots" (Fanon 1965: 8).[9] An individual patient's symptoms are made meaningful in conjunction with stereotypes about North Africans, under the guise of medical objectivity. In this encounter, there is both a conflict over truth—see the reference to lies and malingering earlier—and a disavowal of the qualitative pain that patients may feel. Thus, medical doctors provide interpretations which insist a patient "says he is suffering when we know there are no *reasons* for suffering" (10, emphasis in Fanon).

Even strategies for paying attention to context, such as integrating situational diagnosis, do not lead to a reliable or helpful verdict on the patient's health when trying to apply universal and objective medicine. Fanon rejects the "*diagnostic de situation*" proposed by psychosomatic physicians, showing that the European situational questions are the *wrong questions* when considering the sick North African in France.[10] Erich Stern suggests that we ask about inner tension; Fanon retorts, the patient's "inner tension. Utterly unrealistic! You might as well speak of the inner tension of a stone. Inner tension indeed! What a joke!" (Stern 1949: 12). To note their generalized, vague pains is also to note that their bodies have been worked over and worn down. As Fanon notes, "they have had France squeezed into them wherever, in their bodies and in their souls, there was room" (Fanon 1965: 15).[11] This "forcing into" the body of values and customs results in tension.[12] Including the social is not enough: as Fanon found in his experiments with social therapy, the European notions of sociality and what counts as important cannot be transferred over to Arab and Muslim residents (Fanon and Azoulay 2018).

Further insights can be drawn from "Medicine and Colonialism" (1967). Written during Fanon's time in Algeria, this essay traces both the infrastructural debilitation and the disabling impacts of colonial violence. The fight against illness was explicitly articulated by France as a way toward conquering Algeria, from the 1830s onward: "*il faut instruire et guérir pour conquérir*" (Bayle 1981: 284; Khiati 2000). Colonial medicine therefore operates quite differently from non-colonial medicine. Fanon observes that European medical professionals in Algeria had denied or hid signs of torture, frequently used a "truth serum," and cooperated regularly with colonial police (Fanon 1967: 136–8). Further, "even when the doctor belongs to the dominated people . . . the native doctor is a Europeanized, Westernized doctor" (132). Legal requirements demanded that doctors record names of "suspiciously wounded" Algerians during the revolt (135). In short, the atmosphere in Algeria lends a medical appointment distrust, strain, and significant risk.

The differences in communication, context, and values are crucial for the diagnostic process and present a particular nexus of challenges regarding "mental disorders": "In a non-colonial society, the attitude of a sick man in the presence of a medical practitioner is one of confidence. . . . At no time, in a non-colonial society, does the patient mistrust his doctor" (Fanon 1967: 123). Among others, many disabled people would take issue with this statement. Indeed, disbelief and mistrust surround those with medically unexplained illnesses (Mollow 2014; Wendell 1996). Yet we must heed Fanon's attention to the specificity of colonial environments. The Algerian's refusal to be hospitalized derives from a long-lived mistrust for colonial medical officials that is lived differently. Fanon's white patients, while experiencing distinct pathologies and disabilities themselves, do not have this same hesitation with medical authorities. That is, these reactions also tune into "the problem of the fight against illness, conceived of as an aspect of the French presence" (Fanon 1967: 126), that is, of colonization.

Fanon emphasizes how the colonial doctors, even if they are themselves colonized, often fall into a similar, colonizing medical gaze through habit, searching the body for the truth. Often, "the doctor rather quickly gave up the hope of obtaining information from the colonized patient and fell back on the clinical examination, thinking that the body would be more eloquent. But the body proved to be equally rigid. The muscles were contracted. There was no relaxing" (Fanon 1967: 126–7). We can better understand this dual state of capacitation and resistance through Fanon's many medical and physiological metaphors.

Not Mere Metaphors: Amputation, Refusal, and Tetanization

Fanon's significance for philosophy of disability can be drawn out further by examining the material-metaphorical use of medical and disability terms within his oeuvre. This section elaborates Fanon's underlying philosophy of tetanization by examining the interplay between such terms as *amputation*, *petrification*, *rigidity*, and *tetanization*.[13] Scholars have noticed these terms and their relations to each other for decades (Ficek 2011; Scott 2010; Moten 2008; Macey 2000).

There is good reason to be suspicious of metaphors, especially metaphors that in some way appeal to disability. In *Narrative Prosthesis: Disability and the Dependencies of Discourse* (2000), David Mitchell and Sharon Snyder argue that disabled characters' presence in literature is often reduced to metaphor. As Mitchell and Snyder explain it, "while stories rely upon the potency of disability as a symbolic figure, they rarely take up disability as an experience of social or political dimensions" (Mitchell and Snyder 2000: 48). Disability itself becomes rather a narrative prosthesis, a tool instrumentalized to prop up narratives of abled characters and forms: "The inherent vulnerability and variability of bodies serves literary narratives as a mechanism for that which refuses to conform to the minds desire for order and rationality. Within this schema, disability acts as a metaphor and fleshly example of the body's unruly resistance to the cultural desire to 'enforce normalcy'" (ibid.). Tanya Titchkosky notes how disability "sometimes appears in social justice praxis as an empty nothingness against which is configured the fullness of being of the complete and proper body" of progressive politics (Titchkosky 2015: 4).[14]

Indeed, some disability theorists frame Fanon's use of images of disability and injury as exposing an ableist imaginary. They take off from his discussion at the end of "The Lived Experience of the Black Man" (1986) where Fanon recounts a scene from the film *Home of the Brave* (Robson 1949) and makes a declaration refusing amputation:

> In the interval, just before the film starts, I wait for me. The people in the theater are watching me, examining me, waiting for me. A Negro groom is going to appear. My heart makes my head swim. The crippled veteran of the Pacific war says to my brother, "Resign yourself to your color the way I got used to my stump; we're both victims." Nevertheless with all my strength I refuse to accept that amputation. I feel in myself a soul as immense as the world, truly a soul as deep as the deepest of rivers, my chest has the power to expand without limit. I am a master and I am advised to adopt the humility of the cripple. (Fanon 1986: 140)

At question in this passage is Fanon's relationship to the medical and social models of disability, as well as to cure and healing. Sociologist of disability Mark Sherry (2007) interprets Fanon's work as reinforcing the medical model of disability, both individualized and biologized. Based upon Fanon's diagnosis of colonial pathologies, Sherry concludes that "For Fanon, psychiatric impairments are a sign of the horrors of colonialism. Get rid of colonialism, and we will avoid many disability experiences, and that is unquestionably assumed to be a good thing. Fanon not only assumes that medical diagnoses are objective and scientific, he further assumes that medical responses are unproblematically beneficial" (Sherry 2007: 15). Sherry reads Fanon as exercising the *medical gaze*, "largely ignor[ing] the role of social factors other than colonialism in the creation of disability and impairment" and assuming "that the disability labels which he applies to people reflect objective mental states, rather than subjective interpretations of another person's reality" (ibid.).

Rosemarie Garland-Thomson (2009) reads this passage in a similar manner. Although Garland-Thomson acknowledges Fanon's contribution to staring's functions in upholding and furthering racism, her gloss on Fanon's refusal of amputation mistakenly takes him to be asserting a fixity and unchanging nature to physical disability. She sees Fanon as "recruiting" physically disabled people to displace the marginalization of Blackness. As she writes:

> Fanon recruits disability as the *true mark of physical inadequacy* from which he wishes to differentiate racial marking. A "crippled veteran" tells Fanon's brother to "resign" himself to his color, just as the veteran himself "got used to [his] stump". This comparison outrages Fanon, who claims that racial difference does not make one inferior, but disability does. Fanon defends against the comparison with disability by asserting that his "chest has the power to expand without limit". "I am," Fanon claims proudly, "a master and I am advised to adopt the humility of the cripple". So while Fanon avows "the Negro is not" deserving of subordination, he suggests that "the cripple" is. (Garland-Thomson 2009: 42, emphasis added)

Likewise, in "Disability Rights: Do We Really Mean it?" (2010), Ron Amundson argues that Fanon's famous refusal to be amputated is "an attempt to bargain for racial dignity at the expense of the dignity of people with physical impairments," displacing the dehumanization from the racialized to the disabled (Amundson 2010: 171). Amundson's interpretation (like Garland-Thomson's) reads Fanon as making a comparative and analogical move, fighting stigma by displacing stigma to others. As Amundson argues, "Fanon insists that he is not like a cripple. He says that enforced humility is not deserved by people of African descent in the way that it is deserved by cripples" (ibid.).

Despite the misuses and harms of certain disability metaphors, scholars of disability and race have recently foregrounded the many ways in which metaphors operate. It is crucial to highlight metaphor's functions in Fanon's work because he *both* takes up metaphors that have been used to discipline and police racialized peoples and turns these metaphors on their heads to show their origins and specific harms. Sami Schalk (2018) argues that disability metaphors in and of themselves often can (and do) illuminate the relation between abstract discourses and material results. She foregrounds looking at "the material effects of discourses of (dis)ability" on the Black bodymind both throughout history and at present (Schalk 2018: 44). As such, we have to take account of the metaphors of disability along with the materiality:

> because disability has been used by dominant social discourses to reference, define, and regulate other social systems, it requires reading for the metaphorical, allegorical, or otherwise abstract ways in which its fictional representation is implicated in gender, race, class, and sexuality concerns as both discursive signifier and material effect. (Schalk 2018: 44)

Schalk thus refocuses attention on metaphorical and discursive meanings, while nevertheless highlighting material lived experiences. Schalk's approach may lead us to, as Titchkosky puts it, "treat impairment rhetoric in social justice praxis as a cultural arena in which to explore the meaning of disability within narratives of human life unjustly damaged" (Titchkosky 2015: 10).

Let us return to the metaphor of amputation in Fanon's work since this metaphor is the most contentious to disability scholars. He invokes it several times throughout *Black Skin, White Masks.* Early on, describing a Martinician about to leave for France, he notes that: "He leaves for the pier, and the amputation of his being diminishes as the silhouette of his ship grows clearer" (Fanon 1986: 23). Amputation comes back several times within "The Lived Experience of the Black." Immediately after the train encounter, during his discussion of the schemas, he notes:

> On that day, completely dislocated, unable to be abroad with the other, the white man, who unmercifully imprisoned me, I took myself far off from my own presence, far indeed, and made myself an object. What else could it be for me but an amputation, an excision, a hemorrhage that spattered my whole body with black blood? But I did not want this revision, this thematization. All I wanted was to be a man among other men. (Fanon 1986: 112)

A few pages later, Fanon describes the experience in this way: "I hailed the world, and the world amputated my enthusiasm" (Fanon 2008: 94).[15] As noted earlier, these invocations of amputation peak in his consideration of film. I want, therefore, to reproduce the end of the exchange and Fanon's response:

> The crippled veteran of the Pacific war says to my brother, "Resign yourself to your color the way I got used to my stump; we're both victims." Nevertheless with all my strength I refuse to accept that amputation. I feel in myself a soul as immense as the world, truly a soul as deep as the deepest of rivers, my chest has the power to expand without limit. I am a master and I am advised to adopt the humility of the cripple. Yesterday, awakening to the world, I saw the sky turn upon itself utterly and wholly. I wanted to rise, but the disemboweled silence fell back upon me, its wings paralyzed. Without responsibility, straddling Nothingness and Infinity, I began to weep. (Fanon 1986: 140)

Fanon's articulation of amputation is a discussion of amputation as affective, kin-breaking, world-shattering (though never completely) and *simultaneously* a rejoinder to physical amputation, debilitation, and solidarity. The question at hand is partly, what does refusing amputation mean?

For Fanon, refusing amputation is not refusing an "impaired" or disabled body, nor is it displacing racialization by disability in the scales of the human. Instead, refusing amputation speaks to the injuries and debilitations already at hand as well as the sparsity of options available for healing and modes of living.

Refusal of amputation must be taken up in at least two registers. Many Fanon theorists thus do read the amputation metaphorically, in terms of the relationships between Black cultures and whiteness. Paul Adjei argues that Fanon's refusal of amputation "is denouncing the manner in which the identity of Blackness has been scripted, read, and imposed on bodies of color within the imagination of whiteness. He is also resisting the colonizing knowledge system that constantly pathologizes and criminalizes Blackness and misrepresents it as an agent of malevolent powers there to cause harm to the white world" (Adjei 2010: 88). Walcott argues that "by resisting borders and boundaries, Black cultures refuse to accept what Frantz Fanon called 'amputation.' . . . Acceptance of amputation leads to the imprisonment that accepts the boundaries and borders that state national policies can create" (Walcott 2006: 76). Resistance to amputation, for Walcott, thus "names the process that refuses to allow blackness to be pinned down to specific categories" (ibid.).

These many cultural and symbolic readings of amputation are rich and worthwhile; I do not mean to fault them here. Analysis of the refusal of amputation is ameliorated by taking seriously and examining the relationship to literal injury, modes of debilitation. Recall that Fanon's refusal of amputation comes after watching a scene from *the Home of the Brave* (Robson 1949). Aviva Briefel (2015) notes that Fanon's description of the scene both resonates with and diverges from the actual film, arguing that the representation of the scene in *Black Skin, White Masks* was strategic. She notes the impossibility of reading "Fanon's embodiment of amputation without viewing it as a direct response to the discourse of manual mutilation and race that marked the nineteenth and early twentieth centuries, from the figuratively amputated hands of fingerprinting to the literal ones of corporeal punishment" (Briefel 2015: 152). Bryan Mukandi further draws attention to Fanon's clinical relationship to amputation: "There is a depth of meaning that is opened up by a consideration of the individual who is told that they need an amputation, someone with a gangrenous limb, for example, where refusal almost certainly amounts to death" (Mukandi 2021: 4). Mukandi reads Fanon's response as "both a refusal of the demand to accommodate oneself to an unjust social order and a refusal of that procedure during which the metal teeth of a saw gradually grind their way into, and then through bone" (ibid).[16] Fred Moten connects amputations to the plantation structure and operation that many enslaved Blacks faced. Both the punishments and the working conditions contributed to literal amputations: "There was this ridiculously high incidence of amputations. It was just dangerous work. The cane itself is sharp. People were constantly being cut, and the remedy for the cut was to cut whatever was cut off. So much so that at the sugar mills they would have axes. There was this constant threat of amputation" (Harney et al. 2021).

Titchkosky (2015) has given one of the most thorough discussions of Fanon's amputation metaphor and subsequent refusal. She argues that Fanon is not making a simplistic analogy or displacing the dehumanization from the racialized to the disabled, despite first suspicions that he does so. Rather, Titchkosky understands his interpretation of the film scene as follows:

> The veteran symbolizes the one who conforms to the dominant understanding of amputation as the call of normalcy to stand before the bar, rehabilitate, re-adjust, and re-enter the world, such as it is. The veteran is configured as the one who attempts to guide Fanon to treat amputation as the object that the world imagines it to be, namely, pure disadvantage in need of remedial attention in order to re-enter the world, but again only such as it is. (Titchkosky 2015: 13)

For Titchkosky, Fanon refuses not a disability per se but rather an orientation, a naturalized path of treatment or rehabilitation and an objectification of the body: "he refuses the singular path that allows amputation to stand only for nothingness (i.e., inability, lack, something missing). . . . Within this refusal, amputation becomes other than a diagnostic category. It becomes, instead, a call to respond since it is a place from which Fanon writes and engages his self and the world" (Titchkosky 2015: 14).

If amputation is refused and responded to, part of that response is *physical*. Fanon's metaphors of immobilization, fixity, lead us to a concept of petrification that resonates throughout his work. This state is invoked several times throughout *Black Skin, White Masks*. For example, he states that the Black man who watches a Tarzan film in France is "petrified. There he has no more hope of flight," locked into and homogenized among Black representations (Fanon 1986: 153). Fanon refers to characters in the film *Home of the Brave* (Robson 1949) and the novel *If He Hollers Let Him Go* (Himes 1945) as his "paralyzed" brothers (Fanon 1986: 138). In his conclusion, he notes "There are times when the black man is locked into his body" (225)—literally *enfermé*, closed in. Petrification as a symptom of colonization objectifies or thingifies the colonized as essentially impaired and produces certain relationships to movement and stillness (Ficek 2011: 76; Moten 2008).

In *The Wretched of the Earth*, Fanon emphasizes that any petrification is only a pseudo-petrification, never complete, and always ends in an explosion, a convulsion, or the spasms of hysteria (Fanon 2004: 17, 19). We encounter this (pseudo-)petrification particularly in "Colonial War and Mental Disorders," where he discusses psychosomatic symptoms encountered among patients during the Algerian revolution. One of the major themes is "systemic contraction and muscular stiffness," rigidity that prevents movement in the patients (217–19). It is worth dwelling upon this pseudo-petrification, and asking about the concatenation of movement that leads to tense stillness. To understand petrification better, we can connect it to Fanon's discussions of tetanization and tetanic contractions as disability and debility.

According to *Stedman's Medical Dictionary* (2006), tetanization occurs when a muscle is petrified because of its constant overstimulation, as a result of too much input from the environment or an input that cannot be incorporated. Importantly, some tetanic action is necessary in order for us to bend, move, have actions, relax, and tense (Zoladz 2019). Tetanization is this in *overload*. The first use of this word by Fanon comes shortly after his train encounter: "I rejected all [tetanization] of the emotions. I wanted to be a man, nothing but a man" (Fanon 1986: 113).[17] A few pages later, he notes: "I progress by crawling. And already I am being dissected under white eyes, the only real eyes. I am fixed" (116).

The idea of tetanization resonates throughout Fanon's work, even beyond *Black Skin, White Masks*. Fanon's invocations of tetanization are important because the violences that he traces do not only immobilize the body, and not purely: it is an immobilization from a tension. Although he uses the term to discuss tetanization of affect in *Black Skin, White Masks*, tetanization is a model of how excess spasms and contractions can present as immobility.

Tetanization exists at the material and cultural levels simultaneously. Whitney understands tetanization as a "pathogenic affect . . . not only projected but introjected as a toxic infection that convulses the muscles and disjoints movement, debilitating intentionality not only in its affective but also sensorimotor operation" (Whitney 2019: 507). These interojective movements are also emphasized by Florian Alix (2008) and Al-Saji (2020), inasmuch as they "may look externally like paralysis but . . . hide, in their depth, intense activity and (appropriate) sensitivity to the violence, toxicity, and hostility of the white world" (Al-Saji 2020: 188). Tetanization, the overstimulation of a muscle, sometimes results due to *tetanus infection*, a bacterial cause.[18] However, the numerous ways in which muscles can tetanize—not only through infection but posturally and neurologically—can be considered in a much broader sense. The numerous ways in which muscles can tetanize reflect the diverse ways in which racism and colonialism debilitate and attempt to control.

To be clear, I do not mean to say that overstimulated muscles that are not paralyzed are inherently resistant nor that paralyzed muscles are not resistant. Because muscles require some tetanic contraction and muscle spasms themselves involve both contraction and elongation, taking account of musculoskeletal disability *must go beyond* seeing it as a projection of colonialism alone. Attending to muscles (one of the thematic images found throughout Fanon's writing) and their "disorders" can further reveal dimensions of his views on disability.

The action of tetanization leads us into the way that muscles work and musculoskeletal disability is lived. Though not explicitly thematized, in *The Wretched of the Earth*, muscular tension abounds in Fanon's descriptions of both colonized individuals and the masses. While describing the process of a nation's decolonization, Fanon notes that in the early stages the population confronts and strains against Western values: "the colonized grow tense and muscles seize up . . . [Eventually,] the colonized masses thumb their noses at these very values, shower them with insults and vomit them up" (Fanon 2004: 8). Still after this expulsion of values, Fanon's colonized person is haunted by his muscles. He has muscular dreams, there is an "aggressiveness sedimented in his muscles" that can find temporary release in either dancing or self-destruction (15, 19–20). His muscles remain tensed, always in a state of apprehension, waiting in anticipation for a change to occur (16). The petrifications are never complete (17, 19). These muscular moments are scattered throughout the text: indicating that muscular work is an aspect of many of the stages of decolonization, not a momentary place for a snap but a long-labored site.

Fanon describes muscular dreams, aggression sedimented in muscles, the release of this tension through dance or ritual, and the seizing of muscles in the face of colonial values. The everyday repetition of an atmosphere that creates tense muscles is itself a wearing down, reflected in his case studies. For example, Fanon notes symptoms of rigidity could be identified in a whole group of his psychosomatic Algerian patients:

> There are male patients who slowly have difficulty making certain movements such as climbing stairs, walking quickly, or running . . . walking becomes contracted and turns into a shuffle. Passive bending of the lower limbs is practically impossible. No relaxation can be achieved. Immediately rigid and incapable of relaxing of his own free will, the patient seems to be made in one piece. . . . The patient does not seem to be able to "demobilize his nerves." He is constantly tense, on hold, between life and death. As one of them told us: "you see, I'm as stiff as a corpse." (Fanon 2004: 218–219)

During Fanon's medical career, musculoskeletal disorders came to the fore of medical training and public consciousness. Torsion spasms, dystonias, and hypertonias were the subject of debates about organic and psychic etiologies (Fanon and Lévy 2018). Dystonia, hypertonia, and hypotonia all arise within discussions of general "muscle tone." Contrary to dominant fitness understandings of "toning," muscle tone is instead a way of characterizing a muscle's responsiveness to stress, its contractions and elongations, itself a contentious measure (Cloud and Jinnah 2010). Colonial capacitations of sickness and injury are highlighted in the many meanings of *tetanization*. As observed earlier, tetanization is a tension, a tightness, a stunned state, as well as a mechanism of muscles, a bacterial infection, and an action within stillness. In "Medicine and Colonialism," Fanon states:

> in the very first months of the struggle [the Algerian revolution], the French authorities decided to put an embargo on antibiotics, ether, alcohol, anti-tetanus vaccine. The Algerian who wish to obtain any of these medications was required to give the pharmacist detailed information as to his identity and that of the patient. . . . Numerous families had to stand by powerless, their hearts full of rancor, and watch the atrocious death by tetanus of wounded mujahedin's who had taken refuge in their houses. From the earliest months of the revolution, the directives of the national front were clearly given: any wound, no matter how benign, automatically required an anti-tetanus vaccine injection. . . . But the pharmacists were adamant: the sale of anti-tetanus vaccine was prohibited. Dozens and dozens of Algerians today can describe the slow, frightful death of a wounded man, progressively paralyzed, then twisted, and again paralyzed by the tetanus toxin. (Fanon 1965: 139–40)[19]

In this case, the withholding of medical treatment both maims and kills. This negligence is part of the medical infrastructure of debilitation, one of the ways in which Fanon demonstrates how "colonization turns the bodies of the colonized into instruments against them" (Al-Saji 2020: 185). While this capture and containment regularly occur in colonial states, Puar emphasizes that there are "productive, resistant, indeed creative effects of [the] attempts to squash Palestinian vitality, fortitude, and revolt" in the colonization of Palestinian people by Israel (Puar 2017: 136). So, too, are there creative effects of other colonial violence, even in debilitation.

In fact, we can look to Puar to think through the relationship between so-called "bodily impairments" and "psychosomatic conditions," the relationship of sociogeny to the literal body. Indeed, we can look again to Puar in order to think through Fanon charitably. In "Spatial Debilities," Puar traces "the varied modalities through which many have the logic of containing mobility literalized on their bodies in the form of impairment" in Palestine (Puar 2021: 400). She connects this signification on the body to the production of mobility disabilities through infrastructures (Langan 2001) and carceration (Wang 2018). Furthermore, she signals mobility, disability, and debilitation as sites of solidarity:

> What is the relationship of those who have what is typically referred to as "mobility disabilities" to the gradation of mobility impairment that affects Palestinian mobility generally, regardless of abled or disabled bodily categorization? Reflecting an evolving and convivial notion of disability, by framing differential mobilities as a form of collective punishment we can potentially envision and create new lines of solidarity that link entities through gradations of debilitation rather than sedimenting the self/other binarization that the categorization of disability relies on. It is also . . . the potentiating conduit through which deeper solidarities can be fostered that eclipse "ally" formations perpetuated by disability rights frames of recognition. (Puar 2021: 401)

My argument is that we can read Fanon's disability metaphors and medical work to facilitate such solidarities. Considering "colonial medical and psychiatric facilities as structures of disablement" that transform processes of debilitation and injury, as well as health and health care, Murdock highlights that the occupation and disablement of the land relate: we can make "connections between environmental degradation, lack of infrastructure, police brutality, and racial violence with the increased incidences of illness and premature death in these communities" (Murdock 2022: 106, 118). In the spirit of Puar and Murdock, we can take these invocations from Fanon as invitations (openings?) to solidarity. These debilitations occur across any boundary that might be drawn between disabled/nondisabled: indeed such a distinction becomes a part of the inflicted violence (Puar 2021: 401).

Thinking this way also enables us to connect Fanon's invocations of amputation to contemporary socio-determinants of health and Black pathologization and treatment. In 2020, Lizzie Presser reported on a contemporary amputation epidemic in the Mississippi Delta, that is, an epidemic of Black amputations. The medical establishment, patterns, and experiences of patients reveal "that amputations are a form of racial oppression, dating back to slavery." This epidemic of amputations among Black populations in the American South is an instance of structural disablement and debilitation:

> General surgeons have a financial incentive to amputate; they don't get paid to operate if they recommend saving a limb. And many hospitals don't direct doctors to order angiograms, the most reliable imaging to show if and precisely where blood flow is blocked, giving the clearest picture of whether an amputation is necessary and how much needs to be cut. Insurers don't require the imaging, either. (Presser 2020)

If we are to take Fanon seriously as a theorist and indeed a philosopher of disability (as we should), and work alongside him charitably, we must trace the afterlives of colonialism and slavery through multiple forms and variations of disablement.

Conclusion

Fanon's work, across both philosophy and psychiatry, offers fruitful and provocative points to develop philosophies of colonial debilitation and solidarities. LeRoy F. Moore Jr. and Tamari Kitossa suggest "that ontological and political disablement are twinned and constitute sites of resistance" (Moore and Kitossa 2021: 181). These authors, rather than read Fanon as denying disability, argue that his "refusing to accept amputation does not mean that colonialism is not amputizing [*sic*]—literally and metaphysically—only that the resultant disability is the colonizers' problem, since it is not a self-definition the colonized give themselves" (ibid.). The notions of disability that circulate in tandem with the real injuries and violence lived by the colonized result, for them, in this dual disablement.

Fanon's own life ended with leukemia. He sought treatment first in Russia, then eventually gave in and traveled to the United States, which he called "the nation of lynchers" (Bulhan 1985: 34; Beauvoir 1992: 316). Hussein Abdilahi Bulhan notes:

> He was by then living on borrowed time. Agitation and restlessness dominated his mood and behavior. A treacherous disease, leukemia is characterized by sudden relapses and remissions. Bleeding from the gums, temporary loss of vision, atrocious bruises, marked loss of weight-all these combined with the feeling of hopelessness and helplessness resulting from the knowledge that the disease had little possibility of cure. It was then that his Algerian comrades in struggle urged him to seek treatment in the United States. (Bulhan 1985: 34)

This journey and the decision that led to it were the culmination of years of colonization and liberation struggle, an ongoing debilitation exacerbated by the violence that he experienced prior to treatment. Upon his arrival in the United States, Fanon was at first left untreated. Simone de Beauvoir notes that he was "left to rot in his hotel room for ten days, alone and without medical attention" (Beauvoir 1992: 328). Peter Geismar speculates this neglect was no accident, but rather a calculated choice, that the authorities wanted to "grill the sick man without the interference of a hospital routine" (Geismar 1969: 184). Indeed, these authorities extracted as much information from Fanon as they could: making the body speak. This intentional gap in treatment, with a man so near death, debilitates Fanon. American agents were attempting to capture any utility of his leukemia, his pain, to obtain information. What can this be but an intentional suffering that is put in place as a colonial violence, an abuse of the already-pained body?

Notes

1 For a full biography, see Bulhan (1985).

2 Literature often refers to Fanon as involved in social therapy, institutional therapy, or occupational therapy (used interchangeably in English translations). These names derive from Tosquelles's *psychothérapie institutionnelle*, and his *Groupe de travail de psychothérapie et de sociothérapie institutionnelles*, and the practice of "occupying the time" of residents, but they are translated inconsistently. See Tosquelles (2001).

3 See Wynter (2001) Marriott (2011), and Gordon (2015) for further influential readings of sociogeny.

4 Debilitation enacts a biopolitical right to maim, as opposed to the right to kill or to make live. See Puar (2017) for more details.

5 Puar (2017) describes the right to maim as a particularly neoliberal mode of power. Fanon then highlights a crucial *preformation* of this technique.

6 See Sullivan (2015), Ahmed (2007), and Chebili (2018) on this point.

7 Fanon often worked with psychosomatic disorders. In *The Wretched of the Earth*, he uses the term *corticovisceral* (216–17, see n. 35), which comes from soviet psychiatry and portrays "psychosomatic" issues as material, though not lesion-based. See Chertok (1969) for more.

8 As scholars working in epistemic injustice have noted, the psychiatric or medical encounter often results in epistemic harms for patients. For more see Carel and Kidd (2017).

9 In the original, dead weight is literally "poids mort" (Fanon 1952b: 241).

10 I have substituted *contacts* in translation, as it is more faithful to the original French text (Fanon 1952b: 243).

11 In the original, "*On leur a introduit la France partout*" (Fanon 1952b: 247).

12 "The North African combines all the conditions that make a sick man" (13) In the original, "qui font un homme malade" (Fanon 1952b: 245).

13 For treatments of ankylosis see Al-Saji (2021), Whitney (Fanon 2018, 2019).

14 Titchkosky uses both "disability metaphors" and "impairment rhetoric" in this piece.

15 Here I refer to the Grove Press edition and translation by Philcox, because Markmann significantly alters this line. The original French reads "*Je hélais le monde et le monde m'amputait de mon enthousiasme*" (Fanon 1952a: 112).

16 Wagner (2009) suggests Fanon's refusal of amputation is also a sly reply to Maurice Merleau-Ponty's *Phenomenology of Perception* on phantom limb (Merleau-Ponty 1945: 112).

17 I have edited this to be more truthful to the original, which is "*je refusai toute tétanisation affective*" (Fanon 1952a: 110).

18 Fanon doesn't mention lockjaw or discuss the jaw in particular in any of his works, which indicates that he is thinking of tetanization beyond the bacterial infection alone. For this reason, in part, I look at tetanic action more broadly.

19 See also Khiati (2000: 140).

References

Adjei, Paul (2010), "CHAPTER FOUR: Resistance to Amputation: Discomforting Truth about Colonial Education in Ghana," *Counterpoints* 368: 79–104.

Ahmed, Sara (2007), "A Phenomenology of Whiteness," *Feminist Theory* 8 (2): 149–68.

Al-Saji, Alia (2020), "Frantz Fanon," in T. Szanto and H. Landweer (eds.), *The Routledge Handbook of Phenomenology of Emotion*, 207–14, London: Routledge.

Al-Saji, Alia (2021), "Too Late: Fanon, the Dismembered Past, and a Phenomenology of Racialized Time," in Leswin Laubscher, Derek Hook, and Miraj Desai (eds.), *Fanon, Phenomenology and Psychology*, 177–93, New York: Routledge.

Alix, Florian (2008), "Fanon en movement," *Baobab* 3: 1–17.

Bayle, Jacqueline (1981), *Quand l'Algérie devenait française*, Paris: Fayard.

Beauvoir, Simone de (1992), *Hard Times: Force of circumstance, Vol. II*, trans. Richard Howard, New York: Paragon.

Bell, C. (2017), "Is Disability Studies Actually White Disability Studies?" in Lennard Davis (ed.), *The Disability Studies Reader*, 406–15, New York: Routledge.

Briefel, Aviva (2015), *The Racial Hand in the Victorian Imagination*, Cambridge: Cambridge University Press.

Bruce, La Marr Jurelle (2021), *How to Go Mad without Losing Your Mind: Madness and Black Radical Creativity*, Durham: Duke University Press.

Bulhan, Hussein Abdilahi (1985), *Frantz Fanon and the Psychology of Oppression*, New York: Plenum Press.

Chebili, Saïd (2018), "Fanon and Torture," *L'information Psychiatrique* 94: 281–5.

Chertok, Léon (1969), "Psychosomatic Medicine in the West and in Eastern European Countries," *Psychosomatic Medicine* 31 (6): 510–21.

Clancy-Smith, Julia (1998), "Islam, Gender, and Identities in the Making of French Algeria, 1830–1962," in Julia Clancy-Smith and Frances Gouda (eds.), *Domesticating The Empire: Languages of Gender, Race, and Family Life in French and Dutch Colonialism*, 154–74, Charlottesville: The University Press of Virginia.

Cloud, Leslie J. and H. A. Jinnah (2010), "Treatment Strategies for Dystonia," *Expert Opinion on Pharmacotherapy* 11 (1): 5–15.

Curry, Tommy J. (2011), "The Derelictical Crisis of African American Philosophy: How African American Philosophy Fails to Contribute to the Study of African-Descended People," *Journal of Black Studies* 42 (3): 314–33.

Dhavantari, Sujaya (2020), "The Violent Origins of Psychic Trauma: Frantz Fanon's Theory of Colonial Trauma and Catherine Malabou's Concept of the New Wounded," *Puncta: The Journal of Critical Phenomenology* 3 (2): 33–53.

Erevelles, Nirmala (2011), *Disability and Difference in Global Contexts: Enabling a Transformative Body Politic*, New York: Palgrave Macmillan.

Eromosele, Femi (2020), "Frantz Fanon in the Time of Mad Studies," *World Futures: The Journal of New Paradigm Research* 76 (3): 167–87.

Eromosele, Femi (2022), "Madness, Decolonisation and Mental Health Activism in Africa," in Peter Beresford and Jasna Russo (eds.), *The Routledge International Handbook of Mad Studies*, 327–39, New York: Routledge.

Fabris, E. and K. Aubrecht (2014), "Chemical Constraint: Experiences of Psychiatric Coercion, Restraint, and Detention as Carceratory Techniques," in Liat Ben-Moshe, Chris Chapman, and Allison C. Carey (eds.), *Disability Incarcerated: Imprisonment and Disability in the United States and Canada*, 185–200, New York: Palgrave Macmillan.

Fanon, Frantz (1952a), *Peau noire, masques blancs*, Paris: Éditions de Seuil.

Fanon, Frantz (1952b), "Le syndrome Nord-Africain ," *Esprit* 187 (2): 237–48.

Fanon, Frantz (1961), *Les damnés de la terre*, Paris: La Découverte.

Fanon, Frantz (1965), "Medicine and Colonialism," in *A Dying Colonialism*, trans. Haakon Chevalier, 121–46, New York: Grove.

Fanon, Frantz (1967), "The North African Syndrome," in *Toward the African Revolution*, trans. Haakon Chevalier, 3–16, New York: Grove.

Fanon, Frantz (1986), *Black Skin, White Masks*, trans. Charles Lam Markmann, London: Pluto Press.

Fanon, Frantz (2004), *The Wretched of the Earth*, trans. Richard Philcox, New York: Grove Press.

Fanon, Frantz (2008), *Black Skin, White Masks*, trans. Richard Philcox, New York: Grove Press.

Fanon, Frantz (2018a), "Mental Alterations, Character Modifications, Psychic Disorders and Intellectual Deficit in Spinocerebellar Heredodegeneration: A Case of Friedreich's Ataxia with Delusions of Possession," in Jean Khalfa and Robert J. C. Young (eds.), *Alienation and Freedom*, trans. Steven Corcoran, 203–75, London: Bloomsbury Academic.

Fanon, Frantz (2018b), "Day Hospitalization in Psychiatry: Value and Limits," in Jean Khalfa and Robert J. C. Young (eds.), *Alienation and Freedom*, trans. Steven Corcoran, 473–94, London: Bloomsbury Academic.

Fanon, Frantz and Jacques Azoulay (2018), "Social Therapy in a Ward of Muslim Men: Methodological Difficulties," in Jean Khalfa and Robert J. C. Young (eds.), *Alienation and Freedom*, trans. Steven Corcoran, 353–71, London: Bloomsbury Academic.

Fanon, Frantz and Charles Geronimi (2018), "Day Hospitalization in Psychiatry: Value and Limits. Part Two: Doctrinal Considerations," in Jean Khalfa and Robert J. C. Young (eds.), *Alienation and Freedom*, trans. Steven Corcoran, 495–509, London: Bloomsbury Academic.

Fanon, Frantz and Lucien Lévy (2018), "On a Case of Torsion Spasm," in Jean Khalfa and Robert J. C. Young (eds.), *Alienation and Freedom*, trans. Steven Corcoran, 453–63, London: Bloomsbury Academic.

Ficek, Douglas (2011), "Reflections on Fanon and Petrification," in Nigel C. Gibson (ed.), *Living Fanon*, 75–84, New York: Palgrave Macmillan.

Foucault, Michel (2003), *The Birth of the Clinic*, trans. A. M. Sheridan, New York: Routledge.

Garland-Thomson, Rosemarie (2009), *Staring: How We Look*, Oxford: Oxford University Press.

Geismar, Peter (1969), *Fanon: The Revolutionary as Prophet*, New York: Grove Press.

Gordon, Lewis (2015), *What Fanon Said: A Philosophical Introduction to His Life and Thought*, New York: Fordham University Press.

Harney, Stefano, Fred Moten, Sandra Ruiz, and Hypatia Vourloumis (2021), "Resonances: A Conversation on Formless Formation," *e-Flux* 121: n.p.

Himes, Chester (1945), *If He Hollers Let Him Go*, New York: Doubleday Doran.

Khalfa, Jean (2018), "Fanon, Revolutionary Psychiatrist," in Jean Khalfa and Robert J. C. Young (eds.), *Alienation and Freedom*, trans. Steven Corcoran, 167–202, London: Bloomsbury Academic.

Khiati, Mostefa (2000), *Histoire de la Médicine en Algérie: De l'Antiquité à nos jours*, Paris: Éditions ANEP.

Langan, Celeste (2001), "Mobility Disability," *Public Culture* 13 (3): 459–84.

Macey, David (2000), "Fanon, Politics and Psychiatry: The North African Syndrome," *Free Associations* 8 (3): 463–85.

Marriott, David (2011), "Inventions of Existence: Sylvia Wynter, Frantz Fanon, Sociogeny, and 'the Damned,'" *CR: The New Centennial Review* 11(3): 45–89.

Meekosha, H. (2011), "Decolonising Disability: Thinking and Acting Globally," *Disability and Society* 26 (6): 667–82.

Mitchell, David and Sharon Snyder (2000), *Narrative Prosthesis: Disability and the Dependencies of Discourse*, Ann Arbor: University of Michigan Press.

Mollow, Anna (2014), "Criphystemologies: What Disability Theory Needs to Know about Hysteria," *Journal of Literary and Cultural Disability Studies* 8 (2): 185–201.

Moore, Leroy F., Jr. and Tamari Kitossa (2021), "A Krip-Hop Theory of Disabled Black Men," in Tamari Kitossa (ed.), *Appealing Because He Is Appalling: Black Masculinities, Colonialism, and Erotic Racism*, 177–232, Edmonton: University of Alberta Press.

Moten, Fred (2008), "The Case of Blackness," *Criticism* 50 (2): 177–218.

Mukandi, Bryan (2021), "Picturing Sanity, in Black and White," *Medical Humanities* (Online First, June): 1–7.

Müller-Vahl, Kirsten, Anna Pisarenko, Ewgeni Jakubovski, and Carolin Fremer (2022), "Stop that! It's not Tourette's but a New Type of Mass Sociogenic Illness," *Brain* 145: 476–80.

Murdock, Esme Greene (2022), "Terrortories: Colonialism's Built Environments as Structural Disablement," *Critical Philosophy of Race* 10 (1): 106–27.

Ngo, Helen (2012), *The Habits of Racism: A Phenomenology of Racism and Racialized Embodiment*, Lanham: Lexington Books.

Oliver, Michael (1990), *The Politics of Disablement*, New York: Palgrave Macmillan.

Pickens, Theri A. (2019), *Black Madness: Mad Blackness*, Durham: Duke University Press.

Pitts, Andrea J. (2021), "'That Close and Contagious Death': Symptomatology, Sociogeny, and Structural Oppression," *Theory and Event* 24 (2): 618–24.

Presser, Lizzie (2020), "The Black American Amputation Epidemic," May 19, ProPublica. Available at: https://www.propublica.org/ (accessed July 22, 2023).

Puar, Jasbir K. (2017), *The Right to Maim: Debility, Capacity, Disability*, Durham: Duke University Press.

Puar, Jasbir K. (2021), "Spatial Debilities: Slow Life and Carceral Capitalism in Palestine," *The South Atlantic Quarterly* 120 (2): 393–414.

Robson, Mark, dir. (1949), *The Home of the Brave*. Produced by Stanley Kramer and Robert Stillman.

Schalk, Sami (2018), *Bodyminds Reimagined: Disability, Race, and Gender in Black Women's Speculative Fiction*, Durham: Duke University Press.

Scott, Darieck (2010), *Extravagant Abjection: Blackness, Power, and Sexuality in the African American Literary Imagination*, New York: New York University Press.

Shakespeare, Tom (2010), "The Social Construction of Disability," in Lennard J. Davis (ed.), *The Disability Studies Reader*, 266–73, New York: Routledge.

Sherry, Mark (2007), "(Post)colonizing Disability," *Wagadu* 4: 10–22.

Stedman, Thomas Lathrop (2006), *Stedman's Medical Dictionary*, 28th ed., Philadelphia: Lippincott Williams & Wilkins.

Stern, Erich (1949), "Médecine Psychosomatique," *Psyché* 27–8: 117–36.
Sullivan, Shannon (2015), *The Physiology of Racist and Sexist Oppression*, New York: Oxford University Press.
Taylor, Chloë (2010), "Fanon, Foucault, and the Politics of Psychiatry," in Elizabeth A. Hoppe and Tracey Nicholls (eds.), *Fanon and the Decolonization of Philosophy*, 55–74, New York: Rowman & Littlefield.
Titchkosky, Tanya (2015), "Life with Dead Metaphors: Impairment Rhetoric in Social Justice Praxis," *Journal of Literary and Cultural Disability Studies* 9 (1): 1–18.
Tosquelles, François ([1991] 2001), "Frantz Fanon et la psychothérapie institutionnelle," *Érès "Sud/Nord"* 1 (14): 167–74.
Tosquelles, François and Frantz Fanon (2018a), "On Some Cases Treated with the Bini Method," in Jean Khalfa and Robert J. C. Young (eds.), *Alienation and Freedom*, trans. Steven Corcoran, 285–90, London: Bloomsbury Academic.
Tosquelles, François and Frantz Fanon (2018b), "Indications of Electroconvulsive Therapy within Institutional Therapies," in Jean Khalfa and Robert J. C. Young (eds.), *Alienation and Freedom*, trans. Steven Corcoran, 291–8, London: Bloomsbury Academic.
Tsekoa, L. and E. Mugomeri (2015), "The Phenomenon of Mass Psychogenic Illness Among The Basotho in Lesotho: Proposed Guidelines for Improving the Management of Psychogenic Illness Episode," *Africa Journal of Nursing and Midwifery* 17 (2): 60–74.
Urena, Carolyn (2019), "Decolonial Embodiment: Fanon, the Clinical Encounter, and the Colonial Wound," *Disability and the Global South* 6 (1): 1640–58.
Wagner, Bryan (2009), *Disturbing the Peace: Black Culture and the Police Power after Slavery*, Cambridge, MA: Harvard University Press.
Walcott, R. (2006), "Multiculturally Crazy: Diagnosis in Black," in Roy Moodley and Stephen Palmer (eds.), *Race, Culture, and Psychotherapy: Critical Perspectives in Multicultural Practice*, 27–35, New York: Routledge.
Wang, Jackie (2018), *Carceral Capitalism*, Cambridge, MA: MIT Press.
Ward, L. F. (1898), *Dynamic Sociology or Applied Social Science*, New York: D. Appleton & Co.
Wendell, Susan (1996), *The Rejected Body: Feminist Philosophical Reflections on Disability*, New York: Routledge.
Whitney, Shiloh (2018), "Affective Intentionality and Affective Injustice: Merleau-Ponty and Fanon on the Body Schema as a Theory of Affect," *Southern Journal of Philosophy* 56 (4): 488–515.
Whitney, Shiloh (2019), "From the Body Schema to the Historical-Racial Schema," *Chiasmi International* 21: 305–20.
Wynter, Sylvia (2001), "Towards the Sociogenic Principle: Fanon, The Puzzle of Conscious Experience, of 'Identity' and What it's Like to be 'Black,'" in Antonio Gomez-Moriana and Mercedes Duran-Cogan (eds.), *National Identities and Socio-Political Changes in Latin America*, 30–66, New York: Routledge.
Yancy, George (2008), *Black Bodies, White Gazes: The Continuing Significance of Race*, Lanham: Rowman and Littlefield.
Young, Iris Marion (1980), "Throwing Like a Girl: A Phenomenology of Feminine Body Comportment. Motility and Spatiality," *Human Studies* 3 (2): 137–56.
Zack, Lizabeth (2002), "Who Fought the Algerian War? Political Identity and Conflict in French-Ruled Algeria," *International Journal of Politics, Culture, and Society* 16 (1): 55–97.
Zeiler, Kristin (2013), "A Phenomenology of Excorporation, Bodily Alienation, and Resistance: Rethinking Sexed and Racialized Embodiment," *Hypatia: A Journal of Feminist Philosophy* 28 (1): 69–8.
Zoladz, Jerry A., ed. (2019), *Muscle and Exercise Physiology*, Cambridge: Elsevier.

15 EXEMPTION, SELF-EXEMPTION, AND COMPASSIONATE SELF-EXCUSE

SOFIA JEPPSSON

Moral-Philosophical Introduction

The first section of this chapter sets the stage for my argument by introducing the field of moral responsibility philosophy and its customary representation of Madness. I also briefly discuss some of the field's problems. In the second and third sections, I discuss, in depth, a hitherto ignored problem with traditional philosophical approaches to Madness: it can only be applied to others, not to oneself. In the fourth and fifth sections, I present compassionate excuses and neurodiversity-embracing justifications as preferable alternatives.

Excuses and Exemptions, Participant and Objective Attitudes

Philosophers traditionally distinguish exemptions from excuses. The way that these terms are used in philosophy does not quite map on to how they are used in law, nor how they are used in everyday English—though they are meant to capture a common-sensical distinction. If you have done something bad for which you would normally be blamed, you can be *excused* if you suffered from something like temporary loss of control or if you were innocently ignorant of relevant matters. Suppose that I stepped hard on someone else's foot, but only because I slipped on an ice patch and lost control; or suppose that I kept my neighbor awake all night by blasting loud music because I believed (for understandable reasons) that he was out of town—I might then be *excused* for these behaviors. On the standard philosophical picture, people are *exempted* when they are not intelligent, rational, or generally self-controlled enough to count as responsible agents in the first place; they might, for example, have intellectual disabilities, serious mental disorders, or they might be young children. Despite some notable criticism of the supposed sharp distinction between excuse and exemption, it remains commonplace in moral philosophy.[1]

In texts building on Peter F. Strawson's enormously influential paper "Freedom and Resentment," the distinction is often made by reference to what he identifies as "participant" and "objective" attitudes. When we excuse someone, we retain a *participant* attitude to them: we see them as fellow members of the moral community and as participants in normal human relationships. When we exempt someone, on the other hand, we take an *objective* attitude to them (Strawson 1962/2013: 68–9, 75–6). When you adopt the objective attitude to another person, Strawson writes, you see him as something to be managed, handled, cured, or trained, in your interest, or society's, or even his own (69, 72). You can no longer fight or quarrel with him, nor can you reason with him, although you might pretend to do so (because you may think doing so will have desirable effects) (69, 70). When we see someone as hopelessly "irrational," our anger and resentment against him melt away; when we see him as beyond the reach of argument and quarrels, it does not make sense to blame him either (75–6). Strawson does not merely report common tendencies in how society regards and treats Madpeople; with obvious endorsement, he writes that this is how "civilized" people tend to view the Mad (70).

Now, what is a Madperson, like me, to make of all this?

The Objective Attitude Beyond the Philosophy Seminar

Even though the name "Peter Strawson" is not widely known among non-philosophers, he builds on common and widespread ideas in the aforementioned article, ideas that continue to have wide reach. Therefore, it is problematic that most moral philosophers who write about the subject—some of whom are read by philosophically interested psychiatrists or who in other ways reach outside the ivory tower—continue to defend these ideas.

Tanya M. Luhrmann, in her anthropological study of psychiatrists, writes of how the objective attitude is often seen as an ideal at which to strive. Psychiatrists tell Luhrmann that one must not believe borderline personality disorder (BDP) patients who say that they have been badly treated by other staff members, for that is just "splitting" behavior, something that BPD patients do (Luhrmann 2000: 116–17).[2] One doctor says that it would be easy to control psychosis patients and treat them "like children," if only she could see them as simply "crazy." Her job is made more difficult, however, by the fact that, as she puts it, "I still see that there is a person there" (138).

Important ethical discussions about whether to dismantle coercive psychiatric care altogether become muddled by psychiatrists who do not understand why they should listen to their patients when they talk about their traumas. These psychiatrists hold the Strawsonian belief that patients should be managed and handled rather than included in arguments (Aftab 2021). Many Madpeople have experienced firsthand what it is like to be seen as objects to be handled rather than to be recognized as persons worthy of respect, with all that this recognition entails.

Now, the earlier philosophical tradition is not wholly without criticism in the published literature. For example, Jeanette Kennett writes:

> Kant believed that persons had intrinsic worth and dignity and as such were never to be used merely as means. To treat a person as an object is clearly to mistreat them. The demand for respect and goodwill in our dealings with each other is, in the first place, the demand that we approach each other from within the participant stance. It is minimally the demand that we do not ignore or undermine each other's agency. (Kennett 2009: 111)[3]

Still, it remains commonplace for philosophers who work in the moral responsibility field to assume that Madpeople must either be regarded objectively or be resented and blamed for their Mad behavior. They move from recognizing the latter—resentment or attribution of blame—as unfair to seeing the former as beneficial. But Madpeople who are regarded objectively also suffer injustice.

The Objective Attitude and Injustice

The term *epistemic injustice* was first coined by Miranda Fricker (2007) and describes a previously overlooked aspect of oppression and discrimination: namely, that women and members of various minority groups are often undermined in their capacity as knowers.

I have already touched upon this injustice in the previous subsection: Madpeople, both in psychiatric care and personal relationships, are subjected to one form of epistemic injustice, testimonial injustice, when what they say is perceived as "illness noises" and the content of what they say is ignored (Arpaly 2005; Jeppsson 2021). Furthermore, the academic debate dominated by sane scholars who discuss how "we" should relate to and treat Madpeople is hermeneutically unjust (Leblanc and Kinsella 2016). (Insofar as we distinguish neurodivergence from Madness, this problem arises for neurodivergent scholars as well. [See Anna Stenning 2020 and Robert Chapman 2020]) Sane philosophers who build on Strawson argue, in seminar discussions and conferences, that there is no sanism to be found in his "Freedom and Resentment." The objective attitude is not objectifying, they say, because Strawson recommends that we also take this attitude toward children.[4] The objective attitude is claimed to be compatible with not only fear and repulsion but also pity and some kinds of love. Not "the sort of love which two adults can sometimes be said to feel reciprocally, for each other"—that is out of the question if you are Mad—but with *some* kinds of love (Strawson 1962/2013: 69, emphasis in Strawson). How comforting. The objective attitude need not be cold, but rather can be filled with warm feelings, such as pity, and some kinds of love!

Moving from consideration of epistemic injustice in particular to consideration of injustice in general, we should note that to be seen as irrational and deranged might not protect one from blame and punishment. Strawson *claims* that when "we" (civilized people, that is) see someone this way, our indignation and resentment tend to melt away and, furthermore, we no longer feel inclined to blame them (Strawson 1962/2013: 75–6). This claim, allegedly, embodies an apt description of how our practices largely work, not just a moral ideal, and thus countless later philosophers have accepted—without evidence—that Strawson is correct. In reality, although Black and Indigenous people are often perceived as less rational and as having less self-control than white people, they are simultaneously deemed *more* culpable for criminal behavior and considered fully morally responsible at *younger* ages than their white peers (Ciurria 2020: 122, 146; Hutchison 2018; Atkins-Loria, Macdonald, and Mitterling 2015: 9). The dominance of sane people in philosophical discussions about Madness and moral responsibility is further demonstrated by the ways in which Madpeople are persistently talked about in the third person. Excuses supposedly apply to *us* from time to time, to the writers and readers of philosophy texts, whereas exemptions only apply to *them*.

Autobiographical sidenote: For this reason, it took me a long time to grasp that *I* was one of the "warped and deranged" to whom Strawson refers and one of the people with "mental disorders" that are much discussed in modern philosophy papers. My Madness involves fear of demons, illusions, and hallucinations. I was on antipsychotic medication for many years and have been hospitalized for psychosis. In short, I do not have the kind of Madness of which people might dismissively say "well, we all struggle with that from time to time." Nevertheless, I continued to think of the Madpeople discussed in the philosophical literature as much Madder than me. After all, I was a philosopher: I was one of *us*, not one of *them*. A colleague even told me once that Strawson's objective attitude does not apply to people like me, because I am, quote, "mostly normal."[5]

Of course, these prejudiced us-and-them-formulations abound, not only in philosophy, and not only regarding Madness. Older philosophical texts implicitly assume that everyone is male, though we rarely see this problem in newer texts, which tend to use the singular "they" or alternate between "he" and "she" when discussing people in general. Although the new pronouns do not magically cure philosophy of sexism, they could be inserted without changing the arguments. The problem of only discussing Madpeople in the third person runs deeper than that.

It is problematic—for reasons discussed earlier—for sane people to regard Madpeople objectively, but it remains possible. However, if I am Mad and try to apply this view to myself, it becomes unsustainable and is apt to crumble from the inherent tensions and contradictions.

In the next two sections, I will argue, first, that I cannot consistently see myself as hopelessly unreasonable and uncontrolled and, second, that I cannot consistently regard myself as a causal system that must be managed and handled. In the fourth and fifth sections, I will finally present a more constructive alternative than either angrily blaming or exempting myself.

Applying the Objective Attitude to Myself: Seeing Myself as Hopeless

Below the Rationality Threshold

Let us briefly return to traditional moral philosophy and once again consider its view on moral responsibility. Philosophers disagree about what is required to be morally responsible, but they tend to agree that people need at least the following capacities: they must be able to assess their reasons for action, they must be able to think rationally about their options, and they must have enough control over themselves to act on their decisions.

Most people presumably fulfill these requirements, because rationality and willpower need not be perfect, nor are people required to use them all the time. Sometimes people are blameworthy precisely because they failed to do so when they should have. Nevertheless, these requirements for morally responsible agency explain—or so the traditional view goes—why little children, nonhuman animals, intellectually disabled people, and Madpeople cannot be responsible for their actions. The law makes similar assumptions: only humans above a certain minimum-age limit can be held legally responsible and, in addition, a person might escape conviction in a criminal court on grounds of Madness or intellectual disability. As already noted, people considered irrational and out of control are often subjected to more blame and harsher punishments *in practice*. Nevertheless, many laypeople and legal texts agree *in theory* that if you cannot see reason and/or cannot control yourself and, furthermore, that you cannot do so is not your fault, you are not morally responsible for your actions.

If I feel guilty over Mad things that I have done in the past, I might therefore tell myself that I am not responsible for what happened—because of my Madness, I fall below the rationality threshold. I was too unreasonable and/or too out of control to be blamed. But where exactly is that threshold? The philosophical literature is vague (e.g., John M. Fischer and Mark Ravizza's "moderate responsiveness" [1998]). The common-sense morality of laypeople is, if anything, even vaguer. Even if I had precise criteria at hand, the problem of finding out via introspection whether I fall below the threshold would remain.

This predicament might be why people often make extreme claims when trying to escape blame and feelings of guilt: they categorically state that they had *no* control, *could not* help it, etc. Nevertheless, this view of oneself tends to be unstable because it often clashes with our experiences and memories. We might honestly say that we lack control over being Mad in the first place; yet, claims according to which we lack control over every Mad decision that we have made and every Mad action that we have performed are likely false.

Agency in Everyday Struggles

Let us first look at problems that are common among people who are diagnosed with a wide array of mental disorders. For example, many of us have struggled to make plans and see them through and hence blame ourselves for failing.

Suppose, to borrow an example from sociologist David Karp (1992: 155), that I have repeatedly signed up for college courses only to later drop out. I feel guilty; even if these repeated educational failures hurt only me, I have let myself down. I try to exempt myself by reminding myself that I am diagnosed with one or more mental disorders and, therefore, could not help dropping out. Still, I remember how I read up on yet another college course and had thought to myself that I had good reasons to sign up for it. I remember telling myself that *this* time, I would be more disciplined and persevere. I remember *deciding* to sign up for it and I remember doing so. I further remember what happened later: I thought something like "It's just too much, I can't be bothered! I know I was supposed to pull through this time, but I just can't!" and then dropped out *again*. I recall making decisions based on reasons that seemed to make sense at the time, both when I signed up, and later when I thought "it's just too much" and dropped out again—even though I think, in hindsight, that these decisions and the reasons on which they had been based were shortsighted and weak-willed. I recall acting on those decisions, not being jerked around like a puppet on strings. When these memories hit, so does the guilt.

The earlier scenario is common enough. I might be able to cling to an out of control and therefore blameless self-image for brief stints of time, but soon enough it crumbles in the face of contrary memories.

I do not want to overgeneralize. Sometimes Madpeople do experience a profound loss of control over what they are doing. Wilda White (2021) describes how she, in a state of medication-induced mania, did more and more reckless things and destroyed her own life, feeling almost possessed and helpless to stop herself, despite realizing how destructively she behaved. Nevertheless, it is also common to struggle, and fail, at following through with college courses, getting to work on time, taking care of one's relationships, keeping one's promises, and so on, while retaining enough agency that it would be disingenuous to claim that one should be wholly exempt from responsibility due to loss of control. Even people who suffer from compulsions over which they lack *direct* control can often control the ways in which they deal with them (Gorman 2023).

Agency in Psychosis

Psychosis is often considered the paradigm case of complete non-responsibility. Anyone who has been to a self-help group for psychosis sufferers knows that people often feel guilty over things that they have done in more florid states. People try to tell each other, though, that there is no reason for guilt because, in psychosis, you are both devoid of reason and completely out of control. Nevertheless, if I remember thinking through my (perceived) options, assessing my reasons, making decisions, and acting on them, I will have a hard time accepting these supposed grounds for exemption.

Suppose that I fear demon assassins whom I think hide in my apartment, ready to kill me as soon as I let my guard down. To lose them, I go downtown and mingle with the crowds outside bars and nightclubs. Eventually, I am satisfied that they have lost track of me. I am horribly tired, but if I go back home, they will find me again. I decide to call a friend and ask to stay the night; we are not that close, but they live in the middle of the city, so I can go there without leaving the cover of the crowds. The phone rings for ages before I manage to wake them up—it is 2:00 a.m. on a weekday—but they eventually let me in.

Later, I feel guilty about disturbing my friend, perhaps causing them trouble at work the next day due to lack of sleep. I think that I should not have endangered myself by running through city traffic. I even feel guilty about accepting that the demon assassins were real, or at least about lending that hypothesis enough credibility to act on it.

This set of events might actually be a common type of psychotic experience (Jones et al. 2016; Jones and Shatell 2016; Jeppsson 2021), even though psychiatry at large has failed to catch up. If I tell my psychiatrist that I feel guilty, she likely replies that I have no reason to blame myself; as a matter of fact, she says, psychosis renders a person wholly out of control. Support-group peers will say the same thing, repeating what their own psychiatrists have told them. Nevertheless, that claim contradicts my memories of events: I remember choosing and acting for reasons, albeit under extreme stress and caught up in bizarre experiences.

If you are stalked by assassins, you have *reason* to try to lose them in a crowd. You have *reason* to hide from them. I remained an agent throughout, doing the best that I could in a bizarre and frightening situation. Even "giving in" to psychosis, rather than stubbornly clinging to sane reality, was a choice. Certainly not a free and happy one—more like hanging from a tree branch that I managed to grasp when I fell down a river, feeling the currents pull at me, feeling my arms burn and tremble with lactic acid, eventually thinking that it is not worth the pain and effort, that I might just as well release my grip and let the currents carry me off—but still a choice.

To sum up: It is one thing to see *others*, in Strawson's words, as "hopeless schizophrenics" (or hopeless bipolars, hopeless schizoaffectives, hopeless depressives, etc.) from whom nothing can be demanded. As ethically problematic as this conclusion is, it is at least possible. It might not be similarly possible to take this view on myself when I have lived through all my Mad decisions and actions and experienced them from the inside; when I have seen firsthand that as Mad as I was or am, I was never "hopelessly" unreasonable and out of control.

Applying the Objective Attitude to Myself: A Causal Perspective

There is more to the objective attitude than the idea that Madpeople are "hopeless." Strawson's talk of "managing and handling" presents a picture of Madpeople as causal systems, where one should push the right buttons to produce the desired outcome. However, this picture is also untenable to apply to one's own case.

The Causal Perspective

When we want to stop blaming ourselves for Mad actions, we often take a step back to focus on what presumably caused them. For instance, someone who keeps dropping out of college courses might say that they were caused to do so by some neural dysfunction hypothesized to underlie—or be identical to—their mental disorder. Causation is often not distinguished from constitution in these contexts, but the strategy remains the same if I tell myself that "low serotonin caused me to be depressed which caused me to drop out of college" or "low serotonin/depression caused me to drop out of college." This strategy might temporarily liberate me from guilt by invoking an image of myself as essentially machine-like, a mechanism where input gives output, it is what it is, and there is nothing to judge.

However, that is all that this strategy does. It does not provide an argument for my non-responsibility. As previously noted, Madpeople usually have some agency and control. Hypotheses about underlying neurological dysfunctions, even if they were proven,[6] do not change this state of affairs.

There are different philosophical theories about the mind-body relationship, but no one in the debate believes that the mind can act independently of the brain. All mental phenomena, whether Mad or sane, must have underlying neurological features (Jefferson 2022). If the mere existence of underlying neurological features undermines agency (choice, control, etc.), it does so for everyone, and we arrive at radical skepticism about moral responsibility. However, skeptics tend to argue that although full-blown moral responsibility does not exist, and hence no one can truly *deserve* blame or punishment, certain everyday moral responsibility practices can still be justified (Jeppsson 2022). Thus, if we accept skepticism, we must still figure out whether Madpeople can be apt targets for these practices. If we set skepticism aside and assume that the mere existence of underlying neurological features *does not* undermine agency and moral responsibility, we cannot exempt Madpeople simply by pointing out brain differences. It would have to be shown for each kind of Madness that these specific neurological features undermine agency and thereby responsibility.

Thus, as a Madperson racked with guilt over past Mad actions, actions I remember actively doing for reasons, I cannot turn to biological psychiatry or neurology for proof that I was so beyond reason and so out of control that I should be wholly exempted. But I *can* elicit an intuition or feeling that I lack responsibility for anything that I have done, by thinking of, for example, my neurotransmitters going awry and causing me to do this or that. No responsibility here, just one thing causing another thing causing a third thing, input giving output, it is what it is, and there is nothing to judge.

This strategy is reminiscent of popular thought experiments used in the philosophical moral responsibility debate. Unfortunately, it is far less effective for real people than it is for thought-experiment characters.

The Causal Perspective in Philosophical Thought Experiments

Some philosophers argue that moral responsibility is incompatible with determinism, and perhaps with any way that the universe might plausibly work. They construct thought experiments, in which the main characters are portrayed as causal systems, to pump their audience's intuitions.

In Derk Pereboom's "four-case manipulation argument," Professor Plum murders Miss White. Plum is stipulated to be highly rational: he carefully weighs his options, thinks through his decisions, and then acts in a way consistent with his values and character (Pereboom 2001: ch. 4, 2014: ch. 4). Nevertheless, when we focus on the causal history behind his thoughts and actions—involving, in different versions of the thought experiment, everything from nefarious scientists directly tinkering with his brain to an upbringing in a community that values and encourages selfish behavior—he does not seem morally responsible to us, regardless of how rational and mentally healthy he is.

I have previously argued that other agents' involvement in making Plum the way that he is does *not* play a crucial part in pumping our intuitions. After all, we sometimes read or watch science fiction stories with robots and artificial intelligences (AIs) programmed by engineers, and still think of them as morally responsible agents. I will use Star Trek Voyager's Hologram Doctor as an example; we spontaneously consider him responsible for his actions, even though an engineer programmed him (Jeppsson 2020). But the Hologram Doctor is a fully fleshed-out character, and Professor Plum is not.

> Pereboom's description of Professor Plum draws attention to the way in which he resembles a highly sophisticated vending machine. Insert a coin, out comes a candy bar—insert the scientists' program and the right environmental factors, out comes a murder. We are told that Plum is reasons-responsive, has a first-order will which corresponds to his second-order volitions and so on—but all those agential features seem like nothing but cogs in a sophisticated machine. Even though we are *told* that Plum is a fully-fledged rational agent, it is hard to fully *appreciate* this fact when he is described the way he is. (Jeppsson 2022: 1938, emphasis added)

Even with a rational agent like Plum, we can thus mollify our reactive attitudes if we look at him from a detached, causal angle; if we see him as an *object*, where one step in the causal chain leads to another and eventually results in an action, it is what it is, there is nothing to judge. However, the more that a fictional character/robot/AI is a fleshed-out person, the more likely that we are to see them as a morally responsible agent rather than a causal system.

Although a similar, mechanical, and object-like picture can be painted of real humans if we focus on their genes and neurotransmitters, giving rise to brief non-responsibility intuitions, real humans are always fully fleshed-out persons. Seeing someone *you know* from this perspective is particularly difficult—not to mention seeing yourself this way.

In the internet era, the view that Madness is caused or constituted by imbalanced neurotransmitters and/or hyper- and hypo-activity in various parts of the brain is spread not just by countless popular articles on the subject, but also by Madpeople themselves who share texts and memes on social media. In support groups, people reassure each other that they should not feel guilty, since their failures were caused by faulty neurotransmitters (observed already by Karp [Karp 1992: 154–6]). And yet, the causal perspective does not extinguish our intuitions about guilt and blame as effectively for real people as for Professor Plum. Most philosophers admit to feeling that Plum lacks responsibility when reading the thought experiment; if that feeling does not fit their philosophical theory, they work hard on arguments intended to show that the feeling, albeit strong, is unreliable (McKenna 2008, 2013). When Madpeople try to escape guilt and blame by stressing how we were caused to do what we did, it is often the other way around. We try *so hard* to cling to the non-responsibility view but constantly slide back into seeing ourselves as responsible agents who deserve blame.

There might be several explanations for this outcome, all of which play a part. I already mentioned that we naturally see fully fleshed-out characters as morally responsible. Karp (1992: 156–7) discusses how seeing oneself as a passive victim of faulty neurotransmitters not only feels liberating insofar as one lets go of guilt, but it also makes one feel helpless. Studies indicate that belief in a just world and/or free will can make people more prone to blame mentally ill people (Rüsch et al. 2010; Chandrashekar 2020). I will argue that in addition to other explanations, it is impossible to sustain a strict causal focus on oneself, Mad or not. Therefore, the release from guilt that I can achieve in this manner will always be fragile and fleeting.

The Impossibility of Consistently Seeing Myself from a Causal Perspective

As previously stated, it is easy to regard a briefly described thought-experiment character from a causal perspective; more difficult with a fully fleshed-out fictional character, and very difficult with people that we meet and interact with in real life. If I regularly interacted with Professor Plum or Star Trek's Hologram Doctor, it would soon become unfeasible to stick to an objective, exempting attitude, even if I knew that they had been created and programmed by engineers to be the way that they are (Russell 2010: 158–60).

Strawson similarly writes that we cannot sustain an objective attitude to "normal" people for too long, even though it comes naturally to us when encountering "abnormalities or immaturities" and "the compulsive behaviour of the neurotic" (Strawson 1962/2013: 70). Perhaps there is some truth in what Strawson writes—that is, it might be somewhat less difficult for a sane person to regard Madpeople this way. Madpeople sometimes talk and behave in ways that others find weird, scary, and alienating. Less difficult, but still not easy (remember the psychiatrist that I mentioned in the section "The Objective Attitude Beyond the Philosophy Seminar" who talked about "seeing the person" in her patients). And if I try to take a detached, causal perspective on myself, I will inevitably fail to do so.

Let us reuse Karp's habitual college dropout. Suppose that I want to go back to college again. Still, I hesitate. My mental disorder has caused me to drop out before. Perhaps it will cause me to be too apathetic to enroll in the first place this time. However, if I sit back and wait to see what my disorder will cause me to do, I have effectively decided not to enroll again. As long as I sit and wait for some action or other to emerge, I will remain passive.[7] Suppose, next, that I realize this, but since I still think of myself as a causal system where the right buttons must be pushed for action to happen, I try to push my own buttons—to manage and handle myself, so to speak. I might, for instance, tell other people to encourage me to enroll in college again or try to influence myself to do so by surrounding myself with media portraying the college experience in a positive light.

Nevertheless, eventually, I must decide whether to enroll, or I have effectively decided not to do so. Having my friends encourage me and consuming inspiring media can very well be a good idea, but it cannot replace the actual decision, which I must still make (see also Korsgaard 1996: 162). Furthermore, button-pushing requires a pusher, not just a "pushee." When I try to influence myself by surrounding myself with the right media and people, I already exercise my agency by choosing these methods and implementing them.

The inevitability of exercising my agency—choosing and acting rather than just pushing my own buttons—makes the causal perspective on myself fundamentally unstable.

This instability is true not just for the college dropout but also for more dramatic, psychotic cases where I still have agency. Suppose I once again feel the demons closing in on me. What should I do about it? Should I muster up all my willpower and cling to the belief that I am safe because demons do not exist, despite feeling terrified? If I give up on that endeavor, and let Madness sweep me away, I still have at least two options: I can attempt to flee or to defend myself—perhaps via magical means which make sense from inside my Madness. I cannot just wait and see what my Madness/my genes and environment/my wildly fluctuating neurotransmitters will cause me to do this time. If I try to just wait and see, I have essentially decided to remain passive while my terror rises until it becomes unbearable, at which point I will probably decide to flee anyway. Even in this state, I inevitably exercise my agency.

A More Sustainable Alternative: Compassionate Self-excuse

We cannot consistently regard ourselves objectively. We cannot consistently see ourselves as hopeless cases, too out of control to be responsible for anything that we do; nor can we consistently think of ourselves as causal systems where one thing causes another, input gives output, it is what it is, and there is nothing to judge. People must decide and act. We might find ourselves in situations where all options are terrible, but we must still choose which one to take. This fundamental fact of the human condition does not disappear because I am diagnosed with a mental disorder. Now, it does happen sometimes that people experience themselves as mentally frozen, unable to make a decision or act, or helplessly controlled by alien powers, but this predicament often does not arise, not even in states of florid psychosis.

Nevertheless, I should not beat myself up over Mad things that I have said and done. Compassionate self-excuses offer a more constructive alternative.

Diving in Instead of Stepping Back

Instead of taking up a detached, causal, objective view, I can liberate myself from oppressive feelings of guilt by doing quite the opposite: diving into my own memories and experiences, and fully appreciate how much I have suffered and struggled. When fully appreciating how serious my past difficulties were, I can cultivate *compassion* for myself, and *excuse* myself on compassionate grounds. I might, sadly, suffer from all kinds of psychological hang-ups and obstacles, which make it hard for me to show myself compassion; but unlike seeing myself as a hopeless case or taking up a causal perspective on myself, there is nothing essential about being an agent that prevents compassion. (Nor does one's proximity to a person hinder compassion for them, the way that it hinders seeing them as causal systems. On the contrary, compassion often grows stronger the closer we get to someone.)

When I feel guilty about past wrongdoings, I should try to recall what it was truly like for me when I did wrong. I was, perhaps, stressed out and felt completely overwhelmed by a combination of work tasks and household chores. I was anxious, perhaps downright terrified, about my prospects in a precarious job market.

The full extent of my stress and anxiety might very well be connected to something with which I have been diagnosed; perhaps a sane and neurotypical person in the same situation would have coped better. Diagnoses can have a part to play here insofar as I tend to compare myself to others. They provide some evidence that even if I, say, struggle with common problems like forgetfulness and being easily distracted, I likely have it harder than most. I have only direct access to my own experiences, so if I want to compare myself to others, I must rely on indirect evidence, of which diagnoses can be part.

Nevertheless, what directly matters are my struggles, how I felt and what I experienced, not my diagnoses. I forgot an important promise that I made to one friend and angrily cut off another with a deeply hurtful remark, but I was so overwhelmed and stressed out that it was truly difficult to remember previous conversations and control my impulses. I should show myself compassion, cut myself some slack—perhaps lots of slack—and excuse myself.

Benjamin Kozuch and Michael McKenna (2016) argue that it is better to excuse than to exempt a wrongdoer with a *mild* mental disorder because the objective attitude has serious drawbacks. Yet there is no reason to assume that when moving from milder to more serious mental disorders, we must also move from excuses to an objective attitude and exemption. I may have agency in psychosis, but I am also under a lot of pressure in that state. Letting go of sane reality and allowing myself to be swept away by Madness is comparable to letting go of a tree branch and being swept away by the currents when my arms already tremble and burn from lactic acid. I might have been able to stay at home throughout the night instead of disturbing my friend, desperately clinging to the belief that demons are not real; but doing so would have cost me dearly—that is, cost me in terms of intense mental effort and sheer terror (Gorman 2021). And once I gave in to the belief that supernatural assassins chased me, I did the best that I could in my circumstances, as I experienced them.

We can explain why I ought not to feel guilty or blame myself by invoking common textbook excuses such as acting from a non-culpable false belief and acting under duress. Or we might invoke difficulty and cost directly, appealing to commonsense moral principles according to which blameworthiness is diminished when acting right was very difficult and/or costly (Nelkin 2016; Wolf 1990: 86–7). But to see how ordinary excuses and moral principles apply to me, I must do the opposite of taking up a detached, causal perspective—I should delve into my memories and fully appreciate how hard I struggled.

Diminished Responsibility

A compassionate excuse will often diminish (rather than wholly remove) guilt and self-blame. In this way, a compassionate excuse differs from a causal-perspective-based exemption. For however long I manage to keep up a detached and causal view of myself, I might seem wholly non-responsible in my own eyes; input gives output, it is what it is, there is nothing to judge. But when I remember how I struggled with hard choices and acted under extreme pressure, I keep in mind that I chose and acted. In this picture, I should cut myself some slack—perhaps *lots* of slack—but I do not seem wholly non-responsible. I can still blame myself occasionally, as well as hold myself responsible in a more forward-looking and nurturing manner (Brandenburg 2018). That I can blame myself sometimes is a *feature* of compassionate excuses, not a bug. It allows for nuanced judgments and leaves open the possibility that I might change and improve in various ways.

Seeing myself as a struggling agent who needs compassion and understanding might even hold more potential for self-improvement than seeing myself as fully responsible and guilty (Breines and Chen 2012). Of course, I should not think of myself as a broken thing that needs to be fixed and can be fixed, if only I pull on my bootstraps hard enough; this would be contrary to compassion and understanding. Nevertheless, it is important to recognize the possibility of change, rather than see myself as hopeless (at least unless some external intervention, such as a new medication regime, eventually strikes gold) (Snoek et al. 2021). Complete self-exemption, even if it did provide a stable option for escaping guilt, would close the door to self-improvement; compassionate self-excuse does not have this problem.

I have deliberately spoken rather loosely of what self-compassion entails. I have explained how a compassionate self-excuse differs from attempts to exempt oneself with an objective attitude, but there is still much room for elaboration.

Self-compassion, and compassion overall, is often associated with Buddhist philosophy. However, one need not subscribe to this religion or philosophy to embrace this kind of attitude toward oneself. As Kristin Neff notes, similar ideas can be found in Western psychology too, like Judith Jordan's self-empathy, or Carl Rogers's unconditional acceptance (Neff 2003).

Furthermore, several philosophers discuss holding oneself responsible as a balancing act. Robin Dillon (1992, 2001) writes that true self-respect requires walking the line between excessive self-blame and shrugging off and excusing every wrongful thing one does. Christine Korsgaard (1996: ch. 7) talks of balancing love and respect—harsh blame can be cruel, but constantly shrugging everything off can be disrespectful. These authors do not focus on Madness, but I believe that this balance is as important to find for Madpeople as for others.[8]

Thus, a constructive, loving, and respectfully balanced view of my past wrongdoings and my responsibility for them should go hand in hand with cultivating self-compassion. This balance is complicated because there are no hard and fast principles for determining when I ought to hold myself responsible, and to which extent. But life is complicated, not the least if you struggle with Madness. It is better to acknowledge this complication than to chase in vain for a principled way to separate morally responsible people from those fit only for an objective attitude and exemption.[9]

Compassionate Excuses Versus Justification: A Neurodiversity Perspective

Sometimes, attention to the details of my experience might lead me to judge that what I did was *justified* rather than something that needs to be excused.

An excused wrongful action was still wrong or, at least all things considered, harmful in some way. Excuses merely temper or remove the agent's blameworthiness. A justification, on the other hand, shows that the action was not wrong after all; it might have looked wrong at first glance, but when we know more, we can see that it was not.

Benjamin Kozuch and Michael McKenna (2016) briefly mention the possibility that mental disorders might justify rather than excuse. However, the idea that many of society's norms are unjustifiably tailored to the interests of neurotypical people and ought to change is familiar from the neurodiversity movement (e.g., Singer 1999; Walker 2012).

It is considered nice and polite to look people squarely in the eye when interacting with them. Someone who always looks down, keeps shifting their gaze, and gives only short and stunted replies can be seen as impolite and disrespectful. This interpretation is not wholly unfounded, because the behavior in question *might* signal, for example, that you find the other person boring and therefore try to withdraw from the conversation. For some Autistic or socially anxious people, however, looking someone in the eye and giving long replies might require intense mental effort. In many situations, eating a crunching biscuit among other people would be considered morally neutral, whereas blasting away on a boom box would be wrong. This discrepancy reflects how most people react to sounds—biscuits are easy to ignore, a blaring boom box not—but for a person who experiences misophonia, the biscuit crunching might drive them up the walls.

What should we make of this realization? We cannot create a society perfectly adjusted to everyone, because sometimes needs and preferences legitimately clash. Suppose that one person needs to fidget around to be able to focus, whereas another needs absolute peace and quiet. We should try to avoid situations where these people must work in the same room. Still, it is unlikely that we can create a society entirely free of these kinds of conflicts—both between groups of neurodivergent people and between the divergent and typical ones. The best that we can do, then, is to try to share the burdens of adjustment as fairly as possible (Gorman 2021).

It has been suggested to me that in a society committed to neurodiversity, it might not be considered wrong to wake someone up in the middle of the night because of one's psychotic fears.[10] This suggestion is interesting, but I do not completely endorse it. Sometimes this disruption might be a fair distribution of burdens, but at other times, it might be more damaging for the sane and neurotypical person to have their sleep disrupted—in particular, if it happens repeatedly—than for me to ride out my fears in solitude, or with only a hotline operator for support. It all depends on the details. We should not go from demanding endless adjustments from Mad and neurodivergent people to demanding the same of the sane and neurotypical, because the latter do not have endless energy and resources either. There will always be room for wrongful but largely excusable Mad acts next to the justifiable.

Mad and neurodivergent people are also blamed and made to feel ashamed of behaviors that are not even *prima facie* wrong; behaviors that are harmless, perhaps even beneficial, but that strike other people as weird.

Perhaps I soothe my demon fears by way of little rituals that seem disturbing to sane people—like stuffing my gloves full of moss or arranging the furniture in particular ways. Perhaps, when I cannot so easily soothe my worries, I go down on all fours to avoid seeing my reflection replaced by a mimicking demon in mirrors and windows. Other people might think that it is wrong of me to disturb them with such weird behavior; they might think that they must choose between dismissing me as a hopeless mental case or angrily blaming me. Here, it is reasonable to object that it is not *I* that ought to change, it is *they* who ought to become more tolerant. There is nothing wrong with what I do.

Conclusion

When we exempt someone from responsibility, we take up an objective attitude toward them. We see them as victims of their disorders of whom nothing can be demanded, or as causal systems where one thing leads to another and there is nothing to judge. However, I cannot successfully exempt myself from responsibility in this manner. I cannot stably and consistently look upon myself as either a hopeless case or a mere causal system. Self-exemption is unstable.

Fortunately, the problems of self-exemption do not mean that I must harshly blame myself for failing where sane people succeed and hold myself to impossible standards. Sometimes my Mad behavior is justified—we ought to reject sanist judgments that frame everything weird and unusual as morally wrong. At other times, my behavior was bad or harmful in some way, but I should cut myself some slack by taking my experiences as seriously as they deserve. Rather than take a step back from my actions and look at what might have caused them, I can delve right into my memories and fully appreciate how much I struggled. By showing myself compassion and understanding, I can mitigate my sense of guilt in a more stable manner and excuse myself.

I have focused on how to see myself in this chapter. However, considering how ethically problematic the objective attitude is when applied to other people and the fact that we are social creatures who find it hard to go alone against the flow, partial to full excuses based on compassion and understanding also serve as a desirable alternative to exemption when we relate to other people who struggle with Madness.

Acknowledgments

An earlier version of this chapter appeared as "Exemption, *Self*-Exemption, and Compassionate Self-Excuse," in *The International Mad Studies Journal* 1 (1): 2022. The research for the original article was funded by the Swedish Research Council, grant number 2018-01584. I thank August Gorman and Anneli Jefferson for helpful comments on the first draft of the article.

Thanks to Ida Hallgren for convincing me about the importance of compassion.

Notes

1 Brink and Nelkin (2013: 291–2) write that textbook examples of excuses feature external conditions that rob an agent of responsibility locally and for a short time, whereas likewise standard examples of exemptions feature internal conditions that rob an agent of responsibility for a wide scope of actions and for a long time. However, they write, these three dimensions—internal/external, scope, and duration—need not go together.

2 Fortunately, Day et al. (2018) detect gradually improving attitudes among mental health staff toward BPD patients over time.

3 See also Brandenburg (2022) for criticism.

4 Of course, one might just as well draw the conclusion that Strawson's attitude to children is problematic.

5 A charitable interpretation is that people should only be regarded objectively when they are in a state of florid psychosis. However, Strawson and many later philosophers frequently make blanket statements: people with mental disorders must be regarded objectively and lack moral responsibility. Furthermore, I have written at length elsewhere of how important it is to try to understand and empathize with people *even when* they are psychotic (Jeppsson 2021).

6 The state of evidence for specific brain dysfunctions underlying particular mental disorders is slimmer, patchier, and more complicated than most people

realize. Stephen Stahl's (2018) psychosis research overview, which describes how a simpler dopamine hypothesis gives way to more complicated ones according to which there are different kinds of psychosis involving different neurotransmitters, provides a nice illustration. Even the latest research relies heavily on indirect evidence and inferences from the effects of various drugs.

7 I was challenged on this point by Polaris Koi, who described meditation techniques where you sit and wait for an action to emerge, without actively deciding anything. This might be possible for some people sometimes. Nevertheless, they would still have decided, first, to engage in this kind of meditation. Second, this is something some people do from time to time, not a permanent state in which one can live one's whole life.

8 I have been asked if this also applies to the Madperson's family and friends—whether they should walk a line between holding responsible too much and too little. I think this is in principle right. I also *think* that getting this balance right is even trickier for others; *possibly*, they should err on the side of caution by following the Madperson's lead in what they see themselves as responsible for and to which extent, even if that means excusing them almost all the time. I think it is often *very* difficult to convince someone else that they have more reason, control, and responsibility for what they do than they think they have. But all this is very tentative on my part.

9 I leave it open whether criminal justice requires hard and fast principles for separating the responsible from the non-responsible. The topic of this chapter is solely morality, not law.

10 August Gorman, personal correspondence.

References

Aftab, Awais (2021, June 3), "Global Psychiatry's Crisis of Values: Dainius Pūras, MD," *Psychiatric Times*. Available at: https://www.psychiatrictimes.com/view/global-psychiatry-crisis-values (accessed June 20, 2023).

Arpaly, Nomy (2005), "How it is not 'just like Diabetes': Mental Disorders and the Moral Psychologist," *Philosophical Issues* 15: 282–98.

Atkins-Loria, Sasha, Heather MacDonald, and Courtney Mitterling (2015), "Young African-American Men and the Diagnosis of Conduct Disorder: The Neo-colonization of Suffering," *Clinical Social Work Journal* 43 (4): 431–41.

Brandenburg, Daphne (2018), "The Nurturing Stance: Making Sense of Responsibility without Blame," *The Pacific Philosophical Quarterly* 99 (1): 5–22.

Brandenburg, Daphne (2022), "Diversity and Moral Address," *Journal of Applied Philosophy* 39 (4): 631–44.

Breines, Juliana G. and Serena Chen (2012), "Self-compassion Increases Self-improvement Motivation," *Personality and Social Psychology Bulletin* 38 (9): 1133–43.

Brink, David and Dana Nelkin (2013), "Fairness and the Architecture of Responsibility," *Oxford Studies in Agency and Responsibility* 1: 284–313.

Chandrashekar, Subramanya Prasad (2020), "It's in Your Control: Free will Beliefs and Attribution of Blame to Obese People and People with Mental Illness," *Collabra: Psychology* 6 (1): 29.

Chapman, Robert (2020), "Do Neurotypicals have Intact Moral Agency?" *Critical Neurodiversity*. Available at: https://criticalneurodiversity.com/2020/03/31/do-neurotypicals-have-intact-moral-agency/?fbclid=IwAR0BJRaJlwp5XLwqCCaQ8wk12uT3y26gIlwbOlHMjCaqzT6Cf1b4m9pJUlQ (accessed June 20, 2023).
Ciurria, Michelle (2020), *An Intersectionalist Feminist Theory of Moral Responsibility*, New York: Routledge.
Day, Nicholas J. S., Annalise Hunt, Louise Cortis-Jones, and Brin F. S. Grenyer (2018), "Clinician Attitudes towards Borderline Personality Disorder: A 15-year Comparison," *Personality and Mental Health* 12 (4): 309–20.
Dillon, Robin (1992), "How to Lose Your Self-respect," *American Philosophical Quarterly* 29 (2): 125–39.
Dillon, Robin (2001), "Self-forgiveness and Self-respect," *Ethics* 112: 53–83.
Fischer, John Martin and Mark Ravizza (1998), *Responsibility and Control: A Theory of Moral Responsibility*, New York: Cambridge University Press.
Fricker, M. (2007), *Epistemic Injustice: Power and the Ethics of Knowing*, Oxford: Oxford University Press.
Gorman, August (2021), "Against Ideal Agency," Workshop Presentation: Philosophy of Psychiatry and Lived Experience, Umeå University, April 23.
Gorman, August (2023), "What is the Difference between Weakness of Will and Compulsion?," *The Journal of the American Philosophical Association* 9 (1): 37–52.
Hutchison, Katrina (2018), "Moral Responsibility, Respect and Social Identity," in Katrina Hutchison, Catriona MacKenzie, and Marina Oshana (eds.), *Social Dimensions of Moral Responsibility*, 206–30, New York: Oxford University Press.
Jefferson, Anneli (2022), *Are Mental Disorders Brain Disorders?* London: Routledge.
Jeppsson, Sofia M. I. (2020), "The Agential Perspective: A Hard-Line Reply to the Four-Case Manipulation Argument," *Philosophical Studies* 177 (7): 1935–51.
Jeppsson, Sofia M. I. (2021), "Psychosis and Intelligibility," *Philosophy, Psychology & Psychiatry* 28 (3): 233–49.
Jeppsson, Sofia M. I. (2022), "Accountability, Answerability and Attributability. On Different Kinds of Moral Responsibility," in Dana Nelkin and Derk Pereboom (eds.), *The Oxford Handbook of Moral Responsibility*, 73–88, New York: Oxford University Press.
Jones, Nev and Mona Shattell (2016), "Not what the Textbooks Describe: Challenging Clinical Conventions about Psychosis," *Issues in Mental Health Nursing* 37: 769–72.
Jones, Nev, Mona Shatell, Timothy Kelly, Robyn Brown, LaVome Robinson, Richard Renfro, Barbara Harris, and Tanya Marie Luhrmann (2016), "Did I Push Myself over the Edge? Complications of Agency in Psychosis Onset and Development," *Psychosis* 8 (4): 324–35.
Karp, David A. (1992), "Illness Ambiguity and the Search for Meaning: A Case Study of a Self-help Group for Affective Disorders," *Journal of Contemporary Ethnography* 21 (2): 139–70.
Kennett, Jeanette (2009), "Mental Disorder, Moral Agency and the Self," in Bonnie Steinbock (ed.), *The Oxford Handbook of Bioethics*, 90–113, Oxford: Oxford University Press.
Korsgaard, Christine (1996), *Creating the Kingdom of Ends*, Cambridge: Cambridge University Press.
Kozuch, Benjamin and Michael McKenna (2016), "Free Will, Moral Responsibility and Mental Illness," in Daniel Moseley and Gary Gala (eds.), *Philosophy and Psychiatry*, 89–113, New York: Routledge.

Leblanc, Stephanie and Elizabeth Anne Kinsella (2016), "Toward Epistemic Justice: A Critical Examination of 'sanism' and Implications for Knowledge Generation," *Studies in Social Justice* 10 (1): 59–78.
Luhrmann, Tanya M. (2000), *Of Two Minds: The Growing Disorder in American Psychiatry*, New York: Alfred A. Knopf.
McKenna, Michael (2008), "A Hard-Line Reply to Pereboom's Four-Case Manipulation Argument," *Philosophy and Phenomenological Research* 77 (1): 142–59.
McKenna, Michael (2013), "Resisting the Manipulation Argument: A Hard-Liner Takes it on the Chin," *Philosophy and Phenomenological Research* 89 (2): 467–84.
Neff, Kristin (2003), "Self-compassion: An Alternative Conceptualization of a Healthy Attitude toward Oneself," *Self and Identity* 2 (2): 85–101.
Nelkin, Dana (2016), "Difficulty and Degrees of Moral Praiseworthiness and Blameworthiness," *Noûs* 50: 356–78.
Pereboom, Derk (2001), *Living without Free Will*, Cambridge: Cambridge University Press.
Pereboom, Derk (2014), *Free Will, Agency and Meaning in Life*, Oxford: Oxford University Press.
Rüsch, Nicolas, Andrew R. Todd, Galen V. Bodenhausen, and Patrick W. Corrigan (2010), "Do People with Mental Illness Deserve What they Get? Links between Meritocratic Worldviews and Implicit versus Explicit Stigma," *European Archives of Psychiatry and Clinical Neuroscience* 260: 617–25.
Russell, Paul (2010), "Selective Hard Compatibilism," in Joseph Keim Campbell, Michael O'Rourke, and Harry S. Silverstein (eds.), *Action, Ethics and Responsibility: Topics in Contemporary Philosophy*, vol. 7, 149–73, Cambridge, MA: MIT Press.
Singer, Judy (1999), "'Why Can't You Be Normal for Once in Your Life?' From a 'Problem with No Name' to the Emergence of a New Category of Difference," in Mairian Corker and Sally French (eds.), *Disability Discourse*, 59–67, Buckingham: Open University Press.
Snoek, Anke, Victoria McGeer, Daphne Brandenburg, and Jeanette Kennett (2021), "Managing Shame and Guilt in Addiction: A Pathway to Recovery," *Addictive Behaviors* 120: 106954–106954.
Stahl, Stephen M. (2018), "Beyond the Dopamine Hypothesis of Schizophrenia to Three Neural Networks of Psychosis: Dopamine, Serotonin and Glutamate," *CNS Spectrums* 23: 187–91.
Stenning, Anna (2020), "Understanding Morality through a Study of Autistic Life Writing. On the Importance of Neurodivergent Morality," in Hanna Bertilsdotter Rosqvist, Nick Chown, and Anna Stenning (eds.), *Neurodiversity Studies: A New Critical Paradigm*, chapter 7, 108–24, London: Routledge.
Strawson, P. F. (1962), "Freedom and Resentment," *Proceedings of the British Academy* 48: 1–25. Reprinted in Paul Russell and Oisin Deery (eds.), *The Philosophy of Free Will*, New York: Oxford University Press: pagination refers to this reprint.
Walker, Nick (2012), "Throw Away the Master's Tools: Liberating Ourselves from the Pathology Paradigm," in Julia Bascom (ed.), *Loud Hands: Autistic People, Speaking*, 225–37, Washington: Autistic Self Advocacy Network.
White, Wilda (2021), "Re-writing the Master Narrative: A Prerequisite for Mad Liberation," in Jasna Russo, Peter Beresford, and Kathy Boxall (eds.), *The Routledge Handbook of Mad Studies: Critical Perspectives on Doing Mad Studies*, 76–89, London: Routledge.
Wolf, Susan (1990), *Freedom within Reason*, New York: Oxford University Press.

16 PATHOLOGIZING DISABLED AND TRANS IDENTITIES

HOW EMOTIONS BECOME MARGINALIZED

GEN EICKERS

Introduction

Trans and disabled identities have been subject to vast amounts of pathologization and marginalization (Sauer and Nieder 2019; Baár 2017; McRuer 2006). Pathologization often originates in medical contexts and subsequently contributes to an overall understanding of identities that pathologizes them. In the eleventh edition of the *International Statistical Classification of Diseases and Related Health Problems* (*ICD-11*), a first attempt has been made to provide a de-pathologizing account of what it means to be trans; that is, the *ICD-11* introduces a new definition of gender incongruence in which being trans is no longer classified as a disorder (World Health Organization 2018). Furthermore, the *ICD-11* presents a move away from a binary understanding of trans identities. Rather than define being trans on the basis of a rigid and binary understanding of transition from female to male or male to female, the new *ICD-11* definition is more flexible and explicitly includes nonbinary identities. Nevertheless, the tenth edition of the *ICD* (*ICD-10*) will remain legally authoritative until the *ICD-11* becomes legally binding. In other words, trans individuals will continue to be pathologized under the *ICD-10* classification "transsexualism" and additional *ICD-10* labels that belong to its category of "gender identity disorders" until the *ICD-11* replaces the *ICD-10* (World Health Organization 2004). In short, being trans continues to be considered as a (mental) disorder and to be highly pathologized. Thus, one might, insofar as being trans is considered to be a mental disorder, argue that being trans is pathologized *by way of* the pathologization of disability. Indeed, due to the current conceptualization of being trans as a disorder, medical practices have emerged that gatekeep and further pathologize trans people. The gatekeeping and pathologizing dimensions of these medical practices can range from (for instance) intrusive interrogations and demeaning comments of a medical professional from whom a trans person seeks to receive hormones to more complex problems, such as tensions between a therapist and their patient that had not existed before the patient came out as trans.

Equally, disabled people are also subjected to medical practices that pathologize them. Peter Conrad argues, for example, that categories such as attention deficit hyperactivity disorder (ADHD) or sexual dysfunction are examples of the medicalization and pathologization of behavioral differences (Conrad 2007). As Monika Baár writes: "recent decades have seen the emergence or proliferation of a plethora of new conditions, ones which had not necessarily been categorized in medical terms earlier on. These include autism, attention deficit hyperactivity disorder (ADHD) and depression" (Baár 2017: 294). According to Conrad, this medicalization of behavioral differences results in a narrow focus on the individual that ignores social context and the role of society in the emergence of categories of disorder and disability (Conrad 2007; Baár 2017). By contrast, Baár and other disability scholars consider "disability as part of a larger cultural system which forges bodies into hierarchies and then distributes power and privilege according to arbitrary distinctions" (Baár 2017: 289). This individualization of disability can be understood as part of a broader social and cultural individualization with respect to behavioral differences along lines of gender, sexuality, disability, and other social identity factors. Individualization of this kind often relies on the naturalization of certain phenomena, which may be linked to how the economic interests of pharmaceutical companies and individualized medical practices have played a significant part in the pathologization of behavioral differences (cf. Decker 2013).

To begin to understand the mutually constitutive pathologization of disabled and trans identities, consider these remarks that Robert McRuer has made. McRuer argues that "the system of compulsory ablebodiedness, which in a sense produces disability, is thoroughly interwoven with the system of compulsory heterosexuality that produces queerness: that, in fact, compulsory heterosexuality is contingent on compulsory ablebodiedness, and vice versa" (McRuer 2006: 2). Following McRuer, we can begin to understand the intersections of the diagnostic and social categories of disability and transness, their interdependence, and the social factors that contribute to their mutual pathologization and marginalization by looking at the history of pathologization itself, drawing on the work that Baár, McRuer, and other disability, queer, and trans scholars have already accomplished to do so. We may also do so by looking at marginalization systemically through examination of the specific kinds of marginalization that trans and disabled people experience, which would include analysis of everyday forms of marginalization, such as the often indirect and subtle emotional marginalization that may occur during seemingly innocent everyday social interactions and social encounters. Like disability and transness, emotions—as a phenomenon or the subject of research—have often been considered "natural" phenomena rather than cultural products; thus, the impact of social factors on emotions has often been neglected (Lutz and White 1986; Leys 2017). This failure to investigate the social constitution of emotions ultimately reinforces and reproduces the marginalization of emotions that members of subordinated social groups experience because many of these people may fail to comply with (or may *seemingly* fail to comply with) dominant standards and norms with respect to emotions due to disability, gender performance, gender identity, or other social statuses. For example, someone who is trans might disappoint gendered expectations around emotional behavior; likewise, someone who is disabled might disappoint ableist expectations around emotional behavior.

Emotion theorists and philosophers working on gender, disability, or race have started to analyze and criticize the ways in which we think of emotions such as anger and anxiety (e.g., Srinivasan 2018; Munch-Jurisic 2021; Silva 2021; Archer and Mills 2019). Laura Silva, for example, argues that "anger has been unduly characterized as a hostile emotion" and that "we have reason to take seriously the view that anger is essentially recognitional, that is, that it aims for recognition of harms done" (Silva 2021: 1-2). These (and other) critical approaches to emotion theory point to norms that influence and condition which emotions and emotional displays are deemed to be appropriate and which are deemed to be inappropriate in given situations (Hochschild 1979; Scheman 1980). As suggested earlier, these norms disproportionately impact members of marginalized groups, thereby contributing to their further marginalization (cf. Kurth 2022).

Thus, this chapter will analyze how pathologization and resulting stigma contribute to the emotional marginalization of disabled people and trans people. My argument will proceed in the following way: I will first explain what marginalization is. Then, I will apply the concept of marginalization to emotions and provide a more detailed definition than I have thus far of what emotional marginalization is. In a final step, I will look at specific examples of emotional marginalization that trans and disabled people experience.

Marginalization

Marginalization is a process through which one's access to political, social, and economic goods is limited, as well as one's opportunities to access these goods. This process forces certain people to the peripheries of society. Originally, the concept of marginalization was used to describe experiences of immigration (cf. Park 1928), according to which marginalization meant a "lack of integration and the status as an 'outsider' with respect to dominant cultures" (Bernt and Colini 2013: 14). At present, as noted, however, the term *marginalization* is used to address a broader range of phenomena and considers cultural, social, and structural factors that limit one's access to political, social, and economic goods and push one to the peripheries of society. For example, Iris Marion Young (1990) conceived marginalization with respect to the limited access that one has to economic goods insofar as she considered the lack of access to work as a way to prevent marginalized people from participating in society in meaningful ways. In Young's framework, that is, marginalization is the social practice of exclusion of certain members of society from the workforce which renders them second-class citizens, resulting in material deprivation (Young 1990: 53–5). Marginalized social groups, for Young, include the poor, old people, people of color, disabled people, and everyone who is regarded as "unemployable."

Although an adequate understanding of emotional marginalization requires insight into the derivation of the concept of marginalization and its conceptual development, I will use rather broad conceptualizations of marginalization in this chapter, such as the notion of marginalization that Janet Billson (2005) has articulated. Although Billson explicitly refers to the notion of marginality rather than the notion of marginalization, I think it is fair to assume that a definition of *marginalization* can be derived from the former notion, that is, marginality. Billson (2005) explains that understandings of marginality now include more aspects than cultural marginality, an observation that I note earlier. According to Billson, structural marginality and social role marginality constitute the additional main aspects of marginality. As Billson explains it, "Social role marginality occurs when an individual cannot fully belong to a positive reference group because of age, timing, situational constraints, or when an occupational role is defined as marginal" (Billson 2005: 31). Her examples of social role marginality include women in professions dominated by men and adolescents, insofar as they are in between the social role of an adult and the social role of a child. Structural marginality, Billson writes, "refers to the political, social, and economic powerlessness of certain disenfranchised and/or disadvantaged segments within societies. It springs from location in the socioeconomic structure of society, rather than from cultural or social role dilemmas" (ibid.). In short, authors who write on marginalization regard it as a multidimensional phenomenon. The common ground between these dimensions is the limited access that marginalized people—including trans people and disabled people—have to specific goods, whether social, economic, structural, or some combination thereof.

Since marginalization occurs on all these different dimensions, it would be wrong to argue that only extreme or explicit cases of marginalization are in fact cases of marginalization. Rather, marginalization routinely takes place in subtle ways that may go unrecognized, even by the people marginalized. Members of a specific group do not necessarily know or realize how they perceive out-groups. That is, marginalization is often not based on a deliberate and explicit process; rather, we often contribute to the marginalization of other people through the production of habits and learned behaviors that are common in dominant societal groups. Everyday kinds of marginalization occur because people exhibit social norms and cultural values that have been learned over a long period of time, often unwittingly so. The next section of this chapter considers emotional marginalization in more detail.

Emotional Marginalization

Just as marginalization, in general, can be understood to mean limited access to specific goods (social, economic, structural, etc.), emotional marginalization can be understood as limited access to emotion, that is, limited access to the expression of emotions, the experience of emotions, or the recognition of emotions. For the purpose of understanding how marginalization takes place in and through emotions, let us consider an account that explains how emotion regulation may take place extrinsically. Myisha Cherry (2019) addresses three different stages of extrinsic emotional regulation: identification, selection, and implementation. Identification describes the stage of emotional regulation at which somebody recognizes that a person is "experiencing an emotion and evaluates whether the emotion needs to be regulated" (Cherry 2019: 3). If the evaluation process is concluded by formulating an extrinsic regulation goal—for example, a goal to calm someone down—this evaluation triggers the selection stage. At this stage of extrinsic emotional regulation, the perceiver selects the best strategy for regulating the emotion of the perceived person. We might, for instance, take into account how well we know the perceived person or any prior knowledge that we have about them. What follows next is the implementation stage of extrinsic emotional regulation, which simply describes the execution of the selected strategy (Cherry 2019).

Marginalization may take place at any of the three stages. First, we may ascribe the wrong emotion to the person that we perceive to be emoting, a wrong ascription based on identity factors such as disability, transness, gender, or race. This mistake potentially marginalizes the perceived person emotionally insofar as failure to recognize that they have emoted *X* (rather than *Y*) may thereby limit their access to emotion *X*. At the second stage of emotional regulation, we may respond with a regulation strategy that is based on the wrong emotion ascription or influenced by bias or discriminatory beliefs. We may, for example, decide to ignore an emotional reaction by someone that we perceive to be overreacting or we may react too strongly to someone that we experience as overreacting. Charlie Kurth (2022) argues that the current practices that we exhibit as reactions to the emotions of marginalized people are harmful and contribute to their marginalization. As Kurth writes, "we need to substantively rethink how we appraise and respond to the emotions felt by the marginalized members of our communities" (Kurth 2022: 2).

In addition to Cherry's proposed three stages, we need to take into account how, over a long span of time, social norms contribute to the variety of human emotions that are elicited in the first place. Given the marginalizations that we experience, norms may have an impact on how we express certain emotions, as well as condition which emotions get elicited and how these emotions are experienced. One might ask in what sense emotional marginalization may affect the emotions that we do experience. In classic emotion accounts, emotions are often said to be somewhat universal (for an extensive critique of classic emotion accounts, see Russell 1994, 2003). Surely, social factors affect emotion, but the effects largely revolve around appropriateness conditions, concerning the questions of how and when we express emotions. Nevertheless, some emotion theorists point to a deeper inculcation of norms around emotions, emphasizing that social norms compel us to adjust behaviors on the surface and influence which behaviors that we incorporate into our repertoire in the first place (cf. von Maur 2021). Shiloh Whitney (2018) argues that emotions are embodied and get their meaning through bodily manifestations that impact the felt experiences of others. Marginalized people, according to Whitney, may experience a failure of emotional uptake that involves, "*disabling affective sense-making* . . . by withholding its intercorporeal conditions [and] *dis-integrating the sense and the force of affects* from each other" (Whitney 2018: 495, emphasis in Whitney). Processes that disrupt the sense-making of emotions deprive emotions of their force and, thereby, limit the ways in which the people affected by the disruption (i.e., marginalized people) can experience certain emotions. As I have noted, extrinsic processes of emotion regulation in turn exacerbate this already limited access to emotional experience.

I have now established that emotional marginalization is the process through which one's access to emotions, emotional expressions, and emotion recognition is limited, as well as that emotional marginalization may occur on different levels of an emotion event. In order to understand emotional marginalization more adequately, I will now briefly look at *why* emotional marginalization occurs. The reasons for why emotional marginalization occurs serve to emphasize the long-lasting and deeply penetrating influence of social norms on emotions. In what follows, I will largely attribute the occurrence of emotional marginalization to existing social norms that serve to uphold and reproduce oppressive or marginalizing social structures. Although this methodological technique does not provide a lengthy and detailed answer to the question of why emotional marginalization occurs, it does emphasize the aspects of the question that are important to understand in light of this chapter. In order to proceed in this way, I will focus on examining social norms and their role in upholding social structures by considering a specific kind of social norm: gender norms.

The dominant binary genders of "man" and "woman" provide a structure according to which mainstream society categorizes all gender and sexual identities, a structure that has a tremendous impact on almost all areas of our everyday lives (cf. Butler 1990; Ahmed 2006). Each of the two genders is socialized to occupy roles, motives, goals, and self-schemas specific to it (Brody and Hall 2010), which in turn constitute a set of social norms around gender. Gendered socialization does not entail that someone who is assigned the sex/gender "male" at birth will be socialized as a "man." Rather, gendered socialization points to the systemic socialization that takes place on a societal level, establishing a gender system comparable to a social structure that serves to uphold social norms around gender (cf. also Hall and Briton 1993). People who do not follow these norms, that is, people whose genders do not comply with dominant social norms may be subject to penalties such as social exclusion and differential treatment. In short, they may be subjected to marginalization (cf. Billson 2005). Social norms about gender do not take place merely on an abstract level but rather have real consequences for people who are (seeming) norm subverters. Since social norms manifest in individual psychological processes (which is necessary if they are to be effective), women and men have typically been socialized to have disparate psychological landscapes, including roles, motives, goals, and self-schemas: that is, caretaking roles, intimacy motives, and interdependent self-schemas for women; and provider roles, control motives, and independent self-schemas for men (Cross and Madson 1997; cf. Haslanger 2007). Insofar as gender is present in virtually every aspect of our socialization that manifests in individual psychological processes, gender differences predictably also occur in emotional processes (Fischer 2000;

Fischer and Manstead 2000). Each of the two dominant gender identities gets associated with certain patterns of emotional functioning due to distinct social expectations, display rules, functions, motives, and goals that correspond to each identity. Thus, which emotional process and response occur in a given situation depends on the particular identity that is salient in a given context (Brody and Hall 2010).

Gender stereotypes can generate expectations about our interactions with partners of the same or other genders that, in turn, influence and elicit particular behaviors and emotional expressions (Hall and Briton 1993). For example, studies on blushing show gender differences in blushing frequency and intensity (Eickers 2022c; Crozier 2006; Darby and Harris 2013). Emotions such as "happiness, sadness, and fear are more typically associated with women, whereas anger and pride are more typically associated with men" (Fischer and LaFrance 2015: 23). Gender stereotypes also influence emotion recognition: in accordance with the stereotype that men are more aggressive than women, anger is more readily recognized in men (Becker et al. 2007; Öhman, Juth, and Lundqvist 2010). As Agneta Fischer and Marianne La France point out, "Stereotypes reflect descriptive norms but also generate prescriptive standards . . . about which emotions are seen as appropriate or desirable for whom" (Fischer and LaFrance 2015: 23). The ways in which gender influences emotion expression and recognition are highly dependent on other social and cultural factors insofar as gender norms are part of a larger network of interdependent social norms (cf. Fischer and Evers 2011; Brody, Hall, and Stokes 2016).

Gender norms, as part of a network of social norms that impact and structure our everyday lives, thus, play a role in how emotions are experienced, expressed, and recognized. Since norms around gender and emotion hinge on the respective dominant gender system (i.e., a binary gender system that distinguishes between "men" and "women"), gender norms contribute to the (emotional) marginalization of people who fall outside this binary system and people who fail to comply with the expectations that this system creates. In this context, it is important to note that many trans people occupy binary genders and do not fall outside of the binary system per se. However, they might in some sense fall outside of the binary system according to societal standards about gender. That is, we may speak of a binary and cisgendered gender system. Speaking of a binary and cisgendered gender system does not mean that only people outside of the system are (negatively) affected by the norms prevalent in this system. Quite the contrary: emotional marginalization also affects cis women and men, as my discussion of studies on emotion recognition and expression indicates. Gender norms around emotion, just like other social norms, become prescriptive through the social powers that they inhabit and thus serve to uphold standards around emotion to which many of us fail to comply. The production of conditions for access to, and appropriateness of, emotions fosters emotional marginalization.

In sum, we can roughly identify the following kinds of emotional marginalization:

(1) Emotional marginalization occurs at the stage of elicitation or emotion experience: we may be unable to describe or access our own emotion experience (in accordance with the given norm), or a negative emotion may be elicited due to a discriminatory situation.

(2) Emotional marginalization occurs at the stage of display: emotional display may be different from peers due to disability. That is, we may not display emotion in accordance with what is typically defined as emotion display for emotion *X*, or we may display emotion in accordance with internalized (gender) roles that do not match our outer presence.

(3) Emotional marginalization occurs at the stage of recognition: emotion recognition may be inhibited or filtered through one's marginalization status or experience. That is, an emotion display or performance may be rated as (too) intense, a wrong emotion may be attributed, or an emotion display may not be recognized as an emotion display.

In the following section, I focus on two aspects of social identity—disability and transness—in order to take a closer look at how pathologization of identities serves to uphold systems of normalcy and thereby creates emotional marginalization.

Emotional Marginalization of Disabled and Trans Identities

The specific social norms through which trans and disabled people, in particular, are marginalized vary, depending on a given person's experience of their trans and disabled identity, the intersections thereof, and pertinent intersections with other identity factors. The social norms that are typically relevant in this regard are norms about gender; norms about bodies in general; norms about transness, disability, and race; norms about contributions to social life; and so on. These norms, as I pointed out earlier, also generate more specific norms that manifest in psychological processes such as emotional processes. When reconsidering the historical pathologization of trans and disabled identities, it becomes clear that these norms intersect and serve to uphold systems of normalcy (cf. McRuer 2006). By examining the pathologization and marginalization of trans and disabled identities, we can gain insight into these systems of normalcy.

Let us recall the three different stages of emotion regulation that emotional marginalization comprises: identification, selection, and implementation (cf. Cherry 2019). On the basis of these stages of emotion regulation and the considerations about social norms in a prior section, I categorized emotional marginalization into three different stages: emotion experience, emotional display, and emotion recognition. In what follows, I lay out example cases of emotional marginalization of trans and disabled people in order to address emotional marginalization from an applied perspective. Thereby, I will look more closely at where and how emotional marginalization of trans and disabled identities takes place, as well as whether and how these examples are different from other cases of emotional marginalization, that is, cases that involve cis and nondisabled people. The example cases draw in part on a forthcoming article about emotional injustice that I have co-authored with Arina Pismenny and Jesse Prinz (Pismenny, Eickers, and Prinz, forthcoming). The relationship between emotional marginalization and emotional injustice is complex and deserves proper development. In this chapter, however, I treat these phenomena as related to each other, albeit distinct from each other.

Emotional Marginalization in Emotion Recognition and Display

Emotional marginalization in emotion recognition and display are best analyzed together as they are, ultimately, interdependent. Trans and disabled people may not display emotion in accordance with what is typically defined as the appropriate emotion display for emotion *X* in a given context or situation or may display emotion in accordance with internalized (gender) roles that do not match their outer appearance. In these cases, an emotion display or performance may be rated as (too) intense, a wrong emotion may be attributed, or an emotion display may not be recognized as an emotion display. Thereby, trans and disabled people become emotionally marginalized.

Problems of human interaction arise at the stage of emotion recognition due to the refusal by others to adequately recognize emotions or acknowledge them; that is, everyone may experience situations in which their emotions are not properly recognized or acknowledged. However, people with marginalized identities may experience refusal of emotion recognition more frequently and more starkly precisely due to their marginalization. Some examples may help to illustrate how the refusal of emotion recognition manifests for trans and disabled people. Consider how cis and nondisabled people ignore the emotional costs of behavior—such as unwanted attention and invasive questions (cf. Zurn 2018, 2021)—that objectifies trans and disabled people or discriminates against them in some other way, including pointing out someone's disability or gendered appearance, demanding explanations from trans people about their transness and from disabled people about their disability, and so on. These phenomena are not emotional phenomena per se (like, for example, an anger event); nevertheless, they may, due to their objectifying and discriminatory nature, elicit a negative or unpleasant emotion from a given trans or disabled person who is on the receiving end of them. The degree to which an instance of these phenomena is perceived as emotionally taxing will depend on the situational circumstances of the interaction, whether such interaction is recurring, the affected trans or disabled individual themselves, and so on. Regardless, if a trans or disabled person experiences any instance of such phenomena as emotionally taxing, we should consider the interaction as a part of the complex processes of emotional marginalization which reproduce the historical pathologization and objectification of trans and disabled identities (which are not mutually exclusive).

Unfounded emotion ascription can be identified at the other end of the spectrum of extremes in emotion recognition. Although assumptions about people's emotional or affective states may be made about virtually anyone and occur in all kinds of socio-emotional relations with other human beings, certain kinds of emotions seem to be specifically ascribed to disabled and trans individuals. These specific ascriptions may (and indeed often do) harm disabled and trans people, as well as contribute to their marginalization in other ways or exacerbate it (cf. Cherry 2019; Srinivasan 2018; Scheman 1980). When, for instance, trans and disabled people are framed as inspiring, brave, and courageous (i.e., ascribed a generally positive affective state), this affective ascription too often leads to emotional marginalization at the level of emotion recognition.

For example, disabled and trans people may be regarded as successful, or happy, or to have "made it" *despite* their disability or transness. Indeed, trans and disabled identities are particularly affected by this kind of emotional marginalization. While trans people often experience an ascription of positively connoted "courage" with respect to specific events—such as coming out or being visible—many disabled people experience these positive ascriptions when they perform mundane, everyday activities—such as engaging in conversation, buying groceries, choosing their own clothes, and so on—that nondisabled people had conceived to be impossible for them. In short, disability routinely gets associated with heroism and overcoming adversity (Schalk 2016; Shapiro 1994). Notice that these cases of "positive" ascription implicitly rely upon assumptions according to which disability and transness are considered obstacles or abnormalities that hinder one from leading a worthwhile life. Given that the process of ascribing the wrong emotion to someone or of misrecognizing or ignoring their emotions is often not a one-time event, but rather a longer-term process in which a general affective state of mind (positive or negative) is ascribed, trans and disabled people are routinely, and in an ongoing way, expected to suppress negative emotions and to be courageous, inspiring, and confident (Scott 2006).

Emotional marginalization can, however, take the form of a negative emotional or affective state ascription which may, paradoxically, share features in common with positive emotional/affective ascription. The assumption that trans and disabled people are generally unhappy due to their transness or disability, for example, presupposes the same pathologizing understanding of transness and disability as the unfounded positive emotion ascription, that is, relies on the assumption that trans and disabled people's emotional lives revolve exclusively around their transness and disability, thereby denying them access to a "normal" emotional life. With regard to trans identities, one of the extreme forms of emotional marginalization manifests as what is referred to as "transmedicalism." Transmedicalism assumes a presumptive unhappiness of trans people prior to medical transition because of a dissatisfaction with their own bodies; in other words, transmedicalism assumes that all trans people suffer from gender dysphoria that stems primarily from a hatred of their own bodies. Not a casual misunderstanding, transmedicalism manifests in some countries' laws with respect to trans people. In Germany, for example, health insurance policies stipulate that "suffering" is a criterion that must be met in order for trans people to obtain insurance coverage for trans surgeries and hormone replacement therapy (DGfS 2019). This requirement likely has its origins in the historical pathologization of trans identities in psychiatry.

Emotional marginalization of trans and disabled people is especially evident in overtly pathologizing contexts such as medicine and psychiatry. Generally speaking, marginalized people are more likely to be misdiagnosed in medical or psychiatric contexts (Glavinic 2010; Lev 2004). A famous example is Sigmund Freud's patient Dora. Dora consulted Freud after she was sexually assaulted and began to present various symptoms that she attributed to the assault. Instead of associating Dora's symptoms with the sexual assault (and possible related traumas), Freud diagnosed Dora with hysteria (Gay 2006) and attributed her symptoms to delusion. If we accept that Dora's symptoms were associated with the assault, however, we can identify how Freud misrecognized the cause of her symptoms by providing a naturalizing explanation for them. The explanation that he provided was naturalizing because he ignored the events that led to the symptoms, attributing them instead to Dora's mind itself (cf. Pismenny, Eickers, and Prinz, forthcoming).

Often within medical and psychiatric contexts, emotional processes are considered to be an aspect of someone's illness or disability or become understood as a new development of one's illness or disability. Rarely are the real-life and systemic circumstances that might have led to the emotional processes taken into account. By considering emotions merely as symptoms of certain illnesses or disabilities, the medical and psychiatric gaze distorts emotions. Depression, for example, is often treated as a mere chemical imbalance in the brain rather than as a mental and embodied reply to, say, systemic oppression. In this sense, we may consider certain emotional (phenomenological) experiences—such as specific experiences of depression—to be subject to emotional marginalization. Someone who is depressed may be marginalized because they do not engage in the same emotional display as their peers and by the very experience of depression itself. In the following section, I will look at the emotional marginalization of emotional (phenomenological) experience.

Emotional Marginalization in Emotion Experience

Among the phenomena that emotional marginalization in emotion experience encompasses is the inability to access or describe certain emotional experiences in accordance with a given norm. We may, for example, identify that we feel strange in and strange about a certain situation in which we experience a certain kind of mistreatment for the first time, yet seem to lack the concepts and scripts needed to properly describe the emotional experience that we are having. Some emotional experiences may be so restricted and inaccessible due to social norms that prescribe feeling rules and aptness conditions for a given emotion that we may never have the opportunity to experience the emotion. In addition, emotional marginalization in emotion experience can involve experience of certain negative emotions due to one's marginalization that people who are not marginalized will not experience, including emotions such as shame and guilt that stems from the discrimination that a trans person, disabled person, or other marginalized person experiences in a particular situation or that stems from repeated experiences of discrimination.

As noted, emotional marginalization in emotion experience can occur due to a person's lack of certain concepts or scripts to identify and properly experience certain emotions. Through emotion scripts that guide our emotional behavior, we can conform to the prevalent social norms around emotions (Eickers 2022a). A script for love tells us how love can be expressed, when love is appropriate, and when expressions of love are appropriate. Furthermore, a script for love may include very specific information about how love episodes unfold, such as when to engage in physical contact and when to engage in romantic (inter)action.

For someone whose disability is located in social communication, the lack of a script to identify and experience, say, love, can create problems. If I lack the respective emotion scripts, I need to understand why I am expected to express a specific emotion only in certain situations and not others, which will ultimately influence the way that I experience the emotion. My (unscripted) experience of love may be more encompassing than a socially prescribed script would recommend. For example, I may experience and express love toward the cashier that I see every other day or toward my favorite teacher in school, both of whom are not, according to the standard love script, ordinarily considered to be appropriate objects for expressions of my love. Equally, my experience of love may be less encompassing than a standard love script prescribes. For example, I may not be able to experience and express love toward my partner, yet experience an intimate friendship or experience exhilarating enjoyment in someone else's company. In other words, due to a lack of (insight into) the standard script for emotion *X*, my understanding and, thus, my experience of emotion *X* is different from the standard understanding and experience of emotion *X*. In some situations (such as the situations with the cashier or my teacher), this different experience of emotions may manifest as emotional marginalization: in such situations, my access to the standard experience of emotion *X* is limited and this limited access or non-access to the typical experience of emotion *X* becomes apparent (on a social level), which might, in turn, lead to emotion misrecognition.

The prevalence of a standard love script might also present an issue for someone who cannot identify with or does not match the stereotypical person engaged in romantic love that the love scripts prevalent in our society provide. According to social constructionist conceptions of love, romantic love depends on societal aspects (such as social status and looks) that render a person lovable in society's eyes (Averill 1980, 1985). That is, the standard love script also includes information about who we are supposed to find desirable and lovable (cf. Eickers 2022b; see also Brunning and McKeever 2021; Sedgwick 1990; Behrensen 2018). However, a disabled person might not be seen for who they are but rather as only an object of their disability. Likewise, a trans person might not be seen for who they are but rather only as an object of their transness.

Lenore Manderson and Susan Peake argue that disabled people are often perceived as pre-sexual and ungendered or perceived as a "third gender"

(Manderson and Peake 2005). Trans people, too, are often not implicated in people's sexual identities because they are perceived to be an "extra gender" or, like disabled people, are perceived to be a "third gender" (cf. Eickers 2022b). In other words, trans and disabled people are considered not to be as desirable and lovable as cis people because they are not conceived as implicated in specific sexual identities (such as homosexual or heterosexual). In romantic love and related affective phenomena, that is, marginalized identities may be constructed as an Other. Limited access to romantic love often entails limited access to sex and, thus, desexualization of disabled and trans people (e.g., Siebers 2012). Trans and disabled people may even be perceived as lacking romantic interests and sexual desires.

When we consider a given emotion—for example, romantic love—and affective phenomena that are related to the emotion—for example, sexual and romantic desires—the ways in which transness and disability intersect in addition to their mutual pathologization become especially evident. Manderson and Peake (2005) argue that disabled men often see themselves as less masculine than nondisabled men due to the ways in which gender and the binary gender system are currently constructed. As they explain: "Cultural constructions of masculinity and femininity are reinforced by changes in physicality: male disabled bodies are seen to lose hardness, containment, and control, becoming leaky, . . . indeterminate, liminal and soft, vulnerable to the stares of others" (Manderson and Peake 2005: 234). If disabled men are perceived as feminized due to their disability, gender and disability cannot be conceived as two entirely separate and separable social categories but rather must be seen as interdependent and mutually constitutive. If gender and disability are interdependent and co-constituting, the pathologization of transness is ultimately connected to the pathologization of disability.

Emotional marginalization in emotion experience can mean that one experiences certain negative emotions because of one's marginalization. This feature of emotional marginalization, although not specific to trans people or disabled people, is important to point to because of its connection to pathologization and discriminatory experiences that are likely rooted in pathologization. For example, shame or guilt may be elicited in discriminatory situations or situations that contribute to marginalization. A trans person or disabled person may, for example, feel shame or guilt because they are not considered desirable or they may feel guilty that they are unable to do certain things in accordance with a prevalent social norm. The negative emotional experiences that stem from one's marginalization may have associated long-lasting emotional effects or long-lasting moods and emotional states. For example, Jill Stauffer (2015) identifies a particular kind of loneliness that describes the feeling that one is unheard as a marginalized or mistreated person, especially after an injustice has been inflicted upon them. Stauffer calls this version of aloneness "ethical loneliness." Stauffer describes ethical loneliness in this way:

> Ethical loneliness is the isolation one feels when one, as a violated person or as one member of a persecuted group, has been abandoned by humanity, or by those who have power over one's life's possibilities. It is a condition undergone by persons who have been unjustly treated and dehumanized by human beings and political structures, who emerge from that injustice only to find that the surrounding world will not listen to or cannot properly hear their testimony—their claims about what they suffered and about what is now owed them—on their own terms. (Stauffer 2015: 1)

Stauffer explains that ethical loneliness may be experienced for a range of reasons, that is, can be experienced by someone because they experience some degree of marginalization or feel unheard, as well as experienced by someone who has been persecuted or dehumanized in more extreme ways. Feeling abandoned or pathologized in medical and psychiatric contexts would exemplify the experience of ethical loneliness, as Stauffer characterizes it. Due to their ongoing pathologization and consequent emotional and social marginalization, many trans people and disabled people are subject to ethical loneliness and related emotional phenomena that may intensify their marginalization.

Conclusion

In this chapter, I have examined a common form of marginalization that occurs due to the historical pathologization of trans people and disabled people and injustices that they currently confront, namely, emotional marginalization. I analyzed how the historical and ongoing pathologization of both trans and disabled people (and trans disabled people) through dominant social norms that uphold systems of normalcy contributes to their emotional marginalization. In order to advance my analysis, I identified three different stages at which emotional marginalization may take place, using the different stages of emotion regulation that Cherry (2019) proposes to do so: emotion experience, emotional display, and emotion recognition. Accordingly, emotional marginalization can be understood as limited access to emotion, that is, limited access to the expression of emotions, the experience of emotions, or the recognition of emotions. Trans and disabled people may not experience or display emotion in accordance with norms that define what is typical and apt for a specific emotion. This discrepancy impacts how and if the emotions of trans and disabled people are recognized. Trans and disabled people may lack the scripts or concepts to properly describe and access certain emotions, or their access to certain emotions may be restricted externally (such as lack of access to romantic love). Trans and disabled people may also experience negative emotions due to the specific kinds of pathologization to which they are subject to (e.g., shame or guilt).

If dominant norms about emotion, which disproportionately impact trans and disabled people in negative ways, continue to prevail, then common forms of emotional marginalization will also continue to prevail, including the emotional marginalization that trans and disabled people experience due to the myriad medical, psychiatric, administrative, and everyday practices that pathologize them.

References

Ahmed, Sara (2006), *Queer Phenomenology. Orientations, Objects, Others*, Durham and London: Duke University Press.

Archer, Alfred and Georgina Mills (2019), "Anger, Affective Injustice, and Emotion Regulation," *Philosophical Topics* 47 (2): 75–94.

Averill, James (1980), "A Constructivist View of Emotion," in Robert Plutchik and Henry Kellerman (eds.), *Emotion: Theory, Research and Experience, Vol. 1: Theories of Emotion*, 305–40, Cambridge: Academic Press.

Averill, James (1985), "The Social Construction of Emotion: With Special Reference to Love," in Kenneth J. Gergan and Keith E. Davis (eds.), *The Social Construction of the Person*, 89–109, New York: Springer.

Baàr, Monika (2017), "De-pathologizing Disability: Politics, Culture and Identity," *Neue Politische Literatur* 2: 281–304.

Becker, D. Vaughn, Douglas T. Kenrick, Steven L. Neuberg, K. C. Blackwell, and Dylan M. Smith (2007), "The Confounded Nature of Angry Men and Happy Women," *Journal of Personality and Social Psychology* 92 (2): 179–90.

Behrensen, Maren (2018), "Queer Bodies and Queer Love," in Adrienne M. Martin (ed.), *The Routledge Handbook of Love in Philosophy*, 93–104, New York and London: Routledge.

Bernt, Matthias and Laura Colini (2013), "Exclusion, Marginalization and Peripheralization. Conceptual Concerns in the Study of Urban Inequalities," Working Paper, No. 49, Leibniz Institute for Regional Development and Structural Planning.

Billson, Janet Mancini (2005), "No Owners of Soil. Redefining the Concept of Marginality," in Rutledge M. Dennis (ed.), *Marginality, Power and Social Structure: Issues in Race, Class and Gender Analysis*, 29–47, Amsterdam: Elsevier.

Brody, Leslie R. and Judith A. Hall (2010), "Gender, Emotion, and Socialization," in Joan C. Chrisler and Donald R. McCreary (eds.), *Handbook of Gender Research in Psychology. Volume 1: Gender Research in General and Experimental Psychology*, 429–51, New York: Springer.

Brody, Leslie R., Judith A. Hall, and L. R. Stokes (2016), "Gender and Emotion," in Lisa F. Barrett, Michael Lewis, and Jeannette M. Haviland-Jones (eds.), *Handbook of Emotions*, 4th ed., 369–92, New York: The Guilford Press.

Brunning, Luke and Natasha McKeever (2021), "Asexuality," *Journal of Applied Philosophy* 38 (3): 497–517.
Butler, J. (1990), *Gender Trouble: Feminism and the Subversion of Identity*, London and New York: Routledge.
Cherry, Myisha (2019), "Gendered Failures in Extrinsic Emotional Regulation; Or, Why Telling a Woman to 'Relax' or a Young Boy to 'Stop Crying Like a Girl' Is Not a Good Idea," *Philosophical Topics* 47 (2): 95–111.
Conrad, Peter (2007), *The Medicalization of Society. On the Transformation of Human Conditions into Treatable Disorders*, Baltimore and London: JHUP.
Cross, Susan and Laura Madson (1997), "Models of the Self: Self-construals and Gender," *Psychological Bulletin* 122: 5–37.
Crozier, W. Ray (2006), *Blushing and the Social Emotions. The Self Unmasked*, London: Palgrave Macmillan.
Darby, Ryan S. and Christine R. Harris (2013), "A Biosocial Perspective on Embarrassment," in W. Ray Crozier and Peter J. de Jong (eds.), *The Psychological Significance of the Blush*, 120–46, Cambridge: Cambridge University Press.
Decker, Hannah (2013), *The Making of DSM-III®. A Diagnostic Manual's Conquest of American Psychiatry*, New York: Oxford University Press.
Deutsche Gesellschaft fuer Sexualforschung (DGfS) (2019), *Geschlechtsinkongruenz, Geschlechtsdysphorie und Trans-Gesundheit: S3-Leitlinie zur Diagnostik, Beratung und Behandlung*. Available at: www.awmf.org/uploads/tx_szleitlinien/138-001l_S3_Geschlechtsdysphorie-Diagnostik-Beratung-Behandlung_2019-02.pdf (accessed May 20, 2023).
Eickers, Gen (2022a), "Coordinating Behaviors: Is Social Interaction Scripted?" *Journal for the Theory of Social Behaviour*, 1–15. https://doi.org/10.1111/jtsb.12357.
Eickers, Gen (2022b), "Being Trans, being Loved: Clashing Identities and the Limits of Love," in Arina Pismenny and Berit Borgaard (eds.), *The Moral Psychology of Love*, 171–90, Lanham: Rowman and Littlefield.
Eickers, Gen (2022c), "Approaches to Blushing: Context Matters," *Perspectiva Filosófica* 49 (5): 98–121.
Fischer, Agneta, ed. (2000), *Gender and Emotion: Social Psychological Perspectives*, Cambridge: Cambridge University Press.
Fischer, Agneta and Catharine Evers (2011), "The Social Costs and Benefits of Anger as a Function of Gender and Relationship Context," *Sex Roles: A Journal of Research* 65 (1–2): 23–34.
Fischer, Agneta and Marianne LaFrance (2015), "What Drives the Smile and the Tear: Why Women Are More Emotionally Expressive Than Men," *Emotion Review* 7 (1): 22–9.
Fischer, Agneta and Antony S. R. Manstead (2000), "The Relation between Gender and Emotion in Different Cultures," in Agneta Fischer (ed.), *Gender and Emotion: Social Psychological Perspectives*, 71–94, Cambridge: Cambridge University Press.
Gay, Peter (2006), *Freud: A Life for Our Time*, New York: W.W. Norton and Company.
Glavinic, Tonei (2010), "Research Shows Lack of Support for Transgender and Gender-Nonconforming Youth in U.S. School Systems," *Inquiries Journal* 2 (1). Available at: https://www.inquiriesjournal.com/articles/135/2/research-shows-lack-of-support-for-transgender-and-gender-nonconforming-youth-in-us-school-systems (accessed May 20, 2023).
Hall, Judith A. and Nancy J. Briton (1993), "Gender, Nonverbal Behavior, and Expectations," in Peter D. Blanck (ed.), *Interpersonal Expectations: Theory, Research, and Applications*, 276–95, Cambridge University Press.

Haslanger, Sally (2007), "'But Mom, Crop-Tops Are Cute!' Social Knowledge, Social Structure and Ideology Critique," *Philosophical Issues* 17: 70–91.
Hochschild, Arlie R. (1979), "Emotion Work, Feeling Rules, and Social Structure," *American Journal of Sociology* 85: 551–75.
Kurth, Charlie (2022), "Inappropriate Emotions, Marginalization, and Feeling Better," *Synthese* 2: 1–22.
Lev, Arlene I. (2004), *Transgender Emergence: Therapeutic Guidelines for Working with Gender-Variant People and Their Families*, New York: Routledge.
Leys, Ruth (2017), *The Ascent of Affect: Genealogy and Critique*, Chicago: University of Chicago Press.
Lutz, Catherine and Geoffrey M. White (1986), "The Anthropology of Emotions," *Annual Review of Anthropology* 15: 405–36.
Manderson, Lenore H. and Susan M. Peake (2005), "Men in Motion," in Carrie Sandahl and Philip Auslander (eds.), *Bodies in Commotion: Disability and Performance*, 230–42, The University of Michigan Press.
McRuer, Robert (2006), *Crip Theory. Cultural Signs of Queerness and Disability*, New York: New York University Press.
Munch-Jurisic, Ditte M. (2021), "Lost for Words: Anxiety, Well-Being, and the Costs for Conceptual Deprivation," *Synthese* 199 (5–6): 13583–600.
Öhman, Arne, Pernilla Juth, and Daniel Lundqvist (2010), "Finding the Face in a Crowd: Relationships between Distractor Redundancy, Target Emotion, and Target Gender," *Cognition and Emotion* 24 (7): 1216–28.
Park, Robert E. (1928), "Human Migration and the Marginal Man," *The American Journal of Sociology* 33 (6): 881–93.
Pismenny, Arina, Gen Eickers, and Jesse Prinz (forthcoming), "Emotional Injustice," *Ergo: An Open Access Journal of Philosophy*.
Russell, James A. (1994), "Is there Universal Recognition of Emotion from Facial Expression: A Review of the Cross-Cultural Studies," *Psychological Bulletin* 115: 102–41.
Russell, James A. (2003), "Core Affect and the Psychological Construction of Emotion," *Psychological Review* 110: 145–72.
Sauer, Arn T. and Timo O. Nieder (2019), "We care. Überlegungen zu einer bedarfsgerechten, transitionsunterstützenden Gesundheitsversorgung," in Max N. Appenroth and Maria do Mar Castro Varela (eds.), *Trans and Care: Trans Personen zwischen Selbstsorge, Fürsorge und Versorgung*, 75–101, Bielefeld: Transcript Verlag.
Schalk, Sami (2016), "Reevaluating the Supercrip," *Journal of Literary and Cultural Disability Studies* 10 (1): 71–86. https://doi.org/10.3828/jlcds.2016.5.
Scheman, Naomi (1980), "Anger and the Politics of Naming," in Sally McConnell-Ginet, Ruth Borker, and Nelly Furman (eds.), *Women and Language in Literature and Society*, 22–35, New York: Praeger.
Scott, Catherine (2006), "Time Out of Joint: The Narcotic Effect of Prolepsis in Christopher Reeve's Still Me," *Biography: An Interdisciplinary Quarterly* 29 (2): 307–28.
Sedgwick, Eve K. (1990), *Epistemology of the Closet*, Berkeley: University of California Press.
Shapiro, Joseph P. (1994), *No Pity: People with Disabilities Forging a New Civil Rights Movement*, New York: Times Books.
Siebers, Tobin (2012), "A Sexual Culture for Disabled People," in Robert McRuer and Anna Mollow (eds.), *Sex and Disability*, 37–53, New York: Duke University Press.

Silva, Laura (2021), "Is Anger a Hostile Emotion?," *Review of Philosophy and Psychology*, 1–20.
Srinivasan, Amia (2018), "The Aptness of Anger," *The Journal of Political Philosophy* 26 (2): 123–44.
Stauffer, Jill (2015), *Ethical Loneliness. The Injustice of Not Being Heard*, New York: Columbia University Press.
Von Maur, Imke (2021), "The Epistemic Value of Affective Disruptability," *Topoi* 41: 859–69.
Whitney, Shiloh (2018), "Affective Intentionality and Affective Injustice: Merleau-Ponty and Fanon on the Body Schema as a Theory of Affect," *The Southern Journal of Philosophy* 56 (4): 488–515.
World Health Organization (2004), *International Statistical Classification of Diseases and Related Health Problems (ICD)*, 10th Revision. Available at: https://apps.who.int /iris/ handle /10665 /42980 (accessed May 20, 2023).
World Health Organization (2018), *International Classification of Diseases for Mortality and Morbidity Statistics (ICD)*, 11th Revision. Available at: www.icd.who. int/browse11/l-m/en (accessed May 20, 2023).
Young, Iris M. (1990), *Justice and the Politics of Difference*, Princeton: Princeton University Press.
Zurn, Perry (2018), "Puzzle Pieces. Shapes of Trans Curiosity," *APA Newsletter: LGBTQ Issues in Philosophy* 18 (1): 10–16.
Zurn, Perry (2021), *Curiosity and Power: The Politics of Inquiry*, Minneapolis: University of Minnesota Press.

PART IV

DISABLING NORMATIVITIES

17 A CRIP READING OF FILIPINO PHILOSOPHY

ÉLAINA GAUTHIER-MAMARIL

Introduction

This chapter is my *mestiza* understanding of philosophy of disability, as it is produced at present. The chapter is *mestiza* because I am a disabled Filipinx, a half-Filipina, half-white French Canadian. It is *mestiza* because I have settler privilege. It is *mestiza* because I have "passing" privilege with respect to disability and race. But, mostly, the chapter is *mestiza* because I cannot approach a philosophy of disability, let alone create within it, in any other way. The chapter is my inchoate and exciting contribution to the discourse on what it is to conceive of disability philosophically. I want to draw you, my reader, into this incompleteness, this ambiguity and in-betweenness. Inspired by Gloria Anzaldúa's "*mestiza* consciousness" (Anzaldúa 1987), I echo Filipino philosopher Leonardo N. Mercado's point about lateral thinking (Mercado 1994: 45-6). By working through the complicated questions of "what is crip philosophy?" and "what is Filipino philosophy?" together, I hope to identify and represent some of the many possibilities of dialogue between these hitherto separate domains and open windows on horizons for a crip Filipino philosophy of disability.

The figure of the *mestiza* is complicated and not innocent. In the context of the history of the Philippines, the mixed-race people that resulted from the union between Spanish colonizers, Chinese traders, and American invaders and indigenous peoples have held an ambiguous relationship with power and colonial violence (Tan 1986; Goh 2008). My project in this chapter is, paraphrasing Anzaldúa, to take inventory of what was inherited, what was acquired, and what was imposed when it comes to thinking about the intersection between crip and Filipino philosophy (Anzaldúa 1987: 82). One of the obstacles that philosophy of disability encounters and aims to undermine is the entrenched belief that disability is "natural." On the other hand, the very quest for a "Filipino philosophy" is rooted, though not uncritically, in a nationalistic and naturalizing project. For example, Filipino philosophical traditions call on a "Filipino way" of thinking that depends on contentious anthropological and sociological analyses. As Mercado has pointed out, nevertheless, entertaining a Filipino specificity can be extremely fruitful:

> Does Filipino logic follow lateral thinking? Scientists will have to find out, but we are inclined to suspect that lateral thinking is the answer. Both induction and deduction are complementary ways of arriving at the same truth. The Filipino way of looking at the truth illustrates his [*sic*] intersubjective way of thinking. . . . Objectivism has a totally falsified conception of truth, by exalting what we can know and prove, while covering up with ambiguous utterances all that [we] know and cannot prove, even though the latter knowledge underlies, and must ultimately set its seal to, all that we can prove. In trying to restrict our minds to the few things that are demonstrable, and therefore explicitly dubitable, it has overlooked the a-critical choices which determine the whole being of our minds and has rendered us incapable of acknowledging these vital choices. (Mercado 1994: 45–6)

Philosophy of disability is in many respects wrestling with the ableism of the discipline of philosophy and the attachment of the discipline to Western reason. Filipino philosophy, too, is wrestling with philosophy's attachment to Western reason in addition to the way that it negotiates the colonized history of the geographical region. In this chapter, I want to explore these intersections and divergences.

I endeavor to do so by analyzing Jeremiah Reyes's article "*Loób* and *Kapwa:* An Introduction to a Filipino Virtue Ethics" through a crip reading lens. In other contexts, I have used Reyes's article to discuss power as a virtue, identifying how Reyes's work can be fruitful for an analysis of feminist relational ethics (Gauthier-Mamaril 2022). In this chapter, I engage in a cripistemological dialogue with Reyes's article to demonstrate how Filipino philosophical concepts can contribute to philosophy of disability.

In many ways, Reyes's work represents a long tradition of philosophy in the Philippines insofar as it draws on the writing of Thomas Aquinas. A legacy of the Spanish colonial rule and the presence of Dominican friars on the isles, Thomism continues to leave its mark on Filipino philosophy departments in the present. Like Reyes, I was philosophically raised by Thomists, though thousands of miles away in a small university in Canada run by Dominican friars. Although some of the friars read Aquinas with a Derridean lens, they were Thomists nonetheless. The commonalities between Reyes and I extend even further because Reyes engages with virtue ethics, a task with which I am intimately familiar given my research on feminist theory and bioethics.

If to "do philosophy" is, as Roland Theuas D. S. Pada says, to "engage in philosophical dialogue" (Pada 2014), in this chapter I will "do crip Filipino philosophy" with you, in part through an analysis of Reyes's article. I propose the following roadmap for the chapter: In the first section, I will outline the Filipino notions of *loób* and *kapwa*, as well as argue that they are foundational ontological concepts that allow us to understand individual agency as intrinsically relational within this Filipino context. My aim is to present the onto-ethical framework that *loób* and *kapwa* create as one in which the possibilities of crip agency are accommodated. The second section is devoted to the analysis of four of the five "Filipino virtues" that Reyes derives from the relation between *loób* and *kapwa*. These four virtues address moral relations that range from familial responsibility to political engagement. I will highlight the ways in which each of the virtues both opens possibilities for a critical philosophy of disability and create tensions with the aims of such a way of thinking about disability. Finally, the third section considers the fifth Filipino virtue that Reyes identifies—namely, *lakas-ng-loób/Bahala na*—and the ways in which it can be understood to overlap with the notions of crip hacking and crip time. To increase the accessibility of my chapter, I have provided an appendix that comprises a pronunciation guide of the italicized Tagalog words that appear throughout the chapter.

Loób and *Kapwa*: Finding Relational Common Ground

Reyes identifies the concepts of *loób* (relational will) and *kapwa* (together-with-the-other) as two pillars of Filipino virtues that can be compared and contrasted with Thomistic virtue ethics. I use Reyes's identification of Filipino virtues to discuss the possibilities that are opened and the tensions that are created when we approach Reyes's conceptual taxonomy from a crip perspective. In line with my reading of Spinoza (Gauthier-Mamaril 2021), that is, I join Jasbir K. Puar who writes: "I want cripistemologies to articulate not only alternative epistemologies, but also ontologies, challenging the limits of intersectional analyses and noting the disciplinary character of any subject-driven endeavor" (Puar 2014: 155). In other words, I will treat *loób* and *kapwa* as ontological terms relating to agenthood that have epistemological and ethical consequences.

In the following three subsections of the chapter, I argue that *loób* and *kapwa* explain a kind of relational agency that is relevant to both the elaboration of Filipino philosophy and the practice of philosophy of disability. In the first subsection, I define *loób* and its particular role within the history of thought in the Philippines. I go on to define *kapwa*, drawing the conclusion, in the third subsection, that *loób* and *kapwa* present a fruitful foundation for crip Filipino philosophical reflections.

Defining *Loób*

Reyes tells us that the literal translation of the term *loób* is "inside" (Reyes 2015: 153), which can be used in relation to objects such as pots or cabinets. When the term *loób* is applied to human individuals, it is usually understood as "the will." Yet the history of the concept is important to bear in mind because, as Reyes makes clear, *loób* has evolved from the mixing of tribal animist worldviews and teachings from Spanish Catholicism rather than the Cartesian will, or for that matter, the Kantian will. Because concepts such as body/mind dualism and atomistic individualism did not become widely spread in the Philippines until the end of the nineteenth century when the United States took up the mantle of colonialism in this region from the Spaniards, a Filipino sense of identity and agency was thinkable outside of the category of the (Cartesian) "self." To quote José de Mesa, "*loób* apart from referring to the core of personhood, also states what kind of core that is in relationship. *Loób*, one may say, is a relational understanding of the person in the lowland Filipino context" (De Mesa 1987: 46). In other words, *loób* expresses the concept of relational personhood without appeal to an autonomous or rational self. In fact, *loób* is characterized by becoming-in-relation, that is, by its intrinsic and ontological relationality. This etymology of the term *loób* means, furthermore, that the concept *loób* does not result due to the segregation of emotion and intuition from the realm of rationality. With respect to the concept of *loób*, Reyes notes, no distinction is made between the powers of the soul (including reason) and the appetitive powers of the will and the senses, as is made in Aquinas's moral philosophy (Reyes 2015: 155).

The apparent ambivalence toward reason—which the absence in Filipino philosophy of a distinction between reason and the senses seems to imply—has been used to argue that there is in fact no such thing as Filipino philosophy (Pada 2014). I contend, however, that a more holistic approach to agency and, indeed, to the agent themself resonates with the aims of a critical philosophy of disability. The relational stance of *loób* does not preclude rationality; nor, however, does the stance give rationality automatic priority as we in the West have been trained to do. One's *loób* expresses itself in practice, through the acts of ordinary life, and by living in relationship with others. In this way, the relational stance of *loób* is similar to grassroots feminist ethics that propose ethical norms based on actual human relationships rather than the application of norms to actions in a top-down approach. As much as the *loób* describes the agency of one soul or one individual, it can only be defined in relation with the other, that is, with *kapwa*.

Defining *Kapwa*

Kapwa, like *loób*, is difficult to translate into European languages such as English. It means "others," a term that is laden with mountains of philosophical baggage. Between Emmanuel Levinas's Other, the *autrui* of French existentialists, and Anglo-American individualistic political philosophy, the self/other dichotomy is part of the majority of modern Western philosophical edifices. In the Filipino context, however, *kapwa* does not signal separateness or outsideness but rather expresses the concept of "self-in-the-others" or "together-with-the-person" (Reyes 2015: 156). To evaluate one's *loób* with respect to how well or how poorly it relates to *kapwa* is to take togetherness or relationality as the core priority of ethics. And, given how much *loób* depends on *kapwa* conceptually, I would argue that it presents a core ontological map.

The relationaliity of *kapwa* is not without its drawbacks. As colonized peoples, the native inhabitants of the Philippine Islands were repeatedly depicted as naturally subservient and docile. Even as recently as the 1960s, anthropologist and sociologist Frank Lynch proposed "smooth interpersonal relationship" (SIR) as the highest value of Filipinos (Lynch 1962; Reyes 2015: 155), perpetuating a naturalized conception of Filipinos as upholding the status quo at all cost, prioritizing community harmony over individual agency. This characterization is harmful for multiple reasons, not least: it denies agency to Filipino peoples because they value the recognition of shared identity. In other words, as long as the importance given to *kapwa* is viewed through the lens of a reason-first conception of agency, it will appear as a disadvantage. However, the concept of *kapwa* did not evolve in a context where rationality is the gatekeeper of agency, therefore what it offers us today is a different expression of relational personhood.

Relational Agency is Important to Philosophy of Disability Too

Although it might be difficult to think of agency founded in relationality, it is not impossible and should be understood as a goal of philosophy of disability. Thus, a conceptual framework (like that of Filipino philosophy) in which personhood is defined outside of the usual parameters of rational capacity holds considerable promise for a (Filipino) philosophy of disability. The logic of colonialism encompasses the social and institutional devaluation of marginalized bodyminds, including the bodyminds of disabled people who operate on crip time. I want, therefore, to show that the person-with-others or one-within-otherness version of the agent that the *loób-kapwa* combination proposes can contribute significantly to the elaboration of a philosophy of disability ontology that prioritizes alternative modes of power and agency.

Sources of Possibilities and Tensions

In my *mestiza* reading of Reyes, I was struck by all the possibilities that I envisioned could bloom between Filipino concepts and philosophy of disability. Nevertheless, I also perceived possible points of tension that I want to render in this chapter. The two conceptual pairings that I analyze next, namely, *kagandahang-loób/utang-na-loób* and *pakikiramdam/hiya*, represent two concentric circles of relation: the familial or close kin circle and the larger social circle of the community, respectively. Both my interpretation of Filipino concepts and Reyes's interpretation of them challenge these boundaries. I take my challenge in the direction of crip philosophy and explore how these Filipino concepts interact with crip concerns, whereas Reyes's challenge remains largely wedded to comparisons between Filipino concepts and Thomistic virtue ethics. I think that the tensions and obstacles involved in a union between crip philosophy and Filipino philosophy are not insurmountable. Indeed, my argument is that the four virtues that I outline in what follows can be used in interesting crip ways. I do not wish to have the last word on whether or not the four virtues are completely compatible, but rather hope that my fellow scholars will find this topic important enough to continue research on crip philosophy and the four virtues of Filipino philosophy. My aim in this chapter is a modest one, namely, to give an account of an interaction between these two sets of concepts, regardless of whether that leaves us with some unresolved questions.

Kagandahang-loób and *Utang-na-loób*

The first pairing that I will examine is *kagandahang-loób* and *utang-na-loób*, or, in other, Anglicized words, "beauty of will" and "debt of will." *Kagandahang-loób* and *utang-na-loób* are complementary ethical terms that can be roughly translated as selfless benevolence and indebtedness, respectively. The terms capture the two extreme ends of an asymmetrical power relation. In fact, *kagandahang-loób* is often associated with motherly love and devotion for her child, who, in return, has *utang-na-loób*, an unpayable debt of gratitude, for her. Historically, these terms have been applied to familial and kin links, although Reyes, for one, argues that the Christian tradition sought to widen the ethical reach of the terms (Reyes 2015: 160). Reyes also disagrees with thinkers who dub *kagandahang-loób* as a "feminine" concept akin to Nel Noddings's feminist care ethics (De Castro 2000). For Reyes, this claim ignores the socio-historical context of the term and the concept that it signifies. I agree with Reyes's objection in this context and would add that to approach *kagandahang-loób* through the mother-child lens imposes rather arbitrary limits on what is a selfless definition of responsibility: *kagandahang-loób* is probably neither Kantian disinterestedness nor emotional love. Like everything else related to the *loób, kagandahang-loób* is invested in fostering and protecting a worthwhile relationship through practice, not through moral reflection or feeling.

While responsible devotion is practiced in a relationship by the person in it who has more to give, the receiver of care or vulnerable person in the relationship reciprocates by expressing *utang-na-loób* to their caregiver. An example of this reciprocity is a child's respect for their parents' wishes and their attempt to "make their family proud" by communicating how grateful they are for their life and upbringing. Another example is a debtor who voluntarily pays interest on the loan that they owe a friend as a way to express their gratitude for the relationship of trust that made the loan possible. Just as the mother-child relationship is not the only way to consider *kagandahang-loób, utang-na-loób* need not be understood as unidirectional. Insofar as all of us are in multiple relational webs, there is no one way to care for and be cared for; our relationships with one another are dynamic and they evolve over time and space.

Possibilities

This responsibility-for/gratitude-toward pairing opens up multiple possibilities for philosophy of disability, especially if we explore the different modality of caring relationships beyond blood kin. I want to emphasize the absence of any reference to pure reason or sentimentality in both *kagandahang-loób* and *utang-na-loób*. As I have noted earlier, *loób* does not involve rationality as a core criterion and there seems to be no explicit injunction to be dispassionate in one's relation to *kapwa*. Rather, what is important is that the relation remains harmonious, which might involve reason but does not depend on it. Caring for the *loób-kapwa* relationship also need not be motivated by emotion or affect. One should, for example, express *utang-na-loób* because it is an ethical practice that acknowledges and reinforces community relations rather than because one is grateful. In a way, *kagandahang-loób* and *utang-na-loób* prompt us to consider radical dependence beyond ideas of desert: because we live in community, we all should be responsible for one another and grateful to one another.

Tensions

Like the figure of the *mestiza*, the concepts of indebtedness and gratitude are not innocent. Within the framework of settler colonialism, for example, narratives of the grateful/ungrateful native have been used to justify all kinds of violence and to deny entire peoples agency. From an intersectional feminist perspective, women have, for centuries, been asked to be grateful for their enforced subservient social roles; Black and brown people are supposed to be grateful that they are allowed to exist; and disabled people are expected to rejoice that society diligently tries to discover ways to fix them. The charitable model of disability provides excellent examples of how someone's "selfless sense of responsibility" harms another's agency when unconditional gratitude is expected. Therefore, we must recognize that *kagandahang-loób* and *utang-na-loób* can be used to support disempowering relationships in the name of respecting *kapwa*.

However, this disempowering interpretation of these terms is not inevitable. In the spirit of bringing my *mestiza* inquisitiveness to this topic, I cannot leave at the door my hermeneutical resistance to the concept of uncritical indebtedness. Then again, that is not what *utang-na-loób* implies. Although Lynch's concept of SIR has been used to depict a pliable and docile Filipino identity, placing relationality at the core of personhood and agency does not necessarily require that critical thought be relinquished but rather that we give priority to the shared part of our agency. Giving the shared part of our agency priority over the unique and particular part of it will require that everyone who has long bathed in the waters of atomistic individualism do some deep conceptual reconfiguring. In short, these Filipino concepts do not tell us in advance what kind of relationship is worth protecting other than the relationships that involve vulnerability and dependence beyond transactional relations, a focus that is extremely relevant to the philosophy of disability.

Pakikiramdam and *Hiya*

In this section, I will analyze the concept pairing of *pakikiramdam* (relational sensitivity or prudence) and *hiya* (shame or embarrassment). Reyes links both of these concepts to social self-restraint, empathy, and "emotional intelligence" (Reyes 2015: 163). *Pakikiramdam* in particular concerns "reading the room," that is, one's awareness of or attunement to the social dynamics of a given time or place before one acts. For these reasons, Reyes compares *pakikiramdam* to the Thomist virtue of prudence, a virtue that is useful when one has only indirect access to power. With *pakikiramdam*, we can see, once again, how a Filipino ethical concept that involves a considerable amount of contextual awareness can be (and has been) used to claim that Filipinos are too sensitive and that they care too much about public opinion. Among other things, such a claim disregards the extent to which social praise and blame are important to most ethical theories, including Kant's. Indeed, members of marginalized and socially disempowered groups in philosophy can learn a great deal about how power operates in mainstream philosophy by considering the ways in which prudence is mobilized in ethical theories.

The concept of *hiya* is more difficult to grapple with than the concept of *pakikiramdam*. Reyes makes a distinction between "passive" and "active" *hiya*, or shame that one suffers versus the self-control that motivates us to avoid causing *hiya* to others (Reyes 2015: 164). I consider shame to be a fickle concept: it can be extremely useful, extremely damaging, or both simultaneously. When we consider *hiya* in the context of a relationality that is placed at the core of our ethical practice, we can recognize that *hiya* would serve as a nonrational stopgap to prevent us from destroying community relations out of recklessness or imprudence. One could argue that feeling shamed by one's close friends and family often more effectively motivates behavioral changes than a clear but impersonal rational argument. Historically, however, shame has also been directed at marginalized people in oppressive ways, such as conveying to them that they are defective or dangerous, that they do not belong in public spaces, and that their desires and needs are invalid. Thus, out of all of Reyes's discussions of Filipino concepts, it is the discussion of the concept of *hiya* that gives me the most pause.

Possibilities

With respect to agency, there are (as I have suggested) very interesting points of intersection between *pakikiramdam*, *hiya*, and the aims of a philosophy of disability. Whereas *kagandahang-loób* and *utang-na-loób* are originally directed at immediate relations with the people closest to us, *pakikiramdam* and *hiya* offer the opportunity to think of relationality in a broader sense. Indeed, the concept of *hiya* can be used to discuss our relation to nonhuman animals and the environment by prompting us to consider the strength of all the connections that support our communities. The kind of prudential practices that *pakikiramdam* and *hiya* recommend are less concerned with personal moral valor than with acknowledgment and maintenance of webs of support. This framework is particularly instructive for a philosophy of disability that aims to be anchored in a relational ontology. The framework represents interdependence and the need for mutual aid as the foundation of ethics rather than merely as effective means in special circumstances only. More than that, the framework explicitly values relationality rather than casts it as a weakness or the inability to be a "fully-fledged" agent.

Tensions

One way in which to redeem the concepts of *pakikiramdam* and *hiya* in a crip context is to view them as possible support for solidarity. Both intra-group relationships within disabled communities and inter-group relations with institutions and able-bodied agents require boundary practices. I understand a boundary practice to signify the recognition and expression of the limits of particular instantiations of relationality. In order for me to be in solidarity with blind and visually impaired people, for example, I need to acknowledge that our experiences and needs do not overlap completely. As an Asian-Canadian disabled person who wishes to act in solidarity with Black and Indigenous disabled individuals and communities, I must "check myself" before I act. That is, I must think critically about, for example, whether I have taken up discursive space on their behalf that Black and Indigenous disabled people themselves should have occupied, whether I have misrepresented their issues because of my own social privilege, and so on. Although we can (and often should) conceive of relational sensitivity and shame as mechanisms of assimilation and disempowerment, we can also use them as safeguards against our impulse to center ourselves and overlook critical differences in our effort to create communities for ourselves.

Embracing Uncertainty

In this last section of my chapter, I want to turn to the fifth "Filipino virtue" that Reyes examines, *lakas-ng-loób*. Doing so will enable me to return to a statement that I made at the outset of this chapter, according to which *loób* and *kapwa* should be considered as ontological terms as well as ethical terms. On my understanding of it, the concept of *lakas-ng-loób*, or "strength-of-will," is a worldview, a way of relating to time and becoming by embracing uncertainty. While some philosophers have equated this attitude with fatalism (Bostrom 1968), I want to demonstrate how it can intersect with the concepts of crip time and crip futurism in a way that maps out a different kind of relational agency.

Lakas-ng-loób is often linked to the expression *Bahala na*, which roughly translates into English as "God willing," signifying everything from optimism to fatalism, passing through indifference and irresponsibility. Note that like all of the Filipino concepts that I have discussed in this chapter, the concept of *Bahala na* is a double-edged sword: it can be used as an excuse to reinforce the status quo or as a tool to bring about change. I will not dwell here on the disempowering aspects of fatalism that have been attributed to *lakas-ng-loób* and, by implication, *Bahala na*. Rather, I want to focus on how *lakas-ng-loób* and *Bahala na* can fruitfully intersect with crip ontology.

Lakas-ng-loób can, according to Reyes, be compared to the Thomist virtue of courage, specifically with respect to courage for the *kapwa*, not for ourselves (Reyes 2015: 166). It implies sacrificing oneself for the community in a way that cannot be disentangled from the Christian idea of ultimate sacrifice. This meaning, in and of itself, may not seem appealing to disability theorists or indeed most feminists; there is no shortage of ethical discourses that encourage us to sacrifice ourselves "for the greater good," to view ourselves as a burden, and so on. Yet, *lakas-ng-loób* is primarily directed at the preservation of community relations rather than the agent's moral goodness. In this sense, (self)sacrifice is not a goal in itself, but rather another tool in our relational ethical toolbox. Incidentally, Reyes's examples for this "virtue" relate to the well-being of the nation and thus he names celebrated Filipino revolutionaries and political dissidents José Rizal and Ninoy Aquino, further expanding the scope of ethical webs (167). I will argue that *lakas-ng-loób*, when taken together with *Bahala na* as an ontological worldview, provides us with examples of crip hacking and resistance.

The notion of courage raises alarm bells for my disabled bodymind. It seems dangerously close to "resilience" and the pervasive inspirational supercrip narratives that celebrate disabled peoples' strength (and continued existence) in order to avoid responding to our needs. Given the socio-historical context of *lakas-ng-loób*, however, to have courage can also be understood to mean to be motivated to resist oppressive structures. As much as *loób* and *kapwa*'s emphasis on inherent relationality can be used to justify prioritizing social harmony over change, the *loób*'s effort to benefit the *kapwa* takes shape in *lakas-ng-loób* when the community is threatened. In other words, relationality does not necessarily involve uniformity but rather reminds us that "together-with-others" is our ontological reality and that which to we should aspire, as well as what we should protect. In short, we must resist the forces that threaten our shared selves. As disabled people, we are constantly faced with a world that wants us to change, to leave, to not exist. When we dare to reject the frameworks that deem us essentially unworthy of life, power, and agency, we practice resistance. Although we experience resistance individually, a relational philosophy of disability would argue that *lakas-ng-loób* is both practiced for the good of the community and experienced communally through communal action. Although Reyes heralds the resistance of individuals, we would be justified in thinking that insofar as the agent is intrinsically relational, resistance is also an intrinsically relational endeavor.

If we recall, *pakikiramdam* is an indirect strategy to achieve relational harmony. In other words, *pakikiramdam* relies on empathy and consideration rather than on confrontation, the latter of which is a tool that only the powerful can wield carelessly. If we imagine someone who exhibits *lakas-ng-loób* and *pakikiramdam*, we have the makings of crip hacking. In their "Crip Technoscience Manifesto" (CTM), Aimi Hamraie and Kelly Fritsch (2019) discuss the history of feminist hacking and how the concept of repurposing, diverting, and remaking technology is an important expression of disabled agency. The article also cites Remi Yergeau's (2014) "criptastic hacking" as a "disability-led movement, rather than a series of apps and patches and fixes designed by non-disabled people who cannot even be bothered to talk with disabled people." The CTM is primarily concerned with material hacks or changes to the material world that disabled people have enacted; however, I see no reason why the term *hacking* cannot be applied to social and relational situations as well. In this sense, a disabled person who practices *lakas-ng-loób* and *pakikiramdam* can hack through oppressive situations by drawing upon their crip support systems in order to preserve crip community. The sacrifice (or, at least, the willingness to sacrifice) implied in *lakas-ng-loób* need not be *self*-sacrifice, especially given that there is no *loób* separated from *kapwa*. Rather, the "sacrifice" might be willingness to relinquish oneself of the goodwill and protection of people who uphold oppressive social, political, and institutional norms in order to preserve alternative communities. Crip hacking becomes a necessity because crip lives are systematically deemed disposable in our societies; therefore, hacking is always a rebellious act. I want to suggest that by linking hacking with *lakas-ng-loób* and Reyes's proposal of "Filipino virtues," we can arrive at crip Filipino hacking, which will always be a rebellious *practice*. As Yergeau states, hacking is a dynamic movement that needs to be continuously recharged and renewed. In short, choosing to hack is choosing *lakas-ng-loób* as a way to express community activism and solidarity.

In drawing this chapter to a close, I would like to address the possible conceptual alliance between *Bahala na* and crip time. Both concepts function against or outside of the confines of linear time and theories of progress. *Bahala na* exhibits a trust that the universe will eventually balance itself out and that neither good times nor hard times are eternal. "Crip time," as defined by Alison Kafer, "is flex time not just expanded, but exploded; it requires reimagining our notions of what can and should happen in time, or recognizing how expectations of 'how long things take' are based on very particular minds and bodies" (Kafer 2013: 27). In this sense, *Bahala na* seems to offer a more interesting temporal framework than a progressive capitalist timeline because it accommodates variable, flexible, and dynamic relationships to temporal existence and activity. Although *Bahala na* has been critiqued as a cultural excuse to relinquish agency, this criticism is true only if we assume a very narrow understanding of what is required for one to "take action." For example, disabled life has taught me that more often than not, refusal to act in conformity with "straight time"—for example, by resting—is the most empowering choice that I can make in some situations. *Bahala na* is not necessarily fatalist but rather can be read as determinist, encompassing the belief in a holistic worldview where my acts are importantly embedded in and supported by webs of relations with other humans, rocks, and trees. Much like *pakikiramdam* and *hiya*, *Bahala na* exhorts us to understand our agency within its limits so as to better learn how to flourish in our shared identity.

Conclusion

We have now followed down the path that Reyes carved out for us, examining the essential relationality of the *loób/kapwa* pairing, a conceptual cluster that defies dualistic and individualistic logic to inform onto-ethical relational practices. I have analyzed this enumeration of "Filipino virtues" in ways that highlight when they intersect with and buck against crip philosophical concerns, giving special emphasis to the construction of an agency without the Western self. By considering the virtue of *lakas-ng-loób/Bahala na*, I explained how it provides a useful framework within which to define and explain crip hacking and crip time.

In short, this chapter is the result of a crip reading of concepts in Filipino philosophy, feminist ethics, and virtue ethics; my crip *mestiza* reading. It takes pride in not being definitive or complete. By following Reyes's beats and key concepts, I have introduced you to a few points of entry into Filipino philosophy that I deemed interesting for the purposes of developing a philosophy of disability and contributing a concept of crip relational agency. The choices that I have made throughout this chapter are the result of my own scholarly interest in relational agency and I am sure that I emphasized aspects that others would have neglected because of that bias. I likely emphasized aspects of Filipino thinking and culture that other authors would have neglected. I have done so consciously in defiance of what a philosophy essay is usually designed to be: assertive, confident, and dispassionate. My epistemic position as a disabled *mestiza* philosopher brought me to develop and share an analysis of as-of-yet uncharted territory. Surreptitiously, I have made a bold argument of my own, that is, that my partial investigation should have a ripple effect and prompt other philosophers to excavate further, to build higher, and to sink deeper into the possibilities and tensions between two philosophical cultures. Although it would please me if they were *these*—namely, Filipino and crip—cultures, I hope that my argument has a broader reach.

Appendix

Pronunciation of Tagalog words:

Hiya: Hee-yah

Kapwa: KAH-pooh-ah

Kagandahang-loób: Kah-gahn-dah-hang low-OBB

Lakas-ng-loób: Lah-kahss nang low-OBB

Loób: low-OBB in two syllables

Pakikiramdam: Pah-kee-kee-ram-dam

Utang-na-loób: Ooh-tang nah low-OBB

References

Anzaldúa, Gloria (1987), *Borderlands: The New Mestiza = La Frontera*, 1st ed., San Francisco: Spinsters/Aunt Lute.

Bostrom, L. (1968), "*Filipino bahala na* and American Fatalism," *Silliman Journal* 15 (3): 399–413.

De Castro, Leonardo D. (2000), "*Kagandahang Loób*: A Filipino Concept of Feminine Bioethics," in Rosemarie Putnam Tong (ed.), *Globalizing Feminist Bioethics: Crosscultural Perspectives*. Available at: https://www.taylorfrancis.com/books/9780429500176 (accessed June 24, 2023).

De Mesa, J. M. (1987), *In Solidarity with the Culture: Studies in Theological Re-Rooting*, Quezon City: Maryhill.

Gauthier-Mamaril, Élaina (2021), "Autonomy as a Systemic Virtue: A Spinozist Analysis of Autonomy and Shared Decision-Making in Healthcare," University of Aberdeen. Available at: https://www.academia.edu/51156427/Autonomy_as_a_systemic_virtue_A_Spinozist_analysis_of_autonomy_and_shared_decision_making_in_healthcare (accessed June 24, 2023).

Gauthier-Mamaril, Élaina (2022), "Reframing Patient-Doctor Relationships: Relational Autonomy and Treating Autonomy as a Virtue ," *Journal of Global Ethics* 18 (1): 32–47. https://doi.org/10.1080/17449626.2022.2053188.

Goh, Daniel P. S. (2008), "Postcolonial Disorientations: Colonial Ethnography and the Vectors of the Philippine Nation in the Imperial Frontier," *Postcolonial Studies* 11 (3): 259–76. https://doi.org/10.1080/13688790802226652.

Hamraie, Aimi and Kelly Fritsch (2019), "Crip Technoscience Manifesto," *Catalyst: Feminism, Theory, Technoscience* 5 (1): 1–33. https://doi.org/10.28968/cftt.v5i1.29607.

Kafer, Alison (2013), *Feminist, Queer, Crip*, Indiana University Press. Available at: https://www.jstor.org/stable/j.ctt16gz79x (accessed June 24, 2023).

Lynch, Frank (1962), "Philippine Values II: Social Acceptance," *Philippine Studies* 10 (1): 82–99.

Mercado, Leonardo N. (1994), *The Filipino Mind*. Cultural Heritage and Contemporary Change, 8, Washington, DC: Council for Research in Values and Philosophy.

Pada, Roland Theuas D. S. (2014), "The Methodological Problems of Filipino Philosophy," *Kritike* 8 (1): 24–44.

Puar, Jasbir K. (2014), "Proliferating Cripistemologies: A Virtual Roundtable," eds. Robert McRuer and Merri Lisa Johnson, *Journal of Literary and Cultural Disability Studies* 8 (2): 149–69. https://doi.org/10.3828/jlcds.2014.13.

Reyes, Jeremiah (2015), "*Loób* and *Kapwa*: An Introduction to a Filipino Virtue Ethics," *Asian Philosophy* 25 (2): 148–71. https://doi.org/10.1080/09552367.2015.1043173.

Tan, Antonio S. (1986), "The Chinese *Mestizos* and the Formation of the Filipino Nationality," *Archipel* 32 (1): 141–62. https://doi.org/10.3406/arch.1986.2316.

Yergeau, Remi (formerly known as Melanie) (2014), "Disability Hacktivism," Computers and Composition Online. Available at: https://cconlinejournal.org/hacking/#yergeau (accessed June 24, 2023).

18 RECOGNIZING HUMAN FLOURISHING IN THE CONTEXT OF DISABILITY

JORDAN JOSEPH WADDEN AND TIM STAINTON

Introduction

Throughout the history of philosophy, the term *flourishing* has been intimately tied to definitions of the good life and happiness which have been understood and represented as oppositional to the "cruel," "agonizing," and "suffering" modes of being so often ascribed to disabled people. We argue in this chapter that human flourishing and disability need not, and indeed ought not, be considered opposites. Instead, social understandings and representations of disability must expand in ways that encompass ideas of flourishing. To motivate philosophical discussion about expanded ideas of human flourishing, in the second section we provide a detailed outline of the historical and ethical context of human flourishing. This outline effectively serves as a philosophical basis for the argument about human flourishing in the context of disability that we articulate in the third section of the chapter. Although, as noted, flourishing and disability have been regarded as oppositional in both popular and academic thinking, this dichotomy is contrived. The concepts of disability and flourishing are not mutually exclusive. Furthermore, some disabled individuals flourish in their lives, while some nondisabled individuals do not flourish in their lives. In the fourth section, therefore, we provide an example of how demeaning language affects disabled people and the shift in language that is required to capture both those who flourish and those who do not. In the fifth section, we respond to some criticisms of our argument by highlighting the vast disparities between the perceptions that disabled people have of their own lives and the perceptions that people with no immediate experience of disability have of disabled people's lives.

The History and Ethics of Flourishing

The first stop on our tour of the history of flourishing is the idea that mental and physical pain are equivalent to moral evil or caused by it.[1] The former understanding of pain can be considered a "strong" view of it, while the latter understanding of pain can be considered a "weak" view of it. For an example of the strong view, we can turn to Epicurus's moral philosophy. In his letter *Ad Menoeceum*, Epicurus writes that humans seek the pleasurable because they want to achieve freedom from fear and from pain (Epicurus 1963). This view is a little difficult to work through, however, because, as Panos Dimas (2015) explains, Epicureans believed happiness was something that any human would immediately recognize. In other words, no detailed account of happiness is required because it is self-evident what would help promote flourishing. Later thinkers, such as Cicero (1921), would refine this proclamation somewhat by claiming that pleasure is what humans rejoice in while pain is whatever causes distress.

The strong view—namely, that mental and physical pain are equivalent to evil—could of course be used by an interlocutor to argue that disabled people somehow deserve their conditions because they are evil people or were evil people in a former life. However, we believe that this argument is a misrepresentation of the concept of flourishing due to a superficial understanding of the concept. Cicero's later addition of pleasure as what humans *rejoice in* can instead help make the case for flourishing in the context of disability. Our differences, our limitations, and our experiences with the world can shape what we take pleasure in. Two people with the same condition could have two distinct views on whether they are suffering and why: one of them may believe that they are suffering due to a personal flaw and the other may enjoy their life and who they are but wish for social change with respect to ideas about disability and disabled people. In short, disability does not automatically translate to pain and suffering, as the earlier example of two ways that an individual could view their situation demonstrates.

The weak view (as we have referred to it)—that is, the view that pain is caused by moral evil—can be traced back to Plato's "Myth of Er" and its subsequent uptake in the background of many Neoplatonist and Christian arguments about the good life. In the "Myth of Er," Plato outlines the story of a man who experiences what life is like after death. In this after-death world, souls are given the opportunity to choose their new lives. While everyone has the opportunity to choose a morally good life, not everyone will (Plato 1997). If one leads a life of evil, the choice to do so will manifest in one's mental, physical, or character traits when they are reborn as a direct consequence of this choice. In other words, human flourishing is predetermined: If we suffer from a disability, then we must have chosen this life of "bodily evil" before we were born.

We can turn to Thomas Aquinas (1969) for a more complete evaluation of whether happiness is tied to the selection of moral evil in a prior life. While Aquinas is recognized for his substantial writing about the concept of the Good, many scholars forget about Aquinas's commentary on the body as a vessel toward this goal. In the *Summa Theologiae*, he divides happiness into incomplete Goods and complete Goods—the former can be achieved through the human body, while the latter can only be achieved by one's soul through practical reasoning. This division means that it is possible to flourish regardless of the body that you have, so long as you pursue flourishing intellectually—which for the early Christians, could be done only through coming to know God.[2] Aquinas's views draw on earlier arguments from Augustine (1955) and Boethius (2008) who both argue that happiness comes from the ability to know the Good and cultivate a relationship with it. Now, although this explanation might seem to work against people with intellectual disabilities, in Maimonides's *The Guide for the Perplexed* (1963), we learn that this intellectual pursuit is tied to that which is within one's capacities rather than some arbitrary standard. Incorporating this factor into an expanded conception of flourishing would ensure that we do not accidentally imply that flourishing with disability is possible only for people with physical disabilities.

An alternative to the pain = evil view is embedded in Stoicism. The main teaching of the Stoics is that we must follow the natural order of things if we want to flourish. For the Stoic Seneca (1965), the good life comes from recognizing that life is unchanged by limitations imposed on us. We must avoid fighting against these realities and instead comport ourselves toward an indifference to evils, harms, and pains of the past, present, and future. Marcus Aurelius (1998) expanded on this view by asserting that any pain that does not kill us is tolerable pain. Furthermore, we ought to accept these pains without complaint as there is no benefit to highlighting one's own suffering. To flourish is to live day to day, hour by hour, accepting that whatever happens in life that is out of your control is simply meant to be endured.

In general, the lesson that we can take from Stoicism might be expressed in the form of a cliché: to flourish with disability, we ought to "go with the flow." At one level, this lesson can be helpful. Someone with chronic pain might take comfort in the idea that they can shape their own experience through how they choose to react to their pain. This frame of mind can legitimately lead someone to flourish. On a more general level, however, this outlook could be dangerous. For if we accept the Stoic approach to pain, then we run the risk of creating policy that forces individuals into situations where they cannot flourish. For example, one implication of strict Stoic responses to disability is that no one should feel obligated to make adaptions for accessibility since any given disabled individual can "choose" how they view their circumstance. In short, we run the risk of complacency and stagnation if we abide primarily by Stoic rules. Ultimately, a Stoic response to disability would hinder flourishing.

Another view of flourishing, one that can be identified as early as Aristotle's *Nicomachean Ethics*, considers the pursuit of flourishing to be a continual journey rather than the result of an event or choice. Aristotle believed that happiness and flourishing derived from the habituation of virtue and the use of practical reasoning. He develops this idea while outlining what has become known as virtue ethics, that is, the ethical system that focuses on the continual development of an agent's character rather than on the evaluation of a specific action in isolation. Now, an implication of Aristotle's view that happiness comes from habituation is that a person must be a specific kind of agent to qualify. For example, he argues that children and youth cannot be truly happy because they lack the experience that would make them capable of habituating anything in a meaningful way (Aristotle 2009).

In addition to experience and age, Aristotle identifies six types of moral character which act as indicators of flourishing. These are: brutishness, viciousness, incontinence, continence, virtuousness, and superhuman virtuousness (Aristotle 2009). Someone who flourishes would be in the virtuous or superhuman virtuous categories. It is not easy to achieve placement in one of these categories. Aristotle precludes from the cultivation of fully expressed virtue anyone with intellectual disabilities, illnesses, and even people who have endured tragic life events. For Aristotle, even if one had led a flourishing life but died while enduring a tragedy in their final few moments, then no one could look back on that person's life and say it was a happy life. Instead, these individuals may achieve continence—a roughly beneficial state of being that nevertheless participates in "morbid" states (examples that he provides include madness, disease, and epilepsy). While Aristotle recognizes that these circumstances are beyond an individual's control, he nevertheless believes that they prevent one from flourishing.

Recent developments in virtue ethics have recognized that although Aristotle's focus on the development of character and flourishing might constitute the right approach, his original views are exclusionary, ruling out far too many people from a life of flourishing, including people in tragic dilemmas who cannot "be virtuous" according to his rigid structure. The most famous dilemma of this kind is depicted in William Styron's (1979) novel *Sophie's Choice*, which presents the case of a Polish woman, Sophie, who is forced by a Nazi concentration camp guard to choose which of her two children will live and which one will be killed. If she refuses to choose between the two children, *both* of them will be killed. In short, Sophie has a morally compelling reason to choose one of her children; yet, for each child, she has an apparently equally strong reason to save that particular child. In other words, Sophie is in a situation where no matter what choice she makes, she must act "against virtue" by telling the guard to kill one of her children or by shirking her responsibility to save one of the children.

One method of addressing such tragic dilemmas, which we think seems most appropriate, is to readjust virtue ethics and transform it into a "burdened virtue" theory. Lisa Tessman asserts that burdened virtues include:

> All those traits that make a contribution to human flourishing—if they succeed in doing so at all—*only* because they enable survival of or resistance to oppression (it is in this that their nobility lies), while in other ways they detract from their bearer's well-being, in some cases so deeply that their bearer may be said to lead a wretched life. (Tessman 2005: 95)

For example, on a traditional virtue ethical account, someone who has the virtue of bravery is generally considered to have more opportunities to flourish because they have this virtue. However, if the person's bravery developed because they grew up with abusive parents, then the agent might have been better off if the beneficial virtue had not developed in the first place. In Sophie's case, she might emerge from her tragic dilemma more capable of handling herself and with stronger resolve to fight off the Nazis or come out of it with a stronger desire to protect her remaining child. Both potential traits are admirable, but they come at a significant cost.

Viktor Frankl (1992) presents a similar view that emphasizes finding meaning as a route to flourishing rather than finding happiness as a route to flourishing. He argues that transforming one's personal tragedy into a triumph, or one's predicament into an achievement, is the basis for achieving our individual and unique human potential. His experience with the Holocaust informed his view that suffering shows humanity in its rawest form, highlighting that how we react and develop post-tragedy defines whether we flourish as individuals. In a way, this view can be thought of as blending the virtuous "development" position with the Stoic "do not fight nature" position. Frankl explains that when we can no longer change our situation, such as with significant disease, we are challenged instead to change ourselves. Frankl differs from the Stoics, and therefore better fits in this continual development form of finding flourishing, insofar as he recognizes the need for a progressive development rather than a one-off attitudinal change toward indifference. Rather than avoid conflict with what pains us (Seneca 1965) or live without complaint (Aurelius 1998), we ought instead to explore struggles that confront us and engage with the tragedy that they often entail in order to develop meaning in spite of the pain (Frankl 1992).

It would be remiss to end this section on the history of the concept of flourishing without briefly analyzing how the concept has been constructed in biomedical contexts, especially given how often disabled people find themselves to be the subjects of medical examination or health-care politics. Much of bioethics is founded on the so-called "four principles" of autonomy, beneficence, nonmaleficence, and justice. The principle of autonomy governs the ability of individuals to make decisions for themselves that are free from both controlling interference and limitations that prevent meaningful decisions (Beauchamp and Childress 2013). In medical contexts, the principle of autonomy can be respected by allowing a competent patient to make their own decisions, by providing shared decision-making involving the patient and some other individual, or by using substituted decision-making when the patient is deemed incapable of making their own decisions (Sandman and Munthe 2009).

Although the principle of autonomy is routinely invoked in (among other contexts) legal documents and popular media discussions surrounding disability as a justification for practices that are purportedly designed to enable disabled people to free themselves from suffering, it does not get invoked to support the idea of flourishing with one's disability—an equally valid, autonomous choice. Without recognition that flourishing is possible, jurisdictions run a significant risk of creating and exacerbating situations in which disabled people are not free from external influence or control and hence cannot make autonomous decisions. The very real threat that the autonomy of disabled people will be compromised connects directly to the intended goals of the principle of justice. The principle of justice demands that we consider how we can meet health needs fairly (Daniels 2008). Insofar as health-care policy and legislation focus exclusively on the perceived negative aspects of disability—the putative sufferings and "cruelty" of disability—they do not adequately and fairly meet these needs.

The principles of beneficence and nonmaleficence are sometimes confused with each other since they focus on similar aspects of ethical considerations in healthcare. The former principle—that is, the principle of beneficence—requires that health-care professionals actively benefit the individual, while the latter principle—namely, the principle of nonmaleficence—requires that harms be minimized and mitigated wherever possible (Beauchamp and Childress 2013). Appeals to these two principles can pose problems for human flourishing insofar as such appeals threaten to slide into paternalism or protectionism when they are utilized in the context of significant or high-stakes decisions. Protectionism occurs in health-care settings when health-care professionals overemphasize the principle of nonmaleficence by preventing a given patient from accessing certain procedures, treatments, and so on, that could cause them more harm. Paternalism occurs in health-care settings when health-care professionals overemphasize the principle of beneficence by assuming that they know what is in the best interests of their patients better than the patients themselves do. Both modes of professional and institutional overreach can be recognized in the negative assumptions that currently condition a host of legislative decisions, policies, institutional practices, and popular media communications about disability.

The Argument from Flourishing

Now that we have provided some historical background on the concept of flourishing, we can advance our argument for the implementation and recognition of the concept of flourishing in the context of disability.

First, we believe that a concept of flourishing must be centered on what an individual "rejoices in" rather than be set to some societal or medical metric. Our inspiration for this conviction derives from Cicero's additions to the traditional Epicurean beliefs according to which we all inherently know what it means to flourish. Frankl's explanation of the search for meaning and how it can emerge from pain supplements this requirement. While it may seem as if we already assume that everyone knows what flourishing looks like in today's society, material presented in legal and policy documents implies that once a certain contestable and medically defined threshold is reached, no "happy" options remain for a given individual who is "suffering." If we alter this perspective and formally recognize that difference in experience exists *even for people who are significantly disabled*, then we start to open up the possibility that perhaps disability is not the antithesis to flourishing that we seem to assume it to be.

Second, we believe that a conception of flourishing must recognize that a good life is not tied to a benevolent body. We draw this belief from Aquinas's search for human meaning. It might be tempting to think that if one has enough pain, then it is impossible to flourish—much like Aristotle's original explanation of virtue ethics and a life well lived would have us believe. As others have argued, however, it is a mistake to continue to believe that a disabled body is necessarily a painful or harmful aspect of an "otherwise healthy" individual. Joel Michael Reynolds (2017) has succinctly defined this problematic view as the "ableist conflation," that is, the ableist assumption that disability constitutes a lack of a natural good that necessarily results in pain, suffering, and death. A better understanding of flourishing in the context of disability would necessarily recognize that the body alone is not the reason for one's flourishing or suffering. This recognition requires that language tying disability, treatments, continuing care, and even medical assistance in dying (MAiD) to the body must be altered.

Our definition of flourishing also carefully recognizes the problems with both explicit and implicit protectionism and paternalism that can be found in governmental, academic, and popular discussions about disability. As noted earlier, these problems arise with overreach of the principles of beneficence and nonmaleficence, often done in the name of the principle of justice. Unfortunately, this overreach perpetuates the idea that health-care professionals understand disability better than disabled people themselves. Assumptions according to which health-care professionals, policy-makers, and legislators unquestionably promote each and every disabled person's best interests on the grounds of "the cruelty of life" or "condemned to suffer" are misplaced or openly hostile.

The most significant change to understandings of disability that our conception of flourishing enables is likely the recognition that the combination of disability and flourishing does not constitute a tragic dilemma akin to *Sophie's Choice* and should not be represented as such. Some disabled people who fight for access to interventions such as MAiD may exist within a tragic dilemma. However, we must recognize that this dilemma has arisen due to extenuating circumstances rather than some essential or necessary aspect of disability itself. At minimum, our legislation must not enshrine this tragic-choice model into law and public policy. Indeed, flourishing with disability may be a type of "burdened virtue," in Tessman's sense, because it requires that an individual reject what society expects that disabled individuals will desire. As such, disabled individuals may emerge from these situations stronger, or more resilient, or more determined than they had been, though it would be best if they did not have to struggle to acquire this virtue in the first place. While the burdened virtue approach is therefore not ideal, it does present an avenue to move the language hitherto used to represent disability away from the tragic-choice model and toward something else.

Indeed, recognition of flourishing must actively avoid swapping the negative language used to signify disability for complacency. This concern comes from a recognition that responses to disabled individuals may take a Stoic format along the lines that we have outlined through Seneca and Aurelius. We chose to highlight the arguments of these ancients rather than more modern Stoic arguments because the former arguments provide basic understandings of Stoicism that are better known among the general population. Although more sophisticated Stoicism exists, and many disabled individuals may benefit from sophisticated Stoicism in their own lives, it is the basic form of it that risks complacency.

Applying Flourishing: A Case Study with Medical Assistance in Dying

The practice of MAiD is a natural case study to demonstrate the impact of our *Argument from Flourishing*. In this section of our chapter, therefore, we briefly outline the state of MAiD in Canada and subsequently apply our argument to the introductory paragraph of the original *Carter v. Canada* (2015) decision. This paragraph is probably the most cited part of any authoritative MAiD document in Canada; thus, we believe that it can best demonstrate how language which is informed by the notion of flourishing can assist with the development of legislation and policy, broadly speaking, that does not reproduce the problematic assumptions according to which disability is inherently suffering, negative, or cruel.

Carter v. Canada is a landmark Supreme Court of Canada decision regarding the prohibition of assisted suicide in the country. The legal challenge was focused primarily on two cases: the case of Kay Carter, a woman with degenerative spinal stenosis; and the case of Gloria Taylor, a woman with amyotrophic lateral sclerosis. The unanimous decision in *Carter v. Canada* overturned the Canadian Supreme Court's ruling in *Rodriguez v. British Columbia* (1993) which had denied a right to assisted suicide. The decision in *Carter v. Canada* specifically rules that sections 14 and 241(b) of the Canadian *Criminal Code* had no force to prohibit MAiD. Prior to this case, these sections had provided the most significant legal barrier to anything close to MAiD. Section 14 states that no person is entitled to consent to have someone "inflict death" upon them, while Section 241(b) states that no one may aid in another individual's attempt at suicide (*Criminal Code* 1985). By ruling that these sections have no prohibitive force, *Carter v. Canada* deems that physicians ought to be allowed to assist competent adults to die so long as these individuals clearly consent to the termination of their life and have a "grievous and irremediable" medical condition.

The extremely value-laden language used to draft the ruling has far-reaching implications that are deeply troubling. Consider, for example, the following remarks which can be found at the very outset of the ruling, that is, in the opening lines of the case:

> People who are *grievously and irremediably* ill cannot seek a physician's assistance in dying and may be *condemned* to a life of *severe and*

> *intolerable* suffering. A person facing this prospect has *two options*: she can take her own life prematurely, often by *violent and dangerous* means, or she can *suffer* until she dies from natural causes. *The choice is cruel.* (*Carter v. Canada* 2015: paragraph 1, emphasis added)

Notice the words and phrases that we have highlighted in italics. Clearly, these words and phrases do not convey neutral tones nor do they avoid negative perceptions of and indeed speculations about an individual's quality of life. Instead, these figures of speech present a supposed binary choice: choose to die or live a life in which you are condemned to suffer by your illness. These word choices make it seem as if there is a class of conditions that no rational person would possibly choose to continue to have, that is, there is a class of conditions with which no rational person would wish to continue to live. This subtle, yet dangerous, implication is, in fact, written into the law. Keep this observation in mind, as we return to it later to demonstrate how an *Argument from Flourishing* may alter its language.

Following *Carter v. Canada*, the Supreme Court allowed the Canadian parliament time to develop suitable legislation and enact the ruling. This resulting legislation was Bill C-14 (2016), which provided the necessary exemptions to both sections of the *Criminal Code* cited in the ruling and added definitions and regulations, defining MAiD as:

> **(a)** the administering by a medical practitioner or nurse practitioner of a substance to a person, at their request, that causes their death; or
>
> **(b)** the prescribing or providing by a medical practitioner or nurse practitioner of a substance to a person, at their request, so that they may self-administer the substance and in doing so cause their own death (*Bill C-14* 2016).

The document also included the following: eligibility criteria, discussion of safeguards, discussion of the importance of independent witnesses, and regulations for accessing MAiD.

While many Canadians regarded the introduction of Bill C-14 as a positive legislative addition, others had different reactions to it. The British Columbia Civil Liberties Association (BCCLA), for example, claimed that Bill C-14 was a deeply flawed bill which had been foisted upon the country without critical engagement (BCCLA n.d.). For the BCCLA, the "reasonably foreseeable death" requirement entailed that many Canadians, including Kay Carter herself, would not qualify for MAiD under this legislation. According to the BCCLA, furthermore, Bill C-14 deviates from the *Carter v. Canada* case and therefore will cause more Canadians to suffer insofar as it artificially carves out a significant group who should be able to end their suffering.

Joseph Arvay, the *Carter* lawyer, who testified before a Senate committee that studied Bill C-14, claimed that this piece of legislation would result in more pain because it suggests that disabled people who could otherwise live another twenty years would need to starve themselves to meet the bill's eligibility criteria (Lunn 2016).

Notice, again, the remarkably value-laden terminology used in the bill itself and in reactions to its creation. These antagonistic statements pit MAiD and a "slow and agonizing death" against each other as the only two options for significantly disabled Canadians. Indeed, Arvay's own claims directly make this inference by implying that disabled people would obviously want MAiD and therefore will be compelled to starve themselves in order to receive it. That some disabled individuals would choose to flourish rather than choose to die, if that option was given social uptake, is not a possibility that is seriously entertained.

Recent re-evaluation of the Canadian MAiD program has led to proposed amendments through Bill C-7 (2021), which is informed by the Quebec Superior Court decision in *Truchon v. Canada* (2019), an analysis of Canadian and international studies, and by consultations on MAiD in a Canadian context. The significant proposed changes are: removing the "reasonably foreseeable" requirement for accessing MAiD, the creation of two separate safeguard programs—one safeguard program for people whose death is reasonably foreseeable and the other for people whose death is not reasonably foreseeable—some exceptions to the "final consent" requirement, and amendments to the monitoring and collection of data about people who request MAiD and are assessed for it. By expanding the timeline to include people without a reasonably foreseeable death, Bill C-7 is purportedly designed to provide access to MAiD to people who experience incredible pain and may live for years to come. This amendment initially included a continued prohibition against MAiD where the primary illness is a mental illness but an additional successful Senate amendment requires that mental illness be included in the legislation within two years. In response to *Truchon v. Canada*, Bill C-7 indicates that a "final consent" immediately prior to administration of MAiD would not be required in two situations: first, in cases of advanced consent for people who may lose capacity between the time that they arrange MAiD and the time that they receive it; and second, in cases where a person chooses to self-administer but the process does not result in death, although they lose capacity.

Unfortunately, these changes do not quell our worries about the negative implications of the legal language that is used to discuss MAiD. In particular, Bill C-7 maintains the negatively value-laden terminology and frames within the sections of the *Criminal Code* that cover "life, liberty, and security" as well as "equality." In so doing, Bill C-7 enables the inference that the only way to give people with significant illness or disability access to liberty, security, and equality is to allow them to access faster deaths. As we noted earlier, we do not want to imply that everyone must flourish; nevertheless, we are worried about the ways in which the legal discussions and documents about Bill C-7, in addition to Bill C-7 itself, continue to present a binary choice between dying or living in extreme suffering.

It is now time to consider how the opening paragraph of the *Carter v. Canada* ruling would have been improved with a better understanding of significant disability and explicit recognition that it is possible to flourish with it. We will retain as much of the original phrasing as possible, emphasizing our changes for easy separation. Our version of the paragraph is intended to mirror the phrasing in the original version of it to show how even a quick and rough application of our argument can improve the language used in legislation:

> While some people who are significantly and irremediably ill may live meaningful lives alongside their condition, others may reach a point where they no longer believe that they can flourish in life. If these individuals cannot seek a physician's assistance in dying, they may feel forced into a life of severe and intolerable suffering. A person facing this prospect may believe that they only have two options: they can take their own life prematurely, often by violent and dangerous means, or they can suffer until they die from natural causes. The choice is cruel. (underlines added)

As you can see, the force of the argument for MAiD's permissibility remains as strong in our version of the opening paragraph as it is in the original version with the purely negative language. However, our version of the paragraph, that is, this modified opening statement now no longer forces itself upon everyone living with significant disability. Furthermore, our modified version of the opening statement actively recognizes that people who do not want to use MAiD have not "chosen to suffer" but rather are allowing themselves to flourish.

Combatting Challenges to Our Argument

Some philosophers may read our argument and claim that we tend to glorify disability in a way that does harm to people who are actively suffering. Their view could be grounded in many beliefs, not the least of which is the thought that well-being is simply not possible with illness and disability. This kind of position can be recognized in many places and has been touted by some popular scholars. One of the most prominent in this camp is Peter Singer (2011), who argues that people with disabilities live lives that are less valuable than the lives of "normal" humans. While Singer also recognizes that discrimination on the grounds of disability is wrong, he makes a point to claim that anyone living with a significant condition would do whatever it takes to cure themselves and to prevent the birth of others with their conditions. He firmly claims that disability resides in the body, that is, any argument according to which social factors cause pain, distress, and so on are dismissible on his account of disability. As such, disability is fundamentally negative for anyone, regardless of whether, and how emphatically, a given disabled person states that they do not feel this way about their own body.

When counterarguments based in views like Singer's are advanced, it is incumbent on us to show what many disabled individuals already know, namely, that well-being can be attained with illness and disability. To support this observation and, in addition, close our chapter, we shall briefly turn to the phenomenology of illness.

One method to judge well-being is to simply ask an individual how they perceive their own situation. Erik Angner and colleagues (2009) sought to examine just this question when they conducted their study focusing on the relationship between health and happiness. While they only examine mild chronic pain and various comorbidities (such as asthma, high cholesterol, high blood pressure, diabetes, and heart disease), their study provides a useful starting point for our analysis because of how prevalent the negative public opinion on any illness or disability has become. Angner and colleagues determined that a negative relationship between health and happiness occurs only in the immediate period following the onset of symptoms or the rendering of a diagnosis. After an adjustment period, the happiness and well-being of their research subjects returned to approximately the same levels that they had previously reported, that is, prior to the onset of their symptoms or the rendering of their diagnoses.

This study demonstrates what Gary Albrecht and Patrick Devlieger (1999) have called "the disability paradox." The disability paradox derives from the question that many abled people ask regarding why so many people with persistent and serious disabilities report that they experience anywhere between a good to an excellent quality of life. Albrecht and Devlieger explain that this discrepancy between disabled and abled perspectives highlights the significance of personal experience, individual self-determination, and social relationships. From this paradox, we can discern that members of the abled population tend to significantly underestimate the quality of disabled people's lives because they do not have disabled experiences. Instead, they view these experiences only as othering, at best, or shocking and incompatible with their own understanding of life, at worst.

Havi Carel (2016) explains that one way to interpret the tension between abled individuals—who believe that disability is purely negative—and disabled individuals—who assert that they are happy—is to attend to the differences between insider and outsider perspectives on health. Insider perspectives are first-personal and reflect one's own knowledge, whereas outsider perspectives are fundamentally third-personal. In other words, an outsider's perspective on well-being, happiness, and flourishing in disability is, at best, limited and anecdotal. Without some insider knowledge, or at least some second-personal experience and connections, outsiders can likely never acquire an accurate understanding of disability and illness. Whenever an outsider is asked to anticipate how they would feel if they were disabled, Carel states, the best that they can do is access *imagined experience of illness*.

Carel remarks that we can use phenomenology to think about how illness modifies an ill person's way of being. Recounting her own experiences, she writes:

> The future no longer contains the vague promise of many more decades. Death is no longer an abstract, remote notion. The soft-focus lens is replaced by a sharp magnifying glass through which terminal stages of illness can be viewed in nauseating detail. The future curls in on itself and at once becomes both exposed and radically curtailed. It has a clear end point. (Carel 2019: 171)

This passage might seem to suggest that there is no room for well-being in Carel's illness. If, every day, Carel experiences this "sharp magnifying glass" with respect to her illness, we might think that her life is torturous. However, if we accept this hasty conclusion as the takeaway of her remarks, then we have made the same mistake as other outsiders to her condition because we have accessed only imagined experiences. Carel's insider experience in fact demonstrates that her well-being has returned from its initial sink into despair:

> My body adapted with astonishing alacrity to new limitations. I quickly forgot how things were before. Within a year, my physical habits were entirely different. Whereas in the first months my body would attempt a brisk pace, hurrying up stairs, and physical impatience, these movements have been erased from my bodily repertoire. While my memory still contained images of mountain-top views and the inside of a gym, I could no longer remember what it *felt like* to run, to work out, the euphoric sensations of healthier exertion, or the effortlessness

of being young and healthy. New habits were formed and a new way of negotiating the world was incorporated into my physicality. Blissful forgetfulness of the pleasures of physical movement accompanied them. (Carel 2019: 38)

What the return of Carel's well-being shows is that the human experience comprises adaption and meaning creation. As Carel describes it, through adaption to the reality of her illness, she has changed her conception of happiness. The eventual bodily forgetting of previous activities (such as running or working out) allows Carel's new activities to take their place in the creation of her well-being.

It is through precisely adaption of this sort and creation of meaning that we have grounded our *Argument from Flourishing* in this chapter. Likewise, it is this understanding of one's own conditions, limitations, pains, triumphs, etc. that defeats objections to our claim that flourishing ought to be considered when discussing disability. By creating discussions that do not assume that all disabled people view their situation as inherently negative, we foster discourse that enhances their well-being and flourishing. Moving forward, we believe that discussions about flourishing and disability would greatly benefit from examination and incorporation of Eastern and Indigenous narratives and understandings of flourishing and disability. Most of us live in multicultural societies now, which means that the Eurocentric grounding for the Canadian legislation and practices discussed in this chapter will not represent everyone currently living in Canada. To truly represent flourishing as an individual search for meaning, furthermore, we need to make room for people who do not identify with the authors to whom we have referred in this chapter.

Notes

1 Something we feel needs to be addressed before we begin this section is the fact that we are both based in Canada, which is both a multicultural nation and a colonial nation. Much of the legislation and media we engage with, and which will form the case study in the fourth section, have deep and engrained roots in Western philosophy. Therefore, this section explicitly focuses on the Western canon. While we would have loved to include Eastern and Indigenous conceptions of flourishing, doing so could misrepresent both the Canadian approach as well as these non-Western cultures.

2 For any non-Christian readers, Aquinas's arguments can be translated to be representative of your own religious or secular value system. The Christian God is not a necessary component of the argument for our purposes.

References

Albrecht, Gary L. and Patrick J. Devlieger (1999), "The Disability Paradox: High Quality of Life Against All Odds," *Social Science and Medicine* 48: 977–88.

Anger, Erik, Midge N. Ray, Kenneth G. Saag, and Jeroan J. Allison (2009), "Health and Happiness Among Older Adults: A Community-based Study," *Journal of Health Psychology* 14 (4): 503–12.

Aquinas, Thomas (1969), *Summa Theologiæ vol. 16, Purpose and Happiness (1a2æ. 1-5)*, trans. Thomas Gilby, Cambridge: Blackfriars.

Aristotle (2009), *Nicomachean Ethics*, trans. David Ross, revised by Lesley Brown, Toronto: Oxford University Press.

Augustine (1955), *The De Natura Boni of Saint Augustine*, trans. Albian Anthony Moon, New York: The Coxen Press.

Aurelius, Marcus (1998), *The Meditations of Marcus Aurelius Antoninus*, trans. A. S. L. Farquharson, Toronto: Oxford University Press.

Beauchamp, Tom L. and James F. Childress (2013), *Principles of Biomedical Ethics (7e)*, Oxford: Oxford University Press.

Bill C-7: An Act to Amend the Criminal Code (Medical Assistance in Dying) (2021), *Royal Assent*, March 17, 43rd Parliament, 2nd Session, Ottawa: Public Works and Government Services Canada. Available at: https://parl.ca/DocumentViewer/en/43-2/bill/C-7/royal-assent (accessed July 23, 2021).

Bill C-14: An Act to Amend the Criminal Code and to Make Related Amendments to Other Acts (Medical Assistance in Dying) (2016), *Royal Assent*, June 17, 42nd Parliament, 1st Session, Ottawa: Public Works and Government Services Canada. Available at: https://www.parl.ca/DocumentViewer/en/42-1/bill/C-14/royal-assent (accessed January 5, 2019).

Boethius (2008), *The Consolation of Philosophy*, trans. David R. Slavitt, Cambridge, MA: Harvard University Press.

British Columbia Civil Liberties Association (n.d.), *Carter v Canada: The Death with Dignity Case*. Available at: https://bccla.org/our-work/blog/death-with-dignity-case/ (accessed January 5, 2019).

Carel, Havi (2016), *Phenomenology of Illness*, Oxford: Oxford University Press.

Carel, Havi (2019), *Illness: The Cry of the Flesh*, Third edition, New York: Routledge.

Carter v Canada (2015), SCC 5, [2015] 1 SCR 331. Available at: https://www.canlii.org/en/ca/scc/doc/2015/2015scc5/2015scc5.html (accessed Janury 5, 2019).

Cicero (1921), *De Finibus Bonorum et Malorum*, trans. H. Harris Rackman, New York: G. P. Putnam's Sons.

Criminal Code, R.S.C. 1985, c.46, s.231(6). Available at: https://www.canlii.org/en/ca/laws/stat/rsc-1985-c-c-46/latest/rsc-1985-c-c-46 (accessed January 5, 2019).

Daniels, Norman (2008), *Just Health: Meeting Health Needs Fairly*, Cambridge: Cambridge University Press.

Dimas, Panos (2015), "Epicurus on Pleasure, Desire, and Friendship," in Øyvind Rabbås, Eyjólfur K. Emilsson, Hallvard Fossheim, and Miira Tuominen (eds.), *The Quest for the Good Life: Ancient Philosophers on Happiness*, 164–82, New York: Oxford University Press.

Epicurus (1963), *The Philosophy of Epicurus: Letters, Doctrines, and Parallel Passages from Lucretius*, trans. George K. Strodach, Evanston: Northwestern University Press.

Frankl, Viktor E. (1992), *Man's Search for Meaning: An Introduction to Logotherapy*, Fourth edition, Part one, trans. Gordon Willard Allport, Boston: Beacon Press.

Lunn, Susan (2016), "Lawyer who won Carter Case in High Court Says Assisted-Dying Bill Guts Ruling," *CBC*, May 5. Available at: https://www.cbc.ca/news/politics/joseph-arvay-assisted-dying-1.3568438 (accessed January 5, 2019).

Maimonides (1963), *The Guide of the Perplexed*, trans. Shlomo Pines, Toronto: University of Chicago Press.

Plato (1997), "Republic," in John M. Cooper and D. S. Hutchinson (eds.), *Plato: Complete Works*, trans. Georges Maximillien Antoine Grube, revised by C. D. C. Reeve, 971–1223, Indianapolis: Hackett Publishing Company.

Reynolds, Joel Michael (2017), "'I'd Rather be Dead than Disabled'—The Ableist Conflation and the Meanings of Disability," *Review of Communication* 17 (3): 149–63.

Rodriguez v British Columbia (1993), 3 SCR 519. Available at: https://www.canlii.org/en/ca/scc/doc/1993/1993canlii75/1993canlii75.html (accessed January 5, 2019).

Sandman, Lars and Christian Munthe (2009), "Shared Decision-Making and Patient Autonomy," *Theoretical Medicine and Bioethics* 30 (4): 289–310.

Seneca (1965), *The Stoic Philosophy of Seneca*, trans. Moses Hadas, Gloucester: Doubleday & Company, Inc.

Singer, Peter (2011), *Practical Ethics*, Third edition, New York: Cambridge University Press.

Styron, William (1979), *Sophie's Choice*, New York: Random House.

Tessman, Lisa (2005), *Burdened Virtues: Virtue Ethics for Liberatory Struggles*, Toronto: Oxford University Press.

Truchon c. Procureur General du Canada (2019), QCCS 3792. Available at: https://www.canlii.org/fr/qc/qccs/doc/2019/2019qccs3792/2019qccs3792.html (accessed January 5, 2019).

19 NEURODIVERSITY AND THE ETHICS OF ACCESS

AUGUST GORMAN

Introduction

Some of the most prominent conversations about disability in analytic ethics have been about the degree to which disabled lives are worth living, whether we ought to select against disabled people being born, and the degree to which disabled people might be owed compensation for their "unfortunate" circumstances in life. In real life, and in sharp contrast to this rather bleak theoretical milieu, questions arise not just about us but also *for* us. While other philosophers debate our status as moral agents and moral recipients, we navigate a rich tapestry of social life and experiences, all while mucking our way through complex interpersonal ethical conundrums among ourselves using conceptual resources that we have needed to invent on our own. The current lens with which philosophers tend to think about disability is ableist and blocks the view of this more lively and theoretically rich landscape. The distance between the kinds of questions about disability that are most often discussed in philosophy and the kinds of questions about disability that tend to come up in daily life can be keenly felt in the context of neurodiversity and interpersonal ethics. In this chapter, I aim to illuminate a small part of this terrain, focusing on the normative underpinnings of neurodiversity-related access claims, both their legitimacy and the adjudication of conflicts between them.

Neurodiversity

The word *neurodiversity*, at least as I use it, does double duty. First, the term *neurodiversity* is a descriptive umbrella term that refers to various kinds of cognitive diversity, including, most famously, the kinds of cognitive differences typified by autistic people and people with ADHD (attention deficit hyperactivity disorder), as well as people with diagnoses such as Tourette syndrome, dyslexia, sensory processing disorders, and OCD (obsessive-compulsive disorder). On this usage, phenomena such as the way that an ADHDer experiences time, or the need to avoid certain kinds of tactile stimulation that an autistic person feels, can be described as neurodivergent traits. Second, following Nick Walker and Robert Chapman, *neurodiversity* names a paradigm shift from thinking about these kinds of differences as pathologies to thinking of them as neutrally valanced human differences, where there is no "normal" or "correct" way for an individual mind to be (Walker 2012; Chapman 2019). Although I do not present an argument for the neurodiversity paradigm in this chapter, I nevertheless adopt it in the chapter.

How should we distinguish neurodiversity-type differences from other kinds of personality traits?[1] For example, I consider my ADHD, misophonia, aphantasia, and synesthesia to be related to neurodiversity. Yet I do not consider my vegetarianism, my nosiness, or my artistic ability to be related to neurodiversity. I take this distinction to be somewhat intuitive. In adopting a neurodiversity paradigm, however, we lose two of the ways in which people might have thought that we could explain this distinction. First, inasmuch as we drop the premise that neurodiversity-related traits inherently involve dysfunction, we cannot thereby simply bracket out the things that are typically seen as positive traits, rendering them not potentially related to neurodiversity. Second, inasmuch as we drop the premise that neurodiversity-related traits are caused by distinctive illnesses to be conceptualized by medical diagnosticians, we can no longer bracket out subclinical forms of traits such as inattentiveness or sound sensitivity. Many of these traits are scalar variations in natural human diversity that are not different in kinds from the traits that characterize neurodiversity-related diagnoses. While I take complicating the presumed valence and distinctiveness of neurodiverse traits to be generally good upshots of adopting a neurodiversity paradigm, they complicate the ethics of accessibility insofar as they blur the line between neurodiversity-related traits and other kinds of human difference.[2]

The Ethics of Access

By "disability access," I mean to refer to choices and design of social spaces that do not preclude disabled people from full participation in cultural, social, and political life. In adopting the neurodiversity paradigm, I recognize the site of neurodivergent difficulty as pertaining to the relation between environments and individuals and, in particular, that the availability of certain kinds of access to environments can radically reshape the experience of what it is to have a certain kind of neurodivergence. Genuine accessibility, as many have argued, encompasses more than basic adjustments to inaccessible environments or minor modifications to them that disabled self-advocates themselves have been required to request.[3] Indeed, robust accessibility involves more than the perception that disabled people are misfits to be accommodated with certain discretionary resources to help them—a kind of "consumptive access" (Brewer, Selfe, and Yergeau 2014). In other words, genuine access cannot be achieved by following checklists, since, as Wood et al. put it,

> A checklist approach locates disability over there, isolates disability within the body or mind of one student in one class, freezes disability as a set of symptoms rather than as a social process—or demands that disability be overcome—and allows us to perpetuate the fiction that disability is not me or not now. (Wood et al. 2014: 147)

In short, the ethics of access will require a thoroughgoing interrogation of how our social landscape privileges certain kind of experiencers, on the one hand, and casts aside certain other kinds of experiencers, on the other hand, doing so in ways that are intimately intertwined with the co-construction of our categories of normalcy and disability. As Anita Silvers puts it, working toward genuine accessibility will involve "profound transformation" of the "core conventions that regulate our social interactions" (Silvers 1998: 33).

I want to take a step away from the conversations about costliness, productivity, and legal protections that have so often dominated conversations about access in order to talk about a broader set of ethical issues. Many questions about access involve the literal ability of disabled people to physically enter spaces. This focus is for good reason, as there are far too many places that disabled people still cannot even physically enter. (A snapshot: as of the summer of 2019, only 23 percent of the subway stations in New York City—a city that runs primarily on public transportation—were "accessible" under the terms of the Americans with Disabilities Act [ADA].) Other questions concern whether people can access spaces and experiences in the sense of, for example, the availability of American Sign Language (ASL) interpreters for D/deaf people at talks and concerts. While these basic necessities are, of course, crucial for securing access, I take the normative dimension in these cases to be simple: it is unconscionable to not provide basic access to civic life for all disabled people in society.

In this chapter, I aim to tackle a theoretically thornier set of issues that involve cases in which a person can enter a given space and therein meaningfully participate in some way, though not without significant struggle that could, in theory, be eliminated via some modification. These cases include ones in which a person must exert excessive effort to engage in the social activities themselves, in addition to cases in which the "exhausting labors of passing may make some semblance of presence possible, but with significant hidden costs to the participant" that may manifest themselves at a later time (Hamraie 2016: 261). Examples of cases with such hidden costs include the performance of activities that require concurrently suppressing one's tics or maintaining the sustained performance of non-instinctual eye contact.

Bringing these kinds of cases into focus can help us to see how the ways in which we organize our built environments, social norms, and institutions cater to a mythical "ideal" and thereby, through pathologization, make it difficult for people who do not fit with this ideal to meaningfully access them. As a shorthand, I will call this suite of arranged environments, norms, and institutions our "common social life." Whereas the architect of a new building might be subject to laws requiring the inclusion of ramps and elevators, we are all, collectively, the social architects of our common social life. I take it as given, therefore, that we are subject to the demands of the ethics of accessibility as we go about creating and modifying our social environments. Just about all of us live in societies with entrenched histories of ableism, so we are starting off at a deficit. This observation brings us to the question at hand: given this deeply imperfect status quo, how ought we to navigate claims to modify aspects of our current common social life in order to improve disability access?

In answering this, we will need to grapple with two related questions: one about legitimacy and the other about the adjudication of conflicts.

First, as I have already noted, when looking through a de-pathologized lens, it is more difficult to draw the line between neurodiversity-related access requests and non-neurodiversity-related requests to change some aspect of our common social life. How ought we to think about this difference and demarcate it? What kind of normative weight does the fact that a request is legitimately related to neurodiversity carry with it?

Second, Universal Design (or, UD)—the design of environments accessible to all from the get-go—has been promoted by disability advocates since the 1960s. This movement aims to radically reconceive the default design of spaces, such that maximal accessibility is the norm, with the concept of an ability-neutral space acting as an aspirational idea as well as a sort of creative challenge to the status quo. The fact of the matter is, however, that some environments cannot be made simultaneously accessible to all because the steps that are required to make some aspect of our common social life accessible to a certain set of disability needs may conflict with another set of disability access needs. While this realization is too often used to rationalize inaccessibility, it is also true. Of course, many (or maybe even most?) times such conflicts are merely illusory or contrived—a result of a lack of creativity, understanding, or investment in relevant technologies. Yet even in the most ideal of circumstances, there can be conflicts where what is needed to make some space accessible for one person is precisely the thing that makes the space inaccessible to another person (Barclay 2011). Examples include: access claims to dim lighting and bright lighting (Shakespeare 2006: 46), warmer or cooler room temperatures, the need to stim and misokinesia (a deeply aversive automatic reaction to others' repetitive movements), claims to relax norms about the volume of voices due to an inability to control one's volume, and hypersensitivities to louder voices. Ultimately, there can be no truly "ability-neutral" environment, that is, there can be no environment that does not advantage people with some physical and mental characteristics (Barclay 2011, 2018). If we wish to promote disability justice, how, then, should we mediate these inevitable conflicts between incompatible but legitimately disability-based claims for access?

A Real-Life Illustration

To make concrete the kinds of applications that I have in mind, I will illustrate with a case that stems from lived experience. My spouse is autistic and, for them, this comes with auditory processing differences. In particular, auditory discrimination of spoken word can sometimes be challenging. As they have described it to me, listening is, for them, a two-step process. The words first come to them in a jumbled mess and they must, in turn, disentangle them before they can understand what has been said. For this reason, watching television with subtitles can be very helpful, easing the cognitive burden of unscrambling spoken sentences and making the activity more relaxing. It is not as if they *can't* watch TV otherwise. We communicate in spoken language with each other every day. However, the combination of background music, unfamiliar speakers, and increased difficulty of reading lips makes parsing television even more difficult than other forms of auditory communication.

While subtitles are widely lauded as an accessibility measure with a broad range of benefits, I find it difficult to watch television with subtitles. I tend to avoid watching foreign shows in different languages for this reason and would never choose to watch something with subtitles on my own. For a long time, I could not pinpoint why this was the case, except that I found them distracting. Had I simply thought that captions were a visual eyesore? Was I some sort of television aesthete who thought my immersion was ruined by seeing the words before they were spoken? None of these possibilities seemed right to me; but I knew, my preference was very strong, given that I would usually rather not watch television at all than watch a subtitled show.

I eventually came to discover that my aversion to subtitles was actually rooted in a sensory processing difference of my own, which I did not previously know existed. It turns out that I have a visual processing difference known as ventral simultanagnosia, which entails that whereas I can visually see multiple objects at a time, I can only *identify* one at a time in a complex scene. In retrospect, this diagnosis makes a lot of sense of some of my experiences. For instance, I had to skip all of the questions on the GRE (Graduate Record Examinations) that involved making inferences from graphs; I never could understand the Sunday comics; and I often miss visual cues, which, in television, are frequently used as crucial storytelling devices. Subtitles are difficult for me when I am watching television, I have come to understand, because the presence of written words, which my eyes gravitate toward as more familiar visual signals, exacerbates my tendency to miss crucial visual information.

From the very beginning of our relationship, I was puzzled by the conundrum of whether my spouse and I should put on the subtitles when watching television together. Although my preference was stronger than theirs, the fact that their preference was related to neurodiversity and mine, given what I knew at the time, was not, seemed to make a normative difference. What was it about having the label of "ventral simultanagnosia" that made me come to believe that my access claim now had legitimate normative weight? And, now that we found ourselves in a situation in which we could safely say that both of our claims were related to neurodiversity, we were faced with the problem of two neurodiversity-related claims that conflicted at a fundamental level. How then, I wondered, should we adjudicate *that* kind of conflict?

Perhaps, in the ideal world, the government would invest in supplying my spouse with a pair of captioning glasses and inventing and supplying to me a pair of glasses that superimpose image descriptive tags. But that is not the world in which we live. The world in which we currently live requires that we sometimes navigate the principles of justice on our own in a sub-institutional way. It requires that we navigate our marriage ethically in a way that is consistent with promoting disability justice. But what, exactly, does that require in this case?

In what follows, I provide a preliminary survey of five different approaches that one could take to a situation like ours, as well as to neurodiversity and the ethics of accessibility in general.

Approach 1: Biting the Bullet

One option is to bite the bullet and admit that there is no fundamental difference in kind between access-related preferences and run-of-the-mill preferences after all. As Daniel Putnam et al. (2019) point out, irrespective of any special claim to compensation that one might propose be tied to their disability status, aspects of our common social life might be condemned for being unjustly restrictive. Broadly egalitarian concerns require that we build inclusive environments for the wide range of human variation and that each person's claims to aspects of our common social life be respected in their full weight. On this view, when there are conflicts between two preferences, in general, the stronger preferences ought to win out. As a point in favor of this approach to access conflicts, strength of preference is likely to correspond to willingness to participate, thus honoring stronger preferences is more likely to retain the broadest range of participation, which might be seen as an important aspect of promoting inclusivity.

While it seems that we ought to pay special attention to neurodiversity-related requests due to the privileged status that they have, in this view it is not because they actually have any such status or are more important than any other preferences. One way of explaining why these requests nevertheless seem to be worthy of special attention is that they tend to be subject to significantly more invalidation than other kinds of preferences. We have reason to treat them *as if* they have a special normative status because we are epistemically positioned poorly with respect to their recognition. As a result, we assume that such preferences are much weaker than they in fact are. This view suggests that to adjudicate conflicts, we should look to the relative strength of preferences, but then adjust the weightings in favor of neurodiversity-related claims due to these foreseeable epistemic gaps.

What kinds of epistemic problems might warrant such a norm? First, neurodivergent people are subject to testimonial injustice (Fricker 2007), in which we are systematically wronged in our capacity as knowers, even of, and indeed especially of, our own experience and needs. We are subject to testimonial injustice, that is, credibility deficits on the basis of prejudicial characterizations of people with neurodivergent traits and/or labels. We are socially devalued, as a group, due to our identity group membership, cast as emotionally unstable, cognitively unreliable, or bizarre, as well as dangerous and morally suspicious: features that interfere with the perceived credibility of our characterizations of our own experiences and needs (Jackson et al. 2009: 167–8; Carel and Kidd 2014: 529; Kurs and Grinshpoon 2018). This credibility deficit leads to a second factor that works in tandem—namely, that we are less likely to express our preferences because we face poor outcomes when we do. Given the stigma and the long-standing trope of disabled people as burdens, we tend to downplay our own access needs.

We are also subject to hermeneutical injustice (Fricker 2007). We sometimes simply do not have the words to explain why our preferences are as they are, which can make it less believable that our strong preferences really are as strong as we say that they are. Having only inchoate ways of characterizing one's experience may stem in part from an unjust flaw in shared hermeneutic resources. Neurodivergent people have long been systematically excluded from the institutions that seek to explain and make sense of the phenomena of cognitive diversity, which could very well lead to a failure to develop ways of adequately describing the experience from a first-personal point of view. In academic fields such as philosophy and psychiatry that aim to describe cognitive difference, neurodivergent people are disenfranchised from shaping dominant descriptive models in their likenesses since, as Abigail Gosselin puts it, reasoning capacity "is the currency of power, authority, and privilege" such that self-disclosure threatens one's status (Gosselin 2019). When we do have words to explain our neurodiversity-related difficulties with navigating the world, they are often medicalized to the extent that they imply that the most salient, or perhaps easiest, thing to do would be to fix us rather than to fix the world. Consider, for example, the fact that the frustrated reactions of autistic children whose complex access needs have not been met tend to be reductively described as "meltdowns," which makes these reactions seem disproportionate to the situations that cause them. A tendency to see neurodiversity-related difficulties as personal medical problems dovetails with a form of cultural imperialism that helps to create the illusion that many of the dominant norms that dictate our common social life are important rather than arbitrary (Young 2009).

Yet even if we were to have perfect epistemic access to the relative strength of people's preferences, the bullet-biting approach would lead to some unintuitive results. There are some people who, regarding likes and dislikes, traits, and ideals, just have extremely strong preferences that have nothing to do with what we tend to think of as neurodiversity-related access needs. The aforementioned view predicts that we ought to let such strong desires win out over neurodiversity-related preferences that are strong but not as strong as these non-neurodiversity-related preferences. While it may be easy enough to bite the bullet on this matter regarding a single choice-point or incident, it may be more difficult to do so once we think about the cumulative effects. To illustrate, imagine a person with neurodivergent traits who, when attempting to advocate for their access, always encounters a person with such very strong run-of-the-mill preferences such that this person's desires always win out over theirs. Such people with strong personalities, if positioned in the wrong place at the wrong time, could make it so that every time a neurodiversity-related concern comes up, it never gets acknowledged. The possibility of these sorts of large-scale outcomes seems like a highly unintuitive potential consequence for an ethics of accessibility.

Another potential unintuitive consequence for this approach that is not solved by accounting for epistemic injustice is that some people may grow weary from self-advocacy and become more accustomed to just coping with their discomfort. The concept of access fatigue is relevant here. As Annika Konrad explains, building on scholarship about the impact of accumulation which has been developed in the fields of critical race theory and intersectional feminism, access fatigue is "the everyday pattern of constantly needing to help others participate in access, a demand so taxing and relentless that, at times, it makes access simply not worth the effort" (Konrad 2021: 180). Over time, in recognition of how onerous the self-advocacy process would be to make common social life truly accessible, a person's desire for that change may also dwindle.[4]

Just as the trope of the disabled person as a burden can make us more likely to downplay our needs at the level of what we reveal to others, sometimes this same stigma infiltrates our own self-concept. *I ought to be able to make do with less and deal with more*, we think. Our preferences to modify our common social life can dwindle, while our preferences to *be* different strengthen. Some neurodivergent people will become depressed as a result, which can enshrine self-blame and weaken the strength of their desires in general. At the end of the day, it seems that an ethics of accessibility should be able to secure meaningful access for such people even in the absence of their recognition of their own worthiness. It is unclear whether the bullet-biting approach ever could be made to be compatible with this moral demand.

Approach 2: Suffering/Difficulty

Given that one's own preferences seem to provide a somewhat shaky foundation on which to base an ethics of accessibility, we might instead look for a more objective measure by which we can compare neurodivergent-access claims to the claims of others with strong preferences and by which we might compare the significance of different access claims to each other. Perhaps instead of looking at preferences, we might look at suffering as a basis of comparison. Having run-of-the-mill preferences frustrated can be disappointing but attempting to endure through experiences in environments that are not well-suited to your neurodivergence can be downright painful. Suffering need not be thought of as a property of one's neurodivergence but rather can be thought of as a property of the relationship between one's traits and a particular environment. When faced with two conflicting neurodiversity-related access claims, according to this view, we can see which modifications lead to the elimination of a greater amount of suffering. If it is primarily environments that disable by causing undue suffering, the normative import of questions about access become about the degree of suffering that an environment's arrangement is likely to cause (or alleviate) given its various possible configurations.

A nice feature of this approach is that it helps explain why meeting access needs is not a matter of accommodating wants or appeasing people, but rather is a matter of eliminating needless pain and difficulty that has been propagated by the unexamined conventions of our common social life that exclude neurodivergent people. This approach could therefore work in tandem with the movement to expand our conception of access needs from a model of accommodation to a more broadscale restructuring of an oppressive society. In practice, one proxy for determining the degree of suffering might be a person's willingness to participate in the activity without the modifications requested. Since the people who suffer the most, given the current set-up, are the people who are most likely to be shut out because an activity or event is so inaccessible that it is not even worth participating in, focusing on suffering would prioritize the people who have had the least access to our common social life.

One problem with this view, though, is that it is difficult to assess and compare qualitatively different kinds of struggle. We might wonder how, for example, someone's ability to persist through sensory overwhelm brought about by fluorescent lighting can even meaningfully be compared to another person's difficulty seeing an image in dimmer light.

Another problem with this view is that a person may face not just one but many small struggles that are not especially difficult compared to other kinds of struggles. Nevertheless, these sorts of small struggles could add up. This way of adjudicating competing claims could unjustly privilege the claims of people whose suffering would be great if they tried to participate where that difficulty is limited to only one domain over the claims of people who face a large number of more commonplace struggles when navigating many different aspects of our common social life. Relatedly, it is far from clear even in a case where two people have struggles that are limited to only one domain that it would be fair to privilege, every single time, the claim of the person who would struggle slightly more than the other person.

Furthermore, while the elimination of pain and unnecessary difficulty is a worthy goal that shows how serious claims to access are, focus on this dimension of it might unduly limit the scope of possible societal gains that could be made by making room for neurodivergent thriving. Robert Chapman and Havi Carel note that we should expect there to be a plurality of ways of thriving, many of which have been rendered invisible due to an overly narrow focus on species-standard flourishing (Chapman and Carel 2022: 8). Access, we might think, should not just be about the elimination of suffering but also the promotion of diverse forms of thriving.

It might be possible to habituate to an inaccessible environment over time after repeated exposure such that tolerating it does not feel all that difficult. Nevertheless, the situation is subpar, and neurodiversity advocates might rightly press that we want to build our social environment in ways that go beyond ensuring that they are minimally tolerable. Think, again, of my spouse's willingness to carry on without subtitles. It might be that their preference is not that strong because they have become overly tolerant of suffering. It might, however, be that they have stopped experiencing their difficulty in parsing audio as a form of suffering at all, and instead have come to see it as a tragic fact of life that they will often have to watch things with no subtitles. It may not be especially difficult to carry on and manage trying to enjoy watching television this way because their past difficult experiences may have led them to complacent comfort in the fact that they simply will have to try to piece things together with the scraps that they have—they hardly know any other way. Meanwhile, my level of frustration when attempting to watch television with subtitles, however, might be fairly high. The level of difficulty, in turn, though, could stem from just how novel the situation is for me. I am not accustomed to watching television with subtitles, and there have been only a limited number of circumstances in the past where my visual processing has given me all that much of an issue in comparison to the issues that my spouse's auditory processing gives them. It seems that felt struggle on its own is not sufficient to capture the important relative difference that we have with regard to the situation. This dimension of the case seems to matter morally, but it is unclear that a difficulty-based view has the resources to be able to explain why it should.

Approach 3: Disavowal/Unchangeability

Another approach holds that the degree to which an access claim is legitimate is based upon the degree to which the person's preferences are not held on purpose or the degree to which the person could not change their preferences regarding the scenario. To get at the intuitive idea, suppose there is a clash between the claim of someone who gets overstimulated in loud environments and someone who prefers a loud pizzeria over a quieter one across the street. Even if the second person really likes the pizza at the louder place, they probably could be a little bit more flexible if they tried, whereas someone's susceptibility to auditory overstimulation is unlikely to be as modifiable.

To see why this kind of factor might matter, we can take a page from the literature about the "expensive tastes" objection to welfare egalitarianism in political philosophy. Welfare egalitarianism holds that citizens are entitled to equal levels of welfare in terms of something like happiness or life satisfaction. The expensive tastes objection is this: it seems unintuitive for someone with a born predisposition to require fancy wine for baseline happiness to be entitled to the wine to the same degree as others are entitled to their more reasonable basic necessities for happiness. (For an overview, see Keller 2002). In many ways, the person who just has a strong aesthetic repulsion to subtitles is like the person with expensive tastes. Such a person has a genuine strong preference, but it seems unintuitive that a large entitlement should follow from it, especially one that can bar someone else from what they would otherwise be owed.

One helpful suggestion made in this literature by G. A. Cohen is that the person with expensive tastes, unlike people with deep unmet basic needs, does not disavow their preference and likely could change it if they wanted to (Cohen 1989). Similarly, if I really had only a merely aesthetic distaste for subtitles, we would probably be right to assume that I had acculturated tastes to the visual medium that could be changed if not for my uncritical embrace of my own preferences. My spouse, on the other hand, might wish that they did not need to use the subtitles; it would be easier not only on me but also on them. However, their auditory processing difficulties are not so easily changed. They might turn off a fan in the room or, on a more long-term basis, they might invest in speech or occupational therapy to practice, but most strategies for their auditory communicative success involve modification of the environment.

This suggested difference could help explain the legitimacy question, but it can also be used in much the same way to solve the adjudication problem. We might ask, for example, would it be easier for Person A or Person B to skirt their difficulties by changing their condition? While Person B might not be able to modify their innate visual discrimination any more easily than Person A could change their auditory processing abilities, Person B might be able to consciously acclimate to having the captions on and just not looking at them.

One issue, though, is that some neurodiversity-related traits are, frankly, changeable. It may be easier to take Adderall to improve one's focus than it is to change one's long-ingrained aesthetic preference. With modern pharmaceuticals and therapeutic techniques, there is a range of traits that can be modified and fine-tuned almost in a bespoke manner. Likewise, certain non-neurodiversity-related vicious preferences may be disavowed as part of one's deepest self, and linger precisely because they are difficult to change despite one's hopes.

Furthermore, neurodivergent traits can be, and in fact are, embraced by many people as a source of pride fundamental to one's identity. It would be counterproductive to the aims of neurodiversity acceptance and pride to require a person to disavow their neurodivergence in order to legitimize their access claims. Central to the aims of a neurodiversity paradigm shift is the idea that cognitive diversity benefits human society on an ecological level (Chapman 2021). An ethics of access whose welcome would be overstayed in a world with cures is antithetical to the aims of the neurodiversity movement.

Approach 4: Minority-Group Membership

As we have seen, when considering a metric, there is always the risk that neurodivergent people will downplay or fail to recognize their own legitimate suffering, needs, preferences, and potential to thrive. It might be compelling to explain this self-abnegation by using the concept of internalized oppression, a psychologized acceptance of stereotypes associated with one's minority status that causes people to act in ways that further their own oppression. Internalized oppression can lead to effects as varied as depression, a sense that one lacks agency, and a sense of oneself as fundamentally deviant. Any of these effects can certainly color the way that one perceives one's own access claims (Liebow 2016).

If that observation is correct, then perhaps it is not our own perception of our needs that makes the crucial normative difference between competing claims here, but rather the fact of our oppression itself. To put the thought plainly, even if a white middle-class housewife in the 1950s did not see a need to complain about her lot in life, her possession of this self-understanding did not mean that she was not entitled to liberation. The degree to which her lot in life was proscribed by stereotypes of femininity and the degree to which her autonomy was limited by the patriarchy, we might think, are the kinds of facts that would confer upon her needs special normative merit, above and beyond, say, her husband's strong distaste for cooking and cleaning. Similarly, on a minority group's conception of what disabilities are, the main reason that neurodivergent people encounter difficulties in life is that they face discrimination akin to the kinds faced by other kinds of minorities.[5]

When we conceive of "neurodivergence" as, most fundamentally, a kind of membership in an oppressed minority group, we can recognize that neurodiversity-related access claims are demands to repair systemic and/or historic injustices. On this view, we can answer the legitimacy question by asking whether the person's identity/trait that grounds their access claim is related to righting the wrongs of oppression. Run-of-the-mill preferences about, say, aesthetics or convenience, are not plausibly related to any kind of discrimination or oppression. In this way, the view can offer a justification for distinguishing neurodiversity-related claims from other claims without having to conclude that there is any fundamental kind of difference between neurodiversity-related traits and other traits. It is merely a contingent fact that people who have some sorts of traits rather than others have been subjected to widespread discrimination.

If this thought is correct, then adjudicating between two different neurodiversity-related claims could be a matter of assessing the degree to which people with the relevant traits have been subject to discrimination, or the degree to which a person with the relevant trait tends to experience minority-related impacts that affect various parts of their life. The ethics of access becomes the ethics of righting historic and ongoing wrongs. While this approach may seem appealing, it comes dangerously close to advocating for the establishment of some sort of "Oppression Olympics." There may occasionally be cases in which two conflicting access claims quite obviously stem from very different sorts of minority statuses. Perhaps one person's minority status is rarely relevant to their experience of the world and causes only minor sorts of social friction, while the other person's minority status is a pervasive and intense source of one's ostracization from society. More often, though, we would wade into very murky waters if we tried to determine who is "more" of a minority than someone else. This worry is made worse once we realize that it may not just be difficult to sort out but actually impossible to make such calculations. The theory of intersectionality (Crenshaw 1989), for example, strongly implies that there are no commensurable building blocks of minority status.

The minority-group approach also runs into a potentially vicious circularity when put to use to try to legitimate claims as genuinely related to neurodiversity. Suppose that a person is born with a never-before-seen neurodevelopmental condition. There is clearly no preexisting history of discrimination toward people with her particular profile of cognitive traits. Is it really plausible that her access claims only get validated beyond the status of mere preferences once her exclusion continues along a pattern indicative of oppression until the point at which she is owed recompense? We might think that this problem only arises when we understand belonging to an oppressed minority too narrowly. It is not people who have her particular neurotype that are her fellow minorities, but rather neurodivergent (or even disabled) people as a whole. And neurodivergent people on the whole have certainly been subject to large-scale oppression. But by virtue of what does her nonstandard neurological make-up qualify her as neurodivergent? Taking this tack only serves to reopen the question of what makes the important normative difference between her traits and more run-of-the-mill traits.

For many questions, self-identification or the attribution of a diagnostic label might be good enough to make a person count. Adi Goldiner (2022) argues that identification with a label is sufficient for justifying claims to workplace accommodations because any potential advantage to be gained by aligning oneself with the disabled community is counterbalanced by the stigma that one is sure to face once their behavior is viewed through the lens of their diagnosis. On views like Elizabeth Barnes's (Barnes 2016: 46) to be disabled just *is* to be someone for whom the disability rights movement is fighting. When adjudicating conflicting access claims, though, these pragmatic sorts of sidestepping simply will not suffice. As Leslie Francis says when commenting on the application of Barnes's view to the ethics of access, Barnes would have to argue that accommodations should be available for people when the disability rights movement would make claims of justice for them. Yet this implication, according to Francis, "gets the justification backwards." As Francis puts the problem,

> Instead of the justification being what a rights movement seeks, it should instead be what are the wrongs to be remedied? For disability, they are the wrongs associated with exclusion for supposedly impaired physical or mental function. The wrongs are not the failure to compensate; rather, they are the wrongs of systematic misjudgment of the capabilities of people who function differently. (Francis 2018: 1147)

Approach 5: Going Diachronic

There is at least one other kind of view that is worth considering. This kind of view would admit that many individual choices made between two competing access claims cannot be justified one way or the other, at least not in isolation. These choices may well be examples of what ethicists call "genuine moral dilemmas," that is, situations in which an "agent is required to do each of two (or more) actions; the agent can do each of the actions; but the agent cannot do both (or all) of the actions" and "neither of the conflicting requirements is overridden" by the other (McConnell 2018). How could this be? Perhaps there are multiple normative currencies that matter that are not commensurable with each other. For example: maybe both the alleviation of present-day suffering and the reparation for historical discrimination matter. It could be that there is a way to meaningfully weigh these considerations against each other such that a unique decision is justified in each particular choice. However, it could be the case that there is no fact of the matter about which single factor is more important than the other when they come in conflict. The kind of approach in question would be to admit the latter, namely, that there is no meaningful sense in which these two kinds of factors can be meaningfully compared in a one-off situation.

What, then, can we do? We can move from thinking about the ethics of one-off scenarios to thinking about a just distribution extended over time. One option to consider would involve weighting the claims equally for everyone who meets the legitimacy threshold by any of the previously discussed metrics.[6] In a situation in which the same conflicts will be faced by the same group of people with static access needs, the choices can be distributed to ensure long-term even distribution of claims that are addressed. In situations with changing groups of people or needs, a lottery could be held in which all legitimate neurodiversity claims are chosen at random to be addressed. A related, but distinct, option would be to treat each neurodiverse person's ability to fully participate as equal. The difference between these two approaches concerns people for whom the satisfaction of their access claims entail barring more than one other potential participant from being able to meaningfully participate. If equality of participation rather than of claims is pursued, then such people would have to participate on equal footing less frequently than others in order to allow for fair distribution across neurodiverse participants. It is interesting to note that even when taking this rather neutral kind of approach, some normative choice must be made about whether to prioritize the equality of claims or the equality of participants.

At this point, it might be worth pausing to wonder whether following such metrics might be somewhat alienating for the people with access claims. Independently of whose claim ought to win out in a particular circumstance, thinking about the adjudication of multiple access conflicts over time brings into focus the fact that the adjudication process itself ought to be carried out in an ethical way. I have experienced situations where my access needs were voted on by committee, in addition to situations in which I was left to hash it out with someone who had conflicting access claims. Whether these processes would have led to the fairest distribution of outcomes really took a backseat to the discomfort that I felt about the lack of concern and caring that others displayed about the kind of experience that I would be having. Mia Mingus captures these feelings quite poignantly:

> The fear of being left by the people you love and who are supposed to love you. The pain of staring or passing, the sting of disappointment, the exhaustion of having the same conversations over and over again. The throbbing foolishness of getting your hopes up and the shrinking of yourself in order to maintain. It is an echoing loneliness; part shame, part guilt, part constant apology and thank you. (Mingus 2012)

With this in mind, we might think about moving away from designing procedures to thinking about the kinds of connectedness that we can foster with regard to co-constructing shared social life among neurodiverse people. We might describe this thinking in terms of fostering an ethos of access intimacy. Access intimacy, as Mingus writes of it, involves sensing that one's access needs are anticipated and understood; that instead of being invited into spaces that are not designed for us, people are called upon to inhabit *our* worlds. The hope is that cultivating true access intimacy can foster the kind of creativity to co-construct forms of social life where certain kinds of conflicts are less likely to arise and where the labor of obtaining access is itself distributed more justly. On the other hand, "[s]ometimes access intimacy doesn't even mean that everything is 100% accessible" (Mingus 2011). As Desiree Valentine puts it, access intimacy involves nevertheless "staying-with" the constant struggle of inaccessibility—going through the mess with someone who understands, takes seriously, co-commiserates, and affirms the reality of the situation (Valentine 2020: 84)

While the idea of access intimacy gives us some instructions about how to approach access conflicts, how does this view solve the problem about who gets to count? This view, unlike several of the other views, lacks the resources to make determinations between neurodiversity-related access claims and other claims. That said, perhaps one virtue of this view is that it can be rather maximalist in defining the bounds of neurodiversity. We ought to build access friendships and learn about how people operate in this world regardless of whether their differences are differences that have historically been associated with the neurodiversity movement. Doing so might be seen as a way of respecting the dignity of individuals. The very nature of these friendships will put pressure on us to adapt our preferences, requirements, and assumptions about the operation of various parts of shared social life. One cannot, it would seem, build access intimacy with someone who has auditory processing difficulties without interrogating one's own discomfort with subtitles. Caring about each other can transform—from a zero-sum game into acts of solidarity—the project in which we attempt to recalibrate our preferences, regardless of whether these preferences are related to neurodiversity or not.

While this view offers a promising recasting of the problem landscape within intimate relationships, it may be difficult to scale to smaller and larger units of concern. First, one-off access conflicts will still exist, and embracing this view would require allowing for some level of arbitrariness in how individual conflicts are solved. The view gives no decision procedure for ensuring a justified choice in a given conflict situation. That said, this issue (insofar as it is an issue) is not unique, but rather a familiar feature of virtue ethics and relational ethics. Securing interpersonal relationships of access intimacy is also no guarantee that the right kinds of large-scale societal shifts will be prioritized. The distribution of these connections may itself be unjust and so the ethical questions about conflict will simply come into play at a different moment (see Cordelli 2015). Furthermore, what, on an individual and consensual level is liberatory, can be exhausting, exploitative, and intrusive when the trust required to facilitate emotional vulnerability is absent. In this way, scaling up the model of access intimacy as a framework for the facilitation of larger spaces in an ableist world runs the risk of opening up neurodivergent people to forced intimacy (Mingus 2017).

Conclusion

To sum up, I have posed two interrelated questions to set the stage for a philosophical exploration of neurodiversity and the ethics of accessibility: first, what makes neurodiversity-related claims to access have special normative weight? and second, how should we adjudicate conflicts between two or more legitimate claims? I have surveyed the pros and cons of five general kinds of approaches that one could take: (1) accepting that only epistemic factors make these special cases; (2) adjudicating based on degree of suffering; (3) focusing on the degree to which one's needs are unchangeable; (4) treating the special weight of claims as involving requests to repair systemic discrimination; and (5) refocusing on accessibility as extended across time. While there is something to be said for each kind of approach, I must admit that I find none of them fully satisfactory. Nevertheless, I hope to have demonstrated the existence of a theoretically interesting and practically significant normative terrain to be explored, a philosophical and political challenge that arises wholly from within the lived experience of neurodivergent moral agents who are attempting to build a better world together.

Notes

1 It is outside the scope of this chapter to consider the difficult question of just how far we ought to extend the term to cover various (so-called) mood, personality, addictive and psychotic disorders, developmental disabilities, and brain injuries, although I suspect its usefulness might be quite broad.

2 See also Francis (2018: 1146).

3 For example, see Dolmage (2006), Garland-Thomson (2011), Hamraie (2013, 2016), Price (2014), Tremain (2013), Yergeau (2013).

4 One way to rehabilitate this kind of approach in light of these concerns might be to ask not what you want but what you would want to want, or what you would want if suitably idealized (including being aware of your own oppression). Analogous moves are made in the literatures on relational autonomy and preference-satisfaction forms of well-being.

5 For discussion, see Wasserman and Aas (2022).

6 This approach also presents a potential way to handle cases where there are two or more conflicting claims that are legitimized by one's minority status, if as discussed previously, there may be no sense to make of questions of who is *more* of a minority than someone else.

References

Barclay, Linda (2011), "Justice and Disability: What Kind of Theorizing Is Needed?" *Journal of Social Philosophy* 42 (3): 273–87. https://doi.org/10.1111/j.1467-9833.2011.01533.x.

Barnes, Elizabeth (2016), *The Minority Body: A Theory of Disability*, Oxford: Oxford University Press.

Brewer, Elizabeth, Cynthia L. Selfe, and Melanie Yergeau (2014), "Creating a Culture of Access in Composition Studies," *Composition Studies* 42 (2): 151–4.

Carel, Havi and Ian James Kidd (2014), "Epistemic Injustice in Healthcare: A Philosophical Analysis," *Medical Health Care and Philosophy* 17: 529–40.

Chapman, Robert (2019), "Neurodiversity Theory and its Discontents: Autism, Schizophrenia, and the Social Model," in S. Tekin and R. Bluhm (eds.), *The Bloomsbury Companion to the Philosophy of Psychiatry*, 371–89, London: Bloomsbury.

Chapman, Robert (2021), "Neurodiversity and the Social Ecology of Mental Functions," *Perspectives on Psychological Science* 16 (6): 1360–72. https://doi.org/10.1177/1745691620959833.

Chapman, Robert and Havi Carel (2022), "Neurodiversity, Epistemic Injustice, and the Good Human Life," *Journal of Social Philosophy*, 1–18. https://doi.org/10.1111/josp.12456.

Cohen, G. A. (1989), "On the Currency of Egalitarian Justice," *Ethics* 99: 906–44.

Cordelli, Chiara (2015), "Distributive Justice and the Problem of Friendship," *Political Studies* 63 (3): 679–95. https://doi.org/10.1111/1467-9248.12115.

Crenshaw, Kimberlé (1989), "Demarginalizing the Intersection of Race and Sex: A Black Feminist Critique of Antidiscrimination Doctrine, Feminist Theory and Antiracist Politics," *University of Chicago Legal Forum* 140: 139–67.

Dolmage, Jay (2006), "Mapping Composition," in Brenda Brueggeman and Cindy Lewiecki-Wilson, with Jay Dolmage (eds.), *Disability and the Teaching of Writing: A Critical Sourcebook*, 14–27, Boston: Bedford St. Martin's.

Francis, Leslie (2018), "Understanding Disability Civil Rights Non-Categorically: The Minority Body and the Americans with Disabilities Act," *Philosophical Studies* 175 (5): 1135–49. https://doi.org/10.1007/s11098-018-1067-x.

Fricker, Miranda (2007), *Epistemic Injustice: Power and the Ethics of Knowing*, Oxford: Oxford University Press.

Garland-Thomson, Rosemarie (2011), "Misfits: A Feminist Disability Materialist Concept," *Hypatia: A Journal of Feminist Philosophy* 26 (3): 591–609.

Goldiner, Adi (2022), "Moral Accommodations: Tolerating Impairment-Related Misconduct," *Sixth MAP-Penn Conference: Philosophy of Disability and Illness*, April 8, Philadelphia.

Gosselin, Abigail (2019), "Philosophizing from Experience: First-Person Accounts and Epistemic Justice," *Journal of Social Philosophy* 50 (1): 45–68.

Hamraie, Aimi (2013), "Designing Collective Access: A Feminist Disability Theory of Universal Design," *Disability Studies Quarterly* 33 (4). Available at: https://dsqsds.org/article/view/3871/3411 (accessed July 23, 2023).

Hamraie, Aimi (2016), "Beyond Accommodation: Disability, Feminist Philosophy, and the Design of Everyday Academic Life," *PhiloSOPHIA* 6 (2): 259–71. https://doi.org/10.1353/phi.2016.0022.

"Increasing Accessibility," *New York City Council Website*. Available at: https://council.nyc.gov/data/increasing-accessibility/ (accessed June 20, 2023).

Jackson Lynsey, Jeremy Tudway, David C. Giles, and J. Smith (2009), "An Exploration of the Social Identity of Mental Health Inpatient Service Users," *Journal of Psychiatric and Mental Health Nursing* 16 (2): 167–76.

Keller, Simon (2002), "Expensive Tastes and Distributive Justice," *Social Theory and Practice* 28 (4): 529–52. https://doi.org/10.5840/soctheorpract200228426.

Konrad, Annika M. (2021), "Access Fatigue: The Rhetorical Work of Disability in Everyday Life," *College English* 83 (3): 179–99.

Kurs, Rena and Alexander Grinshpoon (2018), "Vulnerability of Individuals With Mental Disorders to Epistemic Injustice in Both Clinical and Social Domains," *Ethics and Behavior* 28 (4): 336–46.

Liebow, Nabina (2016), "Internalized Oppression and Its Varied Moral Harms: Self-Perceptions of Reduced Agency and Criminality," *Hypatia: A Journal of Feminist Philosophy* 31 (4): 713–29.

McConnell, Terrance (2018), "Moral Dilemmas," in Edward N. Zalta (ed.), *The Stanford Encyclopedia of Philosophy*, Fall 2018 edition. Available at: https://plato.stanford.edu/archives/fall2018/entries/moral-dilemmas/ (accessed June 20, 2023).

Mingus, Mia (2011), "Access Intimacy: The Missing Link," Leaving Evidence (blog), May 5. Available at: https://leavingevidence.wordpress.com/2011/05/05/access-intimacy-the-missing-link/ (accessed June 20, 2023).

Mingus, Mia (2012), "Feeling the Weight: Some Beginning Notes on Disability, Access, and Love," Leaving Evidence (blog), May 8. Available at: https://leavingevidence.wordpress.com/2012/05/08/feeling-the-weight-some-beginning-notes-on-disability-access-and-love/ (accessed June 20, 2023).

Mingus, Mia (2017), "Forced Intimacy: An Ableist Norm," Leaving Evidence (blog), August 6. Available at: https://leavingevidence.wordpress.com/2017/08/06/forced-intimacy-an-ableist-norm/ (accessed June 20, 2023).

Price, Margaret (2014), "Representational Labor: Doing the Work of Race, Disability, and Sexuality in the Academy," Paper presented at National Women's Studies Association, San Juan, Puerto Rico, November 14.

Putnam, Daniel, David Wasserman, Jeffrey Blustein, and Adrienne Asch (2019), "Disability and Justice," in Edward N. Zalta (ed.), *The Stanford Encyclopedia of Philosophy*, Fall 2019 edition. Available at: https://plato.stanford.edu/archives/fall2019/entries/disability-justice/ (accessed June 20, 2023).

Shakespeare, Tom (2006), *Disability Rights and Wrongs*, London: Routledge.

Silvers, Anita (1998), "Formal Justice," in Anita Silvers, David Wasserman, and Mary Mahowald (eds.), *Disability, Difference, and Discrimination: Perspectives on Justice in Bioethics and Public Policy*, 23–146, Lanham: Rowman and Littlefield.

Tremain, Shelley (2013), "Introducing Feminist Philosophy of Disability," *Disability Studies Quarterly* 33 (4). Available at: https://dsq-sds.org/article/view/3877/3402.2014 (accessed June 20, 2023).

Valentine, Desiree (2020), "Shifting the Weight of Inaccessibility: Access Intimacy as a Critical Phenomenological Ethos," *Journal of Critical Phenomenology* 3 (2): 76–94.

Walker, Nick (2012), *Throw Away the Master's Tools: Liberating Ourselves from the Pathology Paradigm*, Neurocosmopolitanism. Available at: https://neurocosmopolitanism.com/throw-away-themasters-tools-liberating-ourselvesfrom-the-pathologyparadigm/ (accessed June 20, 2023).

Wasserman, David and Sean Aas (2022), "Disability: Definitions and Models," in Edward N. Zalta (ed.), *The Stanford Encyclopedia of Philosophy*, Summer 2022 edition. Available at: https://plato.stanford.edu/archives/sum2022/entries/disability/ (accessed September 10, 2023).

Wood, Tara, Jay Dolmage, Margaret Price, and Cynthia Lewiecki-Wilson (2014), "Where We Are: Disability and Accessibility," *Composition Studies* 42 (2): 147–50.

Yergeau, Melanie (2013), "Reason," *Kairos* 18 (1). Available at: https://kairos.technorhetoric.net/18.1/ coverweb/yergeau-et-al/pages/reason/index.html (accessed June 20, 2023).

Young, Iris Marion (2009), "Five Faces of Oppression," in George L. Henderson and Marvin Waterstone (eds.), *Geographic Thought: A Praxis Perspective*, 55–71, New York: Routledge.

20 THE ETHICS OF DISABILITY PASSING AND UNCOVERING IN THE PHILOSOPHY CLASSROOM

JOSEPH A. STRAMONDO

Introduction

In February 2015, Peter Railton, an esteemed professor of philosophy, gave the prestigious Dewey Lecture at the Central Division Meeting of the American Philosophical Association (APA). In the lecture, Railton disclosed that he was a disabled person who had lived with depression for decades. He framed this disclosure with an analogy to the political power that has been leveraged by people coming out as gay, putting it thus:

> The stunning reversal of age-old attitudes toward gay marriage came about, not simply because the heterosexual population became "educated" about homosexuality so that they no longer "thought" it a stain on one's character. It came about, I believe, through experience-based moral learning of the kind Dewey continually emphasized. Enough gay individuals courageously took things into their own hands and came out publicly. (Railton 2015: 13)

In turn, Railton seemed to argue that there is some level of moral obligation for other depressed philosophers to similarly come out in order to help change the hearts and minds of those engaged in professional philosophy and perhaps even the body politic as a whole: "Those whose [*sic*] have dwelt in the depths of depression need to come out as well. Some already have, but far too few adult men (big surprise!), and especially far too few of the adult men who somehow have come to bear the stamp of respectability and recognition, and thus are visible to hundreds of students and colleagues" (Railton 2015: 14).

In this chapter, I will ask whether Railton's call to action was justifiable. That is, I will ask: is there a moral duty to disclose one's disability identity within professional philosophy? In response to this question, I will argue that there is a moral reason for disabled faculty to disclose—or, more accurately, to persistently uncover—their respective disability identities in the philosophy classroom. However, I will also explain that this reason can be, and often is, outweighed by competing prudential reasons. Thus, the duty to uncover is not absolute. Finally, I will conclude the chapter with a discussion of why the mere act of disclosure will not itself fulfill one's limited moral obligation to disclose or uncover disability. Rather, the content of the disclosure—that is, the story that one tells about who they are as a disabled person—also matters to the moral impact of the disclosure.

The Concepts of Passing, Disclosure, Coming Out, and Uncovering

I will begin with a discussion of exactly what it means to pass or disclose one's disability identity in the context of the philosophy classroom, paying careful attention to the adjacent concepts of coming out and uncovering. In his article "Passing as Privileged," Daniel Silvermint defines "passing" as the process whereby "an *x* is perceived as a *y*, resulting in *x* being treated or evaluated as a *y*" (Silvermint 2018: 1), noting that there are many "everyday" examples of ways in which people pass. Indeed, we can imagine passing in relatively harmless ways that make our lives easier, such as allowing one's fellow attendees at a Super Bowl party to wrongly perceive them as a football fan and casual consumer of alcohol. Of course, the advantages of such everyday examples of passing are highly contextual. For example, one may want to pass as lacking interest in football if one is at a meeting of the APA or as abstaining from casual alcohol consumption if one is at a meeting of the Southern Baptist Convention. As Silvermint explains, one can pass either actively or passively, "depending on whether a member of *x* is mistaken for a member of *y* or deliberately presents herself as a member of *y*" (3). The difference between actively passing and passively passing may be the difference between just showing up at the Super Bowl party and making small talk between watching the commercials and studying the two teams the night before the game so that one knows the names of the star players and enough about the game to make some reasonably informed comments about what is happening on the TV screen.

Yet my concern in this chapter with how to navigate disability identity in a philosophy classroom must regard passing as nondisabled in an ableist society as a somewhat different phenomenon than these more innocuous examples. Silvermint helpfully defines this phenomenon as passing as privileged: "attempts by members of oppressed, stigmatized, or discriminated-against groups to improve their lives by being misidentified as members of an advantaged group" (Silvermint 2018: 1). Although everyday instances of passing may make anyone's life go easier in some senses, the sort of passing with which I am concerned is enacted by a disabled person in a context in which they are systemically oppressed and offers them some level of protection from the harms of this oppression. Furthermore, although passing as nondisabled in an ableist society in general and in higher education in particular may help someone avoid the harms of ableist oppression, we need to make an additional distinction so that we do not conflate passing as privileged with acts of collaboration that actively contribute to the harms of this oppression. We should thus reformulate Silvermint's conception of passing as privileged in this way: passing as privileged is enacted when an oppressed, stigmatized, or discriminated-against *x* represents themself as an oppressive, stigmatizing, or discriminating-toward *y*, resulting in *x* being treated or evaluated as a *y* in the context of the oppressive, stigmatizing, or discriminating-toward systems of *y*. In other words, collaboration should be understood as distinct from passing as privileged, where collaboration is enacted when an oppressed, stigmatized, or discriminated-against *x* actively contributes to the oppressive, stigmatizing, or discriminating-toward systems of *y*, resulting in *x* being treated or evaluated in ways that protect them to some degree from these oppressive, stigmatizing, or discriminating-toward systems of.

Given this distinction between passing as privileged and collaboration, we can identify scenarios in which someone passes as privileged but does not collaborate or someone collaborates but does not pass as privileged. For example, a university administrator may present themself as an ally to the neurodivergent community while fighting for policies that accommodate neurodivergent people and celebrating neurodiversity, yet not publicly reveal that they, themself, are neurodivergent. In this case, the university administrator may pass as privileged to protect themself from backlash and leverage the authority that they gain by this mistaken perception of neurotypicality. This case of passing as privileged, I maintain, would not be a case of collaborating. In contrast, someone may be "out" about their neurodivergence but allow other people to tokenize them in a way that obscures or legitimizes the violence perpetrated by an oppressive system. For instance, some autistic people who openly identify as autistic have sat on the board of directors of Autism Speaks, a group that autistic advocates criticize due to its promotion of deeply problematic policies and rhetoric with respect to autism.[1] In the terms of my analysis, these autistic board members of Autism Speaks have collaborated without passing as privileged.

Disclosure is often understood to be the opposite of passing. In the 2013 paper "Disclosing Our Relationships to Disabilities: An Invitation to Disability Studies Scholars," Corbett O'Toole defines the concept of disclosure as "publicly naming one's relationship to disability" (O'Toole 2013). This definition is a good point of departure for my analysis of the concept of disclosure because insofar as it emphasizes one's relationship to disability, it discourages binary thinking about disability identity. There are a wide variety of ways in which one may relate to disability rather than only through one's identification as either disabled or nondisabled. O'Toole, who outlines some of the various ways in which one might relate to disability, perceives a difference between the norms of disability studies and the norms of disability activism with respect to the kind of public disclosure that she would expect of herself and other disabled people. As O'Toole puts it, "My previous work in the disability rights movement taught me the importance of positioning oneself in relation to the lived disability experience, that ableism created different experiences for people with different disabilities, different levels of severity, for people in different close relationships to disabled people. The disability rights movement mandated publicly naming one's relationship to disability" (O'Toole 2013).

To be sure, one may worry that O'Toole's view of disability, with its references to "different disabilities" and "levels of severity," cleaves too closely to the medical model, despite a desire to move away from binary thinking. However, I think that O'Toole is correct to highlight the enormous variety in people's experiences of disability that the sort of disabilities that they have—such as Down syndrome, Deafness, cerebral palsy, or dwarfism—as well as how these disabilities intersect with other aspects of their social identities, in part determine and condition their life circumstances. Siblings, children, and parents of disabled people should, moreover, occupy places in disability politics, even if the details of their respective roles remain contested.[2] Taken in combination, these factors may warrant support for the claim that how one relates to disability should be the subject matter that is disclosed rather than the binary question of whether one is or is not disabled.

Related to the concept of disclosure, some scholars discuss the notion of coming out as disabled by drawing an analogy between disability identity and LGBTQI (lesbian, gay, bisexual, trans, queer, intersex) identity, as Railton has done. The concept of coming out is both narrower and broader than the concept of disclosure. The concept of coming out is narrower insofar as it seems to maintain a sort of binary thinking regarding whether one identifies as disabled or not, unlike O'Toole's view of disclosure. That is, it seems harder to adopt a pluralistic view of what it means to come out than it is to frame the contents of disclosure as multiple and varied. It is harder to make sense of the idea that one may "come out" as a sibling of a disabled person than it is to coherently "disclose" that one is such. Perhaps one might have this intuition that coming out tends to be more binary in this particular way because of how the term originated with LGBTQI identity. It is natural to talk about someone coming out as gay or trans or nonbinary or intersex but it would strike most people as an awkward, or even disrespectful, use of the term to say that one has come out as the parent or sibling of someone who identifies as gay or trans or nonbinary or intersex. One reason someone may hesitate to use the term *coming out* to refer to one's *mere relationship* to LGBTQI identity in this way is that the term seems normatively laden. To come out implies that one accepts taking a certain kind of risk to one's credibility or social status or even personal safety that is just not there for the parent or sibling of someone who holds an LGBTQI identity. So, for these reasons, it seems more natural to talk of disclosing that one has this sort of relationship to another with a marginalized identity, showing that the language of disclosure is more flexible in this regard.

Yet, as Ellen Samuels points out, coming out can also be a broader concept than the concept of disclosure. As Samuels writes:

> In both queer and disabled contexts, . . . coming out can entail a variety of meanings, acts, and commitments. The dual meanings most crucial to my argument can be signified grammatically: to "come out *to*" a person or group usually refers to a specific revelatory event, while to "come out" (without an object) usually refers to the time that one first realized and came to terms with one's own identity. (Samuels 2003: 237, emphasis in Samuels)

Clearly, there is no corresponding dual meaning to the concept of disclosure. Disclosure is always a matter of disclosing information—in this case information about one's identity—to someone else. It would be quite odd to talk of disclosing one's identity to oneself. One of the limits of Samuels's concept of coming out is that in the terms of both definitions that Samuels offers, her articulation of the concept seems tied to a particular event at a particular point in time. After all, coming out *to* is "a specific revelatory event" and coming out without an object "refers to the time that one first realized and came to terms with one's own identity." Of course, Samuels herself attempts to deny this feature of the concept and maintain that coming out in lived experience is not actually a specific event, as she writes,

> Nor is coming out a static and singular event. . . . Certainly, there must be some people who experience such momentous comings out, but I believe that the majority of us find that, even after our own internal shift, and even after a dozen gay pride marches, we must still make decisions about

coming out on a daily basis, in personal, professional, and political contexts. (Samuels 2003: 237)

This explanation seems to involve a contradiction on Samuels's part. Coming out cannot be both "a specific revelatory event" or "the time that one first realized and came to terms with one's own identity" while avoiding being "a static and singular event."

Setting aside this apparent contradiction in Samuel's view, it may be that the concept of coming out is flexible enough to accommodate an ongoing process in which one publicly identifies oneself as disabled or as someone who experiences disability. Since it is contestable whether, or to what extent, the discourse of coming out is flexible enough to track the range of instances in which one may want to reveal or emphasize their relationship to disability identity, I will adopt the term *uncovering* to describe the process by which personal experiences with disability are discussed in the philosophy classroom.

Heather Evans argues that a continuous process of uncovering (which is never complete) is critical for people with invisible or non-apparent disabilities in particular. As Evans explains, "For people with non-apparent impairment, membership in the disability community requires constant, active assertion of one's status, as they can never rest on their status being 'seen' by others" (Evans 2017). For Evans, uncovering is a mode of resistance to oppression by way of "active efforts to resist assimilation into the mainstream of nondisabled norms" (ibid.). Singular events of disclosure or coming out are not enough for invisibly disabled people to resist oppression in this way, they argue, because their "disclosure can quickly become minimized, forgotten, or disregarded as repeated interactions remain interrupted by impairment" (ibid.). As a bulwark against this risk of dismissal, Evans offers the strategy of uncovering which they distinguish from disclosure:

> repeated decisions to un/cover provide space for deepening disability identity and make that identity legible to others in small but normalizing ways. . . . I began to see how these moments differed from disclosure. First-time disclosure carries big risks: changed perceptions based on impairment disclosure can have extremely impactful consequences on social relationships, career opportunities, and personal self-esteem. Un/covering happens in the relatively safe zone after the big risks have already been taken. (Evans 2017)

Uncovering, it seems, is not a solitary revelation of information about who one is or what one's experiences are like, but rather an ongoing process re-emphasizing and reminding others that one relates to disability in a particular way.[3]

Nevertheless, Evans's focus on "invisible" disabilities when discussing the process and benefits of uncovering is flawed in at least two ways. First, as Cal Montgomery argued in *Ragged Edge* magazine as far back as 2001, the very binary distinction of visible and invisible disability is both metaphysically and ethically suspect. In fact, Montgomery worries that this binary harms people with a sort of victim blaming. He writes:

> In the disability community, we speak as if some kinds of disability were visible, and others weren't. Let me suggest a different approach: think about the ways different kinds of disability have become more familiar, and more visible, to you as you've gotten to know more disabled people. . . . Dismissing that which is unfamiliar to us as "invisible" (and suggesting that it cannot be discerned rather than that we have not learned to discern it) is another way of throwing the responsibility for social justice back on the individual who carries the burden of injustice. (Montgomery 2001)

In this way, Montgomery argues that there are discernable signs of all disabilities that we ought to learn to recognize and prioritize with equitable accommodation. For Montgomery, there are no invisible disabilities. For Montgomery, rather, there are disabilities to which we attend and disabilities that we sometimes unintentionally, but at other times, willfully, ignore. If this is the case, and I tend to think that it is, then it is incoherent to believe that uncovering is a process that only people with invisible disabilities can practice. If we acknowledge that the visible/invisible disability binary is incoherent, then we can recognize that the benefits of the process of "uncovering" are available to all disabled people, as are the risks that the process imposes.

Even if Montgomery is correct that the visible/invisible disability binary is false, one might argue that there is a range of disabilities that are more or less frequently or commonly recognized or discerned as such. Even still, uncovering, because it is a matter of emphasis and reminder rather than revelation, is a critically important practice for disabled people with bodies or minds that fit across this entire range of recognizability. Uncovering can be especially important in the classroom. Amber Knight, who was born without a left hand, comments: "In the classroom, as with many other public spaces, my visible disability demands some sort of recognition and explanation" (Knight 2017: 57). Knight explains that although a missing hand is plain to see for most students, the emphasis she gives to her disability in the classroom comes with risks. As she puts it, "Many people—including students—associate neutrality and personal detachment with fairness and epistemological legitimacy. The misguided assumption that education is, or can be, perfectly neutral makes it likely that professors who go against the grain to disclose personal experiences, feelings, and perspectives in the classroom will face criticisms for not giving objective consideration to the course material" (60–1).

Emphasizing one's "visible" disability comes with risk because, despite its visibility, the disability that has been disclosed can, in the words of Evans, "quickly become minimized, forgotten, or disregarded as repeated interactions remain interrupted by impairment" (Evans 2017). This disregard about the fact that one is disabled has happened to me on many occasions, although some of my disabilities are my most easily recognizable traits because I have a form of dwarfism that comes with very, very short limbs and use a bright green power wheelchair. As a semester goes on, my students can become accustomed to my disability identity such that it drops into the background of our interactions to the point that they can be shocked when I re-emphasize it with personal anecdotes that relate to the course material. This shock at the reminder that their instructor is disabled and directly experiences ableism speaks to a need for repeated uncovering of disability in a classroom rather than mere disclosure.

I have now arrived at the central concept of this chapter: uncovering. From this point on, I will develop my argument that there are powerful moral reasons for at least some philosophers to uncover their relationship to disability in their classroom. I will zero in on a particular moral reason to help clarify Railton's thinking that I presented in the introductory anecdote of the chapter: uncovering one's own disability identity in the philosophy classroom can improve the lot of disabled philosophers on the whole by helping to change the socially constructed meaning of disability identity in the profession of philosophy.

Standard Reasons to Pass and Reasons to Uncover

Silvermint offers a detailed discussion of why some people may justifiably pass as privileged, which, as you will recall, we have framed as: when an *oppressed, stigmatized, or discriminated-against x* is perceived as an oppressive, stigmatizing, or discriminating-toward *y*, resulting in the given *x* being treated or evaluated as a *y*. The standard reasons to pass as privileged that Silvermint articulates include prudential reasons—that is, passing as privileged for the sake of one's own interest—and moral reasons—that is, passing as privileged for the sake of the good of others.

With respect to the prudential reasons, one may pass as privileged to protect oneself from oppressive harm as in, for example, when a hard-of-hearing student tries to get by in a classroom without "expensive" accommodations such as captioning or sign language interpretation in order to not be regarded as burdensome to an instructor or their university. In addition, one may pass as privileged to gain access to advantages and privileges that they should not have been denied in the first place. Consider, for example, that an autistic person may learn to suppress their "disruptive" behaviors (such as stimming by hand flapping) in order to avoid the stigmas that may entail and to be more readily accepted as an equal in academic and social life.

Alternatively, one may try to pass as privileged in part because doing so enables them to more effectively interrupt systemic oppression, benefiting others. For example, a university instructor might position themself as an ally to students with learning disabilities and not reveal their own learning disability in order to maintain the perception that they are a competent expert in philosophy pedagogy (a status that their colleagues would question if they revealed this characteristic) who advocates for the implementation of the principles of Universal Design in the philosophy classroom (Silvermint 2018).

In his article, Silvermint also discusses reasons for not passing, or in my preferred terminology, for not uncovering an identity. First, one might feel that passing is a form of deception, that deception is intrinsically wrong, and that it should be avoided, regardless of consequences. Perhaps I am a Kantian who thinks that allowing my colleagues and students to believe that I am entirely neurotypical and that I do not take a selective serotonin reuptake inhibitor (SSRI) to function in a more standard way at work and at home treats the people with whom I interact as "mere means" toward avoiding the stigma and bigotry that I may experience if I were open about my anxiety. Or perhaps someone wishes to avoid passing in order to live a more authentic life. Even if one does not inevitably wrong anyone with the "deception" of passing, one may feel that one owes it to oneself and others to be open about who one really is. So, when teaching a memoir by someone with a spinal cord injury, I may discuss that I have such an injury in addition to my dwarfism and anxiety, so that my students better understand who I am and our relationship in the classroom can be open and authentic.

As Silvermint notes, furthermore, one may uncover an oppressed identity to avoid reinforcing stereotypes and hence doing harm to others who share that identity. We can imagine a professor with multiple sclerosis who talks in class about using accessible parking spaces on campus during a flare-up of symptoms in order to challenge notions that people who "look normal" take advantage of the system and are not entitled to a placard for these parking spaces. In addition, there may in fact be a duty to uncover one's disability as part of a broader duty to resist oppression. Consider that by protecting oneself from both identification as a member of an oppressed group and the mistreatment associated with that identification, one is distancing oneself from, and thus abandoning, the oppressed group to its misery rather than joining the struggle. So, one might uncover as a means of joining the struggle. In the philosophy classroom, this duty may be cashed out by addressing disability oppression in one's teaching and identifying the ways in which one has oneself experienced it (Silvermint 2018).

In addition to these other-regarding moral reasons, Silvermint highlights how some people believe that there is, in addition, prudential reason to disclose or uncover an oppressed identity: by identifying with an oppressed group, an oppressed person can gain emotional, epistemic, and perhaps even material support from that group. This support is a benefit of uncovering that is not at all unfamiliar to disabled people, who borrow community-building strategies (such as Pride parades[4] and literary periodicals[5]) from other social movements. On university campuses, this community-building activity has even taken the form of the establishment of disability cultural centers[6] whose actions go well beyond the disability student services programs that are so common. Students and faculty alike could benefit from this work of culture building by identifying themselves as disabled and ready to give and receive the benefits of participating in acts of disability solidarity (Silvermint 2018).

Knight's essay discusses the positive, distinctly pedagogical, outcomes that are possible when a professor makes themself vulnerable by uncovering their disability identity in a classroom specifically devoted to theory. She explains the methodology of her approach to teaching about disability in this way:

> Ultimately, this essay makes the case that vulnerability can be a pedagogical resource, one that is necessary for disability disclosure to be effective. . . . Drawing from feminist and disability theorists' formulations on pedagogy and epistemology, as well as anonymous feedback from students I taught on disability theory, I argue that disability disclosure has the potential to: (1) personally empower professors and students alike; (2) enrich course material and provide fertile ground for knowledge production; (3) reveal intra-group differences among people with disabilities as an identity-based group; and, (4) teach students how to communicate across social distances. (Knight 2017: 62)

The arguments that Knight makes for specific pedagogical benefits that ensue from uncovering in the classroom are powerful and very much inform my own view in certain ways, as I hope will become clear in the remainder of this chapter. Let me begin to articulate this view by zeroing in on an additional reason why philosophy instructors specifically should, in the context of their classrooms, uncover their own respective relationships to disability, should frequently remind their students about these relationships, and should repeatedly emphasize the importance of these relationships to their students: uncovering our own relationships to disability identity in the classroom can help change the oppressive cultural meaning of disability that is widely accepted in the profession of philosophy and, thus, resist the systemic ableism that pervades the profession.

Relational Narrative Disability Identity and Ableist Oppression in the Philosophy Classroom

In this chapter, I am ultimately trying to make the case that one reason why philosophy instructors should uncover their own relationships to disability identity in the classroom is that uncovering has the potential to challenge oppression by promoting the agency of members of oppressed groups in ways that contribute to the transformation of the identities of those groups. In short, I maintain that uncovering has the potential to transform the group identity of disabled people in academic philosophy through the promotion of their agency. I will start to make this case by laying out my view of what I mean by "disability identity" and explaining how such an identity relates to questions of oppression and agency. To do this, I will draw on Hilde Lindemann Nelson's book *Damaged Identity, Narrative Repair* (2001).

In Lindemann Nelson's view, human identities are most fruitfully understood as narratives that are told relationally, from both the first-person and third-person perspectives. That is, who we are and what we are like is constructed via the stories that we and others tell about who we are and what we are like. From our own perspective, we create who we are "through the loosely connected stories we weave around the things about us that matter most to us: the acts, experiences, and characteristics we care most about, and the roles, relationships, and values to which we are most deeply committed" (Lindemann Nelson 2001: 71). As Lindemann Nelson points out, this is only half the story. Identities are deeply relational insofar as the stories that others tell about us from their third-person perspective are equally impactful on who we are, and sometimes even more impactful, since "other people weave the things about us that matter most to *them* into stories that also constitute our identities" (ibid.). In effect, these third-person stories often act as limiting factors to the stories that we can tell about ourselves, since the first-person and third-person narratives need to agree to a certain extent for a narrative identity to take hold and determine who we are.

No matter how many times that I repeat the claim that I am a talented pianist, this aspect of my identity will not be taken up so long as I continue to struggle to plunk out "Twinkle, Twinkle Little Star." Likewise, I would only continue to be a mostly competent professor of philosophy so long as I perceived myself as such and kept acting like one by teaching philosophy classes, contributing service work to various committees, and writing manuscripts for philosophy journals and presses. In this way, Lindemann Nelson argues, personal identity lies at the intersection of who we understand ourselves to be and who others understand, and perhaps allow, us to be. We need to self-identify in a certain way in order for us to be that way, but we also need other people to affirm that self-identification for it to take hold.

Lindemann Nelson points out that master narratives are of critical importance—from both the first-person perspective and third-person perspective—to the construction of narrative identities. As she argues, "In the course of this narrative construction, we draw on stock plots and character types that we borrow from the familiar stories embodying our culture's socially shared understandings—the stories that I have been calling master narratives" (Lindemann Nelson 2001: 71). These stories that capture socially shared understandings allow us to be intelligible to each other as we do the work of identity construction. For example, if I tell you that I am a die-hard fan of NFL (National Football League) football, you would be shocked if I did not know who was playing in the Super Bowl game and had plans to see a performance of *La bohéme* instead of watching the championship game on TV. This shock derives from the fact that there is a master narrative that pertains to who NFL football fans are and what they are like. By invoking this narrative of "NFL Fan," I have communicated to you something about what you can expect from me and you are surprised when I do not fit that narrative.

While these socially shared understandings are absolutely necessary for doing the work of constructing identities, Lindemann Nelson argues that master narratives can also be profoundly damaging by restricting a person's basic agency as they try to move through the world. Master narratives restrict identity and, thus, agency in two critical ways that correspond to the first-person and third-person perspectives that construct identities, according to Lindemann. Damaging master narratives can produce an "infiltrated consciousness" (Lindemann Nelson 2001: 21) and a "deprivation of opportunity" (20).

Let us take as our example the master narrative of the Elite Philosopher (EP). This master narrative says that the EP is a white, cisgender, straight, nondisabled male from an economically and educationally privileged background who goes to certain "highly ranked" schools, gets letters of reference from certain "well-respected" mentors, publishes in what other EPs have agreed are the most esteemed journals, and, ultimately, correctly navigates the networks of the most powerful EPs in the profession so that he is accepted as one of them, gaining entry into this EP identity. Now, we can examine how the master narrative of the EP might produce the problem of infiltrated consciousness. According to Lindemann Nelson, this problem arises as "a person's identity is twice damaged by oppression when she internalizes as a self-understanding the hateful or dismissive views that other people have of her" (Lindemann Nelson 2001: 21). In this way, a person's aspiration to become an EP could be short-circuited before it is even fully formed. If a student enjoys academic philosophy and is good at it but lacks even one of the major traits that the EP master narrative prescribes, then they may not see themselves as morally worthy to be an EP and may major in another subject or not pursue a four-year degree at all. The distance between the disability identity from the identity of the EP may be enough to infiltrate someone's consciousness so that they do not see themselves as a potential EP. When we combine disability with other identities of race, class, sexuality, gender, and so on, we see how the master narrative of the EP that is widely accepted in the profession may alienate people that deviate from it to the degree that they are alienated from academic philosophy on the whole.

Moreover, we can see how the EP creates a more obviously *structural* oppression in the form of a deprivation of opportunity. Lindemann Nelson describes this deprivation as what occurs when "powerful institutions or individuals, . . . [see] people like her as morally sub- or abnormal, unjustly prevent her and her kind from occupying roles or entering into relationships that are identity-constituting" (Lindemann Nelson 2001: 20). For some disabled people, this deprivation of opportunity can be baked right into the physical space in which the EP operates. The first time that I ever taught a philosophy discussion section as a graduate assistant at a large land-grant university, I arrived to my classroom to find that it was a small amphitheatre-style lecture hall with a podium at the front of the classroom, accessible only by descending the stairs that accompanied the stadium seating. There were spaces for wheelchair users to park at tables at the back of the hall from which stairs descended to space in the front of the room reserved for the instructor; however, there was no way for a chair user to access the position of pedagogical authority at the front of the classroom. Clearly, it was assumed that disabled people who cannot climb up and down stairs may occupy the role of student in such a classroom but did not fit with the master narrative of the EP—or any of its close cousins like the master narratives of the Elite Sociologist or the Elite Historian—and so would never be expected to be a philosophy course instructor at the university.

For me, this close encounter with deprivation of opportunity in the profession of philosophy due to the physical space in which academic philosophy happens was not a one-time occurrence. A year later, at a different public university where I made my first scholarly conference presentation, I confronted a very similar architectural arrangement, even though I had contacted the organizers in advance to tell them that I use a wheelchair. Furthermore, such experiences are not at all limited to wheelchair use. Exclusionary practices and environments are pervasive in academic philosophy and track the expectation that the EP will have the dominant identities of being a nondisabled, white, cis, heterosexual male of economic means.

I would invite you to imagine the kind of feedback loop that exists between the problems of infiltrated consciousness and deprivations of opportunity that the damaging master narrative of the EP creates and maintains. That is, notice how the systematic deprivations of opportunity created by the profession may infiltrate the consciousness of people entering it. The master narrative of the nondisabled EP is communicated to and excludes advanced students of philosophy as they repeatedly encounter, for example, lecture halls with stairs and no hearing loop systems; APA conference cocktail hours with high tables, no chairs, and no universal access policy that accounts for fragrance sensitivity; or "philosophy summer school" social activities centered on hiking and rock climbing. Eventually, many of these students will adopt the view for themselves that people like them are not meant to be an EP and indeed never will be. In this way, the infiltrated consciousness and deprivations of opportunity that are oppressive effects of damaging master narratives, such as the EP master narrative, buttress each other and constrict the agency of many students who wish to enter the field of philosophy, preventing them from doing so or at least erecting significant barriers to their entry.

Classroom Uncovering as a Counterstory of Resistance

The infiltrated consciousness and deprivations of opportunity that identity-damaging master narratives, such as the master narrative of the EP, entail are only some (not all) elements of a pervasive system of oppression that marginalizes disabled people in academic philosophy. To be sure, for a fuller structural understanding of the scope and nature of the oppressive systems that configure the field, one should read Shelley Tremain's *Foucault and Feminist Philosophy of Disability* (2017) and other books and articles that marginalized philosophers have written on this pressing topic.[7] Nevertheless, philosophers must find ways to address the infiltrated consciousness and deprivations of opportunity that the master narrative of the EP produces.

Lindemann Nelson claims that the best answer to an oppressive master narrative is a liberatory counterstory. She points out that if widely shared stories can create a person's identity and constrain their agency by infiltrating their consciousness and depriving them of opportunity, then stories can also serve as a way of "countering the faulty depictions of the members of the oppressed social group so that the members' status as competent moral agents can be affirmed" (Lindemann Nelson 2001: 150).[8] It seems like a counterstory of some kind is needed in response to the master narrative of the EP. Lindemann Nelson argues that counterstories are needed so that we might "root out the master narratives in the tissue of stories that constitute an oppressive identity and replace them with stories that depict the person as morally worthy" (ibid.). My hope is that the wide-scale uptake of a successful counterstory about disabled people and disability can contribute to the subversion of the structural ableism that prevails in academic philosophy by giving both the marginalized minority of disabled people and the dominant group of nondisabled philosophers the narrative tools to imagine a discipline and profession that do not deprive disabled people of opportunity or infiltrate their consciousness in agency constricting ways.

A variety of strategies might be used to craft a counterstory that responds to the master narrative of the EP in ways that enable philosophers whose identities do not fit its very narrow mold to enter into and thrive within philosophy. I want to home in on uncovering their relationship to disability identity as a strategy that instructors can use in their philosophy classrooms to replace excessively narrow and, thus, morally problematic features of the master narrative of the EP with a counterstory about who philosophers are and should be.

Notice that I am calling for a practice of uncovering rather than disclosing or coming out. For a counterstory to effectively resist the master narrative of the EP, it must be told persistently and publicly. As discussed earlier, the disclosure of a feature of one's identity seems to imply a one-off event. In contrast, a counterstory that demonstrates that disabled philosophers deserve an equitable place in the field would be persistently repeated. Uncovering entails a process of re-emphasizing and reminding others of one's identity rather than a singular event with a clearly defined endpoint. For a counterstory to be successful, it must transform an oppressive master narrative, defined as a story "embodying our culture's socially shared understandings" (Lindemann Nelson 2001: 71). Therefore, it is critical that a counterstory be told in a public way that can impact socially shared understandings of identity. This requirement precludes the framing of coming out according to which "to 'come out' (without an object) usually refers to the time that one first realized and came to terms with one's own identity" (Samuels 2003: 237). Uncovering, as a concept, seems less ambiguous and better suited to this work of telling a counterstory than coming out because it is done with an audience in mind and not as part of one's internal reflection.

Furthermore, I am deliberately calling for instructors to uncover their relationship to disability identity rather than uncover their disability identity itself. My hope is that by emphasizing the relational aspect of the process of uncovering, we can head off any tendency to regard disability in an essentialist way that holds it as a static property of a person that can be used to easily place them into a clearly defined and unified metaphysical category. Disability is a deeply contested category and who can or should claim a disability identity is not at all clear. For example, someone may have a serious food allergy that can be disabling for them in some contexts that arise in academic philosophy, including professional conferences that do not take into account a range of dietary restrictions.[9] Insofar as such conditions are not typically taken to be disabilities in the stories "embodying our culture's socially shared understandings" (Lindemann Nelson 2001: 71) of the concept of disability, someone with this sort of disability may feel uncomfortable identifying themself as disabled. If we dispense with the notion of coming out with respect to disability and, instead, prioritize relationships to disability, such a person would be enabled to uncover their relationship with disability as a way in which to tell a story that challenges the deprivation of opportunities and infiltrations of consciousness that impact the prospects of other would-be academic philosophers with similar allergies.

Another advantage of uncovering one's relationship to disability identity in the philosophy classroom rather than uncovering one's disability identity per se is that the approach invites far more nuanced and intersectional analysis of one's position in relation to disability. Consider, for example, if I wanted to uncover my relationship to disability identity as part of my teaching. To do so, I would not merely say whether I ascribe to a binary identity of disabled or nondisabled. Rather, I would discuss how I, as a white, cishet, middle-class man with relatively secure academic employment am affected by different disabling social and physical environments that I encounter in professional academic philosophy. Other philosophers would tell a radically different counterstory to the master narrative of the EP if they were to uncover their particular relationship with disability and its various manifestations and intersections.[10]

It is crucially important to also note that the *content* of these stories matter and not just their bare existence. We must take care to tell an effective counterstory that expands the agency of disabled students of philosophy and does not further reinforce the oppressive aspects of the

EP.[11] To foster appreciation of this point, let us return to the anecdote with which I began this chapter, namely, Railton's Dewey Lecture. Some aspects of Railton's personal narrative might challenge oppressive and exclusionary elements of the EP. For one, Railton suggests that by publicly recognizing and thus normalizing depression, we might take the force out of questions that stigmatize the disability in our own infiltrated consciousness, including: "Would people think less of me? Would I seem to be tainted, reduced in their eyes, someone with an inner failing whom no one would want to hire or with whom no one would want to marry or have children? Would even friends start tip-toeing around my psyche? Would colleagues trust me with responsibility?" (Railton 2015: 14–15). Railton also gestures toward an intersectional analysis in his disability narrative insofar as he recognizes some of his own power and privilege as a man and as a person who is well established in his philosophical career. Finally, and maybe most importantly, Railton suggests that structural interventions be made that normalize medical leave for depressive episodes and prevent negative backlash to these career breaks (15). In short, some of Railton's narrative, with its uncovering of disability, strikes me as exactly the sort of challenge to the master narrative of the EP that we need from philosophers (such as Railton) who have attained enormous status in the profession of philosophy.

At other points in Railton's "counterstory," however, it does not seem like much of a counterstory at all. Throughout his discussion of his disability, Railton frames disability almost entirely through the lens of the medical model. He consistently refers to depression as an individualized and medicalized defect that must be treated—presumably with pharmaceuticals that will normalize a person's psychology—if someone is to even *survive*, let alone thrive in academic philosophy. Thus, one possible worry is that these portions of the speech are actually counterproductive insofar as they further entrench aspects of the EP that sustain structural barriers and alienate disabled people from philosophy. In other words, although there is no single and singular correct counterstory that must be told in answer to the master narrative of the EP, one must take care to uncover one's relationship to disability in a way that does not further oppression and do more harm than good.

Notwithstanding the negative aspects of Railton's story, the way in which it uncovers his relationship to disability identity as a philosophy instructor gives life to the portion of the master narrative of the EP according to which disabled people are not qualified participants in the philosophical community or able to hold positions of authority in academic philosophy. The right kinds of stories, told in unison and with due attention to the intersectional features of each instance of uncovering, might create the comprehensive telling of a counterstory that poses a real challenge to the deprivation of opportunities and infiltrations of consciousness that the master narrative of the EP continues to produce and that continue to constrain the agency of disabled students in philosophy. Tremain's Dialogues on Disability (n.d.), a series of interviews with disabled philosophers, is the best example that I know of this sort of carefully crafted telling of counterstories by way of uncovering. I am calling for us to bring this kind of practice into the philosophy classroom as we emphasize and remind our students about how we as academic philosophers relate to disability identity.[12]

If, in the context of the philosophy classroom, uncovering one's relationship to disability identity actually has the potential to accomplish what I claim that it does, there is a clear moral reason why we *ought* to uncover in this way. Such uncovering is a means toward the good end of greater equity for disabled people in academic philosophy. I want to emphasize, however, that this moral reason is not indefeasible and thus any moral duty to uncover that arises from this reason is also not absolute. There are many legitimate, competing reasons why someone might pass as privileged that can and sometimes do outweigh the moral reason to uncover that I have highlighted in this chapter. These competing reasons to pass as privileged are usually prudential in nature, and typically track the several dimensions of power that exist within the structures of higher education in general and academic philosophy in particular. In short, the moral duty to help tell a counterstory that undercuts the master narrative of the EP is not evenly distributed across the various social locations within academic philosophy because power is not evenly distributed across the various social locations within academic philosophy. Roughly, how weighty the moral reason that one has to uncover their relationship to disability identity in their philosophy classroom is proportional to how much power that they have or do not have within the power structures of academic philosophy. Protection from the harms that uncovering may entail is also proportional to the power that one holds in philosophy.

Knight makes a similar point about the relationship between risk and power when discussing the pedagogical benefits of disability disclosures in the classroom:

> it is important, too, to acknowledge how teachers' social location (i.e. race, gender, sexual orientation) and institutional position (i.e. tenured, graduate student, tenure track, contingent) influences one's ability to take risks, how the act of disclosure is received by others, and the subsequent likelihood that one will experience backlash from students, colleagues, and administrators. Put simply, in a context of social inequality, the risks of disability disclosure are experienced differently. (Knight 2017: 62)

I would add to this intersectional analysis that the kind of disability that one discloses in the university context can determine how the power dynamics of the university operate on them. Although I do not want to imply that I have a medicalized view of disability by suggesting that we focus on one's diagnosis, it is crucial that we not universalize the experience of disability and regard it as a unified monolith.

Some examples could be useful to illustrate this claim. Imagine an associate professor who frequently and enthusiastically uncovers a mobility impairment (such as a spinal cord injury) in professional spaces and who thus might be at increased risk of exclusion from invitations to speak at colloquia given concerns about physical access on university campuses. In a field that cannot seem to relinquish the mind-body dualism and that thus prioritizes the mind and disparages the body, this same person may not be at a disadvantage at all when it comes to invitations to contribute an essay to an edited collection. Although a graduate student may hesitate to uncover their dyslexia while teaching their discussion sections for fear that no faculty member in the department will want to take them on as an advisee, they may not harbor this sort of concern among their cohort and it may not be any more difficult for them to find a roommate among their classmates who wants to split rent on an apartment. Or, maybe an openly autistic junior faculty member is seen as a "boy genius" with respect to philosophy of mathematics or logic but is rarely invited to social gatherings at colleagues' houses because of his "awkward" behavior.[13]

In sum, uncovering disability in the philosophy classroom can contribute to a counterstory that resists various kinds of identity prejudices that the master narrative of the EP perpetuates about disabled people in the field of philosophy and beyond it. Thus, there is a strong moral reason to uncover in this way and do the work challenging the manner in which the master narrative of the EP creates and sustains oppressive power structures through infiltrations of consciousness and deprivations of opportunity. Nevertheless, one's decision about when this moral reason is strong enough to require one to act on it is not a simple matter. Each person's level of duty is mediated by their location in the multidimensional power structures of academic philosophy.

Notes

1 See the Autistic Self Advocacy Network's "Statement on Autism Speaks Board Appointments" and Robison (2020).

2 For an exploration of some of these tensions, see Carey, Block, and Scotch (2020).

3 This is similar to how Samuels tried to frame coming out in real-world practice, despite contradicting the initial view she articulated about the concept of coming out being defined in terms of either "a specific revelatory event" or "the time that one first realized and came to terms with one's own identity."

4 As an example, see the Chicago Disability Pride Parade. Available at: https://www.disabilitypride parade .org/ (accessed May 10, 2022).

5 As an example, see *Wordgathering: A Journal of Disability Poetry and Literature*. Available at: https://wordgathering.com/ (accessed May 10, 2022).

6 For discussion, see Saia (2019, 2022).

7 Some representative examples include: Dotson (2012), Mills (2005), Bettcher (2019), Stramondo (2016).

8 Some may worry that Lindemann Nelson's use of the descriptor "competent" here is ableist, in as far as that term has been weaponized against psychiatric survivors and intellectually disabled people especially. That is, deeming someone as intrinsically and individualistically "incompetent" has been a way to deny their agency in these contexts. However, on my reading, I don't think what Lindemann Nelson means by "competent" here actually tracks the common ableist usage since her work does not reduce competence to a naturalized and individualized phenomenon. Rather, Lindemann Nelson is clear that one is *made* a more or less competent moral agent by infiltrated consciousness and deprivations of opportunity, not some trait intrinsic to their person. That is, her view of agency is as relational as her view of identity.

9 For a detailed discussion of some of these issues, see Huebner and Tremain (2015).

10 For a deeper exploration of these issues of intersectionality in matters of passing and uncovering than I have space for here, see Samuels (2017), Alshammari (2017), Barragan and Nussbaum (2017), Carter et al. (2017), Miller (2017), Seelman (2017), and Harbour et al. (2017).

11 I would like to thank August Gorman for pointing this out.

12 For an understanding of the scope of this work of telling counterstories, see Dialogues on Disability. Available at: https://bio politicalphilosophy.com/dialogues-on-disability/ (accessed May 10, 2022).

13 I would like to thank Daniel Reinholz for helping me think through these differences in how various kinds of disabilities are perceived in higher education.

References

Alshammari, Shahd (2017), "A Hybridized Academic Identity: Negotiating a Disability within Academia's Discourse of Ableism," in Stephanie L. Kerschbaum, Laura T. Eisenman, and James M. Jones (eds.), *Negotiating Disability: Disclosure and Higher Education*, 25–37, Ann Arbor: University of Michigan Press.

Autistic Advocacy Network (2015), "Statement on Autism Speaks Board Appointments." Available at: https://autisticadvocacy.org/2015/12/statement-on-autism-speaks-board-appointments/ (accessed May 26, 2022).

Barragan, Eduardo and Emily A. Nusbaum (2017), "Perceptions of Disability on a Postsecondary Campus: Implications for Oppression and Human Love," in Stephanie L. Kerschbaum, Laura T. Eisenman, and James M. Jones (eds.), *Negotiating Disability: Disclosure and Higher Education*, 39–55, Ann Arbor: University of Michigan Press.

Bettcher, Talia Mae (2019), "What is Trans Philosophy?" *Hypatia: A Journal of Feminist Philosophy* 34 (4): 644–67.

Carey, Allison C., Pamela Block, and Richard K. Scotch, eds. (2020), *Allies and Obstacles: Disability Activism and Parents of Children with Disabilities*, Philadelphia: Temple University Press.

Carter, Angela M. et al. (2017), "Bodyminds Like Ours: An Autoethnographic Analysis of Graduate School, Disability, and the Politics of Disclosure," in Stephanie L. Kerschbaum, Laura T. Eisenman, and James M. Jones (eds.), *Negotiating Disability: Disclosure and Higher Education*, 95–113, Ann Arbor: University of Michigan Press.

Dialogues on Disability (n.d.), BIOPOLITICAL PHILOSOPHY (blog). Available at: https://biopoliticalphilosophy.com/dialogues-on-disability (accessed October 8, 2022).

Dotson, Kristie (2012), "How Is This Paper Philosophy?" *Comparative Philosophy* 3 (1): 3–29.

Evans, Heather Dawn (2017), "Un/covering: Making Disability Identity Legible," *Disability Studies Quarterly* 37 (1).

Harbour, Wendy S., Rosalie Boone, Elaine Bourne Heath, and Sislena G. Ledbetter (2017), "'Overcoming' in Disability Studies and African American Culture," in Stephanie L. Kerschbaum, Laura T. Eisenman, and James M. Jones (eds.), *Negotiating Disability: Disclosure and Higher Education*, 149–69, Ann Arbor: University of Michigan Press.

Huebner, Bryce and Shelley Tremain (2015), "Dialogues on Disability: Shelley Tremain Interviews Bryce Huebner," BIOPOLITICAL PHILOSOPHY (blog). April. Available at: https://biopoliticalphilosophy.com/dialogues-on-disability/ (accessed September 12, 2023).

Knight, Amber (2017), "Feminism, Disability, and the Democratic Classroom," in Stephanie L. Kerschbaum, Laura T. Eisenman, and James M. Jones (eds.), *Negotiating Disability: Disclosure and Higher Education*, 57–73, Ann Arbor: University of Michigan Press.

Lindemann Nelson, Hilde (2001), *Damaged Identity: Narrative Repair*, Ithaca: Cornell University Press.

Miller, Ryan A. (2017), "Complicating 'Coming Out': Disclosing Disability, Gender, and Sexuality in Higher Education," in Stephanie L. Kerschbaum, Laura T. Eisenman, and James M. Jones (eds.), *Negotiating Disability: Disclosure and Higher Education*, 115–34, Ann Arbor: University of Michigan Press.

Mills, Charles (2005), "'Ideal Theory' as Ideology," *Hypatia: A Journal of Feminist Philosophy* 20 (3): 165–83.

Montgomery, Cal (2001), "A Hard Look at Invisible Disability," *Ragged Edge Online* 2. Available at: https://www.raggededgemagazine.com/0301/0301ft1.htm (accessed May 10, 2022).

O'Toole, Corbett Joan (2013), "Disclosing Our Relationships to Disabilities: An Invitation to Disability Studies Scholars," *Disability Studies Quarterly* 33(2).

Railton, Peter (2015), "Innocent Abroad: Rupture, Liberation, and Solidarity," *American Philosophical Association Central Meeting*, February. Available at: https://lsa.umich.edu/content/dam/philosophy-assets/Philosophy%20Documents/Railton%20Dewey%20Lecture%20Central%20APA%202015%20revised.pdf (accessed May 26, 2022).

Robison, John Elder (2020), "My Time with Autism Speaks," in S. Kapp (ed.), *Autistic Community and the Neurodiversity Movement*, 221–32, Singapore: Palgrave Macmillan.

Saia, Toni (2019), *Disability as an Identity: Disability Cultural Centers in Higher Education*, A Dissertation Submitted to the Department of Disability and Psychoeducational Studies at the University of Arizona, Tucson.

Saia, Toni (2022), "Disability Cultural Centers in Higher Education: A Shift Beyond Compliance to Disability Culture and Disability Identity," *Journal of Postsecondary Education and Disability* 35 (1): 17–30.

Samuels, Ellen (2003), "My Body, My Closet: Invisible Disability and the Limits of Coming-Out Discourse," *GLQ: A Journal of Lesbian and Gay Studies* 9 (1–2): 233–55.

Samuels, Ellen (2017), "Passing, Coming Out, and Other Magical Acts," in Stephanie L. Kerschbaum, Laura T. Eisenman, and James M. Jones (eds.), *Negotiating Disability: Disclosure and Higher Education*, 15–23, Ann Arbor: University of Michigan Press.

Seelman, Katherine D. (2017), "Students with Disabilities in Higher Education: Welfare, Stigma Management, and Disclosure," in Stephanie L. Kerschbaum, Laura T. Eisenman, and James M. Jones (eds.), *Negotiating Disability: Disclosure and Higher Education*, 135–47, Ann Arbor: University of Michigan Press.

Silvermint, Daniel (2018), "Passing as Privileged," *Ergo* 5 (1): 1–43.

Stramondo, Joseph (2016), "Why Bioethics Needs a Disability Moral Psychology," *The Hastings Center Report* 46 (3): 22–30.

Tremain, Shelley L. (2017), *Foucault and Feminist Philosophy of Disability*, Ann Arbor: University of Michigan Press.

21 INCLUSIVE ETHICS

A PRECAUTIONARY PRINCIPLE

STEPHANIE JENKINS

A moral anthropology, whether implicit or explicit, undergirds all ethical theories; thus, any attempt to articulate normative principles necessitates an understanding of the sorts of beings to which moral action applies. Critical disability studies and critical animal studies scholars share a common goal of dismantling the disembodied, universal subject that is assumed in traditional ethics. Nearly all the arguments used to justify the domination of nonhuman animals and disabled humans rely on the hierarchical comparison of capacities deemed essential to a meaningful life, including rationality, language use, future thinking, and independence. This "animacy hierarchy" or "scale of relative sentience that places [normate] humans at the very top" (Chen 2012: 89) is produced through the speciesist and ableist "performance criteria" (Bérubé 2010: 100) that define notions of moral status and circumscribe the moral community. Beings who lack, or are perceived to lack, these essential capacities exist outside the protections of moral responsibility.

In this chapter, I argue against the use of performance tests to define the boundaries of the moral community. Contrary to Margaret Somerville, I do not believe that human life is "sacred in some unique and special sense" (Somerville 1996: ix). To the contrary, I contend that attempts to posit such uniqueness ultimately rely upon ableist and speciesist performance criteria. In order to advance my argument, I first review ethical literature on moral status. Then I draw on conceptual tools from critical disability studies and critical animal studies to identify two common approaches used to define moral considerability. These approaches are: The Capacities-Criterion Approach and The Species-Affinity Approach. I argue against these moralities of competition in order to advance an inclusive, embodied ethics that recommends the endorsement of a certain precautionary principle about moral status. I will call the principle: The Precautionary Principle of Moral Status.

The chapter is a project in search of "novel coalitionary possibilities" (Twine 2001: 32) between advocates of nonhuman animals and disabled humans. In what follows, therefore, I focus on disabled humans and nonhuman animals in order to highlight weak points in performance-driven morality. Because many contemporary ethicists use nonhuman animals and people with disabilities as case studies of indeterminate moral status, animality and disability are clear examples of how normative performance criteria undergird moral thought. My aim in the chapter is not to compare disabled humans to nonhuman animals. I do, however, agree with Sunaura Taylor that objections to such comparisons are grounded in speciesism (Taylor 2011: 195; 2017: 145). Nor do I want to propose that ableism and speciesism are equivalent. Both of these conceptual moves artificially homogenize differences among embodiments of diverse origins, etiologies, and experiences, as well as obscure differences among countless species of nonhuman animals. Moreover, such comparisons ignore the ways that (1) ableism and speciesism are mutually constitutive of each other, and (2) ableism and speciesism have disparate context-specific effects.

Delimiting the Moral Community: Who Matters Morally?

In contemporary moral theory, debates about the boundaries of moral consideration typically focus on "moral patienthood" and strive to articulate a "moral taxonomy" (Reinders 2008: 33). In these debates, a moral patient is "an individual who has interests, [and] is diametrically opposed to being considered a resource" (Bernstein 1998: 117). Mark Bernstein continues, "We normally care, as we should, how our actions affect the moral patient itself; its well-being is a concern to us" (177). In the context of these debates, animals and people with disabilities (especially people with cognitive disabilities) are discussed as moral patients because they are regarded as non-contributing dependents.

Moral and political theories presuppose or assert what Michael Sandel calls a "philosophical anthropology" (Sandel 1998: 50), that is, a conception of the person taken to be the subject of its principles. While many moral theories take the subject of ethics for granted (Vetlesen 1994: 7), scholars who examine moral status consider questions about to whom we are responsible, what it is that constitutes a "who," and so on. Such questions get to the heart of philosophical debates over what sorts of beings should be morally considerable. G. J. Warnock formulates the problem this way:

> Let us consider the question to whom principles of morality apply from, so to speak, the other end—from the standpoint not of the agent, but of the "patient." What, we may ask here, is the condition of moral relevance? What is the condition of having a claim be considered by rational agents to whom the principles apply? (Warnock 1971: 148)

From this perspective, we consider not the moral agent who is bound to certain moral principles, but rather the other to whom these principles must be applied. Moral patients populate the moral community and are distinguished from amoral patients to whom we do not hold obligations to protect from harm. Indeed, some philosophers argue that amoral patients, by definition, do not have interests, and thus, cannot be harmed. What is at stake in these theoretical discussions is the moral standing of different kinds of beings who can be found in the world. I prefer the term *moral other* to *moral patient* because it recognizes that moral agents can also be the object of moral perception, judgment, and action. Although all moral patients are moral others, not all moral others are patients. Moreover, this terminology signals that social, cultural, and historical discourses of otherization are at play in the division between moral and amoral others.

According to Mary Ann Warren, moral status can be defined as follows:

> To have moral status is to be morally considerable, or to have moral standing. It is to be an entity towards which moral agents have, or can have, moral obligations. If an entity has moral status, then we may not treat it in just any way we please; we are morally obligated to give weight in our deliberations to its needs, interests, or well-being. Furthermore, we are morally obligated to do this not merely because protecting it may benefit ourselves or other persons, but because its needs have moral importance in their own right. (Warren 1997: 3)

Simply stated, to have moral status in the terms of this ethical discourse means to "matter morally" (Harman 2003: 174) or to have interests that "matter intrinsically" (Jaworska 2010: 369).

Such definitions may appear to offer clear criteria for differentiating between others; however, the limits of the moral community are "imagined," contingent, contested, and indeterminate. Arne Johan Vetlesen states, "At heart the fostering of attentiveness and creation of moral space is a social, indeed a political, issue. And politics means power: the power relations at work between people, and often invisible to them, and the forces of repression at work within the individual" (Vetlesen 1994: 9). For example, as Vetlesen shows, Nazi ideology encouraged a constriction of the moral community. A derealization of the other impeded the affective moral responses of German citizens. In this chapter, I will consider who counts in moral perception, judgment, and action, as well as examine how animals and disabled humans have been denied moral consideration because they fall below the threshold of the "normal human adult." As Bernstein argues, "normal adult human beings . . . have unjustly disenfranchised some individuals from our moral domain" (Bernstein 1998: 3).

Critical animal studies and disability studies advocates seek inclusion in the moral community for their respective moral others. Two main approaches attempt to resolve the ambiguity within the concept of moral status. The first, which predominates the field of animal ethics, I call The Capacities-Criterion Approach. The second, which is more common in disability studies, I refer to as The Species-Affinity Approach. While there are evident nuances between how different thinkers use these strategies, the moral anthropology that underlies both approaches is a normate theory of the human. By demonstrating this common denominator in moral theory, I will put into sharp relief the hegemony of an ableist, speciesist understanding of the moral other in both technical moral thinking and lay moral thinking.

The Capacities-Criterion Approach responds to the shifting nature of the boundaries of the moral community by establishing morally relevant performative criteria for moral standing. This argument is clearest in the work of Russell DiSilvestro who argues that if someone is human, then they have serious moral status. While DiSilvestro's argument may initially appear to represent a version of The Species-Affinity Approach, it is in fact a capacities criterion which stipulates that the justification for moral standing is "the possession of certain capacities" (DiSilvestro 2010: xi). According to this view, personhood—construed as a set of abilities—is the hallmark of moral consideration. Most typically, the ability to reason is taken as the "mark" of personhood and the ground of moral status (Stubblefield 2010: 307; Koch 1998: 32). Other capacities that fulfill the criterion include language use, consciousness, future-oriented thinking, and death awareness.

The Capacities-Criterion Approach has two significant difficulties. The first difficulty is that the use of "performance criteria" (Bérubé 2010: 100) to demarcate the boundaries of the moral community creates "outliers" (Silvers and Francis 2005: 40–76). Ethicists often identify nonhuman animals and people with "severe disabilities" in a group that has contested status (McMahan 2003: 14) and exists in a "moral twilight zone" (McMahan 2003; Singer 1996). According to The Capacities-Criterion Approach, some human animals will meet the standard for moral consideration, while some humans—particularly people with cognitive disabilities—may not fulfill the criterion for moral consideration. This conclusion is the starting point for *The Argument from Marginal Cases*. Proponents of this argument—such as Peter Singer and Jeff McMahan—contend that we have increased moral obligations to nonhuman animals and diminished obligations to disabled humans (McMahan 2003). Some scholars, unwilling to accept this conclusion, reject the use of performance criteria, a move that I will eventually make in this chapter for different reasons.

The second difficulty is that if we accept The Capacities-Criterion Approach, then we are forced to agree with the statement that killing a nonperson is worse than killing a person (Kittay 2008: 137–56). For example, a consequence of this principle would be that it would be worse to kill an adult pig than to kill a human infant. Yet this conclusion violates widely held moral presuppositions. In order to avoid such a conclusion, therefore, many advocates of The Capacities-Criterion Approach posit a modification that it is the *potential* for human capacities, rather than their possession, that is relevant for inclusion in the moral community.

Indeed, The Potential Capacities Approach attempts to include humans who fall below the performance criteria in question by arguing that it is the potential for human capacities, not the actual possession of them, that is the basis for moral standing. This distinction between potential capacities and actual capacities is most salient in the case of human infants. While infants are not persons according to The Potential-Capacities Approach, adherents of this theory argue that infants possess inherent dignity because we must respect that they will meet such criteria in the future. This assumption, as many contributors to the edited collection *Cognitive Disability and Its Challenge to Moral Philosophy* demonstrate, does not afford moral status to human individuals who will never develop the capacity to reason, for example, due to cognitive disability (Kittay and Carlson 2010). Some thinkers respond to this problem by changing the criterion for moral considerability. For example, Agnieszka Jaworska argues that it is the emotional ability to care that should form the basis for moral standing (Jaworska 2010: 369). Jaworska notes, however, that even with this more open criterion, some human individuals will not meet the threshold inclusion in the moral community (Jaworska 2010: 387). Unable or unwilling to settle on a moral "yardstick" (Carlson 2010: 318), some thinkers therefore adopt or presume a version of The Species-Affinity Approach. Jaworska, for example, appeals to "species-typical" capacities in order to include all human beings in the moral community (Jaworska 2010: 387).

The Species-Affinity Approach is in fact the second strategy employed to fix the ambiguous borders of moral consideration. In order to avoid the exclusion of human "outliers" who fall below the threshold of capacities criteria (and to avoid the extension of moral rights to nonhuman animals), adherents to The Species-Affinity Approach argue that all biological humans are members of the moral community. For instance, Eva Kittay holds that moral standing is a result of species membership rather than any particular property that beings possess (Kittay 2010).

The simplicity of this strategy is deceptive insofar as it raises more questions than it answers, that is, the strategy is simplistic because, as Judith Butler points out, it "presupposes that we have first settled the question of who does and does not count as a human" (Butler 2006: 91). As Tom Koch explains, "Membership in the category of protected living humans remains problematic, as does [*sic*] the values defining that membership" (Koch 1998: 25). The Species-Affinity Approach is, in short, The Capacities-Criterion Approach in disguise: it simply shifts the performance criterion from the level of individual capacities to species-typical capacities. In order to restrict moral consideration to *homo sapiens* and justify human moral superiority, defenders of The Species-Affinity Approach must appeal to the capacities of "normal" adult humans. The Species-Affinity Approach is not viable on its own terms; while the argument attempts to displace a performance-based morality, it masks and reifies the capacities-based standard that it explicitly rejects. The Species-Affinity Approach conflates moral status with humanity and, in turn, fails to provide an account of what it means to be human that does not appeal to performance criteria (whether rational or emotional capacities). Therefore, this strategy cannot resolve questions about the moral status of beings who challenge the definition of the human—such as human-animal chimeras, alien life, or artificial intelligence—nor can it provide clear and consistent criteria for the inclusion of moral "outliers" in the moral community.

It should be noted that some theorists rely on a combination of these two approaches, arguing for a "multi-criterial approach" to delimiting the moral community (Warren 2009: 19). This approach does not escape the difficulties detailed earlier, but rather creates additional, more complex, gatekeeping mechanisms. A normative humanism provides the foundation for all three attempts to circumscribe the moral community insofar as each attempt either explicitly or implicitly presumes The Capacities-Criterion Approach. While the selected criteria are intended to be "purely descriptive" of the human species (DiSilvestro 2010: 27), they entrench assumptions about what it means to be human and what kinds of lives are worth living. Nonhuman animals and disabled humans suffer the consequences of this exclusion. In the end, the boundaries of human life "remain shifting and uncertain" (Koch 1998: 33). The aforementioned approaches have limited the ability of moral theorists to fully contemplate the meaning of the indeterminacy inherent within the concept of moral standing because they assume the very criteria for humanness that are under evaluation. No concept of personhood can resolve the "constitutive ambiguities" in moral criteria (Connolly 1995: 232).

DiSilvestro's work exemplifies the normative, performance-driven humanism within moral thought. He contends that moral status is a "placeholder" for the features of "normal adult persons" (DiSilvestro 2010: 12). He discusses people with disabilities as "damaged and disabled human organisms" (55) whose moral standing is based not on our inherent worth, but rather on our belonging to a species that "typically" exhibits high reasoning capacities. From this perspective, our inclusion in the moral community must be addressed in retrospect as a marginal case. To be sure, DiSilvestro does argue that people with mental disabilities have moral standing because they possess the "potential" for higher-order cognitive capacity. However, this claim overextends the meaning of the term *potential* because, as DiSilvestro himself admits, his position assumes technological advances that do not exist. Moreover, there is no reason that his argument could not apply, at the very least, to nonhuman primates or human-animal chimeras with human neurons.

Beyond Performance Criteria

The morality as performance criteria mission that is found in both The Capacities-Criterion Approach and The Species-Affinity Approach must be abandoned. On its own terms, the argument is unable to provide guidance on outlier cases. More importantly, dignity and respect are not moral attributes that must be earned. Performance morality should be accountable for its criteria rather than place the evidentiary responsibility on marginalized others to prove their conformity with a homogenized notion of the moral other. This latter approach guarantees an exclusionary ethics that is powerless to question its complicity with discourses of normalcy.

Performance-based standards for moral consideration engender a morality of competition because the moral community is defined through exclusionary mechanisms. When moral considerability is understood as a zero-sum game, marginalized others compete for space on a moral elevator to raise their group's status on a hierarchy of moral others. This competition reinforces the evaluation of moral others' status via standards of normality and discourages reflection about the deployment of otherizing discourses as a political strategy.

For example, many animal advocates, in their attempt to "graduate" animals to the level of persons, utilize ableist norms to demote people with disabilities. Consider these remarks that McMahan makes in *The Ethics of Killing*:

> I believe that reaching the optimal point of convergence with respect to killing and letting die requires that traditional beliefs about animals be more extensively revised than traditional beliefs about the severely retarded [*sic*]. Killing animals, and allowing them to die, are morally far more serious matters than we have supposed. But allowing severely retarded humans beings to die, and perhaps even killing them, are correspondingly somewhat less serious matters than we have believed. (McMahan 2003: 230)

Some animal activists who use the shaming of deviance from human norms deploy fearmongering to reduce the human exploitation of animals. For example, PETA (People for the Ethical Treatment of Animals) campaigns have deployed techniques such as fat shaming and manipulation of public fears of disability in their advertisements; their "Got Autism?" campaign, which suggests a link between dairy consumption and autism and their "Save the Whales" advertisement—which instructs the public to "lose the blubber" by going vegetarian—are instructive examples of these tactics (Goldstein 2009).

Disability advocates, in vying for membership in the exclusive moral community, may participate in ableist discourses (Salomon 2010: 47–72). Because humans with disabilities are frequently denied moral and political consideration through dehumanization, we must verify our human capacities as unique from and opposed to the capacities of nonhuman animals. For example, Enable, an organization in the United Kingdom (UK) that provides employment training and other services to disabled people, once initiated a campaign that seeks to re-humanize people with disabilities by highlighting the prioritization (in the UK) of animal charities over disability charities (Lake 2007). Such strategies demonstrate how speciesism and ableism coordinate a morality of competition, which places nonhuman animals and human others in opposition to each other.

Insofar as the "Human" is defined in opposition to the "Animal" and, furthermore, since normal human abilities are taken as the mark of moral solicitude, moralities of exclusion, by their very nature, create zero-sum competitions between animal and disabled others. Moral attention is diverted to debates about performance criteria, masking the constitutive role of normalizing institutions. The human, as Butler argues, is not a biologically necessary kind, but a "differential value" that comprises a value and morphology (Butler 2009: 76). Through the competitive exclusion of nonhuman animals and disabled persons in the constitution of the human person, species-typical functioning frames the perception of moral others. As Taylor explains, "At their roots, all arguments used to justify human domination over animals rely on comparing human and animal abilities and traits. We humans are the species with rationality, with complex emotions, with two legs and opposable thumbs" (Taylor 2017: 197). Correspondingly, the determinations of normal human capacity deployed to justify human supremacy devalue the lives of disabled individuals who deviate from performance-based norms.

The project that Singer identifies as clarifying the "basis" of moral status will always result in an exclusive morality defined through performance criteria and, thus, will frame moral consideration as speciesist and ableist. I agree with Warren who argues that there can be no sole criterion for moral standing (Warren 1997: 88). Nevertheless, my analysis departs from Warren's insofar as I also reject her multi-criterial approach. As Steven Best has argued, "the discourse of the 'human' has been constituted in dualistic, speciesist, racist, patriarchal, and imperialist terms" (Best 2009: 15). By combining research in disability studies and critical animal studies, I have demonstrated the importance of including analysis of ableism in an intersectional approach to inquiry, including moral inquiry. Because normal human capacity is conflated with moral status, the interplay of speciesism and ableism is uniquely important to an understanding of the delimitation of the moral community. Unless the mutual constitution of speciesism and ableism in the construction of the moral other is addressed, the fantasized ideal of the human with unique capacities will remain intact. The burden of proof, then, falls on marginalized others to "prove" that they possess the capacities that are prerequisites for moral solicitude. This exclusive view of morality positions animal and disabled human others in competition for the extension of existing moral boundaries to their situations. An effect of this marginalization is that moral reformists may find the deployment of performance criteria as an effective or necessary technique with which to advocate for their inclusion within a morality that is based on the exclusion of abnormal bodies and minds.

If speciesism and ableism are mutually reinforcing oppressions, how can we dismantle this moral double bind? An imaginative, affective, and strategic coalition between advocates of nonhuman animals and disabled humans is crucial to this task. Advocates for both groups will likely be hesitant to entertain this suggestion. People with disabilities may fear that too close an affinity with nonhuman animals will result in our dehumanization. As Licia Carlson notes, people with disabilities—especially of the intellectual variety—have often served as philosophical labor for animals, without receiving any benefit in return (Carlson 2010: 317). However, it is the very mechanism of dehumanization that must be rethought, destabilized, and liquidated. Disability and animal activists, ethicists, and advocates are uniquely positioned to launch such an attack, because of the ways in which the outlier status of these groups has been used to demarcate the moral community and concretize the norm of the species-typical human. Therefore, I concur with Taylor's (2017) and Daniel Salomon's (2010) shared conclusion that we must, as Taylor puts it, "challenge the fields of disability studies and animal rights to take each other seriously" (Taylor 2017: 219). Together we can imagine and create new ways in which to value moral others that normalizing performance criteria do not limit or constrain. Valerie Ann Johnson's work in environmental justice points toward this kind of coalition, arguing that "merging feminist disability studies and environmental justice forces us to confront power dynamics that reinforce a narrow view of 'normal'—one that privileges a particular sense of the human body that is constrictive, not expansive" (Johnson 2011: 5).

An anti-essentialist, inclusive, embodied ethics that opposes the use of performance criteria for moral consideration is needed. Rather than use the model of exclusion for moral considerability, this approach seeks to be inclusive; it begins with the assumption that animate life, whether human or nonhuman, abled or disabled, deserves moral concern. Jacques Derrida explains the transformative power of Jeremy Bentham's displacement of moral prerequisites by asking the question "Can they suffer?" in place of the usual debates about animals' capacities for speech and reason. Rather than the capacity for being-able, suffering is defined by a distinctive passivity or not-being-able (Derrida 2008: 81). Vetlesen adopts a similar perspective, although his analysis remains focused on (nondisabled) humans (Vetlesen 1994: 169). The question "Can they suffer?" highlights our interdependence with all animate beings. To disrupt the question and production of who does and who does not count as human, an inclusive ethics seeks to re-imagine the concept of the right to life (Butler 2009: 18).

In order for an ethics to take into account the production of the human in the determination of the boundaries for moral consideration, it must be able to provide an account of embodied difference as, in Derrida's terms, something other than a privation. Bodily difference must be revalued because, as Jackie Leach Scully (2008) notes, there is an imaginative gap between the worlds of the abled and disabled (and we may add the human and animal) that results in the normalization of ability in ethics. This gap arises because individuals value bodies like their own and only understand physical difference as the lack of an essential component of their own experience. For example, some hearing individuals claim to be unable to imagine a world without music. When thought together, animality and disability, as marginal forms of embodied difference, hold enormous potential with which to challenge essentialist conceptions of the human and articulate difference as productive variation rather than as ontological deprivation (Scully 2008). An inclusive ethics, based on "bodily imperatives" (Weiss 1999: 158) rather than categorical imperatives, calls for recognition of the vulnerability of the other and dissolves speciesist and ableist performance criteria that have historically defined the moral community.

Knowing always has a location and therefore individuals—human or nonhuman, disabled or abled—know the world through embodied perspectives. The situated character of knowledge suggests the possibility of greeting and responding to moral others without privileging essentialist beliefs about the primacy of reason, language, vision, and so on. For example, Derrida asks us to consider how the world would appear and what ethics would look like through the senses of smell or touch. In other contexts, Deaf disability theorist Mairian Corker also sought to disrupt the primacy of the epistemology of vision because she believed that it resulted in a hierarchy between visible and hidden disabilities within disability theory (e.g., Corker 2001: 34–52).

One might object to this embodied, animate, and inclusive ethics by arguing that it will, inevitably, be reterritorialized with new performance criteria. This objection remains within the frames of a competition-based morality. The significance of an inclusive, embodied ethics is not found in replacement criteria, but rather in two ethico-epistemological shifts. The path of the least violence demands "epistemic modesty" (Kittay 2010: 400) insofar as we must recognize the fragmentary, incoherent, and normalizing function of standards for moral status. To the extent that suffering remains a "criterion," it is soft, open, and constantly under question. More significantly, this approach signals a reversal of evidentiary standards. The burden of proof, from this perspective, falls on anyone who would exclude a being from the moral community rather than falling on marginalized others.

Suffering as a standard of incapacity remains under "heightened scrutiny" (Nussbaum 2007: 81). Bodily imperatives engender a *prima facie* duty against killing animate, sentient life. In short, taking a cue from climate ethics, we need a precautionary principle with respect to moral status. Call it: The Precautionary Principle of Moral Status. R. H. Bradshaw, too, has argued for the use of a precautionary principle in the assessment of the moral considerability of nonhuman animals (Bradshaw 1998: 108–44). My recommendation differs from Bradshaw's because Bradshaw analyzes what I consider to be performance criteria. The argument is thus: if there is strong evidence to indicate that a being experiences suffering, then the burden of proof falls on those who seek to deny the being moral status, even if we lack consensus that doing so would constitute a moral harm. A precautionary principle with respect to moral status does not require the inclusion of all biological life in the moral community, as Albert Schweitzer and Kenneth Goodpaster each argue when they present "life" itself as a criterion for inclusion (Schweitzer and Lemke 2009; Goodpaster 1978).

Instead, I have argued that we must both recognize that the goal of an objective, "fundamental account" (Bernstein 1998: 30) of moral considerability is an ableist, speciesist fantasy and relinquish it *as* a goal. The dominance of the performance-driven understanding of the moral other must be challenged in order to weaken the grasp of ableism and speciesism on our moral imaginations. The Precautionary Principle of Moral Status that I recommend offers a tentative understanding of moral status, while recognizing its "viscous porosity" (Tuana 2008: 1998). Such a standard will never offer conclusive, universal determinants of moral status; however, this inescapable uncertainty does not preclude epistemologically modest and responsible "best guesses" that take into account evidentiary caution and moral prejudice. I want to urge disability and animal advocates and theorists to coordinate a sustained, creative, and targeted attack on the use of human species-typical functioning as the mark of moral worth.

Conclusion

Theoretical accounts of moral status are, at their core, ethico-political narratives about belonging: they outline who or what matters. Despite value theorists' attempts to circumscribe the limits of the human, as I have argued, this threshold remains heavily contested, as contemporary debates concerning abortion, premature neonates, euthanasia, and animal rights illustrate. I have examined how speciesism and ableism function as interpretative frames through which liminal others are excluded from the moral community. Because species-typical performance capacities (such as the ability to reason or speak) serve as prerequisites for moral consideration, the limits of moral response are maintained through the mechanisms of ableism and speciesism. As an alternative, The Precautionary Principle of Moral Status that I propose opposes the moral hubris of certainty and purity that Derrida identifies as a target of deconstruction and that Donna Haraway associates with ethical veganism (Haraway 2008: 80).

The attention, within critical disability studies and critical animal studies, to beings who exist at the boundaries of moral considerability exposes the failures of theories of moral status. Rather than base moral consideration on group membership or capacity possession, I envisage a moral relationship that responds to the unknown and unexpected others who transform our understandings of otherness, responsiveness, and moral community. As long as morality is an anthropology in disguise or (in Cary Wolfe's terms) as long as the institution of speciesism and (as I have argued) ableism remain intact, they will "always be available for use by some humans against other humans" (Wolfe 2002: 8), disguising the moral harms done to unrecognized moral beings.

References

Bernstein, Mark H. (1998), *On Moral Considerability: An Essay on Who Morally Matters*, New York: Oxford University Press.

Bérubé, Michael (2010), "Equality, Freedom, and/or Justice for All: A Response to Nussbaum," in Eva Feder Kittay and Licia Carlson (eds.), *Cognitive Disability and Its Challenge to Moral Philosophy*, 97–109, Malden: Wiley-Blackwell.

Best, Steven (2009), "The Rise of Critical Animal Studies: Putting Theory into Action and Animal Liberation into Higher Education," *Journal for Critical Animal Studies* 7 (1): 9–52.

Bradshaw, R. H. (1998), "Consciousness in Nonhuman Animals: Adopting the Precautionary Principle," *Journal of Consciousness Studies* 5 (1): 108–44.

Butler, Judith (2006), *Precarious Life: The Powers of Mourning and Violence*, New York: Verso.

Butler, Judith (2009), *Frames of War: When Is Life Grievable?* New York: Verso.

Carlson, Licia (2010), "Philosophers of Intellectual Disability: A Taxonomy," in Eva Feder Kittay and Licia Carlson (eds.), *Cognitive Disability and Its Challenge to Moral Philosophy*, 315–29, Malden: Wiley-Blackwell.

Carlson, Licia and Eva Feder Kittay (2010), "Introduction," in Eva Feder Kittay and Licia Carlson (eds.), *Cognitive Disability and Its Challenge to Moral Philosophy*, 1–25, Malden: Wiley-Blackwell.

Chen, Mel Y. (2012), *Animacies: Biopolitics, Racial Mattering, and Queer Affect*, Durham: Duke University Press.

Connolly, William E. (1995), *The Ethos of Pluralization*, Minneapolis: University of Minnesota Press.

Corker, Mairian (2001), "Sensing Disability," *Hypatia: A Journal of Feminist Philosophy* 16 (4): 34–52.

Derrida, Jacques (2008), *The Animal That Therefore I Am*, New York: Fordham University Press.

DiSilvestro, Russell (2010), *Human Capacities and Moral Status*, New York: Springer.

Goldstein, Katherine (2009), "PETA's New 'Save The Whales' Billboard Takes Aim At Fat Women,'" *Huffington Post*, September 26. Available at: https://www.huffpost.com/entry/petas-new-save-the-whales_n_261134 (accessed June 24, 2023).

Goodpaster, Kenneth E. (1978), "On Being Morally Considerable," *The Journal of Philosophy* 75 (6): 308.

Haraway, Donna Jeanne (2008), *When Species Meet*, Minneapolis: University of Minnesota Press.

Harman, Elizabeth (2003), "The Potentiality Problem," *Philosophical Studies* 114 (1/2): 173–98.

Jaworska, Agnieszka (2010), "Caring and Full Moral Standing Redux," in Eva Feder Kittay and Licia Carlson (eds.), *Cognitive Disability and Its Challenge to Moral Philosophy*, 369–92, Malden: Wiley-Blackwell.

Johnson, Valerine Ann (n.d.), "Bringing Together Feminist Disability Studies and Environmental Justice," Center for Women Policy Studies. Available at: https://www.peacewomen.org/node/90502 (accessed June 24, 2023).

Kittay, Eva Feder (2008), "At the Margins of Moral Personhood," *Journal of Bioethical Inquiry* 5 (2–3): 137–56.

Kittay, Eva Feder (2010), "The Personal Is Philosophical Is Political: A Philosopher and Mother of a Cognitively Disabled Person Sends Notes from the Battlefield," in Eva Feder Kittay and Licia Carlson (eds.), *Cognitive Disability and Its Challenge to Moral Philosophy*, 393–413, Malden: Wiley-Blackwell.

Kittay, Eva Feder and Licia Carlson, eds. (2010), *Cognitive Disability and its Challenge to Moral Philosophy*, Malden: Wiley-Blackwell.

Koch, Tom (1998), *The Limits of Principle: Deciding Who Lives and What Dies*, Westport: Praeger.

Lake, Howard (2007), "Learning Disabilities Campaign Contrasts Support for Animal Charities," Available at: https://fundraising.co.uk/2007/01/16/learning-disabilities-campaign-contrasts-support-animal-charities/#.XMUKOi-ZPAw (accessed September 12, 2023).

"Learn About the Link Between Dairy Products and the Disorder," *PETA* (blog). Available at: https://www.peta.org/features/got-autism-learn-link-dairy-products-disease/ (accessed April 27, 2019).

McMahan, Jeff (2003), *The Ethics of Killing: Problems at the Margins of Life*, New York: Oxford University Press.

Nussbaum, Martha C. (2007), *Frontiers of Justice: Disability, Nationality, Species Membership*, Cambridge, MA and London: The Belknap Press of Harvard University Press.

Reinders, Hans S. (2008), *Receiving the Gift of Friendship: Profound Disability, Theological Anthropology, and Ethics*, Grand Rapids: William B. Eerdmans Publishing.

Salomon, Daniel (2010), "From Marginal Cases to Linked Oppressions: Reframing the Conflict Between the Autistic Pride and Animal Rights Movements," *Journal for Critical Animal Studies* VIII (1/2): 47–72.

Sandel, Michael J. (1998), *Liberalism and the Limits of Justice*, Second edition, Cambridge: Cambridge University Press.

Schweitzer, Albert and Antje Bultmann Lemke (2009), *Out of My Life and Thought: An Autobiography*, 60th Anniversary Edition, Baltimore: Johns Hopkins University Press.

Scully, Jackie Leach (2008), *Disability Bioethics: Moral Bodies, Moral Difference*, Lanham: Rowman & Littlefield.

Silvers, Anita and Leslie Pickering Francis (2005), "Justice Through Trust: Disability and the 'Outlier Problem' in Social Contract Theory," *Ethics* 116 (1): 40–76.

Singer, Peter (1996), *Rethinking Life and Death: The Collapse of Our Traditional Ethics*, New York: St. Martin's Griffin.

Somerville, Margaret A. (1996), "Genetics, Reproductive Technologies, Euthanasia and the Search for a New Societal Paradigm," *Social Science and Medicine* 42 (12): ix–xii.

Stubblefield, Anna (2010), "The Entanglement of Race and Cognitive Dis/ability," in Eva Feder Kittay and Licia Carlson (eds.), *Cognitive Disability and Its Challenge to Moral Philosophy*, 293–313, Malden: Wiley-Blackwell.

Taylor, Sunaura (2011), "Beasts of Burden: Disability Studies and Animal Rights," *Qui Parle* 19 (2): 191–222.

Taylor, Sunaura (2017), *Beasts of Burden: Animal and Disability Liberation*, New York: New Press.
Tuana, Nancy (2008), "Viscous Porosity: Witnessing Katrina," in Stacy Alaimo and Susan J. Hekman (eds.), *Material Feminisms*, 188–213, Bloomington: Indiana University Press.
Twine, Richard T. (2001), "Ma(r)king Essence- Ecofeminism and Embodiment," *Ethics and the Environment* 6 (2): 31–58.
Vetlesen, Arne Johan (1994), *Perception, Empathy, and Judgment: An Inquiry into the Preconditions of Moral Performance*, University Park: Pennsylvania State University Press.
Warnock, Geoffrey J. (1971), *The Object of Morality*, London: Methuen.
Warren, Mary Anne (1997), *Moral Status: Obligations to Persons and Other Living Things*, Oxford: Clarendon Press.
Weiss, Gail (1999), *Body Images: Embodiment as Intercorporeality*, New York: Routledge.
Wolfe, Cary (2002), *Animal Rites: American Culture, the Discourse of Species, and Posthumanist Theory*, Chicago: University of Chicago Press.

PART V

RESISTING EPISTEMOLOGIES

22 RISKING OURSELVES, TOGETHER

THE POLITICS AND PERSONS OF RISK

MELINDA C. HALL

Introduction

My work in philosophy of disability is informed by critical disability theory. The task of critical disability theory is to analyze disability as a cultural, historical, relative, social, and political phenomenon. Sami Schalk argues that this method of analysis "involves scrutinizing not bodily or mental impairments but the social norms that define particular attributes as impairments, as well as the social conditions that concentrate stigmatized attributes in particular populations" (Schalk 2017). Likewise, I argue that impairment is not the natural or prediscursive foundation of socially constructed disability; rather, both impairment and disability are produced institutionally and discursively. This conviction does not assume that disability and impairment are not real, as the argument's critics routinely charge. On the contrary, this line of thinking follows Shelley Lynn Tremain, who argues that the category of impairment is socially constructed and performatively situated as a naturalized precursor of (the category of) recognizably "social" disability, while disability is in fact a more encompassing and historically relative political apparatus whose material effects are quite tangible (Tremain 2001, 2017). Julie Avril Minich argues that critical disability theory involves the "scrutiny of normative ideologies [that] should occur not for its own sake but with the goal of producing knowledge in support of justice for people with stigmatized bodies and minds" (Minich 2016). In other words, philosophers of disability should work in solidarity, for the purposes of liberation, with people "devalued" or "pathologized" in certain ways, some of whom may not be labeled as disabled or self-identify as such (ibid.).

Given this understanding of the work that philosophy of disability comprises, I want in this chapter to examine the construction of risk and the distribution and attribution of responsibility for it. I am especially interested in the ways in which risk is constructed in bioethics and public health contexts and how responsibility for it is distributed and attributed in these contexts. Risk is tightly intertwined or coincident with constructions of disability in these arenas and, thus, creates a special set of urgent issues for disability justice.[1] I envision my work on risk as both a problematization (in Michel Foucault's sense) of the concept of risk and a reframing of ethical issues with respect to risk that dominant understandings of it present; that is, my work on risk both uncovers how individuals and populations are reductively positioned in dominant discourses as individual subjects at risk or as risk managers and reverses the individualization of risk within these discourses by indicating how orientations toward risk can be collectivized. Within this line of research, I therefore make a critical move by which risk structures themselves can be brought under fresh moral evaluation.

Questions about expert communications tend to dominate when one attempts to swing out to larger portraits of risk. According to Jens O. Zinn and Marcus Müller, "Managing risk well is a technical problem as well as a communicative challenge. Since the way risk knowledge is communicated is central to both public understanding and societal decision-making, a growing body of research and advice literature in risk studies has become concerned with good practice in risk communication" (Zinn and Müller 2022: 271) . In this chapter, I take up a different tactic insofar as I do not assume that the primary challenge in risk management lies in difficulties that experts experience when they attempt to communicate persuasively or objectively about risks.

The chapter proceeds in four stages. In the first and second sections, I acknowledge technical theorizations of risk and begin to sketch a portrait of the political nature of risk. With reference to a set of examples, I claim that risk is a floating signifier and that risk-management discourse is fecund with secondary harms. In the third section, I draw on Foucault to argue that risk-management discourse can count as a productive failure. In these ways, risk discourses can increase harms rather than ease them. In the fourth section, I argue that risk itself is inescapably political and historically contingent. My philosophical position on disability, which I briefly explained at the outset of this chapter, can be understood as the radical view that disability is utterly political—political all the way down. In this regard, I explore the implications of the parallel claim, namely, that risk is utterly political, that is, political all the way down. Throughout the chapter, I consider the many elements of the (political) subjectification of risk; in other words, in addition to the examination of the politics of risk in which I engage in what follows, I consider the constitution of persons of risk, especially with respect to disability and race. I conclude the chapter by identifying opportunities to combat the individualization of risk, to disrupt the harms of risk-management discourses, and to take alternative risks through collective action. I encourage readers to re-imagine and re-fashion risk through radical action as a mode of solidarity—what I will call "risking ourselves." I borrow from Martin Heidegger, while linking the positive picture of my analysis with Foucauldian praxis of refusal, curiosity, and innovation (Foucault 1988: 1). The multi-faceted vision of risk projects that I elaborate is, I argue, aligned with disability justice. In short, the analysis of risk and risk-taking that I offer in the chapter suggests why we should risk ourselves, together, and how we might do so.

Risk as a Floating Signifier

Risk is most familiar in the guise of risk assessment. Indeed, in some settings, *risk* and *risk assessment* are used synonymously (Golding and Tuler 2014: 2873). Sociologist Mary Douglas defined *risk* as the "probability of an event combined with the magnitude of the losses and gains that it will entail" (Douglas 1992: 40). In the assessment of risk, probabilistic rationality engages a value-based orientation toward costs and benefits; one can begin to imagine accompanying tensions between objective theorizations and political and social negotiations. A nonexhaustive list of common arenas of risk assessment would include information technology (Alhawari et al. 2012), construction (Lee et al. 2009), public health (Batterman 2011), property loss and damage, environmental protection,[2] and large-scale conflicts and disruptions (Golding and Tuler 2014: 2873). Risk assessment is a technocratic concern that gives rise to the certification of risk managers in a variety of fields.

As a technocratic science, risk assumes "objective" risk measures and "acceptable" levels of risk (Golding and Tuler 2014: 2876). An example of a postulation of risk in the realm of public health is the equation of risk to a person from chemical exposure with the multiplication of emissions, transport, loss factor, exposure period, uptake, and toxicity factor (Batterman 2011: 1425). For Inmaculada de Melo-Martín, however, such calculations are misleading. She writes:

> Although technical risk-benefit calculations do consider uncertainties, the focus on risks and potential benefits in the ethical analysis of these technologies usually obscures concerns about uncertainties in knowledge and conceals the limits of even the best scientific data. The language of risks reduces issues of uncertainty, ambiguity, and ignorance to the more

controllable and deterministic processes usually associated with risks analysis. (de Melo-Martín 2017: 227)

In other words, risk analysis is a reductionist enterprise that covers over the limitations of data collection. In addition, risk analysis obscures significant arenas of philosophical consideration, including, but not limited to, uncertainty and ambiguity. These problems cannot be overcome via more precise or otherwise improved technical calculations or by communications meant to overcome knowledge gaps. Hence, efforts have been made, in a variety of fields, to nuance—politically and socially—the concept of risk.

In a shift in sociology within what came to be called the "cultural theory of risk" (Kahan et al. 2006), Douglas and Aaron Wildavsky argue that risk analyses are cultural phenomena rather than objective matters related to hazards (Douglas and Wildavsky 1982). Douglas goes even further to claim that risk analysis "makes a spurious claim to be scientific" (Douglas 1992: 14). The cultural theory of risk, overall, "links disputes over environmental and technological risks to clusters of values that form competing cultural worldviews—egalitarian, individualistic, and hierarchical" (Kahan et al. 2006: 1083). As one of its proponents, Douglas believes that at least these features matter for risk analyses: time-span and cultural understanding of it; rumor and risk perception; information authority; blaming; and institutional design (Douglas 1992: 18–19). The cultural theory of risk, then, focuses on the culturally dependent nature of risk interpretation. While this strategy and like interventions aim to interrupt and deepen scholarly conversations around risk, I would like to engage in a more thorough conceptual re-evaluation of risk. After all, Douglas offers that "the risk that is a central concept for our policy debates has not got much to do with probability calculations" (24). This claim mirrors her definition of *risk*, which draws together probabilistic rationality and political values. In practice, this separation of probabilistic rationality and political values means that Douglas and others leave aside a nonpolitical space for more objective probabilistic engagement. By contrast, I assume that such a separation cannot be made.

I shall proceed by focusing on stories that we tell about risk, which, thereby, surface the politics and persons of risk. I am inspired by Sara Ahmed's contention: "Let me repeat: there can be nothing more dangerous to a body than the social agreement that that body is dangerous" (Ahmed 2017: 144). Indeed, as I suggest in this context and further elaborate in the second section, risk discourses are fecund. I use the word *fecund* in this context to refer to the aspects of risk orientations and management practices that occasion new, or secondary, harms. These harms impact already-vulnerable persons along ableist, classist, racist, and sexist lines with intersectional amplification. In this milieu, risk is not an inert description of an orientation toward a hazard, but rather is a floating signifier,[3] one which, lacking a stable referent, attaches itself to entities heterogeneously including, often, to people.

Why claim that risk is a floating signifier? Consider, for example, the marketing strategies of the direct-to-consumer (DTC) testing service 23andMe (Genetics Just Got Personal 2022). With respect to genetic testing for BRCA1 (BReast CAncer gene 1) mutations,[4] several testimonials feature women who describe what they appreciate about the testing. Jill says: "My results allowed me to keep myself healthy." Hilary shares, "I learned something I could be proactive about." And Ann says, "I made a decision about my body from a place of being healthy." Each of these women has interpreted some variety of knowledge about the results of the BRCA1 test as part of their orientation toward risk, but each has separately targeted their risk-management activities, linking knowledge with health in their own cases. Meanwhile, consider Sarah, who is featured with respect to late-onset Alzheimer's disease. Of Sarah, the website claims, "Understanding her own genetic risk helped Sarah feel she had the information she needed to prepare and plan. This in turn has allowed her to be her best self." Note that the language of the self and individual planning is taken as a matter of course in this context, even as some features of the significance of risk shift–in this example, it shifts at minimum from "results" to "knowledge," from "knowledge" to the "body." There is increasing concretization of the information provided by the text, culminating in the idea of a "best self." All of the women featured here understand themselves as subjects in and through their orientations toward the information that they garnered through 23andMe. The ease with which the results of the BRCA1 test becomes attached to the body (Ann: "I made a decision about my body") demonstrates pathways of subjectification. The ease with which Sarah recognizes her "best self" in and through a variety of knowledge about a risk factor further elaborates risk's subjectification. Tellingly, the website that features these testimonials is titled "Genetics Just Got Personal." Throughout the testimonials, risk is ambiguous and malleable.

Police brutality and similar violent encounters make clear the stakes of risk as a floating signifier and begin to point toward risk management as a wider political and social practice with multiple perceived stakeholders and subjects. Aggressors, in order to yield self-defense claims, rely on asymmetrical political understandings of risk landscapes. Specifically, the interpretations of aggressors, according to which unarmed victims nonetheless wield weapons (either on their person or nearby), allows aggressors to ground claims that they felt themselves to be at risk even while committing violent acts. Consider the murder in Sanford, Florida, on February 26, 2012, of a Black youth, seventeen-year-old Trayvon Martin, by George Zimmerman, a neighborhood-watch captain. Eventually charged with second-degree murder for the offense, Zimmerman claimed self-defense and did not take the stand at his trial. Instead, his statements to police were analyzed, along with other evidence, and he was, ultimately, fully acquitted of the charges against him. From the testimony of police and Zimmerman's statements to them, we know that Zimmerman followed Martin in his vehicle as Martin walked home. Zimmerman's lawyer used his client's statements to police to build a legible defense strategy: "Mr. Zimmerman, a neighborhood watch volunteer, claimed that he shot Mr. Martin only after the teenager knocked him to the ground, punched him, straddled him and slammed his head into the concrete—'a weapon,' as his lawyer, Mark O'Mara, called it" (Alvarez 2013). In other words, O'Mara's argument that his client acted in self-defense relied on the claim that Martin was armed by his surroundings. Within the court of law, that is, Martin was identified as a potential threat due to the alleged perception that he would use the sidewalk to harm Zimmerman. In this way, Martin became—that is, was constituted as—a threatening individual, in an asymmetrical fashion that makes evident the political nature of who (and what) counts as a threat.

Consider the murder of another Black youth: eighteen-year-old Michael Brown, who was killed in Ferguson, Missouri, on August 9, 2014, by Darren Wilson, an on-duty police officer. Unlike Martin, who was claimed to be a threat to Zimmerman insofar as Martin could potentially weaponize his immediate surroundings, Brown was claimed to be the embodiment of a threatening weapon and, therefore, to pose an innate risk to Wilson. Wilson, in a court document that includes his list of admissions, articulates this sense of Brown as an embodied threat that put him at risk and justified his violence against Brown as self-defense:

> 39. The holster you carry is designed to prevent someone from easily pulling your weapon from the holster. RESPONSE: Admitted. 40. You eventually decided to draw your gun from the holster and point it at Michael Brown. RESPONSE: Admitted. 41. Before drawing your weapon, Michael Brown had not displayed any weapon. RESPONSE: Objection on the grounds the term "weapon" is vague. To the extent Michael Brown' [*sic*] body (including his fists) constitute "weapons," this is denied. 42. Before drawing your weapon, Michael Brown had not displayed any threatening object. RESPONSE: Objection on the grounds the term "weapon" is vague. To the extent Michael Brown's body (including his fists) constitute threatening objects, this is denied. ("U.S. District Court" 2016, 10; original formatting removed for ease of reading)

The self-defense pleas of both Zimmerman and Wilson constitute sites of risk's racialized construction and its lack of stable referent. Police brutality and adjacent violence encounters are not simply phenomena that carry risks for some populations; rather, these encounters and the larger juridical milieu in which they occur actively construct who or what counts as a threat or whose presence is required to interpret an encounter as risky.

Risk Discourses as Fecund with Secondary Harms

So far, I have considered DTC genetic testing testimonials and the circumstances surrounding the murders of Trayvon Martin and Michael Brown to demonstrate that risk is a significantly malleable concept without stable attachment. In all these examples, risk describes and directs material practices and harm toward specific populations. Thus, I contend that risk is a matter of politics and that the political character of risk should not be obscured by technical understandings of risk. Risk-management discourses deserve political analysis because, as I have indicated, they are fecund in their production of secondary harms.

Responses to viral illness—including the multiple epidemics and pandemic episodes since the turn of the twenty-first century—further demonstrate that risk-mitigation efforts in public health contexts are fecund with secondary harms and drive ableism and racism or are in some way connected to them. In the next section, I turn to COVID-19 to compare individualized and collectivized risk-mitigation strategies. First, however, I want to consider the political character of earlier public health crises of pandemic proportions.

Before the COVID-19 pandemic changed material culture, public discourses, and lexicons of risk mitigation, that is, between 2014 and 2016, Ebola Virus Disease (EVD)—which I will refer to as "Ebola"—emerged in a major outbreak in West Africa (World Health Organization 2022). Researchers have found that racial stigma plays a role in misunderstandings about the transmission and prevention of Ebola (e.g., Davtyan, Brown, and Folayan 2014). I want to point out, furthermore, that risk-mitigation discourse surrounding the phenomena of Ebola racializes risk. In the United States, for example, authoritative public figures and users of social media called for travel bans that would be applied to affected countries, including Liberia, Guinea, and Sierra Leone. These calls for travel bans and related discourse were racially inflected. To take one example, US president Barack Obama was accused of having special ties to West Africa which prevented him from seeing the need for a travel ban (Media Matters 2014). Analysis via Google Trends reveals a correlation between searches for the term *immigration* and searches for the term *Ebola*, with searches for both these terms spiking in the late months of 2015. Other racially inflected cases were reported in October 2014:

> Last month, a cover of *Newsweek* used a chimp to illustrate a story about how bush meat imported from Africa could be a "back door for Ebola." Lawmakers have suggested that Ebola-infected people may stream across the Mexico border. A community college in Texas stopped accepting perfectly healthy students of Nigerian and Liberian descent. Liberian immigrants who live in Texas are getting refused service at restaurants. There are a lot of comparisons being made to AIDS, the last scary disease to come out of Africa that gave rise to similar racial fears and stereotypes. (Culp-Ressler 2014)

As Laura Seay and Kim Yi Dionne, writing for *The Washington Post*, pointed out, "*Newsweek's* use of a chimpanzee to represent a scientifically invalid story about an African disease is a classic case of othering. It suggests that African immigrants are to be feared, and that apes—and African immigrants who eat them—could bring a deadly disease to the pristine shores of the United States of America" (Seay and Dionne 2014). Although President Obama rejected travel bans, he set in place special procedures at airports to screen people traveling into the United States from affected countries.

Some calls for travel bans and screening procedures may be considered unremarkable, given that viral infection is communicable. Yet, panic over the threat of Ebola—partially expressed as panic over the presence, or possible presence, of West Africans and people resembling West Africans—vastly outstripped its potential impacts, especially when compared to far more widespread and deadly viruses prevalent at the time, such as seasonal influenza. In other words, travel bans were not necessary but rather were urged in large part due to racialized panic. According to the Pew Research Center (people-press.org), the 2014 Ebola outbreak in West Africa was at the time the most followed news story since 2010. In October 2014, Pew reported that 77 percent of adults in the United States favored sending troops to West Africa to combat the spread of the virus in the region. (Compare this approval statistic with, in September of the same year, 53 percent approval of President Obama's plan to fight ISIS in Iraq and Syria.) Yet, according to the Centers for Disease Control (CDC), the Ebola outbreak's impact in the United States was limited to only two imported cases and two locally acquired cases.

As the crisis of Ebola subsided in 2015, Zika emerged as a novel threat. Risk discourse surrounding Zika focused on instances of disability among children born of infected women (Huang 2019). Zika was articulated as an "evil" (Sun and Dennis 2016). Women in El Salvador were asked by governmental authorities in 2016 to refrain from having children until 2018 for fear of microcephaly, even though the population, 50 percent of which is Roman Catholic, has a complicated relationship with contraception

(Ahmed 2016). The caution to refrain from reproducing in El Salvador for two years, a nearly unprecedented directive from any government agency, appeared justified by the mere suggestion that reproduction could result in a disabled infant, a claim that outstripped available evidence. This facet of the example of Zika puts into relief how risk and disability are imbricated and, furthermore, that disability is hypostasized as a threat requiring direct governmental intervention on women's reproductive choices. Indeed, studies conducted since the outbreak of Zika show a more nuanced picture: "some 70-80% of pregnant women who get Zika don't transmit the infection to the child"; "while 5-14% give birth to children with signs of congenital Zika syndrome (which can cause developmental issues with their brains and vision), and a 4-6% subset have children with microcephaly" (Haung 2019). In short, the political character of risk discourse is an important area of inquiry for philosophy of disability.

Viral illness mitigation strategies, including in response to Ebola and Zika, are a space in which risk's construction is showcased. Further, we can trace additional layers of risk's subjectification in the context of these events. Public health and popular responses to Ebola referenced race, which called forward identities in and through risk rubrics. These rubrics in turn constructed a population at risk, that is, a risky population, othered by risk managers in control of regulating contact with these risky persons. Public health and popular responses to Zika referenced disability, which called forward identities in and through risk rubrics. These in turn constructed a population at risk, that is, a risky population, positioning reproducers, mostly women, as risk managers. Meanwhile, microcephaly was stigmatized and homogenized—widely varying outcomes were covered over through "the media's persistent depiction of microcephaly as a certain cause of severe debility" (Landman 2016). In epidemic cases, as with the cases of DTC genetic testing and police brutality, orientations toward risk tend to concretize risk in persons, while, at the same time, demonstrating the malleability of risk's signification.

Risk Discourses as Productive Failures

In the first and second sections of this chapter, I began to surface the politics of risk, arguing that risk is a floating signifier. In this section, I further track risk as a mode of subjectification and make use of Foucault's notion of productive failure to perform a more expansive analysis of risk. Foucault analyzed subjectivity as an object or product of power relations. He encouraged the following key questions: "How are we constituted as subjects of our own knowledge? How are we constituted as subjects who exercise or submit to power relations? How are we constituted as moral subjects of our own actions?" (Foucault 1984: 49). For Foucault, Dianna Taylor reminds us, "subjectivity is a mode of self-relation: it provides individuals with a way to understand and relate to themselves and therefore to be understood by and relate to others" (Taylor 2016: 106–7). Taking subjectivity into view as an object of power relations, and as a mode of self-relation, we might identify a multitude of subjects of risk.

Consider the venture capitalist or the business leader who is celebrated for risk-taking.[5] In capitalist societies, dominant public perceptions of them demonstrate that, for some people, orientations toward risk are viewed as a sign of economic success. For many others, careful risk management is valued as responsibility. Responsible citizens are responsive to governmental directives, are compliant with medical professionals, and gather information proactively. As reproduction is a premier site of biopower, combining attention to population and attention to the individual, it is no surprise that responsible risk management is discursively constructed in and through reproductive practices (Savulescu 2001). Parents are meant to be risk managers. Women, in particular, are charged with special duties of risk management in terms of reproduction, including but not limited to responsibility for disability in a future child (Hall 2013, 2016: 127; Waldschmidt 2005). These special duties are indicated even among women who do not intend to have children (Green et al. 2016). As consumers, we are increasingly encouraged to read potential future health risks as direct calls to action, including the call to take or try new medications.[6] The concepts of at-risk populations and risky behaviors are well-worn, politically useful, and even profitable (for instance, through the acquisition of grants and contracts aimed at interventions). Indeed, the calculation of levels of risk for consumers and citizens easily becomes a matter of economic projections and profit, pointing in varied ways to disability itself.[7]

We should notice powerful asymmetries among risk's subjects. A risk manager or responsible citizen is empowered, while at-risk populations are disempowered. Rosemarie Garland-Thomson, in an essay that describes the mutual benefit of working in ways that gather resources from feminist theory and disability theory, has highlighted the question of sexist and ableist representations and their collaborative legitimation of violence (Garland-Thomson 2002: 6–9). In reading Garland-Thomson's analysis, one can articulate a list of traits accorded to people who are privileged by and within racist, sexist, and ableist hierarchies. Within dominant ideologies, ideal subjects are thought to be discrete and autonomous; to conform to binary gender; have bodies that are normal, neutral, and unmarked; have bodies that are unchanging and stable; have bodies that are nondisabled, deracialized, de-ethnicized; and have bodies that are compliant instruments of transcendent will (5–20). Meanwhile, people with non-normative or marked embodiment are thought to be pure body; to embody variation and precariousness; to be deficient and profligate; to be ungovernable, intemperate, and threatening; to be deeply linked with mortality; to be vulnerable and live in contingent ways; and to uniquely need care and assistance (7–21, 34). In these ways, Garland-Thomson's critical analysis of bodily representations in a larger disability-ability machine points to the gulf between at least two products of risk's capacity for subjectification: (1) the subject who manages risk, that is, the risk manager and (2) the at-risk, or risky, subject.

I shall therefore turn now to draw out one aspect of risk's subjectification more completely. This element is the individualization of risk, which serves both the attribution of responsibility and its political neutralization or disempowerment. I have already pointed to this phenomenon in the previous section. Recall the testimonials on the 23andMe website and the ways in which the consumers of 23andMe's DTC genetic testing products begin to understand themselves as responsible subjects. They perceive themselves as exercising responsibility or building better selves through testing. Medical messaging more largely, often mirrored in bioethics literature, similarly situates risk management as a key to better health and medical decision-making, or even as better health itself. Notice that information reported by 23andMe is often not actionable; yet, choosing to use the tests is itself situated as a healthy choice, as "gene therapy" in a different sense.[8] Most frequently, individuals are assigned responsibility for risk—as patients, consumers, citizens, family, and more. Public health messaging, too, is rife with the suggestion that the future is in our individual hands (Tomori et al. 2021).

In *Discipline and Punish* (1977), Foucault notes that prisons have always been criticized for their failure to accomplish the aims that their promoters profess. For authors and thinkers interested in critiquing or understanding the power of prisons, analyzing a prison's failure is, thus, the wrong approach. More illuminating, for Foucault, is inquiring as to what benefit prisons provide—what roles do they serve? Foucault's answers to this question, including his famous analyses of docility and self-surveillance, inform much of his later work (Taylor 2016). In a very different register, Douglas took up a similar approach to questions of risk management: "The manifest intention of any enquiry about disaster is to limit future dangers, but it also has latent functions for the social unit, which need to be understood" (Douglas 1992: 63). For Douglas, the latent social functions related to considerations of disaster include the workings of taboo and sin. The idea that a putative need or overt intention is not met by an institution or discourse, but another need or powerful outcome is indeed met, is invoked with the concept of a "productive failure" (Foucault 1990; Mills 2015; Taylor 2016). Risk-management discourses may fail to mitigate risk, but they do effectively distribute responsibility for risks to individuals. In short, risk discourses are productive failures.

Consider gun violence in schools in the United States as an example of risk management as productive failure. Gun violence is a public health crisis (American Public Health Association 2022). Risk mitigation in response to school shootings exemplifies current modes of risk distribution and the assumptions that produce them. Indeed, there is a diverse array of strategies, responses, and material shifts surrounding school shootings. Changes include (but are in no way limited to): new school architecture, improved locks, curtains, and door stops; specialized defensive school supplies; and activities such as new or modified drills, surveillance, arrests, and counseling. One pattern of responses, typically referred to as the "hardening" of schools, demonstrates the fecundity of risk mitigation particularly well (Walker 2019). This carceral approach can include the arming of teachers in an imagined future and increasing the current police presence on school campuses, both of which responses will contribute to the existing school-to-prison pipeline with obvious discriminatory effects.[9] In the case of school shootings, risk management marginalizes those affected—namely, students—and, paradoxically, seems to increase the severity of the harms to which they are subject; that is, school hardening has directed harm at students and attributed responsibility for risk to them, while simultaneously creating new architectures of power.

One can read the productive failure of risk-management discourses in diverse settings. In the case of Zika's spread in 2015, CDC Zika Health Advisory signs in Florida airports urged pregnant people to protect themselves, saying "Don't let mosquitos bite you."[10] Yet, the threat of mosquitos and our vulnerability to them is largely structural, as it is deeply conditioned by climate change conditions and exacerbated by failed wetlands management and similar environmental policies (Robert, Stewart-Ibarra, and Estallo 2020). When Stoneman Douglas High School students created a national Walk Out protest in response to the 2018 murder in Parkland, Florida, of seventeen people and the injury of an additional seventeen, a countermovement arose to "walk up" to bullies and be kind (Willingham 2018). This countermovement urged personal responsibility as opposed to the gun-control efforts championed by the Walk Out protests. In response to police brutality, some people have underscored why bystanders must film police officers or why body cameras (on police officers) should be used to record encounters, emphasizing the power of individual intervention and surveillance. The impact of bystander films is, however, blunted by possible retaliation and the lack of political action in response to brutality (Ohlheiser 2021). in addition, footage taken by body cameras is often used against victims of police brutality and in favor of aggressors (Lee 2021). Quill Kukla has noted the irony of California's Proposition 65 health warnings on public buildings and spaces, as they are not actionable but rather effectively place liability on the reader of the warnings (Kukla 2013).

Global response to the COVID-19 pandemic, which emerged in early 2020, is deeply instructive with respect to the politics and persons of risks. Our orientations toward COVID-19 are thoroughly responsibilized (Trnka and Trundle 2014). We have seen that early mandates to stay at home and the continuing need to social distance, isolate and quarantine, wear masks, and other activities are not met with the necessary support to make them plausible for most people.

We can, however, take responsibility as a collective with respect to our institutions, decisions, and political landscapes to build more radically open and accessible futures. Consider the following alternative approaches to the harms of COVID-19, which involve risking ourselves collectively rather than individually: mutual aid, decarceration, universal basic income (UBI), debt relief, and online or remote work and learning. Indeed, as I will now argue, risk landscapes can be utterly otherwise.

Is Risk Political "All the Way Down"?

As I indicated earlier, my philosophical position on disability can be described as the radical view that disability is irreducibly political, that is, political all the way down. In this section, I want to track the implications of the parallel claim that risk is political in a similar way. I will therefore work to stay with the thought that risk is political all the way down—in other words, that risk landscapes are mutable and that current landscapes of risk can be utterly otherwise. Other ways of articulating this thought are as follows: risk is produced; risk is a product of choice; or, risk is contingent. As a reminder, the larger project driving me forward is the desire to build, name, and open up obscured or foreclosed opportunities for political action—specifically, projects that collectivize risk. I am inspired by Foucault's commentary on his moral foundations. In an interview, he said, "In a sense, I am a moralist, insofar as I believe that one of the tasks, one of the meanings of human existence—the source of human freedom—is never to accept anything as definitive, untouchable, obvious, or immutable" (Foucault 1988: 1). For Foucault, the mode of problematization is an ethical stance.

As we have already seen, there are more than several ways in which risk is said to be "political." For example, it is often argued that an individual's approach to risk is a matter of one's values and is therefore political (Douglas and Wildavsky 1982). As aforementioned, this type of argument is widely known as the cultural theory of risk (Kahan et al. 2006). "Secondary" or "consequent" risks are thought to be contingent on individual behavior in response to primary risks, making secondary risks political matters (Sunstein 2005). Relatedly, the social amplification risk paradigm (SARP) claims that risk communication elicits affect that shapes how people react to those communications (Pidgeon, Kasperson, and Slovic 2003). Further, "manufactured risks" are thought to stem from risk-mitigation actions, including on the institutional and policy level (Beck 1992). I want to push on these portraits of the politics of risk, since each relies on or refers to a prior naturalized or depoliticized element.

Consider the Douglas and Wildavsky conception of the cultural theory of risk (Douglas and Wildavsky 1982). If an individual's approach to risk is a matter of one's values and is therefore political, then risks remain apolitical (we simply decide how important, or how acceptable, risks are). This, then, is not an irreducibly political picture. Next, consider the secondary risks picture (Sunstein 2005) or the SARP (Pidgeon, Kasperson, and Slovic 2003). In these cases, if secondary or consequent risks are political matters of individual response to primary risks, then primary risks remain apolitical. Finally, consider manufactured risks (Beck 1992). If manufactured risks stemming from risk-mitigation actions are political, then ordinary or original risks remain apolitical.

Yet there are openings to complicate these narrow portraits. Risks are now more frequently viewed as unevenly distributed; for example, a recent study demonstrates that people of color in America breathe more polluted air on average than whites, given the locations of homes in relation to emissions sites (Mikati et al. 2018). In response to the COVID-19 pandemic, it has become commonplace to describe the risks of COVID-19 as directly dependent on the individual's social and political position (including, for example, workplace requirements), which represents shifting attunements to the political nature of risk.

Nevertheless, if we want to stay with the thought that risk is political all the way down, we should push on these complications, too. Consider the increasing discussions of uneven distribution. If risks are unevenly distributed, then a prior or less political distribution is possible. Meanwhile, if the risks of, for example, COVID-19 are dependent on one's political and social position, then, for example, COVID-19 itself can become the individualized or the depoliticized bearer of the concept of "risk." For instance, consider: "If I take this gig, I risk infection"; "others don't face the same COVID-19 risk I do"; and "I am not in the position to avoid this risk." These concerns, while embedded in a larger political structure to which they refer, are not necessarily active. Indeed, they are reminiscent of the CDC's Social Vulnerability Index, which is reactive rather than proactive, and which estimates where support should be directed based on information gathered from the US census (Flanagan et al.

2018, 2020). Overall, the CDC Social Vulnerability Index is not targeted toward proactive or preventative political or social change; rather, the CDC focuses on adequately identifying when or where hazards are most threatening. The Social Vulnerability Index stands, too, to roll ahead with naturalized conceptions of disability, vulnerability, and poverty that are historically embedded in the census and that are thus easily reified.

In the previous section, I argued that risk-management discourses—especially insofar as they individualize responsibility for risk—are political and are productive failures. However, this move to politicize risk-mitigation discourses too may refer to or rely on the naturalization of (some version of) risk. I may have swapped a concept of primary risk for a concept of harm and left room for the type of depoliticization that I aim to critique. In this case, if risk-management discourses are political matters that can harm people, then harms remain apolitical. This putative predicament begins to look like one of the earlier cases: if secondary or consequent risks are political matters of individual response to primary risks, then primary risks remain apolitical; or if manufactured risks stemming from risk-mitigation actions are political, then ordinary or original risks remain apolitical. While I am not ready to dismiss the earlier claim that I make in the chapter, I am committed to staying with the thought that risk is political all the way down.

So, I will now articulate an additional analysis of risk. The concept of risk is political all the way down because risk assessments typically address the probability of a negative outcome within a space of some knowledge and some uncertainty (Hansson 2004). Arriving at the probability of a negative outcome is at least, I claim: (1) a projection or prediction (Golding and Tuler 2014: 2876); (2) an assignment of numerical value (Golding and Tuler 2014: 2876); (3) related to a possible action or investment: (4) contingent; and (5) analyzed from a particular position. Each of these features is political, making risk assessment necessarily political. So, we have strong reasons to view risk assessment as political and, indeed, a marker of power.

Further, risk assessment and risk "itself" have an unstable and leaky relationship; risk assessment creates, describes, and elaborates risk. Risk is not discovered by risk assessment, on this perspective. Meanwhile, it is a short jump from "my actions open me to a possible negative outcome" to "risky behavior," or even "behavioral addiction" (Grant, Odlaug, and Chamberlain 2016). Behavioral addiction is a convenient typology open to diagnosis and regressive psychologizing. Powerfully, "risky behavior" discursively concretizes any potential negative future results within the behavior itself. This performative element of risk means, minimally, that political, social, or imaginative potentialities that a person might enjoy are limited to avoiding (some types of) behavior. Maximally, risks are concretized in persons in a way that calls immediately to mind Foucault's analyses of subjectification.

Sven Ove Hansson (2004) claims that decision-making under risk deals with known probabilities, while decision-making under uncertainty deals with unknown or imprecise probabilities. Building on this account, I want to note that risk assessments are successful on their own terms when they replace uncertainty with "known probabilities" (de Melo-Martín 2017: 227). I argue, then, that there is a powerful incentive toward the expansion of probability and the concretization of risk. This argument lines up with the work of Ian Hacking (1975, 1990), Emily Nacol (2016), and others who describe the emergence and expansion of probabilistic thinking and risk as sciences and attitudes toward the future respectively in historically contingent and political terms.

One may object that the idea that risk is constructed and therefore political is trivial. In other words, one might counter, risk is already calculated in precisely the ways that I indicate—that is, risk is already considered shifting and deeply circumstantial. I would respond, however, that technocratic risk assessment holds the wrong factors in abeyance, that is, the discursive and institutional features of the analysis. What is shifting and deeply circumstantial in risk is not individual behavior or ignorance but shared and political: institutions, discourses, political decision-making, and material conditions.

Conclusion: From Risk Projection to Risk Projects

My primary concerns in this chapter are to analyze risk discourses and to interrupt patterns within these discourses that increase the marginalization of stigmatized people. In the first and second sections, I worked to surface the politics of risk. I claimed that risk is a floating signifier and, in addition, that risk-management discourse is fecund with secondary harms. In the third section, I drew on Foucault to argue that risk-management discourse can count as a productive failure. In the fourth section, I argued that risk itself is inescapably political and historically contingent. Throughout the chapter, I explored many elements of risk's subjectification; in other words, in addition to the politics of risk, I explored the constitution of the persons of risk. The positive project of the chapter is the suggestion that risk can be fundamentally otherwise and that opportunities to disrupt harm and take alternative, collectivized risks can arise. Therefore, in these concluding remarks, I sketch this alternative portrait.

If we shift the meaning of projecting risk away from probabilistic rationality and toward a collective project of risk, that is, making a project of risk, together, we can open powerful, speculative futures for disabled and other marginalized people. These actions can create material differences today and give rise to new coalitions and political solidarity. Again, recall that Foucault has asserted a thin groundwork of moral principles: refusal, curiosity, and innovation (1988: 1). Indeed, as previously mentioned, he stated: "the source of human freedom—is never to accept anything as definitive, untouchable, obvious, or immutable" (1). With Foucault's framing of freedom in mind, I use Heidegger's phenomenological approach to capture the distinction that I want to make between risk projections and risk projects.

What is risk projection? As I set out in the first section, risk is often synonymous with risk assessment, which is a technocratic matter that assigns numerical value in order to create predictions. As a technocratic science, risk assumes "objective" risk measures and "acceptable" levels of risk (Golding and Tuler 2014: 2876). As I set out in the fourth section, risk is political all the way down because risk assessments typically address the probability of a negative outcome within a space of some knowledge and some uncertainty (Hansson 2004). Arriving at the probability of a negative outcome is at least, I claimed, (1) a projection or prediction (Golding and Tuler 2014: 2876); (2) an assignment of numerical value (ibid.); (3) related to a possible action or investment; (4) contingent; and (5) analyzed from a particular position. I then argued that there is a powerful incentive toward the expansion of probability and the concretization of risk. Risk projection is one way of describing the probabilistic rationality at work in these dynamics.

As is well known, Heidegger was interested in meaningfulness as opposed to an objectivist framework. Thomas Sheehan writes: "Heidegger . . . argued that the lived context or world within which things are encountered—the matrix of intelligibility structured by correlative human interests and purposes—was the source of meaning" (Sheehan 2005: 197). Sheehan quotes Heidegger's first lecture course: "The meaningful—that's what is primary, that's what is immediately in your face without any detour through a mental grasp of the thing" (ibid.). In "The Question Concerning Technology," Heidegger described the possibilities of encountering the world through disclosure, or through occasioning, bringing forth, and unconcealment (Heidegger 2008). Yet these possibilities can be covered over, especially through frames of mastery.[11] Indeed, Heidegger suggests that the framing of technology in our encounter with nature covers over meaning rather than discloses it, even while that frame can show us ideas that are, in a sense, correct.

In moving from risk projection to risk projects, I seek to pick up on Heidegger's desire for unconcealment. I would argue that risk projections cover over meaningful future possibilities and that alternative approaches to risk can disclose meaningfulness. Consider, for instance, that risk-assessment sciences cannot inform us about the most crucial aspects of Julian Savulescu's procreative-beneficence argument (Savulescu 2001). This argument holds that we should have the best child of the children that we might have, using available genetic information. Yet, practically, the future is radically unknown, including what traits will be of value, and, morally, assumptions about whole persons based on traits is prejudicial and inaccurate. Risk projections in reproduction that follow Savulescu's procreative-beneficence principle cover over more than they disclose. Indeed, my argument is that prenatal testing technologies generally are engaged in projecting risk in the sense that I seek to capture and, furthermore, that they cover over more than they disclose (cf. Hall 2016; Löwy 2018).

Engaging in reframing well-being and denaturalizing disability, while a collective political and social project with its own destabilizing risks, can open new futures and political opportunities. Futurity is an important thread in critical disability theory, including access to and dreams about the future. As Kelly Fritsch points out, disability is framed as a "future no one wants" (Fritsch 2016: 11). Yet, disability justice activists Patty Berne and Leah Lakshmi Piepzna-Samarasinha, among others, see themselves as dreaming future worlds even in the face of apocalyptic material conditions. Piepzna-Samarsinha writes,

> as disabled people, we know that one of our biggest gifts is the Mad, sick, disabled, Deaf dreams we are always dreaming and have always been dreaming, way beyond what we are allowed to dream . . . I'm talking about the small, huge, everyday ways we dream crip revolutions, which stretch from me looking at myself in the mirror—disheveled and hurting on day five of a major pain flare and saying, You know what, I'm not going to hate you today—to making disabled homes, disabled kinship, and community networks and disabled ways of loving, fighting, and organizing that not even the most talented abled could in a million years dream up. (Piepzna-Samarsinha, quoted in Wong 2020: 253)

Similarly, for Patty Berne: "Even in the moments when we're in pain, when we're uncomfortable, when the task ahead feels overwhelming and we feel defeated by the sheer scope of everything that's wrong with the world, we don't have to give up on life or on humanity. Queer and trans disabled people know that, because that's how we live" (Berne, quoted in Wong 2020: 235). Both activists discuss the dangers and risks of climate change through the lens of collective care and crip kinship, along with alternative ways of living together that open powerful new opportunities for change.

In this chapter, I worked to interrupt patterns in risk discourses that increase the marginalization of stigmatized people or exacerbate existing power asymmetries. I argued that we need strong models of collective responsibility to combat the individualization of risk and to create a habitable future. Rayna Rapp and Faye Ginsburg see the potential to create a habitable future, one in which we "make disability count" for the future rather than "counting disability" (and attempting to eliminate it) to control the future (Ginsburg and Rapp 2015, 2017). Taking up risk as a collective project that interrupts probabilistic thinking (including projecting disability) has the potential to make disability count. Collective-risk projects would ease harms; consider swapping identification and intervention on "at-risk populations" with prison abolition and transformative justice (Kaba 2021). Consider, too, the potential of swapping the work of capturing sea-level rise probabilities for, instead, the work of building new capacities for living on or near water; or, swapping the work of the cost-benefit analysis of novel foods for, instead, dismantling food-distribution structures that waste energy and create malnutrition (Lee 2018). In sum, it was my contention in this chapter that risk landscapes can be otherwise. We can risk ourselves, together, and this risk-taking is valuable. By building alternative risk landscapes, we can refuse a closed future, engaging in our collective potential for radically open and accessible futures.

Notes

1 Consider, for example, Ilana Löwy's analysis of prenatal testing; she writes: "The first 'official' PND [prenatal diagnosis], a direct study of fetal cells obtained through the sampling of amniotic fluid (amniocentesis) was the diagnosis of a risk" (Löwy 2018: 10).

2 Consider, too, Osagie Obasogie's work suggesting the use of environmental impact assessments as a template to assess racialized medicine (2012).

3 A floating signifier is a concept in semiotic theory meant to describe a signifier lacking a referent. Notably, this concept is used by Ernesto Laclau in his study of populism (2005) and by Stuart Hall in his study of race (Obasogie 1996).

4 BRCA1 mutations are associated with higher chances of breast and ovarian cancer (Ford et al. 1994).

5 Consider executive Erin O'Connor, with Cammack Health, speaking as part of a panel on women business leaders: "I've always had this kind of sense of confidence. Like it'll just work out. I'll figure it out very, you know, with five brothers and sisters and one bathroom in our house. I think I learned to negotiate over the bathroom, and I learned to be really resourceful as a young kid. So I always just had this sense that, well, if it doesn't work out, it's not fatal, just and I'll figure it out. And having had the experience of failing in my life, you know, and recovering and failing and recovering got to the point where you know, when we had to invest in this business, I just knew that it was not going to be a problem. I would figure it out, and I trusted my business partner" ('Erin O'Connor Discusses', 2014; text generated from audio transcription).

6 For anthropologist Joseph Dumit, skyrocketing pharmaceutical profits depend on discursive moves whereby "the consumer's felt-sense of health [is] attacked

as not simply mistaken, but dangerous" and consumers are transformed into patients-in-waiting (Dumit 2012: 56).

7 Jasbir Puar argues that the identification of individuals at risk, or the risks related to the reproduction of those individuals, will create new "economic circuits or calculations" based on the scarcity of individuals with low levels of risk (2017: 228). Her analysis offers another layer to the political usefulness of risk calculations in capitalist contexts by suggesting that genetics aids the improvement of human capital.

8 In purchasing a DTC product from 23andMe, consumers often allow 23andMe to store their genetic information in their biobank. 23andMe is currently valued at approximately 1.45 billion dollars, largely due to their value as a biobank of genetic information (2022).

9 For a book-length investigation of the intersectional impacts of the school-to-prison pipeline for black, disabled girls in the United States, see Annamma 2017.

10 Image in author's personal archive.

11 Likewise, Sharon Welch, in her book *A Feminist Ethic of Risk*, posed a logic of control against an ethic of risk in engagement with black thinkers. She writes: "The ethic of risk is characterized by three elements, each of which is essential to maintain resistance in the face of overwhelming odds: a redefinition of responsible action, grounding in community, and strategic risk-taking" (Welch 2000: 46).

References

23andMe Holding Co. (2022), *Yahoo! Finance*. Available at: https://finance.yahoo.com/quote/me/key-statistics (accessed September 29, 2022).

Ahmed, Azam (2016), "El Salvador's Advice on Zika Virus: Don't Have Babies," *The New York Times*. Available at: https://www.nytimes.com/2016/01/26/world/americas/el-salvadors-advice-on-zika-dont-have-babies.html (accessed September 22, 2022).

Ahmed, Sara (2017), *Living a Feminist Life*, Durham: Duke University Press.

Alhawari, Samer, Louay Karadsheh, Amine Nehari Talet, and Ebrahim Mansour (2012), "Knowledge-Based Risk Management Framework for Information Technology Project," *International Journal of Information Management* 32 (1): 50–65.

Alvarez, Lizette (2013), "In Zimmerman Case, Self-Defense Was Hard to Topple," *New York Times*, July 14. Available at: https://www.nytimes.com/2013/07/15/us/in-zimmerman-case-self-defense-was-hard-to-topple.html (accessed September 17, 2022).

American Public Health Association (2022), "Gun Violence is a Public Health Crisis." Available at: https://www.apha.org/-/media/files/pdf/factsheets/200221_gun_violence_fact_sheet.ashx (accessed September 28, 2022).

Annamma, Subini (2017), *The Pedagogy of Pathologization: Dis/Abled Girls of Color in the School-Prison Nexus*, New York: Routledge.

Batterman, Stuart (2011), "Risk Assessment (Public Health)," in Dierdre S. Blanchfield, K. Lee Lerner, and Brenda Wilmoth Lerner (eds.), *Environmental Encyclopedia*, Fourth edition, 1425–8, Detroit: Gale.

Beck, Ulrich (1992), *Risk Society: Towards a New Modernity*, Thousand Oaks: SAGE.

Culp-Ressler, Tara (2014), "The Ugly Racial Undertones in Our Panicked Response to Ebola," *Think Progress*, October 16. Available at: https://thinkprogress.org/health/2014/10/16/3580815/racial-undertones-ebola/ (accessed September 15, 2015).

Davtyan, Mariam, Brandon Brown, and Morenike Oluwatoyin Folayan (2014), "Addressing Ebola-Related Stigma: Lessons Learned from HIV/AIDS," *Global Health Action* Special Issue 7 (November).

de Melo-Martín, Immaculada (2017), *Rethinking Reprogenetics: Enhancing Ethical Analyses of Reprogenetic Technologies*, Oxford: Oxford University Press.

Douglas, Mary (1992), *Risk and Blame: Essays in Cultural Theory*, London: Routledge.

Douglas, Mary and Aaron Wildavsky (1982), *Risk and Culture*, Berkeley: University of California Press.

Dumit, Joseph (2012), "Prescription Maximization and the Accumulation of Surplus Health in the Pharmaceutical Industry: The_BioMarx_Experiment," in Kaushik Sunder Rajan (ed.), *Lively Capital: Biotechnologies, Ethics, and Governance in Global Markets*, 45–92. Durham: Duke University Press.

Films Media Group (2014), "Erin O'Connor Discusses Personal Philosophy on Risk Taking," *Films on Demand*. Available at: digital.films.com/PortalPlaylists.aspx?wID=103003&xtid=163823 (accessed September 26, 2022).

Flanagan, Barry E., Elaine J. Hallisey, Erica Adams, and Amy Lavery (2018), "Measuring Community Vulnerability to Natural and Anthropogenic Hazards: The Centers for Disease Control and Prevention's Social Vulnerability Index," *Journal of Environmental Health* 80 (10): 34–6.

Flanagan, Barry E., Elaine J. Hallisey, J. Danielle Sharpe, Caitlin E. Mertzlufft, and Marissa Grossman (2020), "On the Validity of Validation: A Commentary on Rufat, Tate, Emrich, and Antolini's 'How Valid are Social Vulnerability Models?'," *Annals of the American Association of Geographers* 111 (4): EM-1–EM-VI.

Ford, Deborah, Douglas Easton, Tim Bishop, Steven A. Narod, and David E. Goldgar (1994), "Risks of Cancer in BRCA1-Mutation Carriers," *The Lancet* 343 (8899): 692–5.

Foucault, Michel (1977), *Discipline and Punish: The Birth of the Prison*, trans. A. Sheridan, New York: Vintage Books.

Foucault, Michel (1984), "What is Enlightenment?" in P. Rabinow (ed.), *The Foucault Reader*, 32–50, New York: Pantheon Books.

Foucault, Michel (1988), "Power, Moral Values, and the Intellectual," Interview conducted by M. Bess, *History of the Present* 4 (1–2): 11–13.

Foucault, Michel (1990), *The History of Sexuality Volume I: An Introduction*, trans. R. Hurley, New York: Vintage Books.

Fritsch, Kelly (2016), "Cripping Neoliberal Futurity: Marking the Elsewhere and Elsewhen of Desiring Otherwise," *Feral Feminisms* 5: 11–26.

Garland-Thomson, Rosemarie (2002), "Integrating Disability, Transforming Feminist Theory," *NWSA Journal* 14 (3): 1–32.

"Genetics Just Got Personal" (2022), *23andMe*. Available at: https://www.23andme.com/stories/ (accessed September 8, 2022).

Ginsburg, Faye and Rayna Rapp (2015), "Making Disability Count: Demography, Futurity and the Making of Disability Publics," *Somatosphere*. Available at: https://somatosphere.net/2015/05/making-disability-count-demography-futurity-and-the-making-of-disability-publics.html (accessed September 29, 2022).

Ginsburg, Faye and Rayna Rapp (2017), "Cripping the Future: Making Disability Count," in Juan Francisco Salazar, Sarah Pink, Andrew Irving, and Johannes Sjöberg (eds.),

Anthropologies and Futures: Researching Emerging and Uncertain Worlds, 43–60, London: Bloomsbury.

Golding, Dominic and Seth Tuler (2014), "Risk and Risk Assessment," in Bruce Jennings (ed.), *Bioethics*, Fourth edition, 2873–81, Farmington Hills: Macmillan Reference USA.

Grant, Jon E., Brian L. Odlaug, and Samuel R. Chamberlain (2016), *Why Can't I Stop? Reclaiming Your Life from a Behavioral Addiction*, Baltimore: Johns Hopkins University Press.

Green, Patricia P., Lela R. McKnight-Eily, Cheryl H. Tan, Roberto Mejia, and Clark H. Denny (2016), "Vital Signs: Alcohol-Exposed Pregnancies – United States, 2011–2013," *Morbidity and Mortality Weekly Report* 65: 91–7.

Hacking, Ian (1975), *The Emergence of Probability*, Cambridge: Cambridge University Press.

Hacking, Ian (1990), *The Taming of Chance*, Cambridge: Cambridge University Press.

Hall, Melinda (2013), "Reconciling the Disability Critique and Reproductive Liberty: The Case of Negative Genetic Selection," *International Journal of Feminist Approaches to Bioethics* 6 (1): 121–43.

Hall, Melinda (2016), *The Bioethics of Enhancement: Transhumanism, Disability, and Biopolitics*, Lanham: Lexington Books.

Hall, Melinda (2019), "Critical Disability Theory," in Edward N. Zalta (ed.), *The Stanford Encyclopedia of Philosophy*. Winter 2019 edition. Available at: https://plato.stanford.edu/archives/win2019/entries/disability-critical/ (accessed June 25, 2023).

Hall, Stuart (1996), "Race, the Floating Signifier," Public lecture at Goldsmiths College, transcript made available by the Media Education Foundation. Available at: https://www.mediaed.org/transcripts/Stuart-Hall-Race-the-Floating-Signifier-Transcript.pdf (accessed September 8, 2022).

Hansson, Sven Ove (2004), "Philosophical Perspectives on Risk," *Techné: Research in Philosophy and Technology* 8 (1): 10–35.

Huang, Pien (2019), "Zika: Researchers Are Learning More about the Long-Term Consequences for Children," *NPR*. Available at: https://www.npr.org/sections/goatsandsoda/2019/10/09/768629177/zika-researchers-are-learning-more-about-the-long-term-consequences-for-children (accessed September 22, 2022).

Heidegger, Martin (2008), "The Question Concerning Technology," in D. Krell (ed.), *Basic Writings*, 311–41, New York: HarperCollins.

Kaba, Mariame (2021), *We Do This 'Til We Free Us: Abolitionist Organizing and Transforming Justice*, London: Haymarket Books.

Kahan, Dan, Paul Slovic, Donald Braman, and John Gastil (2006), "Fear of Democracy: A Cultural Evaluation of Sunstein on Risk," *Harvard Law Review* 119; Yale Law School, Public Law Working Paper No. 100; Yale Law & Economics Research Paper No. 317.

Kukla, Quill (2013), "The Relentless Naturalist," Interview with R. Marshall. Available at: https://www.3-16am.co.uk/articles/the-relentless-naturalist (accessed September 29, 2022).

Laclau, Ernesto (2005), *On Populist Reason*, Brooklyn: Verso Press.

Landman, Keren (2016), "Zika is Serious, but Can We Stop Stigmatizing Microcephaly?" *The Dallas Morning News Opinion*, February 12. Available at: https://www.dallasnews.com/opinion/commentary/2016/02/12/keren-landman-zika-is-serious-but-can-we-stop-stigmatizing-microcephaly/ (accessed September 27, 2022).

Lee, Angela (2018), "An Ecofeminist Perspective on New Food Technologies," *Canadian Food Studies* 5 (1): 63–89.
Lee, Hyun-Soo, Hyunsoo Kim, Moonseo Park, Evelyn Ai Lin Teo, and Kwang-Pyo Lee (2009), "Construction Risk Assessment Methodology Using Site Risk Influence Factors," *Korea Journal of Construction Engineering and Management* 10 (6): 117–26.
Lee, Jennifer (2021), "Will Body Cameras Help End Police Violence?" *ACLU of Washington*. Available at: https://www.aclu-wa.org/story/%C2%A0will-body-cameras-help-end-police-violence%C2%A0 (accessed September 29, 2022).
Löwy, Ilana (2018), *Tangled Diagnoses: Prenatal Testing, Women, and Risk*, Chicago: University of Chicago Press.
Media Matters Staff (2014), "Ingraham Calls for Travel Ban in Response to Ebola, Claims Obama's 'Core Ties to the African Continent' Undermine Public Safety." Available at: https://mediamatters.org/video/2014/10/01/ingraham-calls-for-travel-ban-in-response-to-eb/200964 (accessed September 17, 2022).
Mikati, Ihab, Adam F. Benson, Thomas J. Luben, Jason D. Sacks, and Jennifer Richmond-Bryant (2018), "Disparities in Distribution of Particulate Matter Emission Sources by Race and Poverty Status," *American Journal of Public Health* 108: 480–5.
Mills, Catherine (2015), "Resisting Biopolitics, Resisting Freedom: Prenatal Testing and Choice," in S. E. Wilmer and Adronė žukauskaitė (eds.), *Resisting Biopolitics: Philosophical, Political and Performative Strategies*, 109–22, London: Routledge.
Minich, Julie Avril (2016), "Enabling Whom? Critical Disability Studies Now," *Lateral* 5 (1). Available at: https://csalateral.org/issue/5-1/forum-alt-humanities-critical-disability-studies-now-minich/ (accessed July 23, 2023).
Nacol, Emily (2016), *An Age of Risk: Politics and Economy in Early Modern Britain*, Princeton: Princeton University Press.
Obasogie, Osagie K. (2012), "The Return of Biological Race: Regulating Innovations in Race and Genetics Through Administrative Agency Race Impact Assessments," *Southern California Interdisciplinary Law Journal* 22 (1): 1–64.
Ohlheiser, Abby (2021), "The Tactics Police Are Using to Prevent Bystander Video," *MIT Technology Review*. Available at: https://www.technologyreview.com/2021/04/30/1024325/police-video-filming-prevention-tactics/ (accessed September 29, 2022).
Pidgeon, Nick, Roger E. Kasperson, and Paul Slovic, eds. (2003), *The Social Amplification of Risk*, Cambridge: Cambridge University Press.
Puar, Jasbir K. (2017), *The Right to Maim: Debility, Capacity, Disability*, Durham: Duke University Press.
Robert, Michael A., Anna M. Stewart-Ibarra, and Elizabet L. Estallo (2020), "Climate Change and Viral Emergence: Evidence from Aedes-borne Arboviruses," *Current Opinion in Virology* 40: 41–7.
Savulescu, Julian (2001), "Procreative Beneficence: Why We Should Select the Best Children," *Bioethics* 15 (5–6): 413–26.
Schalk, Sami (2017), "Critical Disability Studies as Methodology," *Lateral* 6 (1). Available at: https://csalateral.org/issue/6-1/forum-alt-humanities-critical-disability-studies-methodology-schalk/ (accessed July 27, 2023).
Seay, Laura and Kim Yi Dionne (2014), "The Long and Ugly Tradition of Treating Africa as a Dirty, Diseased Place," *The Washington Post*, August 25. Available at: https://www.washingtonpost.com/news/monkey-cage/wp/2014/08/25/othering-ebola-and-the-history-and-politics-of-pointing-at-immigrants-as-potential-disease-vectors (accessed July 29, 2022).

Sheehan, Thomas (2005), "Dasein," in Hubert L. Dreyfus and Mark A. Wrathall (eds.), *A Companion to Heidegger*, 191–213, Oxford: Blackwell.

Sun, Lena H. and Brady Dennis (2016), "Why Zika is 'Much More Insidious, Cunning and Evil' than Ebola," *The Washington Post*, February 16. Available at: https://www.washingtonpost.com/national/health-science/mysterious-and-fast-moving-zika-virus-has-worlds-health-leaders-scrambling/2016/02/13/c2aac122-d119-11e5-abc9-ea152f0b9561_story.html (accessed September 17, 2022).

Sunstein, Cass (2005), *Laws of Fear: Beyond the Precautionary Principle*, Cambridge: Cambridge University Press.

Taylor, Dianna (2016), "Between Discipline and Caregiving: Changing Prison Population Demographics and Possibilities for Self-Transformation," in Perry Zurn and Andrew Dilts (eds.), *Active Intolerance: Michel Foucault, the Prisons Information Group, and the Future of Abolition*, 105–21, London: Palgrave Macmillan.

Tomori, Cecília, Aziza Ahmed, Dabney P. Evans, Benjamin Mason Meier, and Aparna Nair (2021), "Your Health is in Your Hands? US CDC COVID-19 Mask Guidance Reveals the Moral Foundations of Public Health," *eClinicalMedicine* 38: 101071.

Tremain, Shelley (2001), "On the Government of Disability," *Social Theory and Practice* 27 (4): 617–36.

Tremain, Shelley L. (2017), *Foucault and Feminist Philosophy of Disability*, Ann Arbor: University of Michigan Press.

Trnka, Susanna and Catherine Trundle (2014), "Competing Responsibilities: Moving Beyond Neoliberal Responsibilisation," *Anthropological Forum* 24 (2): 136–53.

"U.S. District Court Document Including Officer Darren Wilson's List of Admissions" (2016), *The Washington Post*, 1–24. Available at: https://apps.washingtonpost.com/g/documents/national/us-district-court-document-including-officer-darren-wilsons-list-of-admissions/2371/ (accessed September 17, 2022).

Waldschmidt, Anne (2005), "Who Is Normal? Who Is Deviant? 'Normality' and 'Risk' in Genetic Diagnostics and Counseling," in Shelley Tremain (ed.), *Foucault and the Government of Disability*, 191–207, Ann Arbor: University of Michigan Press.

Walker, Tim (2019), "School Hardening' Not Making Students Safer, Say Experts," *neaToday*, National Education Association, February 14. Available at: https://www.nea.org/advocating-for-change/new-from-nea/school-hardening-not-making-students-safer-say-experts (accessed August 22, 2022).

Welch, Sharon D. (2000), *A Feminist Ethic of Risk*, Revised edition, Minneapolis: Fortress Press.

Willingham, A. J. (2018), "Walk Out? Father of Parkland Shooting Victim Has Another Idea," *CNN*. Available at: https://www.cnn.com/2018/03/14/us/ryan-petty-walk-up-walk-out-stoneman-douglas-shooting-trnd/index.html (accessed September 28, 2022).

Wong, Alice, ed. (2020), *Disability Visibility: First-Person Stories for the Twenty-First Century*, New York: Vintage Books.

World Health Organization (2022), "Ebola Virus Disease." Available at: https://www.who.int/health-topics/ebola#tab=tab_1 (accessed September 17, 2022).

Zinn, Jens O. and Marcus Müller (2022), "Understanding Discourse and Language of Risk," *Journal of Risk Research* 25 (3): 271–84.

23 DISABLEMENT AND AGEISM

CHRISTINE OVERALL

Discussions of the connections between ageism and ableism and between being old and being disabled are rare in the discipline of mainstream philosophy. As Joel Michael Reynolds remarks, "In philosophical research more generally, there has been relatively little work on aging and even less on disability and aging" (Reynolds 2018: S35). This generalization continues to be correct, as searches of the *Philosopher's Index* and the PhilPapers database will easily confirm. Hence, this chapter seeks to expand theorization about the connections between ableism and ageism and the intersections of disablement and agedness. The chapter has four parts.

I start by outlining my approach to the concepts of, first, ageism, being old, and being aged; and second, ableism, being disabled, and disablement. My aim is to indicate what I take to be some important conceptual relationships among them. I then set out three significant ways in which the ageist conditions of ageing—the material, cultural, psychological, and social environments in which people grow old—produce disablement:

1. by defining oldness as including disablement;
2. by causing old people to acquire the features or conditions of disablement (the ultimate expression of which is physical death); and
3. by wielding double binds that carry unavoidable penalties for old people and that disable by negating the very personhood of the individuals at whom they are targeted.

Clarifying the Concepts

For all the current cultural fables about the joys of getting older, it is evident that ageing is still made into a *social* liability. As I argued in 2006,

> Aging is not a "natural" process; that is, it is in no way outside of culture. . . . [C]ultures *pick out* a certain number of years and *attribute* biological and cultural significance to that number as constituting the state of being old, physically and mentally worn out, no longer in one's prime, and near the end of one's life. (Overall 2006: 129, emphasis in original)

The younger a person is, the earlier they believe that oldness sets in (Chopik et al. 2018).

By "ageing" and being "old," I mean living past the age of, let us say, fifty-nine. That is, in European and North American societies to be "old" is to be aged sixty or more.[1] I will call such persons "ageing" or "old" (though I do not use the adjective *elderly* and I do not refer to older persons with collective nouns such as *the old* or *the elderly*). One could quarrel with where I have placed the boundary for being old—why not sixty-five, or sixty-nine?—nevertheless, the fact is that being considered old (along with the social liabilities that come with it) still sets in fairly early—especially, though not exclusively, for many who are coded as women:

> Your face is lined and your hair is grey, so they think you are weak, deaf, helpless, ignorant and stupid. When they address you they tilt their heads and bare their teeth and adopt a tuneful intonation. It is assumed that you have no opinions and no standards of behaviour, that nothing that happens in your vicinity is any of your business. (Garner 2016: 213)

To be old is to be perceived and treated as being over fifty-nine, and hence valued negatively as varying from the supposed human norm—as being incomplete, abnormal, dysfunctional, or defective. We all know what that norm is: white, slim, disease-free, often athletic, highly productive, heterosexual, gender-sex congruent, middle- or owning-class, with a particular kind of cognitive and psychological functioning, and above all young (though perhaps not too young: culturally speaking, neither a one-year-old nor a twelve-year-old constitutes the norm). The usual assumption is that the state of being old is unpleasant, perhaps even miserable—no matter what old people themselves may say about their lives. The features associated with being old include grey or white hair, wrinkles, a less than upright posture, a slow gait, inactivity, unproductivity, asexuality, slow response time, failing memory, declining sight and hearing, "old-fashioned" views and preferences, frailty, and dependency.

In some cases, the individual may not actually *possess* most of these features; yet, they are assumed to have them due to their age alone, or what is taken to be their age, and are valued negatively as varying from the supposed human norm. As Linn Sandberg and Barbara Marshall point out, to the extent that individuals can avoid these features (I would add: or disguise or hide them), they are considered to age better, to be more successful at getting old, because they are conforming, or clinging, to compulsory able-bodiedness (Sandberg and Marshall 2017: 3). They are expected or encouraged to participate in what Sandberg and Marshall call "new ways of disciplining later life" (4, 5).

Ageism is bias, marginalization, and/or mistreatment targeted at individuals or groups of individuals based on their years lived (age) or perceived years lived. But ageism is not only that. Ageism is also a system of oppression comprised of social practices and institutions that identify and constitute having lived longer than sixty or sixty-five as individual and social problems (Overall 2006: 131).[2] Ageism does not reflect or reveal anything inherent, essential, inevitable, or biologically given about ageing or old people. People at any age can have declining sight or hearing, lose (or never possess) the capacity to walk or to care for themselves, be or become frail and vulnerable, or need medical care or personal support. Yet ageism—as a system—tells us plenty about how to *perceive* old people, what to think about them, how to treat them, and which social policies to choose to govern them. As a result, ageism creates, sustains, and reinforces the actions, policies, resources, conditions, and events that structure the lives of old people. Such people then are "aged"—"aged by culture," to adopt the phrase invented by Margaret Morganroth Gullette (2004), and also aged by institutions, policies, and the material demands of living in the twenty-first century.

For purposes of this chapter, I will use the following definition of the term *disabled*: To be disabled is to be perceived and treated as having a physical, psychological, or cognitive feature, set of features, or a condition that is, within a particular social environment, considered to be an incapacity and is treated as such. Hence, the feature or set of features is valued negatively as varying from the supposed human norm—as being incomplete, abnormal, dysfunctional, or defective. Once again, to be normal is to be white, slim, disease-free, often athletic, highly productive, heterosexual, gender-sex congruent, middle- or owning-class, with a particular kind of cognitive and psychological functioning, and to be young.

People who are designated disabled may be expected or encouraged to conform to "compulsory able-bodiedness" (Sandberg and Marshall 2017: 2), that is, to pass for normal (Overall 1998: 151–71). As in the case of being old, the usual assumption is that not conforming to the norm is unpleasant, perhaps miserable—no matter what disabled individuals themselves may say about their lives. In some cases, the individual may or may not actually possess the feature or set of features or condition that is valued negatively as varying from the supposed human norm. This variant feature or set of features or condition (like *all* features and conditions of human beings) may or may not have been caused by other human beings or social institutions. Furthermore, this variant feature (or features) may or may not involve pain or suffering to the individual herself and may or may not be valued negatively by the individual herself. Indeed, it may also be valued positively.

Ableism is bias, marginalization, and mistreatment targeted at people who are perceived to have (and are treated as having) a physical, psychological, or cognitive feature, set of features, or condition that is both considered to be an incapacity and valued negatively as diverging from the supposed human norm—as incomplete, abnormal, dysfunctional, or defective. Yet ableism is not only these things. Ableism is also a system of oppression that comprises social practices and institutions that identify and constitute certain properties or conditions of individuals as incapacities, as signifying incompleteness, abnormality, dysfunction, or defect, and hence as individual and/or social problems.

The capacities that are regarded as "normal" are those that are called for, in particular social environments; thus, normal capacities vary from one culture to another. In fact, people of all genders, races, classes, and ages, employed or not employed, educated or not, experience varying capacities during their lives. A two-year-old does not have the capacities possessed by a nine-year-old. A thirteen-year-old does not have the same capacities as a forty-year-old. The capacities of a twenty-year-old differ from those of a sixty-year-old. A fifty-year-old has different capacities than an eighty-year-old. Capacities come and go, develop and diminish throughout one's lifetime. For example, my mother, whose native tongue is English, learned to speak French well enough that by her fifties she was able to live and thrive in France. Forty years later, she no longer speaks or understands French. Reynolds and Anna Landre point out that an individual's capacities may also vary over a year, a month, and even a day (Reynolds and Landre 2022: 6). To be a living being is, in part, to have a range of capacities to engage in actions and activities to some degree or other and to have a range of actions and activities that one cannot do, that is, incapacities. Yet not every incapacity is a disability. For example, at ninety-six, my mother is believed to have many disabilities, but the fact that she can no longer speak French is not one of them, as she now lives in an English-speaking environment.

As with ageism, ableism does not reflect or reveal anything inherent, essential, inevitable, or biologically given about the individuals identified as incomplete, abnormal, defective, or dysfunctional. While ableism tells us nothing about individuals themselves, it tells us plenty about how to perceive disabled people, what to think about them, how to treat them, and which social policies to choose to govern them. As a result, ableist media, corporations, governments, and institutions create, sustain, and reinforce the actions, policies, resources, procedures, and events that structure the lives of disabled persons.

I also use the noun *disablement* and the verb *to disable*. When a person, circumstance, policy, or institution disables an individual at any stage of life, the individual loses capacities, skills, know-how, powers, or competences that they either had before becoming disabled, or could have developed, if not for being disabled. Such persons are "disabled," though I do not use the collective term *the disabled*. Disablement is the condition of having been disabled; and it is the result of ableism.

Like the term *the elderly*, the term *the disabled* is both inappropriate and demeaning for two reasons. First, such terms overgeneralize by limiting all members of each group to just one characteristic, as if that is all that they are. Second, such terms erase the personhood of the members of each group by subsuming them under a nominalized adjective.

In order to fully understand how disability results from picking out a diminished or absent capacity or condition and treating it negatively as well as understand how agedness results from picking out a chronological age and treating it negatively, consider the following thought experiments. They are intended to illustrate both that "the prevalent understanding of what disability is does not exist apart from nor prior to the social power relations that are alleged to merely respond to disability" (Tremain 2021: 13) and that the prevalent understanding of what counts as old does not exist apart from nor prior to the social power relations that are alleged to merely respond to ageing.

First, imagine a situation in which being able to sing in a particular way is essential to being a full, functioning member of the society—perhaps because such singing soothes otherwise dangerous animals, or is required by the King and his knights, or communicates with otherwise alien gods. In this society, being able to sing in a particular way is defined as being central to normalcy and full participation in public life. Someone who cannot sing in that way (she simply lacks the capacity, no matter how she tries, perhaps because her vocal cords are structured differently than other people's or for some other reason) is considered and treated as abnormal, defective, incomplete, and not a full person in that society. That person is a target of ableism.

Second, imagine a society in which persons aged fifty to fifty-nine are thought to be dangerous because they are no longer young but are not yet old. They are in a liminal stage, where they cannot be relied on by either those who are young or those who are old. In this society, being either younger or older than that age group is regarded as integral to being a respectable, trustworthy, appropriately knowledgeable citizen. So, then, someone who is fifty-two or fifty-eight is regarded and treated as abnormal, defective, incomplete, and not a full person in that society. That person is a target of ageism.

Now a critic might say that these analogies do not work. Not being able to sing in a particular way does not cause physical pain or suffering. And being fifty-eight does not carry with it the difficulties and challenges that being much older carries. But the non-singer in the first society could very well suffer from her incapacity, just because it is a reason for her exclusion and revulsion. And the fifty-eight-year-old will suffer from her age-based exclusion from mainstream society. Being disabled or old is not about inherent suffering; it is about social oppression and marginalization.

Defining Oldness as Including Disablement

To observe that old people and people with labeled disabilities may often be treated similarly—with ignorance, disrespect, marginalization, isolation, denial of autonomy, institutionalization, physical and psychological violence; in other words, with ableism and ageism—is not new.[3] Members of both groups, that is, both people who are labeled disabled and people considered old, may be regarded as expendable. In addition, the categories of old and disabled "are at least partially constructed by their relationship to work and the economy through what is referred to as 'structured dependency'" (Aubrecht, Kelly, and Rice 2020: 24). That is, people who are designated as disabled and people considered old are seen as economic problems, because they are regarded as unproductive. Because of the stigmas caused by ageism and ableism, furthermore, old people may "resist being classified as disabled and may align themselves with successful and disability-free trajectories to counter the negative implications of age/impairment," while "people who are aging with disabilities may position themselves outside the chronological category of 'old' to resist the narrative of decline" (23).

In a paper that explores the relationship between ageing and disability, Reynolds refers repeatedly to the supposed phenomenon of "becoming disabled *through* aging" or becoming "less abled *due to* aging" (Reynolds 2018: S32, S33, emphasis added). In a more recent co-authored paper, Reynolds and Landre write, "growing old invariably means becoming impaired in various ways" (Reynolds and Landre 2022: 1), using the phrase "becoming impaired through aging" (4). In other words, these authors seem to think that ageing inevitably involves loss of capacities and, therefore, abnormality, frailty, vulnerability, unproductiveness, and dependency, all of which states are commonly regarded as characteristic of disabled people. But the idea that people become disabled simply by virtue of getting older assumes that there is something biologically inherent within living longer that inevitably causes (a) a widespread loss of capacities in such a way that (b) makes one defective, dysfunctional, abnormal, or incomplete. This assumption makes ageing and being disabled merely a matter of one's innate supposedly non-social biology. But (a) is often false, or at least not true at every stage of oldness, and (b) is a socially imposed value judgment.

In media depictions, marketing and advertising, social policies, government edicts, and the popular imagination, to age "successfully" means resisting the markers of disablement. It is assumed that to be old *is* to be disabled. As Katie Aubrecht, Christine Kelly, and Carla Rice note, "whereas disability is isolated as abnormal, age and impairment become conflated as normal and expected" (Aubrecht, Kelly, and Rice 2020: 23). This conflation is made, they say, "irrespective of the ways in which lives have been damaged by factors such as poverty, sub-standard housing, contaminated water, inadequate sanitation, and colonialism" (30), which may well have hastened the loss of capacities. Thus, ageist ideology tells us that the concept of oldness includes ideas of incapacitation.

Is it also true that in dominant North American culture to be disabled *is* to be old? Here, I speculate, the situation is more complex. To be disabled is to be cast out of the normal by virtue of certain sorts of incapacities, and to be normal is (among other characteristics) to be neither very young nor old. To be disabled, especially, but not only, for people between the ages of twenty and fifty-nine, is either to be infantilized, that is, regarded and treated as younger, sometimes much younger, than one is, or to be paternalistically treated as older, sometimes much older, than one is. (Hence the placing of certain disabled people in long-term care homes otherwise populated by people who are old.) I will call the process by which one is treated in these ways being "geriatricized." In some cases, the assumptions of ableist ideology entail that to be disabled is to be geriatricized; in other cases, the assumptions of ableist ideology entail that to be disabled is to be infantilized. Whether infantilized or geriatricized, the results for the individual regarded and treated in these ways can be similar, epitomized by the condescending tone and manner that are often employed to talk to disabled or aged people: loss of autonomy, loss of respect for one's preferences and choices, physical confinement, psychological and cognitive limits on one's activities, expectations about feebleness and fragility, and requirements to conform to rules and regimentation.

Causing Disablement

The view that people become disabled through or due to ageing fails to consider the social context in which human beings get old. Instead, I suggest that *the ageist conditions of ageing*—the material, cultural, psychological, and social environments in which people grow old—are disabling. Ageism is disabling in many ways.

One way involves automatically perceiving and treating old people as disabled. Thanks to ageism, various features or conditions often, but not always, possessed by ageing people, or thought to be possessed by them—including, but not limited to, features and conditions such as grey hair, lined skin, a particular way of moving, a particular way of speaking, a particular posture, balance, or sight or hearing—are perceived and treated negatively as varying from the supposed human norm: as a sign of incompleteness, abnormality, dysfunction, or defectiveness. Because oldness is widely understood to naturally include incapacitation, to be old is automatically to be perceived and treated as being in a state of decline and deterioration (Gullette 2004: 181).

In their paper on the relationship between ageing and disability, Mariska Van der Horst and Sarah Vickerstaff propose that "part of ageism [is] actually ableism" (Van der Horst and Vickerstaff 2022: 1). They suggest that ageism may be "too broadly defined" if it includes ableism within it and, hence, want to see a narrower definition of ageism that distinguishes it from ableism (3). Older workers may be subjected to bias, they believe, either because of "impairments that older people may be more likely to have" (4), or because of stereotypes such as that older workers "are less competent, . . . [have] decreased willingness to participate in training, . . . [or are] less flexible" (3). According to these authors, the former is an expression of ableism, whereas the latter is an expression of ageism.

This approach sounds, unfortunately, like a strategy for reducing the incidence of ageism just by redefining many cases of ageism as manifestations of ableism (and thereby increasing the incidence of ableism). Consider this hypothetical example put forward by Van der Horst and Vickerstaff: "If . . . [an] older worker was not offered [a] career development opportunity because it was assumed that she will not be hearing well enough, especially if the older worker herself also says she is not hearing as well as she used to (as an age effect), this would be ableism rather than ageism" (Van der Horst and Vickerstaff 2022: 5). In a society that somehow is ageist but not ableist, they suggest, such a worker would not be the target of discrimination (6)—at least, not for this reason.

This latter point may be assuming what it is trying to demonstrate: that ableism can always be neatly distinguished from ageism. I think, moreover, that the point underestimates the complexity of the intersections of ableism and ageism. The situation of the worker who is not offered a career development opportunity because it is believed that she will not hear well enough is probably a manifestation of *both* ageism and ableism intertwined, not only ableism. First, the ageist conditions of ageing may very well make employers and their businesses more likely to be on the lookout for so-called impairments in older people and, therefore, more likely to "find" them—and then to regard them as significant and potentially inconsistent with doing the job. When such "impairments" are found in older people, it may be assumed that because these individuals are older, their "impairments" are likely to become even more debilitating. And, furthermore, because these individuals are older, it may be thought less worthwhile for the business to invest in supporting them, by providing ways to enable them to do their work given the physical or cognitive characteristics and conditions that they have. In other words, ageism could predispose employers to see the features of older people in a more negative light than they would see the same features in younger people. If so, then, in many cases of prejudicial judgment and treatment, ageism and ableism may intersect to such an extent that it is impossible to clearly separate them.[4]

But ageism does not merely contribute to the perception that ageing persons belong to the category of disabled persons. Even more important, ageist circumstances and institutions can *cause* ageing persons to acquire incapacities that are seen as varying negatively from the norm and, hence, that become disabilities, and that often in addition involve unnecessary pain or suffering to the individuals who acquire them.

Long-term care institutions provide many examples of ways in which ageism is disabling. For example, in Ontario in 2019—before the COVID-19 pandemic—more than 230 such places "reported either more residents being physically restrained on a daily basis, more potentially inappropriate use of antipsychotic medications, or more residents with pressure ulcers that had gotten worse than reported the same five years ago" (Gibson 2020). Six out of seven long-term care homes in Ontario had repeated incidents of neglect and abuse, with no consequences for their actions (Pedersen, Mancini, Common, and Wolfe-Wylie 2020).[5]

Obvious cases of ageism causing disablement continued during the COVID-19 pandemic. As Ashton Applewhite points out, the social conditions of the pandemic did not necessarily make ageism worse; instead, they "expos[ed] what's been all around all along" (Applewhite 2020). The ageist social response to the pandemic disabled large swathes of the older population, who found their freedom and mobility limited and their well-being and lives threatened by the behavior of other people. Since the start of the pandemic, the treatment of many people who have lived sixty years or more has been seriously, sometimes fatally, disabling, to the point of causing their deaths.

As a particularly egregious example, consider Alessandro and Adelina Busato. Aged ninety-two and eighty-eight, respectively, before the pandemic they had active, autonomous, and social lives at their retirement home. But thanks to the ageist isolation, neglect, separation from family and from each other, and even abuse that they experienced during the lockdown, their "health . . . deteriorated so dramatically they need round-the-clock care." Their ordeal included infections, broken bones, and cognitive changes because of the isolation. When reunited with his spouse of sixty-four years, Mr. Busato no longer recognized her. It was predicted that neither one will regain their ability to walk (Mahoney 2020). As Stephen Archer, a physician in the Queen's University School of Medicine points out,

> [S]eniors in LTCs [long-term care institutions] have already paid twice for the pandemic[;] first we failed to protect them through systemic flaws in our patchwork senior care system (which is not really a "system"). Then in response to our failure and the shocking mortality rates, we locked these facilities down and trapped seniors in isolation, allowing their physical and mental health to deteriorate in ways that have yet to be fully counted. (Archer 2020)

Thus, ageism disabled them.

Yet as Gullette stresses, "Being older is not by itself a death sentence from the virus. Some who survive are over age 65, even over 100: the 'super-survivors,' like Sylvia Goldsholl, who also survived the 1918 flu. . . . People over 65 are not a group doomed to die by our physiology" (Gullette 2020). Nonetheless, the logical outcome of disablement through ageism is to make old people disappear, through a willingness to allow or even encourage them to die.

Well before the pandemic, this idea was already a thread in public and academic discourse as, for example, in John Hardwig's view that old people have a "duty to die" when, or even before, they become a "burden" (Hardwig 2000). But the pandemic made this idea even more explicit. For example, Dan Patrick, the lieutenant-governor of Texas, infamously advocated that "senior citizens" should be willing to die for the sake of preservation of the American economy. He was quoted as saying:

> No one reached out to me and said, "as a senior citizen, are you willing to take a chance on your survival in exchange for keeping the America that all America loves for your children and grandchildren?" And if that's the exchange, I'm all in. And that doesn't make me noble or brave or anything like that. I just think there are lots of grandparents out there in

> this country like me . . . what we care about and what we love more than anything are those children. (Patrick, quoted in Rodriguez 2020)

Toby Young, a British right-wing columnist, argued at the beginning of the pandemic lockdown that "spending £350 billion to prolong the lives of a few hundred thousand mostly elderly people is an irresponsible use of taxpayers' money" (Young 2020). Among academics, this idea is also not uncommon. It has been suggested that the use of triage in apportioning pandemic health care could mean that age on its own is used as "an accepted criterion" for decisions about who lives and who dies in the pandemic (Ayalon et al. 2020). Axel Gosseries, a research professor at Université Catholique de Louvain, writes,

> the age that a person has reached is a key criterion for anyone concerned about *inequalities between short-lived and long-lived persons*, or about improving the situation of short-lived people in priority. The length of one's existence is one of the essential resources that one can dispose of to pursue the projects that give meaning to our lives. Hence, the use of an age criterion in access to life-saving care can be seen as a way of reducing inequalities in longevities, or avoiding to worsen them through health care [*sic*]. From that perspective, if we have to choose between saving a young and an old patient, it does not matter so much whether the young patient is in a better shape than the old one—and whether age is a good predictor for that. (Gosseries 2020, emphasis in Gosseries)

In short, sacrifice the older person; he has already lived his life—even if his life is as medically salvageable as, or more medically salvageable than, that of a young person with the same illness. More than one commentator has pointed out that this cavalier approach is a new form of eugenics (Tremain 2021), assessing old people on their supposed value and "capacity to be productive" (Abraham 2020). Being old, that is, having lived a certain number of years, whether it is ninety, eighty, seventy, or sixty, is the flaw itself, the fatal characteristic that makes them destined for immediate death.

The Role of Double Binds

The cultural construction of double binds is a significant social process by and through which ageism disables people. Forty years ago, feminist philosopher Marilyn Frye wrote, "One of the most characteristic and ubiquitous features of the world as experienced by oppressed people is the double bind—situations in which options are reduced to a very few and all of them expose one to penalty, censure or deprivation" (Frye 1983: 2). To be trapped in a double bind is, according to Frye, to be "caught between systematically related pressures" (3).

In the sense in which I am using the term, a double bind is a forced choice between two (or sometimes more) alternatives, all of which carry heavy penalties. In the case of ageism, double binds are rarely presented explicitly as such; that is, targets of the double bind are not explicitly told that they have only two options and that each of these options results in a penalty. Rather, messages about the options come to the individual under various and different circumstances, in such a way that the targets are less likely to be able to notice and understand their relatedness.

The communication of double binds to people who are old is ubiquitous and repeated. In some cases, such communications may even appear innocuous or well-intentioned. Hence, the situation for the ageing person is likely mystified and mystifying. This fact makes it difficult or impossible for the targets to accurately identify the ageism at work and escape from it. The inescapability of this situation for the ageing person exemplifies Frye's classic bird cage analogy for oppression (Frye 1983: 4–5), in which, as Frye says, each individual wire by itself seems not to limit the bird, but together, as "a network of systematically related barriers" (5), they make escape impossible.

Being in a double bind means a person cannot win, whatever choice she makes or however she decides to act. But double binds have an even more insidious and pernicious consequence. Being the target of a double bind means one cannot fully exist, since each choice negates who one is. One cannot be a full person, with agency and intrinsic value, because the double bind denies these dimensions of personhood. An effective double bind makes its target into a nonperson. Hence, while the most extreme form of disablement by ageism facilitates the physical *death* of old persons (as I argued in the previous section), ageist double binds disable by facilitating the nonexistence of old individuals as persons.

In some ageist double binds, both alternatives are ostensibly positive. In other ageist double binds, one alternative is ostensibly positive and one is negative. And in yet others, both alternatives are clearly negative. But in all ageist double binds, the choices always produce disabling penalties.

Here is an example where the alternatives are both ostensibly positive. On the one hand, targets of ageism are commonly told that old people are privileged to enjoy their leisurely "golden years" without any cares and no longer have to contribute to the society in which they live. On the other hand, targets of ageism are told that they can and should continue to contribute to society by doing volunteer work, by caring for grandchildren or vulnerable relatives or strangers, and by virtue of their supposed wisdom and insight.

The penalty for accepting the first message is accepting a description that says the targets' lives are vacuous and unproductive. And it implies that all those who are not benefiting from a financially secure and leisurely old age either are failures or do not exist. The penalty for accepting the second message is that it sets very high standards for being personally valuable: the old person must be active, giving, contributing, wise. The second message implies that a life not devoted to service lacks value. Meeting those standards can be difficult, painful, or even impossible. The individual is disabled by this double bind because one choice consigns her to the category of parasite, failure, or nonexistence, and the other choice exacts more than most people can do on an ongoing basis. Whichever choice the individual makes, she suffers a disabling penalty and the undermining of the dignity of her own unique existence. In other words, neither choice is existentially tenable.

Some ageist double binds carry a mix of apparently positive and clearly negative messages. Consider, for example, the often-heard remark made to people over sixty that they "don't look their age," that they are not really old, and that they could easily be taken for someone younger. This remark seems, and is often intended, to be a compliment. Old people are exhorted to engage in youthful activities and take on youth-associated values. Hailee M. Gibbons says these pressures aim at "compulsory youthfulness" (Gibbons 2016). Targets who fail to conform to compulsory youthfulness (whether because they cannot or they do not want to) are subjected to overt ageism, including questions about their so-called entitlements, complaints about their present or future burdensomeness, and lack of the kind of respect and autonomy granted to younger people. So, the old individual has the seeming choice of, on the one hand, endeavoring to pass as young, however difficult or distasteful that it might be, and accepting the idea that failing to look and act youthful is bad. Or, on the other hand, refusing to try to pass as young and accepting the ageism and ableism that go along with failing to "age successfully." The double bind negates her existence because either she must pass as what she is not (a conventionally younger person), or she must accept a view of herself as burdensome, undeserving of respect, and a failure.

Here is another example where one alternative is negative and the other ostensibly positive. My 96-year-old mother is losing her vision due to macular degeneration and thus moves using a walker. Along with other residents of so-called retirement homes, she has repeatedly been characterized by the staff at her retirement residence as vulnerable, helpless, and dependent. Yet when it suits the organization, she and the other people who live there are also described as perky, feisty, plucky, and courageous. Both of these characterizations might be interpreted as kindly, well-intentioned, and supportive. After all, it seems important to recognize the vulnerability of people whose physical capacities are gradually changing. And it is good to recognize the courage of people who nonetheless thrive under these conditions. But if a target takes on the characterization as dependent and vulnerable, she runs the risk of accepting and reinforcing her treatment as helpless—although she usually is not. If she takes on the characterization as plucky and brave, she accepts standards that are hard for any human being to instantiate and will face rejection when she fails to be feisty. The double bind is disabling because it stereotypes people such as my mother, emphasizing either weakness and decline or the supposed heroic struggle against them, either of which may be quite inconsistent with the personhood of the old person.

In my final example, both alternatives are unambiguously negative. On the one hand, people who are still engaged in paid work past the age of sixty or sixty-five are often told that they are past their prime and should accept their supposedly age-related disabilities, that they are selfishly withholding jobs from young people, and that they should consider retiring. On the other hand, old people who are *not* engaged in paid work are told that they are a liability, a drag on the social support system, living off state pensions. It is obvious that both of these alternatives are punitive and that both of them depend upon ageist/ableist assumptions. But note, also, that each so-called "choice"—working or not working—is stigmatized in such a way that it negates who the person is: a person of value, with goals, needs, and capacities of her own. Once again, an ageist double bind disables the old individual by undermining and denying her full personhood.

Conclusion

While I cannot offer practical ways to mitigate the contributions of ageism to disablement, I believe that it is useful both to clarify the concepts used to analyze these forms of oppression and to identify some of the specific mechanisms by which ageism contributes to ableism and disablement.

In this chapter, I proposed ways of understanding ageism, being old, and being aged, as well as ableism, being disabled, and disablement, in addition to the conceptual relations among them. I then discussed three significant ways in which the ageist conditions of ageing disable old people. To reiterate, the three ways in which ageism disables old people are: first, by perceiving and treating old people as inevitably and inherently disabled; second, by causing ageing persons to acquire incapacities that are seen and treated as varying negatively from the norm, the ultimate expression of which is precipitating the physical death of the old person; and finally, by means of the imposition of double binds, which always carry unavoidable penalties that disable by negating the very personhood of the individuals at whom they are targeted.

Acknowledgments

I am indebted to Shelley Tremain for inviting me to participate in "Philosophy, Disability and Social Change," the conference that she co-hosted with Jonathan Wolff in December 2020, where I presented an earlier and shorter version of this chapter. I deeply appreciate the encouragement Shelley gave me at that time. I am also grateful to Shelley for her Dialogues on Disability, a series of interviews she is conducting at the BIOPOLITICAL PHILOSOPHY blog. She has interviewed me twice, and I have learned a great deal from the other interviews—far more than can be reflected in this chapter. I have been strongly influenced and inspired by Dr. Tremain's work on disability (2001, 2017, 2021)—although of course I take responsibility for the ways in which I have used it. Finally, I am grateful to Shelley for her close, careful, and sympathetic editing of my chapter.

Notes

1 See Overall (2017) for further discussion of the complexity of defining "old."

2 For further recent discussions of ageism, see de Medeiros (2020); Goldman and Higgs (2021: 71–4); and Hess (2021). Higgs and Gilleard (2020) present a different approach to understanding ageist phenomena. Another form of ageism is directed, in various contexts, at children and young adults (see Gentry Lamb 2021), but for the most part I am not talking about that form of ageism here.

3 See, for example, Sheehan (2003); Akerkar (2020).

4 Van der Horst and Vickerstaff partially concede this (2022: 4) and also suggest that "ableism may depend on age and ageism may depend on dis/ability" (2022: 5).

5 See Tremain (2021) for a close analysis of the pernicious effects of incarceration in Canada's and the United States' "care" institutions.

References

Abraham, Carolyn (2020), "Pandemic Report: Has Ageism Become the New Eugenics?" *Zoomer*, August 25. Available at: https://www.everythingzoomer.com/health/2020/08/25/pandemic-report-has-ageism-become-the-new-eugenics/ (accessed January 25, 2022).

Akerkar, Supriya (2020), "Affirming Radical Equality in the Context of COVID-19: Human Rights of Older People and People with Disabilities," *Journal of Human Rights Practice* 12 (2): 276–83.

Applewhite, Ashton (2020), "Still Kicking—Confronting Ageism and Ableism in the Pandemic's Wake," *This Chair Rocks*, September 25. Available at: https://thischairrocks.com/blog/ (accessed January 25, 2022).
Archer, Stephen (2020), "Dr. Archer's Updates on Covid-19," *Queen's University School of Medicine*, September 14. Available at: https://deptmed.queensu.ca/news/september-14-2020-dr-archers-update-covid-19-response-dom-and-medicine-program (accessed January 25, 2022).
Aubrecht, Katie, Christine Kelly, and Carla Rice (2020), "Aging and Disability: The Paradoxical Positions of the Chronological Life Course," in Katie Aubrecht, Christine Kelly, and Carla Rice (eds.), *The Aging-Disability Nexus*, 21–34, Vancouver: University of British Columbia Press.
Ayalon, Liat, Alison Chasteen, Manfred Diehl, Becca R. Levy, Shevaun D. Neupert, Klaus Rothermund, Clemens Tesch-Römer, and Hans-Werner Wahl (2020), "Aging in Times of the COVID-19 Pandemic: Avoiding Ageism and Fostering Intergenerational Solidarity," *The Journals of Gerontology*, April 16. Available at: https://academic.oup.com/psychsocgerontology/advance-article/doi/10.1093/geronb/gbaa051/5820621 (accessed January 25, 2022).
Chopik, William J., Ryan H. Bremner, David J. Johnson, and Hannah L. Giasson (2018), "Age Differences in Age Perceptions and Developmental Transitions," *Frontiers in Psychology*, February 1. Available at: https://www.frontiersin.org/articles/10.3389/fpsyg.2018.00067/full (accessed January 25, 2022).
de Medeiros, Kate (2020), "A Covid-19 Side Effect: Virulent Resurgence of Ageism," *The Hastings Center Bioethics Forum*, May 14. Available at: https://www.thehastingscenter.org/a-covid-19-side-effect-virulent-resurgence-of-ageism/ (accessed January 25, 2022).
Frye, Marilyn (1983), *The Politics of Reality: Essays in Feminist Theory*, Freedom: Crossing Press.
Garner, Helen (2016), *Everywhere I Look*, Melbourne: Text Publishing.
Gentry Lamb, Erin (2021), "Not Your Grandmother's Ageism: Ageism Across the Life Course," in Andrea Hülsen-Esch (ed.), *Cultural Perspectives on Aging: A Different Approach to Old Age and Aging*, 65–80, Berlin: De Gruyter.
Gibbons, Hailee M. (2016), "Compulsory Youthfulness: Intersections of Ableism and Ageism in 'Successful Aging' Discourses," *Review of Disability Studies: An International Journal* 12 (2 & 3): 70–88.
Gibson, Victoria (2020), "More Than 1/3 of Ontario LTC Facilities Report Increases in Worsening Pressure Ulcers, Chemical or Physical Restraint Use," *iPolitics*, June 2. Available at: https://ipolitics.ca/2020/06/02/more-than-1-3-of-ontario-ltc-facilities-report-increases-in-worsening-pressure-ulcers-chemical-or-physical-restraint-use/ (accessed January 25, 2022).
Goldman, Marlene and Paul Higgs (2021), "Ageism: A Health Humanities Approach," *University of Toronto Quarterly* 90 (2): 71–9.
Gosseries, Axel (2020), "Age in the Coronavirus Age," *Demography, Ethics and Public Policy*, July 18. Available at: https://www.demographyethicsandpublicpolicy.org/posts (accessed January 25, 2022).
Gullette, Margaret Morganroth (2004), *Aged by Culture*, Chicago: University of Chicago Press.
Gullette, Margaret Morganroth (2020), "Being Old is Not a Death Sentence, Even Now," *Los Angeles Review of Books*, August 27. Available at: https://lareviewofbooks.org/short-takes/old-not-death-sentence-even-now/ (accessed January 25, 2022).
Hardwig, John (2000), *Is There a Duty to Die? And Other Essays in Medical Ethics*, New York: Routledge.

Hess, Linda M. (2021), "Queering Ageism," *University of Toronto Quarterly* 90 (2): 207–24.

Higgs, Paul and Chris Gilleard (2020), "The Ideology of Ageism versus the Social Imaginary of the Fourth Age: Two Differing Approaches to the Negative Contexts of Old Age," *Ageing and Society* 40 (8): 1–14.

Mahoney, Jill (2020), "After 64 Years Married, COVID Takes a Toll on One Couple in Long-Term Care," *The Globe and Mail*, August 3. Available at: https://www.theglobeandmail.com/canada/article-after-64-years-married-covid-takes-a-toll-on-one-couple-in-long-term/ (accessed January 25, 2022).

Overall, Christine (1998), *A Feminist I: Reflections from Academia*, Peterborough: Broadview Press.

Overall, Christine (2006), "Old Age and Ageism, Impairment and Ableism: Exploring the Conceptual and Material Connections," *National Women's Studies Association Journal*, Special Issue on *Aging, Ageism, and Old Age* 18 (1): 126–37.

Overall, Christine (2017), "How Old is Old?" in Geoffrey Scarre (ed.), *The Palgrave Handbook of the Philosophy of Aging*, 13–30, London: Palgrave Macmillan.

Pedersen, Katie, Melissa Mancini, David Common, and William Wolfe-Wylie (2020), "85% of Ont. Nursing Homes Break the Law Repeatedly with Almost No Consequences, Data Analysis Shows," *CBC News*, October 23. Available at: https://www.cbc.ca/news/marketplace/nursing-homes-abuse-ontario-seniors-laws-1.5770889 (accessed January 25, 2022).

Reynolds, Joel Michael (2018), "The Extended Body: On Aging, Disability, and Well-being," *Hastings Center Report* 48 (5, Supplement 3): S31–6.

Reynolds, Michael Joel and Anna Landre (2022), "Ableism and Ageism: Insights from Disability Studies for Age Studies," in Marlene Goldman, Thomas Cole, and Kate de Medeiros (eds.), *Critical Humanities and Ageing: Forging Interdisciplinary Dialogues*, New York: Routledge. [Page references in this text are to preprint]

Rodriguez, Adrianna (2020), "Texas' Lieutenant Governor Suggests Grandparents Are Willing to Die for US Economy," *USA Today*, March 24. Available at: https://www.usatoday.com/story/news/nation/2020/03/24/covid-19-texas-official-suggests-elderly-willing-die-economy/2905990001/ (accessed January 25, 2022).

Sandberg, Linn J. and Barbara L. Marshall (2017), "Queering Aging Futures," *Societies* 7 (921): 1–11.

Sheehan, Myles N. (2003), "Disabilities and Aging," *Theoretical Medicine* 24 (6): 525–33.

Tremain, Shelley (2001), "On the Government of Disability," *Social Theory and Practice* 27 (4): 617–36.

Tremain, Shelley L. (2017), *Foucault and Feminist Philosophy of Disability*, Ann Arbor: University of Michigan Press.

Tremain, Shelley Lynn (2021), "Philosophy of Disability, Conceptual Engineering, and the Nursing Home-Industrial-Complex in Canada," *International Journal of Critical Diversity Studies* 4 (1): 10–33.

Van der Horst, Mariska and Sarah Vickerstaff (2022), "Is Part of Ageism Actually Ableism?" *Ageing and Society* 42: 1–12.

Young, Toby (2020), "Has the Government Overreacted to the Coronavirus Crisis?" *The Critic*, March 31. Available at: https://thecritic.co.uk/has-the-government-over-reacted-to-the-coronavirus-crisis/ (accessed January 25, 2022).

24 POWER-KNOWLEDGE AND EPISTEMIC INJUSTICE IN EMPLOYMENT FOR DISABLED ADULTS

JOSH DOHMEN

Disability and Work

A nuanced debate has long taken place in disability studies circles and disability activism about the role of work in the lives of disabled people. While most disability studies scholars and disabled activists agree that existing social and economic benefits for disabled people are appallingly insufficient, there is considerable disagreement about how best to respond to current realities in this regard. The central issues involved in this debate include (1) the extent to which employer accommodations[1] and more accessible spaces can integrate disabled adults into existing workplaces, (2) the stigma placed on disabled people who do not work or who receive welfare support, (3) the role that work plays in one's identity and self-esteem in contemporary industrialized societies, and (4) the absence of meaningful forms of social interaction for those who are not employed. For the sake of clarity and brevity, let me offer three simplified positions that exist on a spectrum of responses to these issues.

Some disability theorists and activists, such as Steven Graby (2015), are influenced by anti-work politics and the autonomist Marxist tradition to advocate against work as a measure of social worth. These authors argue that there should be an unconditional, universal basic income (UBI) that frees individuals to pursue autonomous activities that they find valuable. Absent a UBI, individuals must work to survive, their work compels them to conform to the demands of their employers, and their work is of value to them only insofar as they earn wages by doing it. The implementation of a UBI, they argue, would counteract the negative stereotypes against disabled people who, under systems of disability welfare payments, are stigmatized as "uniquely dependent or 'incapable'" (150). Other disability theorists and activists, such as Michael Oliver (2009) and Colin Barnes (2003), argue that society should, to the greatest extent possible, seek to create forms of employment for disabled adults, even if such employment comes with shorter hours, different expectations, or other sweeping changes to our commonplace assumptions about what constitutes work. The arguments of these disability theorists and activists assume that work is a main source of self-esteem, identity, activity, and social interaction in contemporary industrialized societies. Among the theorists and activists who argue that employment is important for the dignity and respect of disabled people, some emphasize the enforcement of anti-discrimination laws or "naming and shaming" (Barnes 2003) employers who discriminate, while others (e.g., Moss and Malin 1998 and Tororei 2009) argue for state-funded employment supports to alleviate the burdens of accommodations for employers.

A sort of middle ground between a UBI and the expansion of employment opportunities for disabled people is proposed by authors such as Nancy Foley (2006), Sunny Taylor (2004), and Paul Abberley (2002). These authors argue that while seeking accessible employment for as many disabled adults as possible is a worthy goal, paid employment will not be possible for some disabled people regardless of how many accommodations are granted and how accessible workplaces are made. Authors who argue in this way agree with Graby and others who think that it is important to separate our valuation of individuals' activities and lives from paid employment. Foley, for example, writes, "Many injured workers do feel a loss of identity initially. With time, we realize that we still have value apart from our professions. . . . Clearly, we can 'contribute' in ways other than work" (Foley 2006: par. 16–9).

I began this chapter by presenting a range of positions on the subject of disabled people and work in order to note that there continue to be valid disagreements about what constitutes the best response to the role and status that work plays in disabling disabled lives. My aim in this chapter is not to substantively enter this debate and, indeed, I will remain neutral regarding which solution is preferable. Instead, I want to argue that given the concrete realities that they endure and the subordinated social position that they occupy, disabled adults in the United States are presented with a metaphorical minefield of epistemic injustices when they attempt to navigate choices about work. In making this argument, I also have a second, tangential aim: to bring Michel Foucault's analysis of power-knowledge into conversation with existing epistemic injustice literature.

Miranda Fricker, who coined the term *epistemic injustice*, is, I believe, unduly dismissive of Foucault's account of power in her influential book

Epistemic Injustice: Power and the Ethics of Knowing (2007), offering an uncharitable interpretation of this account that I wish to counter. In the context of a discussion about parking enforcement, for example, Fricker argues that we must make a distinction between passive operations of power, such as prevail when people obey parking laws even though they will not be fined for disobeying them, and active operations of power, such as prevail when someone is ticketed. She then suggests that Foucault would disagree, because he says, "Power exists only when it is put into action" (Foucault 2000, in Fricker 207: 10). Yet, this understanding of Foucault's remark misses the point. What Fricker is calling, here, a passive operation of power *is* power in Foucault's sense precisely insofar as it *does* modify the behavior of drivers. Perhaps due to Fricker's reading of Foucault, authors who subsequently use Foucauldian resources to understand epistemic injustice—such as José Medina in his important book, *The Epistemology of Resistance*—have tended to employ Foucault's genealogical method as a way in which to reclaim "subjugated knowledges" (Medina 2013: 286). In this chapter, I argue (contra Fricker) that Foucault's concept of power-knowledge enables an understanding of the ways in which disabled people are subject to control in the world of work and shows how the operations of power-knowledge give rise to epistemic injustices.

This chapter proceeds in three sections. In the first section, I give a brief summary of what Foucault means by "power-knowledge." In the second, I show how this concept can be used to analyze the situations of disabled adults in relation to complex institutions of benefits and employment in the United States. In the third, I argue that disabled adults are often subject to several types of epistemic injustice given these operations of power, including subjection to structural epistemic injustice and forms of epistemic labor.

Power-Knowledge

Beginning with his genealogical work in *Discipline and Punish* (1977 [1975]), Foucault is concerned to develop an account of the relationship between knowledge and power. Knowledge, for Foucault, always has effects of power and power relies on certain forms of knowledge. In fact, knowledge and power are so closely linked that he refers to them together as "power-knowledge." To take a simple example, knowledge of a person's disability enables certain behaviors, it grants power. If the person is a physician, for example, the knowledge of a patient's disability creates the conditions for behaviors such as signing off on documentation for government benefits and supports, prescribing treatments or therapies, and billing an insurance company. But power also enables that knowledge. It is precisely the authority, the power of the physician that grants their claim "my client is disabled" the status of knowledge and, thus, it is the physician's position in matrices of power relations that grants their assignment of disability the status of a truth.

To enable a clear understanding of Foucault's claims about power-knowledge, I want to specify what he means by power. Foucault is emphatic that when he speaks of power, or more commonly, relations of power, he is not speaking solely of top-down relationships of unidirectional influence. Instead, power exists in all relations where a subject has influence over another. Power exists in relationships rather than in individuals themselves. Furthermore, power is the result of a conflict of forces, such that resistance is immanent in these relations, except in cases of the most extreme domination (and perhaps even then). Because power exists in relationships, we must therefore understand that the power emerging in a given interaction is the result of multiple relationships of force that condition it, including the discourses operating, the institutions in which the interaction is embedded, the economic conditions of the exchange, and so on.

Importantly, power should not be understood as only restrictive or repressive. Instead, power is productive. It produces, for example, objects of knowledge, discourses, and individual subjects and forms of subjectivity. Indeed, for Foucault, the question of power and the question of the subject are intimately connected. As he uses it, the term *subject* does not refer solely to a Cartesian thinker but rather evokes dual meanings: to be a subject is to be "subject to someone else by control and dependence, and tied to his own identity by a conscience and self-knowledge" (Foucault 2000: 331). Power-knowledge makes individuals subjects by (1) subjecting them to the control of others and (2) determining the categories through which they are understood, the procedures or "games of truth" (Foucault 1997: 296) for determining what counts as knowledge about them, and thus the self-understandings available to them. By "games of truth," Foucault means the procedures or rules in a given domain (e.g., within medicine, academic philosophy, or the law) that determine what counts as true or false.

Finally, Foucault states that "power relations are both intentional and nonsubjective" (Foucault [1976] 1978: 94), that is, power has certain aims that may not necessarily be the explicit or chosen aims of any given person, not even someone with considerable authority over others. This intentional and nonsubjective character of power is, especially, a feature of the broader networks of power operating in a society as a whole. Foucault says,

> the rationality of power is characterized by tactics that are often quite explicit at the restricted level where they are inscribed, tactics which, becoming connected to one another . . . end by forming comprehensive

systems: the logic is perfectly clear, the aims decipherable, and yet it is often the case that no one is there to have invented them, and few who can be said to have formulated them. (Foucault [1976] 1978: 95)

That is, individual relations of force influence and condition each other in ways that work toward a certain goal, even if no one laid out an explicit, strategic plan for how these individual, tactical relations of force would, overall, work toward that goal. Hence, resistance (which is, after all, the functioning of power) may also be more or less agential. Take, for example, Foucault's discussion of the "tactical polyvalence of discourses." With this phrase, Foucault names the ways in which discourse can both entrench, strengthen, or expand dominant relations of power but also challenge, redirect, or change these relations of power. One of Foucault's most well-known examples concerns sexuality. While nineteenth-century scientific and legal discourses dealing with homosexuality served to further social controls, they "also made possible the formation of a 'reverse' discourse: homosexuality began to speak in its own behalf, . . . often in the same vocabulary, using the same categories by which it was medically disqualified" (Foucault [1976] 1978: 101). Note that because power is intentional but nonsubjective, this reaction can be more or less conscious and more or less explicit: the reverse discourse may be consciously decided upon by a small group of activists who seek to spread it; or, as with homosexuality, the reverse discourse may spontaneously coalesce when people subjected to a form of power take up the pathologized or otherwise despised identity that the form of power produces and reconfigure it in ways that depathologize and even redeem it.

Given these insights about power and the subject, we can now complicate the example introduced earlier. First, we can note that the relation of power between the physician and the patient does not mean that the physician *has* power and that the patient is *powerless*. Rather, this relation of power exists as the nexus of multiple intersecting force relations. For example, the patient may share or not share certain aspects of their experience, influencing the diagnostic options available to the physician. The patient may call upon certain laws protecting their privacy, certain professional codes of ethics, or alternate sources of knowledge (such as disability studies literature or personal narratives). Nevertheless, there is likely an asymmetry of power between the physician and the patient. Given the likelihood that the patient depends upon the physician's decisions and calculations required for the determination of benefits, treatment, or employment—in short, for the production of the patient as a certain *kind* of subject—the physician has greater influence over the options available to the patient than vice versa. The production of the physician as a certain *kind* of subject is possible because of prior assumptions about authority that circulate in a broad range of fields, including the medical field (i.e., in matters of diagnosis and prescription) and the legal field (i.e., in matters that determine what counts as a disability).

In other words, discourses about medicine, the law, and disability; economic and material conditions, such as the inaccessibility of many workplaces, the lack of a universal public health-care system, and the prevalence of poorly funded care and support services for disabled individuals; available subject positions, including patient and physician; forms of knowledge, including knowledge of current medical practice, legal definitions, academic literature, and disability narratives; laws that govern patient privacy, benefits administration, professional licensure, and so on; and games of truth, that is, about what procedures must be followed to be deemed the truth within a certain domain; are co-constitutive of the relation of power that exists in this interaction between patient and physician. Power creates, maintains, and supports these discourses, subject positions, and objects of knowledge, all of which come to exercise power in their own right.

What is the end of power in this asymmetrical relation between the physician and the patient? It seems to be the perceived efficient use of resources, including medical resources, government expenditure, and labor. Consider, for example, that the patient must have their claim of disability verified because the games of truth that operate in our society dictate that what it means for someone to have a disability is that they have certain relationships to work (e.g., they cannot find stable employment or need "accommodations" from an employer) and medicine (e.g., a medical "condition" or "impairment"[2] contributes to their inability to find employment). This subjecting procedure has been established in the legal and medical domains to determine whether it is true that a given person is disabled. We can thus understand the ways in which power-knowledge subjectivizes the disabled person. That is, power gives rise to the disabled subject as under the control of others: the physician, employers, insurers or government benefit agencies, administrators, case managers, and so on. In addition, power constitutes the category of "disabled" as a subject position through which one can understand oneself and be understood by others. In the next section of this chapter, I will focus on the intersection of disability and employment in order to elaborate these claims.

Power-Knowledge and Employment for Disabled Adults

In the complex network of power-knowledge operating today, a person is disabled insofar as they are not perceived to conform to norms of work, study, or health. Robert McRuer, noting that "ability to work" is one definition of "able-bodied" offered by the *Oxford English Dictionary*, points out that labor, that is, the capacity to work, is central to what it means to be disabled under capitalism: "being able-bodied means being capable of the normal physical exertions required in a particular system of labor" (McRuer 2006: 8). Rosemarie Garland-Thomson has similarly argued with respect to the historical and cultural context of the United States that "Nowhere is the disabled figure more troubling to American ideology and history than in relation to the concept of work" (Garland-Thomson 1997: 46).

I agree with McRuer and Garland-Thomson that work is a particularly important locus for understanding disability in contemporary American society. Consider the variety of options with respect to employment from which a disabled American adult can choose at present.

One option is to seek Social Security Disability Insurance (SSDI) by claiming an inability to work. For the purposes of the SSDI program, disability is defined "strictly" as the inability to participate in "substantial gainful activity (SGA)" (Social Security Administration 2022b) understood as making $1,350 or more per month (Social Security Administration 2022a). State agency staff determine whether or not a given person meets these requirements on the basis of information provided by the person's doctors. Such a person may work for a total of nine months at the SGA level in what is called the "trial work period," after which time employment income earned at or above the SGA minimum will lead to a loss of these benefits.

Alternatively, disabled adults may opt to work in a "sheltered workshop." These (so-called) workshops are usually operated by nonprofit organizations for the completion of jobs that other, for-profit companies subcontract to them. The exclusively precarious disabled workforces in these settings are routinely paid subminimum wages. Within the terms of American law, to pay an individual a subminimum wage in such a workshop, the nonprofit organization must demonstrate that the individual (1) is less productive than the average worker performing the same task and (2) is less productive due to a verifiable disability. When that disability is not visibly evident, there must be "medical or psychiatric reports, or psychological tests" on record (U.S. Department of Labor 2018). Since the Supreme Court decision *Olmstead v. L.C.* in 1999, states have been pressured to transition as many workshop employees as possible to community-integrated employment, with several states banning subminimum wages altogether (Association of People Supporting Employment First 2022).

Another option available to prospective disabled workers is to seek employment assistance from a state Vocational Rehabilitation (VR) agency or disability employment agency. These agencies may provide training to help a disabled person find work, help them look for job opportunities, provide "job coaching" to help them succeed on the job or advance in the career, assist them in obtaining assistive technologies, and so on. Under the employment provisions of the amended Rehabilitation Act of 1973, a disability is defined as "a physical or mental impairment that constitutes or results in a substantial impediment to employment" (Rehabilitation Act of 1973 [2016], Sec.7 [9] [A]-[B]).

The fourth option available to disabled adults/prospective workers is to rely on the protections afforded by the Americans with Disabilities Act (ADA). The ADA offers the broadest definition of "disability" of any of the statutes discussed thus far: "The term 'disability' means, with respect to an individual (A) a physical or mental impairment that substantially limits one or more major life activities of such individual; (B) a record of such an impairment; or (C) being regarded as having such an impairment" (Americans with Disabilities Act 2008). Note that this definition is concerned with aspects of one's life that may or may not concern employment directly (A), with disabilities that are intermittent (B), and with social stereotypes that may assume the existence of a disability where, in fact, one does not exist apart from the stereotype or stigma itself (C). The ADA offers disabled Americans two specific employment protections. First, it protects them against unjust discrimination in hiring and promotion as a result of a perceived disability. And, second, it requires employers to provide them with appropriate "accommodations" that make workplaces accessible to them. Should the employer question a request for an accommodation, the disabled employee would be required to provide documentation of their need for the accommodation (U.S. Equal Employment Opportunity Commission 2002). The employer may refuse to make the requested accommodation but may be required to demonstrate that doing so would pose an "undue hardship" on their business, organization, or institution.

By examining these options, we can develop a better understanding of the complex networks of knowledge and power at play in shaping the employment opportunities of disabled adults. In each case, a medical professional is expected to determine the "objective" conditions contributing to a person's disability. In each case, furthermore, people in certain other agencies, including state Disability Determination Services, sheltered workshop operators, state VR offices, Equal Employment Opportunity Commission (EEOC) investigators, and employers, are taken to have knowledge of what constitutes a disability for someone, what should be considered an average or below-average level of productivity for some employee, and what is an undue hardship for a given employer. This knowledge gives each of these parties a considerable amount of control over the lives of disabled adults. As I have indicated, we should not think of this knowledge as existing before or independently of the power that it justifies. Rather, the knowledge itself has a claim to count as knowledge due to the power exercised by, or the authority recognized in, each of the parties. Note, for example, that the range of different definitions of *disability* reveals the extent to which disability is not a prediscursive bodily or mental condition but rather a category that is designed to achieve contextually specific ends.

As in the case of medical treatment discussed earlier, the power operative in this context is not top-down or unidirectional. Instead, the disabled adult may exercise power in the process. Applying for benefits or services, for example, is a way in which to seek engagement with the economic conditions that tie earning a living income to the available employment options. Similarly, protesting an undue hardship determination or discriminatory employment decisions is a way to leverage the power of legal systems in order to exert influence over employers. Power and knowledge are constituted in these complex networks of discourses, legal and medical frameworks, institutions, economic conditions, and actions of employers and disabled adults. Some forces work to amplify one another, such as when legal determinations of disability status give authority to medical professionals. Some forces work to hamper or check one another, such as when employers are forced to provide accommodations through enforcement of the ADA.

From this overview, we can glean some idea of how power, as it operates around disability and employment, is intentional and (more or less) subjective. For example, debates around disability policies make clear that a main goal of this cluster of legislation is to get as many disabled people working as possible without putting too much strain on potential employers. Nevertheless, disabled adults in the United States remain unemployed at almost twice the rate at which nondisabled adults are unemployed (U.S. Bureau of Labor Statistics 2022b). In effect, these policies create a situation in which it is both difficult to find employment and, due to the "strict" definition of disability for the purposes of SSDI, difficult to live without finding employment. The logic of the current state of affairs—according to which disabled lives are worth less than nondisabled lives—is abundantly clear, even if few (say) government officials, medical authorities, or employers dare to articulate it. Indeed, without ever making it their explicit aim, legislators have granted enormous power to medical and mental health professionals, in effect sustaining an individualizing medical model of disability.

In short, a complex and constraining network of medical, juridical, and administrative power creates disabled subjects. First, this network creates conditions under which disabled adults are subject to the control of employers, institutions, medical and mental health professionals, and government agencies. Second, this network creates concepts according to which disabled adults can be understood by others and through which they can understand themselves. Under current social arrangements, that is, to regard a given adult as disabled is to believe that they deserve a subminimum wage, employment protections, or government benefits. Compare this situation to a situation, say, two hundred years ago, in which a person who would be understood as disabled today would, in that earlier social context, have contributed to a family farm. In the latter socio-historical context, the category "disabled," as an epistemic marker that carries the limiting connotations that I have discussed, would make no sense.

Power-Knowledge and Epistemic Injustice in Employment Settings

To this point in the chapter, I have attempted to discuss power-knowledge with regard to disability in neutral, descriptive terms. To be clear, we cannot simply assume that all exercises of power are bad, nor can we assume that exercises of power from people with authority are bad while exercises of power for the purpose of resistance are good. Foucault himself said, "The problem, then, is not to try to dissolve [power relations] in a utopia of completely transparent communication but to acquire rules of law, the management techniques, and also the morality, the *ethos*, the practice of the self, that will allow us to play these games of power with as little domination as possible" (Foucault 1997: 298). He goes on to discuss the example of education:

> I see nothing wrong in the practice of a person who, knowing more than others in a specific game of truth, tells those others what to do, teaches them, and transmits knowledge and techniques to them. The problem . . . is knowing how to avoid the kind of domination effects where a kid is subjected to the arbitrary and unnecessary authority of a teacher. (Foucault 1997: 299)

In other words, the questions that philosophers of disability should ask about power and knowledge include these: when do the uses of power-knowledge constitute domination? When are these practices justified?

I think that the literature on epistemic justice offers resources that are helpful to broach these questions. In general, philosophers discussing epistemic injustice are concerned with the ways in which people are harmed as knowers and as moral agents due to the dominant epistemic practices of a particular society. Epistemology has long been a concern for those seeking social justice, from Marxists' critiques of ideology and positing of a class standpoint, to feminist standpoint theory and criticisms of androcentric ways of knowing and perceiving the world, to race theorists' discussions of double-consciousness and knowledge-production practices. Fricker's *Epistemic Injustice* was pathbreaking, especially insofar as it introduced the notions of testimonial injustice and hermeneutical injustice that she developed by using the language of virtue epistemology. Since the publication of that work, most discussions of epistemic justice that other philosophers articulate are, in one way or another, responses to these terms of reference. This more recent literature, which is to a greater or lesser extent derived from Fricker's work, has two things in common. First, the authors of this subsequent writing on epistemic justice define epistemic injustice in counterfactual formulations, that is, we can recognize epistemic injustice insofar as people in oppressed social positions do not receive the same uptake as people in positions of relative social privilege, even when the former are similar or even better qualified as knowers. Second, these authors identify the specific harms of each form of injustice. In these ways, epistemic justice literature can help us focus on the workings of power-knowledge that constitute domination.

Structural Epistemic Injustice

In this section, I will focus on three concepts of epistemic injustice. The first concept of epistemic injustice that I will address is the epistemic injustice of social institutions, as Elizabeth Anderson has described it. Anderson outlines three ways in which structural injustices in a particular society give rise to structural epistemic injustices. In each case, the injustice arises from the unjustified application of a potentially neutral bias in contexts of structural injustice. For the purposes of my argument, I will focus on two of the three injustices that Anderson discusses. The first case of these injustices is "differential access to the markers of credibility" (Anderson 2012: 169). The idea, here, is that we routinely rely on shared signs—such as level of education or evidence that one is an articulate speaker—to determine whether or not a person should be respected as credible. Use of these markers is not perfect—clearly people with degrees from respected institutions can espouse nonsense, for example—but nor is use of these markers necessarily unjust. Generally, a person with an education relevant to a particular topic is more likely to have well-supported knowledge about that topic than others who are not educated on the topic. Reliance on credibility markers can have epistemically unjust consequences, however, when structural injustices mean that members of particular social groups have inequitable access to those markers. For example, if Black people or working-class people face greater obstacles to gaining a relevant education, then they will also be less likely to be in positions of perceived epistemic authority. The second case of epistemic injustice that Anderson has identified involves the "shared reality bias." This bias is not in and of itself bad. People who interact with each other frequently tend to develop beliefs about and interpretations of the world that align in a way that "helps people coordinate their expectations and behavior with respect to each other, reduces social conflict, and facilitates social bonding and cooperation toward common goals" (170). This alignment becomes a problem, however, when structural social injustices entail that the most advantaged members of society tend to interact among themselves, frequently to the exclusion of members of society who are disadvantaged relative to them. In such cases, the beliefs and interpretations that relatively disadvantaged people have about the world make no sense to people who are relatively advantaged. This phenomenon is related to what Kristie Dotson calls "contributory injustice," which occurs when a dominantly positioned perceiver fails to recognize or learn the alternative hermeneutical resources of the marginalized person(s) whose claims they perceive as incomprehensible (Dotson 2012). Contributory injustice harms the marginalized person's epistemic agency by undermining their ability to contribute their relevant epistemic resources.

Anderson is skeptical that attempts to correct for these biases at the individual level, say, by questioning our unjustified use of markers of credibility or seeking to remain open to alternative interpretations of the social world, will be sufficient to eliminate either type of structural epistemic injustice. Instead, she suggests that structural changes, most importantly social integration, are the remedy. Only by increasing access to the markers of credibility and creating opportunities for more frequent interaction between currently advantaged people and currently disadvantaged people will the resulting structural epistemic injustices be addressed.

How does this conversation apply to disabled adults in relation to work? In a review of research about employer attitudes regarding disabled workers, Song Ju, Eric Roberts, and Dalun Zhang found that "[e]mployers who had previous experiences, especially positive experiences, with workers with disabilities expressed favorable attitudes toward individuals with disabilities and were more willing to hire them" (Ju, Roberts and Zhang 2013: 119). Here, then, we can see one way in which shared reality bias may lead employers to form beliefs about disabled workers that are difficult to challenge, precisely because they do not regularly interact with disabled workers. If a disabled adult were to approach a potential employer who has never before interacted with disabled employees, the employer will likely view the potential employee's claims to be competent for the job with greater skepticism than they would view claims from a similarly qualified applicant who is nondisabled. According to one survey of disabled workers, 36 percent of respondents claimed that employers assumed that they could not perform the required tasks because of their disability (Sundar et al. 2018). An earlier survey found similar concerns among disabled respondents (Freedman and Fesko 1996). In addition, a survey of rehabilitation counselors found that 21.3 percent of respondents believed that employers' "Negative attitudes or stigma" constituted a challenge for cognitively disabled adults seeking employment (Grenawalt, Degeneffe, and

Kesselmayer 2021). Indeed, given the low employment-population ratio (21.3 percent for disabled adults compared to 65.4 percent for nondisabled adults) and the high unemployment rate of working-aged disabled people (7.6 percent for disabled adults compared to 3.5 percent for nondisabled adults), as well as widespread inaccessibility and ableism in society more generally, the absence of regular interactions between employers and disabled adults likely contributes to the dismissal of disabled applicants' claims about their skills and competencies (U.S. Bureau of Labor Statistics 2022a).

In short, we can see how the complex network of power-knowledge discussed earlier produces conditions under which disabled people are in part constituted as subjects precisely through their exclusion from community-integrated employment. In turn, this subject formation gives rise to particular forms of knowledge or lack thereof, such as employers' beliefs about the incompetence of disabled workers, their dismissal of the testimony of disabled applicants who claim to be well-qualified for a job, and their shared reality bias about disabled applicants as less qualified or as incapable. The epistemic consequences of this subject-formation place disabled adults in a double bind: on the one hand, they face the structural injustice of unequal access to employment which leads, on the other hand, to employers committing the epistemic injustices of dismissing disabled applicants' claims to competence and/or rendering their self-interpretations as qualified potential employees incomprehensible.

Epistemic Labor, Epistemic Disavowal, and Testimonial Smothering

A second set of useful concepts for understanding the epistemic injustices that disabled adults confront comprises the notions of epistemic labor, epistemic disavowal, and testimonial smothering. Kamili Posey proposes the term *epistemic labor*, defining it as "a practice of marginalized knowing that involves recognizing the negative stereotypes operating upon us and employing strategies to mitigate those stereotypes in order to gain critical epistemic uptake" for non-epistemic ends (Posey 2021: 23). One example that Posey offers concerns a transgender student who calls their university administration to request that a gender-neutral bathroom be restocked after seventeen days without servicing. The student is met with disbelief: "People like you are always stirring things up" (xiii). In reply, the student says "Maybe I'm wrong about the number of days, sorry. But is it possible for someone to take a look at it?" (ibid.). Notice that the student deflates their own credibility by suggesting that they may be incorrect and then adopts a more submissive tone by apologizing and requesting the same thing in a less assertive way. The student recognizes the stereotype that is acting against them—that "they" are the type to "stir things up"—and adapts their behavior so that at least *part* of their initial testimony receives uptake in hopes that their non-epistemic aim (of a cleaner and sufficiently stocked bathroom) can be achieved. How a person adapts to the negative stereotypes operating in any given interaction can vary: from changing one's tone or temperament, to "testimonial smothering" (Dotson 2011), to accepting the stereotypes and mirroring them back to the relevant audiences for the purposes of the interaction, to letting a dominantly positioned person speak on one's behalf, and to using behavior or dress to counter the stereotypes (27). Posey calls especially severe forms of epistemic labor "epistemic disavowal." In instances of epistemic disavowal, "a marginalized speaker is forced to be complicit in their own self-silencing because of severe non-epistemic threat" (39). In this regard, Posey discusses the use of plea bargains, and specifically the case of Kaleif Browder, who spent three years on Rikers Island before he committed suicide because he refused to offer false testimony. This tragedy reveals the extreme material pressures that are placed on defendants to conform their testimony to the expectations of prosecutors, even when the defendant knows otherwise.

As I have indicated, testimonial smothering constitutes a type of epistemic labor. Developed by Dotson, the term *testimonial smothering* names instances in which (1) a person giving testimony in some way truncates that testimony (2) because they believe that the audience lacks the testimonial competence to adequately understand what they are attempting to communicate (3) as a result of a reliable, harmful ignorance on the part of that audience (Dotson 2011: 244–5). One example that Dotson references is a story recounted by Cassandra Byers Harvin (Harvin 1996). Harvin describes the exchange that ensued in a public library when a white woman asked her what she was researching. In response to the white woman's question, Harvin replied that her research concerned "raising black sons in this society," to which the white woman promptly and indignantly responded, "How is that any different from raising white sons?" (Harvin 1996, in Dotson 2011: 247). Harvin learns that this exchange is a "conversation she couldn't have" (Dotson 2011: 247), such that in the future it would be safer to say something such as "I'm researching how we raise children in this society," if she were to say anything at all (Harvin 1996, in Dotson 2011: 247).

I maintain that a demand is often placed on disabled adults to perform epistemic labor and a threat of testimonial smothering is posed to them when they are asked to share their experiences or preferences regarding employment. To see why this is so, it may be helpful to briefly expand upon the difficult situations that disabled adults face in relation to receiving benefits and/or finding employment.

Programs are in place to provide material support, job assistance, and employment protections for adults with disabilities. However, these supports and protections are poorly funded and insufficiently enforced. In 2020, according to the US Social Security Administration, only 35.2 percent of applicants for SSDI were awarded benefits (Social Security Administration 2021). The average SSDI benefit payment in 2020 was $1,454.33 per month, which translates to about $17,451.96 per year. Consider, for comparison, that the MIT Living Wage Lab estimates that in 2022, a living wage for a single adult with no children in the relatively affordable state of Mississippi is about $33,072 per year (Glasmeier 2022). Recall, furthermore, that after a trial work period, a person receiving SSDI benefits will no longer be eligible if they earn $1,350 or more per month. Seeking employment rarely presents better prospects. Recall that the employment-population ratio of working-aged disabled people is 29.1 percent, while their unemployment rate is 13.4 percent. Moreover, disabled workers are almost twice as likely as nondisabled workers to work part-time (U.S. Bureau of Labor Statistics 2022b).

ADA protections are in place for disabled job applicants. According to the EEOC (2022), however, in 2021 only 2.7 percent of received cases were found to have "reasonable cause" (i.e., the Commission agreed that discrimination had occurred) and only 21.1 percent had "merit resolutions" (where the outcome is deemed favorable to the party charging discrimination). The US Supreme Court has gone so far as to rule, in *Board of Trustees of Univ. of Ala. v. Garrett*, that disabled applicants could not sue states or local governments in federal court for employment discrimination. When disabled workers do find employment, they often continue to live on scarce earnings near the poverty level or below it. Indeed, even a study that concluded that employment is generally cost-efficient for adults with intellectual disabilities noted that those in supported employment earned an average of "$7,485.24 per year, which is well below the poverty line" (Cimera 2010: 129). The author of the study continues, "If supported employment is going to be a viable employment option that promotes both fiscal and physical independence, supported employees must be able to earn a livable wage," either through increased wages, increased hours, or both. And the rise of a new paradigm for the workforce, where workers are expected to be more "flexible" and to work contract "gigs" produces a greater disincentive for employers to invest in accommodations (Wilton 2006). Faced with prospects of unemployment and scant opportunities for socialization in their communities, disabled adults may opt to work in sheltered workshops; as noted earlier, however, most of these "workshops" pay a subminimum wage.

In short, the operations of power-knowledge in our society oppress disabled adults with regard to employment and subsistence. If they cannot work or cannot find work, they will be unlikely to live a healthy, comfortable life on social benefits, which, as I have explained, are dependent upon the knowledge of relevant agencies and medical professionals. If they do work, disabled adults are unlikely to earn a living wage and have to be careful lest their earnings disqualify them for other benefits. Again, any employment supports must be supported by the knowledge of relevant VR and health professionals. If they are seeking work but worry about discrimination or accommodations, they are unlikely to receive support from the EEOC and employers retain the right to claim "undue hardship" in response to requests for accommodations. Absent other employment prospects, sheltered workshops may seem like the best available option for some disabled people in comparison to social isolation.

Given these realities, it is clear that there are myriad non-epistemic pressures that act upon disabled adults in ways that demand epistemic labor. For instance, a common concern among disabled applicants (and job coaches) is when and whether to disclose their disability or need for an accommodation (Sarrett 2017). Some disabled people believe that it is most beneficial to do the work of "demystifying" their disability for potential employers, in part because they worry that if they do not do this, employers will simply not hire them rather than ask them about their need for accommodations (Harpur 2014). Other disabled people avoid discussing their disabilities at all, if possible, particularly if their disabilities are not readily apparent to their employers or coworkers (Pilling 2013). Indeed, if one is disabled in a way that is not readily apparent, one may encounter obstacles to receiving accommodations: such conditions are more likely to be viewed as fraudulent or less legitimate (Valeras 2010; Pilling 2013). Thus, disabled applicants are forced to carefully consider if and how to disclose their disabilities and the accommodations that they require, which itself ought to be recognized as a form of epistemic labor that nondisabled applicants are not called on to perform.

Faced with dismal employment prospects and material insecurity, many disabled adults who are capable of and interested in working are forced to deem themselves "incapable" of supporting themselves through work (National Council on Disability 2005). This form of self-abnegation, I want to argue, is an instance of epistemic disavowal. Recall that epistemic disavowal occurs when a severe non-epistemic threat forces a person in a marginalized social position to self-silence or confirm what oppressive institutions deem true about them. In this case, the threat of poverty may lead disabled individuals to claim an incapacity to work against their truly held belief that they could work if they were given the opportunities and supports that they deserve.

Finally, I would like to discuss two examples of testimonial smothering that occur when disabled adults weigh their employment options. First, consider the experiences of people who work in sheltered employment. Speaking with the *Kansas City Beacon* about the possibility of closing Missouri's sheltered workshops, Sam Crane, the legal director for the national Autistic Self Advocacy Network, noted that "What you often see is people who are really scared that without sheltered workshops people won't have anywhere to go during the day or won't have any options during the day" (Laird 2022). Note that this statement implies that disabled people who work in these sheltered environments may be called upon to defend them because the workshops seem to be the only realistic option available. A person speaking to the press who says, "We believe sheltered workshops need to be replaced by adequately supported employment in the community, supports for independent living, and community integrated day centers" is likely to be heard as saying, "We believe sheltered workshops need to be closed." Thus, the disabled person, rather than encouraged to express the more nuanced view, is compelled to truncate their testimony by emphasizing the positive aspects of workshops (such as opportuities to socialize and be active), while omitting criticisms of them due to fear that they will lose the only opportunities for activity and socialization that are available to them.

Second, consider the pressures that employers of employment specialists and job coaches put on these employees to find employment for their disabled clients. Different states have different funding formulas, but in general, employment agencies for adults with disabilities receive funding from state VR offices (which themselves receive funding from the federal government) based on the services they provide, such as hours that they spend with a disabled client in supported employment, hours that they spend helping a disabled client find work, or successfully finding employment for a client. In other words, there is an incentive for job coaches to place clients as quickly as possible regardless of their clients' preferences. In one survey, for example, some disabled workers expressed that their cases were "closed too quickly" after they had been successfully placed in a job (Freedman and Fesko 1996: 52). Rather than continuing to help disabled clients adjust to their new positions and ensuring that their positions are a good fit for them, agencies consider newly hired disabled clients to be "placed" and move on. Family members who responded to this survey reported similar concerns, worrying that the disabled workers were placed "because there were openings, not because of interest or aptitude for those jobs" (53). The survey of rehabilitation counselors discussed earlier found similar concerns. When asked about obstacles to finding suitable employment for disabled clients, one respondent wrote "high caseloads, strong focus/pressure on closing cases and maintaining paperwork versus helping clients," while another wrote "caseloads are large and successful closure rates [are] pushed when spending more time helps get better rates in the long run" (Grenawalt, Degeneffe, and Kesselmayer 2021: 22;

see also Lidz and Smith 2016). When disabled clients must choose between access to resources for finding and maintaining employment or no access to these resources, pressure is put on them to express approval with whatever services that they do receive. In other words, disabled clients face pressure to truncate their testimony in ways that make the uptake of their testimony more likely among service providers who are expected to quickly find jobs for disabled clients and close cases.

What these concepts help us see is the way in which workings of power-knowledge harm disabled workers as knowers. The existing system creates a class of people who are excluded from the standards of employment to which most adults are expected to conform, a class that is given an identity as disabled and responded to through various other machinations of power, from disability insurance and the attendant claim reviews policed by agency administrators and medical professionals; to discrimination protections and accommodation provisions controlled by agency administrators, medical professionals, and employers; to sheltered workshops controlled by state, nonprofit agencies, and companies who contract out this work; to supported employment controlled by the state agencies, medical professionals, job coaches, and employers. These policies and practices give rise to professional and institutional knowledges that are given credence over other types of knowledge, including the testimony and interpretations of disabled adults.

Society's unwillingness to adequately integrate disabled people into the community in ways that offer them meaningful forms of social interaction and engagement with meaningful tasks creates pressure on their testimony to show appreciation for the scarce resources that do exist, whether poverty-level disability insurance payments, days spent in a sheltered workshop, or placement in any random part-time job. Meanwhile, the purported knowledge of those in positions of relatively greater power is elevated as more "objective," whether that takes the form of quantified placement rates, diagnoses provided by medical professionals, or employers' claims about the qualifications of applicants. Similarly, this asymmetrical relation grants greater credibility to sheltered workshop CEOs (Chief Executive Officers) who may either present employment at a sheltered workshop as a "choice" akin to employment choices made by nondisabled adults or make subtle threats, such as this: "So, if somebody came in today and said, 'You've got to pay them all 15 bucks an hour without additional subsidy,' that group doesn't generate enough margin to support their wage I'd have to pay them. So, they'd be unemployed or underemployed or in a day service" (Laird 2022). In short, power-knowledge works to demand these forms of epistemic labor from disabled adults, while amplifying the knowledge and control of the agencies, professionals, and employers who have power over the lives of disabled people.

Conclusion

In this chapter, I have argued that both Foucault's concept of power-knowledge and the discourse of epistemic injustice are useful for understanding the experiences of adults with disabilities in relation to work. In addition, I have argued that authors writing on epistemic injustice could find valuable resources in Foucault's discussion of power-knowledge, while the discourse of epistemic injustice provides a helpful normative framework for determining when power-knowledge becomes oppressive or threatens domination. It would benefit all of us if society could better attend to the nuanced perspectives of disabled people rather than use the proverbial rock and hard place to coerce testimony from them that reinforces the status quo.

Notes

1 I place *accommodations* in quotation marks to note how this term assumes a standard form of mindedness and embodiment, such that persons who deviate from that standard in any way require some form of modification to the workplace or work expectations. Many disabled activists and disability studies scholars prefer to speak of "accessible" or "inaccessible" public spaces, placing the emphasis on the space and expectations as exclusionary, rather than on the individual as failing to meet a certain standard. Still, the language used in legal, workplace, and medical discussions continues to be "accommodation," in large part because this language is codified in the Americans with Disabilities Act (ADA). For this reason, I will continue to use the term *accommodation* throughout.

2 I put these terms in quotation marks to note that they are contested. Certain accounts of disability, particularly the early social model of disability that Shelley Tremain (2017: 9–12) has called the "British social model," rely on something like an impairment as the underlying feature of an individual's body that when confronted with dis-abling, exclusionary social practices and spaces, gives rise to a disability. I am sympathetic to Tremain's argument that impairments are not prediscursive features, but for the purposes of the argument here, I will continue to refer to "impairments" when this is the language used in existing legal, medical, and mainstream discourse about disability.

References

Abberley, Paul (2002), "Work, Disability, and European Social Theory," in Colin Barnes, Mike Oliver, and Len Barton (eds.), *Disability Studies Today*, 120–38, Malden: Polity.

Americans with Disabilities Act of 2008 (2008), *ADA.gov*. Available at: https://www.ada.gov/pubs/adastatute08.htm#12112a (accessed May 11, 2022).

Anderson, Elizabeth (2012), "Epistemic Justice as a Virtue of Social Institutions," *Social Epistemology* 26 (2): 163–73.

Association of People Supporting Employment First (2022), "2022 State Legislative Watch," April 6. Available at: https://apse.org/state-legislation/ (accessed May 11, 2022).

Barnes, Colin (2003), "Disability, the Organization of Work, and the Need for Change," *Independent Living Institute*, March 6. Available at: https://www.independentliving.org/docs6/barnes20030306.html (accessed May 13, 2022).

Cimera, Robert Evert (2010), "The National Cost-Efficiency of Supported Employees with Intellectual Disabilities: The Worker's Perspective," *Journal of Vocational Rehabilitation* 33: 123–31.

Dotson, Kristie (2011), "Tracking Epistemic Violence, Tracking Practices of Silencing," *Hypatia: A Journal of Feminist Philosophy* 26 (2): 236–57.

Dotson, Kristie (2012), "A Cautionary Tale: On Limiting Epistemic Oppression," *Frontiers: A Journal of Women Studies* 33 (1): 24–47.

Foley, Nancy (2006), "The Stigma of Not Working," *Ragged Edge Online*, May 24. Available at: https://www.raggededgemagazine.com/departments/closerlook/001095.html (accessed May 1, 2022).

Foucault, Michel (1977 [1975]), *Discipline and Punish*, trans. A. Sheridan, New York: Vintage.

Foucault, Michel (1978 [1976]), *The History of Sexuality, Volume 1: An Introduction*, trans. R. Hurley, New York: Vintage.

Foucault, Michel (1997), "The Ethics of the Concern for Self as a Practice of Freedom," in P. Rabinow (ed.), *The Essential Works of Michel Foucault: Ethics, Subjectivity, and Truth*, 281–302, New York: The New Press.

Foucault, Michel (2000), "The Subject and Power," in J. Faubion (ed.), *Essential Works of Michel Foucault: Power*, 326–48, New York: The New Press.

Freedman, Ruth I. and Sheila Lynch Fesko (1996), "The Meaning of Work in the Lives of People with Significant Disabilities: Consumer and Family Perspectives," *Journal of Rehabilitation* 62 (3): 49–55.

Fricker, Miranda (2007), *Epistemic Injustice: Power and the Ethics of Knowing*, New York: Oxford University Press.

Garland-Thomson, Rosemarie (1997), *Extraordinary Bodies: Figuring Physical Disability in American Culture and Literature*, New York: Columbia University Press.

Glasmeier, Amy (2022), "Living Wage Calculation for Mississippi," *Living Wage Calculator*, Massachusetts Institute of Technology. Available at: https://livingwage.mit.edu/states/28 (accessed May 12, 2022).

Graby, Steven (2015), "Access to Work of Liberation from Work? Disabled People, Autonomy, and Post-Work Politics," *Canadian Journal of Disability Studies* 4 (2): 132–60.

Grenawalt, Teresa, Charles Edmund Degeneffe, and Rachel Friefeld Kesselmayer (2021), "Employment and Service System Challenges Affecting Persons with Cognitive Disabilities: A Qualitative Inquiry into Rehabilitation Counselor Perspectives," *Journal of Rehabilitation* 87 (2): 17–27.

Harpur, Paul (2014), "Combating Prejudice in the Workplace with Contact Theory: The Lived Experiences of Professionals with Disabilities," *Disability Studies Quarterly* 34 (1). Available at: https://dsq-sds.org/index.php/dsq/article/view/4011/3544.

Harvin, Cassandra Byers (1996), "Conversations I Can't Have," *On the Issues: The Progressive Woman's Quarterly* 5 (2): 15–6.

Ju, Song, Eric Roberts, and Dalun Zhang (2013), "Employer Attitudes Toward Workers with Disabilities: A Review of Research in the Past Decade," *Journal of Vocational Rehabilitiation* 38: 113–23.

Laird, Skylar (2022), "Missouri Sheltered Workshops a 'Godsend' for Some, Exploitation to Others," *The Kansas City Beacon*, January 23. Available at: https://thebeacon.media/stories/2022/01/23/missouri-sheltered-workshops/ (accessed July 24, 2023).

Lidz, Charles W. and Lisa M. Smith (2016), "Employment Specialists' Perspectives on Implementing Supported Employment with Young Adults," *American Journal of Psychiatric Rehabilitation* 19 (4): 339–52.

McRuer, Robert (2006), *Crip Theory: Cultural Signs of Queerness and Disability*, New York: New York University Press.

Medina, José (2013), *The Epistemology of Resistance: Gender and Racial Oppression, Epistemic Injustice, and Resistant Imaginations*, New York: Oxford University Press.

Moss, Scott A. and Daniel A. Malin (1998), "Public Funding for Disability Accommodations: A Rational Solution to Rational Discrimination and the Disabilities of the ADA," *Harvard Civil Rights-Civil Liberties Law Review* 33: 197–236.

National Council on Disability (2005), *The Social Security Administration's Efforts to Promote Employment for People with Disabilities: New Solutions for Old Problems*, November 30.

Oliver, Michael (2009), *Understanding Disability: From Theory to Practice*, Second edition, New York: Palgrave Macmillan.

Pilling, Merrick Daniel (2013), "Invisible Identity in the Workplace: Intersectional Madness and Processes of Disclosure at Work," *Disability Studies Quarterly* 33 (1). Available at: https://dsq-sds.org/article/view/3424 (accessed June 29, 2023).

Posey, Kamili (2021), *Centering Epistemic Justice: Epistemic Labor, Willful Ignorance, and Knowing Across Hermeneutical Divides*, New York: Lexington.

Rehabilitation Act of 1973 as Amended by WIOA (2016), *U. S. Department of Education*, January 7. Available at: https://www2.ed.gov/policy/speced/leg/rehab/rehabilitation-act-of-1973-amended-by-wioa.pdf (accessed May 11, 2022).

Sarrett, Jennifer (2017), "Interviews, Disclosures, and Misperceptions: Autistic Adults' Perspectives on Employment Related Challenges," *Disability Studies Quarterly* 37 (2). Available at: https://dsq-sds.org/article/view/5524/4652 (accessed June 29, 2023).

Social Security Administration (2021), "Annual Statistical Supplement to the Social Security Bulletin." Available at: https://www.ssa.gov/policy/docs/statcomps/supplement/2021/supplement21.pdf (accessed May 10, 2022).

Social Security Administration (2022a), "Working While Disabled: How We Can Help," January. Available at: https://www.ssa.gov/pubs/EN-05-10095.pdf (accessed May 10, 2022).

Social Security Administration (2022b), "Disability Benefits | How You Qualify." Available at: https://www.ssa.gov/benefits/disability/qualify.html (accessed May 11, 2022).

Sundar, Vidya, John O'Neill, Andrew J. Houtenville, Kimberly G. Phillips, Tracy Keirns, Andrew Smith, and Elaine E. Katz (2018), "Striving to Work and Overcoming Barriers: Employment Strategies and Successes of People with Disabilities," *Journal of Vocational Rehabilitation* 48: 93–109.

Taylor, Sunny (2004), "The Right Not to Work: Power and Disability," *Monthly Review*, March 1. Available at: https://monthlyreview.org/2004/03/01/the-right-not-to-work-power-and-disability (accessed June 7, 2022).

Tororei, Samuel K. (2009), "The Right to Work: A Strategy for Addressing the Invisibility of Persons with Disability," *Disability Studies Quarterly* 29 (4). Available at: https://dsq-sds.org/article/view/973/1174 (accessed June 29, 2023).

Tremain, Shelley L. (2017), *Foucault and Feminist Philosophy of Disability*, Ann Arbor: University of Michigan Press.

U.S. Bureau of Labor Statistics (2022a), "Table A. Employment Status of the Civilian Noninstitutional Population by Disability Status and Age, 2020 and 2021 Annual Averages." Available at: https://www.bls.gov/news.release/disabl.a.htm (accessed May 10, 2022).

U.S. Bureau of Labor Statistics (2022b), "Persons with a Disability: Labor Force Characteristics Summary." Available at: https://www.bls.gov/news.release/disabl.nr0.htm (accessed May 11, 2022).

U.S. Department of Labor (2018), "Field Operations Handbook - Chapter 64 Employment of Workers with Disabilities at Subminimum Wages under Section 14(c)." Available at: https://www.dol.gov/agencies/whd/field-operations-handbook/Chapter-64#b64g00 (accessed May 11, 2022).

U.S. Equal Employment Opportunity Commission (2002), "Enforcement Guidance on Reasonable Accommodation and Undue Hardship under the ADA." Available at: https://www.eeoc.gov/laws/guidance/enforcement-guidance-reasonable-accommodation-and-undue-hardship-under-ada#requesting (accessed May 10, 2022).

U.S. Equal Employment Opportunity Commission (2022), "Americans with Disabilities Act of 1990 (ADA) Charges (Charges Filed with EEOC) Includes Concurrent Charges with Title VII, ADEA, EPA, and GINA) FY 1997- FY 2021." Available at: https://www.eeoc.gov/statistics/americans-disabilities-act-1990-ada-charges-charges-filed-eeoc-includes-concurrent (accessed May 11, 2022).

Valeras, Aimee (2010), "'We Don't Have a Box': Understanding Hidden Disability Identity Utilizing Narrative Research Methodology," *Disability Studies Quarterly* 30 (3/4). Available at: https://dsq-sds.org/article/view/1267 (accessed June 29, 2023).

Wilton, Robert D. (2006), "Working at the Margins: Disabled People and the Growth of Precarious Employment," in Dianne Pothier and Richard Devlin (eds.), *Critical Disability Theory: Essays in Philosophy, Politics, Policy, and Law*, 129–50, Vancouver: UBC Press.

25 "BUT YOU DON'T LOOK AUTISTIC"

EPISTEMIC INJUSTICE AND AUTISTIC IDENTITY

NATHAN MOORE

Introduction

I have two goals in this chapter. I aim to indicate why it is important to recognize both the role of nonpropositional understanding in epistemic oppression and the complexity of fully understanding even a single sort of experience of epistemic oppression. A single sort of experience—such as dismissive "You don't look Autistic" responses to an Autistic person's claims about their Autistic identity, or to their explanations of their needs, or to their explanations of their experiences—often involves a variety of propositional and nonpropositional epistemic injustices.

In the second section, I begin with a cautionary note about why philosophers should avoid, or at least minimize, the epistemic oppression that they could potentially produce when they write about epistemic oppression. I then provide a nonexhaustive overview of varieties of epistemic injustice, focusing on injustices that arise due to credibility or intelligibility deficits. Finally, I describe some metaepistemic injustices that occur at the level of theorizing and writing about epistemic injustice. The third section provides a brief overview of Alexis Shotwell's classification of four kinds of nonpropositional understanding. In fourth section, I examine a variety of epistemic injustices that dismissive "You don't look Autistic" responses to Autistic people's claims can encompass, including widely discussed propositional epistemic injustices and nonpropositional epistemic injustices that have received much less attention. Multiple epistemic injustices occur and interact in even a single instance of epistemic oppression. To fully indicate the complexity and seriousness of the issues under discussion, I examine two sorts of Autistic experiences: the recognition that one is perceived to lack social interest and the denial of appropriate communication options to Autistic nonspeakers. In the fifth section, I discuss four sorts of metaepistemic injustices that play a role in obscuring various features of epistemic injustice that I introduced in the fourth section.

Epistemic Oppression and Epistemic Injustice

Kristie Dotson cautions that "when addressing and identifying forms of epistemic oppression one needs to endeavor not to perpetuate epistemic oppression" (Dotson 2012: 24). *Epistemic oppression*, for Dotson, refers to unwarranted exclusions from epistemic activity that undermine a knower's ability to participate in both knowledge production and the shaping of our epistemic resources. Epistemic oppression can occur when the contributions of particular knowers, including criticisms of shared epistemic resources, are unfairly dismissed. The way to avoid, or at least minimize, epistemic oppression, according to Dotson, is to adopt an "open conceptual structure" (41–2) when theorizing about epistemic oppression. An open conceptual structure does not attempt to fully delimit the scope of our concepts and is thereby explicitly amenable to the possibility of revision. With respect to the concept of epistemic injustice, the use of an open conceptual structure allows for the possibility that new forms of epistemic injustice will be identified and the possibility that previously identified forms of epistemic injustice will be shown to operate in different ways when directed at disparate marginalized social groups.

A related concern involves avoiding what Nora Berenstain calls "structural gaslighting." Structural gaslighting occurs when "epistemologies and ideologies of domination [are invoked] that actively disappear and obscure the actual causes, mechanisms, and effects of oppression" (Berenstain 2020: 734). As Berenstain states:

> Because white feminism fails to situate itself as applicable only in certain contexts and instead masquerades as universal, the underlying message of white feminism is that if it does not fit your lived experience, there must be something wrong with your experience, your interpretation of your experience, or your understanding of reality. This willful misrepresentation of the lack of fit between white feminism and

> the socio-political realities it fails to reflect exemplifies the structural gaslighting at its core. (Berenstain 2020: 736)

Berenstain's claim is not that there is something wrong with accounts about white women's experiences per se, but rather that these accounts should not be universalized. We should be careful about the scope of our claims and recognize the restrictions that any perspective that we take places on this scope. We might understand Berenstain's and Dotson's worries as concerned with two forms of resistance to conceptual revision that result from an overly narrow focus on specific features of experiences of oppression. One of these forms of resistance occurs when a narrow focus on certain features of oppression hides other features of it that should prompt revision of this kind. The other form of resistance occurs when a focus on specific features of oppression leads to overly narrow definitions of concepts.

Before describing varieties of testimonial injustice, I would like to challenge the use of the term *hearers* to refer to people who receive testimony and the term *speakers* to refer to people who give testimony. The use of these terms in the philosophical literature on testimony contributes to the widespread social bias in favor of spoken language that is harmful to various disabled communities. For example, Robert Sparrow writes that "[c]ochlear implant technology represents an attack on the culture of the Deaf, because it seeks to ensure that deaf children grow up to use a spoken language rather than the signed languages of the Deaf" (Sparrow 2005: 136). In addition, the use of these terms in the literature on testimony reinforces the prevalent association made within the Western philosophical tradition and societies in general between speaking and intelligence (Woodfield and Freedman 2021), while obfuscating the importance of access to appropriate communication options for nonspeakers even when competence is presumed (endever* corbin 2021). In this chapter, therefore, I will use the term *recipients* to refer to people who receive testimony and the term *providers* to refer to people who provide testimony.

Miranda Fricker's book, *Epistemic Injustice: Power and the Ethics of Knowing* (Fricker 2007), focuses primarily on what Fricker calls "testimonial injustice." Testimonial injustices, as Fricker conceives them, are injustices in which a recipient gives insufficient credibility, or uptake, to a provider's testimony because of prejudices that the recipient holds. For example, when members of a jury view a Black man's testimony as less credible because he is Black, he has been subjected to a testimonial injustice. To take another example, when an Autistic student has difficulty concentrating on university lectures because of Autistic sensory differences and their request for academic accommodation is denied because they are Autistic, then they have been subjected to a testimonial injustice. Fricker uses the term *pre-emptive testimonial injustice* to refer to another form of testimonial injustice in which prejudice precludes consideration of a potential provider's testimony in the first place. This form of injustice can occur at the level of individual interactions, such as when a potential recipient of a disabled person's testimony directs questions about the disabled person to a personal support worker accompanying the disabled person rather than to the disabled person themself. Pre-emptive testimonial injustice can also arise in structural form, such as when norms of autism research preclude consultation with Autistic people.

Dotson (2011) has identified two additional varieties of testimonial injustice which she describes as "silencing": testimonial quieting and testimonial smothering. For Dotson, testimonial quieting, which she traces to Patricia Hill Collins's work, occurs when a recipient fails to recognize a provider as an epistemic agent and thus fails to recognize the provider's attempt to make an epistemic contribution. Testimonial quieting, understood in this sense, is distinct from testimonial injustice insofar as it seems to be a category mistake for a recipient to apply the concept of credibility to a provider that they do not regard as an epistemic agent. Dotson's use of the terms *silencing* and *quieting* reflects the same bias in favor of spoken language as do the terms *speakers* and *hearers*. I will, therefore, suggest the new term *testimonial rejection* as a replacement for the term *testimonial quieting*. Testimonial smothering, the other form of "silencing" that Dotson identifies, occurs when a provider self-censors their testimony to avoid content that the recipient would misinterpret in a harmful way due to "pernicious ignorance" (Dotson 2011: 244). To illustrate the idea of testimonial smothering, Dotson draws upon Kimberlé Crenshaw's work on Black women's silence about domestic violence, where many people would understand their testimony in this regard as support for harmful, life-threatening stereotypes about Black men.

Fricker uses the term *hermeneutical injustice* to refer to the other significant form of epistemic injustice that she identifies. Hermeneutical injustice, as Fricker construes it, involves a prejudicial intelligibility deficit. That is, hermeneutical injustices, as Fricker conceives them, occur when someone is unable to understand their own experiences or a recipient of testimony is unable to understand a provider's explanations of their experiences due to a lack of hermeneutical (i.e., meaning-making, or interpretive) resources. Thus, one way in which to classify hermeneutical injustices is according to whether the relevant hermeneutical resources exist and, if so, who has them. Trystan Goetze has, for example, classified six species of hermeneutical injustice in this way (Goetze 2018). Nevertheless, the root cause of hermeneutical injustice is that the collective hermeneutical resources to which everyone has access do not include interpretive resources that are needed to understand certain kinds of experiences. Fricker's primary example of this gap in interpretive resources—that is, of hermeneutical injustice—is thus of a woman who is unable to understand her experiences of sexual violence prior to the development of concepts such as "sexual harassment" (Fricker 2007: 6). As Fricker explains it, this gap or lacuna in resources is due to what she calls "hermeneutical marginalization." In short, hermeneutical marginalization denies people with nondominant experiences a role in shaping our collective hermeneutical resources.

Although hermeneutical injustice is inherently structural, it can encompass what Gaile Pohlhaus, Jr. calls "willful hermeneutical ignorance," whereby particular people willfully refuse to acquire various hermeneutical resources (Pohlhaus, Jr. 2012). That is, the willful refusals of individuals to acquire the interpretive resources that marginalized groups create both contribute to and help to maintain the structure that produces hermeneutical injustice. Dotson uses the term *contributory injustices* to refer to hermeneutical injustices that result from these sort of willful refusals (Dotson 2012). Although hermeneutical injustices are structural in character, it can make sense to, in certain respects, hold individuals responsible for them due to the agential nature of contributory injustice and because collective responsibilities for structural injustices can include individual responsibilities (Medina 2013, 2017).

There are issues of ableism and classism tied up with the word *ignorance*, as Shelley Tremain has noted (Tremain 2017: 41–4). Thus, we should keep in mind class- and disability-based barriers to the acquisition of interpretive resources in determining whether to understand a gap in such resources as "pernicious" or as due to a willful refusal to acquire those resources. Knowledge acquisition can be restricted by "levels of literacy, access to education, access to technology, social mobility, access to nutritious food and safe shelter, and involvement in a community or some other kind of social arrangement" (43). Additionally, that an individual does not have certain interpretive resources should not be understood as inherently wrong, unjust, or as indicative of some form of cognitive deficit. Whether there is anything wrong—in any sense of "wrong"—about a specific individual's lack of interpretive resources critically depends on *why* the individual lacks these resources and whether they have a responsibility to acquire these resources.

Fricker discusses semantic and performative aspects of hermeneutical injustices (Fricker 2007) that indicate two ways in which such injustice can be produced (Medina 2017). According to José Medina, hermeneutical injustices are semantically produced when the interpretive resources lack either (1) words and concepts; (2) dominant understanding of words and concepts developed by nondominant groups; or (3) the ability to use words and concepts to express certain meanings (e.g., dismissing racism as a structural and political problem by disallowing the structural component of "racism"). Hermeneutical injustices can also be performatively produced, such as when the intelligibility deficit attributed to a provider is the result of prejudicial assessment of the provider's "communicative performance or expressive style" (Medina 2017: 44). Modes of expression such as body language, accent, facial expression, tone of voice, vocal inflections, or word choice can all lead a recipient to attribute an intelligibility deficit to a provider.

Disabled philosopher of disability Amandine Catala describes varieties of metaepistemic injustice that further underscore why it is important to avoid epistemic oppression in writing about epistemic oppression. As Catala explains it, metaepistemic injustice "occurs at the metalevel of philosophical methodology when theorizing about epistemic injustice, rather than in everyday epistemic interactions" (Catala 2020: 769). Metatestimonial injustice "arises from logocentric assumptions or biases in philosophical methodology, on the part of philosophers theorizing epistemic injustice, about the legitimate scope and holders of epistemic agency" (ibid.). Metahermeneutical injustice occurs because of "an inadequate conceptualization or understanding of the very concepts of epistemic agency and injustice by philosophers theorizing epistemic injustice" (771). This metahermeneutical injustice renders people who do not have propositional epistemic agency or who are assumed to lack it as lacking epistemic agency entirely. This assumption of global lack with respect to epistemic agency results in metatestimonial injustice about how, and to whom, the concept of epistemic agency is applied in discussions of epistemic oppression.

Nonpropositional Understanding

In what follows, I will rely on Shotwell's distinction between four types of nonpropositional, implicit, understanding. I will leave open the question of whether to understand these types of understanding as forms of knowledge or as other kinds of epistemic resources. Shotwell distinguishes between "practical, skill-based knowledge; somatic or bodily knowing; potentially propositional but currently implicit knowledge; and affective or emotional understanding" (Shotwell 2011: xi). Shotwell emphasizes the importance of these epistemic resources and argues that both the narrow focus on propositional knowledge and "the artificial and impoverished focus on thought experiments that actively bracket out much experience relevant to non-dominantly situated knowers" (80–1) perpetuate epistemic injustices.

Skill-based knowledge is the sort of practical knowledge, gained through practice, that is involved in knowing *how* to do something. If I know how to tie my shoes that means, in part, that I *can* tie my shoes. A set of instructions for tying shoes (e.g., "now form that lace into a loop") may be helpful; however, practice is also necessary for me to know *how* to tie my shoes. Nevertheless, know-how and actual ability can come apart. If I have no access to shoelaces to tie or if I become physically unable to tie my shoes, I do not thereby lose my knowledge of how to tie shoes. To be sure, I may eventually lose that knowledge if I am unable to practice tying shoes; but neither a temporary nor permanent loss of actual ability to tie my shoes leads instantly to loss of know-how. Consequently, we should distinguish between the counterfactual ability to tie my shoes when circumstances permit from actual ability to tie my shoes.

Somatic or bodily knowing, which is sometimes also called embodied knowing, is, Shotwell explains, "knowledge people have at the intersection of their bodily and conceptual systems" (Shotwell 2011: xii). This sort of knowledge involves one's own experience of their body, the ways that one moves through the world, and how these movements convey various sorts of information. Somatic knowing can involve body image, knowledge regarding bodily comfort or discomfort, and knowledge of bodily abilities and limits. We use these forms of bodily knowledge in making decisions, for example, about what activities to engage in, when we need rest, and how to relax. Somatic knowing with respect to how one moves through the world is very much connected with how our bodies work and the largely implicit social norms that govern body language. Social norms invest body language with meaning; thus, how one moves through the world is just as much a social and political mattter as it is a bodily matter. Autistic people often mask their differences by attempting to act neurotypical where part of this performance involves suppression of natural Autistic body language such as stimming. Other sorts of bodily knowledge which social norms affect include the self-image that many nonbinary people hold according to which something is wrong with their bodies, a belief that the persistent hegemonic understanding of gender as binary fosters.

The third type of nonpropositional understanding that Shotwell identifies—namely, potentially propositional, or tacit, knowledge—is knowledge that, although currently implicit, could be put in propositional form. This type of knowledge includes much of what we call "common sense." Philosophers of science and psychologists have long known that observation is theory laden; that is, our immediate conscious experience upon observation is already an interpreted experience. Norwood Hanson makes this point succinctly when he remarks "[w]e do not ask 'What's that?' of every passing bicycle. The knowledge is there in the seeing and not an adjunct of it" (Hanson 2009: 442). When we see a bicycle our concept of bicycle is applied prior to our conscious awareness of that visual experience. Thus, tacit knowledge can affect our initial understanding of anything that we encounter in ways that are difficult to counter insofar as tacit knowledge can involve the unconscious application of articulated concepts, such as bicycle, and the unconscious application of unarticulated concepts. Consequently, the way in which dominantly situated knowers conceptualize marginalized identities, for example, can lead to significant differences in treatment even in the complete absence of conscious bias. A police officer seeing a white man and a Black man in identical circumstances may *see* two different circumstances because the act of seeing itself already involves interpretation via concepts such as Blackness.

The fourth and final type of nonpropositional understanding that Shotwell discusses is affective or emotional understanding which involves feelings, including feelings that may not have names and/or may not be expressible (Shotwell 2011: xii). Shotwell is clear that she does not consider affective understanding to be a form of knowledge. Yet affect does play a role in peoples' epistemic lives. For example, affect can play a role in the decisions that we make about what we choose to learn, the sorts of considerations to which we attend and to which we do not attend, and how a change in our epistemic lives impacts us. Affect often plays an explanatory role in how we make sense of our epistemic lives and, as such, cannot be set aside if we want a full understanding of epistemic activity. Medina argues, for example, that epistemic oppression often involves a kind of affective "numbness" in the form of insensitivity to issues of oppression and meta-insensitivity to one's insensitivity to issues of oppression (Medina 2013).

"You Don't Look Autistic": Epistemic Injustice and Autism

It is very common for Autistic people to be told that we "don't look Autistic" when we tell others that we are Autistic. Thus, we find this phrase as part of the title of Michael McCreary's book *Funny, You Don't Look Autistic: A Comedian's Guide to Life on the Spectrum* (McCreary 2019). In addition, the phrase occasionally appears in the scientific literature as, for example, in the case of the title of Kate Seers and Rachel Hogg's article "'You Don't Look Autistic': A Qualitative Exploration of Women's Experiences of Being the 'Autistic Other'" (Seers and Hogg 2021). In some cases, the phrase "You don't look Autistic" is used to indicate disbelief that someone is actually Autistic; in other cases, the phrase is used to express the idea that someone is "not Autistic enough" to have certain experiences of ableism or certain needs. Let's call the experience of being met with a "You don't look Autistic" reaction (regardless of whether that phrase was actually used) "autism denial experiences" and hereafter abbreviate them as ADE.

I have had both sorts of ADE and, although I am multiply neurodivergent and nonbinary, I generally encounter these ADE as a white, Autistic, cisgender man. My ADE usually result from (1) the absence of traits that the recipient believes to be indicative of Autistic identity or (2) the presence of traits, such as having a Ph.D., that the recipient thinks are incompatible with either Autistic identity or with certain kinds of experiences or needs. Other marginalized identities can change both how these cases occur and the underlying explanations for their occurrence. If an Autistic person is marginalized in ways that differ from the ways in which I am marginalized, the ADE that they confront will differ and may be compounded. For example, Autistic women may have ADE due to pervasive beliefs that only men can be Autistic (Seers and Hogg 2021; Sohn 2019). The ADE of nonbinary people will depend on a recipient's assumptions about both the provider's gender and the relationship between autism and gender. Race, too, can condition one's ADE, as is the case when, for example, a Black person's Autistic traits are viewed "as aggression rather than [as] characteristics of autism" (Onaiwu 2020).

A single occurrence of ADE can involve a variety of epistemic injustices and interactions between them. First, the recipient's response often qualifies as testimonial injustice insofar as a provider's testimony is devalued due to a prejudicial credibility deficit. This prejudicial credibility deficit can occur in at least two ways when Autistic identity is the only marginalized identity involved. First, this prejudicial credibility deficit can occur when the recipient views the provider as Autistic and thus dismisses the provider's explanation of, for example, needed accessibility measures due to the belief that the provider is not qualified to identify their own requirements, though certain medical professionals or university administrators would be. Second, this testimonial injustice can occur when the recipient's conception of autism renders the provider (1) unintelligible *as* an Autistic person or (2) intelligible as an Autistic person but unintelligible as a person who would have the kinds of experiences or requirements that the provider describes. In such cases, the testimonial injustice of the ADE results from a hermeneutical injustice. The former kind of hermeneutical injustice can lead to outright rejection of the provider's testimony that they are Autistic, such as, for example, when a recipient who believes only children can be Autistic rejects an Autistic adult's claim of Autistic identity. The latter kind of hermeneutical injustice leads to "You're not Autistic enough" rejections of Autistic peoples' testimony about their requirements and experiences of ableism. For example, when an employer rejects an Autistic employee's testimony about their needs because the employee does not engage in any overtly "anti-social" behavior such as recognizable stimming, the employer's rejection derives from the latter kind of hermeneutical injustice. In this case, the employer's conclusion that the employee is "not Autistic enough" relies on the mistaken conception of autism as something that comes in degrees, where the degree to which someone is Autistic is measured in terms of the degree to which their behavior is considered socially undesirable (Price 2022: ch. 3).

The instances of hermeneutical injustice mentioned earlier can be instances of contributory injustice caused by willful hermeneutical ignorance. Insofar as we consider testimonial exchanges in which an Autistic person attempts to provide information about autism, we can understand that the recipient has consciously and deliberately rejected the sort of testimony that should prompt a change in their conception of autism. Because of the willful hermeneutical ignorance involved in many ADE, furthermore, testimonial smothering can result. It can be unsafe to communicate one's Autistic identity, experiences, or needs to a recipient who is both unable to understand your testimony and unwilling to acquire the hermeneutical resources necessary to do so. In such cases, requests for employment accommodations can be met with sudden dismissal, requests for academic accommodations can be understood as academically dishonest requests for an "unfair" advantage, and requests for understanding of Autistic social differences can damage or destroy relationships. The pervasiveness of hermeneutical injustice, willful or otherwise, and the attendant testimonial injustice are among the factors that lead Autistic people to mask their Autistic traits in order to appear neurotypical. The practice of "masking" is inherently harmful to Autistic people who engage in it; is not fully effective; is often performed unconsciously; and, despite some similarities, should not be confused with code-switching (Price 2022).

In my overview of hermeneutical injustice and in the work on hermeneutical injustice of most of the authors that I have cited thus far, hermeneutical injustice is (as I have explained) characterized as a consequence of a gap in interpretive resources. This characterization suggests that the only deficiency in the available shared hermeneutical resources is that (1) some of the shared interpretive resources are incomplete and/or (2) there are missing interpretive resources in the shared pool of resources. Yet this characterization neglects the fact that existing content within our shared interpretive hermeneutical resources may need to be replaced. Consider, for instance, that these sorts of changes are currently underway in the ongoing process to de-medicalize and de-moralize dominant understandings of gay and transgender identities as medical conditions and moral failings. Being Autistic is not a medical issue and so testimonial injustice that results from a belief that medical practitioners are the best or only people qualified to identify Autistic needs is itself the result of hermeneutical injustice in which autism is mistakenly conceptualized as a medical issue. Medicalizing an identity and recognizing an identity as sometimes in need of medical care are vastly different practices that can entail vastly different outcomes. That autism is, for example, associated with various co-occurring conditions that can require medical care, such as gastrointestinal issues or autoimmune conditions, implies neither that autism is a medical condition nor even that the co-occurring conditions themselves are necessarily medical conditions. The upshot of these observations is that creating an inclusive set of shared hermeneutical resources is as much a matter of determining what needs to be removed as determining what needs to be added.

The four forms of nonpropositional knowledge, or understanding, that Shotwell has identified are also at work in ADE. Part of what is going on with misunderstandings of Autistics stems from a lack of bodymind literacy on the part of neurologically typical people, that is, neurotypicals. Neurotypicals generally lack the know-how to identify many Autistic differences *as* Autistic differences, often rely on tacit knowledge in the form of "common sense" to make credibility judgments or interpret Autistic people's testimony, and rely on their own embodied knowledge and affective understanding to interpret Autistic people's body language and affective states. Although neurotypicals often cannot readily identify Autistic people from mere observation, "research shows there are many subtle markers of our difference that neurotypical people do pick up on" (Price 2022: ch. 6). This limited understanding of Autistic people results in negative social evaluations about them from neurotypicals (Sasson et al. 2017). Margaret Price notes, for example, psychological research that shows an increase in perceived "creepiness" due to "a person having awkward, unpredictable behavior, an unnatural looking smile, laughter that occurred at 'unnatural' times, speaking for too long about a single topic, and not knowing when to end a conversation," which correspond to common misperceptions of Autistic people's behavior (Price 2022: ch. 6). As Price points out, furthermore, research shows that "when a person engages in social mirroring in an even slightly inappropriate way, it skeeves people out, and makes them feel physically colder" (ibid.). In short, conscious or unconscious recognition of Autistic traits, with or without recognition of these traits *as* Autistic traits, can lead to various sorts of negative reactions toward Autistic people.

To reiterate, part of what is going on in ADE is failure of neurotypicals to recognize Autistic differences *as* Autistic differences due to inadequacies in the available hermeneutical resources about Autistics. Nevertheless, certain subtle markers of Autistic difference are present. Tacit knowledge also plays a role insofar as so-called common sense in part determines what counts as socially "appropriate" or "inappropriate" behavior. Indeed, both tacit knowledge and actual propositional knowledge can be involved in the production of ADE as occurs when (1) a recipient consciously takes an Autistic person to be "creepy" due to conscious propositional understanding of some specific behavior as "creepy," but (2) has no idea why they find the behavior creepy since tacit knowledge underlies this judgment. In other words, insofar as a recipient views certain behavior as creepy, they may reject a provider's testimony of their accommodation needs because to do otherwise endorses the "creepy" behavior. The same reaction might not involve propositional knowledge at all if it results from a general, unarticulated, feeling of creepiness on the recipient's part. Embodied knowledge is involved insofar as misapplication of neurotypical embodied knowledge about modes of expression, their meanings, and failure to recognize and understand Autistic embodied knowledge underlies, for example, judgments of Autistic body language and behavior as creepy. Finally, affective understanding is involved insofar as the recipient experiences feelings of creepiness in response to Autistic body language and behavior. For example, the feeling of creepiness may result from a lack of understanding of the affective content of Autistic facial expressions (Moens 2020).

Attention to the interactions involved in instances of epistemic injustice and to nonpropositional forms of knowledge reveals issues that arise from mismatches of knowledge types. Autistic people, for example, possess Autistic embodied knowledge and affective understanding but not neurotypical embodied knowledge and affective understanding. Autistic embodied knowledge and affective understanding are limited as guides to neurotypical body language and affective content. Furthermore, we Autistics understand a lot of neurotypical body language and affective content propositionally in terms of stateable social norms that provide rules and meanings for neurotypical modes of expression. As a result, we often understand neurotypical modes of expression and their nonpropositional content by and through the conscious application of propositional knowledge. Alternatively, it is also true that neurotypical embodied knowledge and affective understanding are limited as guides to Autistic body language and affective content. Neurotypicals must understand and acknowledge this limitation, as well as expend the same sort of cognitive effort in understanding Autistic modes of expression as Autistic people expend to understand neurotypical modes of expression. As I have already stated, Autistic people are harmed when they force themselves to act neurotypical by adopting neurotypical modes of expression. Autistic modes of expression need to be understood rather than eliminated.

The preceding two paragraphs indicate why it is important to recognize and avoid the performative production of hermeneutical injustices. Nevertheless, the issue of hermeneutical injustice with respect to Autistics is not merely due to prejudice against certain modes of expression but rather due to failure to understand the content of Autistic modes of expression and, in some cases, failure to even understand these modes of expression as meaningful.

Recognition of mismatches between knowledge types and, in particular, why such mismatches can be important, reveals more about what is going on in ADE. The reliance of neurotypicals on their own embodied knowledge and affective understanding as interpretive resources results in the perceived unintelligibility of Autistic modes of expression, unintelligibility that comprises both embodied hermeneutical injustice and affective hermeneutical injustice. The inaccessibility, to neurotypicals, of Autistic embodied knowledge *as* embodied knowledge and of Autistic affective understanding *as* affective understanding requires that neurotypicals utilize propositional knowledge. These forms of nonpropositional hermeneutical injustice can lead to propositional hermeneutical injustice as well as testimonial injustice. Included here are what Catala calls "embodied testimonial injustice" and "affective testimonial injustice" in which the communicative content of modes of expression is dismissed or minimized (Catala 2020: 769). We can use this analysis to understand the previously discussed examples of the feeling of creepiness.

Understanding the epistemic injustice involved in even a single sort of marginalized experience can be extremely complicated when we pay attention to the different ways in which that experience can arise. At the outset of my discussion, I pointed out how gender and race can change the details of ADE in important ways. Nevertheless, I did not take gender and race into account in what followed in that context. The complexity of ADE that my discussion has considered pertains to epistemic injustice for Autistic people who are not multiply marginalized. Although a great deal of what I have said will be useful to understand multiply marginalized Autistic experiences, specific attention to the production of multiply marginalized identities with respect to Autistic identity will enable the identification of more ways that epistemic injustices target Autistic people.

Before turning to consider metaepistemic injustice, I will briefly discuss two other sorts of Autistic experiences. First, Autistic people tend to be viewed "as indifferent to social acceptance and their atypical behaviors as indicating a lack of social interest or motivation" (Catala, Faucher, and Poirier 2021: 9014). Tacit knowledge, embodied knowledge, and affective understanding seem to have a central role in instances of epistemic injustice in which an Autistic person's testimony that expresses social interest is dismissed. In such instances, the dismissals of a neurotypical recipient rely on common sense, neurotypical embodied knowledge, and neurotypical affective understanding and misinterpret Autistic modes of expression as indication of a lack of social interest, thereby giving primacy to this misunderstanding in dismissing the Autistic person's propositional testimony to the contrary. The Autistic person appears to be communicating two contrary things—social interest and lack of social interest—and the neurotypical recipient makes a decision (perhaps unconsciously) about which to accept. Yet it is tacit, embodied, and affective hermeneutical injustice that produces misunderstanding of the nonpropositional content of Autistic modes of expression as a lack of social interest. Tension between the neurotypical recipients' propositional and nonpropositional understandings of what is communicated arises from three nonpropositional hermeneutical injustices that, in turn, arise from misapplication of three forms of nonpropositional understanding.

The second sort of Autistic experience that I want to mention occurs when Autistic nonspeakers are denied appropriate augmentative and alternative communication (AAC) options. Lack of access to appropriate AAC options for significant parts of their lives is very common for Autistic nonspeakers. Nonspeaking Autistic Ido Kedar writes in the bio for his blog: "I am an autistic guy with a message. I spent the first half of my life completely trapped in silence" (Kedar n.d.). Similarly, Philip Reyes, in the banner on his blog, writes "This is the story of a boy who could not talk, but learned to make his thoughts known by spelling on a letterboard and typing. This is his path from silence to communication" (Reyes n.d.). The phrase "behavior is communication" is something of a mantra in the Autistic community due to regular dismissals of nonspeaking Autistics' behavior as meaningless (Kim 2014).

Nonspeaking Autistics who are (1) capable of propositional understanding and (2) capable of expressing that understanding with appropriate, but denied, AAC options are not in a position to be subject to propositional forms of epistemic injustice. When we combine the inability to express things propositionally with the tendency to ignore the nonpropositional content of nonspeaking Autistics behavior, we have a situation that we might understand as a hermeneutical counterpart of Dotson's testimonial rejection. The nonspeaking Autistic person is not viewed as a meaning-making subject at all and, thus, we might call this hermeneutical rejection. The inability to communicate with a recipient in part occurs because the provider has not been given necessary tools for communication. So, we might characterize these sorts of cases as involving both hermeneutical rejection and hermeneutical denial. They involve hermeneutical rejection, insofar as meaning-making behavior in which the provider engages is not understood as such; and they involve hermeneutical denial, insofar as the nonspeaking Autistic is denied access to communication tools due to their unintelligibility as an epistemic agent. Hermeneutical rejection also leads to Catala's nonpropositional forms of testimonial injustice (Catala 2020), since not understanding behavior as meaningful leads to dismissal of the communicative content of this behavior. Hermeneutical denial can also play an indirect role in the occurrence of nonpropositional testimonial injustices, insofar as ability to explain the meaning of behavior via AAC could stop the occurrence of these injustices.

Exclusion from Theorizing: Metaepistemic Injustice and Autism

In this last section of my chapter, I will discuss forms of metaepistemic injustice connected to the three sorts of experiences that I consider in the preceding section. I think that with respect to ADE, there are at least two forms of metatestimonial injustice that we can identify, one of which does not involve metahermeneutical injustice. First, a metahermeneutical injustice is involved in conceptualizing hermeneutical injustice in terms of gaps. This metahermeneutical injustice can entail a failure to recognize cases of hermeneutical injustice that do not involve gaps at all, such as a recipient's dismissal of an Autistic person's testimony about their needs because the recipient holds a medicalized understanding of autism, that is, understands autism as a medical condition. This metahermeneutical injustice can also lead to a failure to recognize certain aspects of cases of hermeneutical injustice in which there is both a gap in shared interpretive resources and problematic content that needs to be removed from those shared resources. Arguably, a lot of the hermeneutical injustice that Autistic people face is the latter sort, involving conceptions of autism that are both significantly mistaken and incomplete. This metahermeneutical injustice can lead to metatestimonial injustice in the sense that the failure to recognize certain cases of hermeneutical injustice leads to the absence of discussion of such cases in work on epistemic injustice. This kind of metatestimonial injustice may be an expansion of Catala's notion of metatestimonial injustice, since it does not involve logocentric bias nor does it arise from considerations of who counts as an epistemic agent and instead focuses on what is, or is not, included in discussions of epistemic injustice.

Second, insofar as epistemic injustice is concerned with epistemic marginalization, metahermeneutical and metatestimonial injustice can involve issues that stem from our concept of marginalization or the ways in which we apply that concept, respectively. While we find discussions of both gender and race within feminist philosophy, these discussions are often either (1) general discussions that do not consider differences within these categories or (2) more specific discussions that are (a) not intersectional and universalize (i.e., structurally gaslight) the oppression of (white) women or (b) oversimplify the oppression of Black men and/or Black women. Of course, (nondisabled, cis, white, heterosexual) feminist philosophers do recognize that other social identities, including other gendered and racialized identities, are targets of oppression. Yet there is significant lack of discussion of occurrences of epistemic injustice involving these other identities. Consequently, we have an example of metatestimonial injustice that involves how, or to whom, the concept of marginalization is applied in discussions of epistemic injustice that does not seem to result from metahermeneutical injustice given that writers on epistemic injustice recognize that people excluded from discussion are marginalized. The possibility that a person's claims of group membership may be dismissed or minimized, as in ADE, is not recognized when writers focus on identities that are often assumed to be readily identifiable via visual markers. However, having one's claims of group membership dismissed is a common experience for many disabled people and for many multiracialized people (Song 2020). The experience according to which one is considered not "Autistic enough" or not "disabled enough" to have certain needs or experiences is also missed when discussion focuses on identities that do not come in degrees or are not mistakenly perceived to come in degrees. This metatestimonial injustice results, in part, due to the exclusion of marginalized philosophers from philosophy departments and so is at least culpable insofar as the latter exclusion is culpable. In addition, however, this metatestimonial injustice results from structural gaslighting when philosophers attempt to provide general accounts of epistemic injustice, while excluding consideration of various marginalized groups.

The metatestimonial injustice of applying the conception of marginalized group to only certain groups is prominent in Goetze's classification of hermeneutical injustice according to which group, or groups, have the relevant interpretive resources.[1] Goetze considers the dominant group, a subject that experiences the hermeneutical injustice, that subject's own social group, and the set of nondominant social groups to which the subject does not belong. The dominant group lacks the relevant interpretive resources in each of the six types of hermeneutical injustice that Goetze identifies. Therefore, the classifications differ with respect to which members of the latter three categories possess the relevant interpretive resources. The reason there are six, rather than eight, types of hermeneutical injustice is, as Goetze states:

> I have . . . dropped the permutation where the subject does not have the required tools despite her own social group having them: I am assuming that if a group has the required interpretive tools, then so do all of its members. This is of course an abstraction; certainly, it takes time for interpretive tools to disperse among the members of a discursive group, and its members may disagree. In such cases, however, it suffices to draw the line differently, circumscribing only the subgroup whose members agree. (Goetze 2018: 80–1)

Many people with certain kinds of disabilities—for example, autism—may go through most or all of their lives without even knowing that they are disabled and without understanding their experiences, despite the abundance of interpretive tools that the disabled communities to which they belong have created. For example, I was in my thirties before I discovered that I am Autistic. Goetze recognizes and sets aside a similar sort of case involving the time that it takes for resources under development to be dispersed. Nevertheless, he fails to recognize the actual, very common, and much-discussed case of a member of a given marginalized group who lacks interpretive resources that the larger marginalized community possesses.

The situation is made more egregious by the fact that Goetze considers an example of exactly the sort of case that he fails to recognize and misconstrues it because he does not treat disabled communities as constituting socially salient groups. Goetze describes hermeneutical separation as occurring when a subject and their own social group lack certain interpretive resources and a distinct nondominant social group possesses them. He gives the example of Wendy Sanford, a woman experiencing postpartum depression. Although neither Sanford nor her social circles understand postpartum depression, Sanford attends a feminist consciousness-raising meeting where she learns about it. Although Goetze generally treats marginalized groups as the relevant social groups, he switches to Sanford's personal social circles and a specific group of feminist activists as the relevant social groups in Sanford's case. Yet Sanford is part of a disabled community of people who have experienced postpartum depression. It is only by disregarding Sanford's membership in that community that we can understand her case as a case of hermeneutical separation.

Additional metahermeneutical injustice is involved in how credibility deficits in testimonial injustice tend to be understood. Fricker characterizes credibility deficits as arising from either judgments of insincerity or judgments of incompetence (Fricker 2007). Insofar as the concept of sincerity is involved in our judgments about whether someone is credible as a provider of knowledge, an understanding of sincerity that leads to cases of testimonial injustice that are not recognized as such can be considered a form of metahermeneutical injustice. As the various research noted by Price demonstrates, neurotypicals can judge Autistic people as insincere due to misinterpretation of Autistic behavior (Price 2022, ch. 6). Distrust could, for example, manifest as a result of a recipient's feeling of creepiness in regard to Autistic body language. The way that we conceptualize sincerity and, in particular, what we understand as evidence for insincerity can lead to prejudicial dismissal of Autistic people's testimony. In some instances in which Autistic people's testimony of social interest is dismissed, the recipient's misunderstanding of the provider's body language has created the perception of insincerity. If a neurotypical recipient is consciously aware of the (apparent) tension that they take to be present between the provider's testimony and body language, then the recipient may consciously take the provider's body language as an indication of insincerity, especially if the body language in question is a feature of the dominant propositional understanding of what counts as a marker of insincerity (e.g., lack of eye contact). Consequently, we have a case of metahermeneutical injustice insofar as the dominant understanding of the epistemic concept of sincerity is biased in a way that leads to dismissal of certain cases of testimonial injustice due to the presence of (alleged) markers of insincerity. We also have a case of hermeneutical injustice since the biased concept of sincerity can be directly applied in testimonial exchanges to, for example, render Autistic modes of expression unintelligible as not indicating insincerity.

Examples of Catala's notions of metahermeneutical and metatestimonial injustice, which involve bias in favor of propositional knowledge, are at work in the denial of AAC devices to nonspeakers. Focus on propositional knowledge is entwined with bias in favor of spoken language as the tendency to attribute a lack of propositional knowledge to nonspeaking people demonstrates. When epistemic agency is conceptualized propositionally, both people who do not have propositional epistemic agency and nonspeakers who have propositional epistemic agency, but do not display it, are understood to lack epistemic agency entirely.

Conclusion

Specific instances of epistemic injustice can be incredibly complex. So, too, can be the metaepistemic explanations for conceptual deficiencies or lack of discussion of certain topics in theorizing epistemic oppression. If one narrows their focus too much, they may produce oversimplifications. Some of these oversimplifications will be of the specific sorts that Dotson and Berenstain use as examples in which focus on white women's experiences obscures features of Black women's experiences. In addition, significant oversimplification can occur when a single sort of experience is examined along a single axis of oppression if attention is restricted too narrowly. A narrow focus can obscure both the presence of different kinds of epistemic injustice in a single instance of epistemic oppression and the interactions between epistemic injustices. Focus on propositional forms of epistemic injustice can result in significant oversimplification of even dismissals of propositional testimony by obscuring the role that nonpropositional understanding may play in these cases. Such focus can also lead one to downplay the importance of nonpropositional understanding even when the role that it has played is recognized. The rejection of an Autistic person's propositional claims of social interest seems to be an experience where nonpropositional epistemic injustice has a central role since it often, if not always, explains the propositional epistemic injustice involved. Finally, experiences in which propositional epistemic injustice are absent are understood, incorrectly, as not involving epistemic injustice at all.

Attempts to reduce instances of metaepistemic oppression to a single metatestimonial injustice that a single metahermeneutical injustice may or may not cause can similarly be an oversimplification. Taken together, the metahermeneutical injustice in which hermeneutical injustice is conceptualized in terms of gaps, the metatestimonial injustice in which the concept of marginalization is not applied to disabled communities despite recognition of disabled people as marginalized, the metahermeneutical injustice in which sincerity is conceptualized in a way that favors neurotypical markers of it, and the metahermeneutical injustice in which epistemic agency and epistemic injustice are conceptualized in propositional terms explain the lack of recognition and discussion of aspects of epistemic agency and epistemic injustice that I have raised in this chapter.

Note

1 Goetze's paper, published in *Hypatia: A Journal of Feminist Philosophy*, also includes an awful example of metaepistemic injustice targeted at Indigenous peoples. He provides an explicit reminder of the cultural genocide being carried out against Indigenous communities followed immediately by asking readers to imagine that this process has nearly been carried out to completion to demonstrate a case of what he calls hermeneutical isolation. This lack of concern for Indigenous readers serves to situate Indigenous people as subjects to be written about rather than as colleagues to be engaged with. Additionally, given that Goetze's example would involve epistemicide, the destruction of knowledge, it is significant, but not surprising, that this uniquely colonial form of epistemic oppression is not even mentioned.

References

Berenstain, Nora (2020), "White Feminist Gaslighting," *Hypatia: A Journal of Feminist Philosophy* 35 (4): 733–58.

Catala, Amandine (2020), "Metaepistemic Injustice and Intellectual Disability: A Pluralist Account of Epistemic Agency," *Ethical Theory and Moral Practice* 23: 755–76.

Catala, Amandine, Luc Faucher, and Pierre Poirier (2021), "Autism, Epistemic Injustice, and Epistemic Disablement: A Relational Account of Epistemic Agency," *Synthese* 199: 9013–39.

Dotson, Kristie (2011), "Tracking Epistemic Violence, Tracking Practices of Silencing," *Hypatia: A Journal of Feminst Philosophy* 26 (2): 236–57.

Dotson, Kristie (2012), "A Cautionary Tale: On Limiting Epistemic Oppression," *Frontiers: A Journal of Women Studies* 33 (1): 24–47.
endever* corbin (2021), "Guest Blog: Communication Barriers Faced by AAC Users in Accessing Health Care." Available at: https://communicationfirst.org/guest-blog-communication-barriers-faced-by-aac-users-in-accessing-health-care/ (accessed June 6, 2022).
Fricker, Miranda (2007), *Epistemic Injustice: Power and the Ethics of Knowing*, Oxford: Oxford University Press.
Goetze, Trystan R. (2018), "Hermeneutical Dissent and the Species of Hermeneutical Injustice," *Hypatia: A Journal of Feminist Philosophy* 33 (1): 73–90.
Hanson, Norwood R. (2009), "On Observation," in Timothy McGrew, Marc Alspector-Kelly, and Fritz Allhoff (eds.), *Philosophy of Science: An Historical Anthology*, 432–50, West Sussex: Wiley-Blackwell.
Kedar, Ido (n.d.), "Ido in Autismland." Available at: https://idoinautismland.com/ (accessed June 15, 2022).
Kim, Cynthia (2014), "Behavior is Communication: Are You Listening?" Available at: https://musingsofanaspie.com/2014/04/30/why-behavior-is-communication-is-no-longer-good-enough/ (accessed June 13, 2022).
McCreary, Michael (2019), *Funny, You Don't Look Autistic: A Comedian's Guide to Life on the Spectrum*, Toronto: Annick Press.
Medina, José (2013), *The Epistemology of Resistance: Gender and Racial Oppression, Epistemic Injustice, and Resistant Imaginations*, Oxford: Oxford University Press.
Medina, José (2017), "Varieties of Hermeneutical Injustice," in Ian James Kidd, José Medina, and Gaile Pohlhaus, Jr. (eds.), *The Routledge Handbook of Epistemic Injustice*, 41–53, New York: Routledge.
Moens, Jonathan (2020), "Facial Expressions Between Autistic and Typical People may be Mismatched." Available at: https://www.spectrumnews.org/news/facial-expressions-between-autistic-and-typical-people-may-be-mismatched/ (accessed June 14, 2022).
Onaiwu, Morénike G. (2020), "'They Don't Know, Don't Show, or Don't Care': Autism's White Privilege Problem," *Autism in Adulthood* 2 (4): 270–2.
Pohlhaus, Jr., Gaile (2012), "Relational Knowing and Epistemic Injustice: Toward a Theory of Willful Hermeneutical Ignorance," *Hypatia: A Journal of Feminist Philosophy* 27 (4): 715–35.
Price, Devon (2022), *Unmasking Autism: Discovering the New Faces of Neurodiversity*, New York: Harmony Books. Kindle.
Reyes, Phillip (n.d.), "Faith, Hope, and Love. . .With Autism." Available at: https://faithhopeloveautism.blogspot.com/ (accessed June 15, 2020).
Sasson, Noah J., Daniel J. Faso, Jack Nugent, Sarah Lovell, Daniel P. Kennedy, and Ruth B. Grossman (2017), "Neurotypical Peers are Less Willing to Interact with Those with Autism Based on Thin Slice Judgments," *Scientific Reports* 7: 40700.
Seers, Kate and Rachel C. Hogg (2021), "'You Don't Look Autistic': A Qualitative Exploration of Women's Experiences of Being the 'Autistic Other'," *Autism* 25 (6): 1553–64.
Shotwell, Alexis (2011), *Knowing Otherwise: Race, Gender, and Implicit Understanding*, University Park: Pennsylvania State University Press.
Shotwell, Alexis (2017), "Forms of Knowing and Epistemic Resources," in Ian James Kidd, José Medina, and Gaile Pohlhaus, Jr. (eds.), *The Routledge Handbook of Epistemic Injustice*, 79–88, New York: Routledge.

Sohn, Emily (2019), "Righting the Gender Imbalance in Autism Studies." Available at: https://www.spectrumnews.org/features/deep-dive/righting-gender-imbalance-autism-studies/ (accessed June 14, 2022).

Song, Miri (2020), "Rethinking Minority Status and 'Visibility'," *Comparative Migration Studies* 8 (5): 1–17.

Sparrow, Robert (2005), "Defending Deaf Culture: The Case of Cochlear Implants," *The Journal of Political Philosophy* 13 (2): 135–52.

Tremain, Shelley L. (2017), *Foucault and Feminist Philosophy of Disability*, Ann Arbor: Michigan University Press.

Woodfield, Casey L. and Justin E. Freedman (2021), "Barriers to Knowing and Being Known: Constructions of (In)competence in Research," *Philosophical Inquiry in Education* 28 (2): 177–95.

26 NOCEBOS TALK BACK

MARKED-BODIED EXPERIENCE AND THE DYNAMICS OF HEALTH INEQUITY

SUZE G. BERKHOUT AND ADA S. JAARSMA

Introduction

"Nocebos Talk Back," this chapter's title, invokes a phenomenon that has in recent decades been named and embraced by biomedicine and that, despite this embracing, undermines the mechanistic and individualizing framework of medical research and practice. The "nocebo effect" is a dynamic that takes place in medical and medicalizing contexts—more like a relational exchange than a cause-and-effect mechanism—in which someone experiences a negative symptom, precisely because their bodymind expects such a symptom to emerge in and out of that very situation. "Context matters," nocebo researchers declare (Rossettini et al. 2020), drawing on experimental data in order to underscore an insight long rendered evident by feminist disability studies—namely, that the feedback loops between designs, norms, and practices of spaces and the persons moving and interacting within spaces, hold somatic import, affording exclusionary (in most cases) or accessible (in some cases) experiences that in turn shape future experiences. Although accessible and ease-filled medical scenarios that can yield the positive experience of placebo effects are a well-documented aspect of medical treatment, in this chapter we examine nocebo effects and the many forms of medical and medicalizing exclusions that can serve as nocebos. We offer the phrase "nocebos talk back" in our chapter's title as a way to underscore the importance of the critical examination of nocebo effects for philosophy of disability and feminist disability studies.

Nocebos talk back in the form of nocebo effects, and nocebo effects express feedback loops between persons and the broader structures and practices of biomedicine. These feedback loops, in other words, can draw attention both to individuals ourselves (what "bad outcome" do our bodyminds expect, based on past learnings, that we will then experience?) and to theorists seeking to understand them (what systems and practices lead to these very expectations?). In addition, these feedback loops can implicate the vocational practices of research, as researchers might occupy positions and professions synchronized with authority and power. Indeed, we ourselves work in positions that often reinforce the very kinds of feedback loops that feminist disability studies seek to call out and resist: Suze in psychiatry and both of us in philosophy (Tremain 2020; Jaarsma and Berkhout 2022; Nishida 2018).[1] In the analysis that this chapter comprises, our own respective vocational labor-practices are on the hook in ways that should be generative for other people who likewise inhabit roles in institutions such as universities or hospitals that are inextricably entangled with structural aspects of oppression.

The term *bodymind*, a locution proposed by Margaret Price to subvert the line often drawn between "bodies" and "minds," has become an integral concept in feminist disability studies (Price 2015). This chapter focuses on "the nocebo effect" as a lived example of bodyminds-in-action, testifying (in the words of feminist philosopher Isabelle Stengers) to the myriad capacities for injury in medical contexts (Stengers 2002: 253). Like placebos, nocebos are essentially and importantly biosocial: they differ, from one context to another, and thus can afford a broad transnational examination of the relational exchanges between bodyminds, medicine, and the biosocial meanings that saturate medical contexts.

Given the importance of feedback loops for critical disability studies (Dolmage 2017; Jaarsma 2020), we look to nocebos and nocebo effects as palpable examples of the intersecting, often reinforcing, relations between medicine and harm. Feedback loops can serve as emancipatory resources, drawing attention to exclusions or injury in order to critique and resist injustices. Hence, we want to put nocebo effects forward as palimpsests of past experiences, along the lines that Price and M. Jacqui Alexander suggest (Price 2021: 261; Alexander 2006: 190). Nocebo effects, read through philosophy of disability, are tangible expressions of the "layering and relayering" of time, memories, and embodied movements (Price 2021: 261).

Harm, of course, is precisely what biomedicine seeks to avoid and evade, even as disability studies scholars document, reflect upon, and incisively assess the many ways in which medical treatment can be inextricable from injury, even violence. As we explore in this chapter, nocebo effects are instructive indexes of the porous boundaries between "healing" (a vexed notion for feminist disability studies scholars and philosophers of disability) and harm in biomedical contexts. Even the emergence of the term *nocebo* itself signals an ever-present potentiality for harm in medical research. As we explain in what follows, nocebo effects became salient as a persistent phenomenon in the context of biomedical treatment, so much so that the term *nocebo* was coined to signify the phenomenon, sparking in turn the nascent field of nocebo studies.

Nocebos hold significance for feminist philosophy of disability, in particular, given the ways in which nocebo research can either reinforce or undermine prevailing exclusions in biomedicine, depending on the methodologies and practices of the researchers who engage in it. As we examine throughout this chapter, nocebos make manifest—through traceable and mark-able symptoms and physiological changes—the kinds of inequities that rarely become marked out as such in biomedicine. These inequities stem in part from the sedimented systems and structures of racializing colonial and settler colonialism, which continue to shape and saturate medical institutions. In this way, they align with the call of philosophers such as Desiree Valentine to attend to the processes by which bodyminds become "raced" and "disabled," processes so entangled that Valentine offers the term *racialized disablement* as a structuring concept for engaging with these injustices (Valentine 2022: 337). These racializing and disabling injustices stem from and reflect the norms and normative practices by which some bodyminds get marked out in medical contexts, rendered otherwise from unmarked bodyminds, and, therefore, identified as in need of treatment or intervention. Thus, Valentine's call implicitly instructs us to attend to our own positionalities as authors in this investigation: we are unmarked in certain ways and contexts—for example, whiteness, able-bodiedness—which shapes our experiences within the roles and professional practices that offer critical purchase on our analysis.

This distinction between "marked" and "unmarked" bodies is itself in need of sustained inquiry, according to Sami Schalk and Jina B. Kim, given how the field of feminist disability studies tends to employ methods and canonical texts that bear an "unacknowledged whiteness." In our discussion that follows, we take up Schalk and Kim's call for citational practices and theoretical framings that attend to race as an analytic (Schalk and Kim 2020: 35) by turning to Sylvia Wynter's philosophical work on nocebos. While Wynter's work in decolonial philosophy receives wide-ranging attention across critical race theory, philosophy, and social theory, Wynter's attention to nocebos as an index of oppression is overlooked in otherwise wide-ranging feminist, anti-racist, and decolonial engagement with Wynter's work. By exploring how nocebos "talk back," we bring Wynter into conversation with feminist philosophy of disability and feminist disability studies, tracking and forging the interconnections between the injuries that take place in medical and medicalizing contexts and broader systems of injustice. Wynter solicits attention to the "us/not-us . . . scripts" that animate so many of our social practices and contexts (Wynter and McKittrick 2015: 58). Nocebos and nocebo effects proffer ways to note such scripts, while demonstrating Wynter's call to reckon with the fact that "we are not purely biological beings" (34).

The testimony of nocebo effects underscores the entangled relations between bodyminds, systems and practices, and ideologies of ability, health, and (dis)ability. Schalk suggests using the term *(dis)ability* as a way to foreground "the socially constructed system of norms" categorizing and valuing bodyminds through concepts of ability and disability (Schalk 2017). As Schalk and Kim highlight, feminist-of-color disability studies often expose ideologies and discourses of (dis)ability in situations where the "aboutness" of the events or issues do not immediately appear to relate to disability (Schalk and Kim 2020). In this chapter, we forge links between the nocebo effect and medical injustices in relation to race, gender, and disability (among other identities) in order to critique the ways in which difference, to paraphrase Ehlers and Krupar, is often ontologized as biological truth (Ehlers and Krupar 2019). As biosocial and relational, nocebos, we argue, provide palpable examples of the bodied experience of health inequalities as biosocial dynamics.

In what follows, we outline a general understanding of the nocebo effect from our work tracking research in the field of placebo/nocebo studies. We suggest that, as much as anything, nocebos are a prompt that asks us to consider for whom conventional objects of care (the diploma, the clipboard, the white coat) reflect the pleasures of health versus for whom these putative objects of care demarcate pain, anxiety, and trauma. Which communities have learned—whether personally or through their collective experience—that the health-care system is *not* a place of helping or healing for them? What are the bodied effects of this cut between cure/harm? To address these questions, we consider the notion of marked versus unmarked bodyminds. Heeding Wynter's call to attend to the "us-not-us scripts" at play in concrete contexts, that is, we consider how nocebos reflect a choreography of harming when marked bodyminds attempt to navigate medical spaces. Nocebos and their talk-back effects emerge as sites to think with, especially in terms of the lived intersections between identities, (dis)ability, and the racializing violence of colonial systems.

What Is the Nocebo Effect?

The term *nocebo effect* might not be widely familiar, as it was coined only decades ago; and yet, it refers to scenarios that readers might well have experienced, firsthand. The nocebo effect involves an expectation of adverse, unwanted side effects that in spite of no biochemical or other "actual" property inhering in the treatment itself, arise through symptoms that can be observed or self-described, traced, and empirically studied. In this way, nocebos undermine the very binary between "inert" and "verum" treatments (just as placebos do), which makes them both vexing for biomedical researchers and generative for feminist philosophy of disability.

Researchers, observing that individuals in the placebo-controlled arm of clinical trials could experience adverse side effects despite not themselves receiving the treatment studied, decided to give this widespread pattern a name: the nocebo effect (Enck, Benedetti, and Schedlowski 2008; Hahn 1997; Kennedy 1961). Nocebos, in addition to serving as strange and unwanted interruptions to the protocols of biomedical research, underscore the biosocial significance of these very protocols: participants in trials who are given a placebo undergo the same protocols as participants in them who receive the verum under investigation, including the same sorts of exchanges with clinicians about potential side effects of the verum. In this way, nocebo effects, like placebo effects, make palpable—in measurable and embodied ways—how significant the many varied aspects of medical treatments can be for bodyminds, from the design of a pill to the affects of a clinician. As Elizabeth Wilson puts it in *Gut Feminism*, "having a good drug response seems to go hand in hand with having a good placebo response" (Wilson 2015: 137), so much so that attempts to firmly disentangle them inevitably fail.

The term *nocebo* is a deliberate twist on the centuries-old term *placebo*, referring to harmful, unwanted outcomes that undercut therapeutic goals of medical treatment rather than naming positive outcomes (Evers et al. 2018; Chavarria et al. 2017; Bingel and Schedlowski 2014; Kong et al. 2008). We might say, therefore, that nocebo effects are disloyal to the biomedical endeavor, given how they disrupt the overall framing of medicine as oriented toward "do no harm." We could in addition implicate placebo effects in such disloyalty, given how they wreak havoc with bioethical assumptions about the autonomy of individuals and supposed transparency of knowledge. "Is it ever ethical to prescribe a placebo?" is a question that bioethicists and analytically trained philosophers often pose (Berkhout et al., forthcoming). Placebos, in other words, are also meaningful to think within the context of philosophy of disability, given how they complicate the liberal and humanist paradigm of bioethics. Nocebo effects might be summed up as phenomena "whereby anticipation and expectation of negative outcome may induce the worsening of a symptom" (Benedetti et al. 2007). As we discuss later, these kinds of expectations emerge from many sources, including biomedical practices themselves. As such, nocebo effects pose a threat to the desires, found throughout medicine and every other colonial institution (including the university), for subjects to "please be successful, be pretty, be human" (paperson 2017: 56). Not only are nocebo effects unwanted ramifications of biomedical research and treatment, they draw attention to the concrete, lived injurious effects of such "please be pretty" mandates. As feminist-of-color disability scholars argue, these effects are disproportionately experienced by racialized persons, underscoring the systems-level violence of injustice that Wynter connects with nocebo effects (Wynter and McKittrick 2015: 58, 59, 65, 68).

During the COVID-19 pandemic, nocebo effects have been launched into public consciousness in relation to adverse effects described within studies of COVID-19 vaccinations. A recent systematic review of three SARS-CoV-2 vaccine trials, whose research subjects total roughly 45,000 participants, found high rates of fatigue, headache, and muscle aches and pains reported in the control (placebo) arms of these trials.[2] A larger review of twelve COVID-19 vaccine trials found that nocebo effects accounted for about 76 percent of common adverse reactions after the first dose and approximately 50 percent of adverse reactions after the second dose (Haas et al. 2022). These findings have been widely publicized, contributing to increased public discussion of, and familiarity with, the concept of nocebo effects.

During the pandemic, "the public," as Mel Y. Chen puts it, "has been learning how to think intersectionally" (Chen 2021: 22). Indeed, we take Chen's prompting as an invitation to focus more fully on nocebos *as* intersectional entanglements. A central aim of much disability activism has focused on embracing disability as valuable and desirable (Fritsch 2015), as part of human plurality (Garland-Thomson 2011: 603), and, as Joshua St. Pierre puts it, as a form of biological plurality and a critical opening in systems of power (St. Pierre 2022: 14, 11). Yet, as the work of Schalk and Kim, Ben-Moshe and Magaña, and Hamraie and Fritsch (among others) points out, untangling disability from processes of medicalization and pathologization can be fraught. Many people who are racialized, gendered, and Othered as minorities (via sexual identity, migration status, geography, or social class) experience intense disparities when they attempt to access high-quality health services, often doing so without the benefit of care delivered in spaces that are free from discrimination (Schalk and Kim 2020; Ben-Moshe and Magaña 2014; Hamraie and Fritsch 2019). Moya Bailey and Izetta Autumn Mobley point out that "having access to the healing therapies offered by the medical field is part of addressing the medical field's long disinvestment in Black health" (Bailey and Mobley 2019: 28). Nocebo effects provide ways to read the impact of social power in relation to mutually constitutive, intersectional identities (Cho, Crenshaw, and McCall 2013; Crenshaw 1991), especially in the medicalizing scenarios of a pandemic.

We see nocebo effects most prominently within the practice of informing patients about potential risks of treatments or interventions: through an informed-consent process (meant to protect patients from harm), the expectation of harm can indeed produce the very harms of which patients are warned (Howick 2021; Colloca 2017). As Valentine reminds us, these protocols are fully bound up with race-based systems of violence, pointing to "the atrocities that generated the need for bioethics as a field of study as such" (Valentine 2022: 338). The non-neutral dynamics of bioethics become recognizable, even undeniable, because of the testimony of nocebo effects.

Nocebo effects can, in addition, be revealed within experimental research apparatuses, notably in relation to expectations of pain. Verbal cueing, such as when one is told that a local anesthetic will feel "like a bee sting" rather than told that it will "numb" an area of skin to make a procedure more comfortable, can shape one's experience and intensity of the pain that accompanies the injection (Varelmann et al. 2010). Expectancies are also generated through physical space and context—for example, the familiar smell of the clinic setting or the color of the walls can induce nausea for oncology patients long before a chemotherapeutic agent is given—as well as through the quality of interpersonal dynamics that unfold[3] (Manaï et al. 2019). Furthermore, the clinician's own beliefs and expectancies play a role in the production of nocebo effects and come to matter in the bodymind of the patient-participant. In a dramatic experimental paradigm that demonstrates the relationality and intersubjectivity of nocebo effects, where the experimental administration of placebo versus opiate versus nociceptive (pain-inducing) agent is concealed from both the clinician and patient-participant, the *clinician's belief* about whether an analgesic would be part of the experimental protocol can shift the direction of the patient-participant's pain experience (Gracely et al. 1985). Here, too, we find evidence of Valentine's account of the processes by which racialized disablement takes place (Valentine 2022): rather than inhering in any one particular individual, nocebo effects dramatize how embedded we all are, in our own concrete ways, within the structures of biomedicine and the affective patterns of relating to each other.

Cueing and expectancies that generate negative bodied experiences are not solely pain-related, though pain is the most common experimental paradigm used to examine nocebo effects, including by Wynter. Studies that induce sensations of difficulty or discomfort during breathing (dyspnea), in association with an otherwise neutral cue such as an odor that does not itself impact the airway, likewise generate nocebo effects: an odor that had previously been associated with increased respiratory effort will go on to produce dyspnea by expectation alone. Strikingly, it is not only a sensation of difficulty breathing that is evoked by the neutral odor—differences in neural correlates of dyspnea are also seen on functional magnetic resonance imaging (fMRI) and positron emission tomography (PET) scan (Vinckier et al. 2021).

Nevertheless, detailed study of the physiological endpoints of nocebo effects is a fraught undertaking. Not infrequently, the structure of the experimental apparatus reinforces ableist bifurcations. So-called "healthy volunteers" are regarded as the most ethical participants to willingly and knowingly engage in studies that induce distress, which is one of the reasons that pain paradigms are the most common experimental procedure in nocebo studies—pain can be straightforwardly induced in "healthy volunteers." Inducing additional symptoms or discomfort in individuals who are already experiencing illness is more complex to justify. And although there is a certain logic to this rationale, the division between health/ill, normal/abnormal is sedimented through this structure.

Is there a meaningful takeaway from the experimental apparatus, despite these ontological challenges? Across a range of studies, functional connectivity is thought to be increased between brain areas relating to the perception of sensations inside the body (interoception), autobiographical memory, and neuroanatomical domains that correspond to the specific stimulus (Thomaidou et al. 2021; Schienle et al. 2018). We should attend to the ways in which these connections are importantly biosocial phenomena, linking memory, body sensation, physiology, and self-other relations. Not only do nocebos occur through the cues, verbal scripts, and qualities of the interpersonal interactions and the spatial context, they operate through social forms of learning as well. Observing other people experience pain, discomfort, anxiety, and difficulty to a setting and intervention can likewise produce nocebo effects (Vogtle, Barke, and Kroner-Herwig 2013). In this way, nocebo effects testify to the "basic affectability" that Kristie Dotson and Marita Gilbert argue is part of human experience: as bodyminds, all of us are vulnerable to other people and to our surrounding contexts (Dotson and Gilbert 2014), despite the myriad ways in which some of us, as individuals and as populations, receive shelter from vulnerability and many of us, as individuals and as populations, do not. Personal distress experienced by a research participant as they observe pain or difficulty in another individual similarly influences the magnitude of the nocebo pain that a particular participant themself experiences (Bajcar and Babel 2018). As we will discuss in what follows, this phenomenon has significant implications for feminist philosophy of disability with respect to how we think about harms that are experienced and embodied in the navigation of health-care and medicalized settings.

Research surrounding nocebos (and placebos) tends to describe their ontological implications as "effects": stabilized endpoints or outcomes in a process of production, derived within experimentally controlled situations. But what we also receive from placebo/nocebo studies are stories: stories, we might say, about what we have learned regarding what heals and what harms (Yergeau 2017: 21). The story that much of allopathic medicine tells about itself is that the field comprises equal parts of the benevolent and scientific: a story of healing, affirmed within the experimental paradigms of placebos. Confidence in one's assessment and treatment plan is meant to translate into a story of health-care providers as reassuring, masterful, and expert at controlling the entropy of disease. Another aspect of relationality, indexed by nocebo effects, is this: who is *not* treated with an expertise blanketed by warmth, empathy, and compassion? Put another way, for whom do the degrees upon the wall, the white coat, or the institutional setting demarcate trauma, suffering, and powerlessness? How does *this* relationality impact treatment outcomes and intersect with the affectability of marked-out bodyminds? As noted earlier, research studies that highlight the role that social observational learning plays in relation to nocebo effects make the field of nocebo effects research especially relevant for thinking about intersectional identities, marked-bodied experience, and the impacts of racialized disablement and systemic discrimination in health-care settings.

Marked-Bodied Experience, Health Inequality, and Nocebos

As we write in another context, "nocebos and placebos dramatize the fact that there is no generic body" (Jaarsma and Berkhout 2019) because their effects bear witness to the concrete, contextualized, embedded, and embodied interactions of specific persons. Such "witnessing" runs counter to the presuppositions, upheld by biomedical research protocols and practices, that "the human body" can be generalized, that effects "inhere" in individual persons (Valentine 2022: 337), and that assistive or adaptive technologies reflect standardizable—rather than singular—needs and capacities (Hendren 2020). Whereas the generic human, hailed by the protocols of biomedicine, is of necessity "anonymous," the meaning-responses of nocebo and placebo effects express the scripts of culturally specific, biosocial scenarios (Berkhout and Jaarsma 2018). Nocebo effects help us recognize this tension between the universalizing aims of biomedicine and the specificity of the concrete individuals traversing medical spaces. Critical disability studies scholars often call out this tension in order to lay claim to the resistance and solidarity that emerge out of affirming lived experiences. Alison Kafer, for example, identifies the "system marking some bodies, ways of thinking, and patterns of movement as deviant and unworthy" (Kafer 2013: 89), generating a "self-perpetuating homogeneity" (98). It is not enough, Kafer writes, to replace this system with an alternative one (102); rather, we can open up the very field of possibilities, a kind of opening that depends upon concrete and material scenarios and expressions. Nocebo effects in particular serve as a palpable kind of expression, one that demonstrates the material dynamics and processes by which inequity, injustice, and violence take place.

Kafer's use of the verb *marking* is instructive, underscoring aspects of embodiment that, by definition, often pass unnoticed. As we noted earlier, to be "unmarked," in contexts of colonial and settler colonial institutions, is to move through the world with a lived sense of ease; from first-person experience, in other words, it can seem like a comfort to be taken for granted, occupying space in ways that fit smoothly with its "homogeneity." As Aimi Hamraie explains, even architecture tends to facilitate such fitting between unmarked bodies and spaces, following design principles that heed an "ideology of ability" (Hamraie 2016: 288). In this ideology, disabled bodies are marked out, both on the level of structures (with "accessible" features added on, retroactively) and in lived experience. Disability, Hamraie points out, is cast as needing fixing or cure, in contrast to able-bodied features and movements. As Schalk argues, furthermore, recommending modification of a central term around which disability studies revolves, the term *(dis)ability* has emerged as a concept for the field in order to undermine this "us-not us" bifurcation between disability and ability (Schalk 2017).

Linguistic anthropologists use the term *unmarked* as a way to flag often-otherwise unidentified expressions of whiteness, the hegemonic backdrop of white supremacy resulting from centuries of imperialism (Urciuoli 2011). The violence by which racializing marking out reinforces the hegemony of whiteness perpetuates the power of whiteness, both in a lived sense and on a systems level. Franz Fanon famously captures this entwined violence in his writings, indicting science as one of the forces by which whiteness retains its unmarked status. "Science should be ashamed of itself," he declares (Fanon 2008: 100), given the ways that it upholds a "typical human reality" (6) that reinforces the normativity of white bodies and the exclusions of racialized bodies.

Personal experiences according to which one is marked out as Other are collectively shared, across groups, as people are minoritized by race, gender, sexual identity, socioeconomic or migration status, particularly people whose self-experiences sit in the intersections of these subjecting categories and apparatuses. Because biomedical practices reflect and reinforce systemic patterns of marking out as Other, the lived experiences of individuals in medicalized contexts can include literal, as well as metaphorical, aspects of markedness, as Camisha Russell points out (Russell 2016). Resulting mistrust of medicine—including of the people who practice it, wearing white coats and administering protocols—reflects these injustices, which are essentially connected to colonial and settler colonial systems. Lisa Stevenson's ethnographic work, for example, demonstrates how settler states require citizens to be better patients: in colonial settings, "the patient needed not only to get well, but also to *want* to be the kind of subject or self that got well" (Stevenson 2014: 52, emphasis added), to be "please be pretty, successful, and human," in the words of paperson (paperson 2017: 56). By articulating expectancies as part of normalizing medical treatment, Stevenson prompts us to notice the connections between placebos (anticipating well-being), nocebos (expecting harm), and systems of oppression. Such connections are lived out, in the concrete experiences of bodyminds. Nomy Lamm reminds us, for example, that "the legacy of medical trauma" is a legacy that manifests in personal experiences and that therefore necessitates structural critique and resistance (Lamm 2015). And paperson points out the ever-present capacities for disloyalty, even in colonized settings: the request to be "pretty" and "human" belies the anxiety of the colonizers, imploring, "please do not fail us, reject us, betray us" (paperson 2017: 56).

Wynter brings this knot of connections together by pointing to nocebo effects. As Ashley J. Bohrer notes, Wynter's core commitment is liberation (Bohrer 2020: 529), informed by decolonial and anti-capitalist commitments. The term *nocebo effects* serves, in the critical context of Wynter's work, to demarcate the bundled relations between racializing violence, white supremacy, and lived experiences: nocebo effects refer to the harms, injuries, alienation, anxieties, and other adverse symptoms that stem from colonialism and capitalism. Nocebos are useful, for Wynter, because they cannot be separated from "palimpsestic time," as Alexander puts it (Alexander 2006: 190); tracking nocebo effects in the present turns into a practice of tracing transgenerational injustice and inherited trauma from decades, even centuries, in the past. Second, nocebos are useful, for Wynter, due to their biocultural dynamics, at odds with the attempts of "modern" science to bifurcate biology from culture (Wynter 1987).

Third, Wynter regards nocebos as useful because of their more well-known counterpart, placebos. Wynter invokes the pain-paradigm of nocebo research in order to call out lived differences that might otherwise be unrecognizable because of the unmarked forces of whiteness: notice the contrast, she writes, between whiteness (the "opiate-rewarding" placebo effects of well-being) and racialized experiences ("the opiate-rewarded blocked nocebo terms" of harm) (Wynter and McKittrick 2015: 50). Wynter's account is anti-essentialist, refuting the pseudoscience by which "race" is synced with nonexistent genetic traits or evolutionary trajectories; at the same time, Wynter invites us to consider how we, as human primates, live out our "biology" and our "storytelling capacities" as essentially entangled aspects of who we are as a species (2003).

Fourth and finally, nocebos and placebos gesture toward "flesh and word" as liberatory interrelations. In a recent interview, for example, Wynter rehearses the story of when Frederick Douglass was told about the powers of leaves and plants by a Black person who carried African counter-belief systems over to America: recall, Wynter suggests, "what scientists have told us about neurochemical mechanisms" and consider how "the belief in that leaf giving you power would have also had that literal neurochemical effect" (Wynter, Bennett, Givens 2020: 125). It is precisely because beliefs and stories hold material traction that it matters *which* beliefs and stories enter into the looping patterns that shape our lives, interactions, and social orders.

Understanding nocebo effects as dynamic, relational enactments of harm shifts us away from the mechanizing and individualizing logics of biomedicine. Nocebos make sense of how personal and collective experiences can contribute to harmful feedback loops that further perpetuate health inequality. Simultaneous to the social context that generates inequity on multiple levels (through discriminatory practices and subsequently through the anticipation of such), inequalities in health outcome become naturalized as biology, reinforcing markedness. As Russell articulates, "the view from the margins" (of US health care and biomedicine) means that communities racialized as minorities have a distinct awareness of the historical and contemporary injustices perpetuated through abuses in medical research, reproductive abuse, and health disparities (Russell 2016). The resulting mistrust (as Russell and many scholars of racial health inequality have noted) is far from what biomedicine or philosophy might deem "irrational" (Scharff et al. 2010; Williams and Mohammed 2009). And, as the nocebo literature so clearly outlines, an individual's level of mistrust, apprehension, or negative expectations about a given health-care encounter can be expressed through the physiology and neurobiology of the nocebo effect. Writing before nocebo studies emerged as a field of inquiry, Wynter anticipates the ways in which biochemical reward/punishment mechanisms—experienced on an individual level—reflect much broader systems-level processes: to be marked as "abnormal" is to live out the injuries and injustices of racializing violence, she explains, invoking the term *nocebo effect* to signify these bodymind experiences. Conversely, Wynter explains, to be unmarked in ways that cede to, or benefit from, "normalcy" is to live out the all-too-often unidentified whiteness of placebo effects (Wynter and McKittrick 2015: 50).

Such normalcy extends to the compulsory norms of "health" that underlie ideologies of ability.

Our understanding of nocebo dynamics is thus another way to reference the ways in which communally held stories and memories are lived as bodymind-harms for minoritized, disabled people (Clare 2017). Wide-ranging evidence of race-based health disparities can be understood in part through such disparate experiences of us/not-us within health systems (Varelmann et al. 2010). Nocebo effects, in particular, signal the likelihood that past negative experiences—the discomfort and alienation of being marked out, racialized, or stigmatized—shape the harms and injuries that take place through medical treatment and research (Friesen and Blease 2018b). The field of nocebo studies has begun to consider this explicitly, making links between nocebo effects and health inequities vis-à-vis unequal treatment on the basis of race and ethnicity, (poor) communication, medical mistrust, perceived discrimination, and racial discordance between providers and care recipients (Yetman et al. 2021; Friesen and Blease 2018b). Minoritized recipients of health care have awareness of both their own experiences of suboptimal, dismissive, or low-quality care and the experiences of others in this regard. This awareness creates expectations that, in turn, inform how subsequent interactions with clinicians will be interpreted. This awareness thus has implications for future health-related actions and impacts current health outcomes through a person's acceptance or refusal of interventions (which hails further looping effects related to the very offer of adequate treatment) and the meaning that is made of interventions, shaping capacities for treatment adherence (Yetman et al. 2021; see also Berkhout 2014 and Green et al. 2003).

Medicine and the Choreography of Harming

The nocebo effect reminds us that medical interactions take place in normatively structured social settings. If our presumptions about the starkness of the distinction between what is *curative* and what is *harmful* hinge on our own biosocial travels, then the normative claims of biomedicine can be called out as such: that is, as normalizing ideals rather than treatments that are effective, regardless of context. The qualities of a clinical setting, the interpersonal communication between providers and receivers of care, and the dynamics between them are *themselves* constitutive of health, healing, or its converse. By highlighting how marked bodies have historically been conditioned as such and the fallacy of this naturalization (see Ehlers and Krupar 2019: ch. 2 especially), nocebos make explicit the ontological choreography of harming. By revealing choreographies of harming, furthermore, nocebos disrupt the bifurcated logic of "us/not-us" that underpins markedness/unmarkedness, revealing material impacts of complex intersections of race, class, gender, and disability. Taking these effects of nocebos into account is especially important for thinking about the ways in which disability is perceived to be a natural site of abnormality and disabled people are disqualified on the basis of a negative ontology (Erevelles 2014).

To explore these claims further, we take up the notion of "ontological choreography" from Russell who, in turn, draws on the work of Charis Thompson. An ontological choreography makes reference to the dynamic coordination of the diverse assemblages (be they technical, scientific, gender, racial, legal, financial, kinship, etc.) that produce different kinds of being in a given setting (Russell 2018; Thompson 2005). Thompson and Russell specifically discuss this coordination in relation to assistive reproductive technology (ART). As Thompson describes, referencing ART,

> The term *ontological choreography* refers to the dynamic coordination of the technical, scientific, kinship, gender, emotional, legal, political, and financial aspects of ART clinics. What might appear to be an undifferentiated hybrid mess is actually a deftly balanced coming together of things that are generally considered parts of different ontological orders (part of nature, part of the self, part of society). (Thompson 2005: 8)

Thompson suggests, furthermore, that there is an extent to which this kind of choreography takes place in all spheres of human activity. We can thus think about the ways in which negative outcomes, adverse effects, harm, morbidity, and mortality are medicalized events that likewise have a kind of choreography and, in addition, that "outcomes" such as health inequity can be better understood by attending to the imbrication of the social with the biological.

We want to flag what Thompson calls "strategic naturalizing" as a crucial insight with respect to nocebos and the ontological choreography of harming. Strategic naturalizing concerns the sorting and classifying of some things and not others as biological facts of relevance and the resulting choreography that takes place as different boundaries are drawn around narratives that delineate what is deemed cultural versus natural. Modern medical settings, writes Thompson, regularly produce extended cultural and natural biologies through the coordination of social and natural roles and facts (Thompson 2001, 2005). Relationships are constructed and *then* naturalized (Russell 2018). When we attend to the particularities of nocebo effects, we can appreciate how very real, very material outcomes of discriminatory practices in health care reinscribe further bodied adverse effects, which include under- or un-treated disease, worsened pain, and death, and generated expectancies of disease, trauma, pain, and loss at the individual and community levels. These bodied adverse effects themselves coordinate with treatment algorithms, triage protocols, clinical scoring systems, and the like (Creary and Eisen 2013; Savitt et al. 2014; Roberts 2021), looping back to reinforce exclusionary politics, discriminatory practices, and palpable harms. Nocebos reveal the erasure of the social contexts that drive these feedback loops. By making apparent the individualizing of harms and demonstrating choreographies of harm, nocebos disrupt the bifurcated logic of nature/culture, mind/body, us/not-us.

At this point, a concrete example would be instructive. Consider the ways that medical rationing and triage protocols have been developed and implemented in COVID-19, as well as rightly critiqued from a health-equity perspective. Rationing refers to restrictions on medical supplies, interventions, and care—withholding potentially beneficiary treatments or interventions—from some defined segment of people (Srinivas et al. 2021). Triage protocols are the policies generated by health-care decision-makers that guide how rationing will take place. Globally throughout the COVID-19 pandemic, rationing in both critical and acute care has taken place, including: access to ventilation, to a hospital bed, to medical supplies such as personal protective equipment (PPE), and to therapeutics, particularly during surges of infection and periods of supply-chain interruption (Emanuel et al. 2020; Chen and McNamara 2020; Singh 2020). Triage protocols have been developed in many jurisdictions to address how to distribute "limited" medical resources in a consistent fashion. In some locations, these protocols have been created in reference to "crisis standards of care," which guide how changes in usual health-care operations ought to shift to a level of care that is possible to deliver during pervasive or catastrophic events (Committee on Guidance for Establishing Crisis Standards of Care for Use in Disaster Situations and Institute of Medicine 2012).

Disability scholars from a range of disciplines have flagged care rationing and triage protocols as enforcing discriminatory and unjust practices insofar as ableist assumptions are built into the decision algorithms. For example, the absence of disabled people from the committees that draft these protocols has been noted, as well as the lack of transparent, publicly available treatment-exclusion criteria. Other issues that disability scholars have flagged include the devaluation of disabled lives through metrics such as quality-adjusted life years (QALYs) and biases built into normative concepts such as medical futility (which themselves can be objectivized through the use of enumeration practices) that the protocols incorporate (Chen and McNamara 2020). Underlying conditions such as chronic obstructive pulmonary disease (COPD), chronic kidney disease (CKD), hypertension, asthma, and diabetes, among other bodied experiences, increase the likelihood of worsened COVID-19 outcomes. These conditions are also incorporated into the criteria of clinical predictions related to who will most likely benefit and recover from an intensive intervention.[4] In protocols where an institution aims toward maximizing benefit, people judged to have higher preexisting morbidity are ranked lower in priority for receiving a rationed intervention. In other contexts, even more crude markers (e.g., age alone or the presence or absence of intellectual or cognitive disability) have also been used (Orfali 2020; Bagenstos 2020). Pre-pandemic structural and institutional deficiencies are major contributors to what have been termed "preexisting conditions" in the pandemic, as well as the drivers of poorer health outcomes among disabled people compared to a nondisabled population, especially disabled people who are minoritized across additional axes of social power such as race (Sabatello et al. 2020; Yee et al. 2018). In short, triage protocols act on this inequity and further sediment it. Nocebo effects, as we described earlier, are a part of the looping of harm, biology, and difference that become further entrenched as biology when disabled people are deprioritized or refused care.

Thinking about care-rationing scenarios highlights the tension with which we engaged at the outset of this chapter: namely, between desiring disability and undermining ableist assumptions that intervention is an imperative for any disability, while also calling out the need for *more* medical access, especially to high-quality care delivered in a nondiscriminatory, equitable way. Identifying this tension *as a tension* is not meant to create a false dichotomy between the two positions but rather to draw attention to the ways in which the challenges facing disabled, minoritized individuals in health settings may be more complex than a straightforward revaluing of disability, though as our triage protocol example illustrates, valuing disabled lives *is* a central intervention into making medical spaces less discriminatory. We have named this tension (as a tension) in relation to care-rationing scenarios in order to suggest that our thinking about nocebos in reference to a choreography of harming is a way to think through the material implications of this tension and one of the ways in which it is playing out in a contemporary context.

Concluding Thoughts

As we suggest in our introduction, nocebo effects compel a kind of reflexivity within medicine and with philosophy and other critical, conceptual endeavors, particularly in relation to the ways in which intersecting axes of social power shape roles, spaces, and practices, and how this reflexivity is (and is not) taken up in research practices more broadly. Recognizing the biosocial dynamics of nocebo effects demands, therefore, a far more relational and far less reductive view of how cure and harm work in medicine. As the field of nocebo studies expands its gaze with respect to the implications of its findings, scholarship is urgently needed that brings together insights from across critically engaged fields, such as the work happening within feminist-of-color disability studies.

As much as nocebos might be understood as dramatizing the choreography of harming in medical research and practice, they are also a call to moral and political reckoning far beyond the bounds of medicine or biomedical research. Insofar as nocebos draw our attention to concrete differences across lived experience, attending to the differences aligns with what Kim, responding to Avril Minich, identifies as a critical disability methodology that radiates scholarship outward (Kim 2017). For feminist philosophy of disability, this expansive methodology may require anchoring our work in methodological innovations that radiate our scholarship beyond what is disciplined (and counted) *as* philosophy. As Schalk and Kim note in their own discussion of method, engagement with lived experience through the stories we tell about our own bodyminds is one example (Schalk and Kim 2020). In philosophy, this expansive experiential methodology might look like transdisciplinary research practices, it might include reading more broadly beyond what is typical of philosophical analysis, or it might involve the kind of engagement with the field that Shelley Tremain offers through her long-standing Dialogues on Disability series of open-access interviews with disabled philosophers. Tremain's contributions to the field, which sit beyond the more conventional manuscripts and books/book chapters, are an instance (and there are many others) of what a critical disability methodology might look like (see Tremain n.d.). Following the work of feminist researchers who, in the words of Stengers and Vinciane Despret, find ways to "re-mark what the scientists' claim to universality makes invisible" (Stengers and Despret 2014: 29), nocebo effects invite us to "re-mark" our own methods, our own relational interactions, and our own objects of inquiry.

Notes

1 Shelley Tremain identifies the feedback loop between prevailing methods in philosophy and the practices of hiring committees that maintain and reinforce ableist exclusions in the discipline itself (Tremain 2017, 2020). In an open educational resource, we point to specific ways in which psychiatrists and other clinicians can likewise reinforce exclusionary dynamics within medical contexts (Jaarsma and Berkhout 2022). Akemi Nishida reminds us that academic workers

risk supporting the hierarchies of ableism and the values of white supremacy and settler colonialism (Nishida 2018).

2 The muscle aches and pains denoted as plausible nocebo effects were reflective of generalized myalgias, not specific injection site reactions. One would expect injection site muscle pain to be similar across trials arms given that placebo control participants would also receive an injection (sterile saline) into the deltoid muscle.

3 The nocebo literature suggests that the style and manner of a physician, that is, whether they are experienced as warm and competent versus as cool/distant and with low competence, modifies the extent to which expectancies about an intervention generate nocebo and placebo effects. These findings have cut across different experimental paradigms including in the study of pain as well as the impact of histamine on allergic reaction (See Necka et al. 2021; Howe, Goyer, and Crum 2017).

4 Notably, some underlying conditions have also been demonstrated to reflect racist discriminatory practices through the clinical scores and metrics that define when interventions ought to be offered. As Dorothy Roberts has argued (Roberts 2021), race-based correction of estimated glomerular filtration rate (eGFR) in chronic kidney disease, concretizes worse health outcomes; Elaine Ku et al. have likewise demonstrated how seemingly standard clinical evaluation metrics can result in racial disparities in relation to kidney transplantation, because of racialized assumptions built into practices of standardization (Ku et al. 2021).

References

Alexander, M. Jacqui (2006), *Pedagogies of Crossing: Meditations on Feminism, Sexual Politics, Memory, and the Sacred*, Durham: Duke University Press.

Bagenstos, Samuel R. (2020), "Who Gets the Ventilator? Disability Discrimination in COVID-19 Medical-Rationing Protocols," *Yale Law Journal*. Available at: https://www.yalelawjournal.org/forum/who-gets-the-ventilator (accessed June 19, 2023).

Bailey, Moya and Izetta Autumn Mobley (2019), "Work in the Intersections: A Black Feminist Disability Framework," *Gender and Society* 33 (1): 19–40. https://doi.org/10.1177/0891243218801523.

Bajcar, E. A. and P. Babel (2018), "How Does Observational Learning Produce Placebo Effects? A Model Integrating Research Findings," *Frontiers in Psychology*, 9: 2041. https://doi.org/10.3389/fpsyg.2018.02041.

Ben-Moshe, Liat and Sandy Magaña (2014), "An Introduction to Race, Gender, and Disability: Intersectionality, Disability Studies, and Families of Color," *Women, Gender, and Families of Color* 2 (2): 105–14. https://doi.org/10.5406/womgenfamcol.2.2.0105.

Benedetti, F., M. Lanotte, L. Lopiano, and L. Colloca (2007), "When Words Are Painful: Unraveling the Mechanisms of the Nocebo Effect," *Neuroscience* 147 (2): 260–71.

Berkhout, Suze (2014), "Bad Reputations: Memory, Corporeality, and the Limitations of Hacking's Looping Effects," *Phaenex: Journal of Existential and Phenomenological Theory and Culture* 9 (2): 43–63.

Berkhout, Suze G. and Ada S. Jaarsma (2018), "Trafficking in Cure and Harm: Placebos, Nocebos and the Curative Imaginary," *Disability Studies Quarterly* 38 (4). https://doi.org/10.18061/dsq.v38i4.6369.

Berkhout, Suze G., Ada S. Jaarsma, Maya Morton Ninomiya, and Eva-Marie Stern (forthcoming), "Placebo and Nocebo Keyimages," in Lisa Dietrich and Briana Martino (eds.), *Keywords and Keyimages in Graphic Medicine*, University Park: Penn State University Press.

Bingel, U. and M. Schedlowski (2014), "The Role of Placebo Mechanisms in Pain Therapy," *Aktuelle Neurologie* 41 (5): 287–93. https://doi.org/10.1055/s-0034-1376961.

Bohrer, Ashley J. (2020), "Toward a Decolonial Feminist Anticapitalism: María Lugones, Sylvia Wynter, and Sayak Valencia," *Hypatia: A Journal of Feminist Philosophy* 35 (3): 524–41.

Chavarria, V., J. Vian, C. Pereira, J. Data-Franco, B. S. Fernandes, M. Berk, and S. Dodd (2017), "The Placebo and Nocebo Phenomena: Their Clinical Management and Impact on Treatment Outcomes," *Clinical Therapeutics* 39 (3): 477–86. https://doi.org/10.1016/j.clinthera.2017.01.031.

Chen, Bo and Donna Marie McNamara (2020), "Disability Discrimination, Medical Rationing and COVID-19," *Asian Bioethics Review* 12 (4): 511–18. https://doi.org/10.1007/s41649-020-00147-x.

Chen, Mel Y. (2021), "Feminisms in the Air," *Signs: Journal of Women in Culture and Society* 47 (1): 22–9.

Cho, Sumi, Kimberlé Williams Crenshaw, and Leslie McCall (2013), "Toward a Field of Intersectionality Studies: Theory, Applications, and Praxis," *Signs: Journal of Women in Culture and Society* 38 (4): 785–810. https://doi.org/10.1086/669608.

Clare, Eli (2017), *Brilliant Imperfection*, Durham: Duke University Press.

Colloca, Luana (2017), "Nocebo Effects Can Make You Feel Pain," *Science* 358 (6359): 44. https://doi.org/10.1126/science.aap8488.

Committee on Guidance for Establishing Crisis Standards of Care for Use in Disaster Situations and Institute of Medicine (2012), *Crisis Standards of Care: A Systems Framework for Catastrophic Disaster Response*, Washington: National Academies Press. Available at: https://www.ncbi.nlm.nih.gov/books/NBK201063/ (accessed July 24, 2023).

Creary, Melissa and Arri Eisen (2013), "Acknowledging Levels of Racism in the Definition of 'Difficult'," *The American Journal of Bioethics* 13 (4): 16–18. https://doi.org/10.1080/15265161.2013.767964.

Crenshaw, Kimberlé (1991), "Mapping the Margins: Intersectionality, Identity Politics, and Violence against Women of Color," *Stanford Law Review* 43 (6): 1241–99. https://doi.org/10.2307/1229039.

Dolmage, Jay Timothy (2017), *Academic Ableism: Disability and Higher Education*, Ann Arbor: University of Michigan Press.

Dotson, Kristie and Marita Gilbert (2014), "Curious Disappearances: Affectability Imbalances and Process-Based Invisibility," *Hypatia: A Journal of Feminist Philosophy* 29 (4): 873–88.

Ehlers, Nadine and Shiloh Krupar (2019), *Deadly Biocultures: The Ethics of Life-Making*, Minneapolis: University of Minnesota Press.

Emanuel, Ezekiel J., Govind Persad, Ross Upshur, Beatriz Thome, Michael Parker, Aaron Glickman, Cathy Zhang, Connor Boyle, Maxwell Smith, and James P. Phillips (2020), "Fair Allocation of Scarce Medical Resources in the Time of

Covid-19," *New England Journal of Medicine* 382 (21): 2049–55. https://doi.org/10.1056/NEJMsb2005114.

Enck, P., F. Benedetti, and M. Schedlowski (2008), "New Insights into the Placebo and Nocebo Responses," *Neuron* 59 (2): 195–206. https://doi.org/10.1016/j.neuron.2008.06.030.

Erevelles, Nirmala (2014), "Crippin' Jim Crow: Disability, Dis-Location, and the School-to-Prison Pipeline," in Liat Ben-Moshe, Chris Chapman, and Allison C. Carey (eds.), *Disability Incarcerated: Imprisonment and Disability in the United States and Canada*, 81–99, New York: Palgrave Macmillan US. https://doi.org/10.1057/9781137388476_5.

Evers, Andrea W. M., Luana Colloca, Charlotte Blease, Marco Annoni, Lauren Y. Atlas, Fabrizio Benedetti, Ulrike Bingel, et al. (2018), "Implications of Placebo and Nocebo Effects for Clinical Practice: Expert Consensus," *Psychotherapy and Psychosomatics* 87 (4): 204–10. https://doi.org/10.1159/000490354.

Fanon, Frantz (2008), *Black Skin, White Masks*, trans. Richard Philcox, New York: Grove Press.

Friesen, Phoebe and Charlotte Blease (2018a), "Placebo Effects and Racial and Ethnic Health Disparities: An Unjust and Underexplored Connection," *Journal of Medical Ethics* 44 (11): 774–81. https://doi.org/10.1136/medethics-2018-104811.

Friesen, Phoebe and Charlotte Blease (2018b), "Placebo Effects and Racial and Ethnic Health Disparities: An Unjust and Underexplored Connection," *Journal of Medical Ethics* 44 (11): 774–81.

Fritsch, Kelly (2015), "Desiring Disability Differently: Neoliberalism, Heterotopic Imagination and Intra-Corporeal Reconfigurations," *Foucault Studies*, June, 43. https://doi.org/10.22439/fs.v0i19.4824.

Garland-Thomson, Rosemarie (2011), "Misfits: A Feminist Materialist Disability Concept," *Hypatia: A Journal of Feminist Philosophy* 26 (3): 591–609.

Gracely, R. H., R. Dubner, W. R. Deeter, and P. J. Wolskee (1985), "Clinicians Expectations Influence Placebo Analgesia," *Lancet* 1 (8419): 43–43.

Green, Carmen R., Karen O. Anderson, Tamara A. Baker, Lisa C. Campbell, Sheila Decker, Roger B. Fillingim, Donna A. Kalauokalani, et al. (2003), "The Unequal Burden of Pain: Confronting Racial and Ethnic Disparities in Pain," *Pain Medicine (Malden, Mass.)* 4 (3): 277–94. https://doi.org/10.1046/j.1526-4637.2003.03034.x.

Haas, Julia W., Friederike L. Bender, Sarah Ballou, John M. Kelley, Marcel Wilhelm, Franklin G. Miller, Winfried Rief, and Ted J. Kaptchuk (2022), "Frequency of Adverse Events in the Placebo Arms of COVID-19 Vaccine Trials: A Systematic Review and Meta-Analysis," *JAMA Network Open* 5 (1): e2143955. https://doi.org/10.1001/jamanetworkopen.2021.43955.

Hahn, R. A. (1997), "The Nocebo Phenomenon: Concept, Evidence, and Implications for Public Health – Review," *Preventive Medicine* 26 (5): 607–11. https://doi.org/10.1006/pmed.1996.0124.

Hamraie, Aimi (2016), "Universal Design and the Problem of 'Post-Disability' Ideology," *Design and Culture* 8 (3): 285–309.

Hamraie, Aimi and Kelly Fritsch (2019), "Crip Technoscience Manifesto," *Catalyst: Feminism, Theory, Technoscience* 5 (1): 1–33. https://doi.org/10.28968/cftt.v5i1.29607.

Hendren, Sara (2020), *What Can a Body Do? How We Meet the Build World*, New York: Riverhead Books.

Howe, Lauren C., J. Parker Goyer, and Alia J. Crum (2017), "Harnessing the Placebo Effect: Exploring the Influence of Physician Characteristics on Placebo Response," *Health Psychology: Official Journal of the Division of Health Psychology, American Psychological Association* 36 (11): 1074–82. https://doi.org/10.1037/hea0000499.

Howick, Jeremy (2021), "Unethical Informed Consent Caused by Overlooking Poorly Measured Nocebo Effects," *Journal of Medical Ethics* 47: 590–4.

Jaarsma, Ada S. (2020), "Critical Disability Studies and the Problem of Method," in Carol A. Taylor, Christina Hughes, and Jasmine B. Ulmer (eds.), *Transdisciplinary Feminist Research Practices*, 16–28, New York: Routledge.

Jaarsma, Ada S. and Suze G. Berkhout (2019), "Nocebos and the Psychic Life of Biopower," *Symposium* (*Canadian Society for Continental Philosophy*) 23 (2): 67–93.

Jaarsma, Ada S. and Suze G. Berkhout (2022), "Cartesianism," in P. Ballamingie and D. Szanto (eds.), *Showing Theory to Know Theory: Understanding Social Science Concepts through Illustrative Vignettes*, Ottawa: Showing Theory Press. Available at: https://ecampusontario.pressbooks.pub/showingtheory/chapter/cartesianism/ (accessed June 19, 2023).

Kafer, Alison (2013), *Feminist Queer Crip*, Bloomington: Indiana University Press.

Kennedy, W. P. (1961), "The Nocebo Reaction," *Medical World* 95 (September): 203–5.

Kim, Jina B. (2017), "Toward a Crip-of-Color Critique: Thinking with Minich's 'Enabling Whom?'," *Lateral* 6 (1). https://doi.org/10.25158/L6.1.14.

Kong, J., R. L. Gollub, G. Polich, I. Kirsch, P. LaViolette, M. Vangel, B. Rosen, and T. J. Kaptchuk (2008), "A Functional Magnetic Resonance Imaging Study on the Neural Mechanisms of Hyperalgesic Nocebo Effect," *Journal of Neuroscience* 28 (49): 13354–62. https://doi.org/10.1523/JNEUROSCI.2944-08.2008.

Ku, Elaine, Charles E. McCulloch, Deborah B. Adey, Libo Li, and Kirsten L. Johansen (2021), "Racial Disparities in Eligibility for Preemptive Waitlisting for Kidney Transplantation and Modification of EGFR Thresholds to Equalize Waitlist Time," *Journal of the American Society of Nephrology* 32 (3): 677–85. https://doi.org/10.1681/ASN.2020081144.

Lamm, Nomy (2015), "This Is Disability Justice," *The Body Is Not an Apology* (blog). September 2. Available at: https://thebodyisnotanapology.com/magazine/this-is-disability-justice/ (accessed June 19, 2023).

Manaï, Meriem, Henriët van Middendorp, Dieuwke S. Veldhuijzen, Tom W. J. Huizinga, and Andrea W. M. Evers (2019), "How to Prevent, Minimize, or Extinguish Nocebo Effects in Pain: A Narrative Review on Mechanisms, Predictors, and Interventions," *Pain Reports* 4 (3): e699. https://doi.org/10.1097/PR9.0000000000000699.

Necka, Elizabeth A., Carolyn Amir, Troy C. Dildine, and Lauren Y. Atlas (2021), "Expectations about Pain and Analgesic Treatment Are Shaped by Medical Providers' Facial Appearances: Evidence from Five Online Clinical Simulation Experiments," *Social Science & Medicine (1982)* 281 (July): 114091. https://doi.org/10.1016/j.socscimed.2021.114091.

Nishida, Akemi (2018), "Critical Disability Praxis," in Katie Ellis, Rosemarie Garland-Thomson, Mike Kent, and Rachel Robertson (eds.), *Manifestos for the Future of Critical Disability Studies*, vol. 1, 239–47, New York: Routledge.

Orfali, Kristina (2020), "What Triage Issues Reveal: Ethics in the COVID-19 Pandemic in Italy and France," *Journal of Bioethical Inquiry*, November, 1–5. https://doi.org/10.1007/s11673-020-10059-y.

paperson, la (2017), *A Third University Is Possible*, Minneapolis: University of Minnesota Press.

Price, Margaret (2015), "The Bodymind Problem and the Possibilities of Pain," *Hypatia: A Journal of Feminist Philosophy* 30 (1): 268–84.
Price, Margaret (2021), "Time Harms: Disabled Faculty Navigating the Accommodations Loop," *The South Atlantic Quarterly* 120 (2): 257–77.
Roberts, Dorothy E. (2021), "Abolish Race Correction," *The Lancet* 397 (10268): 17–18. https://doi.org/10.1016/S0140-6736(20)32716-1.
Rossettini, Gioacomo, Eleonora Maria Camerone, Elisa Carlino, Fabrizio Benedetti, and Marco Testa (2020), "Context Matters: The Psychoneurobiological Determinants of Placebo, Nocebo, and Context-Related Effects in Physiotherapy," *Archives of Physiotherapy* 10 (11).
Russell, Camisha A. (2016), "Questions of Race in Bioethics: Deceit, Disregard, Disparity, and the Work of Decentering," *Philosophy Compass* 11 (1): 43–55. https://doi.org/10.1111/phc3.12302.
Russell, Camisha A. (2018), *The Assisted Reproduction of Race*, Bloomington: Indiana University Press.
Sabatello, Maya, Teresa Blankmeyer Burke, Katherine E. McDonald, and Paul S. Appelbaum (2020), "Disability, Ethics, and Health Care in the COVID-19 Pandemic," *American Journal of Public Health* 110 (10): 1523–7. https://doi.org/10.2105/AJPH.2020.305837.
Savitt, Todd L., Wally R. Smith, Carlton Haywood, and Melissa S. Creary (2014), "Use of the Word 'Crisis' in Sickle Cell Disease: The Language of Sickle Cell," *Journal of the National Medical Association* 106 (1): 23–30. https://doi.org/10.1016/S0027-9684(15)30067-5.
Schalk, Sami (2017), "Critical Disability Studies as Methodology," *Lateral* 6 (1).
Schalk, Sami and Jina B. Kim (2020), "Integrating Race, Transforming Feminist Disability Studies," *Signs: Journal of Women in Culture and Society* 46 (11): 31–55.
Scharff, Darcell P., Katherine J. Mathews, Pamela Jackson, Jonathan Hoffsuemmer, Emeobong Martin, and Dorothy Edwards (2010), "More than Tuskegee: Understanding Mistrust about Research Participation," *Journal of Health Care for the Poor and Underserved* 21 (3): 879–97. https://doi.org/10.1353/hpu.0.0323.
Schienle, A, C. Hofler, S. Ubel, and A. Wabnegger (2018), "Emotion-Specific Nocebo Effects: An FMRI Study," *Brain Imaging and Behaviour* 12 (1): 180–7. https://doi.org/10.1007/s11682-017-9675-1.
Singh, Satendra (2020), "Disability Ethics in the Coronavirus Crisis," *Journal of Family Medicine and Primary Care* 9 (5): 2167–71. https://doi.org/10.4103/jfmpc.jfmpc_588_20.
Srinivas, G., R. Maanasa, M. Meenakshi, J. M. Adaikalam, S. Seshayyan, and T. Muthuvel (2021), "Ethical Rationing of Healthcare Resources during COVID-19 Outbreak: Review," *Ethics, Medicine, and Public Health* 16 (March): 100633. https://doi.org/10.1016/j.jemep.2021.100633.
St. Pierre, Joshua (2022), *Cheap Talk: Disability and the Politics of Communication*, Ann Arbor: University of Michigan Press.
Stengers, Isabelle (2002), "Beyond Conversation: The Risks of Peace," in Catherine Keller and Anne Danielle (eds.), *Process and Difference: Between Cosmological and Poststructuralist Postmodernisms*, 235–55, Albany: State University of New York.
Stengers, Isabelle and Vinciane Despret (2014), *Women Who Make A Fuss: The Unfaithful Daughters of Virginia Woolf*, Minneapolis: Univocal Publishing.
Stevenson, Lisa (2014), *Life Beside Itself: Imagining Care in the Canadian Arctic*, Berkeley: University of California Press.

Thomaidou, M. A., K. J. Peerdeman, M. I. Koppeschaar, A. W. M. Evers, and D. S. Veldhuijzen (2021), "How Negative Experience Influences the Brain: A Comprehensive Review of the Neurobiological Underpinnings of Nocebo Hyperalgesia," *Frontiers in Neuroscience*: 652552. https://doi.org/10.3389/fnins.2021.652552.

Thompson, Charis (2001), "Strategic Naturalizing: Kinship in an Infertility Clinic," in *Relative Values: Reconfiguring Kinship Studies*, 175–202, Durham: Duke University Press.

Thompson, Charis (2005), *Making Parents: The Ontological Choreography of Reproductive Technologies*, Cambridge, MA: MIT Press.

Tremain, Shelley (n.d.), "Dialogues on Disability," BIOPOLITICAL PHILOSOPHY (blog). Available at: https://biopoliticalphilosophy.com/dialogues-on-disability/ (accessed June 19, 2023).

Tremain, Shelley L. (2017), *Foucault and Feminist Philosophy of Disability*, Ann Arbor: University of Michigan Press.

Tremain, Shelley Lynn (2020), "Field Notes on the Naturalization and Denaturalization of Disability in (Feminist) Philosophy," *Feminist Philosophy Quarterly* 6 (3). https://doi.org/10.5206/fpq/2020.3.9395.

Urciuoli, Bonnie (2011), "Semiotic Properties of Racializing Discourses," *Linguistic Anthropology* 21 (S1): E113–22.

Valentine, Desiree (2022), "Racialized Disablement and the Need for Conceptual Analysis of 'Racial Health Disparities,'" *Bioethics* 36: 336–45.

Varelmann, Dirk, Carlo Pancaro, Eric C. Cappiello, and William R. Camann (2010), "Nocebo-Induced Hyperalgesia during Local Anesthetic Injection," *Anesthesia and Analgesia* 110 (3): 868–70. https://doi.org/10.1213/ANE.0b013e3181cc5727.

Vinckier, Fabien, Sophie Betka, Nathalie Nion, Laure Serresse, and Thomas Similowski (2021), "Harnessing the Power of Anticipation to Manage Respiratory-Related Brain Suffering and Ensuing Dyspnoea: Insights from the Neurobiology of the Respiratory Nocebo Effect," *European Respiratory Journal* 58 (3). https://doi.org/10.1183/13993003.01876-2021.

Vogtle, E., A. Barke, and B. Kroner-Herwig (2013), "Nocebo Hyperalgesia Induced by Social Observational Learning," *Pain* 154 (8): 1427–33. https://doi.org/10.1016/j.pain.2013.04.041.

Williams, David R. and Selina A. Mohammed (2009), "Discrimination and Racial Disparities in Health: Evidence and Needed Research," *Journal of Behavioral Medicine* 32 (1): 20–47. https://doi.org/10.1007/s10865-008-9185-0.

Wilson, Elizabeth A. (2015), *Gut Feminism*, Durham: Duke University Press.

Wynter, Sylvia (1987), "On Disenchanting Discourse: 'Minority' Literary Criticism and Beyond," *Cultural Critique* 7: 207–44.

Wynter, Sylvia (2003), "Unsettling the Coloniality of Being/Power/Truth/Freedom: Towards the Human, After Man, Its Overrepresentation-An Argument," *The New Centennial Review* 3 (3): 257–337.

Wynter, Sylvia, Joshua Bennett, and Jarvis R. Givens (2020), "'A Greater Truth than Any Other Truth You Know': A Conversation with Professor Sylvia Wynter on Origin Stories," *Souls* 22 (1): 123–37.

Wynter, Sylvia and Katherine McKittrick (2015), "Unparalleled Catastrophe for Our Species? Or, to Give Humanness a Different Future: Conversations," in Katherine McKittrick (ed.), *Being Human as Praxis*, 9–89, Durham: Duke University Press.

Yee, Silvia, Mary Lou Breslin, Tawara D. Goode, Susan M. Havercamp, Willi Horner-Johnson, Lisa I. Iezzoni, and Gloria Krahn (2018), *Compounded Disparities: Health*

Equity at the Intersection of Disability, Race, and Ethnicity, Washington, DC: The National Academies of Sciences, Engineering and Medicine.
Yergeau, Melanie (2017), *Authoring Autism: On Rhetoric and Neurological Queerness*, Durham: Duke University Press.
Yetman, Hailey E., Nevada Cox, Shelley R. Adler, Kathryn T. Hall, and Valerie E. Stone (2021), "What Do Placebo and Nocebo Effects Have to Do With Health Equity? The Hidden Toll of Nocebo Effects on Racial and Ethnic Minority Patients in Clinical Care," *Frontiers in Psychology* 12: 788230. Available at: https://www.frontiersin.org/article/10.3389/fpsyg.2021.788230 (accessed June 19, 2023).

INDEX

CONTRIBUTORS

Suze G. Berkhout is Assistant Professor at the University of Toronto. She is an early career clinician-investigator and a practicing psychiatrist. Her program of research in feminist STS utilizes ethnographic and narrative qualitative methods to explore social and cultural issues impacting access and navigation through health-care systems. She focuses on the epistemic and ontological importance of lived experience in relation to knowledge in/of medicine and related to mental health especially.

Samantha Brennan is Dean of the College of Arts and Professor of Philosophy of the University of Guelph (Guelph, Ontario, Canada). Her primary research interests are in normative ethics and feminist philosophy, and much of her recent work concerns children's rights and family justice.

Licia Carlson is Professor of Philosophy at Providence College. She has published widely in the area of philosophy of disability, and her research interests include feminist philosophy, bioethics, twentieth-century French philosophy, and the philosophy of music. She has co-edited three volumes and is the author of *The Faces of Intellectual Disability* (2009) and *Shared Musical Lives: Philosophy, Disability, and the Power of Sonification* (2022). She is also a violinist with the Longwood Symphony Orchestra.

Amandine Catala is Full Professor in the Department of Philosophy at the Université du Québec à Montréal (UQAM), where she holds the Canada Research Chair on Epistemic Injustice and Agency. She is Senior Research Associate at the African Centre for Epistemology and Philosophy of Science (ACEPS) at the University of Johannesburg. She is an Autistic self-advocate and a co-founder of the Autistic Collective of UQAM, an initiative that aims to bring together and support Autistics who study, work, or teach at UQAM. Her research and teaching focus on feminist, social, and political philosophy and philosophy of disability, which also inform her service.

Robert Chapman is a socially neurodivergent and fiscally communist philosopher. They are currently an Assistant Professor in Critical Neurodiversity Studies at Durham University and have previously worked at Bristol University, Sheffield Hallam, and King's College London. Their first book, *Empire of Normality: Neurodiversity and Capitalism*, is published with Pluto Press, and provides a new history of the normal mind that clarifies precisely how neurodivergent oppression is bound up with the deep logics of capitalism.

Mich Ciurria is a queer, gender-variant, disabled philosopher who works mainly on Marxist feminism and critical disability theory. She completed her Ph.D. at York University in Toronto and subsequently held postdoctoral fellowships at Washington University in St. Louis and the University of New South Wales, Sydney. They are the author of *An Intersectional Feminist Theory of Moral Responsibility* (Routledge, 2019) and a regular contributor to BIOPOLITICAL PHILOSOPHY, the leading blog on critical disability theory.

Tommy J. Curry is Professor of Philosophy and holds a Personal Chair of Africana Philosophy and Black Male Studies at the University of Edinburgh. He is the author of *The Man-Not: Race, Class, Genre, and the Dilemmas of Black Manhood* (2017), which won the 2018 American Book Award. He is the author of *Another White Man's Burden: Josiah Royce's Quest for a Philosophy of Racial Empire* (2018), which recently won the 2020 Josiah Royce Prize in American Idealist Thought. His research explores anti-Black racism and the sexual vulnerability of Black males throughout Western societies.

Josh Dohmen is Assistant Professor of Philosophy at Mississippi University for Women. His research focuses on feminist epistemology, twentieth-century Continental philosophy, and the philosophy of disability as resources for enriching ethical and political thought. Josh is grateful to the students in his Knowledge, Power, Reality seminar for thoughtful discussions related to his contribution to this volume.

Emily R. Douglas recently graduated with a Ph.D. in Philosophy and Certificate in Women's and Gender Studies from McGill University. They teach in the Humanities Department at Vanier College and in the Philosophy Department for Athabasca University.

Gen Eickers is interim professor/lecturer in epistemology at the University of Bayreuth (Germany). Gen's work is mostly concerned with critical philosophy of mind, that is, their work is located at the intersections of philosophy of mind, social epistemology, and social ontology. Their research looks at the contribution of contextual factors and social norms to psychological and epistemological phenomena, and addresses questions around social cognition and social interaction, theories of emotion and emotional expression, and gender and trans philosophy.

Johnathan Flowers is Assistant Professor of Philosophy at California State University, Northridge. Flowers's research areas include African American intellectual history, Japanese aesthetics, American pragmatism, philosophy of disability, and philosophy of technology. Flowers also works in the areas of science and technology studies and comics studies, where he applies insights from American pragmatism, philosophy of race, and disability studies to current issues in human/computer interaction, artificial intelligence and machine learning, and representations of identity in popular culture. His first monograph, *Mono no Aware as a Poetics of Gender*, was published by Lexington Books in 2023.

Élaina Gauthier-Mamaril is a disabled Filipinx philosopher who has a background in feminist interpretations of Spinoza. Her research projects include exploring the intersections between philosophy of disability, Spinoza, and Filipino philosophy. As an interdisciplinary research fellow with the Centre for Biomedicine, Self and Society at the Usher Institute in the University of Edinburgh, Élaina is pursuing cripistemological research on long-COVID. She hosts and produces Philosophy Casting Call, an interview podcast that features underrepresented philosophers, and holds a Ph.D. in philosophy from the University of Aberdeen.

August Gorman is Assistant Professor of Philosophy at Oakland University. They are a disabled philosopher of disability, whose research interests focus on neurodiversity, moral responsibility, well-being, and the philosophy of death. Throughout their publications, they argue for the incorporation of a broader conception of the possibilities of human agency into analyses of ethical concepts.

Lori Gruen is William Griffin Professor of Philosophy at Wesleyan University, where she coordinates Wesleyan Animal Studies. She is the author and editor of more than a dozen books, including *Ethics and Animals: An Introduction* (2011, second edition 2021), *Entangled Empathy* (2015), *Animal Crisis* (2022, coauthored with Alice Crary), *Carceral Logics* (2022, co-edited with Justin Marceau), *Critical Terms for Animal Studies* (2018), *Ecofeminism: Feminist Intersections with Other Animals and the Earth* (2014, second edition 2022, co-edited with Carol J. Adams), and *Ethics of Captivity* (2014). Gruen is one of the faculty founders of the Center for Prison Education at Wesleyan.

Melinda C. Hall (Ph.D., Vanderbilt University) is Associate Professor and Chair of Philosophy at Stetson University. Hall is the author of *The Bioethics of Enhancement: Transhumanism, Disability, and Biopolitics* (2016). Her current book projects focus on risk and a disability history of philosophy. Hall is the author of articles published in *Disability Studies Quarterly*, *International Journal of Feminist Approaches to Bioethics*, *Philosophy Compass*, and the *Stanford Encyclopedia of Philosophy*, among other venues.

Ada S. Jaarsma is Professor of Philosophy at Mount Royal University in Calgary, where she teaches Continental philosophy, critical theory, philosophy of science, queer theory, and feminist philosophy. Her publications include a co-edited collection *Dissonant Methods: Undoing Discipline in the Humanities Classroom* (2020) and *Kierkegaard after the Genome: Science, Existence, and Belief in This World* (2017). She is an associate editor of *Symposium: Canadian Journal of Continental Philosophy*.

Stephanie C. Jenkins is Associate Professor in the School of History, Philosophy, and Religion at Oregon State University. Her research and teaching interests include feminist philosophy, disability studies, critical animal studies, and ethics. In addition to publishing scholarly articles in moral philosophy, she is a co-editor of *Disability and Animality: Crip Perspectives in Critical Animal Studies* (2020), as well as a special issue of the *Public Philosophy Journal* (2022).

Sofia Jeppsson defended her dissertation *Practical Perspective Compatibilism* in 2012. She continued to publish mostly on abstract questions relating to free will and moral responsibility, and to some extent on applied ethics, while holding fixed-term positions at Stockholm University and the University of Gothenburg. In 2018, she was fortunate enough to land a permanent job with good job security at Umeå University, a position she still holds. She then felt safe enough to fully come out as Mad. Although still largely focused on issues of agency and moral responsibility, Jeppsson has turned her attention to madness and psychiatry and openly draws on her own experiences.

Corinne Lajoie is a Ph.D. candidate at the Pennsylvania State University. Their research focuses on disability, access, disorientation, and belonging. Their work has been published in publications such as *The Journal of the American Philosophical Association*, *Hypatia: A Journal of Feminist Philosophy*, and *Chiasmi: Trilingual Studies Concerning the Thought of Merleau-Ponty*.

Julie E. Maybee (Professor, Department of Philosophy, and Coordinator, Disability Studies Minor, Lehman College, City University of New York) is the author of *Making and Unmaking Disability: The Three-Body Approach*; *Picturing*

Hegel: An Illustrated Guide to Hegel's Encyclopaedia Logic; and articles on African philosophy, educational theory, race, and nineteenth-century Continental philosophy. Her work is united by an interest in how socially defined differences (and time and place) shape people's identities, knowledge, and experiences.

Nathan Moore is Site Manager of the Math-Physics Accelerator Help Centre at Western University in Canada. He has a Ph.D. in philosophy from Western University and research interests in neurodiversity, autistic identity, epistemic injustice, nonpropositional knowledge, epistemic responsibility, and the intersection of epistemic responsibility with moral, social, and political responsibility.

Christine Overall is Professor Emerita of Philosophy and holds a University Research Chair at Queen's University in Kingston, Ontario. An elected Fellow of the Royal Society of Canada, she is the author of six books and the editor or co-editor of five, including *Aging, Death, and Human Longevity: A Philosophical Inquiry* (2003), and *Why Have Children? The Ethical Debate* (2012). She has published more than 110 articles and book chapters. Her research and publications are in the areas of procreative ethics, feminist philosophy, philosophy of religion, and philosophy of ageing and death.

Andrea J. Pitts is Associate Professor of Comparative Literature at the University at Buffalo. They are author of *Nos/Otras: Gloria E. Anzaldúa, Multiplicitous Agency, and Resistance* (2021) and co-editor with Mark Westmoreland of *Beyond Bergson: Examining Race and Colonialism through the Writings of Henri Bergson* (2019) and *Theories of the Flesh: Latinx and Latin American Feminisms, Transformation, and Resistance* with Mariana Ortega and José M. Medina (2020).

Kristin Rodier is Assistant Professor of Philosophy at Athabasca University (Treaty 6 territory, Métis Region 4). Her current writing explores a critical phenomenology of the body, intersecting fatness, gender, ability, and race. Her research in feminist philosophy centers conceptions of agency underlying theories of resisting oppression.

Tim Stainton is Professor in the School of Social Work at the University of British Columbia and Co-Director of the Canadian Institute for Inclusion and Citizenship. He has written widely on issues of ethics, history, and policy with regard to intellectual and developmental disability and has been active in the disability rights movement for the past forty years.

Joshua St. Pierre is Canada Research Chair (Tier 2) in Critical Disability Studies and Assistant Professor of Political Science at the University of Alberta. Working at the intersection of critical disability studies, contemporary political theory, and feminist theory, his research focuses on the interplay of communication and disability within information societies. His first monograph is titled *Cheap Talk: Disability and the Politics of Communication.*

Joseph A. Stramondo (he/him/his) is Associate Professor of Philosophy and Director of the Institute for Ethics and Public Affairs at San Diego State University. His research mainly focuses on the intersection of bioethics and philosophy of disability and appears in venues such as *The Hastings Center Report*, *Ethical Theory and Moral Practice*, *Ergo*, *Utilitas*, *Social Theory and Practice*, *Kennedy Institute for Ethics Journal*, and *Theoretical Medicine and Bioethics*.

Shelley Lynn Tremain holds a Ph.D. in philosophy and publishes on a range of topics including ableism in philosophy; Foucault and disability; biopolitics; disability and responsibility; and disability, eugenics, and MAiD. From April 2015, Tremain has coordinated, edited, and produced Dialogues on Disability, the groundbreaking and critically acclaimed series of interviews that she is conducting with disabled philosophers and posts to BIOPOLITICAL PHILOSOPHY, the philosophy blog that she coordinates with Melinda Hall. Tremain is the author of *Foucault and Feminist Philosophy of Disability* (2017), the manuscript for which was awarded the 2016 Tobin Siebers Prize for Disability Studies in the Humanities; the editor of two editions of *Foucault and the Government of Disability* (2005; 2015); and the editor of *The Bloomsbury Guide to Philosophy of Disability* (2023). She is currently writing a book entitled *Disabling Philosophy*.

Desiree Valentine is Assistant Professor of Philosophy at Marquette University. Her research lies at the intersection of critical philosophy of race, critical disability theory, feminist philosophy, and bioethics. Her work has appeared in *Critical Philosophy of Race*, *Journal of Speculative Philosophy*, *Journal of Philosophy of Disability*, *Bioethics*, and *Puncta: Journal of Critical Phenomenology*.

Jordan Joseph Wadden is a bioethicist at Ontario Shores Centre for Mental Health Sciences. He recently received his Ph.D. in philosophy from the University of British Columbia. His primary research areas are: equitable access to health care, disability advocacy in health-care settings, and the ethical implementation of artificial intelligence and machine learning in hospitals. His approach prioritizes the inclusion of patient and family voices and emphasizes the clinical decision-making benefits of being comfortably uncomfortable.

Milton Keynes UK
Ingram Content Group UK Ltd.
UKHW052046150624
444079UK00004B/81

9 781350 268890